Concise Dictionary of British Literary Biography
Volume Four

Victorian Writers,
1832-1890

Concise Dictionary of British Literary Biography
Volume Four

Victorian Writers, 1832-1890

A Bruccoli Clark Layman Book
Gale Research Inc.
Detroit, London

Matthew J. Bruccoli and Richard Layman, *Editorial Directors*
Karen L. Rood, *Senior Editor*

Printed in the United States of America

Published simultaneously in the United Kingdom
by Gale Research International Limited
(An affiliated company of Gale Research Inc.)

∞™ This book is printed on acid-free paper that meets the minimum
requirements of American National Standard for Information Sciences—
Permanence Paper for Printed Library Materials, ANSI Z39.48-1984.

Contents of Volume 4

Authors Included in This Series

Volume 1
Writers of the Middle Ages and Renaissance Before 1660

Francis Bacon
Francis Beaumont & John Fletcher
Beowulf
Thomas Campion
Geoffrey Chaucer
Thomas Dekker
John Donne
John Ford
George Herbert

Ben Jonson
Sir Thomas Malory
Christopher Marlowe
Sir Walter Ralegh
William Shakespeare
Sir Philip Sidney
Edmund Spenser
Izaak Walton
John Webster

Volume 2
Writers of the Restoration and Eighteenth Century, 1660-1789

Joseph Addison
James Boswell
John Bunyan
William Congreve
Daniel Defoe
John Dryden
Henry Fielding
Oliver Goldsmith
Thomas Gray
Samuel Johnson
Andrew Marvell

John Milton
Samuel Pepys
Alexander Pope
Samuel Richardson
Richard Brinsley Sheridan
Tobias Smollett
Richard Steele
Laurence Sterne
Jonathan Swift
William Wycherley

Volume 3
Writers of the Romantic Period, 1789-1832

Volume 5
Late Victorian and Edwardian Writers, 1890-1914

Volume 6
Modern Writers, 1914-1945

Volume 7
Writers After World War II, 1945-1960

Volume 8
Contemporary Writers, 1960-Present

Plan of the Work

The eight-volume *Concise Dictionary of British Literary Biography* was developed in response to requests from school and college teachers and librarians, and from small- to medium-sized public libraries, for a compilation of entries from the standard *Dictionary of Literary Biography* chosen to meet their needs and their budgets. The *DLB*, which comprises more than one hundred volumes as of the end of 1991, is moving steadily toward its goal of providing a history of literature in all languages developed through the biographies of writers. Basic as the *DLB* is, many librarians have expressed the need for a less comprehensive reference work which in other respects retains the merits of the *DLB*. The *Concise DBLB* provides this resource.

The *Concise* series was planned by an eight-member advisory board, consisting primarily of secondary-school educators, who developed a method of organization and presentation for selected *DLB* entries suitable for high-school and beginning college students. Their preliminary plan was circulated to some five thousand school librarians and English teachers, who were asked to respond to the organization of the series. Those responses were incorporated into the plan described here.

Uses for the Concise DBLB

Students are the primary audience for the *Concise DBLB*. The stated purpose of the standard *DLB* is to make our literary heritage more accessible. *Concise DBLB* has the same goal and seeks a wider audience. What the author wrote; what the facts of his or her life are; a description of his or her literary works; a discussion of the critical response to his or her works; and a bibliography of critical works to be consulted for further information: these are the elements of a *Concise DBLB* entry.

The first step in the planning process for this series, after identifying the audience, was to contemplate its uses. The advisory board acknowledged that the integrity of *Concise DBLB* as a reference book is crucial to its utility. The *Concise DBLB* adheres to the scholarly standards established by the parent series; the *Concise DBLB* is a ready-reference source of established value, providing reliable biographical and bibliographical information.

It is anticipated that this series will not be confined to uses within the library. Just as the *DLB* has been a tool for stimulating students' literary interests in the college classroom—for comparative studies of authors, for example, and, through its ample illustrations, as a means of invigorating literary study—the *Concise DBLB* is a primary resource for high-school and junior-college educators.

Organization

The advisory board further determined that entries from the standard *DLB* should be presented complete—without abridgment. The board's feeling was that the utility of the *DLB* format has been proven, and that only minimal changes should be made.

The advisory board further decided that the organization of the *Concise DBLB* should be chronological to emphasize the historical development of British literature. Each volume is devoted to a single historical period and includes the most significant literary figures from all genres who were active during that time.

The eight period volumes of the *Concise DBLB* are: *Writers of the Middle Ages and Renaissance Before 1660; Writers of the Restoration and Eighteenth Century, 1660-1789; Writers of the Romantic Period, 1789-1832; Victorian Writers, 1832-1890; Late Victorian and Edwardian Writers, 1890-1914; Modern Writers, 1914-1945; Writers After World War II, 1945-1960; Contemporary Writers, 1960-Present.*

Form of Entry

The form of entry in the *Concise DBLB* is substantially the same as in the standard series. Entries have been updated and, where necessary, corrected.

It is anticipated that users of this series will find it useful to consult the standard *DLB* for information about those writers omitted from the *Concise DBLB* whose significance to contemporary readers may have faded but whose contribution to our cultural heritage remains meaningful.

Comments about the series and suggestions for its improvement are earnestly invited.

A Note to Students

The purpose of the *Concise DBLB* is to enrich the study of British literature. Besides being inherently interesting, biographies of writers provide a basic understanding of the various ways writers react in their works to the circumstances of their lives, the events of their times, and the cultures that envelop them.

Concise DBLB entries start with the most important facts about writers: what they wrote. We strongly recommend that you also start there. The chronological listing of an author's works is an outline for the examination of his or her career achievements. The biography that follows sets the stage for the presentation of the works. Each of the author's important works and the most respected critical evaluations of them are discussed in *Concise DBLB*. If you require more information about the author or fuller critical studies of the author's works, the references section at the end of the entry will guide you.

Illustrations are an integral element of *Concise DBLB* entries. Photographs of the author are reminders that literature is the product of a writer's imagination; facsimiles of the author's working drafts are the best evidence available for understanding the act of composition—the author in the process of refining his or her work and acting as self-editor; dust jackets and advertisements demonstrate how literature comes to us through the marketplace, which sometimes serves to alter our perceptions of the works.

Literary study is a complex and immensely rewarding endeavor. Our goal is to provide you with the information you need to make that experience as rich as possible.

Acknowledgments

This book was produced by Bruccoli Clark Layman, Inc. Karen L. Rood is senior editor for the *Dictionary of Literary Biography* series. David Marshall James was the in-house editor.

Production coordinator is James W. Hipp. Projects manager is Charles D. Brower. Photography editors are Edward Scott and Timothy C. Lundy. Permissions editor is Jean W. Ross. Layout and graphics supervisor is Penney L. Haughton. Copyediting supervisor is Bill Adams. Typesetting supervisor is Kathleen M. Flanagan. Systems manager is George F. Dodge. The production staff includes Rowena Betts, Teresa Chaney, Miriam E. Clark, Patricia Coate, Gail Crouch, Margaret McGinty Cureton, Mary Scott Dye, Sarah A. Estes, Robert Fowler, Cynthia Hallman, Ellen McCracken, Kathy Lawler Merlette, John Myrick, Pamela D. Norton, Cathy J. Reese, Laurrè Sinckler-Reeder, Maxine K. Smalls, Teri C. Sperry, and Betsy L. Weinberg.

Walter W. Ross and Henry Cunningham did library research. They were assisted by the following librarians at the Thomas Cooper Library of the University of South Carolina: Jens Holley and the interlibrary-loan staff; reference librarians Gwen Baxter, Daniel Boice, Faye Chadwell, Jo Cottingham, Cathy Eckman, Rhonda Felder, Gary Geer, Jackie Kinder, Laurie Preston, Jean Rhyne, Carol Tobin, Virginia Weathers, and Connie Widney; circulation-department head Thomas Marcil; and acquisitions-searching supervisor David Haggard.

Concise Dictionary of British Literary Biography
Volume Four

Victorian Writers, 1832-1890

Concise Dictionary of British Literary Biography

Matthew Arnold
(24 December 1822 - 15 April 1888)

This entry was updated by Suzanne O. Edwards (The Citadel) from her entry in
DLB 57: Victorian Prose Writers After 1867.

See also the Arnold entry in DLB 32: Victorian Poets Before 1850.

BOOKS: *Alaric at Rome: A Prize Poem* (Rugby: Combe & Crossley, 1840);

Cromwell: A Prize Poem (Oxford: Vincent, 1843);

The Strayed Reveller and Other Poems, as A. (London: Fellowes, 1849);

Empedocles on Etna and Other Poems, as A. (London: Fellowes, 1852); republished as *Empedocles on Etna: A Dramatic Poem* (Portland, Maine: Mosher, 1900);

Poems: A New Edition (London: Longman, Brown, Green & Longmans, 1853);

Poems: Second Series (London: Longman, Brown, Green & Longmans, 1855);

Merope: A Tragedy (London: Longman, Brown, Green, Longman & Roberts, 1858);

England and the Italian Question (London: Longman, Green, Longman & Roberts, 1859); edited by Merle M. Bevington (Durham, N.C.: Duke University Press, 1953);

The Popular Education of France, with Notices of That of Holland and Switzerland (London: Longman, Green, Longman & Roberts, 1861);

On Translating Homer: Three Lectures Given at Oxford (London: Longman, Green, Longman & Roberts, 1861);

On Translating Homer: Last Words: A Lecture Given at Oxford (London: Longman, Green, Longman & Roberts, 1862);

Heinrich Heine (Philadelphia: Leypold / New York: Christern, 1863);

A French Eton; or, Middle Class Education and the State (London & Cambridge: Macmillan, 1864);

Essays in Criticism (London & Cambridge: Macmillan, 1865; Boston: Ticknor & Fields, 1865);

On the Study of Celtic Literature (London: Smith, Elder, 1867); with *On Translating Homer* (New York: Macmillan, 1883);

New Poems (London: Macmillan, 1867; Boston: Ticknor & Fields, 1867);

Schools and Universities on the Continent (London: Macmillan, 1868); republished in part as *Higher Schools and Universities in Germany* (London: Macmillan, 1874);

Culture and Anarchy: An Essay in Political and Social Criticism (London: Smith, Elder, 1869); with *Friendship's Garland* (New York: Macmillan, 1883);

St. Paul and Protestantism; with an Introduction on Puritanism and the Church of England (London: Smith, Elder, 1870; New York: Macmillan, 1883);

Friendship's Garland: Being the Conversations, Letters and Opinions of the Late Arminius, Baron von Thunder-ten-Tronckh; Collected and Edited with a Dedicatory Letter to Adolescens Leo, Esq., of "The Daily Telegraph" (London: Smith, Elder, 1871); with *Culture and Anarchy* (New York: Macmillan, 1883);

Matthew Arnold, photographed by Camille Silvy in 1861

Literature and Dogma: An Essay towards a Better Apprehension of the Bible (London: Smith, Elder, 1873; New York: Macmillan, 1873);

God and the Bible: A Review of Objections to "Literature and Dogma" (London: Smith, Elder, 1875; Boston: Osgood, 1876);

Last Essays on Church and Religion (London: Smith, Elder, 1877; New York: Macmillan, 1877);

Mixed Essays (London: Smith, Elder, 1879; New York: Macmillan, 1879);

Irish Essays, and Others (London: Smith, Elder, 1882);

Discourses in America (New York & London: Macmillan, 1885);

Education Department: Special Report on Certain Points Connected with Elementary Education in Germany, Switzerland, and France (London: Eyre & Spottiswoode, 1886);

General Grant: An Estimate (Boston: Cupples, Upham, 1887); republished as *General Grant. With a Rejoinder by Mark Twain*, edited by J. Y. Simon (Carbondale: Southern Illinois University Press, 1966);

Essays in Criticism: Second Series (London & New York: Macmillan, 1888);

Civilization in the United States: First and Last Impressions of America (Boston: Cupples & Hurd, 1888);

Reports on Elementary Schools 1852-1882, edited by Sir Francis Sandford (London & New York: Macmillan, 1889);

On Home Rule for Ireland: Two Letters to "The Times" (London: Privately printed, 1891);

Matthew Arnold's Notebooks (London: Smith, Elder, 1902); republished as *The Note-Books of Matthew Arnold*, edited by Howard Foster Lowry, Karl Young, and Waldo Hilary Dunn (London & New York: Oxford University Press, 1952);

Arnold as Dramatic Critic, edited by C. K. Shorter (London: Privately printed, 1903); republished as *Letters of an Old Playgoer*, edited by Brander Matthews (New York: Columbia University Press, 1919);

Essays in Criticism: Third Series, edited by Edward J. O'Brien (Boston: Ball, 1910);

Thoughts on Education Chosen From the Writings of Matthew Arnold, edited by L. Huxley (London: Smith, Elder, 1912; New York: Macmillan, 1912);

Five Uncollected Essays of Matthew Arnold, edited by Kenneth Allott (Liverpool: University Press of Liverpool, 1953);

Essays, Letters, and Reviews by Matthew Arnold, edited by Fraser Neiman (Cambridge, Mass.: Harvard University Press, 1960).

Collections: *The Works of Matthew Arnold*, edited by G. W. E. Russell, 15 volumes (London: Macmillan, 1903-1904);

The Poetical Works of Matthew Arnold, edited by C. B. Tinker and H. F. Lowry (London & New York: Oxford University Press, 1950);

Complete Prose Works, edited by R. H. Super, 11 volumes (Ann Arbor: University of Michigan Press, 1960-1977);

The Poems of Matthew Arnold, edited by Kenneth Allott (London: Longmans, 1965);

Culture and the State, edited by P. Nash (New York: Teachers College Press, 1965).

OTHER: *A Bible-Reading for Schools: The Great Prophecy of Israel's Restoration (Isaiah, Chapters*

40-66) Arranged and Edited for Young Learners, edited by Arnold (London: Macmillan, 1872); revised and enlarged as *Isaiah XL-LXVI; with the Shorter Prophecies Allied to It, Arranged and Edited with Notes* (London: Macmillan, 1875);

The Six Chief Lives from Johnson's "Lives of the Poets," with Macaulay's "Life of Johnson," edited by Arnold (London: Macmillan, 1878);

The Hundred Greatest Men: Portraits of the One Hundred Greatest Men of History, introduction by Arnold (London: Low, Marston, Searle & Rivington, 1879);

Poems of Wordsworth, edited by Arnold (London: Macmillan, 1879);

Letters, Speeches and Tracts on Irish Affairs by Edmund Burke, edited by Arnold (London: Macmillan, 1881);

Poetry of Byron, edited by Arnold (London: Macmillan, 1881);

Isaiah of Jerusalem in the Authorised English Version, with an Introduction, Corrections and Notes, edited by Arnold (London: Macmillan, 1883);

"Charles Augustin Sainte-Beuve," in *Encyclopaedia Britannica,* ninth edition (London: Black, 1886), IX: 162-165;

"Schools," in *The Reign of Queen Victoria,* edited by T. H. Ward (London: Smith, Elder, 1887), II: 238-279.

A master of both poetry and prose, Matthew Arnold remains significant today for the same reasons that the Victorian age as a whole retains significance. The Victorians—Arnold chief among them—struggled with issues that confront us more than a century later: social injustice, unequal educational opportunity, religious doubt, the uncertain role of the arts in the modern world, the restlessness and confusion of modern man. But Arnold's opinions on these issues differed from those of many of his countrymen. Surrounded by champions of British superiority, Arnold nonetheless refused to be satisfied with the accomplishments of nineteenth-century Englishmen. According to biographer Park Honan, when Arnold was only six months old, he seemed to his impatient father "backward and rather bad-tempered" because he would not lie still in his crib. For the rest of his life, Arnold's critics complained about his refusal to lie still—his unwillingness to be content with the signal achievements of the British.

Arnold's comments on society, religion, and aesthetics remain pertinent primarily because of the critical approach he advocated—an open-minded, receptive, intelligent appraisal of the issues—more than because of specific conclusions he drew or suggestions he proposed. It is this critical method far more than his views on individual controversies that makes Arnold's work enduring. In his essay "Spinoza and the Bible" (collected in *Essays in Criticism,* 1865), Arnold accounts for the genius of men such as Spinoza, Hegel, and Plato and at the same time offers a fitting description of his own genius: "What a remarkable philosopher really does for human thought, is to throw into circulation a certain number of new and striking ideas and expressions, and to stimulate with them the thought and imagination of his century or of after-times." Arnold's own notions of "culture" and "the critical spirit"; of "sweetness and light"; of society divided into "Barbarians, Philistines, and Populace"; of the Christian God as a presence that can be known only as "The Eternal, not ourselves, that makes for righteousness" profoundly influenced his own times and continue to influence ours.

Matthew Arnold, the eldest son of Thomas and Mary Penrose Arnold, was born Christmas Eve 1822 at Laleham-on-Thames in Middlesex. Less than twenty miles west of London, Laleham was a pleasant pastoral spot. There, where his father kept a small school, Arnold spent the first six years of his life. In 1828 Thomas Arnold was appointed headmaster of Rugby School, and the Arnolds moved to the midlands to establish a new home in Warwickshire. Immediately the new headmaster began instituting revolutionary changes. A strict man, Dr. Arnold demanded adherence to a rigid code of morality, establishing for himself the goal of forming Christian gentlemen. His reforms spread into other areas of Rugby life as well. He broadened the traditional classical curriculum to include a more serious study of mathematics and modern languages. Concerned about the low morale of overburdened, underpaid teachers—a concern his son would later share—Thomas Arnold increased teachers' salaries, making it possible for them to relinquish their curacies and to become more committed to the school and to their pupils. And he set himself as a model for the masters as well as for the boys. He not only earned a reputation as a brilliant teacher of history and religion, but he also involved himself in the lives of his students—swimming with them, playing games with them, welcoming them into his home. Dr. Arnold's stellar pupil, and one of the most frequent visitors

Fox How, Ambleside, the Arnold family retreat in the Lake District

to the Arnold home, was Arthur Hugh Clough, who was later to become a poet and Matthew Arnold's closest friend.

Young Arnold himself proved to be a rather poor pupil, however. In 1830 he was sent back to school in Laleham. Eager to be allowed to return home, Arnold applied himself to his studies and showed sufficient improvement to be permitted to come back two years later to instruction under private tutors at his parents' home. In 1836 Matthew and his brother Tom enrolled at Winchester, but Matthew spent only one year there and entered Rugby in 1837. Still a less than devoted scholar, Matthew nevertheless received literary recognition as early as 1840 by winning the Rugby Poetry Prize for *Alaric at Rome*. Otherwise, as Honan points out, the young Arnold "lived in the grandest juvenile defiance of the fact that he

was an Arnold." This defiance manifested itself in his appearance and in his behavior. At age fourteen, he bought and wore a monocle. On one occasion, having been reprimanded by his father for misbehavior in class, he amused his peers by making faces behind Dr. Arnold's back.

The hours Arnold spent in the classroom were offset by many pleasant holidays in the Lake District. In 1831 Dr. Arnold took his family to the north of England and on to Scotland for a vacation. While touring the Lake District, the Arnolds became acquainted with William Wordsworth and Robert Southey. They returned to the lakes for Christmas and again the following summer. The Arnolds became so fond of the spot and of the Wordsworths that they built a holiday house at Fox How in Ambleside, only a short walk from the Wordsworths' home at Rydal

Mount. They stayed there for the first time in the summer of 1834. Thereafter, Fox How was a favorite family retreat, becoming home to Mrs. Arnold after the death of her husband; and years later, Matthew Arnold brought his own children there. Much of the imagery in his landscape poetry was inspired by the spot.

Arnold's poetic landscapes also are indebted to the region around Oxford where, to everyone's surprise, including his own, Arnold won one of two classical Open Balliol Scholarships in 1840. Even at Oxford his carefree attitude persisted. Fishing occupied many of the hours he was supposed to be devoting to his books. He swam nude by the riverbank, enjoyed drinking, lapsed in his regular attendance at chapel, and adopted the airs of the dandy—donning extravagant waistcoats and assuming an affected manner. He delighted in lighthearted pranks. On one occasion, reports biographer Lionel Trilling, a friend named Hawker with whom he was traveling claimed that Arnold "pleasantly induced a belief into the passengers of the coach that I was a poor mad gentleman, and that he was my keeper."

The years at Oxford were marked by sober events as well. Arnold's father died of a heart attack on 12 June 1842, at the age of forty-seven. In the years that followed, Arnold came to see himself as perpetuating many of his father's views on education, social welfare, and religion. In "Rugby Chapel," written more than twenty years after the death of Thomas Arnold, Arnold shows his high regard for his father, remembering him as a son of God, as one of the "helpers and friends of mankind," as a leader worth following:

> . . . at your voice,
> Panic, despair, flee away.
> Ye move through the ranks, recall
> The stragglers, refresh the outworn,
> Praise, re-inspire the brave!
> Order, courage, return.

Arnold came to see his own mission as one of re-inspiring mankind, and he considered it an inherited mission. He wrote to his mother in 1869, "I think of the main part of what I have done, and am doing, as work which he [Thomas Arnold] would have approved and seen to be indispensable."

In the years immediately following his father's death, Arnold grew closer to Arthur Clough, who felt the loss of Dr. Arnold almost as intensely as Matthew himself. Clough and Arnold shared much more than their grief, however. Both were promising, but ultimately disappointing, students at Oxford; both felt strongly attached to Oxford, especially to the countryside surrounding the university; both were restless, unsettled young men. Most significant, both were poets. They criticized one another's work and discussed their developing theories of art.

Despite the sobering effect of his father's death, Arnold continued to shirk his schoolwork. Unprepared for final examinations, he earned only second-class honors in 1844. Yet in 1845 he won a fellowship at Oriel College, Oxford, and spent the next two years reading widely in classical and German philosophy and literature and traveling in Europe as often as he could. At the age of twenty-four, he gave up his residency at Oxford. He took a temporary post as assistant master at Rugby for one term before accepting a position in London as private secretary to Lord Lansdowne, the lord president of the Privy Council.

While holding this position, Arnold wrote some of his finest poems and published them, signed with the initial *A.*, in two separate volumes: *The Strayed Reveller and Other Poems* (1849) and *Empedocles on Etna and Other Poems* (1852). The poems express in verse many of the ideas and opinions that Arnold expressed in his letters to Clough. These letters, collected in 1932 by H. F. Lowry, offer valuable insight into Arnold's thought as it developed from 1845 to 1861, the year of Clough's death. One of the dominant themes of both the letters and the poems is that of the intellectual and spiritual voice Arnold believed to be characteristic of nineteenth-century life. In September 1849 Arnold wrote, "My dearest Clough these are damned times—everything is against one—the height to which knowledge is come, the spread of luxury, our physical enervation, the absence of great *natures*, the unavoidable contact with millions of small ones, newspapers, cities, light profligate friends, moral desperadoes like Carlyle, our own selves, and the sickening consciousness of our difficulties. . . ." For Arnold "this strange disease of modern life," as he called it in "The Scholar-Gipsy," led to disorientation, aimlessness, purposelessness. Looking about him, he witnessed the weakening of tradiional areas of authority, namely the dwindling power of the upper classes and the diminishing authority of the church. Man had no firm base to cling to, nothing to believe in, nothing to be sustained by. Instead, Arnold writes in "Stanzas from the Grand Chartreuse," he finds himself "Wandering between two worlds, one dead, / The other powerless to be born."

Among Arnold's early poems are those love poems about a woman called Marguerite that he grouped under the heading "Switzerland." Although Arnold maintained throughout his life that Marguerite was imaginary, Honan has presented convincing, though not universally accepted, evidence that the poems were inspired by a real woman, Mary Claude, who lived near Fox How, and with whom Arnold fell in love in 1848. In the autumn of 1848 and again in 1849, Arnold traveled in the Swiss Alps and used this setting in the Marguerite poems. Mary Claude apparently did not encourage Arnold's affections, and the romance seems to have ended in 1849. Arnold used the Marguerite poems to explore the effects of modern life on love. In "To Marguerite—Continued," he concludes that the individual is essentially isolated: "in the sea of life enisled. . . . We mortal millions live *alone*." Surely, in the past, there was a sense of community; all men must once have been "Parts of a single continent!" But now each man is an island separated from every other man by "The unplumb'd, salt, estranging sea." Even love lacks the power to unite human beings. In particular, the speaker finds that words fail him. David G. Riede points out in *Matthew Arnold and the Betrayal of Language* (1988) that "Arnold's best love poems are preoccupied with the failure of language to express honest feelings. . . ."

The theme of man's alienation is echoed in later poems as well. In "Rugby Chapel," Arnold asks:

What is the course of the life
Of mortal men on the earth?—
Most men eddy about
Here and there—eat and drink,
Chatter and love and hate,
Gather and squander, are raised
Aloft, are hurl'd in the dust,
Striving blindly, achieving
Nothing; and then they die—
Perish;—and no one asks
Who or what they have been.

And in "Dover Beach" the movement of the ocean calls to mind "the turbid ebb and flow / Of human misery" and "bring[s] / The eternal note of sadness in." The speaker longs for a refuge since the world "Hath really neither joy, nor love, nor light, / Nor certitude, nor peace, nor

help for pain." Arnold's expressed longing for a retreat is not limited to "Dover Beach." For example, he envies the immortal Scholar-Gipsy wandering the hillsides around Oxford who "hast not felt the lapse of hours," who is "Free from the sick fatigue, the languid doubt" inherent in the modern condition. Arnold himself felt acutely the oppression of mortality. At age thirty he wrote to Clough, "How life rushes away, and youth. One has dawdled and scrupled and fiddle faddled—and it is all over."

In spite of such somber poetic reflections, Arnold's demeanor remained persistently cavalier, to the dismay and irritation of his family and friends. When Charlotte Brontë met him in 1850, her first impression was typical. She found him "striking and prepossessing; . . . [he] displeases from seeming foppery. I own it caused me at first to regard him with regretful surprise. . . . I was told however, that 'Mr. Arnold improved upon acquaintance.' So it was: ere long a real modesty appeared under his assumed conceit, and some genuine intellectual aspirations, as well as high educational acquirements, displaced superficial affectations." Even without such testimonies of Arnold's attributes, his poems and letters indicate that he was thinking deeply about the problems of the age and about the role of literature in helping man to cope with those problems.

Arnold's letters to Clough reveal his theory of poetry, particularly his notion of the purpose of poetry. As E. D. H. Johnson points out in *The Alien Vision of Victorian Poetry* (1952), Arnold tried "to reaffirm the traditional sovereignty of poetry as a civilizing agent." In a letter of 28 October 1852, he contended that "modern poetry can only subsist by its *contents:* by becoming a complete magister vitae as the poetry of the ancients did: by including, as theirs did, religion with poetry, instead of existing as poetry only, and leaving religious wants to be supplied by the Christian religion, as a power existing independent of the poetical." Arnold believed that great art, functioning as a civilizing agent to enrich the intellectual and spiritual life of man, had universal application. But his views did not coincide with those of his contemporaries who felt that art should have immediate, practical application to everyday experience.

The critics of Arnold's first two volumes of poems charged that his poetry did not consistently deal with contemporary life. Poems such as *Empedocles on Etna, Tristram and Iseult,* and

"Mycerinus" (the last in *The Strayed Reveller*) seemed to them irrelevant for modern readers. Charles Kingsley's comments, published in 1849 in *Fraser's* magazine, are representative: "The man who cannot . . . sing the present age, and transfigure it into melody, or who cannot, in writing of past ages, draw from them some eternal lesson about this one, has no right to be versifying at all. Let him read, think, and keep to prose, till he has mastered the secret of the nineteenth century." Another complaint voiced by the critics and echoed by Arnold's sister Jane was that his poems expressed dissatisfaction with the age but offered no practical cures for its ills.

Arnold's third volume of verse—the first to bear his full name—appeared in 1853. It included such poems as "Sohrab and Rustum," one of Arnold's personal favorites, and "The Scholar-Gipsy," but it was the preface to the volume rather than the poems it contained that received the most attention. The "1853 Preface" served as both an introduction to the collection and as an answer to the critics of his earlier volumes.

Insisting "not only that it [poetry] shall interest, but also that it shall inspirit and rejoice the reader," Arnold explains in the preface that he has chosen to exclude *Empedocles on Etna* from the 1853 collection because the poem neither inspirits nor rejoices. He has rejected it, not because of readers' objections to the classical subject, but rather because the poem deals with a situation that is, ironically, an especially modern one. For the situation of Empedocles, he maintains, is one "in which a continuous state of mental distress is prolonged, unrelieved by incident, hope, or resistance; in which there is everything to be endured, nothing to be done"; in other words, in Arnold's view, a decidedly nineteenth-century dilemma. This for Arnold is the poem's flaw. In saying so, Arnold is not condemning tragedy in literature. He acknowledges that tragedy can produce high pleasure, but *Empedocles on Etna* is not tragedy; it is pathos. In this respect, then, Arnold agrees with his critics. A poem should not just expose problems or express discontent. Evaluating his own work he wrote to Clough in December 1852, "As for my poems they have weight, I think, but little or no charm." He contends in another letter that people need literature that will "*animate* and *ennoble* them. . . ." He withdrew *Empedocles on Etna* because he believed it failed to do so.

But Arnold vehemently disagrees with critical objections to his use of classical subjects, pointing out that the past supplies subjects that touch "elementary feelings . . . which are independent of time." Arnold defends classical subjects because of their universal relevance. In his edition of Arnold's letters to Clough, Lowry says of Arnold that "The deepest passion of his life was for what is permanent in the human mind and the human heart," and he found this in classical literature. To Arnold, a topic's contemporaneity did not ensure its worth. The important point for the poet to keep in mind was that he should choose a significant subject, whether drawn from the past or the present, for "action" rather than "expression" is the most important part of a poem. In his own *Empedocles on Etna*, there is no action, another sense in which it is "modern." According to Arnold's preface, modern poetry suffers from its emphasis on expression or self-revelation. As Alba Warren explains in *English Poetic Theory* (1950), although he did not make it very plain in the "1853 Preface," "great poetry for Arnold is not lyric, subjective, personal; it is above all objective and impersonal. . . ." In its subordination of expression to action, in its emphasis on the epic and the dramatic, Arnold concludes in his preface, classical Greek poetry is especially praiseworthy. The aspiring nineteenth-century poet, Arnold asserts, can learn much from classical writers.

Although the preface did not quiet his critics, who persisted in echoing their former complaints, Arnold reserved more elaborate development of his position for a lecture he delivered in the autumn of 1857. At the age of thirty-four, he was elected to the poetry chair at Oxford University, a five-year appointment which required him to deliver several lectures each year. Traditionally, the lectures had been read in Latin, but Arnold decided to present his in English. He used the occasion of his inaugural lecture on 14 November 1857 to return to his views about the worth of classical literature and to introduce several other themes which reappear in his later work.

In this first lecture, entitled "On the Modern Element in Literature" and eventually published in *Macmillan's* magazine (February 1869), Arnold advocates a liberal education that features wide-ranging knowledge and the use of the comparative method to build knowledge and to shape understanding. For Arnold, poetry is the "highest literature," and he is confident that comparison among literatures will show that classical Greek poetry is the highest poetry. It is superior to other literatures because it is "adequate," by

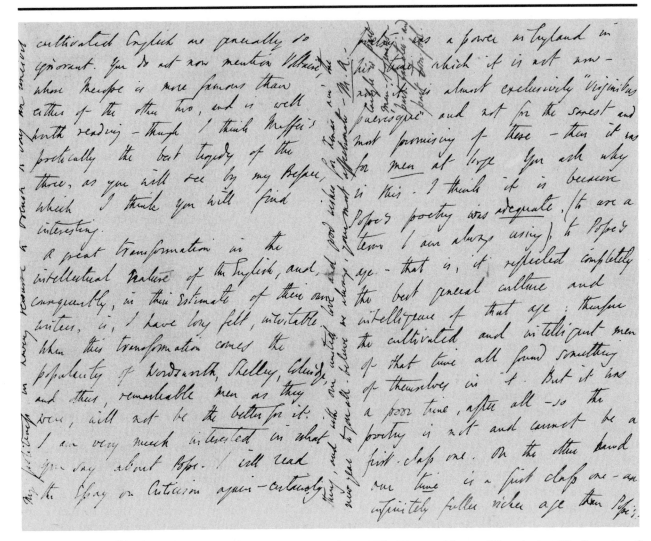

From a December 1857 letter written by Arnold to his brother Thomas (The Pierpont Morgan Library). Arnold's discussion of Pope's poetry as "adequate, (to use a term I am always using), to Pope's age" echoes views he had expressed the month before in the first lecture he delivered as Professor of Poetry at Oxford.

which Arnold means that it "represents the highly developed human nature" of a great age. Arnold believes that "adequacy" is rare because the great writer must be linked with a great epoch for great literature to be produced. In Arnold's opinion, the literature of Pindar, Aeschylus, Aristophanes, and Sophocles matches the greatness of the era in which they lived. Other great ages, such as the period of the supremacy of Rome, failed to produce great poets who were in sympathy with their age. The Elizabethan age was also inferior to classical Greece because the genius of William Shakespeare and John Milton was not matched by a great age; instead, they lived in a time characterized by a lack of religious toleration and by a lack of the critical spirit. As Arnold explains, the climate of the nineteenth century is similarly unconducive to the development

of an "adequate" literature. The view he had expressed in an 1849 letter to Clough remains essentially unchanged in 1857: "how deeply *unpoetical* the age and all one's surroundings are. Not unprofound, not ungrand, not unmoving:—but *unpoetical*." Because of "the enduring interest of Greek literature" founded on its "instructive fulness of experience," it has special relevance for modern man. Classical literature, Arnold argues, can provide the "intellectual deliverance" that modern man needs.

Arnold's next major prose work, *On Translating Homer*, was a series of three lectures given at Oxford in November and December 1860 and January 1861. In these essays, published together soon after the third was delivered, he evaluates selected translations of Homer, noting the strengths and weaknesses of each in an attempt to establish the characteristics of a well-written translation. He criticizes translators who have insisted on imposing "modern sentiment" on the material and is equally impatient with those who have become embroiled in background issues such as establishing the true identity of Homer. He insists that many translators have erred because they do not understand that the true purpose of translation is "to reproduce on the intelligent scholar . . . the general effect of Homer." To achieve that end the translator must retain not only the content or "matter" of the original but also must capture its style or "manner." Arnold warns that style is frequently sacrificed, both by those who translate too literally and by those who embellish the original with quaint, pseudoarchaic language in an attempt to make the translation seem authentic. He proposes that the translator of Homer adopt the characteristics of Homer's poetry: simple but noble diction, plain thought, natural rhythm, and rapid movement. These are the traits inherent in "the grand style" of Homer.

In order to clarify his suggestions, Arnold criticizes illustrative passages from an assortment of translations, using, as Robert H. Super points out in his notes to Arnold's *Complete Prose Works* (1960-1977), the touchstone method of judging poetry that he advocated twenty years later in "The Study of Poetry." These illustrations are central to Arnold's argument in the lectures, for he contends that one must develop a taste for or sensitivity to "the grand style." While the grand style is not strictly definable, it is clearly recognizable to the cultivated reader. He trusts that the reader will note the absence of the grand style from the passages he has condemned and will observe its presence in his own brief model translations.

In these three lectures Arnold drew on his own interest in classical literature, but he also capitalized on widespread contemporary interest in Homeric translation. Most of Arnold's negative remarks focus on a new rendering of Homer, the 1856 translation of the *Iliad* by Francis Newman—a translation marked by contorted diction and meter, and consequently lacking in the "grand style." Newman replied to Arnold's evaluation of his work in a lengthy pamphlet entitled *Homeric Translation in Theory and Practice, A Reply to Matthew Arnold,* published in 1861. Others echoed Newman's long-winded complaints about the faulty meter of Arnold's own translations and about the very premises of his essays, in particular his assertion about the purpose of translation.

For instance, Fitzjames Stephen, in an unsigned appraisal for the *Saturday Review,* agreed with Newman that it was impossible for a translation to produce the same effect as the original "simply because it is not the same thing as the original." Arnold was also criticized, even by members of his own family, for his dogmatic tone. Responding to such a charge from his sister Jane, who had accused him of "becoming as dogmatic as Ruskin," Arnold told her, "the difference was that Ruskin was 'dogmatic and *wrong.*' . . ." On another occasion his reaction was more serious. Writing to Jane in 1861, he reminded her that in his position as lecturer he had to speak with authority, but agreed that use of a "dogmatic" tone would be self-defeating. As Kathleen Tillotson has pointed out in the 1956 article "Arnold and Carlyle," Arnold learned to present himself in future essays and speeches as "regrettably expert."

Arnold's tone was demonstrably modified in his very next lecture. Characteristically, Arnold was not satisfied with leaving his critics unanswered. He replied, primarily to Newman, in *On Translating Homer: Last Words,* a fourth Oxford lecture delivered 30 November 1861 and published the following year. Dismayed that he had so seriously offended Newman, he insisted that his respect for Newman as a scholar was genuine but pointed out that scholarship was not the issue. The issue was Newman's failure to produce a simple but noble "poetic" translation of Homer. He reiterated the major argument of his earlier lectures, dwelling on the characteristics of the grand style. Arnold explained that "the grand style arises in poetry, *when a noble nature, poetically gifted, treats with simplicity or with severity a serious subject.*" He then applied this description not only to translations of poetry but also to poetry itself by examining a wide range of English poets from Geoffrey Chaucer to John Keats, from Milton to William Wordsworth. Just as in the "1853 Preface," Arnold argued in these essays for the importance of the "whole," for the importance of harmony throughout a work.

Finding the time to write and deliver poetry lectures presented a challenge to Arnold, since along with the duties demanded by his honorary title at Oxford were more pressing duties to his family and his job. In 1851 Arnold's appointment as an inspector of schools had provided him sufficient financial security to enable him to marry Frances Lucy Wightman. The marriage was a happy one. Flu, as she was called, frequently accompanied Arnold in his travels and was supportive of his work. According to Arnold, she proved to be "a very good judge of all prose" and criticized his essays and lectures. She provided a liberalizing influence as well, encouraging him to read modern novels and to attend art exhibits and operas. The Arnolds had six children to whom Arnold was a devoted, indulgent father.

During the thirty-five years Arnold spent as a school inspector, he repeatedly complained of his duties: the oppressively long hours, the exhausting travel, and the tiresome bureaucratic system. He spent his days questioning countless schoolchildren and writing endless reports on drainage, ventilation, equipment, teacher performance, and student achievement. Honan reports that in 1855, a "typical" year, Arnold examined 290 schools, 368 pupil-teachers, 97 certified teachers, and 20,000 students. It is little wonder that he claimed to be "worked to death." The depressing conditions he witnessed in the schools affected him deeply. He sympathized not only with ragged, careworn children but with overworked teachers as well. In 1854 he claimed, "No one feels more than I do how laborious is [the teachers'] work . . . men of weak health and purely studious habits, who betake themselves to this profession, as affording the means to continue their favourite pursuits: not knowing, alas, that for all but men of the most singular and exceptional vigour and energy, there are no pursuits more irreconcilable than those of the student and of the schoolmaster."

Still, despite the negative aspects of his job, as Honan points out, Arnold's work exposed him to aspects of English and European life of which he probably would have otherwise remained ignorant, and thus enhanced his credibility as a social commentator: he earned respect as a social critic because he traveled throughout the country and to Europe and daily mingled with people of all levels, especially those of the middle class. The advantages of his job were not clear to Arnold, however. Fatigue and discouragement often overshadowed commitment and enthusiasm. He responded with dismay when people tried to relate his work in education to that of his father. In an 1856 letter to his brother William, Arnold confessed that when he was compared to his father he was tempted to reply: "My good friends, this is a matter for which my father certainly had a specialité, but for which I have none whatever. . . . I on the contrary half cannot half will not throw myself into it, and feel the weight of it

doubly in consequence. I am inclined to think it would have been the same with any active line of life on which I had found myself engaged—even with politics—so I am glad my sphere is a humble one and must try more and more to do something worth doing in my own way, since I cannot bring myself to do more than a halting sort of half-work in other people's way." Arnold's dedication to the improvement of education in England was more clearly indicated by his publications than by his perfunctory performance of routine duties.

On several occasions, Arnold escaped the drudgery of his ordinary assignments to travel in Europe, where he studied foreign educational systems. The first such study took place in 1859 when Arnold was asked by the Education Commission to visit France, French Switzerland, and Holland to examine the elementary schools in those countries. He spent six months, from March through August of 1859, traveling about Europe, observing schools, and consulting with foreign officials. His report, *The Popular Education of France, with Notices of That of Holland and Switzerland,* published in 1861, records his observations and evaluations and his recommendations to England.

The introduction, entitled "Democracy" and later included in *Mixed Essays* (1879), presents Arnold's view that the national government should assume responsibility for educating its citizens. He anticipates middle-class fears of government repression of individual freedom but argues that in England the democratic system is strongly rooted, leaving no danger of loss of liberty if the State assumes control of certain public interests. According to Arnold, the state is the best agent for raising the quality of education. He repeats Edmund Burke's definition of the state as "*the nation in its collective and corporate character.*" The state, because of its authority and resources, can distribute "broad collective benefits" to society at large.

Moreover, the very growth of democracy prompts Arnold to advocate a broad-based, state-supported educational program. Middle- and lower-class people were gaining more and more power of self-government; therefore, Arnold reasons, England must "make timely preparation" for the spread of democracy. This can best be accomplished by adequately educating the middle and lower classes. Upper-class schools were already excellent; it was the schools for the middle and lower classes that needed improvement. Arnold argues that our greatest fear should be of "the multitude being in power, with no adequate ideal to elevate or guide" it. He reminds his reader that "It is a very great thing to be able to think as you like; but, after all, an important question remains: *what* you think." Arnold once again praises ancient Athens, for it was in that society, he says, that people of all classes had "culture." It was in that society that the world witnessed "the middle and lower classes in the highest development of their humanity. . . ." By improving the education of the middle and lower classes, Arnold hoped to see a similar spread of culture in nineteenth-century England.

In the chapters following this important introduction, Arnold offers a detailed explanation of the French educational system and brief overviews of education in French Switzerland and Holland. Arnold finds much to be admired in the French system. While the French have not made elementary education compulsory, they have made it available to all. And while Arnold notes weaknesses in the system and concedes that all do not take advantage of educational opportunities, he finds that "the mental temper" of the French people has shown improvement. He longs for such improvement among the English.

Arnold continues his argument in "A French Eton," which appeared in three installments in *Macmillan's* magazine in September 1863, February 1864, and May 1864. He considered this "one of his most important works to date" and rightly so, for it is in this work that Arnold presents his views on education most concisely and forcefully. He focuses on secondary education, proposing the establishment throughout England of a network of "Royal Schools" (similar to such schools in France) to be distinguished by low fees, regular inspections, and government support. Arnold again voices concern about the existence of a powerful, but inadequately educated, un-"cultured," "self-satisfied" middle class and argues that a school system such as the one he describes would do much to urge "progress toward man's best perfection."

Parliamentary debates over government funding of education motivated Arnold to pick up his pen on other occasions in the early 1860s. Political discussion centered on the Revised Code, proposed by Robert Lowe, the vice-president of the Committee of Council on Education. The Revised Code outlined a plan for appropriating money to schools based on quantifiable "results" achieved by teachers in the classroom. Arnold was appalled by the utilitarian emphasis of the proposal. In "The Twice-Revised Code," an anony-

"Sweetness and Light," Frederick Waddy's caricature of Arnold published in Once a Week, *12 October 1873 (Collection of Jerold J. Savory)*

mous article that appeared in *Fraser's* magazine (1862), he expresses dismay that emphasis is to be placed on reading, writing, and arithmetic to the exclusion of other subjects. Arnold does not deny that many children, especially poor children, are inadequately trained in these subjects but contends that a reductive approach will not ensure better training. He is convinced children need the civilizing influence of a broader, more liberal curriculum. Arnold suggests reorganization of and reduction of the number of school inspectors to cut expenses.

Arnold's belief that all children should receive a liberal education surfaces in other ways, too. In May 1872, for instance, he edited a version of chapters 40 through 66 of Isaiah. Entitled *A Bible-Reading for Schools,* it was widely used as a textbook for children. In 1883 he produced *Isaiah of Jerusalem,* an accompanying version of the first thirty-nine chapters. Arnold believed that schoolchildren ought to study the Bible because, he says, it "is for the child in an elementary school almost his only contact with poetry and philosophy. . . ."

Arnold was sent abroad for seven months in 1865 by the Middle Class School Commission to study middle-class secondary education in France, Italy, Germany, and Switzerland. His report was completed late in 1867 and published in March 1868 under the title *Schools and Universities on the Continent*. Arnold had been among those considered for the position of secretary of the commission. All along he had claimed to have no interest in the position and so was not disappointed when the office went to someone else, but he was distressed that most of those named to the committee were opposed to state control of education. In a 1 December 1865 letter to his mother he confided, "I wish it was a better and more open-minded Commission. But this, like all else which happens, more and more turns me away from the thought of any attempt at direct practical and political action, and makes me fix all my care upon a spiritual action, to tell upon people's minds, which after all is the great thing, hard as it is to make oneself fully believe it so." Arnold used publications such as *Schools and Universities on the Continent* to try to affect people's minds by transforming their attitudes.

In his report Arnold argues for universal educational opportunity. His view of the purpose of education is similar to his view of the purpose of art. He is much more concerned with enrichment and culture than with practicality and relevance. He recognizes that "The aim and office of instruction, say many people, is to make a man a good citizen, or a good Christian, or a gentleman; or it is to fit him to get on in the world, or it is to enable him to do his duty in that state of life to which he is called." But Arnold states emphatically, "It is none of these; . . . its prime direct aim is to enable a man *to know himself and the world.*"

Arnold recommends that the English adopt the trend in foreign schools of mandating the same subjects for all children in elementary school, after which each child may choose between humanistic or natural science curricula, depending on his aims and interests. At the elementary level, the child's education should be a comparative one. In order "to know himself and the world," a child should study other cultures, thereby gaining insight into his own. Convinced of the humanizing effects of literary study in particular, Arnold proposes the study of Greek literature and art, since the Greeks excelled in these areas and since their works speak to all people in all ages; the study of "the mother tongue and its literature"; and the study of the literature of modern foreign languages.

Arnold points out that while the English rave about the high quality of their schools, the schools in Germany, Holland, and Switzerland are clearly superior. Still arguing for a better education for the middle classes, Arnold points again to the stagnation caused by complacency. He claims that the countries he has visited all "have a civil organisation which has been framed with forethought and design to meet the wants of modern society; while our civil organisation in England still remains what time and chance have made it." Because more and more the middle class is actually running industry, commerce, and government, it is especially important that it be well prepared to do so. In an effort to demonstrate the practical advantages of improved education, Arnold's *Schools and Universities on the Continent* draws attention to the dangers of inadequate education. Many professionals in England—engineers, chemists, doctors, teachers, and magistrates—lack proper training and certification. In other countries this is not the case. In France, for instance, those who dispense drugs and those who build bridges must be licensed to do so; but licensing is not required in England. Teachers in France are certified for competency in certain areas, but in England teachers receive a general certification for all subjects. All of society, Arnold maintains, would benefit from the more competent professionals educated by an improved school system.

In order to administer a sound middle-class educational program, an education minister and a Council of Education should be appointed. Those who serve should be experts on education, not political favorites. Local boards would handle regional concerns. Arnold boldly claims that all schools should come under public supervision, including such hallowed institutions as Rugby, Winchester, and Harrow.

Arnold was asked to make a third journey to the Continent to study elementary education at the end of 1885. He completed his travels in March of 1886 and two months later submitted his comments, published in 1886 as *Education Department: Special Report on Certain Points Connected with Elementary Education in Germany, Switzerland, and France*. In 1888 the report was republished for the public by the Education Reform League, an organization which championed universal education. For this edition, Arnold added a one-page preface in which he summarized his long-standing concerns about popular education, namely that the "existing popular school is far too little formative and humanizing, and that much in it, which its administrators point to as valuable *results,* is in truth mere machinery," and that one of the subjects that ought to be taught in elementary schools is religion because it *is* "a formative influence, an element of culture of the very highest value, and [therefore is] more indispensable in the popular school than in any other."

Throughout the 1860s, Arnold composed less and less poetry. As Riede points out, Arnold struggled unsuccessfully to create an authoritative voice. Though he continued to write poems for the remainder of his life, his career as a poet had essentially ended by the close of the decade. His career as a prosodist, however, was just beginning. In his prose works Arnold pursued many of the same ideas he had introduced in his poems, most notably, man's need for spiritual and intellectual fulfillment in a materialistic, provincial society. Already in his Oxford lectures and in his education reports, Arnold had suggested one solution to man's problems—a liberal education. A liberal education would help man develop his critical faculties and would enrich him culturally. As an essayist, Arnold continued to address the subject of intellectual and spiritual growth.

Arnold won fame with his first collection of essays, *Essays in Criticism* (1865), compiled from lectures and reviews written in 1863 and 1864. The essays cover a wide range of topics, as their individual titles indicate: "Maurice de Guérin," "Eugenie de Guérin," "Heinrich Heine," "Marcus Aurelius," "Spinoza and the Bible," "Joubert," "Pagan and Medieval Religious Sentiment," "The Literary Influence of Academies," and "The Function of Criticism at the Present Time." Despite the seeming diversity of the collection, in a 1956 *PMLA* article Robert Donovan has demonstrated the unity of *Essays in Criticism.* As Donovan explains, all the essays are about French writers or are inspired by Arnold's exposure to French literature and culture; all have as a common theme British insularity and complacency; all use the comparative method of argumentation; and all attempt to prove the value of studying literature. In short, Donovan notes, Arnold's major goal was "to introduce the British Philistine to a new realm of Continental ideas."

Arnold was moved to write "Maurice de Guérin" when a collection of the French writer's works appeared in print in 1860. Guérin had died in 1839 at the age of twenty-eight, having published nothing. George Sand was responsible for bringing his work before the public, and it was through her that Arnold first read the little-known Frenchman. In his essay, Arnold not only praises Guérin's writing but also takes the opportunity to express some of his ideas about literature, more specifically, his theory of poetry. He tells us that "the grand power of poetry is its interpretative power; by which I mean, not a power of drawing out in black and white an explanation of the mystery of the universe, but the power of so dealing with things as to awaken in us a wonderfully full, new, and intimate sense of them, and of our relations with them." Guérin succeeded in this in his prose but not in his verse, for Guérin used the alexandrine, which in Arnold's view was not an adequate "vehicle" for the highest poetry. He would have been better served by hexameters or by blank verse. Guérin's prose, however, is exceptional. It is marked by qualities that are usually assigned to poetry: "a truly interpretative faculty; the most profound and delicate sense of the life of Nature, and the most exquisite felicity in finding expressions to render that sense." Arnold elaborates on the interpretative power of literature, saying it is expressed through both the *"natural magic"* of literature and its *"moral profundity."* Only a few writers, such as Shakespeare and Aeschylus, have mastered both. Most great authors master one or the other. Guérin, for instance, excelled in conveying "natural magic" and for this reason deserves to be read.

Arnold continues his attempt to cultivate appreciation of continental writers among provincial English readers in the essay "Heinrich Heine." For Arnold, the great German poet Heine truly possessed the critical spirit. Heine cherished the French spirit of enlightenment and waged "a life and death battle with Philistinism," the narrowness he saw typified in the British. Arnold acknowledges that Heine's assessment of the British was the true one and tries to explain how the British developed in this way. In the Elizabethan age, claims Arnold, England was open to new ideas, but Puritanism crushed them. The English Romantics failed to reinstitute the critical spirit. Samuel Taylor Coleridge turned to opium; Wordsworth grew introspective; John Keats and Sir Walter Scott failed to "apply modern ideas to life." The German Romantic Heine, however, was able to accomplish what the English Romantics could not. "The wit and ardent modern spirit of France Heine joined to the culture, the sentiment, the thought of Germany." This achievement, despite his personal faults, made him a man of genius.

In his essays Arnold sees not only individual authors but also institutions as potentially upholding the critical spirit. "The Literary Influence of Academies" is devoted to praise of the French Academy, which was established to improve French language and literature. The English, he declares, would do well to establish an institution that would uphold standards of taste and help to offset the "materialism, commercialism, [and] vulgarization" of nineteenth-century life. The English, whose "chief spiritual characteristics" are "energy and honesty," in Arnold's view, can learn much from the French, who are noted for their "openness of mind and flexibility of intelligence." Arnold argues that the "retarding" provincialism of English literature would profit from the influence of a "centre of correct information, correct judgment, [and] correct taste. . . ." Though he recognizes that the English are unlikely ever to form an academy like the one in France, English writers, he concludes, should keep in mind such an institution's noble aims.

All of the *Essays in Criticism* essentially deal with the importance of liberal learning, wide reading, and the development of the critical spirit. But the essay best known for its advocacy of these intellectual habits is "The Function of Criticism at the Present Time," which was originally delivered as a lecture at Oxford in October 1864. Arnold presents in this essay a memorable defense of the critical method. Opening with a reference to Wordsworth's disdain for literary criticism, Arnold agrees that "a false or malicious criticism had better never have been written." Admittedly, "the critical faculty is lower than the inventive," yet criticism does have merit; it too may be creative. Its most important function, however, is to create a climate suitable for the production of great art. Arnold repeats the claim he made in earlier lectures, most notably in "On the Modern Element in Literature," that great art depends on great ideas. Artistic genius "does not principally show itself in discovering new ideas." Instead, it works with ideas that are already "current." Arnold contends that "for the creation of a masterwork of literature two powers must concur, the power of the man and the power of the moment, and the man is not enough without the mo-

ment. . . ." The critical power can create an atmosphere in which art can flourish. In Arnold's words, it can "make the best ideas prevail," for criticism "obeys an instinct prompting it to try to know the best that is known and thought in the world. . . ." It is "disinterested," allowing "a free play of the mind on all subjects. . . ." Only by such wide exposure, only by objectivity, can it arrive at the best ideas.

Criticism is not immediately concerned with the practical. It is concerned with the life of the spirit and the mind. Arnold believed that his own age lacked great ideas. It was too complacent, too self-congratulatory to seek anything higher. Arnold quotes two of his contemporaries for illustration—Sir Charles Adderley declaring the English are "superior to all the world" and John Arthur Roebuck, who is prompted by the Englishman's right "to say what he likes" to exclaim, "I pray that our unrivalled happiness may last." How can it be, wonders Arnold, that this same England—the nation of "unrivalled happiness," the nation superior to the rest of the world—is the same nation in which a wretched girl, identified in the newspapers only by her surname, Wragg, strangles her illegitimate child? Criticism can show man the world as it truly exists. The critical spirit can turn man from self-satisfaction to a pursuit of excellence. The aim of criticism, Arnold explains, "is to keep man from a self-satisfaction which is retarding and vulgarising, to lead him towards perfection, by making his mind dwell upon what is excellent in itself, and the absolute beauty and fitness of things."

Arnold develops this view even more fully in *Culture and Anarchy* (1869). As he indicates throughout his works, both poetry and prose, Arnold saw nineteenth-century England as a nation of mechanism and materialism, a nation in which men were content so long as they had the freedom to do as they pleased; in short, a nation marked by intellectual and spiritual anarchy. From Arnold's perspective, the Englishman was more prone to do than to think, and he was losing sight of the fact that action is of little value unless it is preceded by critical thinking. Arnold believed the solution involved the fostering of culture.

Arnold's second term as poetry chair at Oxford University expired in the summer of 1867, and he decided to use culture as the subject of his final address, a lecture he titled "Culture and Its Enemies." Delivered in June, the talk was published the next month as an essay in the *Cornhill Magazine* and aroused widespread critical disapproval.

In the essay, later included in *Culture and Anarchy,* Arnold continues to wage war against complacency. England, he insists, must not rest satisfied with her accomplishments but must continue to develop, and the method of culture—by which Arnold meant the method of liberal learning and objective, critical thought—can help her to do so. For culture signifies to Arnold the process of "getting to know, on all the matters which most concern us, the best which has been thought and said in the world; and through this knowledge, turning a stream of fresh and free thought upon our stock notions and habits. . . ."

Arnold attempts to show that culture and religion are similar forces, though culture is more comprehensive, having as its concern the development of all aspects of man's being; whereas religion is concerned only with the development of man's spiritual aspect. But the aim of culture, says Arnold, is the same as the aim of religion: "human perfection." And perfection is something one moves *toward.* "Not a having and a resting, but a growing and a becoming, is the character of perfection as culture conceives it; and here, too, it coincides with religion." Culture is a combination of "sweetness," or beauty, and "light," or intelligence, and it strives "To make reason and the will of God prevail."

Arnold's views met with considerable scorn. His readers claimed that he was an elitist, a snob, and they labeled his scheme inadequately developed and impractical. Henry Sidgwick, reviewing "Culture and Its Enemies" for *Macmillan's* magazine, found the essay "over-ambitious, because it treats of the most profound and difficult problems of individual and social life with an airy dogmatism that ignores their depth and difficulty." And in a delightfully witty piece for the *Fortnightly Review,* which Arnold good-naturedly claimed made him laugh until he cried, Frederic Harrison asked, "And now, then, how do you get it [culture]? It is very good to tell me how beautiful this is; but if a physician tells me only what a beautiful thing health is, how happy and strong it makes those who possess it, and omits to tell me how I can gain health, or says only, Be healthy, desire, seek after health, I call him no physician, but a quack." If ever culture could be obtained, some still perceived it as worthless. Many asked what good it was. Sidgwick voiced the opinion of many when he pointed out that Arnold's

criticism of action seemed to stem from the fact that the program he advocated, that of culture, was incapable of any action at all. "Culture," Sidgwick maintained, "is always hinting at a convenient season, that rarely seems to arrive."

Arnold responded to his critics in a series of five essays published in the *Cornhill Magazine* in 1868. The series, entitled "Anarchy and Authority," was collected along with "Culture and Its Enemies" to form *Culture and Anarchy.* In the essay series Arnold continues his championship of culture by stressing the present need for it. He criticizes England for having "a very strong belief in freedom, and a very weak belief in right reason. . . ." To justify his claim, he points out that while an Englishman cherishes his right to do as he likes, it never occurs to him that anyone other than an Englishman, and only a middle- or upper-class Englishman at that, ought to be able to do as he likes. Culture demonstrates such inconsistencies and shows that freedom without right reason leads to anarchy. One significant benefit of culture, therefore, would be that people would come "to like what right reason ordains, and to follow her authority. . . ."

To answer questions such as that posed by Frederic Harrison, Arnold suggests that culture is acquired through education, just as he had suggested in his education reports. Culture, he says, is "an endeavour to come at reason and the will of God by means of reading, observing, and thinking. . . ." Literature is one of the principal agents of culture. Arnold firmly believed in the power of literature to enrich and even to transform human life. He wrote in one version of the preface to *Culture and Anarchy,* "one must, I think, be struck more and more, the longer one lives, to find out how much, in our present society, a man's life of each day depends for its solidity and value on whether he reads during that day, and, far more still, on what he reads during it."

In discussing the three principal social classes in "Anarchy and Authority," Arnold finds each one too self-satisfied, too deficient in light, to be the standard-bearer of culture. The Philistines, or members of the middle class, are more interested in the "machinery of business, chapels, tea-meetings, and addresses" from fellow Philistines than in the pursuit of sweetness and light. The barbarians, or aristocrats, are also unsuitable, for they have always belonged to "an exterior culture" which "consisted principally in outward gifts and graces, in looks, manners, accomplishments, prowess," and are, consequently, lacking in light. The populace, or members of the working class, are as yet "raw and half-developed." Since none of the three social classes is a model of human perfection, the individual is left to pursue "right reason" and, thereby, to cultivate his own "best self."

In an effort to understand why true culture is so alien to modern man, Arnold examines the two major tendencies of human development: Hebraism and Hellenism, or energy and intelligence. "The uppermost idea with Hellenism," explains Arnold, "is to see things as they really are; the uppermost idea with Hebraism is conduct and obedience." Although Hellenism is "full of what we call sweetness and light," both are "*contributions* to human development"; neither is sufficient alone. The two must be balanced within a society and within the individual. But in Victorian England, the balance did not exist. Therefore, "the real *unum necessarium* for us is to come to our best at all points."

Arnold contradicts those who have sneered that culture has no practical purpose. Having stated earlier that the motivating force behind culture is "the noble aspiration to leave the world better and happier than we found it," Arnold generalizes about how this will be accomplished. He applies the method of culture to current controversies about the disestablishment of the Irish Church, the real-estate inheritance laws, the concept of free trade, and the legalization of marriage to one's deceased wife's sister to show that the critical approach espoused by culture will enable men to see things as they really are and to make wise decisions. Therefore, he declares, culture is practical because it endorses "a frame of mind out of which the schemes of really fruitful reforms may with time grow." Arnold is not troubled by the slow pursuit of perfection. In fact, to him it is natural that the achievement of progress will take time. He quotes Johann Wolfgang von Goethe's precept "to act is easy, to think is hard." Arnold is able to look to the future with hope, to a time when "man's two great natural forces, Hebraism and Hellenism, will no longer be dissociated and rival, but will be a joint force of right thinking and strong doing to carry him on towards perfection."

In addition to his espousal of literature and education as agents of culture, Arnold also championed religion as a profound cultural force. He wrote four great religious books: *St. Paul and Protestantism* (1870), *Literature and Dogma* (1873), *God and the Bible* (1875), and *Last Essays on Church and Religion* (1877). Arnold had two major purposes in these books: first, to save the church from the dissolution threatened by scientific inquiry, and second, to demonstrate the need for a unified, national church.

Originally published in the *Cornhill Magazine* as a series of three essays in October and November 1869 and February 1870, *St. Paul and Protestantism* was written, in Arnold's words, "to rescue St. Paul and the Bible from the perversions of them by mistaken men." In the first essay Arnold explains that he is principally concerned with Nonconformist religions such as Calvinism and Methodism that have distorted the teachings of St. Paul by claiming that their doctrines were founded on his writings. Arnold contends that a "critical" reading of St. Paul shows that "What in St. Paul is secondary and subordinate, Puritanism has made primary and essential. . . ." He refers to the Calvinist doctrine of election and to the Methodist doctrine of salvation through faith to demonstrate that the denominations are alike in emphasizing "what God does, with disregard to what man does." Paul, on the other hand, focused on man's righteousness. Furthermore, the Nonconformists drew erroneous conclusions because they ignored the poetic, or metaphorical, quality of biblical language. Often Paul spoke figuratively or rhetorically, yet his words were interpreted literally by those eager to justify "preconceived theories."

In the second essay Arnold develops more fully his argument that St. Paul stressed conduct, not doctrine. The Puritans saw Christ as having sacrificed himself to appease a God angered by man's disobedience, thereby winning man's salvation. But St. Paul saw Christ as a model for others to follow in their daily lives. Arnold insists that Pauline theology was not founded on Puritan beliefs about "*calling, justification, sanctification*" but instead on "*dying with Christ, resurrection from the dead,* [and] *growing into Christ.*" Paul believed in both physical and spiritual resurrection, but his emphasis was on the spiritual. According to Arnold, by death Paul meant spiritual death, or "living in sin." The individual must imitate Christ and say "no" to sin, thereby effecting his own "resurrection to *righteousness*" in this life rather than assuming salvation will be his in a life to come.

Arnold presents his concern for religious unity in the third essay. The fragmentation of the Christian church distressed Arnold as it had his father. Arnold hoped that if he adequately demonstrated the weak foundation of Puritan denominations he could help to effect a return of the Nonconformists to the Church of England. The essay states Arnold's belief that the church has to meet the changing needs of the people it serves. The nineteenth-century church itself, he argues, has to change. Because the doctrine of the Church of England has remained open, whereas those of the dissenting churches have been narrow and restrictive, he concludes that the Anglican church "is more serviceable than Puritanism to religious progress...." Arnold reminds his readers that "the Church exists, not for the sake of opinions, but for the sake of moral practice, and a united endeavour after this is stronger than a broken one." In other words, a unified church is more conducive to "collective growth."

A fourth essay, entitled "Modern Dissent," was written to serve as the preface for the publication of *St. Paul and Protestantism* in book form in April 1870. In it Arnold answers the criticisms already voiced by the readers of the serial version of the work. Attacked for his presumption in presenting his views as the "right" ones, Arnold says that his ideas are neither new nor his alone. Asserting that his interpretation of St. Paul is a reflection of the "Zeit-Geist," he insists that: "it is in the air, and many have long been anticipating it. ..." In addition he points out that, unlike the Puritans who claim to possess truth, *the* Gospel, he admits that his "conception" of St. Paul's writings is an evolving one that tends toward truth, but does not pretend to be conclusive. Arnold maintains that he is disinterested; his "greatest care is neither for the Church nor for Puritanism, but for human perfection."

Still, as Ruth Roberts shows in *Arnold and God* (1983), Arnold is guilty of "overingenuity." His argument is not so disinterested as he claims. He often glosses over biblical passages inconsistent with his position. For Arnold, the Bible was literature and must be read as such. What he offers in *St. Paul and Protestantism* is, according to Roberts, "a literary analysis of Scripture." Predictably, this approach elicited objections from many readers. As Super points out, *St. Paul and Protestantism* is a direct development of the arguments presented in *Culture and Anarchy*. Arnold's contemporaries certainly recognized it as such and adopted the phrases made famous by that earlier work in their responses to this most recent one. An anonymous reviewer for the July 1870 issue of the *British Quarterly Review* wrote that "in Mr.

Arnold's culture, perhaps in his nature, the Hellenic element is too exclusive; the Hebraic has scarcely any place. In all that he writes, the purely intellectual predominates over the emotional and spiritual. ... Thus theology is to him merely a system of ethical ideas, and the Church merely a machinery for their culture—a national organization for the comprehension and good order of citizens of all varieties of theological belief." In his book *Culture and Religion* (1870), J. C. Shairp, a contemporary of Arnold's, argued that "They who seek religion for culture-sake are aesthetic, not religious. ..." The same charge was later echoed by T. S. Eliot in *The Use of Poetry and The Use of Criticism* (1933). Eliot found that Arnold had confused "poetry and morals in the attempt to find a substitute for religious faith."

Convinced of the merits of his argument, however, Arnold persisted in defending his case. Of *Literature and Dogma*, his second major work on religion, and by far the best known, Arnold said, "I think it, of all my books in prose, the one most important (if I may say so) and most capable of being useful." Following his earlier practice, *Literature and Dogma* appeared first in the *Cornhill Magazine* in serial installments and was later published as a book. The public must have agreed with Arnold's assessment of the importance of his work. Attesting to its popularity, Mudie's library bought copies for circulation; a less expensive, abridged "popular" edition was printed in 1883; and by 1924 sales of all editions had reached twenty-one thousand copies.

In Arnold's words, "The object of *Literature and Dogma* is to re-assure those who feel attachment to Christianity, to the Bible, but who recognise the growing discredit befalling miracles and the supernatural" because of the influence of science. Arnold sets out to discover, using the method of culture, the "real experimental basis" of the Bible rather than operating from a "basis of unverifiable assumptions." Only culture can supply a valid interpretation of the Bible. In order to be a wise interpreter of the Bible, one must be widely read. According to Arnold, if one knows only the Bible, he does not really know even that. He concedes that applying a critical approach to biblical interpretation is very difficult because we have come to view the Bible "as a sort of talisman given down to us out of Heaven." This inherited assumption makes it even more essential to apply the disinterested critical approach of culture. For, says Arnold, "To understand that the language of the Bible is fluid, passing, and literary, not rigid, fixed, and scientific, is the first step towards a right understanding of the Bible." In Arnold's opinion, as summarized by Basil Willey in *Nineteenth-Century Studies* (1949), it is a "false approach to the Bible which seeks to extract dogma from poetry."

Arnold reminds the readers of *Literature and Dogma* that the Bible is literature, and that biblical terms are literary terms. Even a term such as *God* cannot justifiably be used as if it were a scientific designation with a precise definition. Theologians have aimed at precision by defining God as "the great first cause, the moral and intelligent governor of the universe," when, in fact, such a definition cannot be verified. Instead, Arnold proposes to describe God "scientifically" as "the *not ourselves* which makes for righteousness," as "*the stream of tendency by which all things seek to fulfil the law of their being. . . .*" He admits that these definitions are inadequate, but, in his view, they express all that can be known for certain. While he doubts man's ability to describe satisfactorily the true nature of God, Arnold does not doubt God's existence. He maintains that God's existence is proven—not by the existence of the physical world or by other such tangible evidence—but by man's conscience, which is the guide to God's law. "The idea of *God,* as it is given us in the Bible, rests, we say, not on a metaphysical conception of the necessity of certain deductions from our ideas of cause, existence, identity, and the like; but on a moral perception of a rule of conduct not of our own making, into which we are born, and which exists whether we will or no; of awe at its grandeur and necessity, and of gratitude at its beneficence." All experience proves that God exists. There is something in man that urges him to fulfill the law of his being and that makes him happy when he does so. God is made manifest when man resists the temptation to give in to "the blind momentary impulses" of his weak nature and is subsequently "thrilled with gratitude, devotion, and awe, at the sense of joy and peace, not of his own making, which followed the exercise of this self-control. . . ."

The object of religion is conduct, and conduct, Arnold argues in *Literature and Dogma,* is three-fourths of life. Religion should become "personal," should make us care deeply about conduct. For Arnold, "the true meaning of religion is thus, not simply *morality,* but *morality touched by emotion.*" This was the message of Jesus Christ. Arnold believed that religion had been weakened by the addition of *aberglaube,* or "extra-belief," to

what is provable. These extra beliefs in events such as the Resurrection of Christ or the Virgin Birth undermine religious truth and, for some, become more important than morality, which is the essence of religion.

Arnold asserts that extra belief in and of itself is not harmful and can even be beneficial if it helps one improve his conduct, but eventually the realization will come that there is no proof to support extra belief, and Arnold fears "then the whole certainty of religion seems discredited, and the basis of conduct gone." This is the danger inherent in overemphasizing what cannot be substantiated. Ultimately, religious doubt and uncertainty cannot be avoided. For Arnold, it is "the Time-Spirit which is sapping the proof from miracles,—it is the 'Zeit-Geist' itself." Explaining that the nineteenth century is a questioning age, a scientific age, Arnold concludes that there is no proof of the supernatural events the Bible records. Jesus' miracles were recorded by others; those who reported his actions were merely men, and therefore, fallible. Since most church dogma is founded on an acceptance of the miraculous, many traditional tenets of Christianity have been weakened. But Arnold tells his readers that this is only because the church has drifted so far from the original aims of Christ. "Jesus never troubled himself with what are called Church matters at all. . . ." He dealt with experience, not with theory. Moreover, according to Arnold, there is practically no dogma in the Bible itself. The religious doctrine that it does contain can be summarized by two pronouncements: in the Old Testament, "Obey God!" and in the New Testament, "Follow Jesus!" Arnold asks, "Walking on the water, multiplying loaves, raising corpses, a heavenly judge appearing with trumpets in the clouds while we are yet alive,—what is this compared to the real experience offered as witness to us by Christianity? It is like the difference between the grandeur of an extravaganza and the grandeur of the sea or the sky." Arnold closes, "The more we trace the real law of Christianity's action the grander it will seem."

It was to be expected that *Literature and Dogma* would stir even more controversy than had *St. Paul and Protestantism.* Understandably, many of Arnold's critics were clergymen. John Tulloch, a clergyman reviewing the 1873 volume for *Blackwood's* magazine, was not alone in accusing Arnold of dabbling in "amateur theology." It is true that Arnold was not a theologian, but he did know the Bible. As Roberts points out in *Ar-*

H. Weigall's portrait of Arnold in The Athenæum, London

nold and God, the notebooks Arnold kept from 1852 to 1888 record his reading lists and are filled with quotations from the Bible, in fact with more quotations from the Bible than from any other source. And Arnold had thought long and deeply about his views. Nevertheless, he was stirred to even wider reading and more extensive research in preparation for writing *God and the Bible,* since he conceived it as "a review of objections" to *Literature and Dogma.*

In *God and the Bible* Arnold renews his commitment to making the Bible accessible. "All disquisitions about the Bible seem to us to be faulty and even ridiculous which have for their result that the Bible is less felt, followed, and enjoyed after them than it was before them." Arnold's sole aim is to help the reader *"to enjoy the Bible and to turn it to his benefit."*

In the first three chapters—"The God of Miracles," "The God of Metaphysics," and "The God of Experience"—Arnold justifies the definition of God which he offered in *Literature and Dogma.* He repeats his claims that his definition of God

as *"The Eternal, not ourselves, that makes for righteousness"* is verifiable and that a verifiable definition of God is essential for reading the Bible, a book in which "God is everything." In response to criticism of his refusal to profess belief in a personal God, in other words, a God "who thinks and loves," Arnold says he is unable to affirm or deny this notion of God and, thus, is more comfortable with a verifiable definition.

In three subsequent chapters, "The Bible Canon," "The Fourth Gospel from Without," and "The Fourth Gospel from Within," Arnold discusses current controversy about the biblical canon and the Gospel of John. The resolution of these controversies is "unessential" for enjoyment and appreciation of the Bible, but because some Bible readers ascribe undue importance to such questions, Arnold feels a disinterested appraisal is in order. His critical examination reveals that the positions taken by both popular religion and higher German criticism on these controversies are devoid of light. Both are extremist. Puritans ask no questions and without hesitation accept the Bible as truth while the higher German critics ask too many questions and mislead their followers by presuming that all questions can be answered. In Arnold's view, although there is not enough evidence to ascertain whether the Bible is literally true or false, the absence of certainty should not force one into either blind acceptance or debilitating doubt. "We should do Christians generally a great injustice," Arnold writes, "if we thought that the entire force of their Christianity lay in the fascination and subjugation of their spirits by the miracles which they suppose Jesus to have worked, or by the materialistic promises of heaven which they suppose him to have offered. Far more does the vital force of their Christianity lie in the boundless confidence, consolation, and attachment, which the whole being and discourse of Jesus inspire." Arnold describes his effort in his religious works as "an attempt conservative, and an attempt religious." He assures the reader that he has written "to convince the lover of religion that by following habits of intellectual seriousness he need not, so far as religion is concerned, lose anything."

The year 1877 saw publication of Arnold's *Last Essays on Church and Religion,* a collection of four essays, two of which had originally appeared in the *Contemporary* and two of which had first been published in *Macmillan's* magazine. Arnold was sincere in labeling these papers his "last" words on the subject. At the end of one of the essays, "The Church of England," he explains that he had originally pursued the topic of religion because he had witnessed the damaging effects of dogma and dissent on national religion. "However," he continues, "as one grows old, one feels that it is not one's business to go on for ever expostulating with other people upon their waste of life, but to make progress in grace and peace oneself." Of the four essays in the volume, "The Church of England" and "A Psychological Parallel" are the most important.

In "The Church of England," presented as a lecture before an audience of clergymen at Sion College in 1876, Arnold seeks to explain how it is possible for him to condemn Christian doctrine and yet be an Anglican. His support for the church derives from his view of it as "a great national society for the promotion of what is commonly called *goodness* . . . through the means of the Christian religion and of the Bible." Promoting goodness is the true "object of the Church" and the true "business of the clergy." The basis of religion and the mission of the church are the improvement of conduct, not the promulgation of doctrine. Just as in *God and the Bible*, Arnold insists that men cannot do without Christianity, but "they cannot do with it as it is."

Arnold points out that many working-class people are turning from the Anglican Church because it has failed to support social reform. Clergymen have supplied physical aid to the oppressed but have not shown "a positive sympathy with popular ideals." Instead, the Church is perceived as "an appendage to the Barbarians . . . favouring immobility, preaching submission, and reserving transformation in general for the other side of the grave." Such a position not only alienates the masses from the church, but also alienates the church itself from the true ideals of the active Christian faith as presented in the Bible. "The church of England" ends with the reassurance that the Anglican church "by opening itself to the glow of the old and true ideal of the Christian Gospel, by fidelity to reason, by placing the stress of its religion on goodness, by cultivating grace and peace . . . will inspire attachment . . ." and will endure.

"A Psychological Parallel," is, according to Roberts, "a comprehensive reprise" of Arnold's religious works, for in this essay Arnold contends that whether one accepts or denies the supernatural in religion, one can still be a Christian and a supporter of the church. Arnold first explores the possibility that a man such as St. Paul may be-

lieve in the miraculous and still not be "an imbecile or credulous enthusiast." Arnold compares the belief of St. Paul in "the bodily resurrection of Jesus" to the belief of Sir Matthew Hale, the eminent seventeenth-century judge, in the existence of witches. These "parallel" cases demonstrate that a man may be psychologically influenced by the intellectual atmosphere of the times in which he lives; in other words, by the zeitgeist. Consequently, he "may have his mind thoroughly governed, on certain subjects, by a foregone conclusion as to what is likely and credible." Just as it was commonplace in the seventeenth century to believe in witchcraft, it was commonplace in St. Paul's day to believe in such events as the physical resurrection of the body after death. Arnold explains, "That a man shares an error of the minds around him and of the times in which he lives, proves nothing against his being a man of veracity, judgment, and mental power."

Arnold considers next the possibility that a man may not believe the miraculous and still support the church. He points out that though the zeitgeist of the nineteenth century has caused many Victorians to doubt the literal truth of church teachings, this uncertainty should not prevent their belonging to the church. They must remember that the church is first and foremost "a national Christian society for the promotion of goodness," and they should support it as such. Arnold asserts that the church's emphasis on dogma should be relaxed. He goes so far as to argue that clergymen should not be required to subscribe to the Thirty-nine Articles, for he suspects there are many who cannot profess acceptance of all thirty-nine statements who would nevertheless be committed ministers to the true message of Christianity. Yet Arnold contends that the Book of Common Prayer should be retained because for the masses of Englishmen, "It has created sentiments deeper than we can see or measure. Our feeling does not connect itself with *any* language about righteousness and religion, but with *that* language." In that sense, the prayer book is like the Bible. And Arnold advocates using it as one would use the Bible—accepting the literal truth of part and reading the rest as the poetic "approximations to a profound truth." Arnold concludes, "It is a great error to think that whatever is thus perceived to be poetry ceases to be available in religion. The noblest races are those which know how to make the most serious use of poetry."

Having abandoned the subject of religion after completing his *Last Essays on Church and Reli-*

gion, Arnold focused his writing during the last ten to twelve years of his life on social and literary topics, offering more elaborate or definitive statements of his views on matters that had long held great interest for him. For instance, Super has said of "A French Critic on Milton" from *Mixed Essays* (1879), "As an essay on critical method, it stands in much the same relation to Arnold's later critical essays as 'The Function of Criticism' [does] to the earlier." Just as "The Function of Criticism" instructs man in the application of the critical approach to all aspects of life, "A French Critic on Milton" instructs the reader in the application of the critical approach to the evaluation of literature. Arnold sets about explaining the critical method by comparing several critics of Milton. He dismisses Thomas Babington Macaulay's "Essay on Milton" as popular "rhetoric," as nothing more than a "panegyric" on Milton and the Puritans. He discards Joseph Addison's criticism of Milton as a compilation of conventional platitudes. He also finds Samuel Johnson unsatisfactory as a critic of Milton. Though he avoids the rhetoric and conventionality of Macaulay and Addison, Johnson is not "sufficiently disinterested" or "sufficiently receptive" to judge fairly. However, in Arnold's view there has been an admirable judge of Milton—the French critic Edmond Scherer, who is "Well-informed, intelligent, disinterested, open-minded, [and] sympathetic." Scherer noted the weaknesses of Milton as a man and as an artist. His views were not influenced by Milton's avowed religious convictions or by the religious subjects of his poems. Especially satisfying to Arnold is Scherer's recognition of Milton's "true distinction as a poet"—the greatness of his style. Arnold is convinced that this is the conclusion to which a sensitive yet impartial criticism necessarily leads.

Many of Arnold's other late essays also deal with literature, and more specifically, with sound criticism of literature. The best known of his later collections is *Essays in Criticism: Second Series,* which Arnold began discussing with his publisher in January 1888, but which was not actually printed until November 1888, seven months after Arnold's death. The volume includes nine essays: "The Study of Poetry," "Wordsworth," "Thomas Gray," "John Keats," "Byron," "Amiel," "Count Leo Tolstoi," "Shelley," and "Milton." One of the most important, "The Study of Poetry," first appeared in 1880 as the introduction to *The English Poets,* an anthology edited by T. Humphry Ward. Super reminds the reader that the essay was intended "to give some guidance to a middle-class public not sophisticated in the reading of poetry. . . ." In an opening explanation of the value of literature, Arnold makes grand claims for poetry, saying "we have to turn to poetry to interpret life for us, to console us, to sustain us." In other words, poetry meets the same human needs as religion. Of course, only the best poetry accomplishes so much: "poetry, to be capable of fulfilling such high destinies, must be poetry of a high order of excellence." But "the best poetry will be found to have a power of forming, sustaining, and delighting us, as nothing else can."

Because poetry has so much to offer, Arnold continues, the reader must have some way to recognize the finest poetry. Neither a purely historical nor a purely personal critical method will serve, since each is too biased. Arnold proposes instead a comparative method by which the reader will always have in mind "lines and expressions of the great masters" that he may apply "as a touchstone to other poetry" to help him detect "the presence or absence of high poetic quality, and also the degree of this quality." Arnold maintains that the greatness of poetry is revealed in both substance and style. The substance of great poetry may be recognized by its "truth and seriousness" and the style of great poetry by its "superiority of diction and movement." Beyond these general assertions, Arnold refuses to define, arguing that concrete examples of exceptional poetry will be more helpful than abstract theory or lists of characteristics. He offers a critical overview of the history of English poetry sprinkled with illustrative lines and passages to demonstrate the touchstone method. Arnold begins with Chaucer, whose poetry he deems superior in substance and style, or, to be more exact, in the rich view of human life it presents and in the "divine liquidness of diction" and "divine fluidity of movement" of its manner. These traits make Chaucer "the father of our splendid English poetry"; nevertheless, he does not attain the level of "one of the great classics." Though his poetry has truth, it lacks "high seriousness."

Acknowledging that both Shakespeare and Milton unquestionably belong "to the class of the very best," Arnold moves on to consider the merits of more controversial poets—those of the eighteenth century. In Arnold's estimation, John Dryden and Alexander Pope are masters of prose rather than verse, for the characteristics of their style, "regularity, uniformity, precision,

[and] balance," produce classic prose, not classic poetry. In a separate essay, "Thomas Gray," Arnold maintains that "The difference between genuine poetry and the poetry of Dryden, Pope, and all their school, is briefly this: their poetry is conceived and composed in their wits, genuine poetry is conceived and composed in the soul." "The Study of Poetry" concludes with a discussion of the works of Robert Burns and Thomas Gray. In Arnold's opinion, Burns fails to achieve greatness for much the same reasons Chaucer fails. Like Chaucer, Burns depicts the largeness of life, but he, too, lacks high seriousness. Gray, on the other hand, is a classic—the only eighteenth-century English classic, Arnold thinks. Arnold credits him with achieving such eminence because he gave himself up to a study of the Greeks, absorbing the qualities of exceptional poetry from them.

"The Study of Poetry" no more remained unchallenged than had any of Arnold's other works. Many, including contemporary critics, have disagreed with Arnold's choice of touchstone passages, and many have taken offense at Arnold's pronouncements about the merits of individual authors. Despite such objections, the essay remains an important piece of criticism historically and an important guide to Arnold's own tastes.

The other essays from the *Essays in Criticism: Second Series* that are especially noteworthy are those about the Romantic poets. While Arnold was fully aware of the limitations of purely personal criticism, his assessments of writers did involve some personal commentary. Such subjective evaluations surface in his essays on the Romantics. Coleridge is referred to as a genius "wrecked in a mist of opium," and Shelley is described as a "beautiful and ineffectual angel, beating in the void his luminous wings in vain." In fact, Shelley more than the others troubled Arnold. When Edward Dowden's two-volume biography of the poet was published in 1886, Arnold found the poet's life so scandalous that he claimed the biography should never have been written. Arnold's objections were not restricted to questions of perceived immorality though; he also faulted authors for what he thought to be unattractive character traits. Keats, for example, Arnold considered effusive. He seemed a "sensuous man of a badly bred and badly trained sort" who virtually allowed himself to die young, "having produced too little and being as yet too immature" to achieve greatness. Despite his aversion to some of

their personal qualities, Arnold tried to examine writers' works objectively. Thus, although he considers Keats an immature poet, Arnold commends Keats's celebration of beauty and judges him Shakespeare's equal in the creation of "natural magic" in his poems.

The two Romantics Arnold holds in highest esteem are George Gordon, Lord Byron and Wordsworth, both of whom had failed to receive the serious appreciation Arnold thought they deserved. For some reason, Arnold was able to gloss over Byron's sins though he could not overlook Shelley's. He praises Byron at length for his stand on social injustice. In regard to Byron's poems, he shows special fondness for the shorter pieces and for select sections from the longer works, claiming he "has a wonderful power of vividly conceiving a single incident, a single situation. . . ." Arnold likewise asserts that Wordsworth's best poems are his shorter ones. He considers "Michael" and "The Highland Reaper" poems which afford "a criticism of life," far superior to "philosophical" poems such as *The Excursion* and *The Prelude*. Arnold declares, "Wordsworth's poetry is great because of the extraordinary power with which Wordsworth feels the joy offered to us in nature, the joy offered to us in the simple primary affections and duties; and because of the extraordinary power with which, in case after case, he shows us this joy, and renders it so as to make us share it." For these reasons, Arnold ranks Wordsworth only after Shakespeare, Molière, Milton, and Goethe in his list of the premier poets of "the last two or three centuries."

Of the other pieces Arnold wrote on literature in the last decade of his life, the major one was an essay entitled "Literature and Science." In the autumn of 1880 Thomas Henry Huxley, noted proponent of science and a friend of Arnold's, had presented a lecture in Birmingham on the necessity for scientific knowledge. That address was subsequently published in Huxley's *Science and Culture, and Other Essays* (1881). In it he argues against Arnold's notion that the agent of true culture is humanistic education. Huxley claims, "for the purpose of attaining real culture, an exclusively scientific education is at least as effectual as an exclusively literary education."

"Literature and Science" was Arnold's reply, given as a lecture at Cambridge in June 1882 and published two months later in the *Nineteenth-Century*. In 1883 Arnold delivered the lecture twenty-nine times to eager audiences in the

United States. Arnold is quick to clarify at the beginning of his remarks that in his lifelong insistence on a broad, liberal, classical education and in his advocacy of knowing the best that has been thought and said, he has not meant to suggest that science should be ignored. As Fred A. Dudley points out in a 1942 *PMLA* article, Arnold thought training in science would teach people perception and open-mindedness, qualities he valued highly. Therefore, education should include the study of both science and belles lettres, in Arnold's opinion. Still, in the lecture, he disagrees with Huxley that science is just as valuable in transmitting culture as literature. The study of science, argues Arnold, satisfies only one of the demands of human nature—the need for knowledge. And knowledge in isolation does not fill the needs of the human spirit. According to Arnold, unless knowledge is "put for us into relation with our sense for conduct, our sense for beauty, and touched with emotion by being so put," it will become "to the majority of mankind, after a certain while, unsatisfying, wearying." Literature, both classical and modern, provides the requisite synthesis of knowledge to conduct and beauty. It has "a fortifying, and elevating, and quickening, and suggestive power, capable of wonderfully helping us to relate the results of modern science to our need for conduct, our need for beauty." In that respect, the humanities are not "mainly decorative." Therefore, while men should know both science and literature, Arnold concludes that if one has to choose between the two, he had best choose literature. He acknowledges that the value of studying the classics and belles lettres in general is presently being questioned, yet he predicts, "they will not lose their place. What will happen will rather be that there will be crowded into education other matters besides, far too many; there will be, perhaps, a period of unsettlement and confusion and false tendency; but letters will not in the end lose their leading place. If they lose it for a time, they will get it back again. We will be brought back to them by our wants and aspirations."

In addition to literature, Arnold's later works often treat social topics. In his preface to *Mixed Essays* (1879), Arnold explains that while the essays treat a wide range of subjects they are unified by their concern with the broader subject of civilization. Literature is one aspect of civilization, but only one. Arnold maintains that although literature is "a powerful agency for benefiting the world and for civilising it . . . literature

is a part of civilisation; it is not the whole." Repeating ideas first presented in his lecture "Equality" (February 1878), he defines civilization as "the humanisation of man in society," accomplished primarily by the human need for expansion which manifests itself in the love of liberty and the love of equality. Beyond this, civilization must satisfy man's need for conduct, for intellect and knowledge, for beauty, and for manners. Arnold's social essays examine the success of both England and the United States in fulfilling these needs.

"The Future of Liberalism" (collected in *Irish Essays, and Others,* 1882) provides an elaboration of Arnold's assessment of civilization in Victorian England. Ever critical of the middle class, Arnold asserts that the greatest threat to the future of the Liberal party is its base in Philistinism, for, says Arnold, the Liberals "lean especially upon the opinion of one great class,—the middle class,—with virtues of its own, indeed, but at the same time full of narrowness, full of prejudices; with a defective type of religion, a narrow range of intellect and knowledge, a stunted sense of beauty, a low standard of manners; and averse, moreover, to whatever may disturb it in its vulgarity." In other words, the middle class is virtually uncivilized and will remain so until forced to confront its imperfections. Even with its Philistine foundation, the Liberal party in fostering love of liberty has a more promising future than the Conservatives, who are primarily concerned with keeping order. In order to retain power and influence, the Liberals must not rest satisfied; they must recognize man's continual need for expansion and must work diligently to alleviate the social and political inequality which has resulted in "an upper class materialised, a middle class vulgarised, a lower class brutalised."

Because Arnold perceives Americans to be merely "English people on the other side of the Atlantic," he attributes to American society many of the same weaknesses he notes in British society. American civilization is the topic of "A Word About America," published in the *Nineteenth-Century* in 1882. In this essay Arnold observes that a significant difference between England and the United States is that democracy is more advanced in the United States, leaving fewer citizens members of the barbarian and populace classes. Assuming then that the Philistines comprise "the great bulk of the nation," Arnold suggests for America the same civilizing agents he has repeatedly recommended for the British—improved schools and improved arts.

At the time Arnold wrote "A Word About America," he had never visited the United States, but a year later, in 1883, having received an invitation from the Pittsburgh iron magnate Andrew Carnegie, Arnold, accompanied by his wife and daughter Lucy, sailed to America. The six months spent there were hectic ones, for Arnold was engaged in an extensive and demanding lecture tour in the course of which he met William Dean Howells, Oliver Wendell Holmes, John Greenleaf Whittier, and Mark Twain. Lucy also made new acquaintances, including Frederick Whitridge, whom she married a year later. His daughter's move to New York motivated Arnold to make another trip to the United States just after he retired from school inspecting in May 1886.

Thus Arnold had paid two extended visits to America when he lectured on "Life in America" in January 1888. His remarks, published in April in the *Nineteenth-Century* under the title "Civilisation in the United States," reflect little change in the position he had outlined six years earlier. Arnold argues that while Americans have established a laudable democratic social system and have proven successful in commerce and industry, they have not cultivated beauty. Arnold cites the inferiority of American architecture, painting, and literature as evidence. Even American place names such as Briggsville, Higginsville, and Jacksonville indicate to him an inadequate national regard for the beautiful. He contends, "The Americans have produced plenty of men strong, shrewd, upright, able, effective; [but] very few who are highly distinguished." This situation is hardly surprising, since the democratic system with its "glorification of 'the average man'" makes distinction rare. Arnold is convinced of the value of heritage and established culture and says that Americans apparently desire it, since "all Americans of cultivation and wealth visit Europe more and more constantly." Arnold summarizes: "The human problem, then, is as yet solved in the United States most imperfectly; a great void exists in the civilisation over there: a want of what is elevated and beautiful, of what is interesting."

"Civilisation in the United States" was the last essay by Matthew Arnold to be published in his lifetime. He died of a heart attack on 15 April 1888. John Holloway's remarks on Arnold's style and rhetorical technique in his 1953 book

The Victorian Sage provide a fitting summary of Arnold's prose. Holloway points out that Arnold "had no rigid doctrines to argue for, only attitudes." He argued for the cultivation of "certain habits and a certain temper of mind." Arnold, quite naturally, set himself as a model. It was essential that he present himself as the kind of person he most admired—"intelligent, modest, and urbane." As Holloway observes, in Arnold's prose, it is "his handling of problems" that is more important than his solutions to them. One of Arnold's contemporaries, John Burroughs, writing two months after Arnold's death, claimed that Matthew Arnold deserved to be read extensively, for only then could he be fully appreciated. In the prose, "His effect is cumulative; he hits a good many times in the same place, and his work as a whole makes a deeper impression than any single essay of his would seem to warrant." The modern reader will still find much to savor in the prose of Matthew Arnold.

Letters:

Letters of Matthew Arnold, 1848-1888, 2 volumes, edited by G. W. E. Russell (London: Macmillan, 1895);

Unpublished Letters of Matthew Arnold, edited by Arnold Whitridge (New Haven: Yale University Press, 1923);

The Letters of Matthew Arnold to Arthur Hugh Clough, edited by H. F. Lowry (London & New York: Oxford University Press, 1932);

Matthew Arnold's Letters: A Descriptive Checklist, edited by A. K. Davis, Jr. (Charlottesville: University Press of Virginia, 1968).

Bibliographies:

Thomas B. Smart, *Bibliography of Matthew Arnold* (London: Davy, 1892);

Theodore G. Ehrsam, Robert H. Deily, and Robert M. Smith, eds., *Bibliographies of Twelve Victorian Authors* (New York: Wilson, 1936);

Vincent L. Tollers, ed., *A Bibliography of Matthew Arnold, 1932-1970* (University Park: Pennsylvania State University Press, 1974).

Biographies:

George Saintsbury, *Matthew Arnold* (New York: Dodd, Mead, 1899);

Lionel Trilling, *Matthew Arnold* (New York: Meridian Books, 1939);

E. K. Chambers, *Matthew Arnold: A Study* (Oxford: Clarendon Press, 1947);

A. L. Rowse, *Matthew Arnold: Poet and Prophet* (London: Thames & Hudson, 1976);

Park Honan, *Matthew Arnold, A Life* (New York: McGraw-Hill, 1981).

References:

Warren D. Anderson, *Matthew Arnold and the Classical Tradition* (Ann Arbor: University of Michigan Press, 1965);

Josephine Barry, "Goethe and Arnold's 1853 Preface," *Comparative Literature,* 32 (Spring 1980): 151-167;

E. K. Brown, *Matthew Arnold: A Study in Conflict* (Toronto & Chicago: University of Chicago Press, 1948);

William Buckler, ed., *Matthew Arnold's Books: Towards a Publishing Diary* (Geneva: Droz Press, 1958);

Buckler, *Matthew Arnold's Prose: Three Essays in Literary Enlargement* (New York: A.M.S. Press, 1983);

Buckler, "Studies in Three Arnold Problems," *PMLA,* 73 (1958): 260-269;

Vincent Buckley, *Poetry and Morality: Studies on the Criticism of Matthew Arnold, T. S. Eliot, and F. R. Leavis* (London: Chatto & Windus, 1959);

Douglas Bush, *Matthew Arnold: A Survey of His Poetry and Prose* (New York: Macmillan, 1971);

Joseph Carroll, *The Cultural Theory of Matthew Arnold* (Berkeley: University of California Press, 1982);

W. F. Connell, *The Educational Thought and Influence of Matthew Arnold* (London: Routledge & Kegan Paul, 1950);

Sidney Coulling, *Matthew Arnold and His Critics: A Study of Arnold's Controversies* (Athens: Ohio University Press, 1974);

A. Dwight Culler, *The Imaginative Reason: The Poetry of Matthew Arnold* (New Haven: Yale University Press, 1966);

Carl Dawson and John Pfordresher, eds., *Matthew Arnold: Prose Writings* (London: Routledge & Kegan Paul, 1979);

David J. DeLaura, *Hebrew and Hellene in Victorian England* (Austin: University of Texas Press, 1969);

DeLaura, "Matthew Arnold," in *Victorian Prose: A Guide to Research,* edited by DeLaura (New York: Modern Language Association, 1973), pp. 249-320;

Robert Donovan, "The Method of Arnold's *Essays in Criticism,*" *PMLA,* 71 (December 1956): 922-931;

Fred A. Dudley, "Matthew Arnold and Science," *PMLA,* 57 (March 1942): 275-294;

T. S. Eliot, "Matthew Arnold," in his *The Use of Poetry and the Use of Criticism* (London: Faber & Faber, 1933), pp. 103-120;

Frederic E. Faverty, "Matthew Arnold," in *The Victorian Poets: A Guide to Research,* edited by Faverty (Cambridge, Mass.: Harvard University Press, 1968), pp. 164-226;

Faverty, *Matthew Arnold the Ethnologist* (Evanston, Ill.: Northwestern University Press, 1951);

"The Function of Matthew Arnold at the Present Time," a series of essays by Eugene Goodheart, George Levine, Morris Dickstein, and Stuart M. Tave published as part of a special issue of *Critical Inquiry,* 9 (March 1983);

Leon Gottfried, *Matthew Arnold and the Romantics* (London: Routledge & Kegan Paul, 1963);

W. B. Guthrie, ed., *Matthew Arnold's Diaries: The Unpublished Items* (Ann Arbor: University of Michigan Press, 1959);

John Holloway, "Matthew Arnold," in his *The Victorian Sage* (London: Macmillan, 1953), pp. 202-243;

E. D. H. Johnson, *The Alien Vision of Victorian Poetry: Sources of the Poetic Imagination in Tennyson, Browning, and Arnold* (Princeton: Princeton University Press, 1952);

James C. Livingston, *Matthew Arnold and Christianity: His Religious Prose Writings* (Columbia: University of South Carolina Press, 1986);

Clinton Machann and Forrest D. Burt, eds., *Matthew Arnold in His Time and Ours* (Charlottesville: University Press of Virginia, 1988);

William A. Madden, *A Study of the Aesthetic Temperament in Victorian England* (Bloomington: Indiana University Press, 1967);

Patrick J. McCarthy, *Matthew Arnold and the Three Classes* (New York: Columbia University Press, 1964);

J. Hillis Miller, "Matthew Arnold," in his *The Disappearance of God* (Cambridge, Mass.: Harvard University Press, 1963), pp. 212-269;

Fraser Neiman, *Matthew Arnold* (New York: Twayne, 1968);

David G. Riede, *Matthew Arnold and the Betrayal of Language* (Charlottesville: University Press of Virginia, 1988);

William Robbins, *The Ethical Idealism of Matthew Arnold: A Study of the Nature and Sources of His Moral and Religious Ideas* (Toronto: University of Toronto Press, 1959);

Ruth Roberts, *Arnold and God* (Berkeley: University of California Press, 1983);

Alan Roper, *Arnold's Poetic Landscapes* (Baltimore: Johns Hopkins University Press, 1969);

James Simpson, *Matthew Arnold and Goethe* (London: Modern Humanities Research Association, 1979);

G. Robert Stange, *Matthew Arnold: The Poet as Humanist* (Princeton: Princeton University Press, 1967);

Robert H. Super, *The Time-Spirit of Matthew Arnold* (Ann Arbor: University of Michigan Press, 1970);

Kathleen Tillotson, "Arnold and Carlyle," *Proceedings of the British Academy,* 42 (1956): 133-153;

C. B. Tinker and H. F. Lowry, *The Poetry of Matthew Arnold: A Commentary* (London & New York: Oxford University Press, 1940);

Victorian Poetry, special double issue on the centennial of Matthew Arnold, 26 (Spring-Summer 1988);

Basil Willey, *Nineteenth-Century Studies: Coleridge to Matthew Arnold* (London: Chatto & Windus, 1949);

Raymond Williams, *Culture and Society, 1780-1950* (New York: Columbia University Press, 1958).

Papers:
Major collections of Arnold's papers are at the Beinecke Library, Yale University, and at the University of Virginia. Yale has notebooks, diaries, commonplace books, literary manuscripts, and more than two hundred letters. The Arthur Kyle Davis Papers at Virginia include mainly letters.

Charlotte Brontë

(21 April 1816 - 31 March 1855)

This entry was updated by Herbert J. Rosengarten (University of British Columbia) from his entry in
DLB 21: Victorian Novelists Before 1885.

BOOKS: *Poems by Currer, Ellis, and Acton Bell*, by
Charlotte, Emily, and Anne Brontë (Lon-
don: Aylott & Jones, 1846; Philadelphia:
Lea & Blanchard, 1848);

Jane Eyre: An Autobiography, "edited by Currer
Bell" (3 volumes, London: Smith, Elder,
1847; 1 volume, New York: Harper, 1847);

Shirley: A Tale, as Currer Bell (3 volumes, London: Smith, Elder, 1849; 1 volume, New
York: Harper, 1850);

Villette, as Currer Bell (3 volumes, London:
Smith, Elder, 1853; 1 volume, New York:
Harper, 1853);

The Professor: A Tale, as Currer Bell (2 volumes,
London: Smith, Elder, 1857; 1 volume,
New York: Harper, 1857);

The Twelve Adventurers and Other Stories, edited by
C. K. Shorter and C. W. Hatfield (London:
Hodder & Stoughton, 1925);

*Legends of Angria: Compiled from the Early Writings
of Charlotte Brontë*, edited by Fannie E.
Ratchford and William Clyde De Vane
(New Haven: Yale University Press, 1933);

Five Novelettes, edited by Winifred Gérin (London: Folio Press, 1971);

An Edition of the Early Writings of Charlotte Brontë,
edited by Christine Alexander. *Vol I: The
Glass Town Saga 1826-1832* (Oxford & New
York: Blackwell, 1987).

Collections: *The Life and Works of Charlotte Brontë
and Her Sisters*, Haworth Edition, 7 volumes,
edited by Mrs. Humphry Ward and C. K.
Shorter (London: Smith, Elder, 1899-1900);

The Shakespeare Head Brontë, 19 volumes, edited
by T. J. Wise and J. A. Symington (Oxford:
Blackwell, 1931-1938);

The Clarendon Edition of the Novels of the Brontës, 6
volumes to date, I. R. Jack, general editor
(Oxford: Clarendon Press, 1969-   ).

Charlotte Brontë's fame and influence rest
on a very slender canon of published works: only
four novels and some contributions to a volume
of poetry. Her reputation may be explained in
part by the astounding success of her first novel,
Jane Eyre (1847); it owes much also to the romantic appeal of her personal history, given prominence soon after her death by Elizabeth
Cleghorn Gaskell's excellent biography, a work
preeminent in its genre. Of greater importance,
perhaps, is the recognition by historians of fiction that Charlotte Brontë's work made a significant contribution to the development of the
novel; her explorations of emotional repression
and the feminine psyche introduced a new depth
and intensity to the study of character and mo-

The Reverend Patrick Brontë

Maria Brontë (Brontë Parsonage Museum)

tive in fiction, anticipating in some respects the work of such writers as George Eliot and D. H. Lawrence. Her strength as a novelist lies in her ability to portray in moving detail the inner struggles of women who are endowed with a powerful capacity for feeling, yet whose social circumstances deny them the opportunity for intellectual or emotional fulfillment. Charlotte Brontë was not in any formal sense a proponent of women's rights, but in her writing she speaks out strongly against the injustices suffered by women in a society that restricts their freedom of action and exploits their dependent status. Her protests grew out of her own experience, which provided much of the material for her fiction; though she once insisted that "we only suffer reality to *suggest*, never to *dictate*," her novels include many characters and incidents recognizably drawn from her life, and her heroines have much in common with their creator.

Charlotte Brontë was born on 21 April 1816 at Thornton in the West Riding of Yorkshire. Her father, Patrick Brontë (1777-1861), a native of County Down in Ireland, had risen above the poverty of his family to become an undergraduate at St. John's College, Cambridge, and in 1807 was ordained a priest in the Church of England. In 1812 he met, courted, and married Maria

Branwell (1783-1821), a pious and educated young woman from Cornwall. Their life together was tragically brief; Maria bore six children in seven years (Maria in 1813; Elizabeth, 1815; Charlotte; Patrick Branwell, 1817; Emily Jane, 1818; Anne, 1820), then died of cancer in 1821 at the age of thirty-eight. Her death may have been hastened by the family's move in 1820 from Thornton to Haworth, where Mr. Brontë had been appointed perpetual curate. Beautiful as the landscape might be around Haworth, physical conditions in this rugged little mill town must have been harsh and unpleasant for the parson's delicate wife. The Brontës' new home was a stone-flagged parsonage, standing exposed to the elements at the top of a steep hill and on the edge of the open moors. Its situation was rendered even more unhealthy by its proximity to the overcrowded cemetery of St. Michael's Church. Sanitation in Haworth was primitive: as late as 1850 a government inspector found open sewers and overflowing cesspits on the main street, next to outlets for drinking water. It is hardly surprising that infant mortality rates in Haworth were high or that there were frequent outbreaks of cholera and typhoid. Throughout her life, Charlotte Brontë was to suffer from fevers, colds, and bilious attacks undoubtedly attributable to this

Haworth Parsonage, next to the cemetery that may have contributed to the Brontë sisters' poor health and early deaths

most inhospitable environment.

Nor was there much consolation to be found in the society of Haworth. Its inhabitants, even thirty years later, struck Gaskell as a "wild, rough population" among whom there was "little display of any of the amenities of life." Mr. Brontë won the respect of his parishioners, but there was little social contact between the towns-folk and the family at the parsonage; the Brontë children thus turned to one another for companionship and entertainment. This interdependence was intensified after the death of Mrs. Brontë. The early loss of their mother had a lasting effect on the children, particularly Charlotte; all her published novels are concerned in one way or another with young women who must lead a lonely path through life without the warmth and security of parental love. Not that the young Brontës were uncared for: after Maria's death, her sister Elizabeth Branwell came to live at the parsonage and supervised the household until her own death in 1842. Aunt Branwell was a rather stern, formal woman, however, with rigid and somewhat ascetic religious views; "the children respected her," notes Gaskell, "and had that sort of affection for her which is generated by esteem; but I do not think they ever freely loved her." Yet the children were happy enough:

they played and roamed the moors together; they read widely under the vigorous tutelage of their father, discussed social and political issues of the day, and developed those qualities of intellect and inventiveness that were to flower in the works of their maturity.

In August 1824 Mr. Brontë sent Charlotte to join Maria and Elizabeth at the recently opened Clergy Daughters' School at Cowan Bridge, near Tunstall in Lancashire. This was a charitable institution, where the daughters of poor clergymen might receive an education suited to their station and be prepared for future employment as governesses. Its founder was William Carus Wilson, a well-intentioned but overzealous clergyman who appears to have given little thought to the physical needs of the children in his charge; he imposed a stern regime of ascetic piety and self-denial which, in combination with inadequate attention to proper diet and the unhealthy situation of the school buildings, produced a succession of illnesses among the pupils and an outbreak of typhoid in April 1825. Charlotte Brontë would later give a vivid portrait in *Jane Eyre* of the school and its director; though colored by personal bitterness, her account of "Lowood Institution" is in essentials an accurate depiction of the harshness of life at Cowan

Bridge. Writing to a friend in 1848 concerning the advisability of sending children to the Clergy Daughters' School (then removed to Casterton), Brontë speaks in very matter-of-fact tones of the school's "rickety infancy": "Typhus fever decimated the school periodically, and consumption and scrofula in every variety of form, [which] bad air and water, and bad, insufficient diet can generate, preyed on the ill-fated pupils." Her own sisters were among the victims of such conditions: first Maria, then Elizabeth contracted consumption, were removed from the school, and died at home, Maria on 6 May 1825 and her sister on 15 June 1825. The death of Maria was especially painful to Charlotte; her eldest sister had become a guide and mentor, and Charlotte would later eulogize her patient virtue and premature wisdom in *Jane Eyre* in the portrait of Helen Burns.

After this tragic loss, Mr. Brontë decided to educate his children himself, and for the next six years they lived at home under the watchful eyes of Aunt Branwell and Tabitha Ackroyd, the parsonage servant. More than ever they were thrown upon their own resources; yet, despite their lack of social contact, they were never bored or unoccupied. Mr. Brontë encouraged them to read—and they read voraciously: William Shakespeare, John Milton, John Bunyan, John Dryden, Sir Walter Scott, William Wordsworth, George Gordon, Lord Byron; the *Arabian Nights Entertainments*; Whig and Tory newspapers; monthly magazines, notably *Blackwood's Edinburgh Magazine*; illustrated annuals such as the *Keepsake*. Though their own collection was small, the Brontës had access to the library of the Keighley Mechanics' Institute, less than four miles away, which Mr. Brontë had joined soon after its foundation in 1825. The breadth of their reading attests to their father's liberality of mind; it also helps to explain the curious variety of subjects and techniques displayed in the children's own early writings.

Their apprenticeship to literature had begun before the deaths of Maria and Elizabeth with the composition and performance of little plays under Maria's direction. After the return from Cowan Bridge, Charlotte and Branwell assumed the leadership in devising imaginary worlds populated by romantic figures from myth, history, and high society, whose doings they chronicled in a series of interwoven tales. The first of the series, the "Young Men's Play," originated with Mr. Brontë's gift to Branwell in June 1826

Elizabeth Branwell ("Aunt Branwell"), who raised the Brontë children after their mother died in 1821

of a set of twelve toy soldiers; each of the children took one, naming it after a particular hero (Charlotte called hers after the Duke of Wellington), and made up stories, eventually in written form, about the exploits of the "Twelves." That a group of imaginative children should collaborate in the creation of a fantasy world is by no means unusual; what sets the storymaking of the youthful Brontës apart is that it occupied them all well into adulthood—Emily and Anne were still devising plots for their world of Gondal in 1845—and came dangerously close to an unhealthy obsession from which Charlotte had to free herself in 1839 by a conscious and explicit act of rejection.

The bulk of Charlotte's juvenile writings is concerned with the history of Angria, a kingdom that grew out of her extended collaboration with Branwell. It began as a confederacy of the "Twelves," located in Africa, whose capital was called "Glass Town" and whose rulers were four genii: Tallii (Charlotte), Brannii, Emmii, and Annii. The geography of this new land, first described in Charlotte's tale "The Twelve Adventur-

The Reverend William Carus Wilson, the model for Mr. Brocklehurst in Jane Eyre *(Brontë Society)*

ers" (manuscript dated 15 April 1829), was inspired in part by the Reverend J. Goldsmith's *Grammar of General Geography* (1803) and articles in *Blackwood's Edinburgh Magazine*; its supernatural inhabitants were unmistakably related to their counterparts in the *Arabian Nights* and Ridley's *Tales of the Genii* (1764); its cities borrowed features from those depicted in the extravagant pictures of John Martin, whose work was often reproduced in contemporary annuals; its populace came from the society columns of newspapers or magazines, from portraits of the aristocracy which the young Brontës copied from books, and from the political controversies of the day which they keenly followed and eagerly discussed. This mixture of fantasy and reality is well exemplified by Charlotte's "Tales of the Islanders" (June 1829 - June 1830), an extended narrative set in a fairy-tale world in which her characters debate the political and religious issues of contemporary England, especially the Catholic Emancipation Act of April 1829 and the storm surrounding Arthur Wellesley, the Duke of Wellington. In this story Charlotte also introduced the Duke's sons, the Marquis of Douro and Lord Charles Wellesley, who were to take over from

their father as leading personages in the world of Glass Town.

As the early "plays" gradually merged into the history of the Glass Town Confederacy and the actions of its great notables, the children collaborated in a systematic charting of events and relationships. In January 1829 Branwell began *Branwells Blackwoods Magazine* (subsequently to be called *Blackwoods Young Mens Magazine*), an imitation of the children's favorite periodical reproduced in miniature form, presumably to correspond to the size of their original soldier heroes. Charlotte took over the editorship in August, and under the pseudonym of Captain Tree, or in the characters of Douro or Lord Charles, wrote poems and stories about Glass Town society, frequently alluding to characters or incidents developed in Branwell's manuscripts. The narratives became more complex; Glass Town acquired greater sophistication and became Verreopolis, then Verdopolis; Branwell began to chronicle the military and political upheavals that were to become the focus of his interest in the emerging kingdom of Angria, while Charlotte gave more and more of her attention to the personalities and domestic relations of Verdopolitan celebrities. Her tale of "Albion and Marina" (October 1830) introduced the theme of passionate romantic love that was to dominate her subsequent contributions to the joint saga.

Charlotte's participation in Verdopolitan affairs came to a temporary halt in January 1831 when, with the financial support of her godparents, the Atkinsons, she was sent to Roe Head, a small private school near Mirfield under the direction of Miss Margaret Wooler and her sisters. Here she stayed for a year and a half in much happier circumstances than at Cowan Bridge; indeed, Miss Wooler was to become a lifelong friend, and Brontë would return to Roe Head in 1835 as an assistant teacher. Here also she met the two girls whose enduring friendship was to lift her out of her social isolation at Haworth and to sustain her often in times of emotional duress. Ellen Nussey was a quiet, timid, pious girl whose family lived at Rydings, a big house in Birstall that would later lend some of its features to Thornfield Hall in *Jane Eyre*. Stolid, unimaginative, conservative, Ellen yet possessed a ready fund of sympathy and affection that quickly won a response from Charlotte. Her other newfound friend, Mary Taylor, offered a startling contrast of personality. Mary's father, a cloth manufacturer and banker at Gomersal, had suffered bank-

Charlotte Brontë's watercolor of Glass Town, the capital city of the imaginary African confederacy created by the Brontë children (Brontë Parsonage Museum)

ruptcy in 1825 and spent the rest of his life working to pay off his debts. From him Mary inherited strong Radical views, a blunt outspokenness, and an independence of spirit that would lead her to immigrate to New Zealand. Ellen and Mary became integral parts of Charlotte's life; the three corresponded regularly for more than twenty years, exchanging news about themselves and their families, and Charlotte's visits to their homes provided her with a wealth of impressions which she was to draw on when she came to write her great novels. *Shirley* (1849) is especially indebted to Brontë's memories of the Taylors, who are presented there as the Yorke family; Mary herself appears as young Rose Yorke, as well as lending some of her ideas about society to the novel's eponymous heroine. Ellen's shy and retiring nature contributes something to the depiction of Caroline Helstone; and Shirley's residence, "Fieldhead," is based on Oakwell Hall, an

Elizabethan house near Birstall owned by relatives of the Nussey family. When Mrs. Gaskell came to write the biography of Charlotte Brontë, Ellen Nussey and Mary Taylor provided her with lengthy reminiscences, and Nussey was able to supply her with more than three hundred letters by Brontë which she had kept over the years.

At Roe Head, Charlotte worked hard to make up for the deficiencies in her formal education; Ellen Nussey later recalled that she "always seemed to feel that a deep responsibility rested upon her; that she was an object of expense to those at home, and that she must use every moment to attain the purpose for which she was sent to school, i.e., to fit herself for governess life. . . ." On her return to Haworth in May 1832 Charlotte continued her studies and tutored her younger sisters; but though much of her time was thus occupied, she had not lost interest in the story of Verdopolitan society and renewed her contributions to the saga. In "The Bridal" (August 1832) she enlarged upon the relationship between the Marquis of Douro and his first great love, Marian Hume, filling out the Byronic lineaments of her hero's character and developing the themes of temptation and betrayal, duty and desire that were to recur throughout her juvenilia.

Branwell's writing at this time was mainly concerned with the history and politics of the Confederacy, and his pedantically detailed narratives make dull reading beside Charlotte's lively and melodramatic accounts of romantic intrigue and rival lovers. The children still worked together on the intricate elaboration of their world, and Charlotte's stories assume a knowledge on the reader's part of events described elsewhere by Branwell; but after her return from Roe Head, Charlotte's writing shows a distinct advance in descriptive power and depth of character portrayal. Arthur Wellesley, Marquis of Douro, now Duke of Zamorna, becomes the dominant figure in most of the prose narratives produced by Charlotte after 1832. A compound of moody grandeur, dashing bravery, and sadistic heartlessness, Zamorna wears a mantle woven from Milton and Byron: "O Zamorna! what eyes those are glancing under the deep shadow of that raven crest! They bode no good. . . . Satan gave them their glory to deepen the midnight gloom that always follows where their lustre has fallen most lovingly. . . . All here is passion and fire unquenchable. Impetuous sin, stormy pride, diving and soaring enthusiasm, war and poetry, are kindling their fires in all his veins, and his wild blood

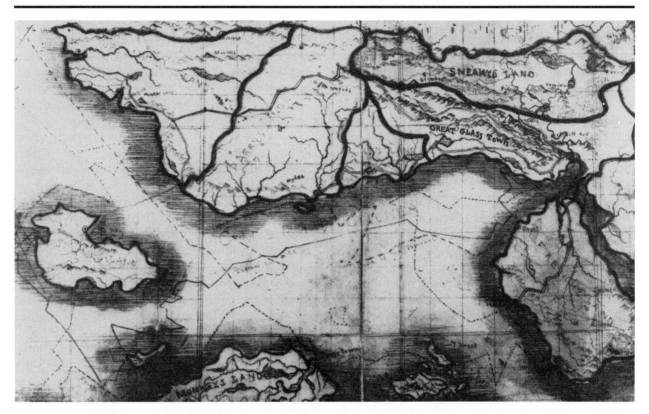

Branwell Brontë's map of the Glass Town Confederacy (British Museum)

boils from his heart and back again like a torrent of new-sprung lava. Young duke? Young demon!" ("A Peep into a Picture Book," May 1834). While Branwell explores Zamorna's political fortunes in the newly created kingdom of Angria (established in the narratives of 1834), Charlotte follows the twists and turns of his unpredictable nature as he torments a succession of beautiful, heartsick women, whose Griselda-like meekness in suffering serves only to arouse his scorn or anger.

The Angrian stories of this period also see the development of a subject touched on in Charlotte's earliest narratives, the antagonism between two brothers. This first appears in the form of Lord Charles Wellesley's hostility toward his older brother Arthur; their rivalry gives way to the deeper rift between Edward and William Percy, the sons of Zamorna's archenemy, Alexander Percy, Earl of Northangerland. The young Percys are first described in Branwell's story "The Wool is Rising" (June 1834); cast off by their father, they establish themselves in the wool trade, but Edward's cold ambition soon leads him to a harsh assertion of mastery over William. Charlotte picked up this theme in several stories ("The Spell," June-July 1834; "My Angria and

the Angrians," October 1834; "The Duke of Zamorna," July 1838; "The Ashworths," 1839-1840); ultimately it would find its way into the first-written of her adult novels, *The Professor* (1857), in the relationship between Edward and William Crimsworth.

Charlotte's absorption in the Angrian world was interrupted in July 1835 when, at the invitation of Miss Wooler, she returned to Roe Head as a teacher. She was accompanied by Emily, who was to receive free tuition as part of the arrangement, but Emily's unhappiness at her exile from Haworth soon led to her replacement by Anne. Despite Miss Wooler's kindness, Charlotte found her duties tedious and distasteful; separated from her creative partner Branwell and allowed little free time, she became increasingly frustrated by the fetters placed on her imagination. A series of diary jottings from this period known as the "Roe Head Journals" show the extent to which the demands of daily routine clashed with powerful inner yearnings. "All this day," she wrote on 11 August 1836, "I have been in a dream half-miserable & half ecstatic miserable because I could not follow it out uninterruptedly, ecstatic because it shewed almost in the vivid light of reality the ongoings of the infernal world. . . . The thought came over me am I to spend all the best part of my life in this wretched bondage forcibly suppressing my rage at the idleness the apathy & the hyperbolical & most asinine stupidity of those fat-headed oafs & on compulsion assuming an air of kindness patience & assiduity?" She recorded waking visions of Angrian scenes which presented themselves to her with frightening vividness; her attempts to repress such imaginings produced feelings of guilt and melancholy. "If you knew my thoughts," she wrote to Ellen Nussey on 10 May 1836, "the dreams that absorb me; and the fiery imagination that at times eats me up and makes me feel Society as it is, wretchedly insipid, you would pity and I dare say despise me."

School vacations brought some relief and allowed Brontë to continue her Angrian narratives. "Passing Events" (April 1836), "Julia" (June 1837), and "Four Years Ago" (July 1837) all develop aspects of the political drama worked out by Branwell, but focus on scene and character rather than on plot. The "infernal world" still exerted its power over her; but Brontë—now past her twentieth year—was moving away from the colorful excitement of simple melodrama toward a maturer exploration of feeling, especially the suffering of women in love. The later Angrian romances reflect this new maturity in their treatment as well as in subject matter. "Mina Laury" (January 1838), in its depiction of Zamorna's heartlessness and Mina's selfless devotion, displays greater unity and coherence than Brontë's earlier stories, and Byronic excess in characterization now gives way to more realistic analysis of character and motive. Setting, too, in these later stories is less exotic, more suggestive of the writer's own environment; in "Stancliff's Hotel" (June 1838) and "Henry Hastings" (February-March 1839) the cloud-capped palaces of Angria are replaced by country houses in a recognizably English landscape. "Henry Hastings" also gives prominence to characters and situations that reemerge in Brontë's adult fiction. The female protagonist, Elizabeth Hastings, is reserved and self-effacing, but her calm exterior conceals intense emotion. Like her yet-distant successor Jane Eyre she is faced with a conflict between duty and desire and is saved from a surrender to feeling by her concern for self-respect. There is an element of autobiography in Brontë's depiction of Elizabeth as "the little dignified Governess" who dresses plainly, values her independence, and loves her degenerate and reckless brother despite his pub-

lic dishonor. Branwell had written several stories in the persona of Henry Hastings; through the story of Elizabeth's loyalty to her reprobate brother, Brontë might express her feelings toward Branwell, whose conduct was already giving evidence of that weakness of character that would lead him to alcoholism and drugs.

Anne's departure from Miss Wooler's school (now relocated at Dewsbury Moor) in December 1837, and her own increasingly depressed spirits, led Charlotte to give up her post and return to Haworth in May 1838. Her respite was brief, however; the family's precarious financial circumstances, made more difficult by Branwell's failure to establish himself as a painter in Bradford, led Charlotte Brontë to seek employment once again, and in May 1839 she became governess to the children of the Sidgwick family of Stonegappe, near Lothersdale. The experience was an unhappy one: the Sidgwicks treated Brontë with what seemed to her to be undue coldness and condescension; the children tormented her by their rudeness and lack of discipline; and after less than three months she was back at home, telling Ellen Nussey that "I never was so glad to get out of a house in my life." Relieved of this burden, Brontë returned to her writing with new vigor and produced "Caroline Vernon" (July-December 1839), the last of her Angrian tales. The account of a young girl's infatuation with her guardian, the Duke of Zamorna, "Caroline Vernon" shows another advance in Brontë's analysis of feminine psychology. Romantic passion is here treated with critical detachment and seen as a destructive force; Brontë does not identify with her heroine, presenting her instead as an inexperienced and undisciplined adolescent, "raw, flighty & romantic."

Sheltered though her own life was in comparison to that of her heroines, Charlotte Brontë discovered to her surprise that she herself was capable of arousing admiration: twice in the same year she received proposals of marriage. The first came from Henry Nussey, Ellen's brother, a curate in Sussex, who wrote in March 1839 to offer Brontë his hand, since "in due time he should want a wife to take care of his pupils." She had no difficulty in turning down this cool suitor, telling Ellen that she could not feel "that intense attachment which would make me willing to die for him; and, if ever I marry, it must be in that light of adoration that I will regard my husband." Her second proposal, the following August, came from another clergyman, an impetu-

Some of the miniature books and magazines produced by the Brontë children. The coin shown is about the size of a U.S. half-dollar (Brontë Parsonage Museum).

ous young Irish curate who was smitten after only one meeting with her; him, too, she refused. The prospects of her finding a man she could truly love seemed remote; "I'm certainly doomed to be an old maid," she wrote to Ellen Nussey; "I can't expect another chance—never mind I made up my mind to that fate ever since I was twelve years old."

The sober awareness that her dreams of passionate love would never be matched by reality may have contributed to her decision to abandon Angria after "Caroline Vernon." In an undated manuscript placed by most scholars at the end of 1839, Brontë announces her desire "to quit for awhile that burning clime where we have sojourned too long—its skies flame—the glow of sunset is always upon it—the mind would cease from excitement and turn now to a cooler region where the dawn breaks grey and sober, and the coming day for a time at least is subdued by clouds." In penning these lines, Brontë was probably thinking about her first venture into realistic prose fiction, which took form in the winter of 1839-1840, and in a revised version of early 1841 culminated in the unfinished story known as "Ashworth." In part, this is a return to old subjects; the central figure, a Yorkshire industrialist named Alexander Ashworth, owes much in character and personal history to Alexander Percy, the Northangerland of Branwell's narratives. Percy's sons Edward and William, already depicted as rivals in the Angrian cycle, reappear as Edward and William Ashworth, and like their ear-

lier namesakes are cast out by their father to make their own way in the world. However, when the story shifts from the Ashworths to a picture of life in a girls' school, focusing on the lonely figure of an orphaned child, the narrative gains new life and interest, and Brontë can be seen moving in the direction of a favorite theme in her later novels. That she regarded "Ashworth" as a serious venture into adult fiction is apparent from her request for an opinion from Hartley Coleridge (son of the poet Samuel Taylor Coleridge), to whom she sent a portion of the manuscript in December 1840, describing her story as a "demi-semi novelette." Coleridge's verdict evidently was unfavorable, since in her reply Brontë promised to commit her protagonists to oblivion. This was not the first time that she had sought advice from a well-known writer; in 1837 she had corresponded with the poet laureate Robert Southey, who had been similarly discouraging, warning her that "literature cannot be the business of a woman's life, and it ought not to be. The more she is engaged in her proper duties, the less leisure will she have for it. . . ."

Under the pressure of "proper duties," Brontë left home once again in March 1841 to become a governess in the White family at Rawdon, near Bradford. The Whites proved to be more amiable employers than the Sidgwicks; but Brontë left them in December to set in motion a plan the family had discussed for six months. This was for the three sisters to open their own school, with financial support from Aunt

Ellen Nussey, who became Charlotte Brontë's lifelong friend
(Brontë Society)

Branwell; as a preliminary step to strengthen their qualifications for such a venture, Charlotte and Emily wanted to spend a half-year in school on the Continent, where they might improve their grasp of foreign languages. Belgium was fixed upon, since there the cost of living was low; also, Mary and Martha Taylor were at school in Brussels and spoke favorably of their experience.

After a short time spent sight-seeing in London (Charlotte Brontë would recall the excitement of this first visit to the capital in both *Villette*, 1853, and *The Professor*, 1857) Charlotte and Emily, accompanied by Mr. Brontë, arrived at the Pensionnat Heger in Brussels on 15 February 1842, there to recommence the lives of schoolgirls at the ages of twenty-five and twenty-three respectively. The school's owner and directress was Claire Zoé Parent Heger, who was thirty-seven years old at the time of the Brontës' arrival in the rue d'Isabelle. In 1836 she had married Constantin Heger, a widower five years her junior, who taught at the Athénée Royal de Bruxelles; after their marriage, M. Heger retained his post at the Athénée, but also assisted his wife in the operation of her school and gave classes there in literature. He was something of a roman-

tic figure, having fought at the barricades during the Belgian revolution of 1830, and displaying a moody impetuousness that undoubtedly had a special appeal for one whose imaginary heroes had been similarly governed by violence of feeling. From the outset, the Hegers showed great kindness to the two strange little Englishwomen. Their lessons in French literature and composition were supervised by M. Heger, who assigned readings in the great French writers and corrected their exercises with comments aimed at sharpening their perception of style. Under Heger's guidance, Charlotte Brontë encountered the works of such authors as Vicomte François Auguste-René de Chateaubriand, Victor-Marie Hugo, and Alphonse-Marie-Louis de Prat de Lamartine and copied out extracts from their writings; she also wrote a variety of devoirs on such topics as "La Justice Humaine," "Le Palais de la Mort," "La Chute des Feuilles," and "La Mort de Napoléon," which, despite the inevitable stiffness of academic set pieces, show commendable fluency and precision. Charlotte Brontë's adult writings in English, characterized by a poetic quality often derived from syntactic inversions, antitheses, and repetitions, would owe much to these exercises performed under the demanding tutelage of Constantin Heger; and her study of French romanticism taught her how to make language convey heightened states of feeling normally expressed in poetic form.

The sisters made few friends at the pensionnat, partly because of their natural shyness and diffidence, partly because of their Protestant suspicion of all things Catholic and their belief in the superiority of all things British. Charlotte Brontë was especially scathing in her comments on the Hegers' Belgian pupils, whose character she described to Ellen Nussey as "cold, selfish, animal and inferior" and whose principles she regarded as "rotten to the core." Nevertheless, Brontë's first year in Belgium was busy and enjoyable; in addition to her own schoolwork, she gave English lessons, visited the Taylor sisters and their cousins, the Dixons, explored art galleries and museums, and saw an exhibition of paintings at the Brussels Salon of 1842 which she was later to recall in an episode in *Villette*. Above all, she found herself drawn more and more strongly to Constantin Heger, an attraction carefully omitted by Gaskell from her biography. Heger's dominant personality, his acute intelligence, his position as mentor and friend, all combined to arouse in Brontë an admiration for one whom

Miss Wooler's school at Roe Head, where Charlotte Brontë spent a miserable three years as a teacher

she could regard as her master. Had she been younger, her feelings might have taken the form of a schoolgirl infatuation, quickly roused and quickly quenched; but at twenty-six she had deeper yearnings, desires which possibly she did not understand herself.

Toward the end of 1842 life in Brussels took on a darker shade. First, in September, came news of the death of William Weightman, Mr. Brontë's attractive young curate since 1839, with whom all the sisters had playfully flirted. An even greater shock was the death of Martha Taylor, who succumbed to cholera in October and was buried at the Protestant Cemetery outside Brussels; the tragedy impressed itself deeply in Charlotte Brontë's mind and would later be alluded to directly in *Shirley*, where Martha appears as Jessie Yorke. A final somber note was struck at the end of October by the death of Aunt Branwell. Charlotte and Emily immediately left for Haworth, taking with them a letter of condolence for Mr. Brontë from Constantin Heger, who expressed the hope that one of the girls, if not both, might be allowed to return.

Charlotte did return, at the end of January 1843; this time, however, she traveled alone (Emily had decided to stay in Haworth), experiencing difficulties much like those she later bestowed on Lucy Snowe, who makes a similar journey in *Villette*. Her second year in Brussels began well; she was warmly received by the Hegers and promoted to the position of salaried teacher. She

gave English lessons to M. Heger and his brother-in-law and continued her own studies in German; she paid frequent visits to her English acquaintances, the Dixons and the Wheelwrights. But without Emily's companionship, and in the absence of Mary Taylor (now in Germany), Charlotte felt increasingly isolated. Her relations with Mme Heger were deteriorating; to Emily she complained of Madame's aversion to her and expressed the belief that she was being spied upon. Allowing for an element of exaggeration in Brontë's complaints, there is little doubt that Mme Heger had become more guarded in her exchanges with the little English teacher; though Brontë never made any avowal of an attachment to Constantin Heger, her feelings must have been quite apparent to the shrewd directress of the pensionnat, who probably sought ways of reducing Brontë's opportunities for social contact with her husband. Brontë found herself in an increasingly "Robinson-Crusoe-like condition," lamenting that M. Heger had "in a great measure withdrawn the light of his countenance." Thrown more and more upon her own resources, Charlotte Brontë withdrew into the childhood world of her imagination; to Branwell, the former partner of her fantasies, she spoke of recurring "as fanatically as ever to the old ideas, the old faces, and the old scenes in the world below." When the school holidays came in mid August, the Hegers left on their vacation, the teachers and pupils went home, and Brontë was abandoned to her own devices until school resumed at the end of September. Her solitude bore heavily upon her, and she entered a state of nervous depression. The feelings of bitter frustration, loneliness, and possibly guilt were too much for her; on 1 September she took the extraordinary step of confessing to a Catholic priest in Sainte Gudule, the collegiate church close to the rue d'Isabelle. Writing to Emily the next day, Charlotte described the incident in full and finally dismissed it as a "freak"; but its details remained clearly impressed upon her memory and provided her with an important scene in *Villette* ten years later.

By the end of the year her loneliness and homesickness had become too much for her, and on 1 January 1844 Brontë left Brussels for the last time. The strength of her feelings for M. Heger, however, was undiminished; the pain she suffered at parting from him was to last for the next two years, as she sought to maintain his friendship by correspondence. Some of her letters to Heger have survived; they were evidently

The Duke of Zamorna and Alexander Percy, two of the characters in the Brontës' Angrian stories, as sketched by Branwell (Brontë Parsonage Museum)

torn up by the recipient, then reassembled by Madame, and now maintain a patchwork existence under glass at the British Library. They reflect a rising desperation in Brontë; in no sense are they love letters, yet they are unmistakably passionate in their pleas for some acknowledgment, some signal of recognition and regard. What Heger thought of all this is not known; there is no evidence that he felt anything but a kindly affection and concern for an apt and hardworking young pupil-teacher. In Brontë's eyes, however, Heger constituted an ideal: cultured, energetic, masterful (she addresses him in one letter as "mon maître"), and there is something of Heger in the heroes of all her mature novels, especially in the figure of Paul Emanuel in *Villette*.

At their parting, Heger had given Brontë a diploma attesting to her experience and qualifications; once back in Haworth, she hoped to make use of this in realizing the sisters' original plan of opening their own school. She set about seeking pupils and in July 1844 sent Ellen Nussey copies of a prospectus she had drawn up, describing "The Misses Brontë's Establishment for the Board and Education of a limited number of Young Ladies." She also wrote to acquaintances to announce her intentions, on one occasion enclosing the diploma she had received from Heger. Her efforts proved fruitless; not one prospective pupil applied, and by the close of the year the plan had been abandoned.

With the failure of the school project, Charlotte Brontë's life seemed to have reached a point of stagnation. She no longer heard anything from Constantin Heger, although she continued writing to him until November 1845. Mary Taylor, her principal source of intellectual stimulation outside her own family, left for New Zealand in March 1845. Ellen Nussey remained always ready to offer friendship and comfort, but she was too limited and unimaginative to provide Brontë with an outlet for her deeper needs and concerns. To make matters worse, in July 1845 Branwell was dismissed from his post as tutor in the Robinson family of Thorp Green, accused of improper conduct toward his employer's wife, and came home to plague the family with his increasingly drunken and irrational behavior. Charlotte, once his closest companion, became bitterly critical of his "frantic folly" and dissipation; her disgust at his moral depravity would shortly find expression in *The Professor*, where her narrator William Crimsworth reflects on the spectacle of "a mind degraded by the practice of mean subter-

Charlotte Brontë about 1838, as painted by J. H. Thompson of Bradford (Brontë Society)

fuge, by the habit of perfidious deception, and a body depraved by the infectious influence of the vice-polluted soul."

Driven closer together by Branwell's progressive deterioration, Charlotte and her sisters now entered a phase of literary production from which their brother was excluded. Its beginnings are chronicled in Charlotte's "Biographical Notice of Ellis and Acton Bell," prefixed to the 1850 edition of *Wuthering Heights* and *Agnes Grey*. In the autumn of 1845, Charlotte "accidentally lighted on a MS volume of verse" in Emily's handwriting and was immediately convinced that the poems merited publication. After Emily's initial reluctance had been overcome, the Brontë sisters set out to realize their long-cherished dream of authorship. They made a small selection of their poems; then, with some of the small legacy left to each of them by Aunt Branwell, they paid the London firm of Aylott and Jones thirty-six pounds, ten shillings to meet the expenses of paper, printing, and advertising. The Brontës became the Bells: Currer (Charlotte), Ellis (Emily), and Acton (Anne). Male-sounding pseudonyms

were preferred, as Charlotte explained in her "Biographical Notice," because "we had a vague impression that authoresses are liable to be looked on with prejudice; we had noticed how critics sometimes use for their chastisement the weapon of personality, and for their reward, a flattery, which is not true praise." *Poems by Currer, Ellis, and Acton Bell* appeared in one volume at four shillings in May 1846; it received several friendly notices, but by June 1847 only two copies had been sold.

Lack of success in their first venture into print did not deter the sisters, however; even before the appearance of the *Poems*, they had already decided to try their hand at publishable fiction. In this they were doubtless encouraged by the enormous popularity of novels with the Victorian public. Thanks to such developments as part publication, cheap one-volume reprints, and subscription circulating libraries, a successful writer might now command a huge audience. The Brontë sisters were certainly impelled by the honorable motive of seeking critical applause, but undoubtedly they also hoped to turn their love of writing to good account and make some money by their pens. To this end each wrote a short novel: *Wuthering Heights* by Emily, *Agnes Grey* by Anne, and *The Professor* by Charlotte. Their intention was to have them published together as a three-volume work, the format imposed on most new fiction by the needs of the circulating libraries. Fair copies of the manuscripts were completed by the end of June 1846 (that of *The Professor* is dated 27 June) and sent to Henry Colburn on 4 July. However, finding an interested publisher proved much more difficult than had been the case with the *Poems*, since the sisters could not meet the costs of production themselves; over the next twelve months, the manuscripts suffered half a dozen rejections. Finally, in July 1847 the London firm of Thomas Cautley Newby agreed to publish *Wuthering Heights* and *Agnes Grey*, provided that the authors contributed fifty pounds toward the cost of production; but Newby flatly refused to include *The Professor*. The sisters accepted these harsh terms, and Charlotte was left to find a separate publisher for her own novel; her search proved fruitless, for though it was instrumental in leading her to the firm that would swiftly accept and publish *Jane Eyre, The Professor* never reached print during her lifetime.

The novel's lack of appeal for prospective publishers is partly attributable to its prosaic subject matter and lack of sensational incident; in-

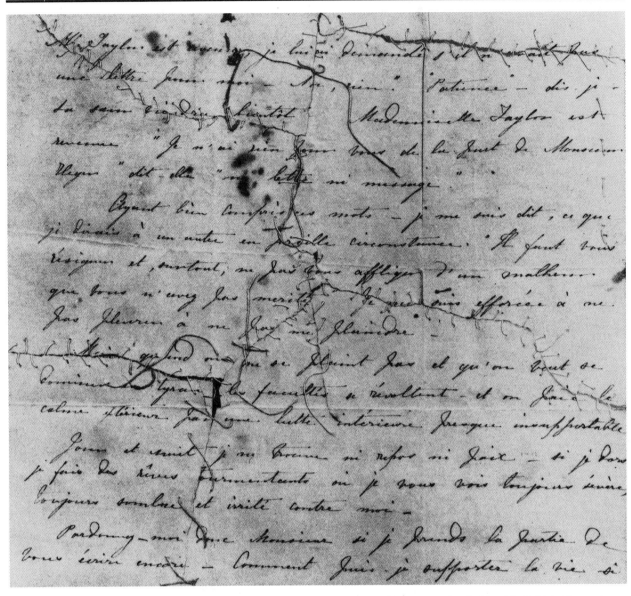

An 1845 letter from Charlotte Brontë to M. Heger, torn up by him and sewn back together by his wife (British Museum)

deed, it was the publisher's objections on this score that led Brontë in her next work (*Jane Eyre*) to the mode of romantic melodrama. *The Professor* suffers also from awkwardness in construction and in the handling of plot: the clumsy opening in epistolary form (a stratagem dropped after the first chapter), the loose arrangement of episodes, the lack of any real suspense, and the anticlimactic ending all make the story seem flat and unexciting. Nevertheless, the book does have real power in its delineation of character and in its exploration of the individual's struggle to find emotional fulfillment despite socially repressive circumstances.

The effectiveness of *The Professor* in depict-

ing strong emotions derives largely from its autobiographical origins; in her portrayal of the love between teacher and pupil in a Belgian girls' school, Brontë drew heavily on her recent experiences in Brussels. She sought to disguise this personal element by making her narrator-protagonist a man, a device she had frequently employed in her Angrian tales; and she revived the Angrian motif of enmity between two brothers, the elder, hardheaded and ambitious, the younger, cultured and sensitive. Like most Brontë protagonists, William Crimsworth is an orphan, in this case the ward of an aristocratic family. He begins his career by rejecting the status of depen-

The prospectus for the Brontë sisters' proposed school, which failed to attract even one application (Brontë Parsonage Museum)

dent and chooses to enter a voluntary servitude as clerk to his elder brother Edward, a blunt and morose mill owner. William's independent nature cannot bear the yoke of his brother's tyranny, however, and he strikes out afresh, becoming a teacher in a boys' school in Brussels. This first part of the narrative is an uneasy mixture of social comedy and melodrama, the tone strained and uncertain; but Brontë succeeds in establishing William as a quirky yet intelligent character, chafing under his bondage to inferior minds and eager to assert his individuality. A related concern is the connection between sexual power and social identity, a theme explored in all of Brontë's subsequent novels; Crimsworth is made painfully conscious that as "a dependant amongst wealthy strangers" he is unattractive to the band of young women who cluster around his prosperous brother. Though there is a self-pitying tone to William's reflections, his emotional vulnerability and sense of failure at this stage are necessary elements in his development; as the novel progresses, he acquires greater confidence and maturity in his relationships with women, until he is ready to take on the dominant role as a lover.

A factor in William's growth is his friendship with the radical and outspoken manufacturer Hunsden Yorke Hunsden, a precursor of

Hiram Yorke in *Shirley*. Hunsden, who encourages William to rebel against Edward, embodies the force of instinctual feeling; this makes him both attractive and dangerous. His association with potentially anarchic impulses is signified by recurring allusions to a demonic element in his nature, and at the end of the novel the mature Crimsworth sees Hunsden's influence as a threat to his son Victor's moral education. The portrait of Hunsden creates some unresolved ambiguities: he is both a capitalist and a critic of capitalism, a cynic and a sentimentalist. He is a friend to Crimsworth, yet subtly undermines the latter's sense of security and self-esteem. Potentially Hunsden is an interestingly complex character, but he lacks the development necessary to make his idiosyncrasies seem wholly credible.

Once the narrative shifts from England to Belgium, Brontë demonstrates much firmer control of her material. The vague industrial setting of a Yorkshire mill town is replaced by the precise topography of Brussels; the melodramatic stereotypes of the early chapters give way to characters with a depth and vividness owing much to real life. Zoraide Reuter, the manipulative directress of the girls' school where Crimsworth is eventually hired to give English lessons, is partly modeled on Mme Heger in her cool efficiency. Through her, and through his encounters with some of her pupils, Crimsworth discovers the superficiality and duplicity of the Catholic system of education. Although Brontë sometimes invites the reader to laugh at her narrator's pompousness or mild vanity, Crimsworth is generally the mouthpiece for her own views; and nowhere is this more evident than in his contemptuous accounts of "Romish wizard-craft" and its victims, the Belgian schoolgirls, who are deceitful, shallow, and "mentally depraved." In making her hero such a bluff proponent of British Protestantism, Brontë intended no irony; she herself had spoken critically of Roman "mummeries" in letters from Brussels in 1842-1843. Nor would her readers have taken exception to such denunciations; despite the political freedom enjoyed by English Catholics since the Catholic Emancipation Act of 1829, Victorian Englishmen regarded Catholics with an undiminished suspicion that was intensified by the Tractarian controversies of the 1830s and 1840s which threatened the hegemony of the Anglican church.

Related to the theme of Catholic treachery is Mlle Reuter's role as seductress and temptress in a struggle with Crimsworth for sexual dominance. Though she is engaged to M. Pelet (Crimsworth's employer at the boys' school) she flirts with the young Englishman, who is saved from imminent folly only by accidentally overhearing her in conversation with Pelet. Henceforth he treats her with a haughty disdain worthy of a Zamorna, which paradoxically serves to make him seem more fascinating in the directress's eyes. This curious turn in their relationship is seen by Crimsworth as further evidence of the degeneration fostered by a despotic religious system; because Zoraïde herself lives by the values of a spiritual tyranny, she respects the manifestation of authority in others. Her new submissiveness arouses Crimsworth to a pleasurable sense of his own power; once he has won recognition of his masculine strength, however, he turns his back on such "low gratification" in favor of the higher charms offered by his Anglo-Swiss pupil Frances Henri.

The comedy of Crimsworth's entanglement with Zoraïde Reuter now gives way to a much more earnest study of a relationship based on intellectual as well as emotional compatibility. There are obvious parallels between Crimsworth's situation in England and Frances's sufferings at the Brussels pensionnat, emphasizing the link between inferior social status and the enforced repression of feeling. Orphaned, poor, and (after her aunt's death) utterly alone, Frances draws Crimsworth's interest by her meekly deferential manner, behind which he perceives flashes of warmth and proud defiance. It is hard to avoid the conclusion that, in her depiction of this relationship, Charlotte Brontë was expressing some of her fantasies about Constantin Heger, her "maître" in Brussels. Through Frances Henri's suffering, and her eventual triumph over the schemes of Mlle Reuter, Brontë could play out a dream of what might have been; here, true merit might defeat hypocrisy, and the professor might clasp his pupil in a warm embrace. Brontë's immersion in the hopes and longings of her principal characters gives conviction to her portrayal of their feelings, but the focus on romantic love costs the novel much of its earlier bite. Through Frances, Brontë adumbrates some of her concerns about the plight of women without money or connections; however, as an idealized embodiment of the author's own yearnings, Frances lacks the depth and complexity needed to carry the burden of such concerns effectively.

Several years after the composition of *The Professor*, when she had won fame as the author of *Jane Eyre* and *Shirley*, Charlotte Brontë again sought its publication and wrote a preface outlining her original intentions. She had sought to create a hero who "should work his way through life as I had seen living men work theirs—that he should never get a shilling he had not earned—that no sudden turns should lift him in a moment to wealth and high station.... As Adam's son he should share Adam's doom, and drain throughout life a mixed and moderate cup of enjoyment." That *The Professor* is sometimes slow, even dull, is perhaps the inevitable consequence of the author's rejection of the sensational in fiction; but her attempt to view life as unromantically as possible, and to focus on the pains and pleasures of a recognizably ordinary life, places Charlotte Brontë at the forefront of developments in modern literary realism.

Even while *The Professor* was going its fruitless round of the publishers, Charlotte was occupied with her next story. In August 1846 she accompanied her father to Manchester, where he underwent an operation for cataracts; and during his convalescence she began *Jane Eyre*. The work continued in Haworth, sometimes with great intensity (as when she wrote the chapters on Thornfield), and aided by critical counsel from Emily and Anne. The book was in its final stages when, on 15 July 1847, the manuscript of *The Professor*, now divorced from its former companions, arrived at the firm of Smith, Elder in London. It was seen by the firm's reader, William Smith Williams, a sensitive and literate man who was to become a close friend of Brontë's. Williams recognized the book's power, but doubted its success as a publication; after consulting with George Smith, he wrote to Brontë, declining *The Professor* but inviting the author to submit a work that might be published in three volumes. Maintaining her pseudonym of Currer Bell, Brontë sent off the manuscript of *Jane Eyre* on 24 August, five days after completing the fair copy. The book was accepted at once; within a month Brontë was correcting proofs; and on 19 October 1847, *Jane Eyre: An Autobiography*, "edited by Currer Bell," was published in three volumes at thirty-one shillings, sixpence.

The book won immediate and widespread acclaim. The *Times* called it "a remarkable production," a tale that "stand[s] boldly out from the mass." The *Edinburgh Review* saw it as "a book of singular fascination," and *Fraser's Magazine* urged its readers to "lose not a day in sending for it." Within three months the novel went into a sec-

A silhouette of Branwell Brontë, whose degenerate behavior grieved and disgusted his sisters (Brontë Society)

ond edition, and a third appeared in April 1848: no small achievement for a three-volume novel by a wholly unknown author. One of its first readers was the novelist William Makepeace Thackeray, who had been sent a copy by William Smith Williams; "exceedingly moved & pleased" by the novel, Thackeray asked Williams to convey his thanks to the author. Touched by this response, Brontë dedicated the second edition to Thackeray and added a preface expressing her admiration for the author of *Vanity Fair* (1848), "the first social regenerator of the day."

In this chorus of praise, there were some discordant notes. The *Christian Remembrancer* for April 1848 commented unfavorably on the "extravagant panegyric" of the preface to the second edition, denounced the novel's "moral Jacobinism," and expressed displeasure at the author's attacks on Christian practice. Even more condemnatory was the unsigned notice in the *Quarterly Review* for December 1848, written by Elizabeth Rigby (soon to become Lady Eastlake). Jane Eyre is here described as "the personification of an unregenerate and undisciplined spirit," exerting the moral strength of "a mere heathen mind which is a law unto itself." The novel is accused of being "pre-eminently an anti-Christian composition," guilty of "a murmuring against the comforts of the rich and against the privations of the poor, which, as far as each individual is concerned, is a murmuring against God's appointment." The prevailing tone, one of "ungodly discontent," allies the novel in the reviewer's opinion to the cast of mind and thought "which has overthrown authority and violated every code human and divine abroad, and fostered Chartism and rebellion at home. . . ."

The plot of *Jane Eyre* might well disturb those to whom the divisions of social rank were sacred, since it follows the progress of a poor orphan from a loveless and humiliating dependence to happiness and wealth as an heiress and the wife of her former employer. Jane is an outcast, a rebel who triumphs over the forces of social convention expressed through caste, religion, and sexual tradition. Victorian readers were disturbed by the novel's suggestion that women need not always be passive or submissive, and by its treatment of love, which, by contemporary standards, seemed coarse and offensive. The supremacy of romantic love is an ancient theme in literature, but in *Jane Eyre* it was presented with a frankness and intensity new to English fiction. That intensity is made possible by Brontë's choice of a first-person narrator. Jane Eyre dominates her world, which exists only as it impinges on her consciousness; every action is filtered through the medium of her sensibility, every character lives only as an actor in the drama of her life. An outline of the plot might suggest that Brontë's novel is little more than a creaky melodrama peopled by crude caricatures, but such is the authority, the conviction with which Jane tells her story that the reader is swept along by the narrative, undisturbed by improbabilities of character or plot.

One version of the novel's origin, related by Gaskell, is that during a discussion with her sisters about the qualities necessary in a protagonist, Charlotte Brontë declared that she would show them "a heroine as plain and as small as my-

JANE EYRE.

An Autobiography.

EDITED BY

CURRER BELL

IN THREE VOLUMES.

VOL. I.

LONDON:
SMITH, ELDER, AND CO., CORNHILL.
1847.

Title page of Charlotte Brontë's first published novel, which was successful with the public and with most of the critics

self, who shall be as interesting as any of yours." Such an intention is evident in the introductory chapters of *Jane Eyre*, where the ten-year-old Jane is seen as a prickly and unappealing child. She is an outsider, excluded by her Aunt Reed from the domestic circle around the hearth (a recurring image in the novel), and markedly different from her handsome but unpleasant cousins. She lacks their external attractiveness and confident air and is looked on with contempt even by the servants; only the solitary world of books and the imagination offers her any comfort, while her yearning for love must satisfy itself with an old doll. Yet the reader is soon made conscious of Jane's inner strength; her fierce assertion of self against the Reeds' cruelty and injustice intimidates even her aunt. Brontë conveys very powerfully the child's sense of alienation, helplessness, and anger in the face of adult oppression. Jane's rebellion at Gateshead against the tyranny of the Reeds is the first step in her progress toward spiritual freedom; at the same time, the wretchedness she feels after her violent outburst against Mrs. Reed reveals the danger of giving "uncontrolled play" to passionate feelings. The destructive potential of passion, imaged in chapter 4 as a fiery heath left "black and blasted," is to become a major theme in the Thornfield section of the novel.

In depicting Jane's search for the warmth and security of familial love, Brontë undoubtedly endowed her heroine with some of her own yearnings; and the autobiographical strain is even more evident in the chapters of *Jane Eyre* describing Lowood Institution, a thinly veiled reminiscence of life at the Clergy Daughters' School at Cowan Bridge. Mr. Brocklehurst, the "black marble clergyman," conveys the tone of William Carus Wilson's evangelical fervor in his speech, but the element of hypocrisy in Brocklehurst's sermonizing probably owes more to Charlotte Brontë's sense of justice than to the truth about Carus Wilson. Unlike his fictional counterpart, Carus Wilson had the welfare of his pupils at heart, but he lacked administrative experience, and his school was plagued in its early days by financial difficulties. Gaskell's description of the Clergy Daughters' School and its director, in the first editon of *The Life of Charlotte Brontë*, seems to confirm the picture given in *Jane Eyre*; but it should be remembered that she had obtained much of her information from Brontë herself, before the latter's death. Under the threat of legal proceedings by Carus Wilson's family (as well as by Branwell's former employer, Mrs. Robinson, now Lady Scott), Gaskell made extensive revisions for the third edition of the biography and presented Carus Wilson in a less unfavorable light.

Gaskell did not, however, soften her account of the cruel treatment suffered by Charlotte's eldest sister, Maria, at the hands of one of Carus Wilson's teachers. Maria was Brontë's model for the character of Helen Burns, Jane Eyre's first friend at Lowood, who achieves almost saintly stature by her meekness and patient endurance of hardship, and who teaches Jane the importance of Christian love and humility. Charlotte Brontë obviously intended to pay tribute to the qualities of her dead sister, but she was artist enough not to be satisfied with a simple portrait from life; Helen Burns teaches Jane the virtues of patience and forgiveness, but her spiritual ardor and otherworldly faith are too intense for one like Jane, whose needs and desires are firmly rooted in this world, and who recoils from the "un-fathomed gulf " of heaven and hell.

At eighteen, Jane leaves Lowood for "a new servitude," to become a governess at Thornfield Hall. Here the novel enters the realm of romance; the realism of character and setting which marks the descriptions of life at Gateshead and Lowood gives way to the mode and materials of Gothic melodrama, a vein that Charlotte and Branwell had mined in their Angrian chronicles. Social concerns are not wholly absent from Thornfield; in her account of Rochester's house party, Charlotte Brontë treats the empty pretensions of the English upper class with the same brand of bitter satire that she directs against Mr. Brocklehurst's religious hypocrisy. For the most part, however, the narrative moves on to a plane where dreams, visions, and presentiments have the force of waking reality: the world of cruel teachers and burned breakfasts gives way to one of mystery, terror, and sudden violence. The master of Thornfield is Edward Fairfax Rochester; like his predecessor, Zamorna, he is a compound of the Gothic villain and the Byronic hero: moody, passionate, overpoweringly attractive to women, burdened by a guilty past. Thornfield itself, with its crenellated front, its dark corridors, its hidden secret on the third story, becomes an English version of the Gothic castle, ruled by a tyrant and haunted by specters. What saves this section of *Jane Eyre* from descending to the level of adolescent fantasy and sensational melodrama is Brontë's concentration on the intensity of Jane's feelings and her use of such conventional materials to reflect and underscore her heroine's emotional turmoil. In the dark confines of Thornfield, Jane's troubled and passionate nature can find a release denied her in the "real" world; Rochester's brooding sexuality offers her the possibility of realizing desires normally forbidden expression. The danger that Jane runs in giving way to such feelings is expressed in language heavily charged with romantic symbolism; images of darkness, storm, and ruin counterpoint the description of the lovers' rising passions, and when Jane accepts Rochester's proposal, Nature herself protests, reminding the reader of the groans and "signs of woe" with which Nature greets the fall of mankind in Milton's *Paradise Lost* (1667). When Jane finally discovers Rochester's secret, the insane wife he has kept hidden at Thornfield for ten years, she is confronted by a frightening projection of one extreme of her own nature; Bertha Rochester is what Jane might have become: a

Norton Conyers at Swarcliffe, a mansion in which a madwoman had been kept locked in an attic room in the eighteenth century. Brontë visited here in 1839, and probably based some aspects of Thornfield on the house.

creature governed by unbridled, irrational passions, stripped of human identity.

The visionary and nightmare qualities of these chapters, strongly suggestive to post-Freudian readers of a disturbed libido, give way to more conventional moral concerns, as Jane rejects Rochester's plea that she live with him as his mistress and flees Thornfield in obedience to the dictates of conscience and self-respect. Here—despite the accusations of the *Quarterly Review*—the novel takes on a distinctly Christian quality, albeit in a somewhat unorthodox mingling of traditional Protestant values and romantic supernaturalism. Jane is seen as a suffering sinner who, like Christian in John Bunyan's *Pilgrim's Progress* (1678), must struggle through the world beset by trials and temptations in search of grace. At moments of intense spiritual crisis she is guided by a benevolent Providence, first manifested in the vision of her mother which tells her to "flee temptation," then sensed as "the might and strength of God" that comes to her rescue in her deepest despair and leads her through the marsh to her cousins' house. Though modern critics, often eager to see in Jane a prototype of the modern liberated woman, rightly emphasize her spirit of independence and self-reliance, it should also be recognized that in her quest for earthly happiness Jane is guided by a simple faith that gives her the inner strength to continue her search. Conviction of the validity of her own feelings is made possible by an unwavering belief in God—not the Calvinistic deity of Mr. Brocklehurst but a loving God expressed in and through nature.

The pattern of trial, temptation, and providential intervention established in the Thornfield episode and echoed in Jane's account of her subsequent wandering on the moors is repeated in the course of her relationship with her cousin, St. John Rivers. Rochester had threatened to destroy Jane's moral nature; St. John, whose powerful will and spiritual ambition almost overwhelm Jane's sense of self, poses an equally serious threat to the passions that give her life. Modeled in part upon Henry Martyn, the devout missionary whom Mr. Brontë had known at Cambridge and who had done much work in India, St. John displays an ardent and eloquent Evangelicalism that is unmistakably sincere. Yet in his pride and ambition he is less than perfect; and the struggle between his sensual nature and his spiritual zeal gives him enough humanity to make him more than just a mechanical foil to Rochester.

Jane is saved from surrendering her will to St. John's only by another providential intervention, this time in the form of Rochester's voice calling to her from afar. Her return to Rochester and their subsequent marriage (made possible by Bertha's fiery demise) is a satisfying conclusion to the story of their troubled love; yet there is a subdued, even anticlimactic quality about the novel's final chapters, perhaps because both Jane and Rochester have lost the spirit of willful defiance that is the basis of their appeal. So much of *Jane Eyre* is pervaded by the language and ideas of romanticism, especially in its emphasis on spiritual rebellion against a corrupt society, that Rochester's retributive maiming and his belated submission to divine law may seem a rather weak surrender to conventional morality. That Jane should now settle into a life of quiet middle-class domesticity also seems a renunciation of the passionate idealism that has hitherto marked her nature. Such an ending, however, reflects a sober recognition that life cannot always be lived at fever pitch. Only those who are prepared to turn their backs on the claims of nature can devote their lives to the unswerving pursuit of an ideal; and significantly the novel's closing paragraphs are concerned with the missionary achievements of St. John Rivers, doomed, like his real-life counterpart Henry Martyn, to an early death in the service of his God.

For *Jane Eyre*, Charlotte Brontë received five hundred pounds: for a first novel, a princely amount indeed, especially in comparison to the terms obtained from T. C. Newby by Emily and Anne, whose advance of fifty pounds toward the cost of production was never refunded. Anne's next novel, *The Tenant of Wildfell Hall*, was also published by Newby; at its appearance in June 1848, Newby sought to profit from the success of *Jane Eyre* by suggesting to the American publisher Harper that *The Tenant of Wildfell Hall* was written by the same author as *Jane Eyre*—that in fact Currer, Ellis, and Acton Bell were the pseudonyms of a single author. This alarmed Smith, Elder, who themselves had already promised Currer Bell's next work to Harper, and who now

asked for assurances that Currer Bell was not acting in bad faith. Accordingly, on a wet evening in July 1848, Charlotte and Anne walked across the moors to Keighley, caught the night train to Leeds, and presented themselves next morning in London to an astonished George Smith, dispelling any doubts the publisher might have had about their separate identities.

Thus began a relationship that was to last until Charlotte Brontë's death seven years later. When they first met, George Smith was twenty-four years old, eight years Brontë's junior, an attractive and energetic young businessman with an open and generous disposition. He and his widowed mother formed a strong attachment to Brontë; they shepherded her around London during her several visits to the capital, introduced her to the literary lions of the day, and on one occasion took her on a brief tour of Scotland. That there was a kind of playful flirtation between them is clear from the tone of Brontë's letters to Smith over the years: there is a lightheartedness, a vivaciousness not apparent in her other correspondence. But Brontë was under no illusion that their friendship might ripen into something deeper: as she told Ellen Nussey in June 1850, "I believe that George and I understand each other very well, and respect each other very sincerely. We both know the wide breach time has made between us; we do not embarrass each other, or very rarely, my six or eight years of seniority, to say nothing of lack of all pretension to beauty, etc., are a perfect safeguard." George Smith was later to tell Mrs. Humphry Ward that he "never could have loved any woman who had not some charm or grace of person, and Charlotte Brontë had none. . . . But I believe that my mother was at one time rather alarmed. . . ."

George Smith was anxious to follow up the success of *Jane Eyre* with another work by Currer Bell, and in December 1847 W. S. Williams suggested that Brontë write a novel for serial publication. She rejected this proposal but revealed that she was already planning a new three-volume novel based on a reworking of the materials she had used in *The Professor*. She made several attempts to begin this new work; one such commencement survives in the undated and untitled manuscript fragment known as "John Henry" or "The Moores," which describes the relationship between an overbearing mill owner and his intelligent, sensitive younger brother. The characters and framework of this story are strongly reminiscent of *The Professor*, but other elements, such as

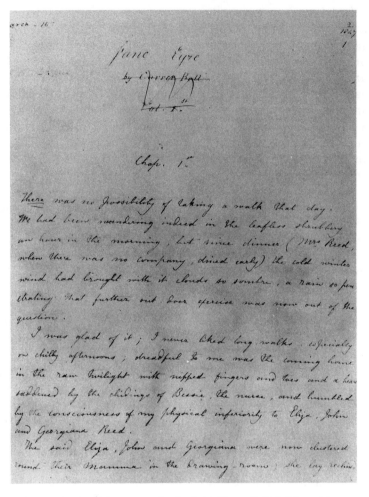

First page of the manuscript for Jane Eyre *(British Museum)*

the characters' names and the younger brother's disdain for superiority based on rank or wealth, point toward *Shirley*. That novel began to take shape early in 1848, and Brontë made such steady progress that the first volume and part of the second were completed before the end of September. Then came a series of tragedies which ended all joy in composition and might well have destroyed the creative impulse in one less strong than Charlotte Brontë.

First, on 24 September 1848, came the death of Branwell. Though he had been declining for a long time, his death still came as a heavy blow to his family. Charlotte, who had been the most angry and embittered at his degenerate conduct, was the one who felt his loss the most deeply, and for several weeks after the funeral she was prostrated by grief and illness. This was succeeded by an even severer shock: Emily fell prey to consumption, and after a brief but heroic struggle, she died on 19 December

1848. More anguish was to follow; even before Emily's death, Anne's health had begun to deteriorate, and now she too suffered a rapid decline. In May 1849 Charlotte and Ellen Nussey took her to Scarborough in the hope that fresh sea air might bring some improvement, but she died there on 28 May, three days after their arrival.

Now, at thirty-three, Charlotte was the sole survivor of the six Brontë children. Grief and solitude weighed heavily upon her, but she pressed on with *Shirley*, finding in work an anodyne for her suffering; as she told William Smith Williams after the novel's completion, "the occupation of writing it has been a boon to me. It took me out of dark and desolate reality into an unreal but happier region." The manuscript of *Shirley* was finished by the end of August 1849. Before sending it off to Smith, Elder, Brontë prepared a lengthy preface in which Currer Bell took to task the hostile reviewer of *Jane Eyre* in the *Quarterly Review*. The peevish tone and somewhat laborious ironies of the intended preface did not please George Smith, and when *Shirley: A Tale* was published in three volumes on 26 October 1849, no preface was included. However, Brontë's angry scorn of the *Quarterly Review* had already found release in the text itself: in Mrs. Pryor's account of her employment as a governess in the Hardman family, the unpleasant Hardmans are made to condemn themselves in words taken verbatim from Elizabeth Rigby's attack on *Jane Eyre*.

In that novel, Brontë had focused on the personal history and emotional experience of an individual; in *Shirley*, she sought to diffuse the interest among more characters and to bring them into contact with the public world of politics and social conflict. The novel is set in the West Riding of Yorkshire during the troubled years of 1811-1812, when the economic hardships ensuing from the war with France, complicated by an embargo on trade with America and the introduction of new machinery, led to massive unemployment and widespread rioting in the wool-producing districts. Much of the novel's action centers on Robert Moore, a local mill owner who is threatened on one hand by bankruptcy and on the other by Luddite machine-breakers. With the help of the militia, he routs a force of workers who had set out to destroy his mill; subsequently, however, he is shot by a religious fanatic and seriously wounded. Alongside this plot of industrial conflict is developed the story of Caroline Helstone, Moore's cousin, and her friendship with Shirley Keeldar, a spirited young heiress and landowner. Caroline, who lives with her guardian, a stern Tory clergyman, falls in love with Moore, but, believing that she has lost him to Shirley, enters into a dangerous decline. She is saved from death by the care of Mrs. Pryor, Shirley's elderly companion, who reveals herself to be Caroline's long-lost mother. Shirley herself is in love with Louis Moore, Robert's brother and her former tutor; despite opposition from class-conscious relatives, Shirley encourages Louis's attentions, and at the novel's conclusion they are married. Caroline and Robert are also united, the latter having recovered from his wound and acknowledged his love for his devoted cousin.

Brontë's choice of a subject so different from that of *Jane Eyre* was governed in part by her response to criticism of that novel's romantic excesses. G. H. Lewes in particular, writing in *Fraser's Magazine*, had mingled praise for the novel's strength of characterization and narrative power with an admonition about the dangers of melodrama. The opening of *Shirley*, with its warning to the reader that he should expect not romance, but "something unromantic as Monday morning," is clearly an answer to that charge and a declaration of solemn intent, though couched in such ironic terms as to make it clear that the author is also mocking her critics. There is certainly a homely realism in much of the first volume, notably in the portraits of the three curates and of the house-proud Hortense Moore, characters drawn with a comic touch that is rare in Brontë's adult fiction. There is no comedy, however, in her description of the hardships of the Yorkshire unemployed, or in her accounts of the bitter confrontations of master and men. Her choice of this grim subject may have been inspired by the Chartist agitation that had troubled England for a decade, reaching its climax with a massive demonstration in London in April 1848. That Brontë should have turned to a historical parallel, the Luddite disturbances, to explore the "Condition of England" question reflects her natural reluctance to become involved in contemporary political controversy; as she told Williams in April 1848, "political partizanship is what I would ever wish to avoid as much as religious bigotry."

Charlotte Brontë took pains to present an accurate picture of the Luddite uprisings in the West Riding. She doubtless recalled stories about this period of Yorkshire history told by Miss Wooler at Roe Head, and by her father, who had known some of the principal antagonists during the time of his curacy at Hartshead-cum-Clifton. To supplement such anecdotal sources, Brontë studied the files of the Leeds *Mercury* for 1811-1813, making copies of some of its reports on Luddite activities. The result in *Shirley* is an authentic re-creation of the period, in which local events are merged with issues of national policy, and fiction is expertly blended with historical fact. The climax of the novel's industrial theme, the attack on Robert Moore's mill, is a reworking of a famous incident in April 1812, when a band of Luddites stormed William Cartwright's mill at Rawfolds, near Hartshead, and suffered a heavy defeat; the assault and its consequences were prominently reported in the Leeds *Mercury*. *Shirley* is not simply fictionalized history, however; Brontë's interest lies primarily in her characters and their relationships, and she adapts or changes historical detail to suit the needs of her narrative. Her treatment of history is also colored to some extent by her Tory partialities: she presents the plight of the workers sympatheti-

The publisher George Smith, to whom Charlotte and Anne Brontë revealed their identities in July 1848 (Brontë Parsonage Museum)

cally, but it is plain that she regards their cause as mistaken, their leaders as rabble-rousers and troublemakers. At the same time, she is critical of the callousness and narrow self-interest of the manufacturers, who exploit the poor with little regard for their misery. The plot of *Shirley* deals in part with the reeducation and rehabilitation of the mill owner Robert Moore, whose contact with the suffering he has helped to create teaches him to value men more than machines. In this respect the novel offers an oblique comment on the need for more tolerant attitudes on the part of the governing class in the England of 1848.

The theme of industrial conflict is interwoven with the stories of Caroline and Shirley, through whom Brontë explores another important social issue: the failure of Victorian society to give women the kinds of opportunities afforded to men to develop their abilities, realize their potential, and exercise some control over their lives. Not unlike the factory workers, women are exploited, their needs ignored, their roles strictly defined by male authority. Shirley, by virtue of her wealth and social station, can successfully challenge this domination, much to the anger and frustration of most of the men she encounters; Caroline, however, poor and unconnected, has few choices: the role of genteel spinster (a forbidding fate, as reflected in the lives of Miss Mann and Miss Ainley), or the servitude of

the governess-trade described with bitter restraint by Mrs. Pryor. Rescue ultimately comes in the only form possible for a woman in Caroline's position: marriage. Yet as Brontë makes clear in a long (and somewhat uncharacteristic) reflection by Caroline in volume two, chapter 11, such salvation does not come to all; and the struggle for success in an overstocked "matrimonial market" all too often leads women into degrading and humiliating competition, making them objects of scorn and ridicule to men. The solution is to give single women "better chances of interesting and profitable occupation than they possess now" and to cultivate girls' minds, not keep them "narrow and fettered." Brontë's feminism lacks the political dimension that marked the growth of the women's movement later in the century, but her call for women's emancipation from domestic slavery puts her at the forefront of that movement and gives *Shirley* added force and interest.

Few of the book's early reviewers, however, found much to praise in Brontë's attempt to branch out into realms of social comment. Only Eugène Forcade, writing in the *Revue des deux mondes* (15 November 1849), voiced approval of the novel's assertion of "moral liberty, the spirit of rebelliousness, the impulses of revolt against certain social conventions," noting that its subtitle might well have been "On the Condition of Women in the English Middle Class." For the most part, critical responses reflected disappointment that *Shirley* was not cast in the same mold as *Jane Eyre*. Reviewers were bored by the characters' lengthy conversations, or offended by the aggressive and unwomanly conduct of the eponymous heroine. While acknowledging the author's descriptive powers, they found the plot slow-moving, the chief male characters unconvincing. There is some basis for such complaints. The narrative lacks focus and unity, in large part because of the almost equal emphasis given to the two heroines and the course of their respective love affairs. The belated introduction of Shirley, who does not appear until the eleventh chapter, gives an awkward wrench to the plot, which has hitherto centered on the relationship between Caroline and Robert. The character of Shirley herself is drawn with mixed success: though she has an appealing liveliness and intellectual vigor, her attractions seem somewhat brittle, and her love for the wooden and uninteresting figure of Louis Moore belies all the positive aspects of her nature. From the account given by Gaskell, it is known that Brontë intended, through Shirley, to portray her

VILLETTE.

By CURRER BELL,

AUTHOR OF "JANE EYRE," "SHIRLEY," ETC.

IN THREE VOLUMES.

VOL. I.

LONDON:
SMITH, ELDER & CO., 65, CORNHILL.

SMITH, TAYLOR & CO., BOMBAY.
——
1853.
The Author of this work reserves the right of translating it.

Title page of the last novel published during Brontë's lifetime

sister Emily as she might have been had she lived. Undoubtedly, Shirley has some of Emily's characteristics—her love of nature, her stoicism, her almost mystical apprehension of experience; but Emily did not have Shirley's dazzling beauty, her aggressive wit and charm, or her ability to dominate all around her. It is likely, rather, that some aspects of Emily's character were grafted onto the portrait of Shirley as the novel was being written; the first volume had been completed before Emily's death in December 1848, and it is possible that when she returned to the novel's composition, Charlotte modified her original conception to include Emily's qualities in the portrayal of Shirley as a kind of posthumous tribute. *Shirley* was an extremely ambitious effort by a young novelist eager to win recognition as a serious writer. It may lack the concentration, the driving force of a single vision that gives *Jane Eyre* its power; but in its treatment of complex social issues and its panoramic study of a turbulent period of English history, *Shirley* ranks with novels

such as Benjamin Disraeli's *Sybil* (1845), Gaskell's *Mary Barton* (1848), or Charles Dickens's *Hard Times* (1854) as a significant contribution to the Victorian debate about the goals and values of industrial capitalism.

Between the publication of *Shirley* in October 1849 and the appearance of *Villette* in January 1853, Charlotte Brontë's life was marked by loneliness, depression, and recurring illness. She occupied herself with household affairs and the care of her father, but the sense of loss weighed heavily upon her, renewed daily by all the associations of the parsonage and the surrounding moors. She found some relief, and an outlet for her creative energies, in editing her sisters' literary remains. At Smith, Elder's suggestion she prepared an edition of *Wuthering Heights* and *Agnes Grey*, together with selections from her sisters' poems. The book was published in one volume at six shillings in December 1850, with a "Biographical Notice" and other prefatory materials by Charlotte which gave the reading public its first glimpse into the lives of the Brontës, as well as dispelling the still-current notion that all their works had been the production of one person. Brontë also emended the text of *Wuthering Heights*, correcting the many errors introduced by its first publisher, T. C. Newby, softening the harsh and incomprehensible dialect of Joseph, and altering the staccato paragraphing to create a greater smoothness of effect. Modern critics have taken her to task for these textual changes; but her introductory comments about Emily's character and about *Wuthering Heights* itself are perceptive and intelligent.

Brontë's widening circle of acquaintances, the result of her literary fame, afforded another source of distraction from her grief. She paid several visits to the Smiths in London and found herself, much to her dislike, the center of eager curiosity and attention. She met Thackeray, for whom her earlier admiration was cooled somewhat by his worldliness and evident enjoyment of fashionable society. She was introduced to G. H. Lewes, with whom she had corresponded since the publication of *Jane Eyre*, and was taken by his remarkable likeness in features to her sister Emily. She also struck up a friendship with Harriet Martineau and became her guest at Ambleside in December 1850; in Miss Martineau's company she met Matthew Arnold, who displeased her by his affected manner and "seeming foppery." In August 1850, staying at Windermere with Sir James Kay-Shuttleworth and his wife, Brontë met her future biographer, Elizabeth Cleghorn Gaskell, and was at once drawn to this warmhearted and sympathetic woman, telling her much that was subsequently to be incorporated into *The Life of Charlotte Brontë*. The most eventful of Brontë's excursions from Haworth was her trip to London at the end of May 1851. Staying as usual at the Smiths', she was taken on numerous outings. She attended four of Thackeray's six lectures on the English humorists; met Richard Monckton Milnes (the future biographer of Keats) and the eminent Scottish scientist Sir David Brewster; breakfasted with the poet Samuel Rogers; and paid five visits to the Crystal Palace, home of the Great Exhibition which had opened on 1 May 1851. In George Smith's company, she attended two performances by the great French tragedienne Rachel, whose acting made her "shudder to the marrow of my bones: in her some fiend has certainly taken up an incarnate home." Smith also indulged her taste for phrenology, the pseudoscience of determining character by examining the conformation of the skull, to which Brontë makes frequent reference in her novels: they visited a Dr. J. P. Browne, whose phrenological study of "Miss Fraser" (her pseudonym on this occasion) resulted in a surprisingly accurate picture of Brontë's character.

Soon after her return to Haworth, Brontë began work on her new novel. The task proved difficult, partly because she could not free herself from the depression that grew out of her solitude. Now thirty-five years old, she saw no prospect of an end to her spinsterhood. For a short time she had received the attentions of James Taylor, George Smith's manager in Cornhill; but he struck her as lacking in intellect and good breeding, and any possibility of a union between them evaporated when Taylor left England in May 1851 to act as Smith's agent in India. Despite the blank prospect that opened before her, Brontë struggled on with her writing; and by the spring of 1852 her creative powers had returned with much of their old strength. After preparing a list of changes and corrections for the new one-volume edition of *Shirley* in March, she worked steadily on *Villette*, sending Smith the last volume in November. A temporary difficulty had been created by her father's wish that the book end happily; Gaskell relates that Mr. Brontë "disliked novels which left a melancholy impression upon the mind." Charlotte would not alter her plan of having Paul Emanuel drown at sea; however, notes Gaskell, she sought "so to veil the fate in oracular

words, as to leave it to the character and discernment of her readers to interpret her meaning." Of greater concern to Brontë was the book's reception by her publisher, not least because she feared that George Smith might take offense at the use she had made of him and his mother in her depiction of the Brettons. She was conscious, too, that the book lacked "public interest" and touched on nothing topical or exciting. Her anxieties were increased by Smith's criticism of the shift in interest from John Graham Bretton to Paul Emanuel in the third volume. Smith seemed reluctant to proceed with the novel's printing; so, unable to bear any further delays or uncertainties, Brontë went up to London to see him. Her visit had the desired effect: whatever objections Smith might have had were overcome, the printing went ahead, and on 28 January 1853 *Villette*, by Currer Bell, made its appearance in the familiar three-volume format at thirty-one shillings, sixpence.

With *Villette* Brontë returned to the autobiographical mode which had given *Jane Eyre* such coherence and conviction despite the implausibility of its plot. This time, however, she avoided an uncritical identification with her heroine: Lucy Snowe embodies much of Brontë's own experience and outlook, and in many respects is a projection of her creator's inner self, but the novel is not simply a fictionalized expression of personal feelings or the enactment of Brontë's secret dreams and fantasies. Despite its obvious connection with the writer's life in Brussels, *Villette* is imbued with a critical irony from which even its narrator is not exempt.

An outline of the plot can scarcely convey the complexity or intensity of the emotional struggles it dramatizes. The reader first meets the heroine, Lucy Snowe, as a fourteen-year-old girl in the household of her godmother, Louisa Bretton, a widow with a sixteen-year-old son, John Graham Bretton. Lucy is joined by little Paulina Home, whose mother has recently died and whose father is going abroad to secure his business affairs. The elfin Polly attaches herself to John Graham, who treats her with an appropriately adolescent mixture of amusement and indifference. Forced by circumstances to support herself, Lucy takes employment as companion to an elderly invalid, Miss Marchmont, whose history of a love frustrated by fate prefigures Lucy's own subsequent experience. At Miss Marchmont's death, Lucy travels to Villette, capital of Labassecour ("little town" and "the farmyard":

Brontë's ironic names for Brussels and Belgium); here she becomes a teacher at the Pensionnat de Demoiselles owned by Mme Beck. In Villette, Lucy meets the Brettons again; John Graham, now ten years older, is a practicing physician for whom the scheming Mme Beck is evidently setting her cap. He seems to encourage Madame's advances, while in reality he is paying court to one of her pupils, the flighty Ginevra Fanshawe. For a time Lucy is herself drawn into "Dr. John's" sphere; however, any chance of his giving her serious attention is ended by the reappearance of Paulina Home, whose father has become the Count de Bassompierre, and who quickly becomes the focus of Dr. John's interest. Lucy herself finds an admirer in Paul Emanuel, Mme Beck's cousin, who teaches literature at the pensionnat; despite his stormy nature and Madame's attempted interference, Paul wins Lucy's love, establishes her in her own little school in Villette, and departs for the West Indies to manage some family affairs. Lucy remains faithful to him during the three years of his absence, but during his return home he perishes in a shipwreck.

In plot and setting, *Villette* has obvious similarities to *The Professor*, but it is not merely a refashioning of the materials used in the earlier work. It is colored even more highly than *The Professor* by Brontë's recollections of her two years at the Pensionnat Heger. The Hegers' school, with its cluster of classrooms and dormitories, its sheltered garden and "*allée défendue*," is re-created in careful detail. The Hegers themselves are unmistakably the models for Mme Beck, the school's calculating directress, and Paul Emanuel, the fiery teacher whose unpredictable temper alternately delights and terrifies his pupils. Even the girls and teachers at Mme Beck's school can be identified with real-life originals Brontë had met in Brussels. Many other aspects of *Villette* are clearly autobiographical; such events as Lucy's journey through London and across the Channel, her visit to an art exhibition and a concert, her attendance at a performance by "Vashti" (Rachel), all are drawn from the writer's own experiences in Brussels and London. Lucy's relationship with the Brettons adumbrates elements of Brontë's friendship with George Smith and his mother. Lucy herself has recognizable similarities to Brontë, from her contemptuous dislike of Belgians and her distrust of Catholicism to her consciousness of physical inferiority and her susceptibility to depression.

Despite the temptation to regard *Villette* as autobiographical, however, the question of Lucy's likeness to her creator must be treated with caution, for Brontë distances herself from her narrator in some ways. Though Lucy speaks with the most authority, she is not always honest with herself or with her reader, and sometimes her interpretation of character or event betrays the biases of a mind warped to some extent by a sense of failure, frustration, and inadequacy. Lucy describes herself as a "looker-on" at life and dreads the revelation of her own feelings; thence springs the agony she feels when asked by M. Paul to take a part in the school play. From her vantage point of seemingly detached observer, she passes caustic comment on the weaknesses or pretensions of those around her. Even as a girl, her determination to avoid emotional involvement is evident in her almost clinical scrutiny of little Polly's suffering at the temporary separation from her father. Writing to George Smith shortly before completing the manuscript, Brontë explained her choice of the heroine's name (she had wavered between "Frost" and "Snowe"): "A *cold* name she must have; partly, perhaps, on the '*lucus a non lucendo*' principle—partly on that of the 'fitness of things,' for she has about her an external coldness." Convinced that fate has decreed that her life be deprived of warmth or love, Lucy is determined to protect herself from rebuff, from the pain that self-exposure might entail; for this reason, she at first conceals from Dr. John (and from the reader) the fact of their earlier acquaintance. She takes a masochistic satisfaction in the contrast between the beauty of her empty-headed young friend Ginevra and her own plainness. Her crusty manner leads Ginevra to call her "Diogenes" or "Timon," nicknames that Lucy enjoys, since they confirm her preferred posture of cynical coldness and spiritual independence.

Yet Lucy is a creature of strong feelings; and inevitably those feelings seek an outlet, first in the morbid depression that leads her to make a confession to a Catholic priest, then in an imagined attachment to Dr. John, who treats her kindly during her illness. This last episode and the subsequent shift of interest to Paul Emanuel have been seen as a structural weakness in the novel; but Lucy's fantasies about Dr. John are a necessary prelude to the real love that awakens in her later. The young Englishman is a kind of conventional novel hero; with his good looks, charming manner, and gentlemanly breeding he presents Lucy with a model of the masculine virtues that, in her longing for love, she can hardly resist. Not until she has buried this romantic illusion (a literal interment, with the burial of Dr. John's letters) can she recognize that love is possible in less conventional, but also less superficial, terms in the hitherto comic form of Paul Emanuel.

The irascible schoolteacher takes Lucy into the last stages of her emotional growth, liberates her from her neurotic repressions, and enables her to find expression for her natural yearnings. From the first he perceives the powerful feelings that Lucy tries to deny, and like Rochester with Jane Eyre, he teases those feelings to the surface by a mixture of insult and kindness. Paul is perhaps the most credible (and likable) of Brontë's male characters: she does not minimize his faults—his jealous pride, his overbearing manner, his pettiness; yet it is he who assumes the role of hero in *Villette*, not the more glamorous John Graham Bretton. He is the "natural" man, incapable of disguise or deceit, whose very weaknesses make him more human and accessible than the polished (and rather superficial) doctor. In the claustrophobic world of the pensionnat, Paul is a breath of fresh air and gives Lucy for the first time in her life a hope of happiness. Like Greatheart in *Pilgrim's Progress*, he becomes her champion, battling for her soul with Apollyon, the redoubtable Mme Beck.

Though cast in the same mold as Zoraïde Reuter of *The Professor*, Modeste Maria Beck is a far more formidable character. The argument as to whether or not she is a just representation of her original, Mme Heger, is irrelevant; her function is to be Lucy's crafty, passionless antagonist, a proponent of spiritual tyranny and Romanist subversion, and for this she is endowed with qualities of intellect and perceptiveness that make her a worthy enemy. Lucy acknowledges her powers and even voices her admiration for her ability to manipulate others. In some respects they are similar in temperament: both are secretive, both conceal their true feelings and assume a persona appropriate to the occasion; but while Mme Beck plays roles systematically as a means of maintaining her power, Lucy does so out of necessity, for fear of giving herself away and losing the mastery over self that protects her from pain.

Punctuating the story of Lucy's struggle with Mme Beck and her own feelings is the recurring motif of the ghostly nun, a Gothic device that turns out to have a somewhat bathetic explanation, but that is nevertheless effective as a means of projecting the turbulence of Lucy's emotions and suggesting the illusory nature of her grasp on reality. The nun in the garden, like the figure of Justine Marie who seems to stand between Lucy and M. Paul, is real enough, yet also a creation of her heated imagination; when she returns from her almost hallucinatory expedition to the park, where she has seen Paul with her imagined rival Justine Marie, Lucy finds the ghostly nun lying on her bed—nothing more than a bolster covered in a black stole. The discovery is a fittingly ironic comment on Lucy's capacity for self-deception and misconstruction.

Distorted though her vision may be at times, Lucy Snowe's painful circumstances are not imaginary. In *The Professor* and *Jane Eyre*, Brontë had already examined the plight of a young woman of feeling and intelligence cast into the world and forced to make her own way. Her own experience had shown her that society placed no premium on inner worth; that happiness was doubtful for those who must earn their own bread; that love, sexual fulfillment, even domestic comfort were achieved by few women. Lucy Snowe tries to detach herself from life out of a conviction that any kind of emotional commitment must bring suffering and humiliation. Even though she wins love in the end, it is a very limited happiness that she is granted, since Paul is snatched away from her at the last moment by a cruel and arbitrary fate. Lucy may have gained maturity of vision and freedom from her neurotic fears of inadequacy, but her creator's pessimism denies her the final reward of romantic reunion: the return to an Edenic garden, permitted to Jane Eyre, is no longer possible.

The intensity of feeling in *Villette*, its concentration on the heroine's yearning and frustration, its veiled and enigmatic ending did not sit well with early readers. Reviewers praised the novel's detailed portrait of school life and found much to applaud in the freshness and vitality of "Currer Bell's" eccentric schoolmaster hero, but there was some dissatisfaction with the novel's emphasis on Lucy's suffering: the *Spectator* felt that Lucy "took a savage delight in refusing to be comforted," and Harriet Martineau protested in the *Daily News* at the "amount of subjective misery," the "atmosphere of pain" that hung about the novel. Readers familiar with the details of the author's life treated *Villette* as a personal revelation; Thackeray saw it as little more than the expression of Brontë's own yearnings for love, while Matthew Arnold declared the novel "disagreeable" because "the writer's mind contains nothing but hunger, rebellion and rage. . . ." Such dismissive judgments, ignoring the book's narrative art and structural ironies, were less than just, yet they reflect an ineluctable truth: the source of the novel's strength, its power to arouse and disturb, does lie in the author's painful attempt to reconcile the conflict between her desires and her sense of inadequacy. *Villette* strikes the modern reader as a successful book because Brontë was able to transform her own "hunger, rebellion and rage" into a dramatic study of a tormented female sensibility, revealing its distortions and excesses as well as its nobility in suffering.

Even before the publication of this, her final work, Brontë's life had entered a new phase that was to bring her, however briefly, the happiness she had sought for so long. On 13 December 1852 she received a proposal of marriage from Arthur Bell Nicholls (1818-1906), her father's dour Irish curate since 1845. She had long suspected his interest in her, but the strength of his feeling took her by surprise. Though his evident suffering and abrupt dismissal by an enraged Mr. Brontë aroused her sympathy, she was not attracted to him, and discouraged his suit. Nicholls persisted in his addresses, however; he and Charlotte entered into a clandestine correspondence, and in April 1854, with Mr. Brontë's reluctant consent, they became engaged. Charlotte's feelings for Nicholls had ripened into respect, but she had no illusions about the brilliance of her prospects, telling Ellen Nussey that "what I taste of happiness is of the soberest order." Fifteen years earlier, she had refused Henry Nussey because he did not inspire in her "that intense attachment which would make me willing to die for him"; experience had cured her of such romantic idealism, and she was now ready to take refuge in the comfort of a relationship promising at least affection and security.

Brontë's increasing preoccupation with domestic affairs and a growing coolness in her relations with George Smith made it difficult for her to apply herself seriously to the task of writing a new novel. She did make several attempts, beginnings which survive in the manuscript fragments "The Story of Willie Ellin" and "Emma." The former, written in the early summer of 1853, represents a return to the theme of two rival brothers which Brontë had first explored in her juvenile stories. Like their many predecessors, the brothers bear the names Edward and William; the elder, Edward Ellin, is a cruel guardian to his ten-year-old brother, whom he intends to apprentice to trade. Willie seeks refuge in the former family house, Ellin Balcony, but is recaptured and whipped for his recalcitrance. The fragments show Brontë experimenting with alternative plot lines, introducing different characters to act as Willie's protectors. One short part presents an unusual narrative point of view: the speaker appears to be a disembodied spirit that haunts the Ellins' ancestral home. The other fragment, "Emma," begun on 27 November 1853, is a more conventional account, about a young girl called Matilda Fitzgibbon who is left by her father as a boarder at a girls' school. At first presumed to be an heiress, she is treated with great partiality; but when the discovery is made that her father had given a fictitious name and address, and that he has disappeared, "Matilda" is confronted by her irate schoolteacher and collapses. The fragment is interesting chiefly for its satirical portrait of Miss Wilcox, the eldest of the sisters who run the school; the chief male character, who takes the rejected Matilda under his wing at the end of the fragment, is called Mr. Ellin. "Emma" was published posthumously in the fourth number of the *Cornhill Magazine* (April 1860), with a laudatory introduction by Thackeray.

With her marriage to Arthur Bell Nicholls on 29 June 1854, Charlotte Brontë's literary activity came to an end. The couple honeymooned in Wales and Ireland, returning at the beginning of August to Haworth (Charlotte could not be prevailed upon to leave her ailing father for long), where Nicholls resumed his duties as Mr. Brontë's curate. For the first time since the deaths of Emily and Anne, Charlotte Brontë found life at the parsonage congenial and satisfying; her new role as a wife kept her active and occupied, and her husband, now reconciled with her father, daily revealed qualities which won her respect and increased her attachment to him. But the pleasures of this domesticity were short-lived. In January 1855 she discovered she was pregnant; she soon began to suffer from extreme nausea and vomiting, a condition which her delicate constitution was unable to bear. Worn out by the struggle, she died on 31 March 1855. Once more the house fell silent. Mr. Brontë remained there until his own death in 1861; Nicholls watched over him in his last years, then returned to his native Ireland, where he remarried in 1864.

Two further publications of importance maintained Brontë's prominence in the literary world after her death. One was Smith, Elder's pub-

The Reverend Arthur Bell Nicholls
(Brontë Parsonage Museum)

lication in March 1857 of Mrs. Gaskell's controversial biography, *The Life of Charlotte Brontë*; this proved so successful that a second edition was required in April, but under the threat of legal action by the families of William Carus Wilson and Lady Scott (formerly Mrs. Edmund Robinson of Thorp Green), Mrs. Gaskell was obliged to make extensive revisions for the third edition, published in September. In her desire to present Brontë as an almost saintly heroine, Mrs. Gaskell had perhaps allowed herself to believe too readily in some of the more exaggerated accounts of the Brontë family's adversities. The same motive doubtless led her to omit any reference to Charlotte's infatuation for Constantin Heger, although she was aware of the letters that Charlotte had written to Heger after her final departure from Brussels. Not until 1913 would the letters and the circumstances surrounding them come into public view, when they were reproduced in the London *Times* by Marion H. Spielmann.

During her research in preparation for the writing of *The Life of Charlotte Brontë*, Gaskell accompanied Sir James Kay-Shuttleworth on a visit to Haworth. They succeeded in persuading Nicholls to lend them unpublished manuscripts,

including that of *The Professor*. Though Gaskell did not think the latter would add to Brontë's reputation, she bowed to Sir James's insistence that the book be published and returned the manuscript to Nicholls with the suggestion that he revise the work for publication. Nicholls did so, making some small changes to remove what Gaskell had called the novel's "coarseness and profanity in quoting texts of scripture," and adding a brief prefatory note dated 22 September 1856. *The Professor* was finally published by Smith, Elder in two volumes in June 1857 and was given a muted reception by its first readers. In his introductory note, Nicholls maintained that *The Professor* and *Villette* were "in most respects unlike," but the reviewers fastened on the obvious similarities and treated the earlier work as little more than a crude sketch of its successor. They regarded it as a literary curiosity; its interest lay in its connection with the career so movingly described by Gaskell, rather than in any claims it might have to serious critical attention. *The Professor* would find its defenders: Peter Bayne praises its vivid character portrayals, thinks the story "full of life," and compares the novel favorably to *Villette*. Even Bayne, however, is forced to acknowledge that it is "by no means a wonderful book." Modern criticism has not sought to reverse that judgment.

In the course of his study, Bayne accords Charlotte pride of place among the Brontë sisters because she had "ten times more power" than Anne and a nature with more geniality and culture than Emily's. Later critics have moved in a different direction, finding Emily to be the greater writer. The stark and mythopoeic qualities of *Wuthering Heights* undeniably reflect a genius and a vision beyond Charlotte's capacities. Yet Emily's enigmatic romance, unique of its kind, was a dead end in English fiction, whereas the painful realism of Charlotte's studies of the human heart gave a fresh impetus and a new direction to the genre of the novel.

Bibliographies:

Thomas J. Wise, *A Bibliography of the Writings in Prose and Verse of the Members of the Brontë Family* (London: Clay, 1917);

G. Anthony Yablon and John R. Turner, *A Brontë Bibliography* (London: Hodgkins, 1978; Westport, Conn.: Meckler, 1978);

R. W. Crump, *Charlotte and Emily Brontë, 1846-1915: A Reference Guide* (Boston: G. K. Hall, 1982).

Biographies:

Elizabeth Cleghorn Gaskell, *The Life of Charlotte Brontë*, 2 volumes, third edition, revised (London: Smith, Elder, 1857);

Thomas J. Wise and John A. Symington, eds., *The Brontës: Their Lives, Friendships and Correspondence*, 4 volumes (Oxford: Blackwell, 1932);

Winifred Gérin, *Charlotte Brontë: The Evolution of Genius* (Oxford: Clarendon Press, 1967).

References:

Christine Alexander, *The Early Writings of Charlotte Brontë* (Oxford: Blackwell, 1983);

Miriam Allott, ed., *The Brontës: The Critical Heritage* (London: Routledge & Kegan Paul, 1974);

Peter Bayne, *Two Great Englishwomen: Mrs. Browning and Charlotte Brontë* (London: Clarke, 1881);

Margaret H. Blom, *Charlotte Brontë* (Boston: Twayne, 1977);

Asa Briggs, "Private and Social Themes in *Shirley*," *Brontë Society Transactions*, 13, part 68 (1958): 203-219;

"Charlotte Brontë's Tragedy: The Lost Letters," *Times* (London), 29-30 July 1913, p. 9;

Mildred G. Christian, "The Brontës," in *Victorian Fiction: A Guide to Research*, edited by Lionel Stevenson (Cambridge, Mass.: Harvard University Press, 1964), pp. 214-244;

Robert A. Colby, "*Villette* and the Life of the Mind," *PMLA*, 75 (1960): 410-419;

Enid L. Duthie, *The Foreign Vision of Charlotte Brontë* (London: Macmillan, 1975);

Rebecca Fraser, *Charlotte Brontë* (London: Methuen, 1988);

Sandra M. Gilbert and Susan Crubar, *The Madwoman in the Attic: The Woman Writer and the Nineteenth-Century Literary Imagination* (New Haven: Yale University Press, 1979);

Robert B. Heilman, "Charlotte Brontë's 'New' Gothic," in *From Jane Austen to Joseph Conrad: Essays Collected in Memory of James T. Hillhouse*, edited by Robert C. Rathburn and Martin Steinmann, Jr. (Minneapolis: University of Minnesota Press, 1958), pp. 118-132;

Jacob Korg, "The Problem of Unity in *Shirley*," *Nineteenth Century Fiction*, 12 (1957): 125-136;

David Lodge, *Language of Fiction: Essays in Criticism and Verbal Analysis of the English Novel* (London: Routledge & Kegan Paul, 1966), pp. 114-143;

Robert B. Martin, *The Accents of Persuasion: Charlotte Brontë's Novels* (London: Faber, 1966);

Pauline Nestor, *Female Friendships and Communities: Charlotte Brontë, George Eliot, Elizabeth Gaskell* (Oxford: Clarendon Press, 1985; New York: Oxford University Press, 1985);

Fannie E. Ratchford, *The Brontës' Web of Childhood* (New York: Columbia University Press, 1941);

Herbert J. Rosengarten, "The Brontës," in *Victorian Fiction: A Second Guide to Research*, edited by George H. Ford (New York: MLA, 1978), pp. 172-203;

Kathleen Tillotson, *Novels of the Eighteen-Forties* (Oxford: Clarendon Press, 1954), pp. 257-313;

Tom Winnifrith, *The Brontës and Their Background: Romance and Reality* (London: Macmillan, 1973).

Papers:

Important manuscript holdings of Charlotte Brontë's prose writings are to be found at the British Library; Brontë Parsonage Museum, Haworth; Harvard University Library; Harry Ransom Humanities Research Center, University of Texas, Austin; Huntington Library; New York Public Library; Princeton University Library; and Pierpont Morgan Library.

Emily Brontë

(30 July 1818 - 19 December 1848)

This entry was updated by Tom Winnifrith (University of Warwick) from his entry in
DLB 21: Victorian Novelists Before 1885.

See also the Brontë entry in DLB 32: Victorian Poets Before 1850.

BOOKS: *Poems by Currer, Ellis, and Acton Bell*, by Charlotte, Emily, and Anne Brontë (London: Aylott & Jones, 1846; Philadelphia: Lea & Blanchard, 1848);

Wuthering Heights, as Ellis Bell (2 volumes, London: T. C. Newby, 1847; 1 volume, Boston: Coolidge & Wiley, 1848).

Collections: *The Life and Works of Charlotte Brontë and Her Sisters*, Haworth Edition, 7 volumes, edited by Mrs. Humphry Ward and C. K. Shorter (London: Smith, Elder, 1899-1900);

The Complete Poems of Emily Jane Brontë, edited by Shorter (New York: Hodder & Stoughton, 1908; London: Hodder & Stoughton, 1910);

The Shakespeare Head Brontë, 19 volumes, edited by T. J. Wise and J. A. Symington (Oxford: Blackwell, 1931-1938);

The Clarendon Edition of the Novels of the Brontës, 6 volumes to date, I. R. Jack, general editor (Oxford: Clarendon Press, 1969-   ).

The biographer of Emily Brontë faces considerable problems. Her slender output of one great novel and some impressive but baffling poems does not give one a great deal upon which to build. Unlike her sister Charlotte, whose works have an autobiographical streak, Emily did not seem to draw upon her own rather humdrum experiences in creating her masterpiece. Attempts to find a real-life Heathcliff in Emily Brontë's Irish forebears or Yorkshire neighbors seem highly speculative. Because Charlotte Brontë won instant fame while she was still alive, far more is known about her life than about Emily's; and it is largely through Charlotte's eyes that Emily is seen: either in incidental references among her correspondence to Ellen Nussey when Emily was alive, or in pious memories when she was dead. Emily Brontë's surviving correspondence is limited to a handful of brief

National Portrait Gallery, London

notes, the diary papers she wrote at four-year intervals with her sister Anne, and some exercises she wrote in French in Brussels.

This pathetic paucity of primary evidence has left biographers free to indulge in wild speculation. The temptation to fill the drab life of a genteel English spinster with the wild power of

60

Wuthering Heights (1847) is certainly great, but the unadorned facts, insofar as they can be ascertained, may serve to make her imaginative achievement more impressive. Emily Jane Brontë was the fifth child and fourth daughter of the Reverend Patrick Brontë, who moved in April 1820 to the village of Haworth eight miles from Thornton, her birthplace. Emily's mother, who had given birth to her youngest daughter, Anne, on 17 January 1820, died in November 1821, having been ill for several months. Like all the Brontë novels, *Wuthering Heights* has more than its fair share of children who have lost one or both parents.

Faced with the care of six motherless children, Mr. Brontë made efforts to marry again, but soon invited his wife's sister, Elizabeth Branwell, to keep house for him. In July 1824 he sent his two elder daughters, Maria and Elizabeth, to Clergy Daughter's School at Cowan Bridge, Charlotte following in August and Emily in November. In the spring of 1825 there was an epidemic of tuberculosis at the school, Maria and Elizabeth died, and Emily and Charlotte were removed from Cowan Bridge. It is difficult to know whether the portrait of Lowood in *Jane Eyre* (1847) is an accurate picture of Cowan Bridge, and although Charlotte clearly was unhappy there, it cannot be known how Emily felt at the age of six. Her subsequent departures from Haworth were brief, and she was not happy away from home.

Emily was indeed at Haworth for the next ten years. In 1826 Mr. Brontë brought home some wooden soldiers, and the precocious children began writing stories about them. With Charlotte and their brother, Branwell, as the main instigators, an imaginary realm in Africa, called Angria, was invented; but at a fairly early stage Emily and Anne broke away and invented their own realm of Gondal, set in the Pacific Ocean. The first of their diary notes, written in November 1834, gives the first mention of Gondal. They continued writing prose and poems about Gondal until the end of their lives. None of the prose has survived, and the poetry, the earliest of which dates to 1836, is difficult to interpret. Various efforts have been made to fit the poems into a coherent saga, but these efforts are probably misguided. Some poems appear not to be about Gondal at all, but rather to reflect Emily's own feelings.

Charlotte had been sent away in 1831 for a year and a half to a school in East Yorkshire run by Margaret Wooler. This school was far more pleasant than Cowan Bridge, and Charlotte made some friends there. In July 1835 Charlotte returned to the school as a teacher, taking Emily with her as a pupil; but this economical arrangement was not a success, and Anne replaced Emily. Emily returned to Haworth and found Branwell there. He had made an equally unsuccessful foray in London in an attempt to earn a living as a painter. With Anne and Charlotte away at Miss Wooler's, Emily and Branwell were thrown into each other's company; and although some of Branwell's influence can be detected in Emily's prose and poetry, the theory that he was the real author of *Wuthering Heights* can probably be discounted.

In spite of her previous failure, Emily made another attempt to leave home, going as an assistant teacher to Law Hill, a school run by Miss Patchett near Halifax. Charlotte wrote a letter complaining of the harsh conditions under which Emily worked. Her lack of formal education (virtually all her lessons having been taken at home), her shy temperament, and her homesickness would seem to have made Emily far from an ideal teacher, but the slighting nature of Charlotte's remarks made Miss Patchett reluctant to discuss her eccentric but distinguished assistant with subsequent biographers. The date and duration of Emily's stay at Law Hill are still in doubt. The recent discovery that Charlotte's letter, dated by most biographers 2 October 1837, is clearly postmarked 2 October 1838 would seem to fix Emily's stay in the winter of 1838 to 1839. Law Hill is regarded as important for *Wuthering Heights* because a house nearby, High Sunderland Hall, is assumed to be the model for the house known as Wuthering Heights, and it has even been suggested that the germ of the story of Heathcliff was to be found in recollections of a local Halifax character, Jack Sharp. The parallels are not exact, and the other main claimant to being the model of Wuthering Heights, Top Withens, near Haworth, certainly has a situation similar to the lonely house of Emily's novel, although Top Withens itself is too humble to be equated with Wuthering Heights.

Returning to Haworth in 1839 at the age of twenty, Emily continued to write poetry. Her sisters made brief and unsuccessful efforts to become governesses, but Emily remained at home, either because she was the most domesticated of the sisters or because she was the least suited to become a teacher. Her July 1841 birthday note is,

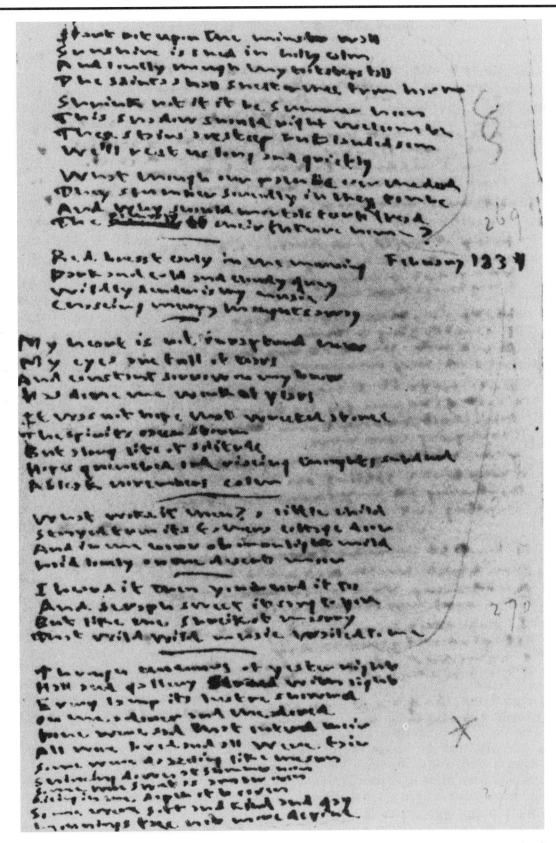

Manuscript of three of Brontë's poems—"Stand not upon the minster wall," "Redbreast, early in the morning," and "Through the hours of yesternight"—written between 1837 and 1839 (John Howell Books, 1982 Anniversary Catalogue)

however, full of enthusiasm for a project that the Brontës should run their own school at Haworth. In order to achieve this the sisters would need foreign languages, and so in February 1842 Emily and Charlotte set out to Brussels; Anne had obtained a post as a governess for the Robinson family at Thorp Green.

The position of the Brontës at the Pensionnat Heger in Brussels was halfway between those of pupils and teachers. Some reminiscences exist of Emily as a teacher, and not surprisingly her forbidding reserve did not attract her pupils to her. On the other hand, M. Heger spoke highly of her intellectual gifts as a student, and her surviving exercises show high imaginative power as well as a good command of French. It is not certain how much German Emily learned; critics have perhaps in too facile a fashion seen the influence of German romanticism behind *Wuthering Heights*.

In November 1842 the Brontës were forced to return home by the death of their aunt. They had previously been shocked by the death of their father's curate, William Weightman, in September, and by the death of their friend Martha Taylor in Brussels. Charlotte returned to Belgium, where she endured much loneliness and the pangs of unrequited love for M. Heger, but Emily remained at home. Their aunt had left the three girls some money, and there are reports of Emily considering the best way of investing it. For most of 1843 Emily was alone with her father, since Branwell had joined Anne at Thorp Green and Charlotte was still in Brussels, from which she returned at the beginning of 1844. In February 1844 Emily copied her poetry into two notebooks, one of which she entitled "Gondal Poems." The other notebook would seem to have contained poetry of a subjective nature.

Emily continued to write poetry in 1844 and 1845, and in a diary note in July 1845 refers enthusiastically to Gondal, although Anne is less sanguine. Branwell Brontë returned home in July 1845 (after being dismissed from his post at the Robinsons for some reason too disgraceful for Victorian prudery to make explicit), and for the rest of his life he was a source of constant anxiety to his family. Mr. Brontë's health was also giving cause for concern. The plan to start a school had foundered in 1844 through lack of pupils, and both Charlotte, who wrote letters to M. Heger which he refused to answer, and Anne, who had been badly shocked by her experiences at Thorp Green, were in low spirits. It was in these unprom-

Law Hill School near Halifax, where Brontë taught in 1838-1839 (Brontë Parsonage Museum)

ising circumstances that Emily wrote some of her greatest poetry and *Wuthering Heights*.

The chronology of the poems and the novel is confusing. Emily continued to write new poems in 1844 and 1845 in both Gondal and non-Gondal notebooks. In the former category can be placed "Remembrance" and "The Prisoner," an extract from a long Gondal poem; and in the latter category belong "The Philosopher" and "Stars." These poems are generally considered to be Emily's finest apart from "No Coward Soul is Mine," written in January 1846. In the autumn of 1845, Charlotte discovered a notebook of Emily's containing poetry which she thought was very impressive. Emily was, however, extremely annoyed by the discovery; it took hours to reconcile her to it, and days to persuade her that the poems should be published. But published they were in May 1846, together with a selection of Charlotte's and Anne's poetry. Gondal references were largely eliminated from the printed selection, which contained both Gondal and non-Gondal poems, including the four famous ones but not "No Coward Soul is Mine," which was presumably written too late for publication. After this Emily wrote only one more poem, in September 1846, which she began to revise in May 1848. Her abandoning of poetry has been variously explained. It has been argued that the fact of publication killed the poetry in her; more prosaically it has been suggested that she was busy with *Wuthering Heights*.

But this explanation has its own difficulties. It is known from a letter of Charlotte's in April 1846 to Aylott and Jones, the publishers of the Brontës' poetry, that the three sisters were well on their way to completing three separate works of fiction, and they had completed these by July 1846. Thus *Wuthering Heights* was finished two years before Emily died, and it is difficult to see what Emily was doing in these two years, when both Anne and Charlotte were busy with second novels. It has been suggested that Emily was also writing a second novel; a more original idea is that she extended *Wuthering Heights* from one-volume length to two volumes when it was decided that Charlotte's novel *The Professor* should try its own fortunes. Eventually the not very reputable firm of Thomas Newby agreed to publish *Wuthering Heights* in two volumes and Anne's *Agnes Grey* in one volume. Newby was dilatory in producing the books, and the terms he offered were not favorable, but the two novels were eventually published in December 1847.

Unlike Charlotte's *Jane Eyre*, which was an immediate success when it was published by Smith, Elder at about the same time, *Wuthering Heights* was received with bewilderment. Reviewers were baffled and shocked by the story, though some paid tribute to its strange power. Perhaps the poor reception of *Wuthering Heights* prevented Emily from embarking on another novel. A letter from Newby, fitting an envelope addressed to Ellis Bell, her pseudonym, and referring to another novel in progress, has been found; but Newby confused all three sisters, and the novel in question may be Anne's *The Tenant of Wildfell Hall*. This novel was published in June 1848, and, though some modern critics have seen it as Anne's answer to Emily's heterodox views, contemporary reviewers saw *The Tenant of Wildfell Hall* as further evidence of the Brontës' coarseness and immorality.

Meanwhile, all was not well with the Brontës' health. Branwell had degenerated badly since 1845, and he died on 24 September 1848. His physical and spiritual welfare must have caused anxiety for all three sisters, and there are stories of Emily, the tallest of the three, bearing the brunt of looking after him and carrying him about. Anne's health had also been worrying Charlotte, but on 9 October Emily was reported as having a cough and a cold. She struggled through her normal household tasks until almost the day of her death, refusing, according to the popular legend, all medical aid. Her death came quickly on 19 December 1848, and she was buried three days later at Haworth.

It is difficult to get any clear impression of Emily's personality or even her personal appearance from the scanty evidence available. Contemporary portraits, not very well authenticated, show Emily in different guises; a certain amount of romanticizing must be allowed for in these pictures. Contemporary accounts suggest that she made no effort to present herself in an attractive fashion. Charlotte Brontë remarked rather oddly that her sister resembled G. H. Lewes, the husband in all but name of George Eliot, although portraits of Emily and Lewes do not seem to bring out the resemblance. Charlotte's memories of her sister, and in particular her remark that the portrait of Shirley in her 1849 novel of the same name was based upon Emily, are likely to have been influenced by a pious wish to speak well of the dead. Emily's originality is borne out by her novel, but tributes to her strength of character ignore the fact that she seemed almost unable to survive outside Haworth. A certain amount of sentimentality must also be allowed for in the picture of Emily working closely in harmony with her two sisters: this picture would seem to be contradicted by the anger of Emily at the discovery of her poems, and by the fact that Anne Brontë, both in her poetry and her second novel, appears to be trying to refute Emily's views. Charlotte's desire to speak highly of her dead sister is of course both understandable and creditable; less creditable has been the refusal of many modern biographers to abandon the hushed superlatives and to admit that Emily, like many great artists, would appear to have had a rather difficult personality.

Her poetry is also difficult to evaluate and to interpret. It was not written for publication, and though she did revise much of her early work in 1844, some of what has been preserved can be discounted as immature early drafts. Gondal is a barrier to the proper appreciation of the poetry. In spite of misguided attempts, notably by Fannie Ratchford in *Gondal's Queen: A Novel in Verse* (1955), to make a coherent pattern of the Gondal saga, the details of the history of this imaginary land cannot be known. Clearly Gondal is a land dominated by dynamic, cruel people prompted by the same violent emotions of love and hate which rule *Wuthering Heights*. One of these characters is called sometimes by her initials, A.G.A., and it is tempting, but not necessarily correct, to say that other female characters in

A medallion of Branwell Brontë, who died three months before his sister Emily (Brontë Parsonage Museum)

the poems who behave in the same Heathcliff-like fashion are A.G.A under different names. Possibly, as in *Wuthering Heights*, more than one generation is involved; it is also possible that Brontë changed the story as she went along. The idea that all poems are Gondal poems seems mistaken in view of Brontë's division of her work into two notebooks. There is also a subjective element in some Gondal poems: in the poem variously entitled "The Prisoner" and "The Visionary," a dreary Gondal tale full of chains that clank and jailers who growl, Brontë appears to have a sudden moment of inspiration and describes the prisoner's vision of release in an impassioned outburst quite unlike anything else in English poetry. This outburst is generally printed in selections from Brontë without its Gondal trappings, and this may be some encouragement to those wishing to appreciate the poems without a knowledge of Gondal.

Much of Brontë's poetry is monotonous and humdrum, achieving its simple effects through narrative force and a clear rhythm. Words such as "drear" and "dark" are too frequent, but even in these poems Emily rises above the level of her sisters by occasionally inserting an unexpected, often a prosaic, word. Her thought, moreover, is clearly highly original. It is in "No Coward Soul is Mine" that one sees best her unorthodoxy as well as her command of sound effects:

Vain are the thousand creeds
That move men's hearts, unutterably vain

Worthless as withered weeds
Or idlest froth amidst the boundless main.

But it is possible to see traces of this brilliance in earlier poems, such as "The Old Stoic," written in 1841:

Riches I hold in light esteem
And Love I laugh to scorn
And lust of Fame was but a dream
That vanished with the morn.

Some poems are—like *Wuthering Heights*—difficult to interpret because the context is not known; nor, as the manuscripts of such poems are sometimes missing, is it always known for certain how to punctuate them. "The Philosopher" is such a poem. Brontë makes one of the speakers talk about three gods warring within his breast, and there is a baffling allusion to three rivers, but it is difficult to see who is speaking to whom, or to what the tripartite division refers. The imagery may be biblical, and is clearly powerful, but it is hard to see where it is leading. It would seem that in her later and finer poems Emily Brontë was slowly working her way to a mystical vision of a universe compared to which all of life's pains and joys were meaningless.

Some sort of commentary on the poems of Emily is provided by Anne's poetry and by *Wuthering Heights*. It would seem that Anne was trying, not very successfully, to counter her sister's philosophy in poems such as "The Three Guides"; in the same way that *The Tenant of Wildfell Hall* has superficial resemblances to *Wuthering Heights*, but a fundamentally different message, so "The Three Guides" would appear to reprimand the unorthodoxy of "The Philosopher." The relationship of the poems to *Wuthering Heights* is a little more difficult to determine. Some work has gone into tracing forerunners of Heathcliff and Cathy in the wild, reckless, amoral inhabitants of Gondal. The rugged landscape in which many of the poems are set resembles the moors in *Wuthering Heights*, both being close to the barren beauty of the countryside near the Brontës' home. In some of the later poems, Brontë seems to be trying to solve some of the metaphysical problems which she raises in her novel. And yet it is a disservice to both the highly practical novel and the deeply philosophical poetry to try to interpret them in the same fashion.

Wuthering Heights begins with the reflections of the narrator, Lockwood, who has come to stay at Thrushcross Grange, but goes to visit his landlord, Heathcliff, at Wuthering Heights. Lockwood, whose name suggests a closed mind, is clearly a fool and makes all kinds of mistakes: he thinks Heathcliff a capital fellow; he suggests that a pile of dead rabbits are domestic pets; and he cannot understand the relationship of Heathcliff to a girl he meets at Wuthering Heights called Catherine Heathcliff, who turns out to be the wife of Heathcliff's dead son. Other inhabitants of Wuthering Heights are a very rough servant, Joseph, and a fairly rough youth, Hareton. Lockwood is forced to stay the night at Wuthering Heights because of bad weather, and he has two bad dreams. One of these involves an almost comic episode in which Lockwood is denounced for yawning at a sermon divided into 491 parts delivered by the Reverend Jahez Branderham. This would seem to be an attack on the folly of conventional moral standards. In the other dream, a child called Catherine Linton is struggling to get in at the window while Lockwood tries to prevent her. This dream has reverberations throughout the novel; Lockwood's cruelty shows that his mind is still closed to the power and pathos of Wuthering Heights in the same way that he tries to keep the window closed.

Heathcliff is awakened by Lockwood's cries after his second dream, and, although considerably disturbed by the episode and by Lockwood's blundering explanations, Heathcliff manages to remain polite to Lockwood. This superficial politeness attracts Lockwood's and the reader's curiosity and sympathy toward Heathcliff, although the reader's judgments will later have to be revised. Lockwood falls ill on his return to Thrushcross Grange and whiles away his convalescence by asking his housekeeper, Nelly Dean, about the previous history of the inhabitants of Wuthering Heights.

Nelly Dean is a more interesting narrator than Lockwood. One obvious reason the story is told at second hand by her rather than by one of the characters principally involved is that the events would seem too violent and melodramatic if narrated directly. It is slightly awkward that Nelly Dean, in spite of her humble status, should have to be so conveniently present at several crises in the novel, and the reader does find himself passing judgment on her. These judgments have, like most pronouncements on *Wuthering Heights*,

been very variable, one critic even finding that Nelly is the villain of the novel. A more balanced view would suggest that Nelly stands for conventional morality, and that her failure to stem or even to understand the tragic passions involved in the story she tells is a further indictment of conventional goodness.

The story Nelly tells is certainly a tragic one. Some thirty years before Lockwood visited Wuthering Heights, Mr. Earnshaw had left the house, inhabited by his wife, son Hindley, daughter Cathy, manservant Joseph, and maidservant Nelly Dean, on a long journey to Liverpool. (Brontë's chronology is very exact, and every event can be dated accurately with no inconsistencies.) On his return Mr. Earnshaw brings not the fiddle his daughter had asked for, nor the whip Hindley had requested, but a dark, Gypsy-like waif he had found abandoned in the streets of Liverpool. His motives for this act of charity do not seem clear; some have suggested that the boy was his illegitimate son, but there is little evidence for this, although the Earnshaws do call him Heathcliff, the name of a son they had lost in infancy. Heathcliff soon gains the affection of Cathy, but Hindley is always hostile to him. One day Mr. Earnshaw presents the boys with two colts, and on finding that his is lame, Heathcliff demands that Hindley make an exchange with him, threatening to report his bullying to Mr. Earnshaw if Hindley refuses.

Mrs. Earnshaw, always a shadowy figure, has died earlier, and shortly after the incident of the colts Hindley is sent away to college. Mr. Earnshaw grows old and dies, much to the grief of Cathy and Heathcliff, who comfort each other with thoughts of heaven. At this stage, Nelly, who is impressed by the children's piety, is definitely on their side, and the reader is inclined to share her sympathy. Hindley returns home after his father's death with a wife, Frances, and Heathcliff is relegated to a menial position. Frances dies after giving birth to a son, Hareton, whom Lockwood has seen at Wuthering Heights, and Hindley takes to drink, maintaining his savage hostility to Heathcliff—who is, however, allowed to run wild together with Cathy.

Cathy and Heathcliff are surprised on an uninvited visit to Thrushcross Grange, home of the Linton family. Cathy hurts her leg in trying to escape and is kept at Thrushcross Grange. The Linton children, Edgar and Isabella, visit Wuthering Heights, and Heathcliff throws a tureen of applesauce in Edgar Linton's face.

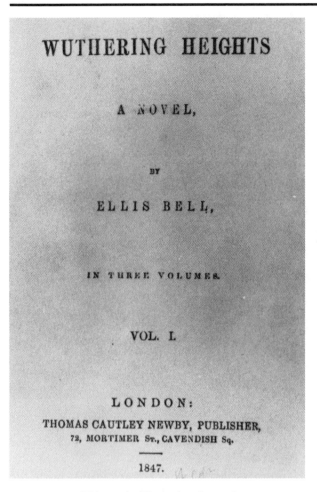

Title page of Brontë's only novel

glides over a subtle change in Nelly Dean's loyalties: hitherto she has been more friendly to the Earnshaws than to the Lintons, and this loyalty has embraced Heathcliff, who seems preferable to the spoiled and cowardly Edgar Linton; on Cathy's marriage, Nelly comes to live with her at Thrushcross Grange, and Edgar begins to appear in a better light. He and his sister are very kind to Cathy, who seems conventionally happy until the point at which Nelly resumes her narrative some six months after the marriage.

The conventional idyll is broken by the return of Heathcliff, who in his absence has contrived to acquire wealth and the manners of a gentleman. It is not clear *how* he has done this; the reason *why* he has done it should be clear when one remembers Cathy's unlucky speech which had impelled him to leave. He uses his wealth to gain a hold over Hindley by gambling with him at Wuthering Heights, and uses his gentlemanly manners to charm Isabella Linton into falling in love with him. No doubt he had intended to become rich to win Cathy, who is at first overjoyed to see him, but becomes distressed when Edgar raises objections and Isabella further complicates matters. Edgar is naturally and conventionally jealous, but it would be a mistake to think of Cathy as being jealous of Isabella. Her distress is not caused by normal sexual possessiveness, as she knows Heathcliff cares nothing for Isabella, but because she is aware that she and Heathcliff, who is intent on his revenge, have lost that fundamental sympathy with each other that they had had in childhood. Cathy's distress leads to mad ravings even before Heathcliff elopes with Isabella.

Heathcliff and Isabella are away for more than two months. During this time Cathy experiences a complete breakdown, but is gently nursed back to partial health by her husband. She is pregnant, having conceived a child at about the time of Heathcliff's initial return. It is uncertain what the implications of this are, or even if Brontë was aware of them. Certainly the love of Cathy and Heathcliff appears to transcend ordinary sexual love, which is much better represented by the feelings of Edgar. In addition, Cathy's daughter when she is born appears to have some Linton characteristics. The latter point is not a very strong one, since Isabella and Heathcliff also have a child who owes nothing to his father. The wedding night of Heathcliff and Isabella is not, and could not be, described, but there are glimpses of its horror when Isabella writes a letter describing her return to Wuth-

Heathcliff is jealous of the attention Cathy gives to Edgar, and Nelly, still vaguely sympathetic to Heathcliff, gives him kindly advice, as she does Cathy, who tells her that Edgar has asked her to marry him. Heathcliff overhears this conversation; and when he hears Cathy say that it would degrade her to marry Heathcliff since Hindley had brought him so low, he leaves—thus not waiting for the end of an impressive speech from Cathy, stressing her total unity with Heathcliff, and including the famous words "Nelly, I am Heathcliff."

Heathcliff in fact leaves Wuthering Heights for more than three years. Cathy rushes desperately onto the moors, becomes severely ill, and is taken in by the Lintons. The Linton parents die, and after an interval of three years, Cathy marries Edgar Linton. Nelly Dean breaks off her narrative at this point, and Lockwood temporarily resumes his. This break does not allow the reader to explore interesting questions such as why Cathy takes so long to make up her mind. It also

ering Heights. She paints a dark picture of the inhumanity of Heathcliff and the squalor of the house. The old servant, Joseph, mocks at Isabella's ladylike airs, and one feels in spite of her misfortunes that Isabella is a little spoiled. Isabella's letter is the nearest approach to a first-person narrative by someone directly involved in the action, and, since it has a melodramatic air about it, is perhaps a sign of how wise Brontë was to tell her strange story through Nelly Dean and Lockwood. Nelly visits Wuthering Heights and finds Isabella looking like a slattern, but Heathcliff flourishing. He is affable to Nelly, but demands with threats that she should carry a letter to Cathy arranging a meeting. As the story reaches its climax, Nelly again pauses in her narrative, and the focus reverts to Lockwood, who foolishly imagines a possible affair between himself and Catherine.

From light comedy, the resumption of Nelly's narrative returns the reader to high tragedy: three days after Nelly's visit to Wuthering Heights, Heathcliff and Cathy meet at Thrushcross Grange while Edgar is at church. They realize that she is near death, and mingle recrimination, anguish, and ecstasy. Although Edgar is just about to return, Heathcliff embraces her passionately. He releases her unconscious as Edgar enters the room, and she dies giving birth to a puny premature daughter, Catherine, without regaining consciousness. Edgar is exhausted, but Heathcliff stays awake in the garden of Thrushcross Grange, savagely dashing his head against the trunk of a tree. After the funeral, Isabella visits her old home to announce that she is leaving for London. With typical violence, she crushes her wedding ring with a poker. She tells of frightening quarrels between Hindley and Heathcliff. Hindley, now a confirmed drunkard, does not outlive his sister very long; on his death it is discovered that he has gambled away all his rights to Wuthering Heights, and Heathcliff now becomes the owner of the house and the guardian of Hindley's son, Hareton. Meanwhile, Isabella has given birth to a son, whom, understandably but confusingly, she calls Linton Heathcliff.

Thirteen years pass, in which young Catherine grows up, lovingly cared for by Nelly Dean and Edgar Linton (who does not, however, play a very active part in the rest of the novel). Isabella dies in London, asking Edgar to look after her son. While Edgar is away, Catherine contrives to visit Wuthering Heights and discovers that

Shibden Hall, near Halifax, the probable model for Thrushcross Grange in Wuthering Heights

Hareton is her cousin. Edgar returns with the sickly Linton, but Heathcliff demands his rights, and insists that the boy come to him.

On her sixteenth birthday, Catherine and Nelly meet Heathcliff and Hareton on the moors, and against Nelly's wishes go to Wuthering Heights. Edgar is feeble and Hareton is uncouth. Heathcliff now begins to plot a grotesque parody of the triangular relationship that had existed between him, Edgar, and Cathy, with the added advantage that if Linton marries Catherine and then dies, he will gain the ownership of both houses. A correspondence between Linton and Catherine is nipped in the bud by Nelly; but the next winter, when Nelly and Edgar are both ill, Catherine visits Linton several times. Encouraged by Heathcliff, the cousins appear to get on well together, although the fundamental difference between them appears when Catherine describes their different ideas of a perfect day, Catherine preferring activity and Linton calm. This passage is sometimes mistakenly linked with the distinction between Wuthering Heights and Thrushcross Grange, seen as representing the forces of storm and calm. In fact, the active landscape Catherine describes is more like that of Thrushcross Grange, and Linton talks of the moors.

When Nelly and Edgar discover what has been happening, they forbid communication between Linton and Catherine. All these events happen in the winter previous to Nelly's narrative, and the past now begins to catch up with the present. A pathetic letter from Linton ensures further meetings with Catherine. Both Edgar and Linton are now dying, and Heathcliff is engaged in a bitter race with death. This he wins by kidnapping Nelly and Catherine and blackmailing Catherine into marrying Linton, forestalling Edgar's efforts to change his will by bribing his lawyer. The feebleness of all the other characters to control their destiny against Heathcliff's wicked designs may seem slightly improbable; but faced with Heathcliff's dynamic energy, the reader, like the other characters, accepts the inevitable.

Linton dies, leaving Catherine's rights as heiress of Wuthering Heights to his father. Modern readers may be shocked that a woman's rights could be bypassed so easily: a contemporary reviewer on the contrary remarked that the book proved that Satan was master of the law of entail. Zillah, the maidservant, acts as temporary narrator at this point, explaining the circumstances which Lockwood found on his visit to Wuthering Heights. Catherine Heathcliff is imprisoned in the house under Heathcliff's control, while her other cousin, Hareton, disgusts her by his boorish ways. Lockwood sees this when he visits Wuthering Heights bearing a letter from Nelly to Catherine. Catherine cannot answer as she has no paper, and accuses Hareton of stealing her books in his efforts to learn to read. Hearing their quarrel, Heathcliff checks his wrath on noticing the strange resemblance of Hareton to Cathy, his aunt. Lockwood departs for London, having tired of Thrushcross Grange, still imagining a possible romance between himself and Catherine.

He returns a year later to hear the end of the story. Nobody is at home at Thrushcross Grange, so he walks up to Wuthering Heights. Here he overhears Catherine and Hareton reading together. Spring is in the air, and flowers are growing in the yard. Nelly Dean tells him the rest of the story. Catherine, after initially rebuffing Hareton, relents, teaches him to read, and falls in love with him. Heathcliff sees this, but seems unable to thwart the destruction of his plans. He is reminded of Cathy and his youth when he sees the pair together, and seems aware

that his death is imminent, although he is still vigorous and in early middle age. His death comes quickly. Catherine and Hareton plan to move to Thrushcross Grange, leaving Wuthering Heights to Joseph and the ghosts of the previous generation. These ghosts are still active, as Lockwood realizes when he hears from Nelly Dean of a small boy blubbering that he has seen Heathcliff walking the moors with a woman, although as Lockwood passes the graves of Edgar, Cathy, and Heathcliff, he piously reflects that he cannot imagine unquiet slumbers for anyone under that quiet earth.

Typically, the novel ends with an ambiguity: it is not clear whether Lockwood is any wiser than at the beginning, and whether the reader is meant to believe that Heathcliff has achieved peace or that he roams with Cathy as a ghost over the moors. Perhaps he does both. Nor is it clear whether the marriage of Catherine and Hareton and their plan to move to Thrushcross Grange represents a defeat for Heathcliff and a rejection of all he stands for, including the wild, stormy atmosphere of Wuthering Heights; or whether Catherine and Hareton are a pale imitation of Cathy and Heathcliff, and their earthly joys are a model of the unearthly ecstasy of Heathcliff once he is united with Cathy.

Heathcliff dominates the novel, and the reader is not really interested in Catherine and Hareton. Catherine does remind one of her mother, and indeed the names "Cathy" and "Catherine" are almost interchangeable in the novel. This confusion (which has been avoided here by arbitrarily calling the elder "Cathy" and the younger "Catherine") is presumably deliberate. When Lockwood visits Wuthering Heights for the first time he finds the signatures of Catherine Earnshaw, Catherine Linton, and Catherine Heathcliff; both heroines have a share in all three names. In spite of these links and in spite of the fact that Catherine is at first sight more admirable than her petulant and selfish mother, the reader seems to be meant to see Catherine mainly as an instrument in Heathcliff's monstrous plan of revenge. Likewise, Hareton's wooing of Catherine by learning to read is not especially exciting, and even slightly ridiculous; what is interesting about Hareton is that he seems oddly fond of Heathcliff, and even, as Charlotte Brontë noted, strikes some sparks of affection in return.

These slight marks of affection for Hareton were said by Charlotte to be Heathcliff's one re-

Top Withens, near Haworth, believed to have suggested the locale of Wuthering Heights *(Yorkshire Post)*

deeming feature. Other critics have been kinder, and certainly Heathcliff's ferocious energy has exercised a strange fascination over most readers. Unlike Milton's Satan or the Byronic hero or even the heroes of German romantic novels, all of which have been seen as possible models for him, Heathcliff is curiously mean and calculating in his villainy. The episode of the exchange of horses shows him in a bad light at an early stage in the novel, and sentimentality about his proletarian origins cannot disguise the fact that in the latter part he behaves like the worst kind of grasping capitalist landlord. Nor can his romantic desire for revenge on Cathy and Hindley and Edgar excuse the deliberate way he warps the lives of Catherine and Hareton and Linton by forcing them to enact a grotesque imitation of the lives of their predecessors. Isabella's treatment is perhaps more excusable, as she brought disaster on her own head, and her shoddy and shallow romanticism deserves to be shown up.

Heathcliff tells the truth even if in rather a savage fashion; this is part of his attraction, and it is also a trait he shares with his creator insofar as one can ascertain anything about Emily

Brontë. Like Cathy, Heathcliff has an immense wealth of unexpected violent—almost Shakespearean—imagery at his command; indeed, rich images, especially those concerned with the weather and the animal kingdom, are a strength of the whole book. Comparison with *King Lear* is inevitable.

Like *King Lear*, *Wuthering Heights* is set in a wild landscape, and it is part of Heathcliff's attraction that he is associated with the landscape and with Wuthering Heights. The opposition between the two houses is an important theme in the book. It is dangerous to see Wuthering Heights through Isabella's eyes as rough and rude in comparison to the civilized luxury of Thrushcross Grange; people do not seem very happy at Thrushcross Grange, which has a cold, formal air about it in contrast to the organic warmth of Wuthering Heights. Lockwood is at pains to stress that Wuthering Heights, both inside and outside, has a certain amount of refinement. Yet one must not be sentimental about Wuthering Heights: it has a fire in summer not just to show organic warmth, but to show that it is cold; the trees outside are warped in the same way as

High Sunderland Hall, near Halifax, on which Brontë based many of the features of the house called Wuthering Heights

Heathcliff warps the lives of other people; and the name "Wuthering" is a local dialect term for the roaring of the wind—attractive to hear at a safe distance, but both frightening and depressing to experience at close quarters.

An attempt has been made to link the two houses and the two generations into some immense cosmic scheme, whereby the two elements of storm and calm are present discordantly in the first generation, but are somehow fused harmoniously with the marriage of Catherine and Hareton. This attempt by Lord David Cecil in *Early Victorian Novelists* (1934) has been very influential, but it is far too schematic. Linton Heathcliff has a stormy father, but it is difficult to see anything but a rather deadly calm in his character; and he is proof, if proof is needed, that in a certain sense storm is better than calm. Thus Cecil's contention that *Wuthering Heights* is an amoral book, refusing to pass judgment on either side in any controversy, seems to fall to the ground if, in spite of all conventional values and the conventional views of Nelly Dean shaping the narrative, the reader still feels drawn to Heathcliff and his turbulent environment.

Few would doubt Cecil's third point, that through the story of Heathcliff and Cathy, Brontë is trying to state some fundamental metaphysical truth. It is the breadth of this ambition which raises *Wuthering Heights* above the level of the poems, which seem to have a narrower scope. In an important 1958 article, "*Wuthering Heights:* The Rejection of Heathcliff ?" in *Essays in Criticism*, 8, Miriam Allott tries to show that Brontë is somehow on Heathcliff's side and believes in what he stands for, but Allott sees the death of Heathcliff and the move to Thrushcross Grange as an elegiac statement of regret at the passing of an impossible dream. More recently there have been more narrowly sociological interpretations of the end of the book by Mrs. Q. D. Leavis in *Lectures in America* (1969) and T. Eagleton in *Myths of Power* (1975). These have seen the triumph of Hareton and Catherine as the triumph of nineteenth-century capitalism over eighteenth-century yeomanry. All these interpretations, although they provide valuable insights, seem to ignore the fact that the end of the novel is a great deal more enigmatic than they make out.

Other modern critical articles on *Wuthering Heights* tend to be eccentric or to deal with only very small sections of the book. Two modern full-length studies of Emily Brontë, by John Hewish and Winifred Gérin, correct the earlier biographical errors of amateur works such as those by Muriel Spark and Derek Stanford, Charles Simpson, and A. Mary F. Robinson, but do not quite clear up the mystery of Emily Brontë's enigmatic personality or offer a definitive interpretation of her famous book. The publication of the Clarendon *Wuthering Heights* (1976) supplies a definite text, but adds little in its introduction apart from some useful information about Newby's imperfections as an editor. Recent critical interest in Charlotte Brontë, an author so much easier to tie down to a definite meaning than Emily, has meant that Emily has slightly lost ground at her sister's expense, although *Wuthering Heights* remains the most popular and the most typical Brontë novel in both academic and popular circles. It is worth remembering that it was only in 1899, with the publication of the Haworth Edition of the Brontë novels, that Emily was finally established as a novelist superior to Charlotte in the introductions of Mrs. Humphry Ward, which remain some of the best prose written on the Brontës.

Emily Brontë remains enigmatic because so little is known about her, and what is known is contradictory. Her life seems one of dreary conformity; her book seems designed to outrage and shock. Even the modern reader, whose susceptibility to shock must be less than that of his Victorian counterpart, is still outraged not so much by the violence of word, deed, and atmosphere as by the sudden surprise to his sensibilities when he finds characters appealing to him in spite of what they do. Perhaps the only certain message of *Wuthering Heights* is that nothing is certain. Brontë's defiance of rigid categories and her refusal to divide people into saints and sinners, gentry and servants, good and bad is very unVictorian, but does not seem out of keeping with what is known of her temperament.

Heathcliff's cruelty and Cathy's selfishness do not prevent them from being attractive. The Lintons are spoiled and weak, but Isabella's and her son's sufferings and Edgar's devotion to his wife win them sympathy. Hindley is profligate and cruel, neglecting even Hareton in a shocking fashion; but Nelly Dean, who is Hindley's foster sister and has an old retainer's loyalty, finds a mournful pathos about his fall and inspires the reader to do the same. Joseph, the servant at Wuthering Heights, is hypocritical, pharisaical, and a believer in hellfire and predestination. Brontë would appear to have believed in truth, tolerance, and universal salvation. Yet it is one of the oddest features of the novel that one feels that Joseph, who is always present at Wuthering Heights, is somehow akin to Brontë in his savage contempt for almost everything and his belief that gloom is good for the soul.

Heathcliff himself, at first sight so straight an unredeemed villain or Byronic hero, acts at times in a surprising fashion. One can never quite make out the significance of the episodes in which he catches Hareton when Hindley drunkenly drops him over the banisters, or in which—spitting and cursing—he prevents Hindley from bleeding to death, although he has threatened to kill Hindley and Hindley has just tried to kill him. It is odd, too, to find Heathcliff offering to make a cup of tea for Nelly Dean and Catherine at a time when he is acting villainously toward both of them. These touches of humanity prevent Heathcliff and *Wuthering Heights* from lapsing into unrealistic melodrama; one is reminded of the sudden unexpected words in Brontë's poetry, and homely glimpses of the authoress of *Wuthering Heights* baking the bread.

Heathcliff stands unredeemed, says Charlotte Brontë in her introduction to the second edition, but qualifies her remark by saying that his affection for Hareton partially redeems him. She then gives a surprising hint about the origins of Heathcliff's name. Most readers will think of a heath as an arid waste, as in *King Lear*, and there are plenty of barren wastes on the moors near Wuthering Heights and in Heathcliff's heart. But there is also a small flower named a heath, and it is to this that Charlotte links the mighty and rugged cliff that stands for *Wuthering Heights*. Emily Brontë would appear to be a wilting flower who created a mighty rock.

Bibliographies:

Thomas J. Wise, *A Bibliography of the Writings in Prose and Verse of the Members of the Brontë Family* (London: Clay, 1917);

G. Anthony Yablon and John R. Turner, *A Brontë Bibliography* (London: Hodgkins, 1978; Westport, Conn.: Meckler, 1978);

R. W. Crump, *Charlotte and Emily Brontë, 1846-1915: A Reference Guide* (Boston: G. K. Hall, 1982).

Biographies:

A. Mary F. Robinson, *Emily Brontë* (London: Allen, 1883);

Charles Simpson, *Emily Brontë* (London: Countrylife, 1929);

Muriel Spark and Derek Stanford, *Emily Brontë* (London: Owen, 1953);

John Hewish, *Emily Brontë* (London: Macmillan, 1969);

Winifred Gérin, *Emily Brontë* (Oxford: Oxford University Press, 1971);

E. Chitham, *A Life of Emily Brontë* (London: Blackwell, 1987);

Katherine Frank, *Emily Brontë: A Chainless Soul* (Boston: Houghton, Mifflin, 1990).

References:

Miriam Allott, "*Wuthering Heights*: The Rejection of Heathcliff ?," *Essays in Criticism*, 8 (1958): 27-47;

Jacques Blondel, *Emily Brontë: Experience spirituelle et création poétique* (Clermont-Ferrand: Presses Universitaires de France, 1956);

David Cecil, *Early Victorian Novelists* (London: Constable, 1934);

E. Chitham, "Almost like Twins," *Brontë Society Transactions*, 85 (1975): 365-373;

C. W. Davies, "A Reading of *Wuthering Heights*," *Essays in Criticism*, 19 (1969): 254-273;

Stevie Davies, *Emily Brontë* (Bloomington: Indiana University Press, 1988);

T. Eagleton, *Myths of Power* (London: Macmillan, 1975);

F. R. Leavis and Q. D. Leavis, *Lectures in America* (London: Chatto & Windus, 1969);

W. D. Paden, *An Investigation of Gondal* (New York: Bookman, 1958);

J. F. Petit, ed., *Emily Brontë* (Harmondsworth, U.K.: Penguin, 1973);

Fannie E. Ratchford, *Gondal's Queen: A Novel in Verse* (Austin: University of Texas Press, 1955);

C. P. Sanger, *The Structure of "Wuthering Heights"* (London: Hogarth Press, 1926);

Mary Visick, *The Genesis of "Wuthering Heights"* (Hong Kong: Hong Kong University Press, 1958);

Irene Cooper Willis, *The Authorship of "Wuthering Heights"* (London: Hogarth Press, 1936);

Tom Winnifrith, *The Brontës* (London: Macmillan, 1977);

Winnifrith, *The Brontës and Their Background: Romance and Reality* (London: Macmillan, 1973).

Elizabeth Barrett Browning

(6 March 1806 - 29 June 1861)

This entry was written by Gardner B. Taplin (Tulane University) for
DLB 32: Victorian Poets Before 1850.

BOOKS: *The Battle of Marathon: A Poem* (London:
    W. Lindsell, 1820);

An Essay on Mind, with Other Poems, anonymous
    (London: Duncan, 1826);

Prometheus Bound, Translated from the Greek of Aeschy-
    lus; and Miscellaneous Poems, anonymous (Lon-
    don: A. J. Valpy, 1833; Boston: J. H. Fran-
    cis / New York: C. S. Francis, 1851);

The Seraphim and Other Poems (London: Saunders
    & Otley, 1838);

Poems, 2 volumes (London: Moxon, 1844); repub-
    lished as *A Drama of Exile: and other Poems,* 2
    volumes (New York: Langley, 1845);

Poems: New Edition, 2 volumes (London: Chap-
    man & Hall, 1850); republished as *The
    Poems of Elizabeth Barrett Browning* (New
    York: C. S. Francis / Boston: J. H. Francis,
    1850);

Casa Guidi Windows: A Poem (London: Chapman
    & Hall, 1851);

Poems: Third Edition, 2 volumes (London: Chap-
    man & Hall, 1853);

Two Poems, by Browning and Robert Browning
    (London: Chapman & Hall, 1854);

Poems: Fourth Edition, 3 volumes (London: Chap-
    man & Hall, 1856);

Aurora Leigh (London: Chapman & Hall, 1857;
    New York & Boston: C. S. Francis, 1857; re-
    vised, London: Chapman & Hall, 1859);

Poems before Congress (London: Chapman & Hall,
    1860); republished as *Napoleon III in Italy,
    and Other Poems* (New York: C. S. Francis,
    1860);

Last Poems (London: Chapman & Hall, 1862;
    New York: Miller, 1862);

The Greek Christian Poets and the English Poets (Lon-
    don: Chapman & Hall, 1863); republished
    as *Essays on the Greek Christian Poets and the En-
    glish Poets* (New York: Miller, 1863);

Psyche Apocalyptè: A Lyrical Drama, by Browning
    and Richard Hengist Horne (London &
    Aylesbury, U.K.: Privately printed, 1876);

New Poems by Robert and Elizabeth Barrett Browning,
    edited by Frederic G. Kenyon (London:

*Elizabeth Barrett Browning (National Portrait
Gallery, London)*

    Smith, Elder, 1914; New York: Macmillan,
    1915);

The Poet's Enchiridion, edited by H. Buxton
    Forman (Boston: Bibliophile Society, 1914);

*Elizabeth Barrett Browning: Hitherto Unpublished
    Poems and Stories, with an Unedited Autobiogra-
    phy,* 2 volumes, edited by Forman (Boston:
    Bibliophile Society, 1914);

*Diary by E. B. B.: The Unpublished Diary of Elizabeth
    Barrett Browning, 1831-1832,* edited by
    Philip Kelley and Ronald Hudson (Athens:
    Ohio University Press, 1969).

Collections: *The Poetical Works of Elizabeth Barrett
    Browning,* 6 volumes (London: Smith, Elder,
    1889-1890);

The Poetical Works of Elizabeth Barrett Browning, edited by Frederic G. Kenyon (London: Smith, Elder, 1897);

The Complete Poetical Works of Elizabeth Barrett Browning, Cambridge Edition, edited by Harriet Waters Preston (Boston & New York: Houghton Mifflin, 1900);

The Complete Works of Elizabeth Barrett Browning, 6 volumes, edited by Charlotte Porter and Helen A. Clarke (New York: Crowell, 1900).

OTHER: "Queen Annelida and False Arcite" and "The Complaint of Annelida to False Arcite," in *The Poems of Geoffrey Chaucer, Modernized* (London: Whittaker, 1841), pp. 237-257;

Richard Hengist Horne, ed., *A New Spirit of the Age,* many anonymous contributions by Browning, 2 volumes (London: Smith, Elder, 1844);

Two versions of "The Daughters of Pandarus," translated from the *Odyssey* by Browning, in Mrs. Anna Jameson, *Memoirs and Essays Illustrative of Art, Literature, and Social Morals* (London: Bentley, 1846), pp. 137-138.

Among all women poets of the English-speaking world in the nineteenth century, none was held in higher critical esteem or was more admired for the independence and courage of her views than Elizabeth Barrett Browning. During the years of her marriage to Robert Browning, her literary reputation far surpassed that of her poet-husband; when visitors came to their home in Florence, Italy, she was invariably the greater attraction. Both in England and in the United States she had a wide following among cultured readers. An example of the reach of her fame may be seen in the influence she had upon the reclusive poet who lived in the rural college town of Amherst, Massachusetts. A framed portrait of Mrs. Browning hung in the bedroom of Emily Dickinson, whose life had been transfigured by the poetry of "that Foreign Lady." From the time when she had first become acquainted with Mrs. Browning's writings, Dickinson had ecstatically admired her as a poet and had virtually idolized her as a woman who had achieved such a rich fulfillment in her life. When Samuel Bowles, a close friend of the Dickinson family and respected editor of the *Springfield Republican,* went to Europe for the first time, he took with him two books: the Bible and Mrs. Browning's *Aurora Leigh* (1857). So highly regarded had she become by

Elizabeth Barrett's father, Edward Barrett Moulton-Barrett (from a painting by H. W. Pickersgill; Collection of Mrs. Violet Altham)

1850, the year of William Wordsworth's death, that she was prominently mentioned as a possible successor to the poet laureateship. Her humane and liberal point of view manifests itself in her poems aimed at redressing many forms of social injustice, such as the slave trade in America, the labor of children in the mines and the mills of England, the oppression of the Italian people by the Austrians, and the restrictions forced upon women in nineteenth-century society.

As a child and a young woman Elizabeth Barrett was extremely fortunate in the circumstances of her family background and environment. Her father, whose wealth was derived from extensive sugar plantations in Jamaica, was the proprietor of "Hope End," an estate of almost five hundred acres in Herefordshire, between the market town of Ledbury and the Malvern Hills. In this peaceful setting, with its farmers' cottages, gardens, woodlands, ponds, carriage roads, and mansion "adapted for the accommodation of a nobleman or family of the first distinction," Elizabeth—known by the nickname "Ba"—at first lived the kind of life that might be expected for the daughter of a wealthy country

Hope End, the Barretts' estate in Herefordshire, where Elizabeth Barrett spent her early childhood

squire. She rode her pony in the lanes around the Barrett estate, went with her brothers and sisters for walks and picnics in the countryside, visited other county families to drink tea, accepted visits in return, and participated with her brothers and sisters in homemade theatrical productions. But, unlike her two sisters and eight brothers, she immersed herself in the world of books as often as she could get away from the social rituals of her family. "Books and dreams were what I lived in—and domestic life only seemed to buzz gently around, like bees about the grass," she said many years later. Having begun to compose verses at the age of four, two years later she received from her father for "some lines on virtue penned with great care" a ten-shilling note enclosed in a letter addressed to "the Poet-Laureate of Hope End."

Before Barrett was ten years old, she had read the histories of England, Greece, and Rome; several of William Shakespeare's plays, including *Othello* and *The Tempest*; portions of Alexander Pope's Homeric translations; and passages from *Paradise Lost*. At eleven, she says in an autobiographical sketch written when she was fourteen, she "felt the most ardent desire to understand the learned languages." Except for some instruction in Greek and Latin from a tutor who lived

with the Barrett family for two or three years to help her brother Edward ("Bro") prepare for entrance to Charterhouse, Barrett was, as Robert Browning later asserted, "self-taught in almost every respect." Within the next few years she went through the works of the principal Greek and Latin authors, the Greek Christian Fathers, several plays by Jean Racine and Molière, and a portion of Dante's *Inferno*—all in the original languages. Also around this time she learned enough Hebrew to read the Old Testament from beginning to end. Her enthusiasm for the works of Thomas Paine, Voltaire, Jean-Jacques Rousseau, and Mary Wollstonecraft presaged the concern for human rights that she was later to express in her poems and letters. At the age of eleven or twelve she composed a verse "epic" in four books of rhyming couplets, *The Battle of Marathon*, which was privately printed at Mr. Barrett's expense in 1820. She later spoke of this product of her childhood as "Pope's Homer done over again, or rather undone." Most of the fifty copies that were printed probably went to the Barretts' home and remained there. It is now the rarest of her works, with only a handful of copies known to exist.

At the age of twenty Barrett offered to the public, with no indication of authorship, a slender volume entitled *An Essay on Mind, with Other Poems* (1826). Long afterward, in a letter to an American critic, she called the book "a girl's exercise, nothing more nor less!—not at all known to the public." The poem for which the volume was named was a pretentious and frigid effort to survey in some eighty-eight pages the history of science, philosophy, and poetry from ancient Greece to the present. The other fourteen poems were occasional pieces or verses of a personal nature which did not yet display the author's authentic voice. Of the two journals which noticed the volume, one objected to its obscurity of language and its "barren themes," and the other advised the poet to come down from the heights to look more closely at nature.

Shortly after the publication of this volume Barrett entered into one of the most important friendships of her life. Hugh Stuart Boyd, a totally blind, middle-aged dilettante scholar with private means, had published at his own expense several volumes of translations from the Greek patristic writings. Since the author of the "Essay on Mind" lived not far from him, he was eager to become acquainted with a poet of such extraordinary erudition. From his home in Malvern Wells he sent her copies of his works and invited her to pay him a visit. Starved as she was for intellectual companionship, she eagerly began to correspond with him and before long was making frequent visits to Ruby Cottage, where he lived with his wife and daughter. It was entirely owing to Boyd's influence that Barrett's enthusiasm for Greek studies was rekindled. During this period she read an astonishing amount of classical Greek literature—Homer, Pindar, the tragedians, Aristophanes, and passages from Plato, Aristotle, Isocrates, and Xenophon—as well as the Greek Christian Fathers Boyd had translated.

In 1832 the peaceful, secure lives of the Barretts in their Herefordshire retreat came to a distressing close. For years the Jamaican plantations of the Barrett family had been mismanaged and Mr. Barrett had suffered serious financial losses. With the prospect of a greatly reduced income he could no longer afford to maintain the Hope End estate and suffered the embarrassment of its having to be sold at a public auction to satisfy creditors. The eleven children and their father (Mrs. Barrett had died in 1828) went to live temporarily in Sidmouth, on the southern coast of Devonshire. The reason for the choice of this town in the south of England may have been Mr. Barrett's concern for Elizabeth's health. At

An 1823 drawing of Barrett by her mother

the age of fifteen she had injured her spine when she was attempting to saddle her pony. Seven years later the breaking of a blood vessel in the chest left her with a weakened constitution and a chronic cough. During the period of the Barretts' stay in Sidmouth, Boyd lived for a year and a half within a few minutes' walk from their home. To the detriment of her own poetic career she went to him daily and helped him to see through the press a bizarre volume on his favorite subject, Greek Christian Fathers. By the time she left Sidmouth, Barrett's feelings toward Boyd had changed: she now saw him as limited, naive, and even pathetic. The one volume that she produced while at Sidmouth was *Prometheus Bound, Translated from the Greek of Aeschylus; and Miscellaneous Poems,* published anonymously in 1833. Twelve years later in a letter to Boyd she called the translation "that frigid, rigid exercise," and after her marriage she made amends by writing a vastly improved version. The "miscellaneous poems" are all immature in content and expression and give little promise of their author's future distinction.

After living for three years in several rented houses in the coastal town, the Barretts moved in 1835 to London, which was to remain their permanent place of residence. At first Elizabeth missed the fresh sea breezes and the sound of the waves, and disliked her new setting because of the ever-

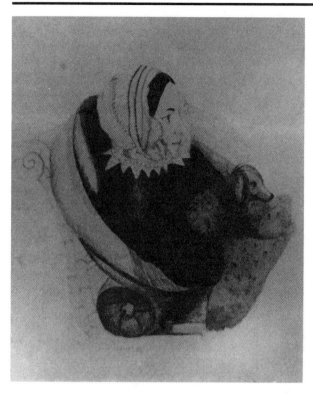

A drawing of Barrett by her brother Alfred (Collection of Edward Moulton-Barrett)

present soot and fog and the long, narrow streets lined with attached stone or brick houses which all looked alike. But before long she was content to be living in a great metropolis, the center of the nation's literary and artistic activities. Barrett made her name known in literary circles with *The Seraphim and Other Poems* (1838). Except for the privately printed *Battle of Marathon*, this was the first work with her name on the title page. She said that the volume, despite some shortcomings, was "the first utterance of my own individuality." The many reviews that appeared both in England and America almost all hailed her as a young poet of extraordinary ability and still greater promise. The long poetic drama of seventy-eight pages for which the volume was named presents the conversation of two angels in the heavens retelling portions of the Old and New Testaments, and commenting on the Crucifixion then taking place. Although most of the critics considered the poem too mystical and too high-flown to be successful, they generally praised the shorter poems, most of which now seem sentimental and trite. A poem that soon became a great favorite with both professional critics and the general public was "Isobel's Child," with its depiction of the death of a three-month-old baby who has

been lying all night in the mother's arms. The well-known critic John Wilson ("Christopher North") declared that there was beauty in all the poems and that some were "altogether beautiful."

Just as Barrett was being recognized as one of England's most original and gifted young poets, she was in such poor health because of the weakness of her lungs that her physician recommended that she move away from London and live for a while in a warmer climate. Torquay, on the south coast of Devonshire, was selected, and there, together with various members of her family who took turns living with her, she remained for three years as an invalid under the watchful care of her physicians. Seriously ill as she was, she suffered a sudden shattering blow that left her prostrated for months. The death by drowning on 11 July 1840 of her favorite brother, Edward, who had been with her constantly at Torquay, was the greatest sorrow of her life. The memory of that tragic event remained with her as long as she lived and was so painful that she could never speak of it even to those closest to her.

When she returned to the family home at 50 Wimpole Street after the three terrible years at Torquay, she felt that she had left her youth behind and that the future held little more than permanent invalidism and confinement to her bedroom. For the following five years she remained mostly in her room, which she decorated with busts of Homer and Geoffrey Chaucer and later with engravings of Browning (whom she had not yet met), Alfred, Lord Tennyson, Thomas Carlyle, Harriet Martineau, and Wordsworth. Yet despite her frail health she was more fortunate in her circumstances than most women writers of her time. Thanks to inheritances from her grandmother and her uncle, she was the only one of the brothers and sisters who was independently wealthy. As the eldest daughter in a family without a mother, she normally would have been expected to spend much of her time supervising the domestic servants, but her weakness prevented her from leaving her room. Thus the members of her family came to visit with her and to bring her everything she desired. Relieved of all household burdens and financial cares, she was free to devote herself to reading English and French fiction and memoirs and to writing letters, essays, and poetry. Since the prospect of meeting strangers made her nervous, only two visitors besides her family had the privilege of seeing her in her room: John Kenyon, a minor poet and friend of many English poets, and the well-known writer Mary Russell Mitford. During her last year or two at Wimpole Street she also received the Reverend George B. Hunter, whom she had come to know during her years at Sidmouth, and the art critic Anna Jameson.

Protected from the outside world and surrounded by a loving family, Barrett resumed her literary career, which had been partially interrupted during her serious illness at Torquay. In addition to producing a continuous flow of poems for publication in both English and American journals, she wrote a series of articles on the Greek Christian poets and another series on the English poets, the latter originally begun as a critique of a recently published anthology of English verse. Also, in collaboration with the playwright Richard Hengist Horne, she made many anonymous contributions to a book of critical essays on eminent literary figures edited by him and entitled *A New Spirit of the Age* (1844). Within three years after her return to Wimpole Street she had many new poems in manuscript and others already published in journals, and she believed that the time was ripe for their appearance in book form—the first since *The Seraphim and Other Poems* of 1838. The critical reception of her *Poems,* published in two volumes in 1844, was such that the author was no longer merely a promising young poet but had suddenly become an international celebrity. On both sides of the Atlantic the leading journals came out with substantial reviews, and almost all found much to praise; Elizabeth Barrett was now acclaimed as one of England's great living poets. The poem which found least favor with the critics was "A Drama of Exile." For 119 pages the drama recounts the conversations and events of the first day's exile from Eden, as various spirits alternately rebuke and console the fallen pair. In the judgment of most reviewers the drama was lacking in coherence, the language was obscure, and the characters were unreal.

None of the shorter poems caught the public fancy more than "Lady Geraldine's Courtship: A Romance of the Age." A young poet with slender financial resources falls in love with the daughter of an earl; but since her life is filled with luxuries, he has little hope that his love will be returned. Despite the social barriers, however, the romantic conclusion has the girl responding to her suitor's ardor. Another poem much admired by sentimental readers was "Bertha in the Lane." The heroine, though apparently in good

The Barretts' home at 50 Wimpole Street, London

health, dies after learning that her lover has jilted her in favor of her younger sister. The most influential poem in the volumes, and one of the best-known of all her works, was "The Cry of the Children," which had first appeared in *Blackwood's* a year earlier. Having read the reports from the parliamentary commissioners of the terrible conditions of children's employment in mines, trades, and manufactures, she tells of the hopeless lives of the boys and girls who are the victims of capitalist exploitation. Even though Barrett was a bookish, sheltered, upper-middle-class unmarried woman far removed from the scenes she was describing, she gives evidence here of her passionate concern for human rights. The critics reviewing *Poems* praised her for her intellectual power, originality, and boldness of thought; but most agreed that her weakness lay in her frequent vagueness of concept and obscurity of expression.

The two volumes found their way into the home of Robert Browning. Upon seeing a handsome tribute paid to him by name in "Lady Geraldine's Courtship," Browning in January

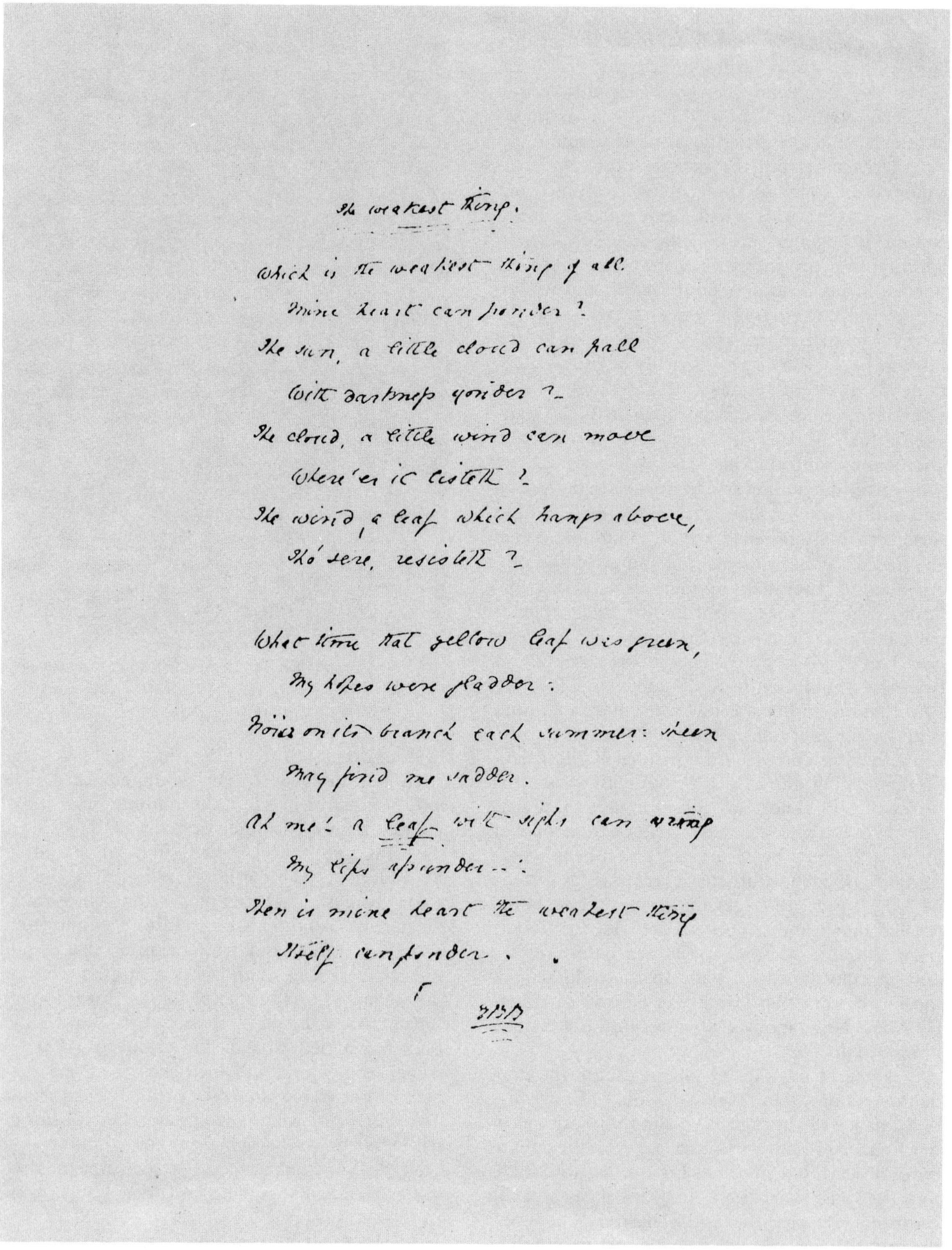

The weakest thing.

Which is the weakest thing of all
  Mine heart can ponder ?
The sun, a little cloud can pall
  With darkness yonder ?—
The cloud, a little wind can move
  Where'er it listeth ?
The wind, a leaf which hangs above,
  Tho' sere, resisteth ?—

What time that yellow leaf was green,
  My hopes were gladder :
Now on its branch each summer: seen
  May find me sadder.
Ah me ! a leaf with sighs can wring
  My lips asunder—:
Then is mine heart the weakest thing
  Itself can ponder .

                                    EBB

Manuscript page for one of the poems published in Barrett's The Seraphim and Other Poems *(American Art Association/ Anderson Galleries auction catalogue, sale number 4098, 4-5 April 1934)*

1845 wrote a letter which began, "I love your verses with all my heart, dear Miss Barrett." When Browning wrote that first of the many letters that were to be exchanged between the two poets, Barrett had already won an admiring public and was maintaining an extensive correspondence with writers and artists in England and the United States. Browning, on the other hand, was bitterly discouraged because his poetical career was not prospering and his productions on the London stage had proved to be hopeless failures. Six years younger than Barrett, he had abundant energy and good health, dressed as a young man of fashion, and enjoyed going to dinners and receptions where he conversed with many of the leading figures of the literary world. For almost all of his life he had been living at home with his parents and his sister—all three of whom adored him—and was financially dependent upon his father, since none of his volumes of verse had repaid the expenses of publication.

The courtship progressed despite the objections of Mr. Barrett, who wished his children to remain totally dependent on him. During the period of the exchange of letters and of Browning's visits to her room, she was composing the poems later to be named "Sonnets from the Portuguese." Most of the world's great love poetry has been produced by men; what is new about the sonnets is that the coming of love into the writer's life is described from the point of view of the woman. Among the finest love poems ever written by a woman, they are her most enduring poetic achievement. A chronic invalid, worn down by a succession of griefs, robbed of the bright-hued cheeks and resilience of youth, living without hope that a new life might someday be hers outside of her virtual prison, she expresses in the sonnets her sense of wonder that her life has been so transfigured. Filled with gratitude for her suitor's offer of love, she at first tells him that they must remain no more than friends because of the disparities in health and age. Marriage, she says, would place a severe burden upon him, for the care of an invalid wife six years older than he would necessarily take him away from the varied social life he has been enjoying. Will love that has come so quickly not fade just as quickly? Is her lover's suit based merely on pity? If she will promise to give up her home and the day-to-day associations with father, brothers, sisters, and friends, will he in turn be everything to her so that she will never miss the life she leaves behind? From the earnest look of her

lover's eyes she finds the answers to these and other questions, so that her doubts and hesitations are dispelled. With the full assurance of the depth of his feelings for her, she responds to his love in the most inspired sonnet of the cycle, "How do I love thee? Let me count the ways."

The clandestine marriage ceremony took place on 12 September 1846 at St. Marylebone Parish Church, which was not far from the Barretts' house. Almost immediately the couple left for Italy, where they hoped the warmer climate might help Elizabeth to regain some of her strength. After one winter they moved to Florence, which was to remain their home until Elizabeth's death. Despite the responsibilities of marriage and motherhood—their only child, Robert Wiedemann Barrett Browning, called "Pen," was born in 1849—Mrs. Browning had no intention of discontinuing her literary career. Her first task was to revise her volumes of 1838 and 1844 for publication in a new edition.

For the three years following her marriage Mrs. Browning had kept the forty-four sonnets in a notebook; she did not show them to her husband until the summer of 1849. He was so impressed with their beauty that he insisted on their appearing in her forthcoming new edition of *Poems* (1850). In order to make it appear that the poems had no biographical significance, the Brownings selected the ambiguous title "Sonnets from the Portuguese," as if they were translations. "Catarina to Camoens," the poem immediately preceding the sonnets in the second volume of *Poems*, tells of the love of Catarina for the Portuguese poet Camoens. Since first reading "Catarina to Camoens" in Elizabeth's *Poems* of 1844, Browning had associated Elizabeth with the Portuguese Catarina. Most of the reviews of the *Poems* of 1850 paid little attention to the sonnets, but a writer in *Fraser's* magazine immediately appreciated their distinctive quality: "From the Portuguese they may be: but their life and earnestness must prove Mrs. Browning either to be the most perfect of all known translators, or to have quickened with her own spirit the framework of another's thought, and then modestly declined the honour which was really her own." The sonnets gradually gained critical acceptance and have become the most beloved of all Mrs. Browning's works.

Besides the "Sonnets from the Portuguese," the other major new work in the volumes was the retranslation of *Prometheus Bound*. This new version was an enormous improvement over the translation that had been published in 1833; it is faithful to the original without being pedantic and is expressed in lively, idiomatic English. The two volumes were fairly well received in England, where the reviewers praised her for the depth of her intellect, the earnestness of her thought, and the "pathetic beauty" of the romantic ballads. They believed, however, that Mrs. Browning's poetry still retained some of the deficiencies of her earlier books, such as diffuseness, obscure language, and inappropriate imagery.

Mrs. Browning had developed a passionate interest in Italian politics; during her first year in Italy she had written "A Meditation in Tuscany" and sent it to *Blackwood's*. The editor had declined it and returned the manuscript to her, and it became the first part of *Casa Guidi Windows* (1851). The poem deals with political events as seen by the poet from the windows of Casa Guidi, the great stone palace in Florence where the Brownings had an apartment. In 1846 the newly elected Pope Pius IX had granted amnesty to prisoners who had fought for Italian liberty, initiated a program looking forward to a more democratic form of government for the Papal State, and carried out other reforms so that it looked as though he were heading toward the leadership of a league for a free Italy. Progressive measures had also been instituted in Tuscany by Grand Duke Leopold II, who arranged for a representative form of government and allowed the people to have a free press and to form their own civic guard. The first half of *Casa Guidi Windows* had been written when Mrs. Browning was filled with enthusiasm and was hopeful that the newly awakened liberal movements were moving toward the unification and freedom of the Italian states.

In the second half of the poem she voices her disillusionment and her bitter disappointment that liberalism had been crushed almost everywhere in Italy. Pope Pius had fled in disguise from the Vatican in the face of agitation for a republican government and had taken refuge at Gaeta under the protection of the king of Naples. Leopold, whom Mrs. Browning had at first admired, had proved to be a coward; and, rather than agree to the formation of a constituent assembly of the Italian states in Rome, he had left his Florentine palace and joined the exiled pope in Gaeta. Several months later the Austrian troops had occupied Florence, and Leopold had returned under their protection. In her poem Mrs. Browning expresses her disappointment with the pope, the grand duke, the English

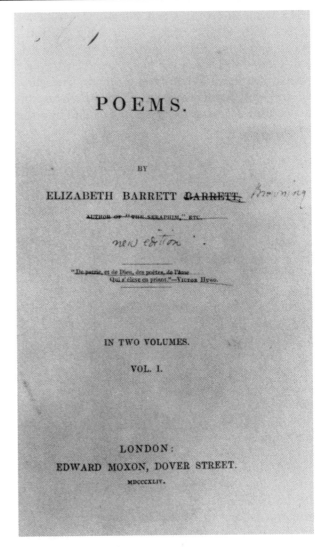

Title page for the volume of poems that made Barrett an international celebrity. After her marriage, she crossed out her maiden name and substituted "Browning."

government for its failure to intervene on the side of the Italian patriots, and the Florentines themselves because they had been unwilling to make the necessary sacrifices. By the middle of 1849 the liberal impulses had been crushed; except for Piedmont all the Italian states were under the domination of Austria and the papacy. For the next ten years there were no more uprisings or wars, and in the absence of stirring political events Mrs. Browning began the composition of a completely different kind of poem from anything she had written up to then.

As early as 1845 she had written to Browning that it was her intention to write a sort of novel-poem "running into the midst of our conventions, & rushing into drawing-rooms & the like 'where angels fear to tread'; & so, meeting face to face & without mask the Humanity of the age, & speaking the truth as I conceive of it, out plainly." For several years events in her own life and in the world about her distracted her from her purpose, so that the first mention of her new work appears in a letter written in 1853 to her friend Anna Jameson. Her poem would fill a volume when it was finished, she said; it was the romance she had been "hankering after so long, written in blank verse, in the autobiographical form." Named after the heroine of the poem, *Aurora Leigh* was published in 1857. In the dedication to her lifelong friend and benefactor John Kenyon she wrote that it was "the most mature of my works, and the one into which my highest convictions upon Life and Art have entered." In a narrative of some eleven thousand lines the heroine tells of her birth in Italy, her early years in rural England, her successful literary career in London and later in Florence, and at the end her marriage to her one true love.

Orphaned at an early age and brought up by an aunt in the western county of Shropshire, the youthful Aurora finds herself in a cultural desert, with no one to share her enthusiasm for literature. Aurora's description of the kind of education imposed upon her by her conventional aunt illustrates the restricted, anti-intellectual attitudes of the English middle classes toward the upbringing of their daughters. Aurora memorizes the Collects of the Anglican Church; takes lessons in music and dancing; is given some superficial instruction in French, German, history, and geography; and is taught sewing and embroidery. Not only were young women discouraged from learning Greek and Latin and from reading "controversial" books, but they were denied a university education. Aurora has to seek her education at home, whereas her cousin Romney Leigh is sent to a university. Rebelling against her aunt's narrow regimen, Aurora finds her true life in the world of books. Discovering her father's private library hidden away in the attic, she reads widely in Greek and Latin literature and English poetry and begins to compose verses of her own.

At the age of twenty she rejects a proposal of marriage from Romney Leigh, who asks her to be his wife for the sole reason that he needs her to help him in his philanthropic activities. Women, he tells her, are lacking in the higher imaginative qualities that would enable them to be great writers or artists. Aurora moves away from the rural community which has so stifled her and makes her home in London, where she

A somewhat inaccurate portrait of Robert Browning from R. H. Horne's A New Spirit of the Age *(1844); it hung on Barrett's wall at Wimpole Street. Before they met, this picture gave Barrett her only conception of Browning's appearance.*

will be independent and strive for literary success. By dint of steady application she wins within six or seven years a place for herself in the London literary world. To help support herself she writes articles for encyclopedias and journals, but she finds her chief satisfaction in the publication of her volumes of poetry. The heroine of this novel-poem serves as Mrs. Browning's mouthpiece when she declares that the most fitting subjects for poetry are to be found in contemporary settings and that a poet should not reject her own times to seek inspiration from earlier civilizations. Aurora, though still in her middle twenties, has already produced books of poetry which are reaching a wide and admiring public.

In contrast to Aurora, who has lived a serene and rather sheltered life, the main figure of the subplot is a pathetic victim of the abuses of society. Marian Erle is the only child of an ignorant and abusive migrant farm worker and a wife cowed into submission by his drunken rages. The girl runs away from her parents in fear of their vio-

Casa Guidi, the palace in Florence where the Brownings had an apartment

lence, is rescued from destitution by Romney Leigh, and even receives from him an offer of marriage. As a radical socialist he thus proposes to put into practice his utopian ideal of the destruction of the barriers that separate the rich from the poor and the educated from the ignorant. The marriage, however, does not take place, for Marian is treacherously spirited away from England by a woman who believes herself to be in love with Romney. Marian is taken to a house of ill repute in Paris, where she is drugged and sexually assaulted. As a result of this act of violence she becomes pregnant and after much ill-treatment gives birth to a son.

After nine years in London, Aurora suddenly gives up her apartment and establishes a new home for herself in a villa in Florence. On the way she stops in Paris, where she encounters Marian and hears her story; she takes Marian and the baby to Florence with her. A few months after her arrival Aurora is asked once again by Romney to be his wife. This time, however, he is

blind and much humbled by his misfortunes. Leigh Hall, which he had converted into a utopian community, had been set on fire and destroyed by the very people whom he had been aiding. At the time of the fire he had been struck on the forehead and blinded by a falling beam. Romney now sadly admits that doctrinaire socialism is a failure, for the people will rebel against any restrictions and reforms imposed upon them. Aurora says that she too has been wrong in her proud independence and her belief that her life could be complete without the companionship of a loved one. They pledge themselves to each other and look forward to a life of shared responsibilities. In the meanwhile Marian has told them that she will never marry and that when her child no longer needs her care she will devote herself to helping the "outcast orphans of the world."

In this long narrative poem Mrs. Browning has dealt with some of the major social problems of her age. In Victorian England an educated

John Kenyon, friend and benefactor of the Brownings
(The British Museum)

woman with unusual talents had almost no opportunity to make use of her skills in a world that was dominated by men. Nevertheless, as the poem shows in the example of its heroine, it was possible for a woman with great energy and sense of purpose to live by herself in London and become renowned on the strength of her own unaided efforts. Professional success alone, however, is not sufficient, for nothing can give more meaning to a woman's life than enduring love in marriage. Another theme is Mrs. Browning's distrust of the theories of contemporary French socialists, such as Charles Fourier, who advocated the division of society into communistic units. She believed that in the kind of state envisioned by the radical socialists there would be no place for artists and poets. Nothing stirred up more controversy than her frank treatment of the plight of "the fallen woman"—a subject that was considered by the Victorian public to be outside the purview of the serious novelist or poet. In mid-nineteenth-century England, standards of sexual conduct were so rigid that any woman who bore a child out of wedlock, even if she had been a victim of male aggression, was shunned by "respectable" people and condemned to a life

of penance and mortification. Eighteenth-century readers had allowed their novelists more freedom to depict sexual irregularities, but the great Victorian novelists dealt obliquely, or not at all, with such subjects. One of Mrs. Browning's most fundamental convictions was that sexual activity outside of marriage was immoral, but she believed that society should be more compassionate in its treatment of women who had been victims of seduction or sexual attacks. It is not surprising that the story of Marian Erle shocked women readers, some of whom were reported to have said that the reading of *Aurora Leigh* had endangered their morals.

Most of the Brownings' literary friends were delighted with the poem and accorded it the highest praise; Algernon Charles Swinburne, Leigh Hunt, Walter Savage Landor, John Ruskin, and Dante Gabriel Rossetti all spoke of it with unrestrained enthusiasm. From a commercial point of view it proved to be by far the most successful of Mrs. Browning's works; by 1885, twenty-eight years after its first publication, it had gone through nineteen editions. Despite its great popularity with other poets and with the general public, it found little favor with professional reviewers. Most were in agreement that the poem was too long and lacking in coherence, that the characterization was weak, that the plot was melodramatic and implausible, that the imagery was often inappropriate and discordant, and that some of the material was so vulgar that it offended good taste. One reviewer declared that the coarseness of its language made Mrs. Browning's book "almost a closed volume for her own sex." The notices in the most influential journals, however, granted that despite its shortcomings the poem gave evidence of its author's vigorous intellect, her earnestness, and her wide and humane sympathies.

Two years after the publication of *Aurora Leigh* Mrs. Browning again became absorbed in current political events as the Italians, after a decade of truce, began once more their struggle for independence and unity. In June 1859 Italian troops under the leadership of King Victor Emmanuel of Piedmont, joined by Napoleon III, who had come to northern Italy with substantial French forces, won two battles against the Austrians in Lombardy. Then early in July, Napoleon surprised and bitterly disappointed the Italians by agreeing at Villafranca to an armistice which would leave Venice under the domination of Austria. In response to these events Mrs. Browning's

Poems before Congress was published in the spring of 1860; but by the time the volume appeared the title was misleading, for the congress of the leading powers that was to have been held in January had been indefinitely postponed. Seven of the eight poems deal with Italian politics, while the other, "A Curse for a Nation," is an antislavery poem that had earlier been published in an abolitionist journal in Boston. Although Mrs. Browning felt betrayed when she first heard of the truce initiated by the emperor, whom she had long admired, she expressed her continuing faith in him in two of the poems, "A Tale of Villafranca" and "Napoleon III in Italy." In her view the emperor was not at fault, for his noble aims had been frustrated by selfish and small-minded statesmen. In "Italy and the World" Mrs. Browning prophesies that the states of central Italy in revolt against Austria will join Piedmont and Lombardy to form a united and independent kingdom, but the triumphant conclusion of the Italian cause will owe nothing to the English government, which she berates for its failure to provide military aid. The notices in the leading English journals were uniformly unfavorable toward the volume, which they found offensive because of its strident tone and anti-British bias.

In the spring of 1860 Mrs. Browning continued to write poems on the Italian situation, which to her great delight appeared to be moving toward a victorious outcome. Central and northern Italy had become a united kingdom under the leadership of Victor Emmanuel of Piedmont and his prime minister, Count Camillo Bensodi Cavour. The theme of "King Victor Emmanuel Entering Florence, April, 1860" is the great joy of the people of Tuscany and their expressions of gratitude toward the king for the part he has played in helping them to their freedom. The tone of "Summing up in Italy," however, is bitter; here Mrs. Browning utters her fears that although the great powers of Europe will ratify the creation of the new kingdom of Italy, they will discredit its chief architects. Besides her political poems, at this time she wrote "A Musical Instrument," which has become one of her best-known poems. Based on the myth of Pan and Syrinx, the verses exemplify the doctrine that the true poet is destined to suffer much hardship and pain in the practice of her art.

Despite her extreme frailty Mrs. Browning followed with feverish excitement the rapidly unfolding events of the winter of 1860-1861. The

Elizabeth Barrett Browning in 1858

peoples of Sicily, Naples, and the States of the Church had voted for annexation with Victor Emmanuel's new kingdom. With most of the Italian states united, a national parliament met at Turin early in 1861. Mrs. Browning felt that her faith in the Italian leaders had been justified. "There are great men here, and there will be a great nation presently," she declared. She had been in poor health for several years, suffering from weakness of the lungs and heart, and her obsession with Italian politics further weakened her nervous system. The final blow, which prostrated her emotionally and physically, was the unexpected and premature death on 6 June 1861 of Count Cavour, the great patriot who had been chiefly responsible for bringing the disparate states into a unified and independent kingdom. "I can scarcely command voice or hand to name *Cavour*," Elizabeth wrote; "if tears or blood could have saved him to us, he should have had mine." For the next two weeks she remained in seclusion, never going out and seeing almost no one at home. Then on 20 June she was stricken with a severe cold, cough, and sore throat, and was confined to her bed; she died in Browning's arms early in the morning of 29 June. Within a month Browning left Florence with his son to make his permanent home in London.

The many journals which reported Mrs. Browning's untimely death all spoke of her as the greatest woman poet in English literature. The highly respected *Edinburgh Review* expressed the prevailing view when it said that she had no equal in the literary history of any country: "Such a combination of the finest genius and the choicest results of cultivation and wide-ranging studies has never been seen before in any woman." In America the most extravagant of the obituary notices appeared in the *Southern Literary Messenger,* which called her "the Shakespeare among her sex" and placed her among the four or five greatest authors of all time. A year after her death Browning collected and arranged for publication her *Last Poems,* which included translations from Greek and Latin poetry, personal lyrics, and poems on Italian politics. In the same year the fifth edition of her *Poems* was published. Both works were warmly received by the leading literary journals on both sides of the Atlantic as they reviewed her poetic career from its beginning and concluded that her gifts had been of the highest order. A writer in the *Christian Examiner* of Boston said that Tennyson's *In Memoriam* (1850) and Mrs. Browning's *Aurora Leigh* were the two greatest poems of the age and that the "Sonnets from the Portuguese" were the finest love poems in English: "Shakespeare's sonnets, beautiful as they are, cannot be compared with them, and Petrarch's seem commonplace beside them."

In the decades following Mrs. Browning's death her poetry began to lose much of the appeal it had held for readers during her lifetime. The consensus of late-Victorian critics was that much of her writing would be forgotten in another generation but that she would be remembered for "The Cry of the Children," a few of the romantic ballads, such as "Isobel's Child" and "Bertha in the Lane," and most of all for the "Sonnets from the Portuguese." During all this period and for the first three decades of the present century, *Aurora Leigh* largely dropped out of sight. In 1930, however, Virginia Woolf in an article in the *Times Literary Supplement* deplored the fact that Mrs. Browning's poetry was no longer being read and especially that *Aurora Leigh* had been forgotten. She urged her readers to take a fresh

look at the poem, which she admired for its "speed and energy, forthrightness and complete self-confidence." "Elizabeth Barrett," Woolf wrote, "was inspired by a flash of true genius when she rushed into the drawing-room and said that here, where we live and work, is the true place for the poet." In Woolf's view, the heroine of the poem, "with her passionate interest in social questions, her conflict as artist and woman, her longing for knowledge and freedom, is the true daughter of her age."

Notwithstanding Woolf's enthusiasm for *Aurora Leigh,* the poem continued to be ignored by the general public and by scholars until the recent advent of feminist criticism. None of Mrs. Browning's poems has received more attention from feminist critics than *Aurora Leigh,* since its theme is one that especially concerns them: the difficulties that a woman must overcome if she is to achieve independence in a world mainly controlled by men. In her *Literary Women* Ellen Moers writes that *Aurora Leigh* is the great epic poem of the age; it is "the epic poem of the literary woman herself." It now looks as though Mrs. Browning's literary reputation will remain secure with future critics who view her work from a feminist perspective. One may also prophesy that for the general public the "Sonnets from the Portuguese," despite some Victorian quaintness of imagery, will continue to hold their place among the most-admired love poems of world literature.

Letters:
Letters of Elizabeth Barrett Browning Addressed to Richard Hengist Horne, 2 volumes, edited by S. R. Townshend Mayer (London: Bentley, 1877);

The Letters of Elizabeth Barrett Browning, 2 volumes, edited by Frederic G. Kenyon (London: Smith, Elder, 1897);

Letters to Robert Browning and Other Correspondents by Elizabeth Barrett Browning, edited by Thomas J. Wise (London: Privately printed, 1916);

Elizabeth Barrett Browning: Letters to Her Sister, 1846-1859, edited by Leonard Huxley (London: Murray, 1929);

Letters from Elizabeth Barrett to B. R. Haydon, edited by Martha Hale Shackford (New York: Oxford University Press, 1939);

"Twenty Unpublished Letters of Elizabeth Barrett to Hugh Stuart Boyd," edited by Bennett Weaver, *PMLA,* 65 (June 1950): 397-418;

Elizabeth Barrett Browning's tomb in the English Cemetery, Florence

"New Letters from Mrs. Browning to Isa Blagden," edited by Edward C. McAleer, *PMLA*, 66 (September 1951): 594-612;

Elizabeth Barrett to Miss Mitford: The Unpublished Letters of Elizabeth Barrett Barrett to Mary Russell Mitford, edited by Betty Miller (London: Murray, 1954);

Elizabeth Barrett to Mr. Boyd: Unpublished Letters of Elizabeth Barrett Browning to Hugh Stuart Boyd, edited by Barbara P. McCarthy (New Haven: Yale University Press, 1955);

Letters of the Brownings to George Barrett, edited by Paul Landis with the assistance of Ronald E. Freeman (Urbana: University of Illinois Press, 1958);

The Letters of Robert Browning and Elizabeth Barrett Barrett, 1845-1846, 2 volumes, edited by Elvan Kintner (Cambridge, Mass.: Harvard University Press, 1969);

Invisible Friends: The Correspondence of Elizabeth Barrett Barrett and Benjamin Robert Haydon, 1842-1845, edited by Willard Bissell Pope (Cambridge, Mass.: Harvard University Press, 1972);

Elizabeth Barrett Browning's Letters to Mrs. David Ogilvy, 1849-1861, edited by Peter N. Heydon and Philip Kelley (New York: Quadrangle/New York Times Book Co. and the Browning Institute, 1973);

The Brownings' Correspondence, 8 volumes to date, edited by Philip Kelley and Ronald Hudson (Winfield, Kans.: Wedgestone Press, 1984-1990).

Bibliographies:

H. Buxton Forman, *Elizabeth Barrett Browning and Her Scarcer Books* (London: Privately printed, 1896);

Thomas J. Wise, *A Bibliography of the Writings in Prose and Verse of Elizabeth Barrett Browning* (London: Privately printed, 1918);

Wise, *A Browning Library. A Catalogue of Printed Books, Manuscripts, and Autograph Letters by Robert Browning and Elizabeth Barrett Browning, Collected by T. J. Wise* (London: Privately printed, 1929);

Theodore G. Ehrsam, Robert H. Deily, and Robert M. Smith, *Bibliographies of Twelve Victo-*

rian Authors (New York: Wilson, 1936), pp. 48-66;

Warner Barnes, *A Bibliography of Elizabeth Barrett Browning* (Austin: University of Texas Press, 1967);

William S. Peterson, *Robert and Elizabeth Barrett Browning: An Annotated Bibliography, 1951-1970* (New York: Browning Institute, 1974);

Philip Kelley and Ronald Hudson, eds., *The Brownings' Correspondence: A Checklist* (New York & Arkansas City, Kans.: Browning Institute & Wedgestone Press, 1978).

Biographies:

Jeannette Marks, *The Family of the Barrett: A Colonial Romance* (New York: Macmillan, 1938);

Dorothy Hewlett, *Elizabeth Barrett Browning: A Life* (New York: Knopf, 1952; London: Cassell, 1953);

Gardner B. Taplin, *The Life of Elizabeth Barrett Browning* (New Haven: Yale University Press, 1957; London: Murray, 1957);

Edward C. McAleer, *The Brownings of Casa Guidi* (New York: Browning Institute, 1979);

Rosalie Mander, *Mrs. Browning: The Story of Elizabeth Barrett* (London: Weidenfeld & Nicolson, 1980).

References:

Deirdre David, *Intellectual Women and Victorian Patriarchy: Harriet Martineau, Elizabeth Barrett Browning, George Eliot* (Ithaca, N.Y.: Cornell University Press, 1987);

Alethea Hayter, *Mrs. Browning: A Poet's Work and Its Setting* (London: Faber & Faber, 1962; New York: Barnes & Noble, 1963);

Gladys W. Hudson, *An Elizabeth Barrett Browning Concordance*, 4 volumes (Detroit: Gale, 1973);

Mary Jane Lupton, *Elizabeth Barrett Browning* (Old Westbury, N.Y.: Feminist Press, 1972);

Dorothy Mermin, *Elizabeth Barrett Browning: The Origins of a New Poetry* (Chicago: University of Chicago Press, 1989);

Ellen Moers, *Literary Women* (Garden City, N.Y.: Doubleday, 1976);

Virginia L. Radley, *Elizabeth Barrett Browning* (New York: Twayne, 1972);

Patricia Thomson, *George Sand and the Victorians: Her Influence and Reputation in Nineteenth-Century England* (New York: Columbia University Press, 1977).

Papers:

There are important collections of Elizabeth Barrett Browning's manuscripts and books at the Wellesley College Library, in the Berg Collection at the New York Public Library, the Huntington Library, the British Library, the Folger Library, the Harvard University Library, the Yale University Library, the Pierpont Morgan Library, the Library of the University of Texas, the Armstrong Browning Library at Baylor University, and the Boston Public Library.

Robert Browning

(7 May 1812 - 12 December 1889)

This entry was updated by Thomas J. Collins (University of Western Ontario) from his entry in
DLB 32: Victorian Poets Before 1850.

BOOKS: *Pauline: A Fragment of a Confession*, anonymous (London: Saunders & Otley, 1833);

Paracelsus (London: Wilson, 1835; edited by C. P. Denison, New York: Baker & Taylor, 1911);

Strafford: An Historical Tragedy (London: Longman, Rees, Orme, Brown, Green & Longmans, 1837);

Sordello (London: Moxon, 1840);

Bells and Pomegranates. No. I.—Pippa Passes (London: Moxon, 1841);

Bells and Pomegranates. No. II.—King Victor and King Charles (London: Moxon, 1842);

Bells and Pomegranates. No. III.—Dramatic Lyrics (London: Moxon, 1842; edited by J. O. Beatty and J. W. Bowyer, New York: Houghton, 1895);

Bells and Pomegranates. No. IV.—The Return of the Druses: A Tragedy in Five Acts (London: Moxon, 1843);

Bells and Pomegranates. No. V.—A Blot in the 'Scutcheon: A Tragedy in Five Acts (London: Moxon, 1843; edited by W. Rolfe and H. Hersey, New York: Harper, 1887);

Bells and Pomegranates. No. VI.—Colombe's Birthday: A Play in Five Acts (London: Moxon, 1844);

Bells and Pomegranates. No. VII.—Dramatic Romances & Lyrics (London: Moxon, 1845);

Bells and Pomegranates. No. VIII.—and Last. Luria; and A Soul's Tragedy (London: Moxon, 1846);

Poems: A New Edition, 2 volumes (London: Chapman & Hall, 1849; Boston: Ticknor, Reed & Fields, 1850);

Christmas-Eve and Easter-Day (London: Chapman & Hall, 1850; Boston: Lothrop, 1887);

Two Poems by Robert Browning and Elizabeth Barrett Browning (London: Chapman & Hall, 1854);

Men and Women (2 volumes, London: Chapman & Hall, 1855; 1 volume, Boston: Ticknor & Fields, 1856);

Dramatis Personae (London: Chapman & Hall, 1864; Boston: Ticknor & Fields, 1864);

The Poetical Works of Robert Browning, 6 volumes (London: Smith, Elder, 1868);

The Ring and the Book (4 volumes, London: Smith, Elder, 1868-1869; 2 volumes, Boston: Fields, Osgood, 1869);

Balaustion's Adventure, Including a Transcript from Euripides (London: Smith, Elder, 1871; Boston: Osgood, 1871);

Prince Hohenstiel-Schwangau, Saviour of Society (London: Smith, Elder, 1871);

Fifine at the Fair (London: Smith, Elder, 1872; Boston: Osgood, 1872);

Red Cotton Night-Cap Country; or, Turf and Towers (London: Smith, Elder, 1873; Boston: Osgood, 1873);

Aristophanes' Apology, Including a Transcript from Euripides: Being the Last Adventures of Balaustion (London: Smith, Elder, 1875; Boston: Osgood, 1875);

The Inn Album (London: Smith, Elder, 1875; Boston: Osgood, 1876);

Pacchiarotto and How He Worked in Distemper, with Other Poems (London: Smith, Elder, 1876; Boston: Osgood, 1877);

La Saisiaz, and The Two Poets of Croisic (London: Smith, Elder, 1878);

Dramatic Idyls (London: Smith, Elder, 1879);

Dramatic Idyls: Second Series (London: Smith, Elder, 1880);

Jocoseria (London: Smith, Elder, 1883; Boston & New York: Houghton, Mifflin, 1883);

Ferishtah's Fancies (London: Smith, Elder, 1884; Boston: Houghton, Mifflin, 1885);

Parleyings with Certain People of Importance in Their Day (London: Smith, Elder, 1887; Boston & New York: Houghton, Mifflin, 1887);

Asolando: Fancies and Facts (London: Smith, Elder, 1889; Boston & New York: Houghton, Mifflin, 1890).

Collections: *Complete Poetic and Dramatic Works of Robert Browning*, Cambridge Edition, edited by G. W. Cooke and H. E. Scudder (Boston & New York: Houghton, Mifflin, 1895);

The Complete Works of Robert Browning, Florentine Edition, 12 volumes, edited by Charlotte Por-

National Portrait Gallery, London

Robert Browning.

ter and Helen A. Clarke (New York & Bos-
ton: Crowell, 1898);
The Works of Robert Browning, Centenary Edition,
10 volumes, edited by Frederic G. Kenyon
(London: Smith, Elder / Boston: Hinkley,
1912);
*New Poems by Robert Browning and Elizabeth Barrett
Browning*, edited by Kenyon (London:
Smith, Elder, 1914; New York: Macmillan,
1915);
The Complete Works of Robert Browning, 9 volumes
to date, edited by Roma A. King and others
(Athens: Ohio University Press, 1969-1991);
Robert Browning: The Ring and the Book, edited by
Richard D. Altick (London: Penguin / New
Haven: Yale University Press, 1971);
Robert Browning: The Poems, 2 volumes, edited by
John Pettigrew, supplemented and com-
pleted by Thomas J. Collins (London: Pen-
guin / New Haven: Yale University Press,
1981);

The Poetical Works of Robert Browning, 3 volumes, edited by Ian Jack and Margaret Smith (Ox-
ford: Clarendon Press, 1983-1991);
The Plays of Robert Browning, edited, with an introduction, by Thomas J. Collins and Richard
Shroyer (New York: Garland, 1988).

OTHER: John Forster, *Lives of Eminent British
Statesmen*, volume 2, undetermined contribu-
tion to biography of Thomas Wentworth,
Earl of Strafford, by Browning (London:
Longman, Orme, Brown, Green & Long-
mans, 1836);
Letters of Percy Bysshe Shelley, introduction by
Browning (London: Moxon, 1852), pp. 1-44;
The Agamemnon of Aeschylus, translated by Brow-
ning (London: Smith, Elder, 1877);
Thomas Jones, *The Divine Order: Sermons*, introduc-
tion by Browning (London: Isbister, 1884);
"Sonnet: Why I Am a Liberal," in *Why I Am a Lib-
eral*, edited by A. Reid (London: Cassell,
1885).

Robert Browning, with Alfred, Lord Tennyson, is considered one of the two major poets of
the Victorian age. His life (1812-1889) and the
chronological span of his publishing career (from
Pauline in 1833 to *Asolando* in 1889) place him
firmly in the context of Victoria's reign (1837-
1901); his major poetic achievements, including the development of his themes and techniques, simultaneously reflect and dominate the
period in which he wrote. Although his early poetry was generally either ridiculed or ignored, as
the century progressed Browning gained recognition for his mastery of the dramatic monologue
form, for his skillful and penetrating method of
character analysis, and for the enunciation of important Victorian themes—especially progress, imperfection, and optimism. Like Tennyson, Browning not only reflected his culture, but because
he seemed to offer a sense of the stable and the enduring in a dynamic and ever-changing world, he
became an object of culture. Thus, by the early
1880s, members of the newly formed Browning
Society thought of Browning not only as a major
poetic force, but also as a prophet and a teacher
who bore an inspired message to an unbelieving
and materialistic age.

When one is faced with such a huge bulk
of poetry, such major artistic achievements, and
such varied and frequently contradictory reasons
for admiration of the canon, it is prudent to engage in careful discriminations. From a twentieth-

century perspective, Browning's development of the techniques of the dramatic monologue form is regarded as his most important contribution to poetry. His use of diction, rhythm, and symbol directly influenced Ezra Pound, T. S. Eliot, and Robert Frost, to cite only a few examples. But the dramatic monologue, although the most successful of Browning's endeavors, does not exhaust the variety or the scope of his creative efforts.

Browning was born in 1812 in Camberwell, a middle-class suburb across the Thames from the main part of nineteenth-century London, to Robert Browning, Sr., and Sarah Anna Wiedemann Browning. Mrs. Browning, of German-Scottish descent, was a musician, a lover of nature, and a devout evangelical Christian. She was no doubt the stronger of the two parents in guiding her son through his developmental stages. A woman of common sense and stability—qualities inherited by Browning's sister, Sarianna, who was born in 1814—she was later characterized by Thomas Carlyle as "the true type of Scottish gentlewoman." Like his father before him, Browning's father was employed as a clerk in the Bank of England. Robert Browning, Sr., a rather passive man, quietly labored at the bank and pursued his cherished interests in the home environment. He was an artist, a scholar, a collector of books and pictures, and an antiquarian. His rare book collection of more than six thousand volumes included works in Greek, Hebrew, Latin, French, Italian, and Spanish.

It is believed that Browning was already proficient at reading and writing by the age of five. He was then sent to a local dame school, but was asked to leave after a short time, apparently because he was superior to the other students. He studied at home until the age of seven and about that time was sent to the lower school at Peckham, run by the Ready sisters. When Browning was ten he passed from the lower school to the classes of the Reverend Thomas Ready, studying writing, arithmetic, English, history, Latin, and Greek. This narrow, conservative, and traditional training was doubtless augmented by the vast store of materials in Browning's father's library, in which the boy was encouraged to read; among the works consumed by the young Browning were Nathaniel Wanley's *The Wonders of the Little World* (1678) and the fifty-volume *Biographie Universelle*. The esoteric nature of the library and his father's wide-ranging interests make it hardly surprising that Browning's poetry is so richly allusive. From fourteen to sixteen, the aspiring poet

was educated at home, attended to by various tutors in music, drawing, dancing, and horsemanship. Since he was ineligible to attend Oxford or Cambridge because he was not a member of the Church of England, he attended London University for about one year, during which he was enrolled in a regular program of study in Greek and Latin, and also in beginning German. His sudden departure in 1829 perhaps indicates a firm decision to turn his attention to poetry as a vocation.

Given the circumstances of Browning's education, it is not surprising that he was especially precocious in his poetic development. At the age of twelve he wrote a volume of Byronic verse entitled "Incondita," which his parents attempted, unsuccessfully, to have published. The two poems which survive, "The Dance of Death" and "The First-Born of Egypt," clearly reflect the Byronic influences on and impulses of the early-adolescent Browning. The most momentous occurrence for the young Browning was in 1825, when he was given a copy of Percy Bysshe Shelley's *Miscellaneous Poems* (1826) by his cousin, James Silverthorne. This volume, which contained poems pirated from Mrs. Shelley's edition of *Posthumous Poems* (1824), included all of the most important of Shelley's lyrics except "The Cloud" and "Ode to the West Wind." At his request, Browning's mother purchased most of Shelley's other works for his birthday that same year, thus enabling Browning to immerse himself in the Shelley canon. At the age of thirteen, Browning, strongly under the influence of Shelley, became a vegetarian and an atheist. As Mrs. Sutherland Orr, a confidante in his later years and one of his first biographers, records, he "gratuitously proclaimed himself everything that he was, and some things that he was not."

Browning seems to have written no poetry between the ages of thirteen and twenty; then, in 1832, he composed his first major published work, *Pauline*. Few details are available concerning the period leading up to the publication of *Pauline*, but it is evident from the poem that sometime during this period Browning had come to terms with Shelley's influence; by 1832 he no longer accepted the apocalyptic impulse as the most important, and he also rejected Shelley's atheism and returned to more orthodox Christianity.

Published anonymously in 1833, *Pauline*, slightly more than one thousand lines in length, is, as its subtitle states, *A Fragment of a Confession*.

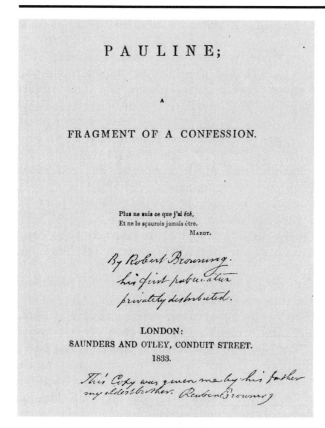

Title page for Browning's first published work, on which his name did not appear (Anderson Galleries auction catalogue, 13-16 May 1918)

The poem falls roughly into three divisions: in the first and third, the speaker addresses the imaginary Pauline, with whom he appears to be deeply infatuated, and complains that he can no longer be productive poetically, that he is in a state of deep depression and sadness, and that he wants desperately to try to understand his fragmented state. In the initial section, the speaker celebrates the influence upon his life and poetry of the "Sun-treader," whom most scholars identify as Shelley:

> Sun-treader, life and light be thine for ever!
> Thou art gone from us; years go by and spring
> Gladdens and the young earth is beautiful,
> Yet thy songs come not, other bards arise,
> But none like thee.

The "Sun-treader" has had an important influence on the speaker's early years, but that influence is now diminished; and the speaker sets out in the second third of the poem to try to understand the course of his own development. This section is heavily autobiographical, referring specifically in various places to aspects of Browning's youth and adolescence. The speaker then moves into a long lyric passage near the beginning of the third segment of the poem in which he attempts to revivify himself by traveling through nature with the fictional Pauline. He resolves his doubts and difficulties by affirming his faith in God and in the necessity of offering some allegiance to the spirit of orthodox Christianity, rather than to the spirit of his former poetic mentor. However, as the poem closes, the speaker yokes Shelley and God:

> Sun-treader, I believe in God and truth
> And love; and as one just escaped from death
> Would bind himself in bands of friends to feel
> He lives indeed, so, I would lean on thee!

Consequently, the reader is left wondering whether or not the personal problems which evoked the poem's utterance have indeed been solved. John Stuart Mill, who was sent a copy of *Pauline* for review by Browning's friend W. J. Fox, wondered about precisely this. In the copy of the book sent to him (now housed in the Victoria and Albert Museum in London) Mill wrote: "With considerable poetic powers, the writer seems to me possessed with a more intense and morbid self-consciousness than I ever knew in any sane human being." His lengthy comments, many of which reflect this attitude to the poem and its speaker, have served as the focus of a good deal of the discussion about Browning's early work, particularly *Pauline, Paracelsus* (1835), and *Sordello* (1840).

Fox gave his copy of *Pauline,* with Mill's comments, to Browning shortly after publication. Browning added his own remarks to those of Mill by way of reply and explained, presumably in an attempt to downplay the autobiographical nature of the work, that the poem had "for its object the enabling me to assume and realize I know not how many different characters;— meanwhile the world was never to grasp that 'Brown, Smith, Jones, and Robinson' . . . the respective authors of this poem, the other novel, such an opera, such a speech etc. etc. were no other than one and the same individual." A similar explanation is added in the preface to the poem which Browning wrote for its republication in 1868. It is generally believed that Browning reacted with acute embarrassment to the self-revelation of *Pauline.* Deeply hurt by Mill's comments, he resolved to distance himself from the poem, and to protect himself in the future by turn-

PARACELSUS.

BY ROBERT BROWNING.

LONDON:
PUBLISHED BY
EFFINGHAM WILSON, ROYAL EXCHANGE.

MDCCCXXXV.

Title page for Browning's second published book (American Art Association/Anderson Galleries auction catalogue, sale number 4320, 14 April 1937)

ing from lyrical expression to more dramatic forms. There is little doubt that Browning attempted to divorce himself from the persona of the poem, and there is equally little doubt that the poem is highly personal. And although the contention that his subsequent movement to more dramatic forms resulted solely from Mill's comments is an oversimplification, the attitude expressed by Mill was perhaps one of several factors which influenced his decision in his next published work, *Paracelsus*, to employ at least the external trappings of drama.

Paracelsus, a poem of more than four thousand lines, is divided into five sections which seem to function as scenes. Browning provides each scene with a specific time, cast of characters, and dialogue. But nothing of an external nature really happens in the poem. The minor characters, Festus and Michal, are simply foils for Paracelsus as he reflects upon the events of his life and on his problems in coming to an understanding of himself, his ambitions, and the nature of reality.

While *Paracelsus* is no greater a technical success than *Pauline*, there is one important point of contrast between the two poems. The ideas in *Pauline* are unclear, irresolute, and incomplete; in *Paracelsus*, the ideas are relatively clear, certain, and complete. This difference is significant, for in *Paracelsus* Browning is dealing with basically the same problems which concerned him in *Pauline*. Browning's development is described in *Pauline* as a series of stages: he desires greatness, pursues a utopian dream, fails, becomes a cynic, and finally announces that he is saved. But the conclusion of the poem, its religious resolution, is problematical and contradictory. In *Paracelsus*, Browning is one step removed from his problems and thus can work out, with a greater degree of objectivity, the moral dilemma left unsolved in *Pauline*: what is man's relationship to God and to his fellowman; how can unlimited aspiration be reconciled with limited ability; how can man reach God without succumbing to the fruitless idealism of Shelley; and how does one serve the human race without being dragged down into the quagmire of reality? Through the poem's five parts, each of which represents a different stage in the life of Paracelsus, Browning explores these problems; in Canto V, he offers solutions.

The character Paracelsus is based upon a real historical figure, a German who lived from 1490 to 1541. The original Paracelsus is only vaguely present in the poem; Browning recreates the character to suit his own particular purposes. The basic problem of Paracelsus is his desire to possess a kind of godhead, to obtain some form of perfect knowledge. These desires are outlined in the expository first canto. In the second section of the poem, Paracelsus meets a poet, Aprile, modeled on Browning's conception of Shelley; Aprile explains that he, too, has tried to possess an absolute—perfect love—but that he has failed and has come to understand the nature of the imperfect world in which man must live and which man must accept. Paracelsus mistakes Aprile's message and sets off to combine the aspiration for perfect knowledge with the aspiration for perfect love, and thereby to possess the whole of existence. He is, of course, unable to realize his ambition, and inevitably falls into despair and cynicism.

It is only in Canto V, following his philosophical and personal setbacks, that Paracelsus is able to come to terms with his problems. He under-

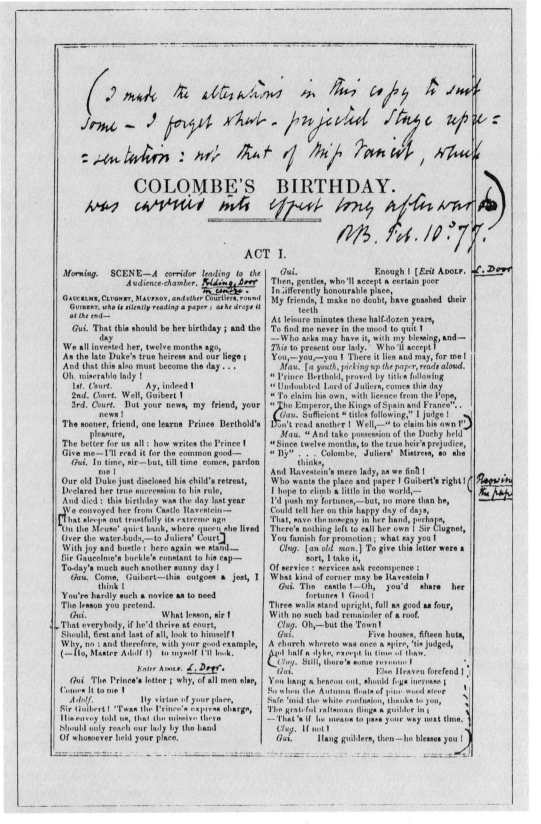

First page of Part VI of Browning's Bells and Pomegranates *(1844), with notations by Browning*
(David Magee/Antiquarian Books, Victoria Catalogue*)*

stands that infinites are unattainable to man in his present state of imperfection; that imperfection, qualified by the necessity and the inevitability of progress, is the law of life; and that progress depends upon the recognition that the flesh is not a snare but a temporal element which can contribute to man's ultimate perfection. Finally, he learns that God rejoices and resides in all aspects of His creation, even to the extent of allowing man, in his weakness, to reflect His grandeur. Through *Paracelsus,* Browning is able to reconcile himself to the nature of limited aspiration, and is also able to work out some of the basic elements of his reflective thought on the fundamental problems of humanity.

Like *Pauline, Paracelsus* was an experimental poem. It was not well received critically, although some reviewers noted the presence of an embryonic dramatic talent. And Browning's dramatic impulse would soon be allowed to surface. Browning first met the great actor W. C. Macready at the home of W. J. Fox on 27 November 1835. On 16 February 1836 he visited Macready to discuss an idea for a play. This meeting was unproductive, but on 26 May of the same year Browning met Macready again, with Walter Savage Landor and William Wordsworth, at a dinner given by Sir Thomas Talfourd in honor of the success of his play *Ion.* Macready is reported to have said to Browning, "Will you not write me a tragedy, and save me from going to America?" Browning took the challenge seriously and wrote a historical play, *Strafford,* which ran for five nights in 1837. That Browning was not to become the savior of the Victorian stage is clear in the failure of *Strafford;* this historical play could not engage its audience because, while Browning was able to deal skillfully with the internal conflicts of human beings, he was unable to represent on the stage the public, external drama of men acting and conflicting in the world of politics and business. This is true as well of the various plays published between 1841 and 1846 in the *Bells and Pomegranates* series. But in 1837 Browning had another major project in mind.

Sordello was published in 1840, but it had been in the process of composition since 1833. During this period, the poem underwent four distinct stages of composition: the first stage, between March of 1833 and March of 1834, concerned the development of a poetic soul. The second period began after the completion of *Paracelsus* and continued into 1837. During this stage, the poem probably focused on events connected

with war and passion. In the third stage, from September 1837 until the middle of April 1838, Browning added the historical element to the poem. In the final stage, which began in August 1838 and lasted until May 1839, Browning concentrated upon a dedication to humanity and the extension of his earlier Shelleyan liberalism. As a result of this constant revision, the poem became a conglomeration of psychology, love, romance, humanitarianism, philosophy, and history.

Upon publication, *Sordello* was regarded as a colossal failure. Harriet Martineau was so wholly unable to understand it that she supposed herself ill. Douglas Jerrold reportedly read *Sordello* when he was recovering from an illness and thought that he was going mad; and Jane Carlyle is said to have read it through without being able to ascertain whether Sordello was a man, a book, or a city. However, *Sordello* is worth brief comment because in it Browning enunciates theories of the poet and poetry which further refine statements made in *Pauline* and *Paracelsus.*

As in *Paracelsus,* the main character in the poem is historical in origin but adapted by Browning for his own purposes. Sordello is primarily a poet, and a most important aspect of the poem is his attempt to understand his role as a poet and the nature of poetic expression. Central to both of these elements in the poem, and most important for Browning's own career, is the recognition that poets must always temper their idealism with an understanding of reality, and that language as the vehicle for poetic expression can never adequately enunciate the poet's vision:

> Piece after piece that armour broke away,
> Because perceptions whole, like that he sought
> To clothe, reject so pure a work of thought
> As language: thought may take perception's place
> But hardly co-exist in any case,
> Being its mere presentment—of the whole
> By parts, the simultaneous and the sole
> By the successive and the many.

Participating in the poem as narrator who comments upon Sordello and the action of the work, Browning explains that the true poet can never accomplish what he desires in this grimy, imperfect society; he must not only find beauty in the ugly, the whole in the broken, but he must also be content to accomplish partial good. Similarly, poetry itself can never be perfect; at best it will be an inadequate verbal instrument which only partially expresses the total poetic vision. Sordello fails to grasp either of these principles. He is broken, rather than usefully changed or educated, by his attempt to bypass these restrictions on both the poet and his poetry. But Browning is clear about these ideas and they are, perhaps, the most central and important of the poem's various concerns.

Browning's three early long poems were not successes by any conceivable standard of judgment. But they are important for understanding Browning's poetic aspirations and for the opportunity they provide the reader to trace Browning's developing philosophy and his developing poetic techniques. In these poems Browning has learned to temper the Romantic idealism of Shelley, and has also begun to develop the techniques of representing action in character which would find their fruition in the dramatic monologue. In the work of the 1840s following the publication of *Sordello,* the impulse to a combination of dramatic and lyric expression can be traced.

Whatever the effect of Mill's comments about *Pauline,* the reaction to *Sordello* was so extremely negative that it must have caused Browning to reassess his poetic aims. Comments such as the following help explain why the damage done to Browning's reputation by the publication of *Sordello* was so severe: "the sins of [Browning's] verse are premeditated, willful, and incurable"; "the song of the bard falls dull and muffled on the ear, as from a fog"; and, perhaps more to the point in terms of mid-Victorian standards of taste, one critic complained that the poem is "offensive and vicious . . . apparently grounded on some conceited theory, at utter variance with all the canons of taste and propriety." When Browning moved with his family from Camberwell in December 1840 to New Cross Hatcham in Surrey, he turned his attention to the publication of a series of pamphlets entitled *Bells and Pomegranates.* Browning explained the meaning of his title for these pamphlets (the idea for them was suggested by Edward Moxon, the publisher of *Sordello*) between the two parts of *Bells and Pomegranates* number VIII: "I only meant by that title to indicate an endeavour towards something like an alternation, or mixture, of music with discoursing, sound with sense, poetry with thought; which looks too ambitious, thus expressed, so the symbol was preferred."

This series contains *Pippa Passes* (1841), *Luria* (1846), and *A Soul's Tragedy* (1846), all of which are closet dramas, and four other plays written expressly for the stage: *King Victor and King*

Charles (1842), *The Return of the Druses* (1843), *A Blot in the 'Scutcheon* (1843), and *Colombe's Birthday* (1844). In addition, the third and seventh numbers in the series, *Dramatic Lyrics* (1842) and *Dramatic Romances & Lyrics* (1845), contain collections of short poems. Of all this work, the first number in the series, *Pippa Passes,* deserves particular attention, as do some of the short poems in the 1842 and 1845 collections. But the dramas written for the stage were unsuccessful, as *Strafford* had been in 1837, and for very much the same reason: Browning understood—and was able to represent with great skill—action in character, but he did not understand nor could he present effectively character in action. Taken as a collection, however, the seven plays show Browning experimenting with syntax, imagery, diction, and rhythm, gradually developing the techniques of characterization fully evident in the other monologues and, in the process of this development, confirming his growing sense that his true talent lay solely in character delineation. It is in *Pippa Passes* and two of the shorter poems written during this period that this experimentation becomes most clearly focused.

The numerous connections between *Pippa Passes* and *Sordello* indicate that *Pippa Passes* was written immediately after *Sordello* was completed on 1 May 1839, and that it was a direct byproduct of the longer poem. Browning's travels in northern Italy in June 1838 had taken him to Asolo, and his observation of life there contributes to the materials which make up *Pippa Passes.* The topography of Asolo, the conditions in the silk mills, church and political affairs, as well as such character types as mill owners, workers, peasants, policemen, and itinerant students, all appear in the poem. An even more significant link between the two works is to be found in the relationship between Sordello and Pippa. They are both solitary individuals, both stolen children who are the offspring of wealthy parents, and both poets. Sordello's problem is that he attempts to involve himself too fully as a reformer both as a politician and as a poet. It is as a result of his failed aspirations that he learns about the necessity of compromise in life. *Pippa Passes* seems to be a turning away from *Sordello* in terms both of the nature of the poet figure and the techniques involved in presenting such figures.

Pippa, the poor young silkwinder, sets out on New Year's morning, her only holiday of the year, to wander through her environment. She seems committed to nothing except singing short

Registration of the Brownings' marriage at St. Marylebone Parish Church

lyrics from time to time, as she wanders from location to location. She does, however, have a striking effect as an instrument of God's mercy and justice on the lives of the various individuals who hear her songs. Each of the four parts of the poem—Morning, Noon, Evening, and Night—involves characters at points of crisis in their lives, who are moved to make significant moral decisions on overhearing Pippa's songs. In these specific episodes Browning can be observed honing his dramatic skills and developing his verbal techniques.

The first scene involves Ottima and Sebald, lovers who have been responsible for the death of Ottima's husband Luca. Pippa's song seems to move them to feel some degree of guilt and perhaps even to suicide; there is, at any rate, a recognition on the part of the lovers that they have sinned. The second scene concerns Jules, a sculptor, and Phene, a young model whom he has recently been tricked into marrying. Phene recites a poem composed for the occasion by a group of Jules's confederates which informs him about the sham of his marriage; Pippa's song is heard immediately afterward. Rather than rejecting Phene, as his peers had anticipated, Jules resolves to be loyal to her and to help her develop the fullness of her humanity. The two following scenes, one involving the revolutionary Luigi and his mother, and the other the Monsignor and the Intendant, are also concerned with moments of decision. The four scenes are connected by episodes which reflect on the action which has preceded or anticipate that which is to follow. In these linking episodes, Browning pays particular attention to the rhythms of conversation.

Of the short poems published in 1842 and 1845, the most important are "My Last Duchess" from the first collection and "The Bishop Orders His Tomb at St. Praxed's Church" from the sec-

ond. "My Last Duchess," a poem of fifty-six lines in rhyming couplets, has been much discussed as an example of Browning's ability to concentrate and distill experience in the brief dramatic-lyric form. The speaker of the poem, the Duke of Ferrar, is overheard coolly explaining to an individual, who remains unidentified until near the end of the poem, the subject of a painting—his recently deceased wife. It becomes evident that the duchess had displeased her husband by her generous behavior toward others and also by her failure to recognize his superiority in even the most trifling of matters, and that this led to his order to have her executed:

> Oh sir, she smiled, no doubt,
> Whene'er I passed her; but who passed without
> Much the same smile? This grew; I gave commands;
> Then all smiles stopped together. There she stands
> As if alive.

The reader learns at the end of the poem that the duke is addressing his remarks to the envoy from the count whose daughter he next plans to wed. The duke treated his wife as an art object in life, and disposed of her when she displeased him; it is implied that he will treat his next wife the same way.

Robert Langbaum, in *The Poetry of Experience* (1957), explains that this poem represents an important aspect of Browning's technique in the dramatic monologue; the poet is able to achieve in the reader a suspension of judgment concerning the odious behavior of the duke, and a degree of sympathy is engaged which allows the reader to attempt to understand the duke's character. This relationship between sympathy and judgment is accepted by most students of Browning's poetry as an important principle in understanding the dramatic monologue form. Other aspects of the dramatic monologue are also typified by "My Last Duchess": it has a single speaker who is not the poet, addressing an unspeaking audience within the poem. There is a psychological interplay between the speaker and the audience which, in various subtle ways, influences the progression of the speaker's thought patterns, which he then verbalizes. In addition, the poem is set in a particular place at a specific time. Most of Browning's successful mature monologues contain some combination of these elements.

It is, however, in "The Bishop Orders His Tomb at St. Praxed's Church" (1845) that Browning hits upon the synthesis of technique and form that he was later to exploit so fully in the dramatic monologues of *Men and Women* (1855). This poem, the first blank-verse dramatic monologue, concerns the dying bishop's pleas to his assembled nephews concerning his placement in the church upon his death, and the particular kind of tombstone he desires. His "nephews" are, of course, really his children, and his reactions to their facial expressions strongly suggest that they view both him and his wishes with some degree of disdain. As the poem unfolds, the bishop's mind wanders over his career and his relationship with his competitor in love and life, Fra Gandolf:

Draw round my bed: is Anselm keeping back?
Nephews—sons mine . . . ah God, I know not!
 Well—
She, men would have to be your mother once,
Old Gandolf envied me, so fair she was!

The poem offers brilliant insights into the psychology of a once lively and powerful, but now dying and dispirited, individual.

During this period in the early 1840s, Browning's correspondence indicates that while he might attempt to gain an audience by writing for the theater, he knew full well that his talents, and the possibility of gaining a larger audience, would probably have to result from different kinds of endeavors. Thus, in May 1842 he wrote his friend Alfred Domett that "these things [the dramas] done . . . I shall have tried an experiment to the end, and be pretty well contented either way." Similarly, in 1844 he wrote Domett that, having seen the publication of most of his dramas, he will "begin again. I really seem to have something fresh to say." That is, following the recognized failures of his long poems in the 1830s and of the dramas in the early 1840s, he was resolved to concentrate his efforts on shorter

poems. But some considerable time was to elapse, and events of momentous importance were to occur, before this ambition could be realized.

When Browning was traveling in Italy in 1844, Elizabeth Barrett's *Poems* was published. In "Lady Geraldine's Courtship," she links Browning with Wordsworth and Tennyson and praises his humanity: "or from Browning some 'Pomegranate,' which, if cut deep down the middle, / Shows a heart within blood-tinctured, of a veined humanity." Browning first wrote Barrett on 10 January 1845, and was allowed to see her on 20 May. The Robert Browning and Elizabeth Barrett Browning letters of 1845-1846, collected and fully annotated in the Harvard edition, are important documents which detail the development of their growing love relationship and of their mutual concern over issues of the day and their own poetic endeavors.

In his second letter, on 13 January, Browning proclaimed: "You *do* what I always wanted, hoped to do. . . . I only make men & women speak—give you truth broken into prismatic hues, and fear the pure white light, even if it is in me." He explains on 11 February that he has never undertaken "R. B. a poem." These letters indicate Browning's tendency to self-effacement in his poetry, as well as his parallel tendency to adopt poetic personae and have characters other than himself articulate the poems. Elizabeth continually urges him to speak out in his own person; but despite her encouragement, Browning seemed to be facing an artistic impasse at this time.

As he prepared the collection of *Dramatic Romances & Lyrics* for publication in 1845, Browning complained to Elizabeth that he was not satisfied with a poetic fragment, "Saul," which he felt unable to complete. In the first nine stanzas of the poem, David, the young singer, is sent to attempt to cure Saul's physical and spiritual inertia. David celebrates the natural joys of living and the stature and grandeur of the king as the pinnacle of natural creation; but Browning could not move the poem to a redemptive solution which would lead to a full spiritual regeneration for Saul. He sent the poem to Elizabeth, and she commented, in a letter of 27 August, that he should have no doubts about the poem. She suggested that he either allow it to be published in its partial state or complete it without fully revealing the nature of the cure which is achieved for Saul's spiritual malaise. Browning chose the former alternative; the poem would not be finished until sometime after

A letter from Browning to his sister-in-law, Henrietta Moulton-Barrett, announcing the birth of his son
(American Art Association/Anderson Galleries auction catalogue, sale number 4320, 14 April 1937)

1852, when Browning had come to terms with religious and poetic problems with which he was grappling during the late 1840s.

It was the influence of Elizabeth which doubtless assisted him in the resolution of these difficulties. Following their marriage in September 1846, against the wishes of her autocratic, overbearing father, the Brownings traveled to Pisa; they lived there for six months before moving to an apartment in the Casa Guidi in Florence, where they were to live for fourteen years. During this period their activities included reading, writing, visiting galleries and churches, and entertaining visitors from the United States and England. Robert Wiedemann Barrett Browning ("Pen") was born on 9 March 1849. His birth, after several miscarriages, brought joy and comfort to both the Brownings.

Browning's first collected edition appeared in 1849; it significantly omitted *Pauline* and *Sordello*. The poet's only original work during this period includes *Christmas-Eve and Easter-Day* (1850) and the "Essay on Shelley" written in 1851 and published in 1852. *Christmas-Eve and Easter-Day* represents a serious approach on Browning's part to religious problems he had neglected in his poetry up to this time. In these poems Browning considers an assortment of religious approaches —Evangelicalism, Roman Catholicism, and Biblical criticism in *Christmas-Eve*; and the cynical, relaxed approach to Christianity and its opposite, the narrowly aesthetic approach which stresses the difficulty of belief, in *Easter-Day*—and singles out from these analyses elements of belief he could accept. The results of this liberal Christian survey by Browning may be summarized as follows: belief in the divinity of Christ and the power of divine love; the realization that through human love man in some way partakes of God's love; a growing awareness of the limitations of the power of reason, which, in *Paracelsus,* had been equated with the power of love; and finally, an understanding that the world must be seen not as an end in itself but as a means to a higher goal.

The "Essay on Shelley," in contrast, represents Browning's articulation of poetic principles which, coupled with the consolidation of his religious views, would release his poetic energies in the two most important collections of short poems in his career: *Men and Women* in 1855 and *Dramatis Personae* in 1864. Browning begins the essay by defining and distinguishing between the terms *objective* and *subjective*. The objective poet is one who essentially deals with reality, while the subjective poet concerns himself with the ideal. The objective poet appeals to the "aggregate human mind" and so depicts the actions of men. Conversely, the subjective poet, who appeals to the "absolute divine mind," dwells on external appearances which serve to draw forth his own "inner light and power." There is an important function for each of the two kinds of poets, and the best poetry is that which fuses the objective and subjective modes. This combination of the real and the ideal, of the dramatic and lyric, is found in what Browning calls the "whole poet." He cites Shakespeare as an example of the objective or dramatic poet; judging from the depiction of the Shelleyan visionary tendency depicted in *Pauline* and *Paracelsus,* one might expect that Browning would name Shelley as an example of the subjective poet. However, he now seems to contradict the ideas enunciated in his youthful poetry, and he even appears to forget that he has unequivocally stated in the essay itself that there has never been an adequate fusion of the seer-fashioner roles. Shelley has, by some incomprehensible transformation, become the "whole poet." Browning seems to be identifying Shelley with himself: it is Browning, not Shelley, who will combine the roles of the objective and subjective poets, who will learn how to fuse the real and the ideal in his poetry, and who will unite the dramatic and lyric modes in the dramatic monologue form. The "Essay on Shelley" exhibits

Browning working through his problems as a poet and coming to an understanding, even if a misrepresentation, of how poetic unity and some degree of redemptive vision can be achieved.

All of the available evidence indicates that Browning wrote no short poems between 1845 and 1852. By the latter date, having worked through the most important of his religious and poetic problems in the two long poems published in 1850 and in the "Essay on Shelley," Browning seems to have achieved a sense of balance which enabled him to turn his attention once again to the shorter form. Early in 1852 he completed "Women and Roses," "Childe Roland to the Dark Tower Came," and "Love among the Ruins." On 24 February 1853 he wrote to his friend Joseph Milsand from Florence: "I am writing—a first step towards popularity for me—lyrics with more music and painting than before, so as to get people to hear and see.... Something to follow, if I can compass it." Browning was at this time preparing poems for the two volumes of *Men and Women* to be published in 1855.

With the possible exception of *The Ring and the Book* (1868-1869), *Men and Women* is the most highly regarded of all Browning's works. Now agreed to be one of Victorian England's most distinguished poetic accomplishments, it had little impact at the time: of the fairly small pressrun of about two thousand, many copies were still available a decade later, and there was no second edition. Browning continued to be known as his wife's husband. However, in the fifty-one poems contained in these volumes, Browning achieved his widest ranging accomplishments in terms of characterization, techniques of presentation, psychological insight and penetration, ambiguity, irony, and topicality. The many excellent poems in these volumes include the completed "Saul," "Fra Lippo Lippi," "Andrea del Sarto," "Childe Roland to the Dark Tower Came," "Bishop Blougram's Apology," "Cleon," and "Karshish." They are among the most anthologized works in the Browning canon.

It was probably the completion of the fragmentary "Saul," first published in 1845, which helped Browning to achieve the full poetic release which enabled him to compose the other poems in *Men and Women*. He had been unable to complete "Saul" in 1845 because he was unsure of how to achieve the poem's religious and poetic resolution; the work's original version ended with a naturalistic celebration of the joys of life and praise of Saul as the epitome of creation, but could not move beyond that level. Having achieved the sense of certainty that resulted from his work between 1845 and 1852, Browning was able to effect a sense of resolution in "Saul" that was not possible earlier. David the singer, in the first version, acted primarily as a fashioner; he dealt with the real world and with things of everyday life. In the stanzas added in 1852 or 1853, David assumes the role of the subjective poet; he undergoes a revelatory experience culminating in a prophetic foreshadowing of the Incarnation:

> "He who did most, shall bear most; the strongest shall stand the most weak.
> 'Tis the weakness in strength that I cry for! my flesh, that I seek
> In the Godhead! I seek and I find it. O Saul, it shall be
> A Face like my face that receives thee; a Man like to me,
> Thou shalt love and be loved by, for ever: a Hand like this hand
> Shall throw open the gates of new life to thee! See the Christ stand!"

In this yoking of the concerns of the objective and subjective poets, and in the acceptance of Christ as a poetic symbol of the reconciliation of the real and the ideal, the human and the divine, the flesh and the spirit, Browning comes to understand how he can most effectively operate as a "whole poet." Similar concerns are explored in "Fra Lippo Lippi" and "Andrea del Sarto," both poems about artists.

"Fra Lippo Lippi" is one of Browning's finest character portraits. The poem concerns a licentious monk caught out late at night in streets "where sportive ladies leave their doors ajar." His amicable confrontation with the city guards causes the good monk to explain in some detail his past and present circumstances. With the auditors in the poem, the reader learns that at an early age he was taken by his aunt to a monastery and pressed into service. As he matured, his superiors discovered that he had artistic talents, and they instructed him to paint vague and spiritual pictures for the edification of the viewers. He has been instructed to paint "soul," but Fra Lippo Lippi knows that this view of art is invalid. The monk explains that his purpose in painting is not to glorify the flesh, but to employ it as a means through which man can more easily perceive soul. This view of art reflects his view of life. Fra Lippo celebrates the physical, and yet clearly understands the nature of the relationship between

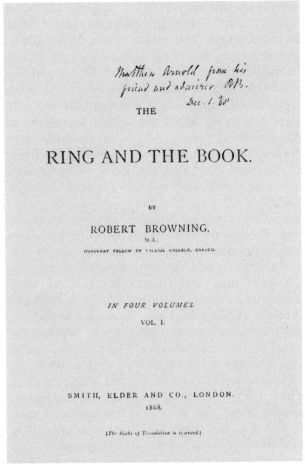

Title page for Browning's poem based on an actual seventeenth-century murder case, with an inscription by Browning to Matthew Arnold (American Art Association/Anderson Galleries auction catalogue, sale number 4255, 30 April 1936)

the physical and spiritual. He may paint, at times, as directed by his superiors, but he cannot, and does not, suppress the impulse toward the physical evident in his own life. Fra Lippo Lippi is both intriguing and beguiling. Despite his apparent self-indulgence, most readers view him as a sympathetic and entertaining character. Such is not the case with Andrea del Sarto.

This individual, called "The Faultless Painter" in the poem's subtitle, creates work which presents a perfect pictorial image of flesh but which has no soul. Andrea is a fine draftsman, but his work has no insight and no depth. The cause of his failure is his complete devotion to his wife, Lucrezia, who has proven herself to be a negative source of inspiration. His painting, for which Lucrezia always serves as the model, exactly parallels in its strength and its weakness the physical beauty and spiritual emptiness of his wife. Having sacrificed all for this empty spiritual vessel, he is now on the verge of losing her to the "cousin" who waits for her at twilight outside their residence. Andrea's present is empty of meaning, and his future is devoid of hope. But he is resigned.

Four other poems depict a wide range of character types. In "Childe Roland," which seems to reflect a terrifying nightmare experience, the speaker feels that both man and nature are conspiring against him. As he journeys across a barren and sterile wasteland, Roland believes that he is guided by fate or the devil and that he has no hope of success in his quest. However, he persists through adversity, and the poem closes with his ringing assertion of self-identity, which shows that he has been able to overcome the obstacles thrown up by his own mind in his pursuit of self-knowledge.

Bishop Blougram has, perhaps, too much self-knowledge. In this long and complicated poem, Blougram converses with an individual whom he considers a third-rate journalist, Gigadibs. The argument of the poem concerns the nature of reality and the nature of the faith which is necessary to sustain oneself in the face of that reality. In his effort to assert his intellectual and moral superiority, Blougram offers lengthy disquisitions on each of these subjects and the manner in which they relate to his own accomplishments.

Gigadibs is an absolutist who insists that one must possess total faith or none at all, while the bishop explains that both life and faith are compromises and that absolutes simply cannot be grasped. The poem is highly ironic. Blougram is easily able to overcome the journalist in argumentation and takes considerable pride in doing so. But he has not deflated or demoralized the journalist as he had intended, nor does Gigadibs succeed in gathering information with which to embarrass the bishop publicly. Instead, as the poem closes the poetic speaker reveals that Gigadibs has been converted to Christianity and is setting off for a new life abroad:

He did not sit five minutes. Just a week
Sufficed his sudden healthy vehemence.
Something had struck him . . .
Another way than Blougram's purpose was:
And having bought, not cabin-furniture
But settler's-implements (enough for three)
And started for Australia—there, I hope,
By this time he has tested his first plough,
And studied his last chapter of Saint John.

"Cleon" and "Karshish" are unique in the Browning canon because they are epistolary monologues. Each of the title characters writes a letter to his superior describing his most recent experiences. With his highly trained intellect, Cleon, the Greek philosopher, has delved into the fundamental problems of existence and discovered the answer to the contradiction posed by the theory of progress which, for the non-Christian, can end only with regression and death. His answer to the questions of Protus concerning the nature of existence is that there is no final and clear answer. Cleon, the most highly gifted of Greek philosophers and poets, will die like Protus, and his works will serve only to mock him in death, not to grant him immortality. He explains that he has recently heard of doctrines being proposed by "a mere barbarian Jew" named "Christus," which offer hypothetical answers to the questions raised by Protus; but Cleon believes that "their doctrine could be held by no sane man." Karshish, the Arab physician, reports on his travels to his medical and academic superior, Abib. Wearied by his long and difficult journey from Jericho to Bethany, yet eager to share the experiences he has had, he records his thoughts haphazardly, as they come to him. He details matter of immediate interest, particularly pertaining to medical observations, and then proceeds to a discussion of the strange case of a man named Lazarus who, after being dead for three days, was cured by some medical means unknown to Arab science, and is now in good health. A trained observer should not become a superstitious gossip, so Karshish dismisses the matter, but not without some hopeful speculation that there might be some truth in the story. The poem thus closes on a somewhat more positive note than that struck by "Cleon."

The poems in *Men and Women* are chiefly concerned thematically with art, religion, and love. The characters depicted are fascinating in their variety and their complexity, and the nuances of language and tone render these poems among Browning's finest. But the remaining years of the decade were not to be highly productive for Browning. From 1855, when they visited London in order that Browning could oversee the publication of *Men and Women,* to June 1861, when Elizabeth died, the two poets and Pen lived a quiet social and literary life in Florence. Some poems might have been written by Browning during this period, but none were published.

In 1856 the Brownings were granted a degree of financial independence as a result of a bequest made to them by their friend John Kenyon. It was Kenyon who had encouraged Browning to write to Elizabeth in 1845. After Elizabeth's father had abandoned the management of her financial affairs because of her marriage, Kenyon had assumed those duties; following Pen's birth in 1849, Kenyon generously sent the poets an annual gift of £1100. Although Elizabeth's poetry produced some funds which helped them to maintain their livelihood during the 1850s, and they also received £1170 a year from English government bonds, Kenyon's bequest upon his death provided the first real relief for the Brownings from financial concerns. The £111,000 which he willed to them provided an income of about £1550 per year.

Elizabeth Barrett Browning died in June 1861. Browning and Pen left Florence in August; after a holiday in France, they settled in London in October. Browning and his son moved into a house at 19 Warwick Crescent, where the poet resided for the next twenty-six years. Arabel Barrett, his wife's sister, was a neighbor with whom he visited frequently. Pen and his father were joined at 19 Warwick Crescent in 1866 by Browning's sister Sarianna, who was to remain with Browning until his death. These years prior to the publication of *Dramatis Personae* in 1864 were primarily devoted to raising Pen. Browning strove to give the boy a masculine sense of identity by changing the rather feminine haircut and clothing which had been imposed upon the child by his mother. The period is also marked by Browning's increasingly active social life. Perhaps the most mysterious event during this period was the offer to Browning in 1862 to succeed William Makepeace Thackeray as the editor of the *Cornhill* magazine. This was a financially advantageous opportunity, and considerable stature went with the position; but for some unknown reason Browning declined.

A good deal is known about the years from 1861 to the early 1870s because of Browning's letters to Isabella Blagden. Miss Blagden had been a close friend of the Brownings in Florence and had greatly assisted Browning in his bereavement in 1861. Following Elizabeth's death, Browning and Isa Blagden agreed to write each other regularly, she on the twelfth of each month and he on the nineteenth. These informative letters cover a period of ten years up to Blagden's death. During this time Browning began to make

Browning with his son, Pen, in 1870

plans for another collection of poems like *Men and Women,* and also to work on the "old yellow book" he had purchased from a bookstall in June 1860 in Florence.

Dramatis Personae contains important poems but is more abstract, less pictorial, more speculative, less vibrant, and more meditative than *Men and Women.* Nonetheless, it was the first of Browning's publications to go into a second edition. Sales were relatively good; in his fifties, Browning was beginning to attract a fair number of readers. (In 1868, however, Chapman and Hall still had 550 copies on hand.) This work, including such important pieces as "Abt Vogler," "Rabbi Ben Ezra," "A Death in the Desert," and "Caliban upon Setebos," was the last successful collection of Browning's short poems to be published.

From the publication of *Dramatis Personae* to the end of the 1860s, Browning especially concerned himself with three activities: the raising and education of his son; the composition of the poem considered by many to be his major contribution to English literature, *The Ring and the Book*; and the increasing social whirl, which Browning seemed to enjoy immensely.

Browning assiduously attempted to prepare his son for Balliol College, Oxford, but without much success: Pen was adept at drawing, fencing, and riding, but not at learning. He finally sat for matriculation on 2 April 1868, but failed. Browning's dream of sending his son to Balliol College was not realized, but Pen was finally matriculated at Christ's Church, the most popular and least demanding of the Oxford colleges at the time. Browning's disappointment might have been partially offset by his progress with the old yellow book which he was transforming into *The Ring and the Book.*

The collection of materials which Browning had acquired in Florence in 1860 included legal briefs, pamphlets, and letters relating to a case involving a child bride, a disguised priest, a triple murder, four hangings, and the beheading of a nobleman. He resolved in October 1864 that he would write twelve books of the poem in six months, but by July 1865 he had completed only 8,400 lines, about a third of the eventual total. When it was finally printed in 1868-1869, its reception was better than that of any other work of Browning's published to that time. The *Athenaeum* for 20 March 1869 called it "beyond all parallel the supremest poetical achievement of our time ... the most precious and profound spiritual treasure that England has produced since the days of Shakespeare."

The title of the poem contains multiple associations. It points to the poem's source, the old yellow book; to the pattern of the monologues, which is circular; to Browning's initials; and, in the ring, to the memory of Elizabeth. In the first and last books of the poem, the speaker, usually identified with Browning, addresses the British public and describes how he uncovered in a Florence bookstall a book concerning a seventeenth-century Italian murder trial. He explains why its subject attracted him, and how he has since imaginatively re-created every moment of the trial of Count Guido Franceschini, which took place in the courts of Rome in January and February 1698. The speaker portrays himself as a master craftsman who will fashion a poem out of the raw stuff of his old document.

Introducing the actors in the original case, he offers to bring them back to life through a poetic reproduction of their voices. He continually asserts the factual nature of his rendition, identifying himself with the skilled artist who shapes the metal (the facts), made malleable by the addition of an alloy (the poet's own fancy), until with the re-

moval of the alloy the ring stands triumphant as a completed work of art. The speaker suggests that it is through the withdrawal of his personality that the truth emerges through the voices of the characters in the drama. While he insists upon the facts, he also indicates that the truth to be perceived by the reader lies beyond the simple factual level. Browning presents the basic material and its meaning three times in the opening book and says that he has found Guido guilty as charged; consequently, the reader is not to concern himself with who is right and who is wrong but is to examine the ten monologues with a view to understanding why objective reality appears so differently to different eyes.

In 1693 Guido Franceschini, a relatively poor nobleman of inferior rank, married a young woman, Francesca Pompilia, who had been raised in Rome by a couple named Comparini. When the Comparinis visited Guido's home in Arezzo three years after the marriage, they found that Guido had misrepresented his financial condition at the time of the marriage and, consequently, brought suit against him for the return of Pompilia's dowry. Violante Comparini had revealed to her husband that Pompilia was really the daughter of a whore, and that she had claimed her as her own in order to gain an inheritance left to them on condition of their having a child. As a result of their action, Guido became an even more impossible husband than he had been previously. Pompilia attempted to flee many times; she was eventually successful in escaping and taking flight for Rome with the assistance of a young canon, Giuseppe Caponsacchi. Guido followed, and Pompilia and her companion were captured about fifteen miles from Rome. According to the documents, Caponsacchi was charged with "adultery," and found guilty of "seduction" and of having "carnal knowledge" of Pompilia. Pompilia was sent during further inquiry to a nunnery for penitent women. But she was pregnant, and was shortly thereafter sent to the house of the Comparinis in Rome. Eight months after her flight from Arezzo, she gave birth to a boy, who was named Gaetano. Shortly after, Guido came with four of his henchmen pretending to bear a message from Caponsacchi, murdered and mutilated the Comparinis, and left Pompilia for dead with twenty-two wounds in her body. She died four days later. Guido was captured, charged with the crime, and tried.

There was no question that Guido had committed the deed; the legal quandary was whether a husband should be allowed to kill his adultress wife and her accomplices without incurring the ordinary penalty. This reopened the question, which the courts had never considered settled, as to whether or not Pompilia had committed adultery with Caponsacchi. Thus, the conduct and the characters of the Comparinis, Guido, Pompilia, and Caponsacchi were thrown open in order that the court might arrive at a decision as to whether Guido was justified in any way whatsoever in his triple murder. In February 1698 the court decided against Guido and condemned him to be beheaded and his fellow conspirators hanged. But Guido, who held a minor office in the church, appealed to Pope Innocent XII to set aside the judgment. The pope refused the appeal, and Guido and his companions were executed on 22 February 1698. Shortly thereafter, Pompilia was declared innocent, and Gaetano was declared the rightful heir to her property.

Browning took these materials, cast over them the light of his own imaginative power, and transmuted them into *The Ring and the Book.* Book I serves as the explanatory introduction. In Book II, "Half-Rome," the speaker is the first of three anonymous commentators upon the crime which Guido has committed. He is an older man who is having difficulty with his wife, and his sympathies are with Guido. The speaker in Book III, "The Other Half-Rome," is a younger man with finer instincts than those of "Half-Rome." He speaks on behalf of Pompilia. The speaker in Book IV, "Tertrum Quid," is relatively neutral. He sums up, weighs, and arranges the evidence of the two speakers who have gone before him, and of the whole case. In Book V, "Count Guido Franceschini," Guido's first monologue occurs just a few days after the crime. Guido is speaking to his judges and cleverly defends himself by reviewing his life, eliciting the sympathy of the hearers, and blaming the faithlessness of his wife for his present sorry condition. In Book VI, "Giuseppe Caponsacchi," the young priest addresses the judges about four days after the murders, while he is still in the throes of grief over the slaughter of Pompilia. His speech reflects his love for Pompilia, his hatred for Guido, and his scorn for the judges. Book VII is "Pompilia": in her deathbed monologue, Pompilia attempts, with considerable difficulty, to reconstruct the events which have led to her present situation. She tries to explain her life to herself as well as to her confessor, Fra Celestino. Books VIII and IX present the two lawyers, Dominus Hyacinthus

Browning in his later years

de Anchangelis and Juris Doctor Johannes-Baptista Bottinus, the former the defender of Guido, and the latter his prosecutor. These monologues provide some humor, striking a note of relief following the intense monologues of Pompilia and Caponsacchi, and preceding the monologue of the pope in Book X, "The Pope." It has been generally assumed that the pope speaks on Browning's behalf, and this is to some extent true. The judgments rendered by the pope on Guido, Pompilia, and Caponsacchi are similar to those offered by Browning's speaker in Books I and XII of the poem. In the eleventh monologue, "Guido," Guido is given a second chance to defend himself immediately before his death. He sheds the hypocritical mask worn in Book V and reveals that he has, all the time, been motivated by hatred of his superiors, of the church, and above all of Pompilia. The poem's final book, "The Book and the Ring," reintroduces the speaker closely identified with Browning himself. The poem concludes with important comments on the nature of art and on the uses of indirection and obliqueness in poetry, and offers the proposition that, although the poet employs facts, the meaning lies beyond them: "So write a book shall mean, beyond the facts, /Suffice the eye and save the soul beside." In the final few lines the poet makes reference to his "Lyric Love," Elizabeth, and to her gold ring of verse which links England and Italy:

> And save the soul! If this intent save mine,—
> If the rough ore be rounded to a ring,
> Render all duty which good ring should do,
> And, failing grace, succeed in guardianship,—
> Might mine but lie outside thine, Lyric Love,
> Thy rare gold ring of verse (the poet praised)
> Linking our England to his Italy!

The Ring and the Book combines the most important of Browning's thematic concerns—the nature of truth, the value and validity of human perception, the nature of poetry and poetic expression—with his greatest technical achievement in the extended monologue form. Most critics of Browning's poetry, as well as the general public, agree that *The Ring and the Book* represents the apex of Browning's career. He continued to write until his death in 1889, however, and many of the works published during this period are of considerable interest to Browning specialists because of the experiments with technique and form he undertook in them.

Of particular interest in this regard are *Prince Hohenstiel-Schwangau, Saviour of Society* (1871) and *Parleyings with Certain People of Importance in Their Day* (1887). *Prince Hohenstiel-Schwangau* is a long, complex interior monologue; the speaker is modeled on Napoleon III. The poem is basically one of self-examination and the contemplation of life's possibilities before the speaker decides upon a course of political action. Section I, to line 1,231, focuses on the intellectual convolutions of the prince's attempt to explain himself to himself; in the second section, from line 1,231 to the end of the poem, the prince posits and then undercuts an ideal conception of self. The characterization is precise although complex, and the style is dense, elliptical, and full of nuances. In its difficulty, it is representative of much of Browning's poetry after *The Ring and the Book*. The essentially negative public reaction to it typifies the reaction to much of the poetry Browning wrote during this period.

Just as Browning's poetry during the last twenty years of his life was not as successful as he would have wished, so too his personal life, despite outward appearances, was not as happy as he might have desired. In 1870, at the age of

A photograph of Browning taken the year of his death

twenty-one, Pen disappointed his father by failing the exams at Christ's Church. In a letter to George Barrett in June 1870, Browning remarks, somewhat despairingly, "the poor boy is simply weak." Browning's perception of Pen's weakness would not be contradicted by his son's activities in the 1870s and 1880s. In 1874 he was sent to Antwerp to study painting and, aided by his father's rather shameless patronage, achieved some minor success as a painter-sculptor. But he was, finally, not much more than a dilettante, despite his father's affection and attention.

During the final two decades of his life Browning wrote, traveled, and became very much a part of the London social scene. As Henry James suggests in his short story "The Private Life" (1892), there seemed to be two Robert Brownings inhabiting one person during this period. James was especially fascinated by the contrast between the Browning who wrote poems and the Browning one met socially. It was difficult to reconcile the person who wrote the dense, difficult, and frequently high-sounding poetry with the plump, garrulous gentleman in white waistcoat who was such a favorite at London dinner parties. Although *Parleyings with Certain People of Importance in Their Day* offers a mental biography of the poet by delineating seven men who represent the seven major interests in Browning's life—philosophy, history, poetry, politics, painting, the classics, and music—this problem of Browning's double image remains unresolved.

But many of Browning's contemporaries regarded the poet as a sage who deserved recognition and praise in his declining years. In 1881, for example, Frederick James Furnivall, founder of the Early English Text Society (1864), the Chaucer and the Ballad Societies (1868), and one of the initial planners of the *Oxford English Dictionary*, instituted the Browning Society. He circulated a prospectus which read, in part: "The Browning student will seek the shortcomings [of Browning's obscure style] in himself rather than in his master. He will wish . . . to learn more of the meaning of the poet's utterances; and then, having gladly learnt, 'gladly wol he teche,' and bring others under the same influence that has benefited himself. To this end *The Browning Society* has been founded." Browning was understandably flattered by the formation of a society in his honor, but he was also rather skeptical about the intelligence and motivation of some of its members. He was much less reluctant about accepting the symbolic status conferred by honorary degrees from Oxford University in 1882 and the University of Edinburgh in 1884.

As these events suggest, Browning's final decade was active. In 1887 he was forced to vacate Warwick Crescent as a result of demolition by the Regent's Canal Bill; he moved with Sarianna to 29 DeVere Gardens, across the street from Henry James at No. 32. He continued to travel. He and Sarianna were in Venice in the fall of 1888, with Pen and his wife Fannie, to visit and inspect the Palazzo Rezzonico, a colossal derelict structure soon to be purchased and refurbished for Pen by Fannie, using her inheritance. Early in August 1889 Browning was quite ill, but he was sufficiently recovered by the end of the month to undertake a trip with his sister to Asolo, Italy, to be followed by another visit with Pen and Fannie. November and December were cold and damp months in Venice in 1889, and the poet's previous illness and advanced age made him particularly susceptible. He contracted a cold in late November and died during the evening of Thursday, 12 December. Browning was buried on 31 December in Westminster Abbey in the Poet's Corner, an appropriate and final public honor.

Browning's career falls roughly into three divisions. His early poetry of development to 1845 reflects his growing awareness of his own powers as a poet; it also illustrates the method by which he refined his poetic techniques in order to reach the stage during which he could perfect the dramatic monologue as a poetic form. From 1845 to 1869 Browning wrote the poems for which he is most popular today. The last part of his career involved a falling off poetically and was a time of much less personal satisfaction than the years of his marriage.

Browning's importance as a poet of the nineteenth century is unquestionable, as is the extent to which he influenced the major poets of the twentieth century, such as Ezra Pound and T. S. Eliot. Since the 1950s there has been an upsurge of critical activity aimed at coming to an understanding of all aspects of Browning's work. Significant advances have been made in the perception and elucidation of Browning's technical achievements, and in the relationship of these achievements to his aesthetic concerns.

Letters:

Letters of Robert Browning Collected by Thomas J. Wise, edited by Thurman L. Hood (New Haven: Yale University Press, 1933);

Robert Browning and Julia Wedgwood: A Broken Friendship as Revealed in Their Letters, edited by Richard Curle (London: Murray & Cape, 1937);

New Letters of Robert Browning, edited by William Clyde DeVane and Kenneth Leslie Knickerbocker (New Haven: Yale University Press, 1950);

Dearest Isa: Browning's Letters to Isa Blagden, edited by Edward C. McAleer (Austin: University of Texas Press, 1951);

Browning to His American Friends: Letters between the Brownings, the Storys, and James Russell Lowell, 1841-1890, edited by Gertrude Reese Hudson (London: Bowes & Bowes, 1965);

Learned Lady: Letters from Robert Browning to Mrs. Thomas FitzGerald 1876-1889, edited by McAleer (Cambridge, Mass.: Harvard University Press, 1966);

The Letters of Robert Browning and Elizabeth Barrett, 1845-1846, 2 volumes, edited by Evan Kintner (Cambridge, Mass.: Harvard University Press, 1969);

*The Palazzo Rezzonico, Venice, where Browning died
(Wellesley College Library)*

The Brownings to the Tennysons, edited by Thomas J. Collins (Waco, Tex.: Armstrong Brown Library, Baylor University, 1971);

"Ruskin and the Brownings: Twenty-five Unpublished Letters," edited by David J. DeLaura, *Bulletin of John Rylands Library,* 54 (1972): 314-356;

The Brownings' Correspondence, 8 volumes to date, edited by Philip Kelley and Ronald Hudson (Winfield, Kans.: Wedgestone Press, 1984-1990).

Bibliographies:

Warner Barnes, *Catalogue of the Browning Collection at The University of Texas* (Austin: University of Texas Press, 1966);

William S. Peterson, *Robert and Elizabeth Browning: An Annotated Bibliography, 1951-1970* (New York: Browning Institute, 1974);

Philip Kelley and Ronald Hudson, eds., *The Brownings' Correspondence: A Checklist* (New York & Arkansas City, Kans.: Browning Institute & Wedgestone Press, 1978).

Biographies:

Mrs. Sutherland Orr, *Life and Letters of Robert Browning,* revised by F. G. Kenyon (London: Smith, Elder, 1908);

W. Hall Griffin and Harry Christopher Minchin, *The Life of Robert Browning* (London: Methuen, 1910);

Betty Miller, *Robert Browning: A Portrait* (London: Murray, 1952);

Maisie Ward, *Robert Browning and His World,* 2 volumes (London: Cassell, 1967-1969);

William Irvine and Park Honan, *The Book, the Ring, and the Poet: A Biography of Robert Browning* (New York: McGraw-Hill, 1974);

John Maynard, *Browning's Youth* (Cambridge, Mass.: Harvard University Press, 1977).

References:

Isobel Armstrong, "Browning and the Grotesque Style," in *The Major Victorian Poets: Reconsiderations,* edited by Armstrong (London: Routledge & Kegan Paul, 1969), pp. 93-123;

G. K. Chesterton, *Robert Browning* (New York & London: Macmillan, 1903);

Thomas J. Collins, *Robert Browning's Moral-Aesthetic Theory 1833-1855* (Lincoln: University of Nebraska Press, 1967);

Eleanor Cook, *Browning's Lyrics: An Exploration* (Toronto: University of Toronto Press, 1974);

A. Dwight Culler, "Monodrama and the Dramatic Monologue," *PMLA,* 90 (May 1975): 366-385;

William Clyde DeVane, *A Browning Handbook,* second edition (New York: Appleton-Century-Crofts, 1955);

DeVane, "The Virgin and the Dragon," *Yale Review,* new series 37 (September 1947): 33-46;

Edward Dowden, *Robert Browning* (London: Dent, 1904);

Philip Drew, *The Poetry of Browning: A Critical Introduction* (London: Methuen, 1970);

F. J. Furnivall, ed., *The Browning Society's Papers,* 3 volumes (London: Browning Society, 1881-1891);

Mary Ellis Gibson, *History and the Prism of Arts: Browning's Poetic Experiments* (Columbus: Ohio State University Press, 1987);

Roy E. Gridley, *The Brownings and France: A Chronicle with Commentary* (London: Athlone, 1983);

Donald S. Hair, *Browning's Experiments with Genre* (Toronto: University of Toronto Press, 1972);

Constance W. Hassett, *The Elusive Self in the Poetry of Robert Browning* (Athens: Ohio University Press, 1982);

Park Honan, *Browning's Characters* (New Haven: Yale University Press, 1961);

Robert Langbaum, *The Poetry of Experience* (New York: Random House, 1957);

William S. Peterson, *Interrogating the Oracle: A History of the London Browning Society* (Athens: Ohio University Press, 1970);

F. A. Pottle, *Shelley and Browning: A Myth and Some Facts* (Chicago: Pembroke Press, 1923);

Robert O. Preyer, "Robert Browning: A Reading of the Early Narratives," *ELH*, 26 (December 1959): 531-548;

Preyer, "Two Styles in the Verse of Robert Browning," *ELH*, 32 (March 1965): 62-84;

William O. Raymond, *The Infinite Moment and Other Essays in Robert Browning*, second edition (Toronto: University of Toronto Press, 1965);

Clyde L. Ryals, *Becoming Browning: The Poems and Plays of Robert Browning, 1833-1846* (Columbus: Ohio State University Press, 1983);

Ryals, *Browning's Later Poetry: 1871-1889* (Ithaca, N.Y.: Cornell University Press, 1975);

W. David Shaw, *The Dialectical Temper: The Rhetorical Art of Robert Browning* (Ithaca, N.Y.: Cornell University Press, 1968);

Lionel Stevenson, "Tennyson, Browning, and a Romantic Fallacy," *University of Toronto Quarterly*, 13 (1944): 175-195;

Arthur Symons, *An Introduction to the Study of Browning*, revised edition (London: Dent, 1906);

Michael Timko, "Ah, Did You Once See Browning Plain?," *Studies in English Literature*, 6 (Autumn 1966): 731-742;

Herbert F. Tucker, *Browning's Beginnings: The Art of Disclosure* (Minneapolis: University of Minnesota Press, 1980).

Papers:
There is no central depository for Robert Browning's papers. A listing of all manuscripts and their locations can be found in *The Browning Collections* by Philip Kelley and Betty A. Coley (Winfield, Kans.: Wedgestone Press, 1984).

Lewis Carroll
(Charles Lutwidge Dodgson)

(27 January 1832 - 14 January 1898)

This entry was updated by Kathleen Blake (University of Washington) from her entry in
DLB 18: Victorian Novelists After 1885.

SELECTED BOOKS: *A Syllabus of Plane Algebraical Geometry, Part I*, as Charles Lutwidge Dodgson (Oxford & London: Parker, 1860);

The Formulae of Plane Trigonometry, as Dodgson (Oxford & London: Parker, 1861);

A Guide to the Mathematical Student, Part I, as Dodgson (Oxford: Parker, 1864);

The New Method of Evaluation as Applied to π, anonymous (Oxford, 1865);

The Dynamics of a Parti-cle, anonymous (Oxford: Vincent, 1865);

Alice's Adventures in Wonderland (London: Macmillan, 1865; New York: Appleton, 1866);

An Elementary Treatise on Determinants, as Dodgson (London: Macmillan, 1867);

The Fifth Book of Euclid Treated Algebraically, as Dodgson (Oxford & London: Parker, 1868);

Phantasmagoria and Other Poems (London: Macmillan, 1869);

Through the Looking-Glass, and What Alice Found There (London: Macmillan, 1872; Boston: Lee & Sheppard / New York: Lee, Sheppard & Dillingham, 1872);

The New Belfry of Christ Church, Oxford, as D. C. L. (Oxford: Parker, 1872);

The Vision of the Three T's, as D. C. L. (Oxford: Parker, 1873);

The Blank Cheque: A Fable, as D. C. L. (Oxford: Parker, 1874);

Suggestions as to the Best Method of Taking Votes, as C. L. D. (Oxford: Hall & Stacy, 1874); revised as *A Method of Taking Votes on More than Two Issues*, anonymous (Oxford, 1876);

The Hunting of the Snark: An Agony in Eight Fits (London: Macmillan, 1876; Boston: Osgood, 1876);

Euclid and His Modern Rivals, as Dodgson (London: Macmillan, 1879; New York: Dover, 1973);

Doublets: A Word-Puzzle (London: Macmillan, 1879);

Rhyme? And Reason? (London: Macmillan, 1883);

Lewis Carroll at age twenty-four (Morris L. Parrish Collection, Princeton University)

Supplement to "Euclid and His Modern Rivals, as Dodgson (London: Macmillan, 1885);

A Tangled Tale (London: Macmillan, 1885);

Three Years in a Curatorship, by One Who Has Tried, as Dodgson (Oxford: Baxter, 1886);

The Game of Logic (London: Macmillan, 1886; New York: Macmillan, 1886);

Alice's Adventures Under Ground (London: Macmillan, 1886; New York: Macmillan, 1886);

Curiosa Mathematica, Part I: A New Theory of Parallels, as Dodgson (London: Macmillan, 1888);

The Nursery Alice (London: Macmillan, 1889);

Sylvie and Bruno (London & New York: Macmillan, 1889);

Eight or Nine Wise Words about Letter-Writing (Oxford: Emberlin, 1890);

Syzygies and Lanrick: A Word-Puzzle and a Game (London: Clay, 1893);

Curiosa Mathematica, Part II: Pillow-Problems, as Dodgson (London: Macmillan, 1893);

Sylvie and Bruno Concluded (London & New York: Macmillan, 1893);

Symbolic Logic, Part I: Elementary (London & New York: Macmillan, 1896);

The Lewis Carroll Picture-Book (London: Unwin, 1899); republished as *Diversions and Digressions* (New York: Dover, 1961);

Feeding the Mind (London: Chatto & Windus, 1907);

Further Nonsense Verse and Prose, edited by Langford Reed (London: Unwin, 1926; New York: Appleton, 1926);

The Collected Verse of Lewis Carroll (London: Macmillan, 1932; New York: Macmillan, 1933); republished as *The Humorous Verse of Lewis Carroll* (New York: Dover, 1960);

For the Train, edited by Hugh J. Schonfield (London: Archer, 1932);

The Rectory Umbrella and Mischmasch (London: Cassell, 1932; New York: Dover, 1971);

Lewis Carroll, Photographer, edited by Helmut Gernsheim (London: Parrish, 1949; New York: Dover, 1969);

Diaries of Lewis Carroll, edited by Roger Lancelyn Green, 2 volumes (London: Cassell, 1953; New York: Oxford University Press, 1954);

Useful and Instructive Poetry (London: Bles, 1954; New York: Macmillan, 1954);

Mathematical Recreations of Carroll, 2 volumes (New York: Dover, 1958; London: Constable, 1959);

The Annotated Alice: Alice's Adventures in Wonderland and Through the Looking-Glass, edited by Martin Gardner (New York: Potter, 1960);

Symbolic Logic, Parts I and II, edited by William Warren Bartley (New York: Potter, 1977).

Collections: *The Complete Works of Lewis Carroll* (London: Nonesuch, 1939; New York: Modern Library, 1939);

The Complete Illustrated Works of Lewis Carroll, edited by Edward Guiliano (New York: Avenel, 1982).

Lewis Carroll (the Reverend Charles Lutwidge Dodgson) was a Victorian nonsense writer for children whose works hold enduring fascina-

Photograph by Carroll of Alice Liddell, the inspiration for Alice's Adventures in Wonderland

tion for adults as well. His *Alice's Adventures in Wonderland* (1865) and *Through the Looking-Glass* (1872) are classics of the English language, vying with the Bible and William Shakespeare as sources of quotation, and they have been translated into virtually every other language, including Pitjantjatjara, a dialect of Aborigine. Alice's story began as a piece of extempore whimsy spun out to entertain three little girls on a boating trip on the river Isis in 1862, and it continues to delight children and to excite the responses of psychoanalysts, philosophers, mathematicians, linguists, semioticians, and Victorianists; historians of children's literature and of childhood; those studying the sources of the parodies, the genre of nonsense, and the development of Victorian humor; along with biographers and literary critics of eclectic interests. Next to the Alice books, Carroll's *The Hunting of the Snark* (1876) attracts the most attention and admiration as a nonsense epic in verse, an absurdist quest poem, a *Moby-Dick* of the nursery. Carroll wrote humorous works for children and some for his Oxford colleagues, as well as publishing many puzzles and games. Among these, the letters written over the years to his child-friends strike the classic nonsense note. The long, late novels *Sylvie and Bruno* (1889) and *Sylvie and Bruno Concluded* (1893) have risen in critical regard to the status of interesting failures for their mixture of fantasy and society-novel realism. Their high seriousness contrasts strikingly with the nondidacticism that makes the Alice books and *The Hunting of the Snark* seem light, dry, problematical, and "modern," even "postmodern." Interesting as period pieces, the *Sylvie and Bruno* novels also prefigure twentieth-century experimentations in form.

Quite different from these literary works are mathematics and logic studies by Carroll. These products of his career as a professor at Christ Church, Oxford, run the gamut from the purely academic—*An Elementary Treatise on Determinants* (1867)—to the wittily serious—*Euclid and His Modern Rivals* (1879), *The Game of Logic* (1886), and *Symbolic Logic, Parts I and II* (1896, 1977). They also cover a range of scholarly significance from negligible to considerable. The recovery of Carroll's last work, Part II of *Symbolic Logic*, confirms his claim to importance in his academic field. Of the academic studies, the most notable are not the most serious in tone but are leavened with humor, so that it is too simple to insist on any absolute split in style or character. However, another aspect of Carroll's work seems very separate and yet bears relation to the rest; the collection of his photographs in *Lewis Carroll, Photographer* (1949) demonstrates his excellence in this area. Yet the children who inspired the photographer inspired the storyteller and letter writer as well, and they kindled or rekindled the spirit which filled the logic text with nonsensical examples and an awareness that sense itself is a made-up thing, like a child's game.

Carroll divided himself up into two names, Lewis Carroll and the Reverend Charles Lutwidge Dodgson. He frequently insisted on the division because he detested lionization as the children's author while carrying on his very regular, donnish life at Oxford. He sometimes refused to receive fan mail addressed to Lewis Carroll at Christ Church. In one letter to a child-friend he gives an amusing account of the meeting of his two selves. Still, just as most of the letters to children and the major children's books are signed Lewis Carroll, so is *Symbolic Logic*. Some have viewed him as a split personality, and yet there is much that comes together in the life and works of Lewis Carroll; one may use a single name to refer to him.

A great deal is known about Carroll's life from *The Life and Letters of Lewis Carroll* (1899) compiled soon after his death by his nephew, and from important editions of his extensive diaries and letters. But enough remains enigmatic about a man so varied in interests and output, whose best friends were little girls, to inspire new biographical interpretations. He was born on 27 January 1832, the eldest son in a clergyman's family of eleven children living in less-than-affluent circumstances at the parsonage of Daresbury, Cheshire. In 1843 the family moved to Croft in Yorkshire to enjoy a more capacious parsonage and a better living. The boy had a multitude of sisters, and he was the master of their ceremonies, inventor of games, magician, marionette theater manager, editor of the family journals. His mother was sweet, lovable, and much loved; she died just as her son turned nineteen. The letters make more reference to the father than to the mother. His father died when Carroll was thirty-six, and he called this the saddest blow he had known. The elder Reverend Charles Dodgson was an upstanding Christ Church and Church of England man and paterfamilias, who instilled in his son religious faith and a belief in earnest endeavor strong enough to make Carroll sometimes feel slack in his work and tardy in his progress despite his lifelong habits of discipline and labor. But his father was not only an earnest Victorian; he also had humor to pass on, judging from this letter to the seven-year-old Charles: "you may depend upon it I will not forget your commission. . . . I WILL have a file and a screw driver, and a ring, and if they are not brought directly, in forty seconds, I will leave nothing but one small cat alive in the whole town of Leeds. . . . Then what a bawling and tearing of hair there will be! Pigs and babies, camels and butterflies, rolling in the gutter together—old women rushing up the chimneys and cows after them—ducks hiding themselves in coffee cups, and fat geese trying to squeeze themselves into pencilcases."

Carroll was a writer from the earliest age. From the floorboards of the nursery at Croft has been recovered a cache he apparently left there for posterity when a new floor was laid, containing, among other things, a white glove, a child's left shoe, and the intriguing words, "And we'll wander through the wide world / and chase the buffalo." More of the writer's funny juvenilia have survived, such as the poem "Rules and Regulations" from the family magazine *Useful and Instructive Poetry*:

Don't push with your shoulder
Until you are older.
Lose not a button.
Refuse cold mutton
Starve your canaries.
Believe in fairies. . . .
Moral: Behave.

After his education at home and at Richmond and Rugby schools (1844-1849), Carroll matriculated at Christ Church, Oxford, in 1850 and entered into residency in 1851. He passed from a studentship through bachelor and master of arts degrees to a mathematics lectureship, and even after he resigned his teaching post in 1881, he functioned as curator of the Senior Common Room (1882-1892) and remained a member of the house for a total of forty-seven years until his death. In choosing Christ Church he followed in the footsteps of his father but did not, like him, go on to marry or to become a practicing minister. He became a deacon of the Church of England in 1861 but chose not to go further. After he had lost both parents he became the head of his family in that he provided a home for his unmarried sisters at Guildford in Surrey. His life came to be geographically defined by residency at Oxford, holiday visits to his family home, frequent trips to London, and summer seaside vacations most often at Eastbourne and Sandown. He departed from his usual track by making a trip to Russia with a friend in 1867. He had a gentle face and a thin, erect figure and looked "as if he had swallowed a poker." He was abstemious in eating and drinking. His habits were extremely methodical: for instance, among his many other records, he maintained information on his dinner guests, what they had been served and where they had sat, so as to avoid repeating the same arrangements.

During the period of his studies and early teaching career, in the years leading up to the writing of *Alice's Adventures in Wonderland*, Carroll led a lively artistic and intellectual life, became a devoted playgoer, contributed to humorous journals, and created the pen name Lewis Carroll for the *Train* (in 1856). Based on a Latin translation of the author's first and second names, the pseudonym was chosen by the *Train*'s editor, Edmund Yates, from a list of four submitted. Also during this period Carroll took up his photographic hobby. This avocation was closely linked with his cultivation of child-friends, first and foremost of whom was Alice Liddell, instigator and auditor of the famous tale and the model for its heroine.

Photography satisfied Carroll's artistic instincts and his love of gadgets and children. It also provided an alternative to drawing: while he never gave up sketching, he became convinced of his limitations in this area. The great art critic John Ruskin took a discouraging view of his talent and persuaded him against pursuing this interest seriously. Many have felt, however, that Carroll's illustrations of early works and of the manuscript of *Alice's Adventures Under Ground* (1886) possess a grotesque, surreal power that offsets their lack of professional polish. For that matter, Carroll's aesthetic awareness was not so unformed as one might suppose. A Pre-Raphaelite influence is discernible in his drawings of Alice. He had purchased a painting by Arthur Hughes at about the time that he was illustrating his manuscript, and he was personally acquainted with such artists as Dante Gabriel Rossetti, John Millais, Holman Hunt, and G. F. Watts. He always took great interest in the decoration of his books and made many suggestions to his illustrators—John Tenniel, Henry Holiday, A. B. Frost, Harry Furniss, and Gertrude Thomson. Carroll found in photography the fullest expression of this strong visual interest. In addition, the technical challenge and advantages of the new collidion or wet-plate process helped attract him to the hobby. His invention-loving Uncle Skeffington Lutwidge introduced him to the camera in 1855, and Carroll was soon going to many lengths to capture distinguished sitters, such as Alfred Tennyson; he ran after the famous in a way that he came to dislike when he became famous himself. But it was not long before his interest shifted and settled on portraiture of children. Along with Julia Margaret Cameron, he has been hailed as one of the great portraitists in this new medium, "the most outstanding photographer of children in the nineteenth century." He lacked interest in landscape but could felicitously place a figure in a simple, expressive setting, and he excelled at composition. He made children look natural, despite the strain of having to hold still for the camera for a long time.

His camera brought him into contact with many young girls, most importantly Alice Liddell. She makes her first appearance in Carroll's diary in an entry of 25 April 1856, concerning a photographic venture. Carroll had sought to photograph Christ Church Cathedral from the deanery, where he had met the three little daughters of the dean of the college and had turned his lens on the girls. Alice was then almost four

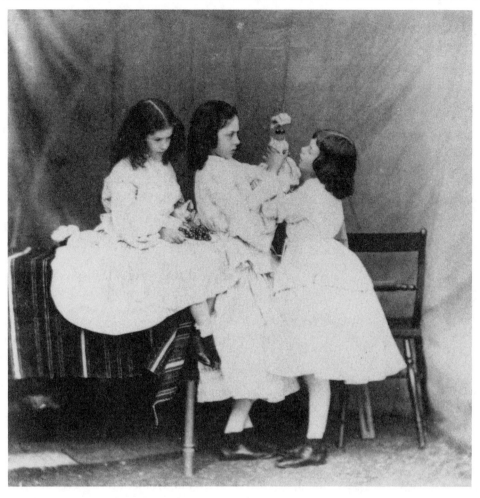

The Liddell sisters, Edith, Lorina, and Alice, for whose amusement Carroll created the story of Alice
(Morris L. Parrish Collection, Princeton University)

years old. The sisters were impatient sitters, but the entry concludes with the phrase Carroll reserved for his best times, "Mark this day with a white stone." On 5 June he is boating with two Liddells and marking the day as "Dies mirabilis." The entry for 14 November conveys an initial hint of the coolness from Mrs. Liddell which has intrigued biographers but eluded clearcut interpretation: she wished the children to be photographed as a group, not separately. But photographing at the deanery continues to be noted. The diaries covering the period between 1858 and 1862 have disappeared, but they pick up in time to record the famous boating expedition of 4 July 1862 on which Carroll told Lorina, Alice, and Edith Liddell the story of Alice's adventures; Alice was ten years old. Here is an account by the grown-up Alice, Mrs. Hargreaves: "I believe the beginning of 'Alice' was told one summer afternoon when the sun was so burning that we had

landed in the meadows down the river, deserting the boat to take refuge in the only bit of shade to be found, which was under a new-made hayrick. Here from all three came the old petition, 'Tell us a story,' and so began the ever-delightful tale. Sometimes to tease us—and perhaps being really tired—Mr. Dodgson would stop suddenly and say, 'And that's all till next time.' 'Ah, but it is next time,' would be the exclamation from all three."

Carroll's method of composition for children followed one of the three ways described by C. S. Lewis. Like J. M. Barrie, Kenneth Grahame, and Beatrix Potter, he created for one or more particular children rather than for a child audience in the abstract, or, as Lewis himself did, for the sake of writing in a children's literary form. Carroll's particular child was Alice; she was the one who pressed him to put the story on paper. On the train the day after the river trip

Photograph by Carroll of George MacDonald and his daughter Lily, who urged publication of Alice's Adventures in Wonderland

he wrote out headings, and while the work gestated he corrected proof sheets for his "Circular to Mathematical Friends." He met with the Liddell children for walks and croquet and heard them sing "Beautiful Star," which got into the book as the Mock Turtle's song on "Beautiful Soup," one of the many parodies of well-known songs and poems. Carroll records an all-day, all-night session grading exams, followed the next day by more work on *Alice's Adventures Under Ground*. At the same time he sensed some ebbing of his intimacy with the children. He suspected that Lorina would no longer be able to join their expeditions. By 21 November 1862, he records his surprise at an invitation by Mrs. Liddell to visit with the children. Yet 10 March 1863 was spent enjoying the wedding festivities of the Prince of Wales with the Liddells and was marked by a white stone.

The manuscript of *Alice's Adventures Under Ground* had been written out by 10 February 1863, and Carroll sent it to a friend, the writer George MacDonald. His children responded favorably, and the MacDonalds urged Carroll to publish the book. He took his time completing his illustrations for the manuscript, which was not sent to Alice until 26 November 1864. Meanwhile, Carroll expanded *Alice's Adventures Under Ground* to form *Alice's Adventures in Wonderland* and arranged for Tenniel to illustrate it. By this time Carroll had registered Mrs. Liddell's desire that he keep his distance—no great hardship, it seems, for he found Alice much changed and hardly for the better, according to a diary entry of 11 May 1865. On 4 July 1865, three years after he first told the tale, he sent thirteen-year-old Alice Liddell a special vellum-clad copy of the first edition. This edition ran into difficulties due to the fastidiousness of illustrator and author. Tenniel complained about the printing of the pictures, and so Carroll insisted that the book be recalled. The unbound sheets were sold to Appleton of New York and published in 1866 as a second issue of the first edition. A second edition came out in 1865, though dated 1866. These complications have made early copies of *Alice's Adventures in Wonderland* rare items, prized and paid royally for by later book collectors. This publishing history also illustrates Carroll's perfectionist standard and his concern for the beauty of the physical book.

The tremendous success of *Alice's Adventures in Wonderland* led to the writing of its sequel, *Through the Looking-Glass, and What Alice Found There*, begun in 1867 and published in 1872, also illustrated by Tenniel. Alice Liddell inspired this work only retrospectively, for by the time she received her copy she was a young lady with whom Carroll had virtually no contact. While these two novels are separate creations, they may be discussed together. *Alice's Adventures in Wonderland* concerns a seven-year-old Alice whose curiosity causes her to follow the White Rabbit down the rabbit hole into a dream world which she finds both wondrous and exasperating. In the course of her adventures she seeks out the key to the beautiful garden, nearly drowns in the pool of her own tears, eats and drinks one thing and then another, growing and shrinking, so that once she is so big she gets stuck in the White Rabbit's house and has to stick one foot up the chimney, and another time she is so small her chin strikes her foot. She does get into the garden, having encountered a gallery of eccentrics such as the Cheshire Cat with his grin, the Caterpiller on his magic mushroom who asks, "Who are you?,"

60

at the Great Northern Hotel, & dined with the Burnetts.

July 29 (Sat.) From London to Croft.

Aug 2 (W.) Finally decided on the re-print of "Alice," & that the first 2000 shall be sold as waste paper. Wrote about it to Macmillan, Combe & Tenniel. The total cost will be — drawing pictures — 138.. cutting ———— 142 printing (by Clay) 240 binding + advertising (say) 80 ——— 600

i.e. 6/ a copy on the 2000 — If I make £500 by sale, this will be a loss of £100, & the loss on the first 2000 will probably be £100 leaving me £200 out of pocket.

But if a second 2000 could be sold it would cost £300, & bring in £500, thus squaring accounts, & any further sale would be a gain: but that I can hardly hope for.

A page from Carroll's diary, noting his decision to recall the first edition of Alice's Adventures in Wonderland *because the illustrations had been poorly reproduced*

Sir John Tenniel

the Mad Hatter gathered with the March Hare and the Dormouse at the Mad Tea-Party, the Queen of Hearts presiding over a croquet game gone berserk and a trial that requires "Sentence first—verdict afterwards." This madcap world loses its appeal the more it becomes a downright mad one: Alice is not pleased to hear it when the Cheshire Cat says, "We're all mad here." She stands up for sense, finally condemning the nonsense of Wonderland, disrupting the trial of the Knave of Hearts, and waking from her dream. She may be seen as the sensible child not to be taken in by grown-up insanity; or, since she grows physically at the end, she may be seen as maturing to leave a childishly anarchic world behind her. Her character may seem unimaginative and priggish, or gallantly sane, depending on the reader's attitude toward sense and nonsense.

If Alice grows older in *Alice's Adventures in Wonderland*, she has to do it over again in *Through the Looking-Glass*, for she is no more than seven and a half in the later book, and she passes through the mirror to an analogous series of confrontations with anarchy, which she finally rejects

and leaves. She finds herself a Pawn in a fascinating but mad game of chess, and as she passes across the board to the Eighth Square—meeting up with the authoritarian Red Queen and the dissociated White Queen—she learns, among other things, to run as fast as she can to stay in place and to believe six impossible things before breakfast. She gets to know nursery-rhyme characters such as Tweedledum and Tweedledee, but she does not like it when they question whether even her tears make her a real child, rather than just a figment in a dream. Humpty-Dumpty gives her a lecture on language, showing how made-up and confusing it really is. Throughout, Alice has trouble reciting songs and verses that won't come out right; "Jabberwocky" is the epitome of the nonsense poem that seems to mean something, though it is never clear quite what. This strange looking-glass land holds a charm for a very curious child, and Alice enjoys some companionship with the White Knight, a mad inventor, with anklets for his horse to keep off sharks and stakes for the head, up which hair can be trained to grow to keep it from falling out. Yet, finally, Alice can stand no more a dream-game world she cannot comprehend, and she wakes. There is a subtle difference between this and the earlier *Alice's Adventures in Wonderland*: the reader is made more aware of the implications of loss and mortality in the growing-up process. In one chapter, Alice is likened to a flower whose petals have already begun to fade; and according to the dedication poem, the voice of time

> Shall summon to unwelcome bed
> A melancholy maiden!
> We are but older children, dear,
> Who fret to find our bedtime near.

Carroll suggests that maidenhood ends in the sexual bed, life in the bed of the grave. It seems likely that an Alice Liddell no longer a child somewhat saddened the tone of *Through the Looking-Glass*.

Other reflections of Carroll's personal experience appear in the books: the pool of tears no doubt derived from a wetting undergone by Carroll and the Liddell children on one of their outings, to give just one instance. Carroll—Dodgson— was the Dodo. Self-portraiture has also been seen in his characterization of the White Knight, the Gnat, and—since the rediscovery of a canceled sequence of *Through the Looking-Glass* known as "The Wasp in a Wig"—in the Wasp. Political and

Specimen illustrations by Sir John Tenniel for the 1866 London edition of Alice's Adventures in Wonderland

cultural allegory has been sought in the books: some evidence of veiled allusions to Oxford politics may be mustered; the likeness to Benjamin Disraeli of the Man in White Paper brings the national political scene into view—though this caricature is Tenniel's, after all, not Carroll's. Some commentators recommend bearing in mind the Victorian context: for instance, remembering Darwin's ideas about evolution while considering the creatures emerging from the pool of tears. Carroll's work is placed in a historical context by those concerned with nonsense as a genre and with Victorian humor, and especially by historians of children's literature and of childhood. Growing interest in fairy tales and fantasy characterized the early nineteenth century and flowered in Carroll's writing. The Alice books marked an emancipation of children's literature from heavy-handed didacticism. They also epitomized important developments in the concept of the child: Carroll expresses a romantic view of childhood in his introductory poem to *Through the Looking-Glass*, dedicated to the "Child of the pure unclouded brow." At the same time the novels present a less-than-perfect heroine; not all readers like her. She has her good and bad points, plucky but also prim, polite but sometimes aggressive. This little girl likes to play "let's pretend" with her nurse—"Let's pretend that I'm a hungry hyaena and you're a bone!" Such a characterization of a girl in an age inclined to idealize the female is historically notable and of interest to feminists. Alice's brow is not conventionally unclouded: the dream adventures go on in *her* sleep and *her* head, and considerable darkness tinges tales told "all in the golden afternoon."

In their own time, the Alice books were mostly regarded as sparkling whimsy, and there are still those who decry an intellectual approach intent on discovering darker depths. But in this century, stress has fallen on those depths. William Empson's essay of 1935, "Alice in Wonderland: The Child as Swain," and Martin Gardner's 1960 edition of *The Annotated Alice* initiated consecutive waves of serious analysis. Freudian commentators have heightened awareness of the level of anxiety in the books, the eating and being eaten, the threats to bodily integrity implicit in radical size changes and such grotesque incidents as the lengthening of Alice's neck till it rises to the treetops and the near knocking of her chin on her foot as she shrinks. They have pointed out Alice's claustrophobia when she is stuck in the Rabbit's house, her frustration when she runs with-

out getting anywhere, and, above all, the repeated crises of identity which she faces. She is unable to answer the Caterpillar's "Who are *you*?," she loses her name in the nameless woods, she is disquieted by death jokes. At the extreme, Paul Schilder finds these tales too frightening to be fit fare for children. A Freudian approach also raises questions about the author's mental and emotional fitness. His interest in children and children's literature may signal nostalgia and regression. His devotion to Alice's real-life model may indicate sexual immaturity, if not perversion. His pleasure in nonsense may hint of escapism, or, alternately, his heroine's preference for sense may reveal anal-retentive compulsiveness. Carroll's exploration of assaults on life and identity raises questions about his control of his own aggressions and about his own wholeness as a man. At the extreme, Peter Coveney characterizes the author as "almost the case-book maladjusted neurotic." Reacting against a normative Freudian approach which stands in judgment of "unhealthy" aspects of the work or author are those who value Carroll's treatment of the integrity of self and world under radical stress; so viewed, Carroll seems to belong almost more to the twentieth century than to his own. Thus, the Alice books have been compared with the works of T. S. Eliot, James Joyce, Hermann Hesse, and Vladimir Nabokov; they have been analyzed in terms of game theory, linguistics, semiotics, and the philosophy of Ludwig Wittgenstein. A 1966 essay by Donald Rackin bears the characteristic title "Alice's Journey to the End of Night." Nightmare dissolution of coherence threatens Alice in various ways, for instance in the many identity problems, in the incoherence of the games—cards, croquet, chess—which figure in both books, in the logical conundrums, and in the many perplexities of language. "Things flow about so here," says Alice plaintively. Stability of being, consistency of rules to allow fair play, rational constructs, and even words themselves flow about amidst riddles, puns, conversational misconstructions, and constant plays upon semantic and grammatical anomalies. For the reader, like Alice, many statements seem to make no sense at all, and yet they are certainly English. Meaning threatens to dissolve in the flow.

It is worth turning to Carroll's personal attitude toward language, the vehicle of meaning. He had a lifelong attraction-repulsion to words. A letter written when he was a schoolboy shows his fascination and dismay; he had been reading

Lewis Carroll (Dodgson Family Collection)

cal: he said it was their nature to be ambiguous. This was the reason why from 1861 until his death he kept a register of all letters received and sent, the last entry numbering 98,721. A précis allowed him to assure himself, and sometimes his correspondent, of what exactly had been said in case of later misunderstanding. By such recording he sought to secure verbal reliability, without altogether expecting to succeed. His *Eight or Nine Wise Words about Letter-Writing* (1890) humorously explores the proposition that if anything can misfire in communication, it will. Compared to natural language, mathematical/logical symbol systems are a great deal more certain. In his revealing preface to *Curiosa Mathematica, Part I: A New Theory of Parallels* (1888), Carroll praises pure mathematics for "the absolute certainty of its results: for that is what, beyond almost all mental treasures, the human intellect craves for. Let us only be sure of something." Concerning the uncertainty of language, it is interesting to compare Carroll to his friend and fellow writer of children's fantasies George MacDonald. MacDonald reveled in ambiguity, for in his view this increased suggestiveness, while Carroll was bothered as well as intrigued.

Carroll's decision not to proceed to full holy orders may be understood partly in terms of his doubts about language as a carrier of meaning. Religion offers the ultimate source and ground of meaning, and Carroll met with uncertainties here, too. A minister customarily advises members of the flock troubled in their faith, and Carroll once said he felt his utter incompetence in such a situation to convince anybody of anything. Furthermore, he had been a stammerer from childhood, which intensified his distrust of words. He did lecture and preach on occasion, but the occasions could be painful, and so it may be understandable that he never committed himself to a career of Sunday sermonizing and pastoral care and that he also gave up regular teaching at Christ Church when the sale of his books allowed him the privilege of lecturing as little as he liked. (He did do some teaching later; for instance, he presented a logic class at an Oxford senior girls' school.)

Other reasons have been proposed for Carroll's decision not to take full holy orders. These involve speculations about his unorthodoxy or even religious doubts. He had been advised by his bishop about the impropriety of playgoing in a clergyman, and this may have checked his advancement in the clergy, while it

Thomas B. Macaulay's *History of England from the Accession of James II* (1849-1861): "one passage struck me when 7 bishops had signed the invitation to the pretender, and King James sent for Bishop Compton (who was one of the 7) and asked him 'whether he or any of his ecclesiastical brethren had had anything to do with it?' He replied after a moment's thought, 'I am fully persuaded, your majesty, that there is not one of my brethren who is not as innocent in the matter as myself.' This was certainly no actual lie, but certainly, as Macaulay says, it was very little different from one. On the next day the King called a meeting of all the bishops. . . . He then for form's sake, put the question to each of them 'whether they had had anything to do with it?' Here was a new difficulty, which Compton got over by saying, when it came to his turn, 'I gave your majesty *my* answer yesterday.' It certainly showed talent, though exerted in the wrong direction." Carroll continued to find words problemati-

did not check his playgoing. Also, the preface to his *Curiosa Mathematica, Part II: Pillow Problems* (1893) contains the remark that mathematical puzzles may help divert the mind from irreverent thoughts on sleepless nights. No one knows what thoughts troubled him and how irreverent they were, but it is clear that he did not like to be troubled in this way. He sometimes complained about irreverent jokes. He had a better memory than was quite comfortable, for when some biblical phrase he had heard used in a joke was cited in a sermon, he became the victim of verbal associations. However, when Carroll declared his faith, as in one letter to a young lady, he showed his real reverence at the same time that he revealed his sense of religious paradox: no realm, he says, is as certain as mathematics or logic. The letter indicates his awareness of contradictory views of God—if all-powerful, then how also all-good? He considers this problem as one incapable of rational resolution and explanation, yet resolvable in psychological terms: he says that one must simply choose the view that enables one to live a moral life, and so he chooses to believe in a good God. Carroll lacked the flexibility of temperament to live at ease amid uncertainties; for that matter, John Keats did not say it was easy either. He did what he could to live with certainties in his academic field and to minimize close encounters with religious uncertainties—he did not evade his own, but he could avoid the perplexities of parishioners. At the same time, he bowed out of careers demanding perpetual verbal explanation and did what he could to firm up the certainty of his own use of language.

In the Alice books, certitude—linguistic and ontological-religious—remains unobtainable: Alice is not certain that Humpty-Dumpty can make words mean what he says they mean; neither is she sure of the status of the reality to which words so uncertainly refer. *Through the Looking-Glass* ends with an open question about the dreamer of the dream. Who dreamed it all, Alice or the Red King? What if he woke? The attitude expressed toward these quandaries—the degree of affirmation at the ends of *Alice's Adventures in Wonderland* and *Through the Looking-Glass*— remains a matter of dispute, though there is little reason to doubt Carroll's own affirmation of language despite everything. He was a writer, after all, glorying in words with all their unruliness, enjoying the giddy flirtation of sense with nonsense. One might as well be gleeful as rueful about the teetering of certitude. Nor is there rea-

Self-caricature by Lewis Carroll

son to dispute Carroll's own religious affirmation. He was a devout member and deacon of the Anglican church and found a personal faith, even if he doubted his capacity to persuade others to believe. Still, his next major literary work, *The Hunting of the Snark*, ends in a way that is quite inconclusive and discomforting. Its last line came to Carroll first: "The Snark *was* a Boojum, you see." The meaning of this line is only darkly hinted at in the course of a long poem of eight parts, subtitled *An Agony in Eight Fits. The Hunting of the Snark* describes the voyage quest of a ship's company of incongruous characters linked only by the fact that their names all begin with a B. The Snark is an elusive prey:

> They sought it with thimbles, they sought it with care;
> They pursued it with forks and hope;
> They threatened its life with a railway-share;
> They charmed it with smiles and soap.

They have not much to go by. Having dispensed with merely conventional guidelines, they navigate by means of a blank map. Shipboard conflicts and foreboding dreams afflict them. The Barrister's dream resembles the "Mouse's Tale" and the courtroom scene of *Alice's Adventures in Wonderland*, for it involves a travesty trial, with the Snark as defense lawyer, jury, and judge, who eventually condemns and sentences his own client. Also carrying over from the Alice books is an obsession with assaults on identity: the success of the quest means the end of the Baker; upon discovering the Snark to be a Boo—, he vanishes in mid word. This poem is gaining more and more attention and regard for its casting of certain characteristic themes of the Alice stories into a new, even more purely nonsensical and poetic form.

The Hunting of the Snark was dedicated to Gertrude Chataway, a little girl Carroll met in 1875, one of the many child-friends who took the place of Alice Liddell over the years. He met Gertrude at the seaside. This was one good place to strike up acquaintances with children; other opportunities came by way of railway journeys, backstage introductions to child actresses, and his photographic hobby, as well as meetings with the families of friends and colleagues. Carroll's letters to these child-friends offer nonsense in the best *Alice* and *Snark* veins, and they reveal his strange and very special relationship with children. Here is a letter concerning a visit to Carroll by a certain wax doll:

> she sat on my knee, and fanned herself with a penwiper, because she said she was afraid the end of her nose was beginning to melt.
>
> "You've no *idea* how careful we have to be, we dolls," she said. "Why, there was a sister of mine—would you believe it?—she went up to the fire to warm her hands, and one of her hands dropped right off! There now!"
>
> "Of course it dropped *right* off," I said, "because it was the *right* hand."
>
> "And how do you know it was the *right* hand, Mister Carroll?" the doll said.
>
> So I said, "I think it must have been the *right* hand, because the other hand was *left*."
>
> The doll said, "I shan't laugh. It's a very bad joke."

The letter is striking for its cleverness, its tinge of the grotesque in the joke about melting body parts, and the tartness of the response to the joke, suggestive of the teasing between Carroll and his young friends. The tone is unsentimental. In a real sense, Carroll communicated with children on their level; he did not confine himself to what a parent might entirely approve. For instance, one letter to Hallam Tennyson expresses regret that the knife given by Carroll should have been confiscated by the family authorities, " 'till you are older.' However, as you *are* older now, perhaps you have begun to use it by this time [and] I hope that if Lionel ever wants to have *his* fingers cut with it, you will be kind to your brother, and hurt him as much as he likes."

Perhaps symptomatically, Carroll pictures a brother at the receiving end of a sharp knife and a sharp-edged joke. He also gave Kathleen Tidy a penknife and advice about the convenient way it could be run into the hands and faces of her brothers. Carroll did have some friendships with boys, such as Hallam Tennyson, but his preference for girls was pronounced. One letter to a little girl concludes, "My best love to yourself—to your Mother my kindest regards—to your small, fat, impertinent, ignorant brother my hatred." Carroll explained that he was not impartial when it came to children: "With little *boys* I'm out of my element altogether." He did not like all little girls, nor too many at once, but he was not exclusive and kept up a variety of child contacts. Part of his interest was that of a collector. He sometimes expressed a generalized romantic notion of the purity of children as being closer to God than are adults. At other times he revealed more specific, personal tastes. He liked spontaneity, provided this combined with good manners. He applied physical standards and looked for beauty in little girls to please his artist's and photographer's eye. A class bias occasionally appeared in remarks about the lesser looks of lower-class children.

Of course, one wonders whether this response to physical beauty implies a sexual element. None of the children or their families have left any record of being scandalized. This does not mean that all regarded Carroll's ways as quite conventional. He said of himself that he lived upon the frowns of Mrs. Grundy. He knew that he risked offending this mythical figurehead of respectability when it came to kissing girls who were not so young as they looked, or taking nude photographs of certain children, or inviting child-friends of rather advanced age—teenagers and even young ladies—to spend holidays with him at the seaside. He sought to avoid outraging Mrs. Grundy by doing nothing behind her back: he scrupulously discussed the kissability of daughters with their mothers, and also went over the family view of nude photographs and the particu-

Specimen illustrations by Tenniel for the 1872 edition of Through the Looking-Glass, and What Alice Found There

A preliminary sketch made in 1887 by Carroll of a scene from Sylvie and Bruno Concluded *(1893)*
(Lilly Library, Indiana University)

lar child's attitude. Carroll did not wish to provoke the least bit of shyness in a girl. When he invited young ladies to spend time with him at the seaside, he declared his sense of propriety in doing so but asked them to make sure of their own feelings. Carroll could casually liken one such visit to a honeymoon and himself to a bachelor unused to têtes-à-têtes with young females. It is hard to interpret the implications here. Is it important that he should raise the erotic issue, or unimportant in that he raises it so casually? Anne Clark's biography of Carroll (1979) suggests that he loved Alice Liddell in the romantic sense that he wanted to marry her. This idea remains controversial. There is no clear evidence of romance in his life, whether involving a girl or a woman. One may speculate about his affection for the actress Ellen Terry, which lasted from her childhood into her full adulthood. Some of his friend-

ships did last in this way, and the older Carroll became, the more often a child kept him as a friend as she grew up. Sometimes Carroll joked about a girl's growing too old to be interesting, more often about her growing too old to care for him. The letters contain a great deal of byplay about gradually cooling forms of address and the evolution from intimacy to formality to be seen in ways of signing a name. Carroll certainly felt the loss of many friends to time, but he took his losses gracefully and found great satisfaction in his friendships with children, and he avoided catastrophe. Whatever one may make of Carroll's child-friendships in a post-Freudian age, one must recognize his own freedom from conscious guilt or regret and admire his success in living as he chose to live. In any period it is unusual to care for children so much. It may be especially unusual to love them as children, without even a sexual element to explain it. Most people like only their own children and do not socialize with other people's. The romanticism of the nineteenth-century could glorify the rare ability to maintain the heart of a child, while today this may seem regressive and immature. Carroll joins J. M. Barrie as a children's writer open to such a range of praise and blame. C. S. Lewis would like to grant manhood to writers such as these: as he says, one need not lose touch with childhood in the process of also developing beyond it.

When Carroll gave up his photography and his lectureship in 1880-1881, the likely reason was his desire to devote all his time to his writing, and indicating the two main tracks of his interest are the two major works produced in this last portion of his life—the children's novels *Sylvie and Bruno* (1889) and *Sylvie and Bruno Concluded* (1893), and the treatise *Symbolic Logic*. The inception of the Sylvie and Bruno books dates back to 1867, when Carroll published the story of "Bruno's Revenge." Several letters indicate his desire to write something of a more serious nature for children than the Alice books and *The Hunting of the Snark*. Over the years Carroll brought together various bits and pieces into his two-volume work of "litterature." These novels have struck most readers as overserious and disjointed. The story divides into two narrative lines, one realistic and edifying, the other fantastic. According to the first story line, the grown-up, real-life Lady Muriel Orme ends her engagement to her suitor Eric, who lacks religious faith, to marry another suitor, Arthur. He departs one hour after the wedding to risk his life doctoring epidemic-stricken villagers. Following a report of his death, it turns out that a reformed Eric has rescued Arthur, who reappears to be nursed back to health by his loving wife. The other narrative line tells of Lady Muriel's fairy double, the child Sylvie, and her adventures with her brother Bruno (Carroll *could* create a positive boy character) tracing their lost father and saving the throne of Outland from usurpation by the Vice-Warden and his son Uggugg. Linking these stories are the appearances and good works of Sylvie and Bruno amid the real-life characters and the knowledge of their doings in both England and fairyland by a narrator capable of "eerie" as well as ordinary states of consciousness. There is some interest in the narrative oddity here and in the interpenetration of dream and reality. Fine nonsense enlivens the fairy sequences, such as this from "The Pig Tale":

Lewis Carroll's grave, Guildford Cemetery

Little Birds are bathing
    Crocodiles in cream,
      Like a happy dream:
Like, but not so lasting—
Crocodiles, when fasting,
      Are not all they seem!

These lines provide the title for a one-actor dramatic rendering of Carroll's life by David Horwell and Michael Rothwell, *Crocodiles in Cream* (1976), and they signal the importance of aggression and the unimportance of righteousness in much of his nonsense. This is the Carroll who, when pressed to comment, said Alice was about malice. In the Sylvie and Bruno books Carroll notes that "live" spells "evil" backwards. And yet these last books affirm life more decisively than anything earlier. The theme song about love strikes the serious note which Carroll sought. Some find it sentimental and "Victorian":

For I think it is Love
For I feel it is Love,
For I'm sure it is nothing but Love!

Like the last children's work, Carroll's last academic work, *Symbolic Logic*, has been valued for good bits and historical interest more than for classic status. But with the recovery and publication of Part II by William Warren Bartley, its historical interest has grown and surpassed that of the Sylvie and Bruno books. The treatise has been persistently honored by quotation in later logic texts because of the ingenuity and charming presentation of its logical problems—the Jack Sprat problem, the Pig and Balloon problem, the problem of the Pork-Chop-Eating Logicians. According to Bartley, some innovation appears in Part I (enough to prompt the praise of Bertrand Russell), and Part II confirms and strengthens Carroll's standing as an original thinker. (For instance, his truth tables prefigure those developed by Wittgenstein in the 1920s.) Yet Carroll was not really a father of modern logic. Rather, his merit lies in synthesizing the Boolean logic of his day, an algebraic form which superseded syllogistic Aristotelian logic and has since been superseded by Russell's brand of mathematical logic. This synthesis is noteworthy first because Carroll went beyond anything being done in the logical backwater of Oxford to concern himself with the forefront of thought in his field, and second because he defined a logical system that was so soon revolutionized as to have left no other comprehensive text.

The volumes of *Symbolic Logic* reflect Carroll's lifelong attraction to certitude in the face of imponderables. According to a letter to his sister, he turned from a prospective book on religious difficulties to devote himself to this work, for which he felt more fitted. Thus in the works of his last years, Carroll affirmed as much as he could as clearly as he could—love in *Sylvie and Bruno*; in *Symbolic Logic*, sense. But, as Sylvie realizes that to love matters more than to be loved, Carroll's logic presents sense as something made, not given. As a logician he was very much a formalist. The earlier *The Game of Logic* prepares the way for Carroll's statement in *Symbolic Logic* that "the rules, here laid down, are *arbitrary*." Throughout his life and works Carroll was concerned with the very difficult, very necessary task of making meaning enough to live by. He lived well by his own rules, loving little girls and God as he saw fit, as systematic in his mind and ways as the uncertainty of things would allow. If he was eccentric or, more harshly, neurotic, he knew how to make the best of eschewing the norm. The Alice books strike most critics today as explorations of

nightmare reaches beyond sense and security. And yet Alice does not lose her pluck or her mind (as she does in Andre Gregory's Manhattan Project dramatization of 1970). She perhaps grows or even triumphs; at least she emerges from her dreams. Mathematician, logician, photographer, the greatest nonsense writer in English and possibly any language, as indispensable to adults as to children, Carroll remained healthy and active to the end; in the last year of his life he thought nothing of an eighteen-mile walk. He died at the age of sixty-five, of bronchitis taken after a cold, at his sisters' home in Guildford.

Letters:

A Selection from the Letters of Lewis Carroll (The Rev. Charles Lutwidge Dodgson) to His Child-friends, edited by Evelyn M. Hatch (London: Macmillan, 1933);

The Letters of Lewis Carroll, 2 volumes, edited by Morton Cohen with the assistance of Roger Lancelyn Green (London: Macmillan / New York: Oxford University Press, 1979).

Bibliographies:

Sidney Herbert Williams, Falconer Madan, Roger Lancelyn Green, and Denis Crutch, *The Lewis Carroll Handbook* (Folkestone, U.K.: Dawson, 1979);

Edward Guiliano, *Lewis Carroll, An Annotated International Bibliography 1960-1977* (Charlottesville: University Press of Virginia / Sussex, U.K.: Harvester Press, 1980).

Biographies:

Derek Hudson, *Lewis Carroll: An Illustrated Biography* (London: Constable, 1976; New York: Potter, 1977);

Anne Clark, *Lewis Carroll: A Biography* (London: Dent / New York: Schocken, 1979).

References:

Nina Auerbach, "Alice and Wonderland, A Curious Child," *Victorian Studies*, 17 (1973): 31-47;

Kathleen Blake, *Play, Games, and Sport: The Literary Works of Lewis Carroll* (Ithaca, N.Y. & London: Cornell University Press, 1974);

Harold Bloom, ed., *Lewis Carroll* (New York: Chelsea House, 1987);

Stuart Dodgson Collingwood, comp., *The Life and Letters of Lewis Carroll* (London: Unwin, 1899);

Teresa De Lauretis, *Alice Doesn't Feminism Semiotics Cinema* (Bloomington: Indiana University Press, 1984);

Gilles Deleuze, *The Logic of Sense*, translated by Mark Lester and Charles Stivale (New York: Columbia University Press, 1990);

William Empson, "Alice in Wonderland: The Child as Swain," in *Some Versions of Pastoral* (London: Chatto & Windus / New York: New Directions, 1935);

Martin Gardner, ed., *The Annotated Alice* (New York: Potter, 1960);

Jean Gattégno, *Lewis Carroll: Fragments of a Looking-Glass*, translated by Rosemary Sheed (New York: Crowell, 1976);

Donald J. Gray, "The Uses of Victorian Laughter," *Victorian Studies*, 10 (1966): 145-176;

Edward Guiliano, ed., *Lewis Carroll: A Celebration* (New York: Potter, 1982);

Guiliano, ed., *Lewis Carroll Observed: A Collection of Unpublished Photographs, Drawings, Poetry, and New Essays* (New York: Potter, 1976);

Guiliano and James R. Kincaid, eds., *Soaring with the Dodo: Essays on Lewis Carroll's Life and Art* (Charlottesville: Lewis Carroll Society of North America/University Press of Virginia, 1982);

Michael Hancher, *The Tenniel Illustrations to the Alice Books* (Columbus: Ohio State University Press, 1985);

Alice Hargreaves and Caryl Hargreaves, "Alice's Recollections of Carrollian Days," *Cornhill Magazine*, 73 (1932): 1-12;

Daniel Kirk, *Lewis Carroll, Semeiotician* (Gainesville: University of Florida Press, 1962);

Florence Becker Lennon, *Victoria Through the Looking-Glass* (New York: Simon & Schuster, 1945);

William Madden, "Framing the *Alices*," *PMLA*, 101 (1986): 362-373;

Cornelia Meigs, et al., *A Critical History of Children's Literature: A Survey of Children's Books in English*, revised edition (London: Macmillan, 1969);

Barry Moser, *Illustrations for "Alice in Wonderland"* (Berkeley: University of California Press, 1982);

Moser, *Illustrations for "Through the Looking-Glass and What Alice Found There"* (Berkeley: University of California Press, 1983);

Graham Ovenden, ed., *The Illustrators of Alice* (London: Academy / New York: St. Martin's Press, 1972);

George Pitcher, "Wittgenstein, Nonsense, and Lewis Carroll," *Massachusetts Review*, 6 (1965): 591-611;

Robert Phillips, ed., *Aspects of Alice: Lewis Carroll's Dreamchild As Seen Through the Critic's Looking-Glasses 1865-1971* (New York: Vanguard / London: Gollancz, 1971);

Robert M. Polhemus, "Carroll's *Through the Looking-Glass*: The Comedy of Regression," in *Comic Faith: The Great Tradition from Austen to Joyce* (Chicago & London: University of Chicago Press, 1980);

Elizabeth Sewell, *The Field of Nonsense* (London: Chatto & Windus, 1952);

Linda Shires, "Fantasy, Nonsense, Parody, and the Status of the Real: The Example of Carroll," *Victorian Poetry*, 26 (1988): 267-283;

Robert D. Sutherland, *Language and Lewis Carroll* (The Hague: Mouton, 1970);

Warren Weaver, *Alice in Many Tongues: The Translation of Alice in Wonderland* (Madison: University of Wisconsin Press, 1964).

Papers:

Collections of Lewis Carroll's papers are held at the British Museum; Castle Arch Museum, Guildford, England; Christ Church College Library, Oxford; Houghton Library, Harvard University; National Portrait Gallery, London, Photographic Division; Berg Collection, New York Public Library; New York University Library; Pierpont Morgan Library; Morris L. Parrish Collection, Princeton University Library; Rosenbach Foundation, Philadelphia; and Harry Ransom Humanities Research Center, University of Texas, Austin.

Wilkie Collins

(8 January 1824 - 23 September 1889)

This entry was written by Jeanne F. Bedell (Wentworth Institute of Technology) for
DLB 70: British Mystery Writers, 1860-1919.

See also the Collins entry in DLB 18: Victorian Novelists After 1885.

BOOKS: *Memoirs of the Life of William Collins, Esq., R.A.,* 2 volumes (London: Longman, Brown, Green & Longmans, 1848);

Antonina; or, The Fall of Rome (3 volumes, London: Bentley, 1850; 1 volume, New York: Harper, 1850);

Rambles Beyond Railways; or, Notes in Cornwall Taken A-foot (London: Bentley, 1851);

Mr. Wray's Cash-Box; or, the Mask and the Mystery: A Christmas Sketch (London: Bentley, 1852); republished as *The Stolen Mask; or, the Mysterious Cash-Box* (Columbia, S.C.: De Fontaine, 1864);

Basil: A Story of Modern Life (3 volumes, London: Bentley, 1852; 1 volume, New York: Appleton, 1853; revised edition, London: Sampson Low, 1862);

Hide and Seek, 3 volumes (London: Bentley, 1854); revised as *Hide and Seek; or, the Mystery of Mary Grice,* 1 volume (London: Sampson Low, 1861; Philadelphia: Peterson, 1862);

The Holly-Tree Inn, by Collins and Charles Dickens, *Household Words* (Christmas 1855); (New York: Dix & Edwards, 1855);

After Dark, includes material by Dickens, 2 volumes (London: Smith, Elder, 1856; New York: Dick & Fitzgerald, 1856);

The Wreck of the Golden Mary, by Collins and Dickens (London: Bradbury & Evans, 1856);

The Dead Secret, 2 volumes (London: Bradbury & Evans, 1857; New York: Miller & Curtis, 1857);

The Two Apprentices. With a History of Their Lazy Tour, by Collins and Dickens (Philadelphia: Peterson, 1857); republished in *The Lazy Tour of Two Idle Apprentices. No Thoroughfare. The Perils of Certain English Prisoners* (London: Chapman & Hall, 1890);

The Queen of Hearts (3 volumes, London: Hurst &

Wilkie Collins, 1873 (photograph by Napoleon Sarony, New York; Houghton Library, Harvard University)

Blackett, 1859; 1 volume, New York: Harper, 1859);

The Woman in White (3 volumes, London: Sampson Low, 1860; 1 volume, New York: Harper, 1860);

No Name (3 volumes, London: Sampson Low, 1862; 2 volumes, Boston: Fuller, 1863);

My Miscellanies (2 volumes, London: Sampson Low, 1863; 1 volume, New York: Harper, 1874);

Armadale (2 volumes, London: Smith, Elder, 1866; 1 volume, New York: Harper, 1866);

No Thoroughfare. A Drama in Five Acts, by Collins, Charles Fechter, and Dickens (New York: DeWitt, n.d.); republished in *The Lazy Tour of Two Idle Apprentices. No Thoroughfare. The Perils of Certain English Prisoners* (London: Chapman & Hall, 1890);

The Moonstone (3 volumes, London: Tinsley, 1868; 1 volume, New York: Harper, 1868);

Black and White, by Collins and Fechter (London: Whiting, 1869);

Man and Wife (3 volumes, London: Ellis, 1870; 1 volume, New York: Harper, 1870);

Poor Miss Finch: A Novel (3 volumes, London: Bentley, 1872; 1 volume, New York: Harper, 1872);

Miss or Mrs?: And Other Stories in Outline (London: Bentley, 1873; revised edition, London: Chatto & Windus, 1877);

The New Magdalen (2 volumes, London: Bentley, 1873; 1 volume, New York: Harper, 1873);

The Dead Alive (Boston: Shepard & Gill, 1874); republished as *The Frozen Deep and Other Stories*, 2 volumes (London: Bentley, 1874);

The Law and the Lady (3 volumes, London: Chatto & Windus, 1875; 1 volume, New York: Harper, 1875);

The Two Destinies (2 volumes, London: Chatto & Windus, 1876; 1 volume, New York: Harper, 1876);

My Lady's Money and Percy the Prophet (Leipzig: Tauchnitz, 1877); *Percy the Prophet* republished (New York: Harper, 1877); *My Lady's Money* republished as *My Lady's Money: An Episode in the Life of a Young Girl*, 2 volumes (New York: Harper, 1878);

The Haunted Hotel, A Mystery of Modern Venice (Toronto: Rose-Belford, 1878); republished as *The Haunted Hotel, A Mystery of Modern Venice, to Which is Added: My Lady's Money*, 2 volumes (London: Chatto & Windus, 1879);

The Fallen Leaves (3 volumes, London: Chatto & Windus, 1879; 1 volume, Chicago: Rose-Belford, 1879);

A Rogue's Life: From His Birth to His Marriage (London: Bentley, 1879; New York: Appleton, 1879);

Jezebel's Daughter (3 volumes, London: Chatto & Windus, 1880; 1 volume, New York: Munro, 1880);

The Black Robe (3 volumes, London: Chatto & Windus, 1881; 1 volume, New York: Munro, 1881);

Heart and Science (1 volume, New York: Munro, 1883; 3 volumes, London: Chatto & Windus, 1883);

"I Say No"; or, the Love-Letter Answered (New York: Harper, 1884); republished as *"I Say No,"* 3 volumes (London: Chatto & Windus, 1884);

The Evil Genius: A Domestic Story (3 volumes, London: Chatto & Windus, 1886; 1 volume, New York: Harper, 1886);

The Guilty River (Bristol: Arrowsmith, 1886; New York: Harper, 1886);

Little Novels, 3 volumes (London: Chatto & Windus, 1887);

The Legacy of Cain (1 volume, New York: Harper, 1888; 3 volumes, London: Chatto & Windus, 1889);

Blind Love, by Collins and Walter Besant (3 volumes, London: Chatto & Windus, 1890; 1 volume, New York: Appleton, 1890);

Under the Management of Mr. Charles Dickens: His Production of "The Frozen Deep," by Collins and Dickens, edited by Robert Louis Brannan (Ithaca, N.Y.: Cornell University Press, 1966).

PLAY PRODUCTIONS: *The Lighthouse*, by Collins and Charles Dickens, London, Tavistock House, 15 June 1855; London, Olympic Theatre, 10 August 1857;

The Frozen Deep, by Collins and Dickens, London, Tavistock House, 6 January 1857; London, Olympic Theatre, 27 October 1866;

The Red Vial, London, Olympic Theatre, 11 October 1858;

A Message from the Sea, London, Britannia Theatre, 7 January 1861;

No Thoroughfare, by Collins, Charles Fechter, and Dickens, London, Adelphi Theatre, 26 December 1867;

Black and White, by Collins and Fechter, London, Adelphi Theatre, 29 March 1869;

The Woman in White, London, Olympic Theatre, 9 October 1871;

Man and Wife, London, Prince of Wales's Theatre, 22 February 1873;

The New Magdalen, London, Olympic Theatre, 9 May 1873;

Miss Gwilt, London, Globe Theatre, 15 April 1876;

The Moonstone, London, Olympic Theatre, 17 September 1877;

Ranks and Riches, London, Adelphi Theatre, 9 June 1883.

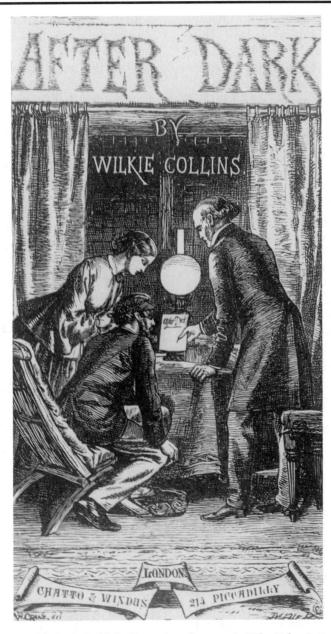

Cover, with E. G. Dalziel's illustration of a scene in "The Stolen Letter,"
for a paperback edition of Collins's 1856 collection of short stories

Although best known to modern readers as the author of *The Woman in White* (1860) and *The Moonstone* (1868)—which T. S. Eliot and Dorothy Sayers have called the best English detective story—Wilkie Collins made contributions more substantial than his current reputation indicates to the development of mystery and suspense fiction. As early as 1865 Henry James noted that Collins had "introduced into fiction those most mysterious of mysteries, the mysteries which are at our own doors." Writing before the detective story had become established as a genre and be-

fore it had hardened into formula, Collins (like other mid-Victorian authors who emphasized secrecy, mystery, and crime in their fiction) was considered by contemporary reviewers a sensation novelist, and James's comment singles out an innovation crucial to the creation of modern suspense fiction. Sensation fiction, generally viewed as domestication of the Gothic romance, established an atmosphere of mystery and terror in realistic settings and relied upon factually accurate detail and believable characterization to give verisimilitude to often lurid plots. Collins shared the Victorian belief that fiction should be true to nature; and in the "Letter of Dedication" to *Basil* (1852) he wrote that he founded the novel "on a fact within my own knowledge" and stressed his adherence to the "actual" and to "everyday realities." In simultaneously emphasizing his reliance upon experience and retaining his prerogative to exercise his imagination and to include "those extraordinary accidents and events which happen to few men" as "legitimate materials for fiction," Collins fused the romantic and the realistic and provided a model for subsequent suspense and mystery fiction. His plotting, called by a contemporary "almost as ingenious as the knot of Gordius," was intricate and closely meshed. Praised for his skill in "the gradual unravelling of some carefully prepared enigma" and his ability to make "every circumstance subordinate to his leading idea," Collins established plot techniques of such obvious importance to detective fiction that without his contributions, as Sayers maintains, "the English novel of intrigue would either never have developed at all or would have developed much later and upon much narrower and more Gothic lines," and "the modern English detective story could never have risen to its present position of international supremacy."

Collins's own background, which combined the artistic with the practical, proved ideal for his future career as an author. Born 8 January 1824, the first son of William Collins, R.A., and Harriet Geddes Collins, William Wilkie Collins spent his childhood in London in the parish of Marylebone. William Collins, who had been elected to the Royal Academy in 1820, was a successful painter but definitely not a bohemian. To his sons Wilkie and Charles, born 25 January 1828, he emphasized the importance of religious piety, filial obedience, and aristocratic connections. Wilkie was apparently an obedient son—his first book (1848) was a laudatory biography of his father—but the scathing attacks in his novels upon religious hypocrisy and social pretentiousness reveal divergence from his father's principles. His powerful portrayal in *Hide and Seek* (1854) of the rigors of an English Sunday and the effects of narrow religiosity upon a sensitive child may be partly autobiographical, but there is no real evidence that Collins's childhood was unhappy or that it differed markedly from that of other middle-class Victorian children. In fact, his notable eye for landscape and his skill in descriptive writing can be attributed to his familiarity

with painting and to the occasional sketching expeditions on which he accompanied his father. His appreciation of art was enlarged and deepened during the years 1836-1838, which the family spent in travels through Italy. While William Collins studied Italian masterpieces, the adolescent Wilkie savored not only the beauties of art but also the contrasts between Italy and England. His enchantment with Rome is evident in the Roman setting of his first novel, *Antonina* (1850). His exposure to Italian culture gave him, at an impressionable age, a vivid and fascinating alternative to the narrow rigidity of Victorian society and perhaps provided a basis for the critical attitude toward that society he was later to display.

The journey to Italy interrupted Collins's formal education, begun at Maida Hill Academy in 1833; on his return to England it was continued at a private school in Highbury. In 1841 he was apprenticed to Antrobus and Company, a large firm of tea merchants. Aside from giving him a distaste for a business career, described in *Hide and Seek* as "nine hours of the most ungrateful labour," Collins's five years with Antrobus seem to have had little influence upon his development. An expedition to Scotland and the Shetland Islands with his father in the summer of 1842 and a trip to Paris with Charles Ward in the early autumn of 1844 broke the monotony of his business career, as did the writing to which he devoted his leisure time. His first verifiable publication, "The Last Stagecoachman," a short lament for the disappearance of stagecoaches as a consequence of railway expansion, appeared in the *Illuminated Magazine* of August 1843. Collins was fortunate to attract the attention of the magazine's editor, the popular author and playwright Douglas Jerrold, who became a lifelong friend. Jerrold introduced him to the theater and to theatrical melodrama, a style of importance in the development of his literary technique.

In 1846 Collins was released from his apprenticeship with Antrobus and entered as a law student on the rolls of Lincoln's Inn. Although he qualified for admission to the bar in November 1851, Collins did not pursue his law studies seriously after the death of his father in February 1847. Their effect upon his writing is, however, significant. The number of characters associated with the legal profession, plots which turn on detailed knowledge of law, and the narrative structures of *The Woman in White* and *The Moonstone*—both of which are designed to resemble the methods by which evidence is presented in

The amateur cast for the 1857 production of The Frozen Deep *included the play's authors, Charles Dickens (reclining at center) and Collins (kneeling with head on hand), and various friends and family members.*

court—reveal the impact of Collins's tenure as a law student.

The death of his father actually marks the beginning of Collins's literary career. Freed by inheritance of the necessity to earn a living, he first carried out William Collins's request that he write a memorial of his life. *Memoirs of the Life of William Collins, Esq., R.A.* was published by subscription in 1848 and attracted favorable attention for its young author. The reception of this book undoubtedly owed more to the reputation and popularity of its subject than the skill of the biographer, but Collins wrote in a pleasant, unpretentious style and made ample use of diaries and letters to reveal his father's personality. Detailed discussions of his father's paintings offered good practice in descriptive writing, an ability for which he became justly known.

Once his filial obligations had been completed, Collins returned to the historical romance on which he had been working for years. *Antonina*, written under the influence of Sir Walter Scott and Edward Bulwer-Lytton, did not display his talents to advantage. Turgid, inflated prose and a plot which moves with soporific slowness combine to produce a novel Sayers appropriately calls "impossibly melodramatic and impossibly dull." In depicting the adventures of a

pure-minded and beautiful adolescent girl during the Gothic invasion of Rome, the religious fanaticism of her father, the opposing fanaticism of a pagan high priest, and the consuming desire for vengeance of a Gothic woman whose husband and children were massacred during the sack of Aquileia, Collins produced a blood-drenched but implausible narrative. Surprisingly, the novel was favorably reviewed by critics who found its portrayal of Roman life accurate and moving. A warning note, however, was sounded by H. F. Chorley in the *Athenaeum*. Chorley, later one of Collins's most virulent critics, warned him "against the vices of the French school—against the needless accumulation of revolting details—against catering for a prurient taste by dwelling on such incidental portions of the subject as, being morbid, ought to be treated incidentally." The commentary is significant as a harbinger of the attacks on the morality of Collins's fiction which became commonplace with the publication of his next novel, *Basil*, and continued throughout his career.

Both professionally and personally, mid century proved an exciting and influential period for Collins. Through his brother Charles's association with the Pre-Raphaelite brotherhood, he met such artists as William and Dante Gabriel Ros-

Wilkie Collins, circa 1865

setti, William Frith, J. E. Millais, Augustus Egg, and Holman Hunt. In 1849 he submitted a landscape to the Royal Academy; it was accepted, probably out of respect to his father's memory, but hung near the ceiling, where it was practically invisible to viewers of the exhibition. According to Hunt, Collins later kept the painting in his study and narrated its history to guests with ironic self-mockery.

The reception of his painting convinced Collins that his future lay in literature, and a walking tour of Cornwall with his new friend, artist Henry C. Brandling, in the summer of 1850 led to the writing of *Rambles Beyond Railways*, published in 1851. An anecdotal travelogue of the sort popular with mid-Victorian audiences, *Rambles* is slight but charming and shows that Collins possessed a sense of humor and a talent for humorous characterization not indicated by *Antonina*.

Early in 1851 Collins's passionate interest in amateur theatricals led to his first meeting with Charles Dickens. Learning of Collins's ability as an amateur actor from their mutual friend Egg, Dickens wrote to ask him to take a small part in

Bulwer-Lytton's *Not So Bad As We Seem*. The first performance of the play was given 14 May 1851 at Devonshire House in the presence of Queen Victoria and Prince Albert. This auspicious beginning led to a close personal and professional relationship which lasted until the death of Dickens in 1870. A bachelor and bon vivant twelve years Dickens's junior, Collins became a favored companion for dinner, theater parties, and extended rambles about London. Dickens's biographer John Forster says that Collins was "one of his dearest and most valued friends," and although the friendship apparently cooled in the late 1860s, it proved profitable, in both financial and literary terms, to both men. Collins became a paid contributor to Dickens's *Household Words* in 1853 (the same year in which he toured Switzerland and Italy with Dickens and Egg) and an editor in 1856. The encouragement of Dickens, who considered Collins the most promising young writer of his time, and the association with *Household Words* were influential in shaping both his approach to fiction and his career as a popular author.

The first evidence of Dickens's influence appears in *Mr. Wray's Cash-Box* (1852), a Christmas tale published in *Household Words* in December 1851. The story features Reuben Wray, a retired actor, and the theft of his most prized possession, a bust of Shakespeare; it concludes with a Christmas feast and is notable only for its use of Collins's experience in amateur theatricals (material presented to better effect in *No Name*, 1862) and in its contemporary setting. Collins's forte, as he himself realized, was not the historical novel, and in his next book, *Basil*, his most significant novel of the 1850s, he turned to the present.

The reality in *Basil* was too strong for many contemporary critics who found in it the "aesthetics of the Old Bailey" and condemned it because it did not "elevate and purify." Collins referred to these criticisms in prefatory remarks to the revised 1862 edition of the novel:

> On its appearance, it was condemned off-hand, by a certain class of readers, as an outrage on their sense of propriety. Conscious of having designed and written my story with the strictest regard to true delicacy ... I allowed the prurient misinterpretation to assert itself as offensibly as it pleased, without troubling myself to protest against an expression of opinion which aroused in me no other feeling than a feeling of contempt.

Collins's contempt for middle-class morality and the limitations it imposed on the artist, only thinly disguised here, was to culminate in later references to the "clap-trap morality of the present day." He refused to accept "young people as the ultimate court of appeal in English literature" or to succumb to "this wretched English claptrap" which forbade a writer to "touch on the sexual relations which literally swarm around him."

Collins's appreciation of human sexuality is evident in *Basil*, where his depiction of sensuality is remarkably candid for the early 1850s. Its hero is a young man of aristocratic background, the second son of a father whose pride in his lineage is fanatical. In pursuit of realistic detail about human nature for a historical romance he is writing, he boards a London omnibus and becomes immediately infatuated with one of the passengers: "I had helped to hand her in, as she passed me; merely touching her arm for a moment. But how the sense of that touch was prolonged! I felt it thrilling through me—thrilling in every nerve, in every pulsation of my fast-throbbing heart." The young woman under whose sexual spell he falls is Margaret Sherwin, the daughter of a linen draper. Basil knows that she is an unsuitable wife (that he cannot introduce her to his father or sister), but his desire for her is so great that he consents to a secret marriage and even accepts the stipulation of Margaret's father that the marriage not be consummated for a year. He feels "guilty" and "humiliated" and comes to see "certain peculiarities in Margaret's character and conduct, which . . . gave me a little uneasiness and even a little displeasure." Margaret, as the reader understands at once, is vain, shallow, and materialistic; she feels no affection for Basil and is interested only in his wealth and social position. The uneasy and unnatural situation of Basil, who calls on his wife in the evening and is chaperoned during the visits, is further complicated by the appearance of Mr. Sherwin's clerk, the mysterious Robert Mannion, a reticent and sinister figure whose relationship with Margaret creates a sense of foreboding. Basil's humiliation becomes complete when, shortly before the year is up, he follows Margaret and Mannion to a seedy hotel and learns that they are lovers. Infuriated, he attacks Mannion and permanently disfigures him.

Despite a melodramatic conclusion in which Mannion tries to murder Basil and is himself killed, the novel is successful. The anonymous critic of *Bentley's Miscellany* who found "a startling antagonism between the intensity of the passion,

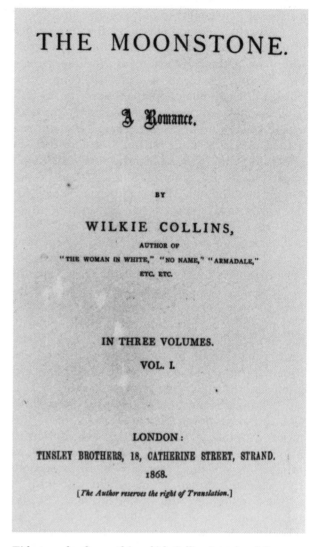

Title page for the novel in which Collins introduced Sergeant Cuff, whom T. S. Eliot called "the ancestor of the healthy generation of amiable, efficient, professional but fallible inspectors of fiction among whom we live today"

the violent spasmodic action of the piece, and its smooth, commonplace environment" identifies Collins's achievement: he uses crime, passion, and domesticity in "the secret theatre of home," employing the technique he was to put to such masterful use in *The Moonstone* and *The Woman in White*. Secrecy and crime in a mundane suburban villa bring suspense and terror close to the reader's own experiences and prove more frightening and more significant than similar crimes committed in the ruined castles so commonplace in the Gothic romance. Like Dickens, Collins was able to see "the romantic side of familiar things." *Basil* also anticipates Collins's future work in its use of letters and journals (to vary the narrative) and dreams (to express unconscious feelings and give a sense of inevitability to plot action).

Morally, *Basil* is ambiguous: the hero's older brother, a man of the world with a mistress whom he jokingly refers to as "the morganatic Mrs. Ralph," presents an implicit contrast to Basil, whose humiliating experiences are, as William Marshall rightly observes, caused by "the honorable quality of his intentions.... Had he not wished to marry Margaret but to seduce her—in effect, to follow that aristocratic ethic that Ralph himself has consistently personified—had he not sought to enter with Margaret the state which for the Victorian bourgeois was at the center of all social order—then he would have avoided all his difficulties." In simultaneously criticizing the aristocratic ethic in his portrayal of the arrant snobbery of Basil's father, and affirming its value in his depiction of the competent and practical manner in which Ralph straightens out the mess Basil had made of his life, Collins neglects to provide the consistent moral focus so important to Victorian critics, but he has presented a realistic portrait of a young man caught between two value systems, both of which have obvious flaws.

Although much less powerful than *Basil*, Collins's next novel, *Hide and Seek* (1854), was more favorably received by critics who found its morality unobjectionable and who praised its humor. In creating Valentine Blyth, a second-rate painter devoted to an invalid wife and an adopted daughter who is a deaf-mute, Collins put to good use his knowledge of the art world. The basic plot, which turns on the parentage of the deaf-mute Madonna, relies too heavily on a series of improbable coincidences, but the novel is noteworthy for containing Collins's first piece of sustained detection and for the characterization of Matthew Grice, also known as Mat Marksman. An eccentric wanderer who has spent most of his life in the wilds of North America and had been scalped by Indians, Grice is derived from James Fenimore Cooper's Leatherstocking. Dickens considered him "admirably done," as well he might, since Collins had clearly profited from studying Dickens's own touch with eccentricity. Grice's detection is admirable for its pertinacity rather than its skill. His search for his lost and ruined sister and his discovery of her death and subsequent identification of her seducer and her child, especially the detailed reconstruction of past events, indicate the approach Collins was to follow in later novels. *Hide and Seek* also displays his antipathy toward narrow religiosity and the association of morality with respectability, attitudes at variance

with his own moral vision, which consistently emphasized charitableness and forgiveness.

Because of the outbreak of the Crimean War at the time of its publication, *Hide and Seek* failed to attract a large audience. Although Collins was discouraged by readers' temporary preference for newspapers over fiction, he persevered in his work and was rewarded by the serialization of his next novel, *The Dead Secret* (1857), in *Household Words*. As the title indicates, Collins was moving closer to sensation fiction, a genre Kathleen Tillotson has aptly christened the "novel-with-a-secret." Once again the discovery of a young girl's parentage is the focal point of the plot, but the secret itself, evident in the early chapters of the novel, is less important than the characterization of the custodian of the secret, Sarah Leeson, and its effect upon her mental and physical health. Her weak heart and mental instability establish her as a precursor of Anne Catherick, the title character in *The Woman in White*. Collins's sympathetic treatment of her and her illegitimate daughter, Rosamund Frankland, as well as Leonard Frankland's dismissal of class distinctions when he learns that his wife is the daughter of a lady's maid and a miner, embody Collins's divergence from usually strict Victorian attitudes toward sexual morality and social stratification.

Two volumes of short fiction (largely pieces previously published in *Household Words*), *After Dark* (1856) and *The Queen of Hearts* (1859), display an increasing preoccupation with suspense and an innovative approach to detection. Collins provided a frame narrative for both collections, but the main interest in each lies in the short stories and novelettes collected. "A Terribly Strange Bed," usually considered Collins's best short story, appears in *After Dark*, as do "Sister Rose," a short novel set during the French Revolution and a possible influence on Dickens's *A Tale of Two Cities* (1859), and "The Yellow Mask," which features a Machiavellian priest—a character type developed at greater length in *The Black Robe* (1881). "A Terribly Strange Bed" is a horror story of considerable merit with debt to Edgar Allan Poe's "The Pit and the Pendulum" and the tradition of Gothic haunted-chamber fiction. Two young Englishmen in Paris visit a shady gambling house where the narrator breaks the bank at *rouge-et-noir* and overindulges in champagne in celebration. Persuaded to spend the night at the house instead of risking robbery during the return to his hotel, he is unable to sleep and lies in his canopied four-poster bed watching "a dark old pic-

Publicity poster by Frederick Walker for the 1871 production of Collins's dramatic version of the novel that a decade earlier had inspired "Woman in White" cloaks, bonnets, perfumes, waltzes, and quadrilles

ture" on the opposite wall. Gradually he realizes that his view of the picture has changed and that the canopy of the bed is descending. Paralyzed with fear, he rolls off the bed, "just as the murderous canopy touched me on the shoulder," he says. Macabre though it is, the story builds suspense through careful revelation of detail and the somewhat befuddled mental condition of the narrator, which make the slow realization of his plight more terrifying and more believable.

Generally, the stories in *The Queen of Hearts* are better than those in *After Dark*. The frame narrative—in which three elderly men tell stories to amuse a young woman who, by her father's will, must spend six weeks each year with her guardian at an isolated Welsh estate—is more convincing. "Mad Monkton," which Dickens had declined for *Household Words* because he thought its theme of hereditary insanity might offend read-ers, is an interesting study of an abnormal mental condition and the impact of family legend upon an unstable personality. "The Dream-Woman," in which a man's dream precisely predicts future action, maintains a feeling of inescapable doom. "The Biter Bit," an epistolary tale usually considered the first humorous detective story, features an inexperienced policeman who is consistently misled by the thief he has set out to catch. The reader is (or, ought to be) aware of the criminal's identity, a circumstance which adds to the story's ironic humor. "Anne Rodway," though sentimental, has an unusual heroine-detective, a poor seamstress who succeeds in finding the murderer of her friend after the incompetent police have failed to find a single clue. Collins's always ambivalent and frequently critical attitude toward the official police figures prominently here. The chief investigator is a "big, thick-voiced, pompous man, with a horrible unfeeling pleasure in hearing himself talk before an assembly of frightened, silent people."

Collins's attempts throughout his life to make a career in the theater were not successful. Many of his attempts to dramatize his own novels failed either to find a producer or to hold an audience, but the theatrical experiments were beneficial to his work as a novelist and contributed to the effectiveness of such superb set scenes as the opening of *The Woman in White* and the dramatic intensity with which he maintains suspense in the major novels.

No doubt the most important personal event of the late 1850s was Collins's liaison with Caroline Graves, a widow with a child. As related by John G. Millais in his biography of his father (1899), their meeting was dramatic: in the late summer of 1855, as Collins, his brother, and John Everett Millais were walking to Millais's studio in Gower Street in north London, they were startled by a woman's scream from the garden of a nearby house:

> It was evidently the cry of a woman in distress; and while pausing to consider what they should do, the iron gate leading to the garden was dashed open, and from it came the figure of a young and very beautiful woman dressed in flowing white robes that shone in the moonlight. She seemed to float rather than to run in their direction, and, on coming up to the three young men, she paused for a moment in an attitude of supplication and terror. Then, suddenly seeming to recollect herself, she suddenly moved on and vanished in the shadows cast upon the road.

Collins ran after the woman and did not reappear until the next day, when he told his friends that she had been kept prisoner for several months by a man who used "threats and mesmeric influence" to prevent her escape. Whatever truth there may be in this story, and it resembles the opening chapter of *The Woman in White* far too closely to be accepted without reservations, Collins's meeting with Caroline, however it may have occurred, effected significant change in his life. Cautiously, he remained living at home with his mother and brother until 1859, when he set up housekeeping with Caroline and her daughter, Lizzie. The move restricted Collins's extensive social life—his mother was a noted hostess—because his friends, although sympathetic, did not introduce Caroline to their wives. Millais concluded his account of her with typical Victo-

rian reticence: "Her subsequent history, interesting as it is, is not for these pages." The conspiracy of silence with which Collins's friends and acquaintances treated his affair and the absence of letters to Caroline or his later mistress, Martha Rudd, account for the paucity of information about his private life. In 1868 Caroline married Joseph Clow, a plumber, and Collins formed a liaison with Rudd, who became the mother of his three children (born in 1869, 1871, and 1874). Caroline's marriage was apparently unsuccessful, and by the early 1870s she was again living with Collins. At his death he left the income from his estate divided between Caroline and Martha and their three children, who were acknowledged in his will. It seems fairly certain that Collins's sympathetic fictional treatment of illegitimacy and the problems of fallen women, as well as his frequently caustic comments about those who confused morality with respectability, reflect his personal situation and his sensitivity to the difficulties faced by the two women in his life. The reasons for his personal antipathy to marriage are not known, but both his long and lively bachelorhood and the rheumatic gout from which he began to suffer in the mid 1850s, and which led to an eventual addiction to laudanum, may have produced an aversion to the responsibilities of marriage and sustained domesticity.

The contributions of his relationship to Caroline to his career are purely conjectural, but the decade of the 1860s did mark the end of his apprenticeship and inaugurated the period of his greatest success. *The Woman in White*, serialized in *All the Year Round* (successor to *Household Words*) from 26 November 1859 to 25 August 1860, and published in book form by Sampson Low in August 1860, was his most popular book and one of the most popular novels of the century. The first impression sold out on the day of publication and was followed by six impressions in the next six months. Public acclaim was shared by such notable figures as Prince Albert (who sent a copy to Baron Stockmar), William Gladstone, William Thackeray (who read it straight through), and Dickens, who told Collins that he found it "a very great advance on all your former writing." "Woman in White" cloaks, bonnets, perfumes, waltzes, and quadrilles became the rage. This gratifying popular acclaim was, however, diminished by negative critical responses to the novel. While most critics agreed that *The Woman in White* was "in point of intricacy a masterpiece" and praised its maintenance of suspense, many agreed with

*The evil count and Lady Laura, drawing by an unknown artist of a scene
from the 1871 dramatic version of* The Woman in White

the *Saturday Review* that Collins was "an admirable story-teller . . . not a great novelist." The Victorian distinction between the novel of incident and the novel of character worked to Collins's disadvantage, and although he himself professed contempt for such criticism, it is significant that in the preface to *The Moonstone* he wrote that he was attempting "to trace the influence of character on circumstances" rather than "the influence of circumstances upon character" as he had previously done. Modern criticism, following Henry James, sees plot and character as inseparably interrelated and is perhaps better able to understand Collins's achievement than either he or his contemporaries. This is especially true of the narrative technique used in both *The Woman in White* and his second masterpiece, *The Moonstone*. Contemporaries recognized that multiple narrators contributed to the dramatic development of the story and to its "lifelike" quality without, apparently, seeing that Collins—in making subjectivity and the peculiarities of perception central to his method—had made not only a major advance in the possibilities of narrative, but had also devised a method for the revelation of personality that is inextricable from plot.

The Woman in White contains two secrets: the first, of secondary importance, is the identity of Anne Catherick (the title character); the second, and chief motivation for the novel's main action, is the illegitimacy of Sir Percival Glyde. Sir Percival marries Laura Fairlie to gain access to her income and then, when that proves insufficient to meet his debts and because he thinks she knows his secret, imprisons her in a private asylum under Anne Catherick's name and buries the dead Anne under Laura's name. In these nefarious activities he is aided, or, one might better say, masterminded, by the most engaging villain in Victorian fiction, the Italian Count Fosco, and opposed by one of its most fascinating heroines, Marian Halcombe, who "has the foresight and the resolution of a man," and Walter Hartright, the drawing master whose love for Laura and desire to restore her identity make him an amateur detective of outstanding ability. Collins's use of a witness as narrator not only enriches the novel but emphasizes the legal predicament of Laura and the desperate position of married women who were, as John Stuart Mill said, "legal slaves." It is the fat and charming Fosco, surrounded by his pet white mice, who presents Collins's indictment of Victorian marriage; in defense of his wife's part in his Machiavellian schemes he says, "I ask if a woman's marriage obligations in this country provide for her private opinion of her husband's principles? No! They charge her unreservedly to love, honour, and obey him." Fosco too reminds Marian that "English Society . . . is as often the accomplice as it is the enemy of crime. . . ." Even the contrast between the pathetic Laura, a typical Victorian heroine in her submissive and dutiful attitude toward her father's memory, and the "masculine" but effective Marian reveals the independence of Collins's approach to female characterization. *The Woman in White* is indeed superb suspense fiction; but, like all major Victorian novels, it embodies serious comment on contemporary society. The law, as Walter Hartright says in the opening narrative, is "the pre-engaged servant of the long purse," and the novel displays a knowing appreciation of the problems of the powerless and their lack of protection under the law. Suspense and social significance are soundly embedded in character. The haunting figure of Anne Catherick, weak and terrified after her escape from an asylum, appears to Hartright on Hampstead Heath and establishes immediately an atmosphere of secrecy and fear. The mystery of her paternity, her resemblance to Laura, and the relationship between her hypocritical, selfish mother and Sir Percival link past and present. Mrs. Catherick, whose desire for social acceptance and financial security has made her the ally of Sir Percival, shares with him and Fosco a facade of respectability which cloaks an unscrupulous nature. Deception is the key here as it is in *No Name* (1862) and *Armadale* (1866). Seemingly prosperous Blackwater Park is debt ridden, the suave and gentlemanly Count Fosco is villainous, and Laura's beloved father is an adulterer. In *The Woman in White* Collins questions definitions of reality and shows how the limitations of personality entrap and mislead; people see, he says, not what *is* but what *seems* to be or what they *wish* to see.

Disguise, deception, and legal injustice are the mainsprings of the action in *No Name*, where Collins once again describes a world where reality blurs, shifts, and alters. Life itself is an amateur theatrical where characters play out assigned or chosen roles. The placid and happy Vanstone family of Combe-Raven is legally no family at all; an unfortunate early marriage precluded Mr. Vanstone's marrying the woman he loves and with whom he lives in perfect amicability for a quarter century. Because of the ability of "Mrs."

Vanstone "to resolve firmly, scheme patiently, and act promptly," they are able to live publicly as man and wife. They are eventually able to marry, but since Mr. Vanstone is killed in a train wreck before he can change his will, and she dies in childbirth, their two daughters are disinherited, and his fortune passes to his brother. The elder daughter, Norah, becomes a governess, and she accepts her fate. Her younger sister, Magdalen, who shares with other heroines of sensation fiction a marked deviation from acceptable models of female behavior and an exceptional talent as an actress, joins forces with a swindler named Captain Wragge. She does this to earn money through a series of dramatic performances and then marries, under an assumed name, her cousin and thus regains possession of her name and her father's fortune. Her conspiracy fails when her husband discovers her identity and disinherits her; but Magdalen, who is perhaps the most spirited and attractive of all Collins's heroines, is charming even when deceitful. Wragge, a comic and successful scoundrel, his slow-witted and childishly affectionate wife, and the pusillanimous Noel Vanstone (Magdalen's miserly cousin) contribute to the success of *No Name*, which blends humor, pathos, suspense, and social commentary.

Although some reviewers felt that Magdalen did not suffer severely enough for her sinful activities, critical response to *No Name* was reasonably favorable and its popular success so great that Collins was given a five-thousand-pound advance for his next novel, *Armadale* (of which T. S. Eliot said, "it has no merit beyond melodrama, and it has every merit melodrama can have"). It is the most intricately plotted of Collins's novels. While some contemporary critics objected to the foreshadowing dream which gives the novel its basic structure as arbitrary and unbelievable, a view shared by Eliot, who called the technique one of "spurious fatality," most attacked the book's morality. The characterization of Lydia Gwilt, a beautiful, scheming, criminal heroine, bore the brunt of critical attack: H. F. Chorley asked, "What artist would choose vermin as his subjects?" The *Spectator* called her "fouler than the refuse of the streets" and accused Collins of overstepping "the limits of decency" and revolting "every human sentiment." Far too complicated to summarize with any accuracy, the plot involves two young men both named Allan Armadale, the foreshadowing dream which indicates that one will, like his father before him, be murdered, and the involved

*"The Master of Sensation," caricature of Collins by
Adriano Cecioni (* Vanity Fair, *February 1872)*

plans of Miss Gwilt to marry one and become a
rich widow. Modern readers, who tend to share
Victorian critics' feelings that the novel is
overplotted, find Lydia Gwilt fascinating; as
twentieth-century critic Julian Symons puts it, she
may be " 'wild and strange' . . . yet she is drawn
with a conviction and assurance that compel belief."

In 1868 the second of Collins's great novels,
The Moonstone, appeared. No novel considered a
detective story has received such praise or held
its public over such a period of time. Again using
multiple narrators, Collins limited the focus of
this novel to one event, the disappearance of the
fabulous Indian diamond of the title. Through
skillful revelation of detail, varied and consistently interesting characterization, and a highly original denouement, he constructed a perfectly plotted fiction, which is (as modern criticism has
demonstrated) also a study of the unconscious
mind and the limitations of individual perception. From the opening scene in India where the
diamond is stolen from a Hindu temple, to the discovery of the villain murdered in a squalid East
End rooming house, every clue has been fairly
given, but each clue is so enmeshed in the per-

sonal peculiarities of its narrator that the reader
is apt to misinterpret its importance. Collins sub-
verts the old maxim that seeing is believing and
shows that truth is more complex and reality less
easily discernible than the reader may have
thought.

The characters in *The Moonstone* are individuals. The heroine, Rachel Verinder, is a vivacious
and independent-minded young woman who is described by family steward Gabriel Betteredge as
her own worst enemy and her own best friend because of her "secrecy" and "self-will." The hero
is Franklin Blake, whose dogged pursuit of evidence that will clear him of suspicion of theft
impresses the reader. Betteredge's devotion to
Robinson Crusoe, his jaundiced view of matrimony,
and his understanding that "Gentlefolks have a
very awkward rock ahead in life—the rock of
their own idleness" distinguish him from the
usual family retainer. Collins's sympathy for the
lower classes is evident in all his portrayals of servants but appears nowhere more compellingly
than in Rosanna Spearman, the lame former
thief whose hopeless love for Blake is both dignified and pathetic and whose suicide in the Shiver-
ing Sand is one of the most memorable moments
in the story. Religious fanatic Drusilla Clack is a
paradigm of her species, a frustrated spinster
who sees sin everywhere and whose excessive admiration for philanthropist Godfrey Ablewhite
first warns the reader of Ablewhite's true nature.
Collins's satirical view of organized charity is presented with humor, but his critical attitude toward it is nonetheless clear. Miss Clack says of
the Select Committee of the Mothers' Small-
Clothes-Conversion Society, "The object of this excellent Charity is . . . to rescue unredeemed fathers' trousers from the pawnbroker, and to
prevent their resumption on the part of the irre-
claimable parent, by abridging them immediately
to suit the proportions of the innocent son."
Ablewhite, though not as original a villain as
Fosco, is a smooth-tongued hypocrite and ideally
suited to his part; like most of Collins's villains,
he presents a respectable facade to conceal his
criminal activities. Few novels present such an
abundance of memorable characters, but perhaps
in terms of subsequent influence Sergeant Cuff,
the detective, is most important. Astute, experienced, and devoted to the culture of roses, Sergeant Cuff is, as T. S. Eliot says, "the ancestor of
the healthy generation of amiable, efficient, professional but fallible inspectors of fiction among
whom we live today." Cuff 's failure to solve the

crime is oddly appealing. Ezra Jennings, the doctor's assistant who is an opium addict and whose experiences parallel Collins's own, discovers the series of clues which reveal the identity of the criminal through a process closely approximating Freudian word-association techniques. Contemporary critics, obtuse as usual, repeated their praise of Collins's ingenuity and puzzle-making ability without understanding either the originality of his narrative method or his psychological perceptiveness.

Integrating suspense and social criticism proved a difficult and often impossible feat for Collins in his later years. He had made a reading tour of the United States and Canada in 1873-1874 in order to take advantage of his considerable popularity there. The tour was only moderately successful—Collins did not possess Dickens's histrionic talent nor his ability to hold an audience—and a continued decline in his health, constant pain relieved only by laudanum, and the effects of long-term addiction resulted in increasing reclusiveness in the late 1870s and 1880s. His association with Charles Reade, who replaced Dickens as a close friend and important influence after Dickens's death in 1870, is at least partially responsible for the inferior quality of his later work. The impact of Reade's melodramatic didacticism can be seen in the increasingly propagandistic tone of Collins's novels, as well as in their treatment of specific social grievances. It is also possible that critics' failure to appreciate the seriousness of his work and their dismissal of him as a mere entertainer encouraged the erroneous belief that attention to social problems might strengthen his reputation. The results were unfortunate. Swinburne's famous couplet, while unfair, sums up what many critics, contemporary and modern, have seen as the central flaw in the novels that followed *The Moonstone*:

> What brought good Wilkie's genius nigh perdition?
> Some demon whispered—Wilkie! have a mission.

Margaret Oliphant, one of the more intelligent Victorian commentators on Collins, expressed a similar view: his "strength, which lies in plot and complication, does not lend itself to polemics."

In *Man and Wife* (1870), Collins's novel after *The Moonstone*—and one showing the weakening of his talent—he addresses himself to three actual public grievances: the inconsistency and ambiguity of the Irish and Scottish marriage laws; the English property laws which gave a husband con-

trol of his wife's earnings and possessions; and the cult of athleticism. The most powerful portion of the novel concerns Hester Dethridge, a working-class woman who, after years of abuse, murders her husband in order to keep control of her wages. The weakest portion of the novel concerns Geoffrey Delamayne, a famous athlete who seduces Anne Sylvester and, when their Scottish marriage by intent is proved valid, plots to murder her in order to marry a woman with an income of ten thousand pounds a year. Collins offers no explanation for Delamayne's decline from public hero to would-be murderer except his devotion to sports. In his condemnation of athleticism Collins badly overstates his case: "The manhood and muscle of England resemble the wool and mutton of England in this respect; that there is almost as much variety in a flock of athletes as in a flock of sheep." His discussion of marriage laws, treated in the relationship between Delamayne and Anne Sylvester, is preceded by analysis of the situation of Anne's mother. Her husband, desirous of finding a wife who could aid his aspirations to a parliamentary career, found a loophole in the Irish statutes under which they were wed and disowned her and their child. The involvement of both mother and daughter in similar predicaments strains credibility, but Collins's characterization of women, as usual, is good, and the portrayal of Hester Dethridge's long struggle to survive the brutal treatment of a drunken husband is moving, even though the method which she uses to murder him detracts from the intensity of her sufferings.

In subsequent novels Collins wove plots around such topical subjects as the fallen woman, divorce, antivivisection, the relationship between heredity and environment, and a woman's place in the business world. *Poor Miss Finch* (1872), written to demonstrate that physical handicaps could be a source of happiness, has what is perhaps the most implausible plot in English fiction: Lucilla Finch, blind since early childhood, when she developed a morbid horror of dark colors, falls in love with Oscar Dubourg. She recovers her sight shortly after a series of medical treatments have turned him dark blue. Fortunately, Lucilla's blindness returns, Oscar's twin brother's plot to win her hand is foiled, and she finds happiness since she cannot see her lover. The novel was popular with the public, as Collins's novels continued to be. His outstanding failure was *The Fallen Leaves* (1879), which features a hero called Amelius Goldenheart and his love for a redeemed prosti-

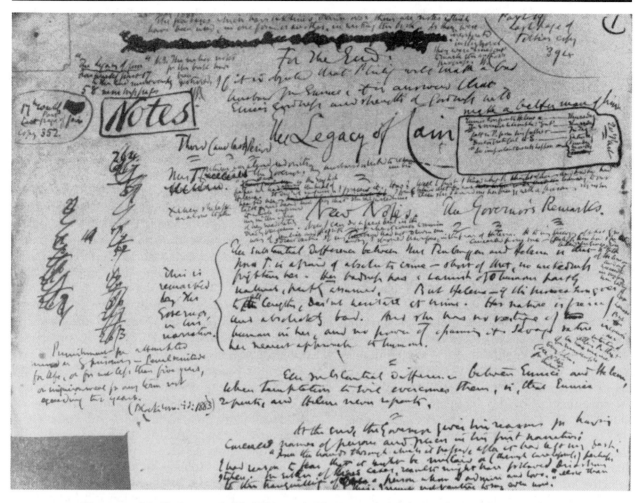

First page of Collins's notes for his 1888 novel, The Legacy of Cain *(Durham University Library)*

tute named Simple Sally; Swinburne found it "ludicrously loathsome." *The New Magdalen* (1873) employs the deception theme; Mercy Merrick, a former prostitute, assumes the identity of Lady Janet Roy and, despite exposure, wins the affection of her employer and the hand in marriage of Julian Gray, a renowned preacher. The novel is weakened by too sharp a contrast between the fallen woman and her respectable foil, Grace Rosenberry, whose only virtue is chastity. Collins's rejection of conventional morality is clear, but he sacrifices sound characterization to promulgate his message. Similar criticism can be made of *Heart and Science* (1883), where an oversimplified attack on vivisection yields an implicit though unintentional condemnation of scientific inquiry, and *The Legacy of Cain* (1888), where Collins's misunderstanding of Darwinian theory creates an untenable hypothesis—that the daughter of a murderess will inherit her criminal tendencies—and a forced contrast between the evil daughter of a

minister and the good daughter of the murderess.

Among the most interesting of the later novels is *Jezebel's Daughter* (1880), which, although marred by a melodramatic conclusion in the Frankfurt deadhouse, offers a striking portrait of a frustrated woman whose natural abilities have no outlet. Unhappily married to a physician who has devoted himself to chemical research in a provincial German town, Madame Fontaine finds her social ambitions thwarted and chafes at the restricted boundaries of her life. She writes to a friend: "Gossip and scandal, with an eternal accompaniment of knitting, are not to my taste, and while I strictly attend to my domestic duties, I do not consider them as constituting, in connection with tea-drinking, the one great interest of a woman's life." She sublimates her frustrations first in purchasing expensive goods and then in becoming a poisoner. When Madame Fontaine first administers poison, she says, "The Power that I have dreamed of is mine at last!" By contrasting her unfulfilled life with that of Mrs. Wagner, who becomes on her husband's death "sole successor" and senior partner in his import-export firm, Collins gives explicit form to his long-held aversion to the social and economic restrictions placed on women. His sympathetic presentation of a socially ostracized divorced woman in *The Evil Genius* (1886) expresses his continuing concern with the destructive effects of an uncharitable moral code. Collins's discussion of the problems of women and his portrayals of independent, capable women who defy the Victorian stereotype irritated many of his contemporaries who found his unconventional approach immoral, but these things have been singled out as two of his major achievements by modern critics tired of the pallid, insipid heroines so common in Victorian fiction.

Of special interest to readers of mystery fiction are two late novels. *The Law and the Lady* (1875) is the first English detective story with a female protagonist. Valeria Woodville, with the help of a family lawyer, successfully undertakes the investigation of the death of her husband's first wife. *My Lady's Money and Percy the Prophet* (1877), although weakly plotted, reveals the influence of Émile Gaboriau in its detective, Old Sharon, modeled upon Père Tabaret, the elderly detective of his *The Widow Lerouge* (1873), and it is unique in that the vital clue is discovered by a dog. Of the later novelettes, "Mr. Policeman and the Cook" deserves mention. Written in confessional form, the story follows a young policeman through the investigation of his first murder case. His admirable determination to solve the murder after his superiors have given up produces an ironic result: the criminal is his own fiancée.

Despite the inferior quality of Collins's later works, he continued to be popular with the public and was widely reviewed in influential periodicals and newspapers. His last years, marred by deteriorating eyesight and the constant pain of rheumatic gout, were not happy, but he continued working until his death, on 23 September 1889, from a stroke. He was buried at Kensal Green Cemetery. The inscription on his tombstone reads, by his own direction, his full name, the dates of his birth and death, and the words "Author of the Woman in White and Other Works of Fiction."

The obituaries which followed Collins's death emphasized his skill as a storyteller and expressed gratitude for the delight which he had given audiences for forty years. Swinburne called him a "genuine artist" of the second rank, comparable in merit to Anthony Trollope and Charles Reade. Although his reputation, like that of many other Victorian writers, was in eclipse during the early twentieth century, it began to revive in the 1920s, when T. S. Eliot turned critical attention to his work. Today his reputation is secure with both academic critics and the mystery-story reading public.

The lasting significance of Collins's work, aside from its intrinsic merit, lies in its fusion of the romantic and the realistic and its creation of suspense and terror in ordinary, middle-class settings. In *The Moonstone* Gabriel Betteredge questions the intrusion of crime into "our quiet English house": "Whosoever heard of it—in the nineteenth century, mind, in an age of progress, and in a country which rejoices in the blessings of the British constitution?" The most cursory familiarity with mystery and detective fiction, from Sir Arthur Conan Doyle through Agatha Christie and Sayers to the present, reveals the crucial importance of Collins's domestication of criminal activities and the great debt which subsequent authors owe to his emphasis upon the actual. By integrating accurate depiction of contemporary manners and customs with the secrecy and romance of crime, he established a pattern which modern writers of mystery fiction still follow.

Bibliography:
Kirk H. Beetz, *Wilkie Collins: An Annotated Bibliography* (Metuchen, N.J. & London: Scarecrow Press, 1978).

References:
R. V. Andrew, "A Wilkie Collins Check-List," *English Studies in Africa*, 3 (March 1960): 79-98;
Robert Ashley, *Wilkie Collins* (New York: Roy, 1952);
Ashley, "Wilkie Collins," in *Victorian Fiction: A Second Guide to Research*, edited by George H. Ford (New York: Modern Language Association, 1978);
Ashley, "Wilkie Collins and the Detective Story," *Nineteenth-Century Fiction*, 6 (June 1951): 47-60;
Bradford A. Booth, "Wilkie Collins and the Art of Fiction," *Nineteenth-Century Fiction*, 6 (September 1951): 131-143;
Robert Louis Brannan, ed., *Under the Management of Mr. Charles Dickens: His Production of "The*

Frozen Deep" (Ithaca, N.Y.: Cornell University Press, 1966);

Nuel Pharr Davis, *The Life of Wilkie Collins* (Urbana: University of Illinois Press, 1956);

T. S. Eliot, "Wilkie Collins and Dickens," in *Selected Essays* (New York: Harcourt, Brace & World, 1964);

S. M. Ellis, *Wilkie Collins, LeFanu, and Others* (London: Constable, 1931);

Winifred Hughes, "Wilkie Collins: The Triumph of the Detective," in her *The Maniac in the Cellar: Sensation Novels of the 1860s* (Princeton: Princeton University Press, 1980), pp. 137-165;

Albert D. Hutter, "Dreams, Transformations, and Literature: The Implications of Detective Fiction," *Victorian Studies*, 8 (1975): 181-209;

Clyde K. Hyder, "Wilkie Collins and The Woman in White," *PMLA*, 54 (March 1939): 297-303;

Walter M. Kendrick, "The Sensationalism of *The Woman in White*," *Nineteenth-Century Fiction*, 32 (1977): 18-35;

U. C. Knoepflmacher, "The Counterworld of Victorian Fiction and *The Woman in White*," in *The Worlds of Victorian Fiction*, edited by Jerome H. Buckley (Cambridge, Mass.: Harvard University Press, 1975), pp. 351-369;

Gavin Lambert, *The Dangerous Edge* (London: Barrie & Jenkins, 1975);

Lewis Lawson, "Wilkie Collins and *The Moonstone*," *American Imago*, 20 (Spring 1963): 61-79;

Sue Lonoff, "Charles Dickens and Wilkie Collins," *Nineteenth-Century Fiction*, 35 (1980): 150-170;

Dougald B. MacEachen, "Wilkie Collins and British Law," *Nineteenth-Century Fiction*, 5 (1950): 121-139;

MacEachen, "Wilkie Collins' *Heart and Science* and the Vivisection Controversy," *Victorian Newsletter*, no. 29 (Spring 1966): 22-25;

William Marshall, *Wilkie Collins* (New York: Twayne, 1970);

C. H. Muller, "Incident and Characterization in *The Woman in White*," *Unisa English Studies*, 11, no. 2 (1973): 33-50;

Muller, "Victorian Sensationalism: The Short Stories of Wilkie Collins," *Unisa English Studies*, 11, no. 1 (1973): 12-24;

Ian Ousby, "Wilkie Collins and Other Sensation Novelists," in his *Bloodhounds of Heaven: The Detective in English Fiction from Godwin to Doyle* (Cambridge, Mass.: Harvard University Press, 1976), pp. 111-136;

Norman Page, ed., *Wilkie Collins: The Critical Heritage* (London: Routledge & Kegan Paul, 1974);

Walter C. Philips, *Dickens, Reade, and Collins: Sensation Novelists* (New York: Columbia University Press, 1919);

John R. Reed, "English Imperialism and the Unacknowledged Crime of *The Moonstone*," *Clio*, 2 (June 1973): 281-290;

Kenneth Robinson, *Wilkie Collins, A Biography* (London: Bodley Head, 1951);

Charles Rycroft, "A Detective Story: Psychoanalytic Observations," *Psychoanalytic Quarterly*, 26 (1957): 229-245;

Dorothy L. Sayers, *Wilkie Collins: A Critical and Biographical Study*, edited by E. H. Gregory (Toledo, Ohio: The Friends of the University of Toledo Libraries, 1977);

Jenny Bourne Taylor, *In the Secret Theatre of Home: Wilkie Collins, Sensation Narrative, and Nineteenth-Century Psychology* (London & New York: Routledge, 1988).

Papers:

Princeton University Library holds letters, manuscripts, and other papers of Wilkie Collins. Columbia University Library holds the correspondence of Collins and Henry Rider Haggard in a collection of Haggard papers.

Charles Dickens

(7 February 1812 - 9 June 1870)

This entry was updated by George H. Ford (University of Rochester) from his entry in
DLB 21: Victorian Novelists Before 1885.

See also the Dickens entries in DLB 55: Victorian Prose Writers Before 1867 *and* DLB 70: British Mystery Writers, 1860-1919.

BOOKS: *Sketches by Boz, Illustrative of Every-Day Life and Every-Day People* (first series, 2 volumes, London: Macrone, 1836; second series, London: Macrone, 1837); republished as *Watkins Tottle and Other Sketches Illustrative of Every-Day Life and Every-Day People*, 2 volumes (Philadelphia: Carey, Lea & Blanchard, 1837) and *The Tuggs's at Ramsgate and Other Sketches Illustrative of Every Day People* (Philadelphia: Carey, Lea & Blanchard, 1837);

The Village Coquettes: A Comic Opera in Two Acts, as "Boz," with music by John Hullah (London: Bentley, 1836);

The Posthumous Papers of the Pickwick Club, Edited by "Boz" (20 monthly parts, London: Chapman & Hall, 1836-1837; 26 monthly parts, New York: Turney, 1836-1838);

The Strange Gentleman: A Comic Burletta, in Two Acts, as "Boz" (London: Chapman & Hall, 1837);

The Life and Adventures of Nicholas Nickleby (20 monthly parts, London: Chapman & Hall, 1837-1839; 20 monthly parts, Philadelphia: Lea & Blanchard, 1839);

Sketches of Young Gentlemen, Dedicated to the Young Ladies (London: Chapman & Hall, 1838);

Memoirs of Joseph Grimaldi, Edited by "Boz," 2 volumes (London: Bentley, 1838; Philadelphia: Carey, Lea & Blanchard, 1838);

Oliver Twist; or, The Parish Boy's Progress, by "Boz" (3 volumes, London: Bentley, 1838-1839; 2 volumes, Philadelphia: Carey, Lea & Blanchard, 1839);

Sketches of Young Couples, with an Urgent Remonstrance to the Gentlemen of England (Being Bachelors or Widowers), on the Present Alarming Crisis (London: Chapman & Hall, 1840);

The Old Curiosity Shop (2 volumes, London: Chapman & Hall, 1841); published in part as *Mas-*

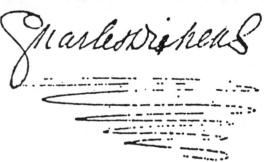

ter Humphrey's Clock (Philadelphia: Lea & Blanchard, 1840); republished in full as *Master Humphrey's Clock* (Philadelphia: Lea & Blanchard, 1841);

Barnaby Rudge: A Tale of the Riots of 'Eighty (London: Chapman & Hall, 1841; Philadelphia: Lea & Blanchard, 1841);

American Notes for General Circulation (2 volumes, London: Chapman & Hall, 1842; 1 volume, New York: Harper, 1842);

The Life and Adventures of Martin Chuzzlewit (20 monthly parts, London: Chapman & Hall, 1842-1844; 1 volume, New York: Harper, 1844);

A Christmas Carol, in Prose: Being a Ghost Story of Christmas (London: Chapman & Hall, 1843; Philadelphia: Carey & Hart, 1844);

The Chimes: A Goblin Story of Some Bells That Rang an Old Year Out and a New Year In (London: Chapman & Hall, 1845; New York: Harper, 1845);

Pictures from Italy (London: Bradbury & Evans, 1846); republished as *Travelling Letters: Written on the Road* (New York: Wiley & Putnam, 1846);

The Cricket on the Hearth: A Fairy Tale of Home (London: Bradbury & Evans, 1846; New York: Harper, 1846);

The Battle of Life: A Love Story (London: Bradbury & Evans, 1846; New York: Wiley & Putnam, 1847);

Dealings with the Firm of Dombey and Son, Wholesale, Retail, and for Exportation (20 monthly parts, London: Bradbury & Evans, 1846-1848); 20 in 19 monthly parts (parts 1-17, New York: Wiley & Putnam, 1846-1847; parts 18-19, New York: Wiley, 1848);

The Haunted Man and the Ghost's Bargain: A Fancy for Christmas-time (London: Bradbury & Evans, 1848; Philadelphia: Althemus, 1848);

The Personal History of David Copperfield (20 monthly parts, London: Bradbury & Evans, 1849-1850; Philadelphia: Lea & Blanchard, 1851);

A Child's History of England (3 volumes, London: Bradbury & Evans, 1852-1854; 2 volumes, New York: Harper, 1853-1854);

Bleak House (20 monthly parts, London: Bradbury & Evans, 1852-1853; 1 volume, New York: Harper, 1853);

Hard Times: For These Times (London: Bradbury & Evans, 1854; New York: McElrath, 1854);

The Holly-Tree Inn, by Dickens and Wilkie Collins, *Household Words* (Christmas 1855); (New York: Dix & Edwards, 1855);

Little Dorrit (20 monthly parts, London: Bradbury & Evans, 1855-1857; 1 volume, Philadelphia: Peterson, 1857);

After Dark, by Collins, includes material by Dickens, 2 volumes (London: Smith, Elder, 1856; New York: Dick & Fitzgerald, 1856);

The Wreck of the Golden Mary, by Dickens and Collins (London: Bradbury & Evans, 1856);

The Two Apprentices. With a History of Their Lazy Tour, by Dickens and Collins (Philadelphia: Peterson, 1857); republished in *The Lazy Tour of Two Idle Apprentices. No Thoroughfare. The Perils of Certain English Prisoners* (London: Chapman & Hall, 1890);

A Tale of Two Cities (London: Chapman & Hall, 1859; Philadelphia: Peterson, 1859);

Great Expectations (3 volumes, London: Chapman & Hall, 1861; 1 volume, Philadelphia: Peterson, 1861);

The Uncommercial Traveller (London: Chapman & Hall, 1861; New York: Sheldon, 1865);

Our Mutual Friend (20 monthly parts, London: Chapman & Hall, 1864-1865; 1 volume, New York: Harper, 1865);

Reprinted Pieces (New York: Hearst's International Library, 1867);

Hunted Down: A Story, with Some Account of Thomas Griffiths Wainewright, The Poisoner (London: Hotten, 1870; Philadelphia: Peterson, 1870);

The Mystery of Edwin Drood (6 monthly parts, London: Chapman & Hall, 1870; 1 volume, Boston: Fields, Osgood, 1870);

A Child's Dream of a Star (Boston: Fields, Osgood, 1871);

Is She His Wife?, or, Something Singular: A Comic Burletta in One Act (Boston: Osgood, 1877);

No Thoroughfare. A Drama in Five Acts, by Collins, Charles Fechter, and Dickens (New York: DeWitt, n.d.); republished in *The Lazy Tour of Two Idle Apprentices. No Thoroughfare. The Perils of Certain English Prisoners* (London: Chapman & Hall, 1890);

The Life of Our Lord (New York: Simon & Schuster, 1934);

The Speeches of Charles Dickens, edited by K. J. Fielding (Oxford: Clarendon Press, 1960);

Under the Management of Mr. Charles Dickens: His Production of "The Frozen Deep," by Dickens and Collins, edited by Robert Louis Brannan (Ithaca, N.Y.: Cornell University Press, 1966);

Uncollected Writings from Household Words, 1850-1859, 2 volumes (Bloomington: Indiana University Press, 1968; London: Allen Lane, 1969);

Charles Dickens' Book of Memoranda: A Photographic and Typographic Facsimile of the Notebook Begun in January 1855, transcribed and annotated by Fred Kaplan (New York: New York

Public Library; Astor, Lenox and Tilden Foundations, 1981).

Collections: *Cheap Edition of the Works of Mr. Charles Dickens* (12 volumes, London: Chapman & Hall, 1847-1852; 3 volumes, London: Bradbury & Evans, 1858);

The Charles Dickens Edition, 21 volumes (London: Chapman & Hall, 1867-1875);

The Works of Charles Dickens, 21 volumes (London: Macmillan, 1892-1925);

The Works of Charles Dickens, Gadshill Edition, 36 volumes (London: Chapman & Hall / New York: Scribners, 1897-1908);

The Nonesuch Edition, edited by Arthur Waugh and others, 23 volumes (London: Nonesuch Press, 1937-1938);

The New Oxford Illustrated Dickens, 21 volumes (Oxford: Oxford University Press, 1947-1958);

The Clarendon Dickens, edited by Kathleen Tillotson and others, 7 volumes, ongoing (Oxford: Clarendon Press, 1966-   ).

PLAY PRODUCTIONS: *The Strange Gentleman*, London, St. James's Theatre, 29 September 1836;

The Village Coquettes, London, St. James's Theatre, 6 December 1836;

Is She His Wife?, or, Something Singular, London, St. James's Theatre, 6 March 1837;

The Lighthouse, by Wilkie Collins and Dickens, London, Tavistock House, 16 June 1855; London, Olympic Theatre, 10 August 1857;

The Frozen Deep, by Collins and Dickens, London, Tavistock House, 6 January 1857; London, Olympic Theatre, 27 October 1866;

No Thoroughfare, by Collins, Charles Fechter, and Dickens, London, Adelphi Theatre, 26 December 1867;

The Battle of Life, London, Gaiety Theatre, 26 December 1873;

The Old Curiosity Shop, London, Opera Comique, 12 January 1884.

The life story of Charles Dickens is, from several perspectives, a success story. Generally regarded today as one of the greatest novelists in the English language, Dickens had the unusual good fortune to have been recognized by his contemporaries as well as by posterity. He was not one of the neglected artists such as John Keats, doomed to wait for later generations to discover his stature. Instead, Dickens's *The Posthumous Papers of the Pickwick Club* (1836-1837), which began publication when he was twenty-four years old,

was a phenomenally popular success on both sides of the Atlantic. Before he was thirty, when he had already produced five vastly scaled novels, he came to America for a visit and was accorded the most triumphant reception ever staged for a foreign visitor. As the newspapers reported, even the enthusiastic reception of General Lafayette in 1824 did not equal the way Dickens was received. His success was also reflected in his earnings: in the 1850s Dickens was making as much as eleven hundred pounds for one of his novels, a figure to be contrasted with the mere six hundred pounds earned in a year by his eminent contemporary and fellow novelist William Makepeace Thackeray. After his death the success story continued. During the more than 120-year period since then there have been times, of course, when his status among critical readers declined markedly, as during the decades following his death and during the early years of the twentieth century. Since 1950, however, the curve of his reputation has shot upward so high that recently there has been more written about Dickens each year than about any other author in the English language except William Shakespeare.

In the history of novel writing, Dickens's early start stands out as especially unusual. Poets and musicians often create significant compositions in their youth. Novelists, contrariwise (at least major novelists), are generally late starters, perhaps because novel writing calls for perspectives of a special sort. The explanation for Dickens's early start is provided by the all-purpose word *genius*, with which the young man was evidently abundantly endowed. But genius in novel writing needs experiences to work with, painful experiences as well as pleasant ones. It was Dickens's fortune to have encountered both sorts while still a youth. Dickens's ancestry included a mixture of servants and office workers. His paternal grandfather, who died before Dickens was born, had been a steward in an aristocratic estate where Dickens's grandmother (who died when the boy was twelve) had been the housekeeper. One of her two sons, John Dickens (1785-1851), who had grown up on this country estate, obtained employment in London at the pay office of the British navy, a position that necessitated his moving to other localities from time to time. John Dickens was to be immortalized many years later by his son's portrait of him as Mr. Micawber. He reputedly resembled Micawber in loquaciousness and in pseudoelegance of man-

Charles Dickens's parents, Elizabeth Barrow Dickens and John Dickens (Dickens Fellowship)

ner, as well as in his fondness for libations—all of which make him sound like the father of another literary genius, James Joyce. In 1809 John Dickens married Elizabeth Barrow (1789-1863), whose father also worked in the pay office. Years later she, too, would be the model for one of her son's characters, the fast-chattering Mrs. Nickleby. With two such talkers for parents, the son was to have a more than adequate early exposure to the spoken voice.

Eight children were born to John and Elizabeth, the first, Frances (Fanny), in 1810, and the second, Charles, more than a year later. His birthplace was a house in Portsmouth, a town to which his father had been transferred some time previously. Except for a short stay in London, Dickens's boyhood was passed in towns on the south coast of England, especially in the twin towns of Rochester and Chatham, where the family settled when he was five. This pocket of preindustrial England had a powerful impact on Dickens's attitudes. He is conventionally thought of as the novelist of the big city, which he was; but it is noteworthy that during the last ten years of his life he chose to live not in London but near the town of Rochester, in Kent, in the region where he had spent his boyhood. Here in the town of Chatham he had attended a good school; discovered his favorite novelists, such as Tobias Smollett; and generally enjoyed himself.

He did suffer from bouts of ill health; and sometimes he was afraid to go to bed after listening to the hair-raising bedtime stories inflicted on him by the nurse, especially a story called "Captain Murderer." Nevertheless, these first eleven years were happy ones.

This idyll was shattered after his family moved to London, where his father's casual mismanagement of his income finally led to his imprisonment for debt and to his twelve-year-old son's being sent to work in a blacking warehouse. The boy's job consisted of pasting labels on bottles of black shoe polish, this menial job being performed near a window within sight of passersby on the street. Living alone in cheap lodgings and nearly starving, Charles was overwhelmed with a sense of having been willfully abandoned by his parents and sentenced to remain in a rat hole for life. That his novels would be full of characters who are orphans is not surprising. The blacking warehouse experience lasted in reality only about twelve months, but to the boy, and to the grown man in retrospect, the time seemed endless. As he wrote in his autobiography more than twenty years later: "I never had the courage to go back to the place where my servitude began. . . . My old way home by the borough made me cry, after my eldest child could speak." Eventually he was rescued by his father, who had acquired some funds, and was sent to a school in London

149

Old Hungerford Stairs, near the blacking warehouse where Dickens spent several miserable months of his boyhood

from the ages of twelve to fifteen. His mother, strangely unaware of her son's feelings, wanted him to stay at work rather than resume school, and Dickens never forgave her for her failure to provide the love and understanding he most desperately needed. A further twist of the knife had occurred before the ordeal was over. His older sister, Frances, had been fortunate enough to be enrolled in the Royal Academy of Music before her father was imprisoned and to continue her studies there while Charles worked in the warehouse. In June 1824 she was awarded a silver medal for her excellent playing and singing. Her young brother was present at the awards ceremony, and, as he later wrote, he "felt as if my heart were rent. I prayed . . . that night, to be lifted out of the humiliation and neglect in which I was."

The importance of these unhappy experiences, especially in a career so seemingly happy and successful, cannot be exaggerated; it set up in Dickens's mind a specter of insecurity that was never to disappear. These experiences may also have contributed to his zealous resolution to excel and to his almost ruthless energy in all his pursuits, in particular his writing. As he noted in a letter of 1855: "Whoever is devoted to an art must be content to deliver himself wholly up to it, and to find his recompense in it." Dickens has often been characterized as the great recorder of life in the Victorian age, or as one of its major critics, but he was also, in his energetic pursuit of his goals, the embodiment of his age, the archetypal Victorian.

With the dark world behind him, Dickens began attending school at Wellington Academy in London. It was not as good a school as the one he had attended in Chatham, but it served his purposes, and at the end of his three years there he was head of his class and the winner of a prize for Latin. At fifteen he had finished his formal education and begun a lifetime of work. The possibility that he might go on to a university was apparently never considered by anyone. One of Dickens's sons, Henry, would attend Cambridge, but he himself was to acquire learning on his own; his college was the great library of the British Museum in London, where he was admitted as a reader on his eighteenth birthday. Here he soaked himself in works of history and literature (especially Shakespeare) that would make up a storehouse of knowledge to draw upon during the busy years ahead. In sum, Dickens's education, formal and informal, did not equip him to

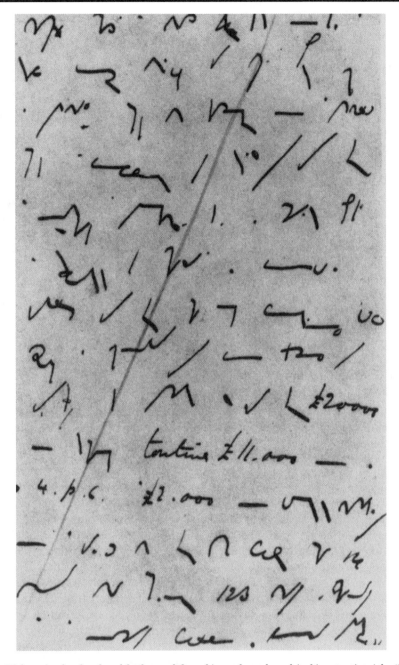

A page of notes by Dickens in the shorthand he learned from his uncle and used in his reporting jobs (Dickens Fellowship)

edit a learned journal such as the *Westminster Review* (of which George Eliot, the most erudite of novelists, would be an editor), but it did equip him to write novels. Perhaps a more extensive exposure to learning would have enabled him to write a better version of his embarrassingly crude potboiler *A Child's History of England* (1852-1854), but it is doubtful that it would have enabled him to write a better novel than the one he was writing at the same time, his great masterpiece *Bleak House* (1852-1853).

During the seven years after leaving school, the young Dickens lived at home with his family (although he was sometimes absent on trips). His experience during this apprentice period included exposure to the worlds of law, politics, journalism, and the theater. For the first two years he was a clerk in a law office, and it is remarkable how often in his novels he sets up scenes, usually comic ones, portraying the antics of junior clerks in lawyers' offices. For the next four years his employment involved the preparation of shorthand reports for lawyers who worked in Doctors' Commons. He had learned shorthand from one of his uncles, John Henry Barrow, an experienced reporter, who eventually obtained for Dickens a position as shorthand reporter in Parliament. Dickens's mastery of shorthand gained him some notoriety both for his speed and his accuracy, and these skills continued to be of use to him in his next position, that of a news reporter on the staff of the *Morning Chronicle*, which he joined in 1834. In this new role, he was frequently sent on journeys to report on election speeches in distant places. From his two years as a reporter of political events as well as from his years covering Parliament, Dickens acquired an extraordinary amount of information about the political life of his country during a crucial period following the passage of the Reform Bill of 1832. He also acquired from these experiences a realization that political oratory is often absurdly empty. During the rest of his life he was appalled at times by the ineptitude of some political leaders, but his more typical response was to find them funny, especially in their public speeches (of which he had listened to thousands). In an early sketch, "The House," he likened the House of Commons to a pantomime that was "strong in clowns." The members of Parliament, he comments, "twist and tumble about, till two, three and four o'clock in the morning; playing the strangest antics, and giving each other the funniest slaps on the face that can possibly be imagined, without evincing the smallest tokens of fatigue." The members, he adds, are "all talking, laughing, lounging, coughing, oh-ing, questioning, or groaning; presenting a conglomeration of noise and confusion, to be met with in no other place in existence, not even excepting Smithfield [the cattle market] on a market-day, or a cock-pit in its glory."

This awareness of political absurdities appears very early in Dickens's writings. In his first month as a news reporter, he had been sent to Edinburgh to report on a banquet being given in honor of Earl Grey, the retiring prime minister. Dickens's amusement on this occasion was prompted not by Grey's address but by the behavior of the dinner guests, who had become impatient because the guest of honor had not arrived on schedule. One of these guests, he reports, was so impressed by the fare available at the banquet, the "cold fowls, roast beef, lobster, and other tempting delicacies (for the dinner was a cold one)," that he decided "the best thing he could possibly do, would be to eat his dinner, while there

An illustration of a London pawnshop by George Cruikshank for Sketches by Boz

was anything to eat. He accordingly laid about him with right good-will, the example was contagious, and the clatter of knives and forks became general. Hereupon, several gentlemen, who were not hungry, cried out 'Shame!' and looked very indignant; and several gentlemen who were hungry cried 'Shame!' too, eating, nevertheless, all the while, as fast as they possibly could. In this dilemma, one of the stewards mounted a bench and feelingly represented to the delinquents the enormity of their conduct, imploring them for decency's sake, to defer the process of mastication until the arrival of Earl Grey. This address was loudly cheered, but totally unheeded; and this is, perhaps, one of the few instances on record of a dinner having been virtually concluded before it began." Dickens was only twenty-two years old when he composed this report from Edinburgh, but already developed are some of the characteristic earmarks of his mature prose style, especially the imperturbable jocularity of tone with which the absurd episode is suffused—a jocularity enhanced when, as here, the episode involves man as a political animal.

In addition to his experiences as a journalist during this period between leaving school and becoming a creative writer, the young Dickens was also deeply involved with the theater, both as a spectator and as a potential actor. If in the day-time he were committed to the law or to journal-ism, it was to the world of the footlights that he was committed at night. At the age of twenty, in fact, he decided to become an actor and wrote a let-ter to the manager of Covent Garden Theatre rec-ommending himself as endowed with "a natural power of reproducing in his own person what he observed in others." The letter led to his being in-vited for an audition to offer a sample of his histri-onic talents. When the day came, however, Dick-ens was stricken with a cold so severe that he had to excuse himself, proposing that he would reap-ply the following season. He never did reapply. Nevertheless, this incident of the audition usually prompts any admirer of Dickens's writings to a moment of reflection. Suppose the stagestruck young man had not been ill that day? Suppose that he had made a triumphant appearance? Might he have been lost to literature? As he him-self remarked in a letter: "See how near I may have been to another life." And in his novel *Great Expectations* (1861) almost thirty years later, there is a passage about how one day in our lives can make changes lasting a lifetime. His protagonist Pip reflects about having spent his first day with the beautiful girl Estella: "That was a memorable day to me, for it made great changes in me. But it is the same with any life. Imagine one selected day struck out of it, and think how different its course would have been." Happily, the young man was, of course, not lost to literature; in fact, it was only a few months after that memorable day of the nonaudition that he was to send his first literary effort to a publisher.

In 1830 Dickens was introduced into the household of George Beadnell, a prosperous banker, and his wife and their three daughters. The youngest daughter, Maria, was twenty years old, and with her the eighteen-year-old Dickens fell overwhelmingly in love. Writing to her three years later, Dickens still affirmed: "I never have loved and I never can love any human creature breathing but yourself." The relationship devel-oped happily for some time, and at the outset, Maria was apparently encouraging with her teen-aged suitor. But by 1832 her parents began to dis-courage his attentions, perhaps having heard re-ports about his father's unreliability, or perhaps on the grounds that Dickens himself did not seem to have suitable prospects. In any event, Maria was sent abroad to a finishing school in

Catherine (Kate) Dickens, drawn by Daniel Maclise shortly after her marriage to Dickens (Dickens Fellowship)

Paris, and after her return, her interest in Dick-ens had cooled altogether. In March 1833 he re-turned all the letters she had written to him, la-menting his fate and reminding her, with a flourish, that she had been "the object of my first, and my last love." The infatuation lasted four years, and the frustrations of the relation-ship were even more painful for Dickens to look back upon than were his experiences in the black-ing warehouse. His best friend and biographer, John Forster, at first found this story of Dickens's adolescent love to be incredible, especially incredi-ble being the importance that the mature Dick-ens ascribed to it in his development. Only gradu-ally did Forster come to realize how hurt his friend had been by a sense of social inferiority in this thwarted early love affair. The depth and long-lasting quality of these feelings are evident in the fact that while Dickens decided to share with Forster the autobiographical fragment he had written about his blacking warehouse experi-ences, he could not bring himself to share what he had written about the Maria Beadnell epi-sode; and a few years later, he simply burned it.

One of the lasting effects of the thwarting

A page from the manuscript for The Pickwick Papers. *The chapter should be numbered XXXVII; the error appeared in the serial publication but was subsequently corrected (Sotheby's auction catalogue, 23 November 1971).*

was its influence on his desire to succeed and to become financially secure, just as David Copperfield, in his novel, would be impelled to strenuous efforts to succeed. As Dickens explained to Forster: "I went at it with a determination to overcome all the difficulties, which fairly lifted me up into that newspaper life, and floated me away over a hundred men's heads." When at last Dickens tried his hand at literature, the same driving energies persisted: with his pen he would show those unseeing banking Beadnells (by heaven!) what a paragon they had missed being allied to. But first he had to pass through his liter-

ary apprenticeship as he had passed through his earlier apprenticeships to law, journalism, and the stage. During the three years before launching his first full-length novel, Dickens was learning the craft of literature by writing occasional short pieces which he called sketches. Some of these pieces tell a story; others are simply descriptions of London localities such as Newgate Prison or Monmouth Street (the shopping center for secondhand clothing); and others offer portraits of picturesque characters such as a cabdriver or a circus clown.

The first sketch, "A Dinner at Poplar Walk," was submitted for publication in late 1833, when

Dickens was twenty-one, and appeared in the *Monthly Magazine* in January 1834. Later in life he looked back upon the excitement he had felt on those occasions. This first sketch, he recalled, had been "dropped stealthily one evening at twilight, with fear and trembling, into a dark letter-box, in a dark office, up a dark court in Fleet Street." Some weeks later, when he bought a copy of the magazine and saw his sketch "in all the glory of print," he was overcome with emotion. "I walked down to Westminster Hall, and turned into it for half-an-hour, because my eyes were so dimmed with joy and pride, that they could not bear the street, and were not fit to be seen there." The emotional satisfaction of seeing his sketch in print was the only reward Dickens received for this publication; indeed, he received no payments whatever for the first nine of his sketches, which were all published in the *Monthly Magazine*. Thereafter, having established his literary credentials, he was able to require payments for his efforts when they appeared in magazines or newspapers and receive further payments when the sketches were collected and published in volumes in 1836. There were some sixty sketches in all, making up two volumes entitled *Sketches by Boz*. The pen name of Boz, used for this first publication, continued to be used to refer to Dickens by affectionate readers throughout his lifetime, even though the true identity of Boz had been established by the summer of 1836. The name was borrowed from the nickname that Dickens devised for his youngest brother, Augustus, calling him "Moses" after one of the Primrose children in Oliver Goldsmith's *Vicar of Wakefield* (1766). Augustus mispronounced this name as "Boses," which was shortened to "Bose" and eventually to "Boz" (which is pronounced as rhyming with "laws" rather than with "foes").

Sketches by Boz was well received by reviewers and had an encouraging sale. The favorable reception was partly attributable to the witty illustrations provided by George Cruikshank (1792-1878), the most popular illustrator of the period and an artist whose established reputation was especially helpful for a hitherto unknown writer. Many years later the two men became estranged, but in this earlier period they were good friends. Cruikshank was also Dickens's illustrator for *Oliver Twist* (1838-1839) and *Memoirs of Joseph Grimaldi* (1838). In any event, the initial collaboration worked well, and the *Sketches by Boz* caught the eye of several well-pleased reviewers. One of

the first of these recommended it in particular to American readers because the volume would "save them the trouble of reading some hundred dull-written tomes on England, as it is a perfect picture of the morals, manners, habits of a great portion of English society." He added: "It is hardly possible to conceive of a more pleasantly reading book." Another reviewer noted that although parts of the book picture the "wretchedness" of London's slums, the writer's disposition "leads him to look on the bright and sunny side of things." Most acutely, this reviewer described Dickens as "a close and acute observer of character and manners, with a strong sense of the ridiculous."

This review, appearing in the *Morning Chronicle* on 11 February 1836, gave Dickens a special degree of pleasure because of its having been written by George Hogarth, his prospective father-in-law. Hogarth (1783-1870) was a cultivated man of many talents. After working some years as a lawyer in Edinburgh, where he had connections with Sir Walter Scott, he gave up law for journalism and moved to England as a newspaper editor. He was also an accomplished musician and the author of books and articles about music. In 1834 he and Dickens came to know each other at the offices of the *Morning Chronicle*, and Dickens was soon a frequent visitor at Hogarth's house, where he met the eldest daughter, Catherine (1815-1879), who was called Kate. George Hogarth was an admirer of the *Sketches by Boz* (as his review indicated), knowing them "by heart," as Dickens remarked. Dickens, in turn, became an admirer of Hogarth's pretty daughter. Early in 1835 he became engaged to her, and in April 1836 they were married. Kate's appearance at this time was described by a woman who had known her: she was "plump and fresh-coloured; with . . . large, heavy-lidded blue eyes." Her mouth was "small, round and red-lipped, with a genial smiling expression of countenance, notwithstanding the sleepy look of the slow-moving eyes." During the year of their engagement, however, there were many occasions when Kate's expression must have been no longer genial and smiling, for her hardworking fiance was frequently too busy to visit her. The curious letters he wrote to her during this period almost always involve his reporting that in order to meet some publisher's deadline, he must defer the pleasure of a visit; and if she complained of such neglect, she was likely to receive an admonishing lecture in Dickens's next letter, urging her to change her ways. One such admonishment concluded by his sounding rather like his own Mr. Pecksniff: "You may rest satisfied that I love you dearly—far too well to feel hurt by what in any one else would have annoyed me greatly." These letters to Kate are sometimes affectionate and playful, but are clearly different in tone from the passionate infatuation that Dickens had expressed during his earlier courtship of Maria Beadnell. In defense of Dickens, it may be added that his repeated references to overwork during his courtship seem altogether justifiable. To obtain and furnish suitable living quarters demanded strenuous efforts from Dickens in his various employments. By Christmas 1835 he was able to rent a suite of three rooms in Furnival's Inn, where the young couple resided for their first year of marriage. Here at Furnival's Inn, his first child was born some nine months after his honeymoon; and here, too, he completed writing his first novel, which had been taking shape during the last months of his courtship.

Dickens's shift from being a writer of sketches to a writer of novels was effected in a remarkably haphazard way. A few days after his twenty-fourth birthday in 1836, he received a proposal from Chapman and Hall, who were planning to bring out a book of illustrations by a well-known comic artist, Robert Seymour (1798-1836). What the publishers wanted from Dickens was a series of comic stories and sketches that could provide materials for Seymour to illustrate. The series would eventually appear as a book, but its first appearance would be in twenty monthly installments. Dickens at once set to work, and by late March, within a day of his marriage to Catherine Hogarth, the first installment appeared of *The Posthumous Papers of the Pickwick Club*, later to be known simply as *The Pickwick Papers*.

Seymour's guiding idea was to portray the inept antics of a group of Londoners who had organized a hunting and fishing club, a "Nimrod Club," as he called it. Dickens tried to adapt his text to Seymour's idea by including some sporting transactions in the early installments—as when one of the Pickwickians, Mr. Winkle, is ignominiously unseated by a rented horse or when he goes shooting at a country estate and bungles his handling of his gun. Such episodes were what Seymour wanted for his illustrations; but there were not to be many of them, for as Dickens had forewarned his publishers, he "was no great sportsman" even though he had been "born and partly bred in the country." As publication got under

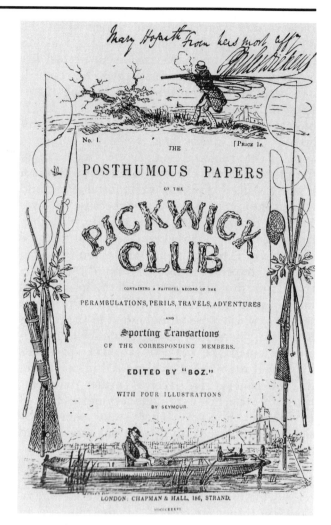

Cover of the first monthly part of Dickens's comic masterpiece, with an inscription by Dickens to his sister-in-law (Dickens Fellowship)

way, it became evident that the novelist and the illustrator were in disagreement not only about how much emphasis was to be on the comedy of country sports. Dickens gradually began taking over as manager of the whole Pickwick project, with the twenty-four-year-old novelist, not the thirty-eight-year-old illustrator, calling the shots. Otherwise, as Dickens saw it, the tail would be wagging the dog. For Seymour, who was in a state of depression, the relationship with Dickens was intolerably galling, and in April, he shot himself. One of the illustrators who applied to be Seymour's replacement was William Makepeace Thackeray, later to be Dickens's rival as leading novelist of the age, but Thackeray was passed over in favor of Hablôt Browne (1815-1882). Browne was even younger than Dickens, and there was never any question from this time on that the novelist was fully in charge of the production.

One important legacy of his having started working with Seymour was the distinctive method of publication in monthly numbers that they had adopted. As a way of publishing novels, this was an innovation, and one that gradually came to be looked upon with favor by the early Victorian reading public. All of Dickens's novels were to be published in installments; and for thirty-five years or so after *The Pickwick Papers*, other novelists, such as Thackeray, would also publish in monthly numbers. An interesting feature of serial publication was its enabling the novelist to get an early impression of how the work was being received by the public. *The Pickwick Papers* looked at first like a loser: the opening chapters failed to attract attention, and only five hundred copies of the second installment were printed. Some months later, the publishers were frantically trying to print enough copies to meet the demands of thousands of *Pickwick Papers* enthusiasts. Of the final number (October 1837) some forty thousand copies were printed. What was the reason for this turnaround? Most of Dickens's contemporaries traced the change to the fourth number, in which he had introduced two strikingly colorful Cockney characters: Sam Weller and his father, Tony, the fat coachman. Sam's mixture of impudence and warmheartedness, and his worldly wise anecdotes purveyed in a lively Cockney accent, made him an ideal foil for Mr. Pickwick's innocent and well-intentioned benevolence. By having Sam become Mr. Pickwick's servant, Dickens had re-created an endearing pair like Sancho Panza and Don Quixote, and his readers greeted the combination with a level of enthusiasm rarely to be matched in the history of literature. *The Pickwick Papers* ended up as the most sensational triumph in nineteenth-century publishing. For a full-scale account of this triumph, the opening chapter of *Dickens and His Readers* (1955), by George H. Ford, may be consulted. As Ford shows, one of the most striking aspects of the popularity of *The Pickwick Papers* was that it appealed to all classes of readers, the highly educated as well as the poorly educated. In June 1837 one early reader, Mary Russell Mitford, recommended *The Pickwick Papers* to a friend in a letter: "It is fun—London Life—but without anything unpleasant: a lady might read it all *aloud.* . . . All the boys and girls talk his fun . . . and yet they who are of the highest taste like it the most." As an example of high taste, Miss Mitford cited a judge, Lord Denman, who "studies *Pickwick* on the bench while the jury

are deliberating." This letter provides several clues to account for the success of Dickens's first novel. That it could be read aloud, as she noted, without offensive references to sexual exploits, was an important element of Dickens's recipe. *The Pickwick Papers* was still being published in the year Victoria became queen, and its appearance coincided with a change of attitudes toward the laxity and lewdness that had been such prominent features of life and literature in the 1820s. There is plenty of hearty drinking and eating in *The Pickwick Papers*: in one scene even the saintly Mr. Pickwick imbibes so much cold punch that he passes out and awakes to find himself on exhibition in a village pound. But there are no comparable bedroom incidents in this rollicking tale, and in general the benevolence and warmheartedness of the protagonist tone down the rough horseplay of some of the scenes which resemble the so-called "novel of high spirits" written by Dickens's immediate predecessors, such as Pierce Egan (1772-1849).

Miss Mitford's mentioning of how the lord chief justice enjoyed *The Pickwick Papers* is a reminder of one of the many triumphs of this novel: its presentation of the lawyers and judges encountered by Mr. Pickwick on the occasion of his being sued for breach of promise by his landlady, Mrs. Bardell, a widow. The funniest of many funny scenes in the novel is the trial scene of *Bardell* v. *Pickwick*, featuring Mrs. Bardell's lawyer, Serjeant Buzfuz, whose ludicrously eloquent speech for the plaintiff is a magnificent parody of legalese and of courtroom tactics. After Mr. Pickwick loses the case he chooses to go to prison rather than pay the settlement, and in the scenes of life behind bars there is, of course, much less opportunity for comedy. In this part of the novel there is a sad seriousness that anticipates the prison scenes of some of the later novels, such as *Little Dorrit* (1855-1857). In fact, some solemn readers misread *The Pickwick Papers* by arguing that the prison episode is the key to the whole book and that the funny parts are finally subordinate. To reinforce their argument, they point to some of the strangely melodramatic short stories interspersed throughout the novel, such as "A Madman's Manuscript," as further examples of seriousness unmixed with comedy. Such arguments may provide a useful corrective, but a fair-minded rereading of the whole novel would suggest its limitations. Humor is the chief quality of Dickens's first novel, as his own contemporaries recognized. In his later life, after his vision had be-

Illustrations for The Pickwick Papers *by the original artist for the series, Robert Seymour (left), and by his replacement, Hablôt Browne ("Phiz")*

come a much more somber one, many of his readers wished he would return to the vein of pure comedy in which they believed *The Pickwick Papers* to have been written. Despite the successes he was to achieve with other kinds of novels, it was this early sunshine-studded tale that was probably his best-liked book among Victorian readers. In the second half of the twentieth century this evaluation no longer holds. Most admirers of Dickens now would not recommend newcomers to his work to try their teeth first on *The Pickwick Papers*; instead, they would urge postponing a reading of it until one has enjoyed some of the later writings, in which the artist is more surefooted. *The Pickwick Papers* was a kind of slapdash production, and the result, as even Miss Mitford remarked, was "rather fragmentary." The artful construction evident in such a novel as *Bleak House* is not yet developed. What is already fully developed and abundantly present in dozens of episodes is a brilliant prose style—or styles, rather— and a command of dialogue, which variously combine for delightful comic effects unsurpassed by other novelists and even by Dickens himself. "The Inimitable," as he sometimes referred to himself in fun, had earned the right to his title at

the early age of twenty-four.

Also at the age of twenty-four, Dickens began to earn enough from his writing of fiction so as to be able to give up working for the *Morning Chronicle*, which he did in November 1836. It was well that he could do so, for at this time he was absurdly overcommitted to a long list of literary projects and deadlines. Sparked by the dizzying success of *The Pickwick Papers* and by a youthful faith that his energy was unfathomable, and also aware of his new responsibilities as husband and father-to-be, Dickens had signed one agreement after another with three different publishers during 1836. The *Sketches by Boz* would be completed, fortunately, in December, but *The Pickwick Papers* was only halfway complete at this date, and an installment had to be written for every month until November 1837. Dickens had also made a loose agreement with another publisher that he would have completed a novel, "Gabriel Vardon," by November 1836! Of this novel there was no sign at this date. Indeed, it did not surface until four and a half years later, in 1841, and then with a different publisher and different title (*Barnaby Rudge*). With Richard Bentley, another publisher, he had made even more extensive commitments late in 1836: he had contracted to write two novels and also to take on the role of editor of a new magazine, *Bentley's Miscellany*—a position he held until January 1839. In late 1836 he had also tried his hand at writing the libretto for a comic opera, *The Village Coquettes*, which was performed in December and was well received for a few weeks.

One review of the opera reported that the first-night audience insisted that Boz appear onstage at the end of the performance, and there was much astonishment among those who were seeing him for the first time. They seem to have expected that he would look like one of the Pickwickians or even like Tony Weller! Instead, they saw a thin young man, of medium height, modest in manner, but with long, wavy dark hair and wearing a flamboyantly colorful dandy-style vest. His expression was one of amiability and good humor. What the audience saw that night was the Dickens still visible today in the fine portrait painted three years later by his friend Daniel Maclise (1806-1870).

The following year, 1837, was a little less frantic. It opened with the publication of the first of the twenty-four monthly installments of his second novel, *Oliver Twist*. Unlike *The Pickwick Papers* and most of Dickens's other novels, which appeared first in separate numbers with each number having its own cover, the installments of *Oliver Twist* were part of a magazine, *Bentley's Miscellany*. Although there were four more installments than had been used for *The Pickwick Papers*, each installment was considerably shorter; so the whole novel, although appearing over a period of more than two years, was also considerably shorter than *The Pickwick Papers*. But there were more significant differences between the two novels than the differences in their forms of serialization. For readers who had grown fondly accustomed to the fun and frolics of successive numbers of *The Pickwick Papers*, this new novel by Boz must have prompted a sense of shock. Most of the adventures of the young protagonist consist of a succession of encounters with the worlds of brutality and crime. The story opens with the death of Oliver's mother in a dark, cold workhouse where she has given birth to him, and the child is raised in this bleak environment under the stern management of Mr. Bumble, the beadle. As a young boy, Oliver escapes to London, where he is initiated into a gang of criminals headed by Fagin, a Jew, who has organized a group of boys into a team of pickpockets, the

George Cruikshank's illustration of Oliver Twist asking for more porridge

most expert of whom is the Artful Dodger. Fagin also receives other kinds of stolen property provided by the housebreaker and robber Bill Sikes, who lives with Nancy, a prostitute. Fagin's gang seeks to make Oliver work for them, but the boy escapes and eventually obtains protection in kindly households in the country. The novel ends with the gruesome death of Sikes after his brutal murder of his mistress and a scene of Fagin in his condemned cell in Newgate prison following his capture by the police. *Oliver Twist* thus exposes its readers to a world of crime and meanness, a dog-eat-dog world that is altogether different from the jolly world of *The Pickwick Papers*. To emphasize the difference further, this dark and sordid world is presented by Dickens from the perspective of an orphan, a lost child whose sense of bewilderment and fright reminds one of how the twelve-year-old Dickens had himself responded to the soul-crushing experiences of the blacking warehouse.

Dickens's decision to write in a mode so different from one that had already proven in his hands to be triumphantly successful must have taken a lot of nerve, for the expectation of a reading public is for the novelist to repeat. On this point there is a sympathetic comment by another successful and popular novelist, Angus Wilson, in his 1966 introductory essay on *Oliver Twist*. An "anxious question which would have pressed upon Dickens," Wilson notes, was "would his second novel maintain the fantastic popularity of *Pickwick Papers*? Every novel is a hurdle for the popular novelist, but certainly the second is the most alarming."

Dickens, however, seems to have had some good reasons for being less alarmed than might have been expected. He had chosen to write a kind of novel that had already become established as highly popular in the hands of his immediate predecessors, the so-called Newgate novel, such stories of crime and punishment as Edward Bulwer-Lytton's *Paul Clifford* (1830) or Harrison Ainsworth's *Rookwood* (1834). Indeed, it was this school of fiction that seems to have attracted him for models before he became immersed in the world of Mr. Pickwick. When he was only twenty-one, he spoke in a letter of "my proposed novel." One scholar, Kathleen Tillotson, argues persuasively that what Dickens was referring to at that date was not *The Pickwick Papers* but an incipient *Oliver Twist*, and that his second novel was, in effect, his first.

In any event the gamble paid off, by and large. Inevitably, he did lose some readers who found the whole criminal scene to be "painful and revolting," as one of them said. Another, Lady Carlisle, commented loftily: "I know there are such unfortunate beings as pick-pockets and street walkers . . . but I own I do not much wish to hear what they say to one another." A different kind of reader was put off by the prominence of the social criticism in the opening chapters, in which Dickens exposes the cruel inadequacies of workhouse life as organized by the New Poor Law of 1834. This law had been the brainchild of the Utilitarians, and anyone attacking it would call down the ire of such Utilitarian readers as Harriet Martineau. After these exceptions are granted, however, there can be no doubt that this second novel was another extraordinary success. Its greatness was different from that of *The Pickwick Papers*, but it was still incontestably greatness. In the twentieth century it has remained one of Dickens's most popular and best-known novels; as Angus Wilson said of it: "perhaps more than any other it has a combination of sensationalism and sentiment that fixes it as one of the masterpieces of pop art." As proof of this comment, one may cite the remarkable popular success of Lionel Bart's musical comedy version, *Oliver!* First staged in 1960, this work established a London record for its more than six

Portrait by Hablôt Browne of Mary Hogarth, Dickens's sister-in-law, whose death at age seventeen shattered Dickens. She was the inspiration for Little Nell in The Old Curiosity Shop *(Dickens Fellowship).*

years of performances. The film version of *Oliver!* was seen by vaster audiences, although how much the status of Dickens benefited from the film is difficult to assess inasmuch as the only reference to *Oliver Twist* occurs in the long list of credits with which the film opens. There, in the midst of the names of technicians, costume designers, and suchlike is a line in small letters announcing that the production has been freely adapted from a novel by Charles Dickens! Nevertheless, the film does have a virtue in reminding one that in the midst of the nightmare of Dickens's story there is also a good deal of comedy. In chapter 17 of *Oliver Twist*, Dickens himself comments with amusement about the combination: "It is the custom on the stage, in all good murderous melodramas, to present the tragic and the comic scenes, in as regular alternation, as the layers of red and white in a side of streaky bacon." Although his comment is only half serious, it is evident that he follows the streaky-bacon recipe in this novel by its effective appeal to both the reader's sense of humor and his sense of fear. The beadle, Mr. Bumble, for example, is on one level the despicable petty tyrant in uniform who flourished in Hitler's Germany and still flourishes in other countries. He is like the nameless master of the workhouse from whom Oliver asks for "more," and who (according to Arnold Kettle, a Marxist critic) "is not anyone in particular but every agent of an oppressive system everywhere." But as Dickens presents Bumble, he is not only frightening but also a figure of fun, as in the scene of his proposing marriage to Mrs. Corney—a hilarious incident. In the later parts of the novel, Mr. Bumble becomes the stock comic figure of the henpecked husband with the domineering wife. When told that "the law supposes that your wife acts under your direction," Mr. Bumble comments: "If the law supposes that, the law is a ass—a idiot." An even more distinctly sustained comic scene is of the Artful Dodger in court demanding his "priwileges" as an Englishman and admonishing his judges that "this ain't the shop for justice." The humor in the presentation of Fagin is more complex, at least for later readers, in view of the repeated references to him as "the Jew." Responding to accusations of anti-Semitism, Dickens pointed out that at the time of the action of *Oliver Twist* all of the fences in London were Jewish, and, more important, that the most villainous characters in his novel are Sikes and Monks, rather than Fagin. In any event, the memorable early scenes of the Merry Old Gentleman, with his toasting fork and handkerchief tricks, are funny as well as vivid.

The successful launching of *Oliver Twist* inspired Dickens in the spring of 1837 to rent a terrace house at 48 Doughty Street in Bloomsbury, where he lived for the next two and a half years before moving to a larger house on Devonshire Place. Of the three houses in London in which he lived, only the Doughty Street one has survived (although the bomb damage it suffered in World War II required considerable restoration). In 1925 it was bought as a museum by the Dickens Fellowship, and, especially recently, it has become one of the most successful literary museums in London, attracting every year thousands of visitors for a tour of its twelve small rooms, including a little back room displaying the desk on which *Oliver Twist* and *Nicholas Nickleby* were written.

The Doughty Street household consisted not only of Dickens and Kate and their child but of Kate's younger sister, Mary Hogarth, who had sometimes stayed with them earlier at Furnival's Inn to help her sister during pregnancy and to

Tombstone of George Taylor in Yorkshire, which gave Dickens the idea for the character of Smike in Nicholas Nickleby

be a companion for her brother-in-law—a not unusual arrangement in nineteenth-century families. What was unusual was the intensity of Dickens's feelings about this seventeen-year-old girl, whose animated company he had come to depend upon, and whose sweet innocence represented an ideal spirit, a shining lamp in a world of darkness. On 7 May 1837 the lamp was suddenly put out forever. After attending an evening showing of *The Village Coquettes*, the two sisters and Dickens had returned in high spirits to Doughty Street, where Mary was suddenly stricken with some unidentified illness, and the next day she died in his arms. After the funeral, he and Kate went to a country retreat for some weeks, and the numbers of both *The Pickwick Papers* and *Oliver Twist* were suspended from publication for a month.

The shock of Mary's death had profound effects on Dickens as a man and as a novelist. Until the day of his own death he wore the ring she had been wearing when she died. It was his wish that, like Heathcliff in Emily Brontë's *Wuthering*

Page from the manuscript for Nicholas Nickleby *(Sotheby's auction catalogue, 23 November 1971)*

Heights (1847), he would be buried beside her (which proved to be impossible). And for ten months he dreamed of her every night, the dreams ceasing only after a visit to Yorkshire during which he wrote to Kate about them. According to a Freudian critic, Steven Marcus, the extraordinary cessation of these nightly visions may have been prompted not merely by his reporting the phenomenon to his wife but by an experience he had in Yorkshire at this same time, of his coming across the gravestone of a boy "eighteen long years old" who, Dickens said, had "died at that wretched place. I think his ghost put Smike into my head upon the spot." Thoughts of Smike, the boy who was to die in his projected novel *The Life and Adventures of Nicholas Nickleby* (1837-1839), may thus have affected thoughts of Mary and purged the vision. For the novel following *Nicholas Nickleby*, there can be no doubt how Dickens's feelings about the life and death of Mary Hogarth shaped Little Nell's portrait and the story of her dying. As he tried to write her death scene in *The Old Curiosity Shop* (1841), he confessed in a letter: "I shan't recover from it for a long time. . . . Old wounds bleed afresh when I only think of the way of doing it. . . . Dear Mary died yesterday, when I think of this sad story." In later novels there are other young women characters who seem to be modeled on Mary Hogarth, even though they do not die. Of these women, several of whom are seventeen—Mary's age when she died—it was remarked by John Greaves, usually a most indulgent reader of Dickens, that they are "perhaps rather colourless creations."

Dickens was soon back at his desk, completing *The Pickwick Papers* late in 1837 and *Oliver Twist* in spring 1839; and then, before he was thirty, he published three more full-length novels: *Nicholas Nickleby, The Old Curiosity Shop*, and *Barnaby Rudge*. It was an extraordinary performance, and all of these novels were (*Barnaby Rudge* less so) popular and critical successes.

The main plot of *Nicholas Nickleby* involves some stock characters, heroes, and villains in stock situations of fortunes lost and found. The chief villain is a miserly businessman, Ralph Nickleby, who schemes to frustrate the career of his young nephew, Nicholas, who has come to London to seek his fortune after the death of his father. Ralph hates Nicholas and arranges for him to take a low-paying job as a teacher in Yorkshire, a job which the young man eventually quits after exposing corruption at the school. For a time Nicholas makes a living with a troupe of traveling actors headed by Mr. Vincent Crummles. On his travels Nicholas is accompanied by a crippled youth, Smike, whom he had defended at school. Later, Nicholas gets a good job in London in the office of two benevolent businessmen, the Cheeryble brothers; they introduce him to a wealthy heiress whom he finally marries. On various occasions, Nicholas prevents his uncle from carrying out wicked schemes—as, for example, his attempt to sell Kate, Nicholas's sister, to her aristocratic admirer, Lord Verisopht. Wicked Uncle Ralph finally loses his fortune and is driven to hang himself after he discovers that Smike, the unfortunate youth whom he had tried to persecute, was his own son.

In one of the best critical essays on this novel, Michael Slater admitted in 1978 that this main plot "is largely a lifeless bore" featuring some "crashing melodramatic cliches." A similar complaint was made by Dickens's best friend, John Forster, who, in reviewing the novel in 1839, contrasted its clumsy plot with Henry Fielding's *Tom Jones* (1749): "A want of plan is apparent in it from the first, an absence of design. The plot seems to have grown as the book ap-

peared by numbers, instead of having been mapped out beforehand." Both critics have put their fingers on the weakest aspect of Dickens's early novels, one that continues to be evident even in *The Life and Adventures of Martin Chuzzlewit* (1842-1844). In his later novels, fortunately, Dickens would toil to correct his clumsy construction and to shape and plan his narratives. Yet it is misleading to cite Slater and Forster on Dickens's plot without remarking that almost everything else they have to say about *Nicholas Nickleby* is enthusiastic. What sustains this novel, as they and other critics have found, is its gallery of colorful characters whose vitality charges it with energy. The best known of these was and is Wackford Squeers, the semiliterate proprietor and master of a school in Yorkshire. As with *Oliver Twist*, part of the appeal of *Nicholas Nickleby* was its exposure of some contemporary corrupt institutions. Dotheboys Hall, as Mr. Squeers's school is aptly called, was modeled in part on schools visited by Dickens in preparation for writing his novel. Also memorable is Nicholas's mother, said to have been modeled in part on Dickens's own mother. Mrs. Nickleby's loquacious monologues are full of most delightful absurdities, as are the speech and actions of some of the members of the theater troupe. Overall, *Nicholas Nickleby* is Dickens's most theatrical novel, and the theatricality is not limited to the scenes onstage. Perhaps its staginess may account for its having received "little attention from modern criticism," as Slater's essay notes. Perhaps the same quality might account for the remarkably successful stage version of *Nicholas Nickleby* put on in London and New York in 1980-1981, each two-part performance lasting a total of eight hours! Critics were astonished by how effective this awesome experiment turned out to be.

The statement about little attention being paid to *Nicholas Nickleby* in modern criticism is equally applicable to *The Old Curiosity Shop*, and, in this instance, stage or screen treatment does not modify the situation. (The 1970s film musical *Quilp* was an embarrassment.) Much of the discussion of this novel has been historical, such as George Ford's chapter "Little Nell: The Limits of Explanatory Criticism," which deals with the striking contrast between how Dickens's contemporaries responded to the life and death of Nell and how later generations have rejected that story as an absurdity. Her impact on early readers was simply overwhelming, and her death sent thousands of households into a state of mourning. Francis

Dickens in 1839, at the height of his fame, as painted by Maclise. An engraving from this portrait was used as the frontispiece to Nicholas Nickleby *(National Portrait Gallery, London).*

Jeffrey, a sophisticated and sometimes severe literary critic, was so moved by the story that he likened the young novelist to Shakespeare as a writer of great tragedy. There had been "nothing so good as Nell since Cordelia," Jeffrey affirmed. Sales figures—soaring to an unprecedented one hundred thousand copies—indicate what a hit Dickens had made. Little Nell became Dickens's trademark, a household word in England and America and also in the Russia of Fyodor Dostoyevski. In the late Victorian period there occurred a distinct shift of taste whereby Nell was no longer appreciated. Even Algernon Charles Swinburne, who idolized Dickens's writings, asserted that Nell was about as real as a child with two heads; and Oscar Wilde capped the reaction by observing that one must have a heart of stone to read the death of little Nell without laughing. In the twentieth century it has been Wilde's verdict on Nell, rather than Francis Jeffrey's, that has prevailed. A once-familiar formula for achieving success with novel readers was: "Make 'em laugh; make 'em shudder; make 'em cry." Dickens's first novel fitted the first category, and his second fitted the second. *The Old Curiosity*

Shop, his fourth novel, is best known for fitting the "cry" category, and because of what seems today to be an ineffective use of pathos in this early novel, its other qualities have tended to be overlooked. This neglect is to be regretted, for Little Nell is not the only character in *The Old Curiosity Shop*. Indeed, Nell's situation leads to her being connected with some of the most colorful characters ever created by Dickens. At the age of fourteen, she discovers that her grandfather, keeper of the Old Curiosity Shop in London, has become a maniacal gambler. In order to get him away from the moneylenders who have him in their power, the girl persuades the old man to join her on a journey on foot through the English countryside. Such a journey, as in *Nicholas Nickleby*, leads to encounters with all sorts of characters on the road, such as Mrs. Jarley, the owner of a traveling waxworks show. Nell works for Mrs. Jarley for a time before becoming ill and dying in a remote hamlet, where her repentant grandfather soon follows her into his own grave. Even more memorable than the characters encountered on the road are the persons associated with Nell and her grandfather back in London. The chief moneylender, Daniel Quilp, is a dwarf with the head of a giant, a combination of prankster and villain, a creature who participates in some haunting scenes of terror and fun. Quilp's gouging of his victims is aided by the legal research of his lawyer, Sampson Brass, and Sampson's awesome sister, Sally—these three make a striking trio of gargoyles. In a different vein, there is the song-singing Dick Swiveller, a law clerk who works in the offices of the Brasses. Dick and his illiterate companion, a servant girl he calls "The Marchioness," provide a combination of fun with tender affection. The endearing scenes between these two outcasts show how beautifully Dickens can handle tender relations when he avoids the heavy mawkishness that mars his accounts of the affectionate nature of Little Nell.

His fifth novel, *Barnaby Rudge*, again demonstrates his versatility. In it he tries his hand at a historical novel (his other venture in this vein would be *A Tale of Two Cities* almost twenty years later). *Barnaby Rudge* is also a murder mystery, the murderer being a former servant named Rudge, who had been employed at an estate in the country. His son, Barnaby, is a picturesque half-wit, devoted to his mother and to a pet raven named Grip. During the Gordon Riots of 1780, a central incident in the novel, Barnaby is induced to join one of the mobs in London which burned and pil-

TABLEAUX VIVANS.

BOZ BALL.

February 14th, 1842.

ORDER OF THE DANCES AND TABLEAUX VIVANS.

1.—GRAND MARCH.

2.—TABLEAU VIVANT—"Mrs. Leo Hunter's dress *déjeûné*."

" ' Is it possible that I have really the gratification of beholding Mr. Pickwick himself?' ejaculated Mrs. Leo Hunter. ' No other, ma'am,' replied Mr. Pickwick, bowing very low. ' Permit me to introduce my friends—Mr. Tupman—Mr. Winkle—Mr. Snodgrass—to the authoress of the ' expiring frog.' "—*Pickwick Papers.*

3.—AMELIE QUADRILLE.

4.—TABLEAU VIVANT—" The middle-aged lady in the double-bedded room."

"The only way in which Mr. Pickwick could catch a glimpse of his mysterious visiter, with the least danger of being seen himself, was by creeping on to a bed, and peeping out from between the curtains on the opposite side. To this manœuvre he accordingly resorted.— Keeping the curtains carefully closed with his hand, so that nothing more of him could be seen than his face and night-cap, and putting on his spectacles, he mustered up courage, and looked out.— Mr. Pickwick almost fainted with horror and dismay. Standing before the dressing-glass, was a middle-aged lady in yellow curl-papers, busily engaged in brushing what ladies call their ' back hair.' It was quite clear that she contemplated remaining there for the night; for she brought a rush-light and shade with her, which, with praiseworthy precaution against fire, she had stationed in a basin on the floor, where it was glimmering away, like a gigantic lighthouse in a particularly small piece of water.'

5.—QUADRILLE WALTZ—selections.

6.—TABLEAU VIVANT—" Mrs. Bardell faints in Mr. Pickwick's arms."

" ' Oh, you kind, good, playful dear,' said Mrs. Bardell, and without more ado she rose from her chair and flung her arms round Mr. Pickwick's neck, with a cataract of tears and a chorus of sobs. ' Bless my soul !' cried the astonished Mr. Pickwick. ' Mrs. Bardell, my good woman—dear me—what a situation—pray, consider—Mrs. Bardell, don't—if any body should come !—' —' Oh ! let them come,' exclaimed Mrs. Bardell, frantically ; ' I'll never leave you— dear, kind, good soul.' And with these words, Mrs. Bardell clung the tighter. ' Mercy upon me,' said Mr. Pickwick, struggling violently ; ' I hear somebody coming up the stairs. Don't—don't, there's a good creature don't !' But entreaty and remonstrance were alike unavailing ; for Mrs. Bardell had fainted in Mr. Pickwick's arms ; and before he could gain time to deposit her in a chair, Master Bardell entered the room, ushering in Mr. Tupman, Mr. Winkle and Mr. Snodgrass."

Program page for the Boz Ball given in Dickens's honor in New York during his first visit to America (Harry Ransom Humanities Research Center, University of Texas, Austin)

laged the houses and property of Roman Catholic citizens. For his part in the rioting Barnaby is sentenced to death, although he is finally granted a reprieve. This story of civic anarchy had a special appeal for Dickens's contemporaries because of its relevance to political and economic conditions in England during the 1840s. A severe economic depression during the "Hungry Forties," together with the spread of the radical Chartist movement, inspired among the ruling classes a dread of violent rioting. *Barnaby Rudge* was thus a topical novel and fared well. In recent decades it has not continued to do so. In 1970, for example, a survey was made of publishers in the United States and England to discover the sales figures for Dickens's novels: *Barnaby Rudge* was at the bottom of the list of fifteen novels in both countries. Nevertheless, a few critics have made high claims for it: Angus Wilson's opinion is that it represents "the turning point in Dickens's growth from an extraordinary to a great novelist." Wilson's comment also dates from 1970, and perhaps this novel will be treated to fresh reappraisals in future decades.

Mention needs to be made of the distinctive way in which *Barnaby Rudge* was published. Like *The Old Curiosity Shop*, it appeared in weekly installments in *Master Humphrey's Clock*, a special kind of periodical that Dickens had launched in April 1840. Early in the previous year he had given up being editor of *Bentley's Miscellany*, but the urge to run a periodical remained with him and, if done successfully, would—he hoped—enable him to take a rest from writing novels. The rest, however, was very short-lived. His original aim with *Master Humphrey's Clock* had been to feature assorted sketches, essays, and episodes, rather than to provide another full-length novel; it was to be somewhat in the vein of Joseph Addison's *Spectator* papers—much beloved by Dickens. But the scheme did not find favor with the public, and Dickens found himself back at his novelist's desk. His hoped-for rest from the labors of novel writing had to be postponed until January 1842, when he and Kate sailed to America, leaving their children with friends. For the next five months, the only writings he would turn out were letters home to friends and family.

After his tour of America, Dickens claimed that he had traveled some ten thousand miles. The exaggeration was pardonable, for he and Kate did cover a lot of territory. After landing in Boston, they spent considerable time on the eastern seaboard in New York, Philadelphia, and Washington, followed by a brief excursion into the slave states ending at Richmond, Virginia. More adventurously, they traveled west by riverboat from Pittsburgh to Saint Louis, where they saw a prairie. The return route included crossing Ohio by coach, a visit to Toronto and Montreal, and back to New York via Lake Champlain. What Dickens was seeking was a rest from novel writing and also, presumably, some materials for a travel book to be written at a later date. He did not come to America to lecture or, as he did in 1868, to offer paid public readings. In 1842 he spoke at only a few banquets, and such performances were not for pay. On this first visit he came simply to see and to be seen.

Maclise's sketch of Dickens reading The Chimes *to his friends at John Forster's house in London, December 1844*
(Dickens Fellowship)

His reactions to the American scene changed dramatically during these five months. In January and February he was as enthusiastic about America as Americans were enthusiastic about him. By June he was almost totally disillusioned. Because his two books about America were written after disillusionment had set in, they do not give a reliable account of the change in his opinions. The most effective way of following what happened is to read Dickens's letters and to watch a love match gradually turning sour. When he arrived in Boston he was an ardent pro-American, full of great expectations. Politically, Dickens is always hard to categorize, but at this stage he could be described as a Liberal-Radical, impatient with the whole English establishment of aristocratic privilege. In a letter he speaks of the "swine-headed" obstinacy of George III and notes how lucky Americans are to live in a "kingless country freed from the shackles of class rule." A self-made man, Dickens rejoiced to be in a country in which the self-made man seemed to be king. The *New York Herald* responded by asserting: "Dickens's mind is American—his soul is republican—his heart is democratic." But within two months the honeymoon was over, and Dickens's letters are full of laments about the failure of the American ex-

periment. Slavery appalled him, and so did Congress: Washington, he said, is where one encounters "slavery, spittoons, and senators." Above all, American newspapers appalled him. In an early speech, he had ventured to make a reasonable plea for international copyright, whereupon many newspapers set about attacking him viciously. Upon reading such "unmanly" attacks Dickens commented: "I have never in my life been so shocked and disgusted." Despite his enjoyment of hospitality and many friendly encounters (his closest friendship was with Cornelius Felton, a professor of classics at Harvard), Dickens's overall response to America was one of keen disappointment. On the ship from New York back to England he encountered some steerage passengers who had tried living in America and had found the environment hostile. "They had gone out to New York," Dickens says, "expecting to find its streets paved with gold; and had found them paved with very hard and very real stones." Metaphorically at least, Dickens's own experience during his five-month visit resembled the experiences of these returning immigrants.

Dickens landed in England on 29 June 1842. After six months of vacation he was eager to resume his writing schedule. Following a happy reunion with children and friends in London, the family moved to Broadstairs for the summer. This "little fishing town on the sea coast," as Dickens described it in a letter, had become since 1837 a favorite summer locality in which to rent a house for himself and his family. Ideal working conditions were combined at Broadstairs with the relaxations of long walks and sea bathing. Here he began work on his two-volume travel book *American Notes for General Circulation*, which he completed in a burst of speed and published in October 1842. The book sold well and was usually reviewed with approval. Thomas Hood observed that the work would please any readers who could be "content with good sense, good feeling, good fun, and good writing." Nothing in the book, he said, had been "set down in malice." This verdict might be generally shared by later readers. Knowing from his letters how critical he had eventually become about America, one can watch his efforts to tone down his disappointment and to be fair. About the American newspapers, however, there was no pulling of punches, and with good cause. On 11 August there appeared on the front page of a New York paper a forged letter purportedly written by Dickens consisting of diatribes against his American hosts, and many Americans were taken in by it. The effect of this scurrilous trick was to give edge to Dickens's attacks on American journalism in the *American Notes*. The press in America responded predictably to Dickens's criticisms, as did some private individuals. Most of Dickens's American admirers, however, accepted the book as a fair sketch, although many of them would not accept what he was to say about America in his next novel, *The Life and Adventures of Martin Chuzzlewit*.

Martin Chuzzlewit is the first novel by Dickens that is unified by a theme, although this unification is only loosely sustained. Its theme is selfishness. As originally conceived, the novel would confine its examples of selfishness to the English scene. The young protagonist, Martin, suffers from a mild infection of selfishness, but he is finally cured of it and thereby reaps his reward by becoming heir to his Grandfather Chuzzlewit's fortune. Other characters infected with selfishness are represented as incurable. The most striking of these are Seth Pecksniff and Jonas Chuzzlewit. Pecksniff professes to be a teacher of architecture (Martin is one of his students for a time), but in this role, as in all others, he is a colorful and eloquent fraud, the arch-embodiment of the hypocrite—and also, it must be added, a great comic creation. Jonas Chuzzlewit is much less a

comic figure. A greedy man of business who murders his father, Jonas has as his motto: "Do other men, for they would do you." Less clearly allied to the theme is a gin-drinking nurse, the immortal Mrs. Gamp, who fulfills her need for praise by inventing an imaginary spokesman, Mrs. Harris, whom she quotes with pleasurable relish. Her praises are also voiced by the undertaker, Mr. Mould, who observes that Mrs. Gamp is the sort of woman one would bury for nothing, and do it neatly, too.

Although Mrs. Gamp and Pecksniff are two of Dickens's most memorable creations, the novel in which they appear was not well received. Some years earlier a reviewer had said of the author of *The Pickwick Papers* that "he has risen like a rocket, and will come down like the stick." Not until this sixth novel, however, did the prediction seem to come true. Sales of the early installments were alarmingly poor, and reviews were alarmingly hostile. In an effort to give his failing novel a turnaround with his public, Dickens hit upon a scheme to have his protagonist seek his fortune in America, where further exhibits of selfishness would be abundantly available. The American scenes in *Martin Chuzzlewit* are open-stopped satire, beginning with Martin's arrival in America and encounter with the shouting newsboys: "Here's this morning's New York Sewer! Here's this morning's New York Stabber! . . . Here's the New York Keyhole Reporter!" The scenes of Martin in the swampy land development called Eden bring to mind Gulliver among the Yahoos. But however powerful as satire, even these American episodes did not generate satisfaction with the work on the part of the English reading public; and in America, as Thomas Carlyle said in his picturesque vein: "All Yankee-Doodle-Dum blew up like one universal soda-bottle."

In the midst of these discouragements in 1843, Dickens found a way to restore his sagging self-confidence. Instead of beginning another novel, he tried his hand at a short fable also dealing, like *Martin Chuzzlewit*, with the theme of selfishness. It was the first and best of his Christmas books, *A Christmas Carol*, which caught on at once and has become his most widely known piece of writing. It illustrates most effectively his theory that a Christmas fable should exhibit what he called "fancy" in ways that would be inappropriate in the more realistic world of a long novel. These fanciful ways include the three memorable ghosts who show Scrooge the past, present, and future.

Tavistock House, Bloomsbury, Dickens's home from 1851 until 1858

Despite the reassurance provided by the reception of his *Christmas Carol*, Dickens was ill at ease about his finances. To increase his income, he shifted to a new firm, Bradbury and Evans, who promised him more profitable contracts. But more drastic measures were required to enable him to make up for the various drains upon his earnings. One of these drains involved looking after his parents: his father, an inveterate sponger, had run up heavy debts while Dickens was in America. One of John Dickens's letters seeking a loan from Charles's bankers at this time glitters with Micawber-like flourishes: "Contemporaneous events place me in a difficulty which without some anticipatory pecuniary effort I cannot extricate myself from." The extricating was later to be performed, of course, by his son. More significant expenditures were called for by Dickens's household of wife and five children, a household recently enlarged by the addition of Kate's sixteen-year-old sister, Georgina Hogarth (1827-1917). At times Georgina reminded him strongly of Mary Hogarth, then dead for seven years—"her spirit shines out in this sister," he wrote. But Georgina was not to suffer Mary's fate; she was a

member of his household and his intimate companion until his death. "Aunt Georgy," as she was called by the children, who adored her, soon became a crucially important member of the family, reliable and energetic in ways her indolent (and frequently pregnant) sister Kate seemed unable to manage. But she, like all members of the household, needed to be provided for, and one efficient way of doing so, in Dickens's view, was to sublet his London house and to move his "whole menagerie" to the Continent for a year's residence, where living expenses would be less than half what they were in England. In July 1844 they settled in Genoa, traveling there via Paris and Marseilles. This year in Italy was devoted primarily to sight-seeing and traveling. Eventually, it would provide materials for his second travel book, *Pictures from Italy*, published in May 1846. On the whole, it was a period of rest for Dickens. His only significant writing was his second Christmas book, *The Chimes* (1845), a short fable relating to the "Condition of England Question" with emphasis upon the inhumanity of Utilitarian theories of social and economic relationships. In November he returned to London to try out the

An illustration by "Phiz" for Bleak House

story by reading it aloud to a group of his friends, who were overwhelmed by his performance.

In July 1845 the whole family returned to England. During the next eleven months, Dickens continued to abstain from writing novels; instead, he completed his Italian travel book and also his third Christmas story, *The Cricket on the Hearth* (1846). Much of his time was taken up with other pursuits. In October he accepted the editorship of a newly founded liberal newspaper, the *Daily News*. Hardly had the paper begun publication in January 1846 when Dickens resigned from the editorship, having discovered that he was temperamentally unsuited for the position. Much more successful were his ventures into amateur acting. In 1845 he and a group of friends successfully produced Ben Jonson's *Every Man in his Humour* with Dickens playing Bobadil, as well as being director and stage manager. Dickens reveled in this chance to act before an audience, and for the rest of his life he welcomed opportunities to throw himself into performing in farces and tragedies.

In the summer of 1846 Dickens again moved his whole family to the Continent, this time to Switzerland. One of the worst of his Christmas stories, *The Battle of Life* (1846), was written during this period, and also one of his better novels, *Dombey and Son* (1846-1848). There is a noteworthy gap of four years between his launching of this novel and the start of his previous novel, *Martin Chuzzlewit*. His pace of writing was thus strikingly different from the sprawling productivity of his earlier years, and this restraint affected the quality of his art as a novelist. Philip Collins notes that there is today a "critical consensus" that *Dombey and Son* is Dickens's "first mature masterpiece." It is also the first of his novels in which the action occurs at about the same date as when it was published, rather than being set in earlier decades: in *Dombey and Son* the characters travel by railroad rather than by stagecoach. Indeed, as Steven Marcus states in his brilliant chapter on this novel, the railroad is one of the two "massive images" around which the story is organized, the other being the sea. Both images are associated with change—overall change in social and economic life, and, in particular, change in the life of a family, "a single and rather small family as it persists through time." The head of this family, Mr. Dombey, is a proud man of business and the

Mrs. Maria Winter, the former Maria Beadnell, Dickens's first love and the model for Flora Finching in Little Dorrit *(Dickens Fellowship)*

widowed father of two children. The younger child, Paul, is doted upon by his father; the older child, Florence, who herself dotes on her father, is strangely resented by him and treated with an icy coldness that chills the whole household. Mr. Dombey suffers a terrible blow when little Paul dies shortly after beginning school, and a further blow when his second wife, Edith, runs away from home to have an affair with one of his employees. Finally, his family business, the House of Dombey, collapses into bankruptcy. At the end, having his eyes opened by such adversities, Dombey learns the real value of his daughter's steady devotion to him; with her and her husband, Walter Gay, he will spend the rest of his days. Perhaps the title might more appropriately have been "Dombey and Daughter," for it is the complex relationship between Florence Dombey and her father that is the central concern of this mature novel.

The generally high regard in which the story of Mr. Dombey and his children is held by modern critics was anticipated by its reception among its first readers. After the relative failure of *Martin Chuzzlewit*, the response to *Dombey and Son* was reassuring to Dickens. The critical reaction was generally enthusiastic, and the sales were like earlier days. In fact, after this novel, the gnawing anxieties about financial survival

which had plagued him in the early 1840s were no longer a serious issue. From this time forward, to all intents and purposes, he was secure.

In April 1847, in the midst of writing *Dombey and Son*, he had again returned to England from the Continent but this time was disinclined to write his expected Christmas story (which he postponed until 1848, when it would appear under the title *The Haunted Man and the Ghost's Bargain*, the last of these stories). Much of his energy was expended in 1847 upon a charitable project fostered by Baroness Burdett-Coutts, a wealthy heiress. The project aimed to provide a friendly shelter for prostitutes seeking rehabilitation. Urania Cottage, as the shelter was named by Dickens, also served as a refuge for other women in distress. Urania Cottage was but one of several good works participated in by Dickens in his role as responsible citizen. He was also concerned with such problems as water pollution, as in his speeches before the Metropolitan Sanitary Association in the 1850s, and with popular education, as advocated in his speeches to working-class audiences. He served as a trustee of a fund to assist retired actors, and he was a founder of the Guild of Literature and Art. Some of these causes called for unobtrusively working behind the scenes; others called for more conspicuous performances as a public speaker, and all reports indicate that Dickens was a superb speaker and an extraordinarily effective advocate. (The collection of his speeches edited by K. J. Fielding in 1960 gives some idea of his powers of persuasion.)

Despite these diversions, his principal efforts during the two remaining decades of his life were expended on the writing of novels. Following the final number of *Dombey and Son* there was a rest period of about a year before the fresh and delightful opening number of *The Personal History of David Copperfield* was published in May 1849. It was an immediate hit, and after seven months, Dickens could report in a letter: "I think it is better liked than any of my other books." According to Edgar Johnson, it is still today "the best-loved of all Dickens' novels" and it was Dickens's own "favourite child." Part of its appeal depends on its use of the first person, an innovation in the Dickens canon, which is handled with consummate skill, especially in the scenes of David's childhood. George Orwell reports that when he first began reading this novel at the age of nine, its mental atmosphere was "so immediately intelligible" that he thought it must have been written "by a child." Also innovative, for Dickens, is that

Dickens (on the ground) acting in a play he coauthored with Wilkie Collins, The Frozen Deep, *as depicted in the* Illustrated London News, *17 January 1857*

here is a true Bildungsroman; the protagonist changes and develops and learns, as contrasted with the static character of Oliver Twist. Perhaps most skillful of all is how Dickens combines personal history with imagined characters and events. The core of the novel is the autobiographical fragment about his experiences in the blacking warehouse, and in those blacking scenes of *David Copperfield* it could be said that David *is* the boy Charles. But most of the novel is not based on historical correspondence. Even in the character of the protagonist there are marked differences from that of his creator: combined with his demonstrated tenderness there was in Dickens a hard, almost ruthless streak which is omitted entirely from the character of his consistently gentle hero. This difference in character results, in turn, in a different attitude toward the exposure of the wrongs of social institutions. There is hence less crusading in this work than in most of Dickens's novels—except, perhaps, *Great Expectations*, his other first-person Bildungsroman, which also features a gentle protagonist as narrator.

David Copperfield is one of Dickens's novels that is commonly read in childhood. Among

other qualities it has the virtues of a children's classic: it is memorable because of the special kind of fears it arouses, as in the scenes with Mr. Murdstone or Mr. Creakle, or even the gargoylelike menacings of Uriah Heep; it is memorable, too, for its fun. But *David Copperfield* is also a classic for adults; and while continuing to respond to its frightening parts and its wonderful humor, one may find, as George Ford suggests in an essay, upon rereading it as grown-ups, that this is a sadder book than one had remembered it to be. "Dickens himself recognized its predominant tone when in later years he was looking back over his own life from the lonely pinnacle of the monumentally successful man, and asked: 'Why is it, that as with poor David, a sense comes always crushing on me now, when I fall into low spirits, as of one happiness that I have missed in life, and one friend and companion I have never made?' All the steam that rises from Mr. Micawber's delectable hot rum punch cannot obscure the nostalgic impression, in almost every chapter, of roads not taken and of doors that never opened."

If satirical exposures of institutional inadequacies were kept to the minimum in *David*

Ellen Ternan, the actress who became Dickens's mistress, around the time of their first meeting, in 1857 (Enthoven Collection, Victoria and Albert Museum)

Copperfield, Dickens seems to have decided to make up for his restraint when he began writing his next novel, *Bleak House*. This work seethes with discontents sometimes expressed in fiery invectives, discontents which are also prominent in others of his novels of the 1850s and 1860s: *Hard Times* (1854), *Little Dorrit*, and *Our Mutual Friend* (1864-1865). This group, anticipated by *Dombey and Son*, was labeled by Lionel Stevenson as Dickens's "Dark Period" novels, and the term seems apt. What is strange about the chronology, however, is that the 1850s and 1860s, economically and in other areas, were not a dark period, but rather a rare bright one. These were decades when the English seemed at last to have solved some of the big problems that had looked to be insoluble in the 1830s and 1840s. As the historian G. M. Young has said: "Of all the decades in our history, a wise man would choose the eighteen-fifties to be young in."

Dickens evidently would not have agreed with Young's cheerful report; he preferred to write as an angry outsider, critical of the shortcomings (as he saw them) of mid-Victorian values. Predictably, these Dark Period novels cost him some

readers who felt that the attacks on institutions were misguided, unfair, and finally, tiresome. Such a reader was Fitzjames Stephen, whose irritated response to Dickens's account of the Circumlocution Office (in *Little Dorrit*) led to his writing the nastiest review of a Dickens novel ever to appear in England during Dickens's lifetime. According to Stephen, Dickens's literary fare was simply "puppy pie and stewed cat." More temperate and representative was an article of 1857 titled "Remonstrance with Dickens," lamenting all the Dark Period novels. "We admit that Mr. Dickens has a mission," writes this critic, "but it is to make the world grin, not to recreate and rehabilitate society." Citing in particular what he calls the "wilderness" of *Little Dorrit*, he adds: "We sit down and weep when we remember thee, O *Pickwick*!" Obviously not all of Dickens's contemporaries felt likewise, for among the reading public, from *Bleak House* onward, the Dark Period novels fared well, as they have continued to do in the second half of the twentieth century. In fact, these are the novels that have been chiefly responsible for the remarkable "Dickens boom," as Hillis Miller called it, of the 1960s and after. Among this group it is *Bleak House* that seems to have been most highly regarded by modern criticism.

During the thirteen-month interval between the final number of *David Copperfield* and the great opener of *Bleak House*, Dickens had been engaged in various other activities. Most important was his effort to make a success as editor of a new weekly magazine—a success that had hitherto eluded him. This time, as both owner and editor, he made it, and handsomely. *Household Words*, founded in January 1850, flourished exceedingly, with an average sale of forty thousand copies a week. Its title page announced that it was "conducted" by Charles Dickens. What this meant was that all contributions would appear anonymously, no matter how eminent the contributor, including those by Dickens himself. "Conducted" also meant the assurance for readers that Dickens had approved the contribution, whether it was a sketch, an installment of a novel, or some journalistic report on current issues such as sewage disposal or juvenile illiteracy or the role of detectives in the expanding metropolis. In his role as citizen, as well as editor, Dickens became increasingly involved with such issues during the 1850s. In 1852, in fact, he was asked to run for Parliament but decided that he could do more good for the world by sticking to his journalism in *Household Words* and to his craft as a nov-

Kate Dickens at the time of her separation from Dickens in 1858 (Gernscheim Collection)

elist in *Bleak House*. Also during this thirteen-month interval, he moved his family into a larger residence, Tavistock House, where the tenth and last of his children was born (his infant daughter, Dora, had died a few months earlier).

The narrative technique of *Bleak House* is much more experimental than that of *David Copperfield* and involves the use of two narrators. Half the book is told in the first person and is again, like *David Copperfield*, the story of one character's growing up and self-discovery—in this case the story of a girl, Esther Summerson, an illegitimate child. The other half of the novel, told in the third person, deals with lives and institutions which variously relate to Esther's story, such as what happens to her mother, Lady Dedlock, and how legal delays, enacted in the fogbound Court of Chancery, cripple the spirits and empty the pockets of generations of litigants who have been involved with the "mighty maze" of a law case known as "Jarndyce and Jarndyce." As G. K. Chesterton observes (alluding to *Hamlet*): "The whole theme is what another Englishman as jovial as Dickens defined shortly and finally as the law's delay. The fog of the first chapter never

lifts." But *Bleak House* is not only a novel of social criticism; it is also a detective novel, perhaps the first detective novel in English. The shooting death of Mr. Tulkinghorn, a lawyer, leads to a relentless hunt for the murderer directed by a colorful detective, Inspector Bucket. Among Bucket's suspects is Esther's mother, Lady Dedlock, who, although innocent of the murder, dies from exposure and exhaustion during the pursuit and finds her resting place at the grave of her former lover, Captain Hawdon. Meanwhile, Inspector Bucket tracks down the true murderer, Hortense, a Frenchwoman who had been Lady Dedlock's maid. Esther is thereafter free to marry Alan Woodcourt, a surgeon, and to reside with him in a house that is, despite its name—"Bleak House"—a generally cheerful and happy home for her and for her family.

The closing number of *Bleak House* was written in France at a house near Boulogne that Dickens had rented for the summer. In the autumn he took a two-month vacation trip to Italy and returned to Tavistock House in time for Christmas. His plan had been not to think about writing another novel until the next summer, but special circumstances once again put him back to work at an earlier date. Late in 1853 it was noticed that the circulation of *Household Words* was for the first time slipping, and Bradbury and Evans proposed to Dickens that a rescue operation might be effected if he would bring out a new novel to appear in its pages as a weekly serial. In January he reluctantly started writing, and on 1 April 1854 the first chapter of *Hard Times* was published. Although the rescue operation worked, with the circulation of *Household Words* doubling after the novel began appearing, Dickens found that the task of writing short weekly installments was formidably difficult. He felt hemmed in; the lack of adequate space was, as he said in a letter, "crushing." As a result of this mode of publication, *Hard Times* is Dickens's shortest novel (117,000 words as compared with the 350,000 words of *Bleak House*). Its shortness may account for its having some resemblances to Dickens's fables, such as *A Christmas Carol*, in its making prominent an anti-Utilitarian moral, and even in the names of some of the characters, such as the bullying factory owner, Mr. Bounderby, or the fact-crammed school teacher, Mr. M'Choakumchild. The central drama in *Hard Times* is the conflict between the world of Mr. Gradgrind, a hardware merchant who believes in the exclusive values of fact and rational calculation, and the world of affec-

Gad's Hill Place, Dickens's final home, and the chalet there where he did much of his writing after 1865

tion and imagination. The latter includes the enjoyment of poetry (which Gradgrind despises) but is more prosaically represented by the entertainments of Mr. Sleary's circus and its horse riders. Such an account unduly emphasizes the abstract aspects of *Hard Times*, for despite the prominence of its fable, its core is distinctly realistic, as was illustrated in the excellent television version of 1977 (which was shown on national networks in the United States as well as in Great Britain). This vivid and sensitive interpretation was filmed in an industrial area of the English Midlands like the town of Preston, near Manchester, which Dickens had visited to report on a strike in January 1854, and which served as the model for Coketown in his novel.

Because of its hard-hitting social criticism, *Hard Times* was a favorite for such readers as George Bernard Shaw and John Ruskin; others, such as George Gissing, found its bleakness so harsh as to make the book unreadable. A similar harshness marks Dickens's next novel, *Little Dorrit*, although the effect of it is different because of a difference in length. Dickens was forty-three years old when he began *Little Dorrit*, about the same age as his protagonist, Arthur Clennam, whose unhappiness seems to reflect his creator's unhappiness at this time. The action takes place almost thirty years earlier, but significantly the principal setting of this novel is a debtors' prison, the Marshalsea, where Dickens as a boy used to visit his imprisoned father during the blacking warehouse period of his life. That had been in 1824; the novel opens in 1826. As John Holloway said of the characters in this book, "the present is imprisoned in the past"; his statement also seems applicable to Dickens himself in 1855. For in *Little Dorrit* Dickens was looking back not only to the shameful memories of the Marshalsea days but also to the painful memories of his frustrated love for Maria Beadnell. In February 1855 Maria had written to her former admirer, and a meeting was arranged by him with the now forty-four-year-old wife and mother. Dickens was crushed with disappointment when they met, an experience which he drew upon almost literally when he described Arthur Clennam's reunion with Flora Finching, "his old passion." Not only had Flora changed physically (once a "lily" and now a "peony"), she had become a bore; everything she said was "diffuse and silly." The coyness in her manner that had allured him when she was twenty was still there but was now intolerable to him. So Clennam's "old passion," like

Dickens's, "shivered and broke to pieces." For these and other reasons, *Little Dorrit* is the saddest of Dickens's novels, a quality which did not prevent its being admired by its early readers (it sold more copies than *Bleak House*) and by later critics. Two important appreciations are Lionel Trilling's classic essay and a chapter by F. R. Leavis, who discovered Dickens's greatness late in life and came to the conclusion that *Little Dorrit* is "his greatest book."

The financial rewards from *Little Dorrit* and from *Household Words* enabled Dickens, as he was finishing the novel, to realize a dream of his early boyhood. Gad's Hill Place, a beautiful eighteenth-century brick house on a hill outside of Rochester, which he had admired during walks with his father, came up for sale, and he bought it. (The owner had been one of his contributors for *Household Words*, Mrs. Lynn Linton.) It had plenty of room for guests (it is today a boarding school for girls), attractive gardens, and a surrounding landscape ideal for walks. Dickens lived there for the final ten years of his life (he sold Tavistock House in 1860). This happy realization of a boyhood dream coincided with an opposite kind of development: the gradual breaking up of his marriage, culminating in a legal separation from Kate in May 1858.

Hints of his growing dissatisfaction as a husband can be detected in his letters of the early 1850s in references to his "miserable" marriage, and in his report to Forster: "Poor Catherine and I are not made for each other, and there is no help for it." But the formal break did not occur until Dickens had met an attractive eighteen-year-old actress, Ellen Ternan, who eventually became his mistress. They first came to know each other in 1856-1857, when Dickens had once again thrown himself into amateur theatricals in order to raise funds for charities. In a new play, *The Frozen Deep*, cowritten with his young friend Wilkie Collins, Dickens made a hit playing the leading role. This production led to Dickens's making acquaintance with a professional acting family consisting of Mrs. Ternan, a widow, and her three daughters, of whom Ellen was the youngest. Although some twenty-seven years younger than Dickens, Ellen fascinated him from the outset, and this infatuation confirmed his resolve to set Kate up in a separate establishment with Charlie, their eldest child. The rest of the children, and also Georgina Hogarth, remained with him at Gad's Hill. According to accounts of his relationship with Ellen published during the past fifty

Dickens giving a reading from one of his works
(Dickens Fellowship)

years, Dickens was also responsible in the 1860s for a third household, having bought a residence for the Ternans in London and later at Peckham. This arrangement put more than financial strains upon Dickens, for he knew that it would be disastrous to his reputation as a writer, especially as a proponent of family and home and editor of *Household Words*, if his relationship became public knowledge. During his lifetime there were rumors, of course; at the time of the separation there was an abundance of gossip. At the Garrick Club some members were overheard by Thackeray airing a story that Dickens was having an affair with his sister-in-law. Thackeray corrected them by affirming, instead, that the affair was with an actress! Dickens became so enraged by such talk that he wrote letters to the newspapers denying all whispered reports of any amorous relations with "a young lady for whom I have great attachment and regard." His gesture of protest was certainly misguided but fortunately did not lead to any disclosures in the press. However, he came dangerously close to public exposure in the summer of 1865: returning from a visit to

France with Ellen and her mother, Dickens was sharing a train compartment with them when a serious wreck occurred, one extensively reported in the news. Afterward, the possibility of publicity must have haunted Dickens, like Banquo's ghost, for anxious months. But for the most part, this skeleton in his closet remained hidden from his public while he was alive and also for more than sixty years after his death. In the 1920s his daughter Kate Perugini decided that the truth about her father ought to be known and reported the Ellen Ternan story that appeared in *Dickens and Daughter* by Gladys Storey in 1939. In some quarters the disclosures were dismissed as scandalmongering, but further evidence kept surfacing that seemed to substantiate them. There was even a story that Dickens had had a son by Ellen Ternan, a story most emphatically denied by dedicated Dickensians. Yet in some newly discovered papers left after her death by Gladys Storey, and published in 1980 in the *Dickensian*, there is fresh evidence that the story was probably true.

At the earlier stage, in 1858, incidents involving the Ellen Ternan story led to a quarrel between Dickens and his publishers Bradbury and Evans and to his starting a new periodical to replace *Household Words*. Published by Chapman and Hall, *All the Year Round* was another success with the reading public, reaching a circulation of one hundred thousand in the 1860s. Part of its success is attributable to Dickens's publishing in its pages two of his best-known novels: *A Tale of Two Cities* (1859) and *Great Expectations* (1861). The first of these has been one of his most popular novels, especially in the United States, where, in 1970, more copies were sold than of any other novel by Dickens. Philip Collins suggests that its popularity may be due to its shortness and to its having been "dramatized with notable success." This explanation is helpful, but it should be remarked that the popularity of *A Tale of Two Cities* may also derive simply from its being an exceptionally lively story, full of fast-paced action. Like *Barnaby Rudge*, it is a historical novel set in the 1770s and 1780s in a period of riot and violence, this time the French Revolution. It was a period that had always fascinated Dickens; he once remarked that he had read Carlyle's *The French Revolution: A History* (1837) "five hundred times." In his *Tale of Two Cities*, London and Paris are linked through a relatively small cast of characters, in particular through Sydney Carton, a London lawyer who falls in love with a young French-

A READING.   39

It was a ghastly figure to look upon. The murderer staggering backward to the wall, and shutting out the sight with his hand, seized a heavy club, and struck her down. !! *Action*

The bright sun burst upon the crowded city in clear and radiant glory. Through costly-coloured glass and paper-mended window, through cathedral dome and rotten crevice, it *Mystery* shed its equal ray. It lighted up the room where the murdered woman lay. It did. He tried to shut it out, but it would stream in. If the sight had been a ghastly one in the dull morning, what was it, now, in all that brilliant light!!! / *Terror to the End* /

He had not moved; he had been afraid to stir. There had been a moan and motion of the hand; and, with terror added to rage, he had struck and struck again. Once he

Page of the prompt copy of one of Dickens's readings, Nicholas Nickleby at the Yorkshire School *(1868), with stage directions written in by Dickens (Suzannet Collection)*

woman, Lucie Manette. Carton's love is a hopeless one, for, although talented, he is a confirmed drunkard and knows he is unworthy of his beloved. Instead, she marries his look-alike, Charles Darnay, a former French aristocrat who immigrated to London before the revolution. Back in France, Darnay's family members are doomed to be guillotined if captured. Darnay nevertheless takes the risk of returning to France on a mission. As might have been predicted, he is captured there and would most certainly have suffered the fate prescribed for his family had he not been rescued by Carton, who substitutes himself for Darnay and gives up his life in order to save the husband of the woman he loves. Confronting death, Carton affirms his credo: "It is a far, far better thing that I do, than I have ever done."

Despite its popularity, *A Tale of Two Cities* has never received much serious attention from critics. On the other hand, his next novel, *Great Expectations*, has been both popular and a favorite topic for critical discussions. Many of his Victorian readers welcomed this novel for its humor; after the Dark Period novels, *Great Expectations* seemed to them a return to the good-hearted vein of *The Pickwick Papers*. Consonant with this seemingly cheerful vein was Pip's growth from "ugly duckling" into a "proud swan." As Barry Westburg noted in 1977, "The mode of consciousness that defines Pip is 'expectation'—his mind is typically directed toward the future rather than toward the past"—as contrasted with David Copperfield, for example. Most critical discussions since 1950 argue that the Victorians were misled by some of its great comic scenes, such as Mr. Wopsle's playing Hamlet, and also by Pip's career (the alternate endings not affecting the point). Unlike the Victorians, modern critics see *Great Expectations* as a brilliant study of guilt, another very sad book—another Dark Period novel, that is— and one of Dickens's finest in any vein. David Lean's successful screen version, first shown in 1946 and many times revived, has no doubt added to the popularity of this novel, but its critical status is so firmly based as not to require any reinforcements from the camera.

At the time of Dickens's changing his publishers, his career underwent another and more important change: in April 1858 he finally decided, after much hesitation, to start a tour during which he would do readings from his own writings, such as *A Christmas Carol* and the trial scene in *The Pickwick Papers*. At this date he was already

Dickens in 1868, on his second American tour
(Dickens Fellowship)

an experienced and highly successful reader, but heretofore his performances had been to raise money for charities. Now, instead, he was billed as a professional, raising money for himself. Yet it is evident that he took on this new career not just to earn money; he needed the direct contact with vast audiences of his readers in order to compensate for a sense of loneliness and dissatisfaction which afflicted him powerfully in these late years. The readings exhausted him (his first tour called for eighty-seven performances), but they also exhilarated him. Another result of his readings was one that Forster had predicted when he had urged Dickens not to engage in them—his productivity as novelist inevitably suffered. After finishing *Great Expectations* in the summer of 1861, he was soon launched on another season of readings, and it was three years before he started another novel, the last that he would live to complete: *Our Mutual Friend* (1864-1865). About this novel, there would be no mistaking the tone, as Victorian readers had done with the previous one. *Our Mutual Friend* is grim and bleak, with an air of darkness even more oppressive than that of *Bleak House*. What humor there is is predominantly in a satirical vein, as in the memorable dinner-party scenes at the homes of Mr. and Mrs. Podsnap and of Mr. and Mrs. Veneering. Many readers, from Dickens's generation onward, find that the creaky plot—involving the presumed death by drowning of the hero, John Harmon, and an elaborate sequence of deceptions about his hidden inheritance—makes the book hard to read. Such readers might even agree with a review by the young Henry James, who called it "the poorest of Mr. Dickens's works. . . . And it is poor with the poverty not of momentary embarrassment, but of permanent exhaustion." James's insights were shrewd, for it is now known that Dickens *was* exhausted while writing this novel; but a writer's state of exhaustion does not necessarily lead to a failure of his art. In fact, some critics today, who have given *Our Mutual Friend* a serious and close reading, find it to be his most impressive creation, praising it for its unified presentation of the theme of money and for its brilliant use of recurring images of dust and foul water to evoke a sense of death in modern life.

After completing *Our Mutual Friend* in November 1865, Dickens resumed his reading tours and occasionally wrote some short fictions. It was four years before he tried his hand again at a novel—the longest break between novels in his career and a marked contrast to his pace in the 1830s. Not that he was idle during the interval. In late 1867 he sailed to America for a scheduled tour of eighty readings, which netted him a vast sum of money and a further chance to bask in the warm receptions of enthusiastic audiences in New York, Boston, Baltimore, and Buffalo. (On this visit he limited his travels almost entirely to the eastern seaboard.) On 22 April 1868 he sailed for home. It had been a triumphant visit, and the bad feelings of the *Martin Chuzzlewit* phase of his relations with America had been erased after the passing of twenty-six eventful years. The triumph had, however, been a costly one. Most of the readings had been performed when Dickens was ill with colds and an assortment of other ailments. His determination to continue to meet his engagements, instead of retiring to a sickbed, impressed those of his friends who knew what he was going through but also impressed others that his behavior was suicidal. Back in England, he continued to drive himself. In October he began a projected series of a hundred readings, of which he had completed eighty-

Cover of the American edition of one of Dickens's readings
(Dickens House Museum)

six by April 1869. In this series he introduced for the first time the scene of Nancy's murder in *Oliver Twist*. His final series of readings, early in 1870, ended in March with a brief farewell: "From these garish lights I vanish now for evermore."

Some months earlier he had started writing *The Mystery of Edwin Drood*, which was scheduled to be published in twelve monthly numbers, of which he completed six. The early numbers, starting in April 1870, had a sale of fifty thousand copies, "outstripping," as he was pleased to note, "every one of its predecessors." Not much significant criticism has been written about *The Mystery of Edwin Drood*: as Philip Collins noted wittily in 1978, "Recent Dickens critics seem to have worn out their brains by the time they arrive at 1870." This is not to say that little has been written about this tantalizing fragment: there are shelfloads of books with *The Mystery of Edwin*

Drood as their subject, but they are not critical studies; instead, they are attempts to solve the mystery by conjecture or by simply inventing six more books of the story as Dickens might have written them. (One of the more successful attempts in the latter mode was by Leon Garfield in 1981.) Like Keats's urn, the mystery of Drood doth tease us out of thought, for what is involved is not just the mystery of what happened to Edwin Drood and his uncle but the mystery of how the ailing novelist achieved in this book some of the most extraordinary stylistic feats of his whole career. Graham Greene spoke once of Dickens's "secret prose" with its "music of memory" in *David Copperfield*, and when Dickens writes of time passing and the crumbling cathedral of Cloisterham in *The Mystery of Edwin Drood*, he most tellingly illustrates Greene's comments about his stylistic wizardry.

The last completed page of *The Mystery of Edwin Drood* was written at Gad's Hill on the afternoon of 8 June 1870. That evening Dickens was stricken with an aneurysm in the brain and died the following day without regaining consciousness. Even though he had wanted to be buried in the Rochester area which was so deeply associated with both his lost childhood and with recent triumphs and losses, his wish had to be overruled in favor of Westminster Abbey. On 14 June, in a private ceremony, he was buried in Poet's Corner, which the London *Times* described on this occasion as "the peculiar resting place of English literary genius."

Letters:

The Letters of Charles Dickens, Pilgrim Edition, 5 volumes, edited by Nina Burgis, Kenneth J. Fielding, Madeline House, Graham Storey, and Kathleen Tillotson (Oxford: Clarendon Press, 1965-1981).

Biographies:

John Forster, *The Life of Dickens*, 2 volumes (New York: Scribners, 1905);

Edgar Johnson, *Charles Dickens: His Tragedy and Triumph* (2 volumes, New York: Simon & Schuster, 1952; 1 volume, revised and abridged, New York: Viking, 1977; London: Lane, 1977);

Norman MacKenzie and Jeanne MacKenzie, *Dickens: A Life* (New York: Oxford University Press, 1979);

Michael Allen, *Charles Dickens' Childhood* (New York: St. Martin's Press, 1988);

Dickens reading to his daughters Mary and Kate at Gad's Hill Place (Dickens Fellowship)

Fred Kaplan, *Dickens: A Biography* (New York: William Morrow, 1988);

Peter Ackroyd, *Dickens* (London: Sinclair-Stevenson, 1990).

References:

Arthur Clayborough, *The Grotesque in English Literature* (Oxford: Clarendon Press, 1965);

Philip Collins, "Charles Dickens," in *Victorian Fiction: A Second Guide to Research*, edited by George H. Ford (New York: Modern Language Association, 1978), pp. 34-114;

Collins, ed., *Charles Dickens: The Public Readings* (Oxford: Clarendon Press, 1975);

Collins, ed., *Dickens: The Critical Heritage* (London: Routledge & Kegan Paul, 1971);

H. M. Daleski, *Dickens and the Art of Analogy* (New York: Schocken, 1971);

Dickens Studies Annual (New York: AMS Press, 1980);

K. J. Fielding, *Charles Dickens* (London: Longmans, Green, 1963);

George H. Ford, *Dickens and His Readers* (Princeton, N.J.: Princeton University Press, 1955);

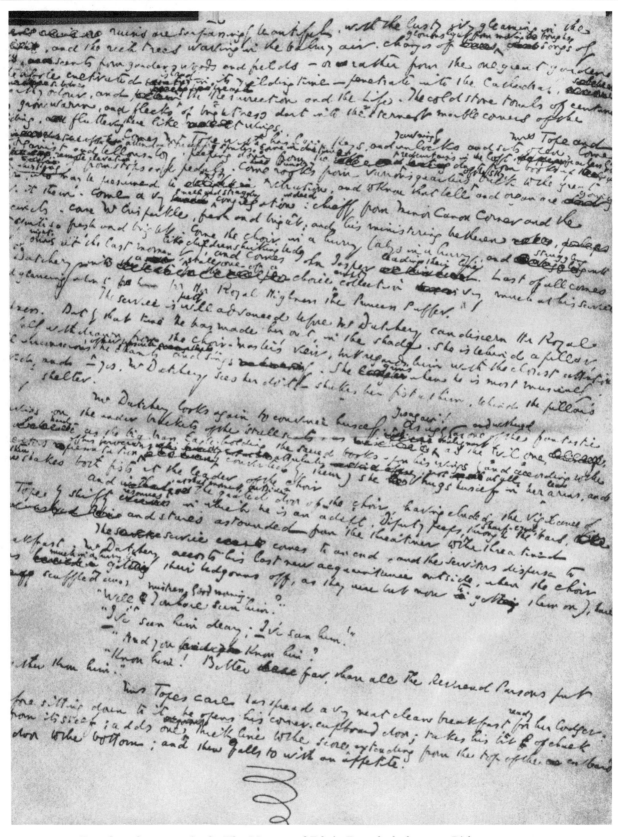

Page from the manuscript for The Mystery of Edwin Drood, *the last page Dickens ever wrote*
(Forster Collection, Victoria and Albert Museum)

Ford and Lauriat Lane, Jr., eds., *The Dickens Critics* (Ithaca, N.Y.: Cornell University Press, 1961);

Leon Garfield, *The Mystery of Edwin Drood* (New York: Pantheon, 1981);

John Greaves, *Dickens at Doughty Street* (London: Hamish Hamilton, 1975);

John Gross and Gabriel Pearson, eds., *Dickens and the Twentieth Century* (London: Routledge & Kegan Paul, 1962);

Alfred Harbage, *A Kind of Power: The Dickens-Shakespeare Analogy* (Philadelphia: American Philosophical Society, 1975);

Barbara Hardy, *The Moral Art of Dickens* (New York: Oxford University Press, 1970);

Humphry House, *The Dickens World* (London: Oxford University Press, 1941);

James R. Kincaid, *Dickens and The Rhetoric of Laughter* (Oxford: Clarendon Press, 1972);

Mark Lambert, *Dickens and the Suspended Quotation* (New Haven: Yale University Press, 1981);

F. R. Leavis and Q. D. Leavis, *Dickens the Novelist* (London: Chatto & Windus, 1970);

Steven Marcus, *Dickens from Pickwick to Dombey* (New York: Simon & Schuster, 1965);

Juliet McMaster, *Dickens the Designer* (London: Macmillan, 1987);

Sylvère Monod, *Dickens the Novelist* (Norman: University of Oklahoma Press, 1967);

Harland S. Nelson, *Charles Dickens* (Boston: Twayne, 1981);

Ada Nisbet, "Charles Dickens," in *Victorian Fiction: A Guide to Research*, edited by Lionel Stevenson (Cambridge, Mass.: Harvard University Press, 1964), pp. 44-153;

Nisbet and Blake Nevius, eds., *Dickens Centennial Essays* (Berkeley: University of California Press, 1971);

Robert Patten, *Dickens and His Publishers* (Oxford: Clarendon Press, 1979);

Michael Slater, *Dickens and Women* (London: Dent, 1983);

Slater, ed., *Dickens 1970* (London: Chapman & Hall, 1970);

Slater, ed., *Dickens on America and the Americans* (Austin: University of Texas Press, 1978);

Garrett Stewart, *Dickens and the Trials of Imagination* (Cambridge, Mass.: Harvard University Press, 1974);

Taylor Stoehr, *Dickens: The Dreamer's Stance* (Ithaca, N.Y.: Cornell University Press, 1965);

Harry Stone, *Dickens and the Invisible World* (Bloomington: Indiana University Press, 1979);

Claire Tomalin, *The Invisible Woman: The Story of Nelly Ternan and Charles Dickens* (London: Viking, 1990);

Lionel Trilling, *The Opposing Self: Nine Essays in Criticism* (New York: Viking, 1955), pp. 50-65;

Alexander Welsh, *The City of Dickens* (Oxford: Clarendon Press, 1971);

Welsh, *From Copyright to Copperfield* (Cambridge, Mass.: Harvard University Press, 1987);

Barry Westburg, *The Confessional Fictions of Charles Dickens* (DeKalb: Northern Illinois University Press, 1977);

Angus Wilson, *The World of Charles Dickens* (New York: Viking, 1970).

Papers:

Most of the surviving manuscripts of Dickens's novels are in the Forster Collection at the Victoria and Albert Museum, London. In the Pierpont Morgan Library, New York, are the manuscripts of *Our Mutual Friend* and several of the Christmas books as well as some 1,360 autograph letters by Dickens. The Dickens House (48 Doughty Street, London) also has a valuable collection of letters, which was augmented in 1971 by assorted manuscripts from the great collection of the Comte de Suzannet. The Berg Collection of the New York Public Library has 500 letters and several important manuscripts, including a notebook used by Dickens when planning his novels. Manuscripts of Dickens's sketches and essays are included in collections at the Beinecke Rare Book and Manuscript Library, Yale University; the Huntington Library, San Marino, California; and the Free Library of Philadelphia, which also has a collection of more than 1,000 of Dickens's letters.

George Eliot
(Mary Ann Evans)
(22 November 1819 - 22 December 1880)

This entry was updated by Joseph Wiesenfarth (University of Wisconsin) from his entry in
DLB 21: Victorian Novelists Before 1885.

See also the Eliot entries in DLB 35: Victorian Poets
After 1850 and DLB 55: Victorian Prose Writers
Before 1867.

BOOKS: *Scenes of Clerical Life* (2 volumes,
Edinburgh & London: Blackwood, 1858; 1
volume, New York: Harper, 1858);

Adam Bede (3 volumes, Edinburgh & London:
Blackwood, 1859; 1 volume, New York:
Harper, 1859);

The Mill on the Floss (3 volumes, Edinburgh & London: Blackwood, 1860; 1 volume, New
York: Harper, 1860);

Silas Marner: The Weaver of Raveloe (2 volumes,
Edinburgh & London: Blackwood, 1861; 1
volume, New York: Harper, 1861);

Romola (3 volumes, London: Smith, Elder, 1863;
1 volume, New York: Harper, 1863);

Felix Holt, The Radical (3 volumes, Edinburgh &
London: Blackwood, 1866; 1 volume, New
York: Harper, 1866);

The Spanish Gypsy: A Poem (Edinburgh & London:
Blackwood, 1868; Boston: Ticknor & Fields,
1868);

How Lisa Loved the King (Boston: Fields, Osgood,
1869);

Middlemarch: A Study of Provincial Life (8 parts,
Edinburgh & London: Blackwood, 1871-
1872; 2 volumes, New York: Harper, 1872-
1873);

The Legend of Jubal and Other Poems (Edinburgh &
London: Blackwood, 1874; Boston: Osgood,
1874);

Daniel Deronda (8 parts, Edinburgh & London:
Blackwood, 1876; 2 volumes, New York:
Harper, 1876);

Impressions of Theophrastus Such (Edinburgh & London: Blackwood, 1879; New York: Harper,
1879);

Quarry for Middlemarch, edited by Anna T. Kitchel
(Berkeley: University of California Press,
1950);

George Eliot in 1860, drawn by Samuel Laurence

Essays of George Eliot, edited by Thomas Pinney
(New York: Columbia University Press,
1963; London: Routledge & Kegan Paul,
1963);

*Some George Eliot Notebooks: An Edition of the Carl
H. Pforzheimer Library's George Eliot Holograph
Notebooks, Mss. 707, 708, 709, 710, 711* [the
Daniel Deronda notebooks] edited by William Baker (Salzburg: Universitat Salzburg,
1976);

George Eliot's Middlemarch Notebooks: A Transcription, edited by John Clark Pratt and Victor

A. Neufeldt (Berkeley: University of California Press, 1979);

A Writer's Notebook, 1854-1879, and Uncollected Writings, edited by Joseph Wiesenfarth (Charlottesville: University of Virginia Press, 1981).

Collections: *The Works of George Eliot*, Cabinet Edition, 24 volumes (Edinburgh & London: Blackwood, 1878-1885);

The Novels of George Eliot, Clarendon Edition, 5 volumes to date (Oxford: Clarendon Press / New York: Oxford University Press, 1980-).

TRANSLATIONS: David Friedrich Strauss, *The Life of Jesus, Critically Examined*, 3 volumes, translated by Evans from the fourth German edition (London: Chapman, 1846);

Ludwig Feuerbach, *The Essence of Christianity*, translated by Evans from the second edition, Chapman's Quarterly Series VI (London: Chapman, 1854).

The most learned and respected novelist of the late Victorian period, George Eliot suffered a decline in reputation after her death and into the early twentieth century because the biography stitched together by her widower, John Walter Cross, left out the most interesting parts of her life. "It is not a Life at all," said William Gladstone. "It is a Reticence in three volumes." Although her contemporaries Anthony Trollope and Henry James saw her as the first psychological realist in the English tradition, readers of *George Eliot's Life as Related in Her Letters and Journals* (1885) saw her as the sibyl of a dying age. A revival of interest in George Eliot's novels began on the centenary of her birth, with an essay in the *Times Literary Supplement* by Virginia Woolf, and crystallized with the publication of F. R. Leavis's *The Great Tradition* in 1949. Since then she has been at the center of literary study, and *Middlemarch* (1871-1872) is now regarded as one of the outstanding masterpieces of nineteenth-century fiction.

George Eliot was born Mary Ann Evans at five o'clock in the morning of St. Cecilia's Day, 22 November 1819, at South Farm, Arbury, Warwickshire. Her father was Robert Evans (b. 1773) and her mother was his second wife, Christiana Pearson (b. ca. 1788), whom he had married in 1813. Mary Ann had a half brother, Robert (b. 1802); a half sister, Frances (b. 1805), called Fanny; a sister, Christiana (b. 1814), called Chrissey; and a brother, Isaac (b. 1816), who was

to be the most important sibling in her life. George Eliot described her father as a man who "raised himself from being an artisan to be a man whose extensive knowledge in very varied practical departments made his services valued through several counties. He had a large knowledge of buildings, of mines, of plantations, of various branches of valuation and measurement—of all that is essential to the management of large estates." These varied activities are telescoped in the word "business," which Caleb Garth, an idealized version of Robert Evans, uses to describe his work in *Middlemarch*. The Pearson family was considered socially superior to the Evans family, and Robert was thought to have done well in marrying Christiana four years after the death of his first wife, Harriet Poynton, in 1809. After the birth of Mary Ann, however, Christiana—the sharp-tongued model of the invalid Mrs. Poyser of *Adam Bede* (1859)—was not in good health; indeed, she lost sickly ten-day-old twin boys in 1818. Consequently, she sent her children to school when they were quite young. When Mary Ann was four months old, the family moved to "a charming red-brick ivy-covered house on the Arbury estate" of Sir Francis Parker-Newdigate, which Robert Evans managed. Griff House was the place George Eliot was most attached to: "my old, old home," she later affectionately called it. There Mary Ann saw her father manage the Newdigate property much in the manner that Adam Bede did the Donnithorne woods. There she came to hear the clucking of the relentlessly respectable Pearson sisters, her maternal aunts, whom she later immortalized as the rich and righteous Dodson sisters of *The Mill on the Floss* (1860). The neat and trim Chrissey was the apple of their aunts' eye and the disheveled Mary Ann the bane of their existence. Mary Ann was, however, her father's favorite child, while her mother preferred Isaac to her daughters. It was Robert Evans who gave Mary Ann *The Linnet's Life* (1822, by the Reverend Isaac Taylor and his family), her first book, which she kept until her death.

When she was sent to join Chrissey as a boarder at Miss Lathom's school at Attleborough, Mary Ann was separated from Isaac, who had hitherto been her constant companion. Perforce she turned from fishing, marbles, and top spinning to reading and was deeply immersed in the imaginative world of Sir Walter Scott's *Waverley* (1814) by the time she was eight years old. In 1828 the sisters transferred to Miss Wallington's school in

South Farm, Arbury, George Eliot's birthplace

Nuneaton, where Maria Lewis, the chief governess, became Mary Ann's intimate friend. It was under Miss Lewis's tutelage that the child became an ardent Evangelical, although her parents were traditional Anglicans. Having learned French and become adept at music, Mary Ann, age thirteen, exhausted the accomplishments offered by Miss Wallington's school and transferred to the Misses Franklin's school in Coventry. Daughters of a Baptist minister, the Misses Franklin sharpened the dogmatic tendencies of Mary Ann's mind, giving a Calvinist tint to its Evangelical shade. The girl dressed so severely that one visitor mistook her for a schoolmistress. At Nuneaton, nonetheless, Mary Ann learned to excel as a pianist under the guidance of a local church organist. With a year of Parisian experience, Rebecca Franklin—a prototype of Esther Lyon in *Felix Holt, The Radical* (1866)—brought Mary Ann to proficiency in French, and she won Blaise Pascal's *Pensées* (1670) as a prize for excellence in the language during her first year at school. Under Miss Franklin's guidance she also lost her provincial pronunciation and learned to speak English faultlessly in a strikingly modulated voice that was to become a marked characteristic of George Eliot as well as

of her principal heroine, Dorothea Brooke, whose voice was like that "of a soul that had once lived in an Aeolian harp." Immersion in historical romances combined with a gift for composition led Mary Ann to write a story in imitation of G. P. R. James: the hero is "an outcast from society, an alien from his family, a deserter, and a regicide." "Edward Neville" is the title Gordon S. Haight has given to this first extant fragment of fiction from George Eliot's pen.

Mary Ann left the Coventry school at the end of 1835; her mother died the following February. After Chrissey married in May 1837, Mary Ann became mistress of Griff. In addition to attending to the housekeeping and caring for her father, she continued her intellectual pursuits. She studied German and Italian with a tutor and made progress in Latin and Greek. She published her first poem in the *Christian Observer* in January 1840; untitled, though beginning with a quotation from 2 Peter 1: 16, the poem's first stanzas are indicative of its religious fervor:

As o'er the fields by evening's light I stray,
I hear a still, small whisper—"Come away!
Thou must to this bright, lovely world soon say
    Farewell!"

The mandate I'd obey, my lamp prepare,
Gird up my garments, give my soul to pray'r,
And say to earth and all that breathe earth's air
Farewell!

As her religious commitment intensified, she proposed composing a chart of ecclesiastical history from the birth of Christ to the Reformation. She was given unlimited use of the Arbury Hall library and read widely in scriptural commentary, the Oxford *Tracts for the Times*, church history, and the edifying biographies of eminent Christians. When, after her "deconversion," the Birmingham theologian Francis Watts visited her in 1842 with the hope of bringing her back to the faith, he could not. Commenting on her extensive reading on religious subjects, he said quite simply, "She had gone into the question."

Robert Evans retired as manager of the Newdigate estate in 1841 and in March moved with his daughter to Bird Grove, a large house on the Foleshill Road, just outside of Coventry. There, in November, Mary Ann found in Charles and Caroline Bray and Caroline's sister and brother, Sara and Charles Christian Hennell, friendship and an intellectual community far different from any she had known previously. Bray was a ribbon manufacturer by trade but a philanthropist and freethinking philosopher by preference. Hennell was the author of *An Inquiry Concerning the Origin of Christianity* (1838), a copy of which Evans bought and read. Hennell had written the *Inquiry* at Caroline's request to substantiate—contrary to her husband's contention—that Christianity was a divinely revealed religion. After a thorough study of the Gospels, Hennell concluded that truth of feeling, not divine revelation, shows itself in the "beautiful fictions" at the origin of Christianity. He affirmed that the New Testament account of Jesus' life could not pass the test of history and that the Gospels were a compilation of myths expressing man's deepest thoughts and feelings. Evans met the Brays and Hennells, as Charles Bray later remarked, at a point in her life when she was "turning towards greater freedom of thought in religious opinion." Consequently, Hennell's treatise acted as a catalyst in a mind prepared for change by reading in Scott, William Wordsworth, Thomas Carlyle, and their contemporaries in literature and science. On 13 November 1841, eleven days after meeting the Brays at their Rosehill home, Evans wrote to Maria Lewis: "My whole soul has been engrossed in the most interesting of all enquiries

for the last few days, and to what result my thoughts may lead I know not—possibly to one that will startle you, but my only desire is to know the truth, my only fear to cling to error."

Shortly thereafter she abandoned her Evangelical faith, denied divine revelation, affirmed the truth of feeling, and cast off taboos associated with fundamentalist belief. For her as for Hennell, Christianity changed from a divinely revealed religion to one of human origin which leads to "the finer thoughts and feelings of mankind" that "find a vent in fiction." In January 1842 Mary Ann refused to attend church, and her outraged father threatened to put her out, sell Bird Grove, and live elsewhere by himself. Only the timely intervention of Fanny, Isaac, Chrissey, and family friends prevented a complete rupture. Mary Ann finally agreed to accompany her father to church as long as she could think as she pleased while she was there: "I have nothing to say this morning, my soul as barren as the desert; but I generally manage to sink some little well at church, by dint of making myself deaf and looking up at the roof and arches." She lived on with her father at Foleshill—"I and father go on living and loving together as usual, and it is my chief source of happiness to know that I form one item of his"—and she came to regret her failure to tolerate his intolerance during the crisis in their lives, because for her "*truth of feeling*" was, finally, "the only universal bond of union." The large tolerance that would become characteristic of George Eliot's narrative voice first finds expression in those words addressed to Sara Hennell in 1843. The novelist who was later to say that her realistic fiction was meant "to call forth tolerant judgment, pity, and sympathy" found that she had allowed intellectual conviction to run roughshod over filial feeling. George Eliot found in the "Holy War" with her father the *truth of feeling* that would be the hallmark of her fiction.

Through the Brays, Evans met Rufa Brabant, who, when she became Charles Hennell's fiancée, abandoned the project of translating David Friedrich Strauss's *Das Leben Jesu (The Life of Jesus*, 1835), having completed only two chapters. Evans assumed the task. Strauss argues that Christian myth represents the truth of feelings and aspirations which are an expression of the *idea*, in the Hegelian sense of the word, that divinity and humanity are eventually to be reunited. "Proved to be an idea of reason, the unity of divine and human nature must also have an histori-

Griff House, George Eliot's favorite home during her childhood

cal existence." The Jesus of the Gospels is seen as the product of his disciples' idea that he was the heaven-sent Messiah promised in the Old Testament. Jesus, however, was only the *symbolic* anticipation of a Divine Humanity, which is the *real* goal toward which all creation actually strives. Evans was immersed in the translation of this relentlessly analytical book from January 1844 to June 1846. Toward the end of her task, she told Caroline Bray that she was "Strauss-sick" because "it made her ill dissecting the beautiful story of the crucifixion, and only the sight of her Christ-image and picture made her endure it." While this work of translation sapped her energy, she also cared for her aging father, whose health began to fail in 1846. He died after a prolonged illness on 1 May 1849. "What shall I be without my Father?" she asked the Brays. "It will seem as if a part of my moral nature were gone. I had a horrid vision of myself last night becoming earthly sensual and devilish for want of that purifying restraining influence." Something of that fear was undoubtedly grounded in the attraction she had felt to Rufa's father, Dr. Robert Brabant, who had toyed with her affections to the extent that his wife, though blind, had discovered enough to

order Mary Ann out of her house in November 1843. A similar lack of emotional stability had manifested itself in what she called "my unfortunate 'affaire.' " Having accepted the suit of an engaging young picture-restorer in March 1845, she had changed her mind and sent him away: "I did meditate an engagement," she wrote Martha Jackson, "but I have determined, whether wisely or not I cannot tell, to defer it, at least for the present." Shortly she was to become involved more compromisingly with the publisher John Chapman, and more desperately with the philosopher Herbert Spencer.

In her last years in Robert Evans's house, Mary Ann had worked on a translation of Benedict de Spinoza's *Tractatus Theologico-Politicus* (1670) at the suggestion of Chapman, who had published the *Life of Jesus.* Although her admiration for Spinoza amounted to adulation—Spinoza "says from his own soul what all the world is saying by rote"—she did not complete the translation. From December 1846 to February 1847 she published five essays under the rubric "Poetry and Prose, From the Notebook of an Eccentric" in the Coventry *Herald and Observer,* a newspaper which Charles Bray had bought in June 1846.

Charles and Caroline Bray and Sara Hennell, three of George Eliot's closest friends (Coventry City Library)

The most notable of three known reviews from that period was one she wrote of James Anthony Froude's *The Nemesis of Faith* (1849) for the *Herald*. Froude's novel had been publicly burned at Exeter College, Oxford, where he was a fellow; nevertheless, Evans praised his book as one that makes us feel "in companionship with a spirit who is transfusing himself into our souls and so vitalizing them by his superior energy, that life, both outward and inward, presents itself to us in higher relief, in colours brightened and deepened." Exhausted by her father's illness and devastated by his death, she could, however, do no further intellectual work. With a legacy of one hundred pounds in her pocket and an annuity of approximately ninety pounds to support her, she set out with the Brays for the Continent, taking the route of the grand tour.

When they arrived in Geneva in July 1849, Evans decided on a protracted stay in the city of Jean-Jacques Rousseau, whose *Confessions* (1781, 1788), she had told Ralph Waldo Emerson at Rosehill in July 1848, "first wakened her to deep reflection." She lived for a time in a pension, the Compagne Plongeon, where a Piedmontese noblewoman insisted that she change her hairstyle: "The Marquise . . . has abolished all my curls and made two things stick out on each side of my head like those on the head of the Sphinx." She moved in October to the house of the Francois D'Albert-Durades: "I like these dear people better and better—everything is so in harmony with one's moral feeling that I really can almost say I never enjoyed a more complete bien-etre in my life than during the last fortnight." She came

quickly to call Madame "Maman," and she loved Monsieur "as if he were father and brother both." He was "not more than 4 feet high with a deformed spine," but he was an accomplished painter. With an excellent singing voice as well, D'Albert-Durade was the model of Philip Wakem, the hunchbacked musician-painter of *The Mill on the Floss*. Whether—like Philip—he loved a Maggie in "Minnie," as he called Evans, remains an unanswered question. A salon was held each Monday evening, and Evans mixed with a cultivated Genevese society that admired the plain-looking young lady from England. She sat for a portrait by D'Albert-Durade which she carried back to England, where he escorted her in March 1850. Finding her family uncongenial companions, Marian, as she now called herself, settled with the Brays at Rosehill until January 1851, when she went to London to make her career in journalism and took up residence at John Chapman's house.

The ground floor of 142 Strand housed the offices of Chapman's bookselling and publishing business, and the rest of the building was home for his wife; his two children; and his mistress, Elizabeth Tilley, who was ostensibly the children's governess. The house was large enough to accommodate boarders. Having first met Chapman in 1846, Evans had seen him again at Rosehill in October 1850, when he discussed with Charles Bray his intention to buy the *Westminster Review*. She had just written an excellent notice of R. W. Mackay's *The Progress of the Intellect* (1850) for that periodical when she arrived in London. It was not long before she aroused the ire of Elizabeth Tilley, who saw Chapman trying to ensnare Evans in his far-flung amorous net. Evans left London in late March and stayed at Rosehill until May, when Chapman, soon to purchase the *Westminster Review*, invited Evans to edit it; she returned to 142 Strand on 29 September 1851, Chapman having convinced his wife and mistress that her presence was required for business reasons. She served as editor of the *Westminster Review* from January 1852 to July 1854, living at Chapman's until 17 October 1853.

During her years at the Chapman house, Marian Evans met many of the eminent intellectuals of the day, who passed through the offices of the *Westminster Review*. The two who became most important to her were Herbert Spencer, to whom she proposed marriage; and George Henry Lewes, who made her his lifelong companion. Evans and Spencer enjoyed each other's companionship in conversation, on walks, and at the theater and opera until she fell very much in love with this handsome confirmed bachelor: "I want to know if you can assure me that you will not forsake me, that you will always be with me as much as you can and share your thoughts and feelings with me. If you become attached to someone else, then I must die, but until then I could gather courage to work and make life valuable, if only I had you near me. I do not ask you to sacrifice anything—I would be very good and cheerful and never annoy you. But I find it impossible to contemplate life under any other conditions," Evans wrote Spencer in July 1852. Although, as she said, "all the world is setting us down as engaged," Spencer found it impossible to return her affection: "Physical beauty is a *sine qua non* with me," Spencer wrote in his *Autobiography* (1904), "as was once unhappily proved where the intellectual traits and the emotional traits were of the highest." George Henry Lewes was a friend of Spencer's, and Evans had been introduced to him by John Chapman at Jeff's bookshop in the Burlington Arcade on 6 October 1851. At first Evans did not like Lewes's manner and thought him very ugly as well. But he became a regular visitor at 142 Strand; and one day, visiting there with Spencer, he stayed behind with Evans after his friend left. By 28 March 1853, she found Lewes "as always, genial and amusing. He has won my liking, in spite of myself." As the drama critic of the *Leader*—Lewes wrote his column under the name of Vivian—he had entrée to the theaters and began taking Evans there with him. In addition, one contribution or another of

Robert Evans, George Eliot's father, around the time of their disagreement over religion in 1842

Lewes's appeared in almost every edition of the *Westminster Review* that she edited. They were frequently together; and on 17 October 1853, when Marian moved from the Strand to 21 Cambridge Street, Hyde Park, they may have begun to live together as well. Their intimacy almost certainly dates from this time.

During this period Evans was translating Ludwig Feuerbach's *Das Wesen des Christentums* (*The Essence of Christianity*, 1841). Her love for Lewes and Feuerbach's deification of love intersected at precisely the right moment for her. Lewes was a married man whose wife had been notoriously unfaithful to him by the time he met Evans. Agnes Jervis Lewes had borne Thornton Leigh Hunt two children by then, would bear another before Evans and Lewes left for Germany, and yet another after that. Lewes had registered the first child as his own, thus legally condoning the adultery and making it practically impossible to get a divorce under English law. When the second bastard was born, Lewes considered his marriage terminated morally, if not legally. Marian

Evans endorsed this interpretation, and Feuerbach gave her the theoretical ground for doing so. He argued that Christian dogma was the symbolic expression of man's conscious and unconscious needs; thus man has "no other definition of God than this; God is pure, unlimited, free Feeling." Man must become conscious of God as "a loving, tender, even subjective human being." Only love enables him to attain that consciousness. "Love is the middle term, the substantial bond, the principle of reconciliation between the perfect and the imperfect, the sinless and the sinful being, the universal and individual, the divine and the human. Love is God himself, and apart from it there is no God." Consequently, "that alone is a religious marriage which is a true marriage, which corresponds to the essence of marriage—of love." In April 1854 Evans wrote Sara Hennell—who was proofreading this translation as she had the Strauss—"With the ideas of Feuerbach I everwhere agree"; in June she corrected the last proof and inserted her name, Marian Evans, on the title page; and in July she left for the Continent with Lewes, representing herself as his wife. In marked contrast to Maggie Tulliver in *The Mill on the Floss*, she did not turn back.

The Leweses, as they became known, went to Weimar to follow the tracks of Johann Wolfgang von Goethe, whose biography Lewes was writing. Evans wrote the first of a series of articles for the *Westminster Review*. She also wrote to Chapman telling him of the joy she had found in her union with Lewes: "Affection, respect, and intellectual sympathy deepen, and for the first time in my life I can say to the moments, 'Verweilen sie, sie sind so schon.' " Meanwhile, Charles Bray was defending her character back in England, where spicy gossip garnished delicious rumor: "She must be allowed to satisfy her own conscience. . . . I have known her for years and should always feel that she was better by far than 99/100 of the people I have ever known." Very few felt that way, and the Lewes-Evans liaison was roundly condemned. After a sojourn in Berlin, where Evans worked on a translation of Spinoza's *Ethics* (1677) while Lewes continued with *The Life and Works of Goethe* (1855), they returned to England in March 1855, eventually taking up residence in Richmond. From July 1855 to January 1857 Evans wrote the "Belles Lettres" section of the *Westminster Review* in addition to a series of often brilliant essays that marked her path to fiction. Her article "Evangelical Teaching: Dr.

Cumming" convinced Lewes of her genius, and her review "The Natural History of German Life" outlined her theory of realism in art: "Art is the nearest thing to life; it is a mode of amplifying experiences and extending our contact with our fellow-men beyond the bounds of our personal lot. All the more sacred is the task of the artist when he undertakes to paint the life of the People. Falsification here is far more pernicious than in the more artificial aspects of life. . . . The thing for mankind to know is, not what are the motives and influences which the moralist thinks *ought* to act on the labourer or the artisan, but what are the motives and influences which *do* act on him." This is the beginning of a credo on art that is enacted in George Eliot's fiction beginning with "The Sad Fortunes of the Reverend Amos Barton," which she started to write on 23 September 1856.

In "How I Came To Write Fiction" (1857), Marian Evans says that Lewes urged her to try her hand at a novel, certain of her ability in every way but the writing of dialogue and dramatic scenes. Once he had read what she had written, his enthusiasm and encouragement never waned. He sent the manuscript of "Amos Barton" to William Blackwood and Sons, Edinburgh, saying only that the author, whose work was unsigned, was a friend of his. John Blackwood accepted the story and sent fifty guineas as payment. *Scenes of Clerical Life* was now established, with "Amos Barton" making its way into print and "Mr. Gilfil's Love-Story" being written. "Janet's Repentance" was meant to be the penultimate story, but Blackwood's dislike of the first two parts of it discouraged the author, and the series was concluded. The first installment of "Amos Barton" appeared in *Blackwood's Magazine* in January 1857 and the last part in the February issue. Responding to John Blackwood's cover letter for the second installment, Marian Evans signed her name "George Eliot" as "a tub to throw to the whale in case of curious inquiries." She later said that she took this name because "George was Mr. Lewes's Christian name, and Eliot was a good mouth-filling, easily pronounced word." Since Marian Evans was a name held in scorn because of her liaison with Lewes, she was forced to find a pen name that would give her fiction a fair hearing. "George Eliot" was born of scandal to live in honor. The last two stories of *Scenes of Clerical Life* appeared in the next nine issues of *Blackwood's Magazine*, and all three were published as a book in two volumes under

*Portrait of George Eliot by François D'Albert-Durade, 1849
(National Portrait Gallery, London)*

the pseudonym "George Eliot" on 5 January 1858.

Scenes of Clerical Life is written out of George Eliot's recollections of the Midlands. People in Warwickshire began immediately to relate fact to fiction: the Reverend John Gwyther of Chilvers Coton Parish Church to the Reverend Amos Barton of Shepperton, his wife Emma to Milly Barton, Christiana Evans to the sharp-tongued Mrs. Hackit, and the Newdigate family to the Oldinports. Further identifications were made not only in "Amos Barton" but in each of the stories to follow. George Eliot was forced to protest that "no portrait was intended" and that "the details have been filled in from my imagination." But these first stories showed how close to the quick her imagination cut. They were also evidence of a realism that transcended local color to express the tragedy, pathos, and humor of life generally.

The sad fortunes of Amos Barton stem from selfishness and misunderstanding, and George Eliot is keen on purging her readers of such faults by letting them see these qualities in others. The two most misunderstood people in the town of Milby are Amos and the Countess Czerlaski. They are both persons whom their neighbors want to misunderstand: Amos is so com-

monplace that they do not want to believe that anyone could possibly be so dull; the countess is so beautiful that they do not want to believe that she could possibly be good. When Amos gives a home to the uncommonplace countess, Milby makes her his mistress. Two unlikely lovebirds are thus killed with one unpleasant fiction. And so is Amos's loving wife Milly, who, isolated from her friends and worn out by children and childbirth, dies—redeeming her husband in his parishoners' eyes: could anyone who grieved as deeply as Amos have ever loved anyone but his lovely, lamented wife?

George Eliot shows her readers how the town's dislike of Amos and the countess has led it to invent reasons for its scorn by creating damaging fictions about them. The townspeople enjoy their own fiction more than the truth they refuse to admit: "the simple truth ... would have seemed extremely flat to the gossips of Milby, who had made up their minds to something much more exciting." George Eliot is hinting here that readers of her story who object to its being about commonplace people—"But my dear madam, it is so very large a majority of your fellow-countrymen that are of this insignificant stamp"—are like the gossips of Milby who would rather have excitement than truth. If the reader recognizes his own lack of sympathy with the truth in Milby's lack of sympathy with it, he has a better chance to accept the truth the next time either life or art presents it to him. "Amos Barton" stands forth as a story about the dangers of failing to apprehend the truth of life and about the need for sympathetic understanding to get at that truth.

George Eliot defends her choice of an old gin-sipping parson as the hero of a romance in "Mr. Gilfil's Love-Story": "Dear ladies, allow me to plead that gin-and-water, like obesity, or baldness, or the gout, does not exclude a vast amount of antecedent romance." Just as in "Amos Barton," an unlikely hero is here justified in terms of life as the reader knows it. Gilfil is the remnant of a highly intelligent and sensitive man who, through the lack of these qualities in others, has lost the one woman he passionately loved. Maynard Gilfil, who loves Caterina Sarti, can marry her only after she has been physically and emotionally weakened by her passion for Captain Anthony Wybrow. Sir Christopher Cheverel (whose beautifully restored manor house George Eliot modeled on the Newdigates' Arbury Hall) knows nothing of his nephew Anthony's flirtation

*The philosopher Herbert Spencer, object of George Eliot's
unrequited love*

and tries to force him into the arms of an heiress
and Maynard into the arms of Caterina. All this
eventually proves too much for Caterina, who
dies in childbirth as Gilfil's wife: "the delicate
plant had been too deeply bruised, and in the
struggle to put forth a blossom it died." Something in the sensitive and stalwart Gilfil dies with
Caterina: "Tina died, and Maynard Gilfil's love
went with her into deep silence for evermore."
The gin-sipping parson survives into old age—
just, generous, sympathetic as well as loved and
respected—but only as the gnarled trunk of what
had promised to be a splendid tree. "Mr. Gilfil's
Love-Story" is a study of the effect of the loss of
love on human growth at the same time that it is
a study of the selfishness that surrounds Gilfil
and Tina and takes life and love from them. In
the dramatization of Anthony Wybrow as a Narcis-
sus who lets his lover turn into an Echo and finally loves himself to death, and in the presentation of Maynard Gilfil as an Orpheus who cannot
bring his Eurydice back from death, George Eliot

tells her story of selfishness and selflessness, giving mythical resonance to the love story of an
ordinary-looking clergyman who likes his dogs
and his drink. In this second of the *Scenes of Clerical Life* George Eliot begins to give extraordinary
dimension to ordinary lives.

This continues in "Janet's Repentance,"
where a Christlike clergyman, Edgar Tryan, struggles with a diabolical drunken lawyer, Robert
Dempster, for the soul of Dempster's wife Janet,
who is herself an alcoholic. Janet is presented as
the lost sheep that the Good Shepherd must find
and save. Mythically, in Dempster and Tryan,
Christ faces Satan; psychologically, the spoiled
child faces the self-possessed man. The story centers on Janet, the action being her repentance. It
portrays her moving out of an atmosphere of nega-
tivity and hate, centered in Dempster, and into
one of affirmation and love, centered in Tryan.
It shows how her life is changed by substituting
the gospel which Tryan preaches, one emphasizing the efficacy of sorrow, for the one she early es-
pouses: "That is the best Gospel that makes everybody happy and comfortable." This change leads
to the "recognition of something to be lived for beyond the mere satisfaction of self, which is to the
moral life what . . . a great central ganglion is to animal life." The conversion concerns the town, "a
dead an' dark place," as well as Janet. Milby
turns from the narrow, self-satisfied way which
Dempster's bullying drunkenness exemplifies to
the way of self-surrender which is Tryan's Christian message. The narrator penetrates the mys-
tique of heroism by entering minutely into the
character of Tryan to understand him by feeling
with him: "I am on the level and in the press
with him, as he struggles his way along the stony
road through the crowd of unloving fellow-men."
What George Eliot said of Julia Kavanagh's *Rachel Gray* (1856) can aptly be said of "Janet's Repentance": "It undertakes to impress us with the every-
day sorrows of our commonplace fellow-men,
and so to widen our sympathies."

Reflecting on *Scenes of Clerical Life*, Mathilde
Blind fixed on its realistic portrayal of the commonplace by speaking of George Eliot's "power
of rendering the idiom and manners of peasants,
artisans, and paupers, of calling up before us the
very gestures and phrases of parsons, country
practitioners, and other varieties of inhabitants of
provincial towns and rural districts." This homely
domestic realism, combined with psychological
penetration of character, added up to a new kind
of fiction. Shortly before the publication of *Scenes*

Isaac Pearson Evans, who was so outraged by his sister's relationship with G. H. Lewes that he did not speak or write to her for twenty-three years

of *Clerical Life*, George Eliot lamented that Charles Dickens could only give "with the utmost power . . . the external traits of our town population"; she went on to say, "if he could give us their psychological character—their conceptions of life, and their emotions—with the same truth as their idiom and manners, his books would be the greatest contribution Art has ever made to the awakening of social sympathies." What Dickens could not do George Eliot began doing in *Scenes of Clerical Life*. Adapting a program of realism from John Ruskin's *Modern Painters* (1843-1860), George Eliot insisted that art had the moral purpose of widening man's sympathy with his fellowman and that this could only be achieved by presenting a true picture of life. "The truth of infinite value" that Ruskin teaches, she says, "is *realism*—the doctrine that all truth and beauty are to be attained by a humble and faithful study of nature, and not by substituting vague forms, bred by imagination on the mists of feeling, in place of definite, substantial reality." By the "thorough acceptance of this doctrine" George Eliot began to remold the English novel.

"There can be no mistake about *Adam Bede*," wrote the reviewer for the *Times*. "It is a first-rate novel, and its author takes rank at once among the masters of the art." George Eliot began writing *Adam Bede* on 22 October 1857 and completed it on 16 November 1858. It was published in three volumes on 1 February 1859. A year later it had gone through four editions with four printings of the last edition; had been translated into French, German, Dutch, and Hungarian; had spawned a sequel; and had brought forward a Warwickshire eccentric named Joseph Liggins who claimed to be George Eliot. *Adam Bede* sold sixteen thousand copies in a year and earned George Eliot £1,705 in 1859. "In its influence," Lewes wrote to his son Charles, "and in obtaining the suffrages of the highest and wisest as well as of the ordinary novel reader, nothing equals *Adam Bede*."

"The germ of 'Adam Bede,'" George Eliot wrote in her journal, "was an anecdote told me by my Methodist Aunt Samuel (the wife of my Father's younger brother): an anecdote from her own experience. . . . It occurred to her to tell me how she had visited a condemned criminal, a very ignorant girl who had murdered her child and refused to confess—how she had stayed with her praying, through the night and how the poor creature at last broke out into tears, and confessed her crime." George Eliot turned the condemned criminal into Hetty Sorrel, while "the character of Dinah grew out of my recollections of my aunt," and "the character of Adam, and one or two incidents connected with him were suggested by my Father's early life; but Adam is not my father any more than Dinah is my aunt." They are "the suggestions of experience wrought up into new combinations."

Adam Bede presents two levels of society as one century gives way to another in 1799. The gentry are represented by Arthur Donnithorne, and the workers by Adam Bede. Their lives intersect in various ways, but especially at the Hall Farm on the Donnithorne estate, which is in the capable hands of the Poyser family. Mrs. Poyser's two nieces live with her. Hetty Sorrel catches the attention of both Arthur and Adam, while Dinah Morris is courted ineffectually by Adam's brother Seth. The more Adam finds himself in love with Hetty, the more Hetty finds herself in love with Arthur, who seduces her in a wood that is under Adam's management. She becomes pregnant, runs away, bears a child, and so neglects it that it dies. Imprisoned for murder, Hetty is visited by

Dinah, who brings her to confession and repentance. Adam, who has been sorely tried by the death of his father, now finds himself broken by the infidelity of the woman he loved and the friend he admired. Only the very gradual realization of his love for Dinah and her willingness to marry him allows him to grow whole again.

In these bare details of its plot, *Adam Bede* seems not to be realistic or subtly psychological. It is for this very reason that George Eliot refused to give an outline of the story to John Blackwood, who asked for one after reading the first volume of manuscript. "I refused to tell my story before," she wrote, "on the ground that I would not have it judged apart from my *treatment*, which alone determines the moral quality of art." *Adam Bede* develops in a tragicomic pattern. The tragic element is the idea that a man cannot escape the results of his actions: "Consequences are unpitying," says Mr. Irwine, the novel's excellent clergyman. "You can never do what's wrong without breeding sin and trouble more than you can see," Adam tells Arthur, to no avail. The happier side is the gospel of love that Dinah Morris preaches, with Jesus as her model. As for Jesus, so for Adam: the man of sorrows becomes the loving man. The process requires the self-righteous Adam to get his heartstrings bound around erring creatures—his father, Arthur, and Hetty—all of whom seriously disappoint his expectations. This involves him in suffering and leads him into fellow feeling with these sinners. It also eventually leads him to Dinah, whose attachment to him deepens her own fellow feeling and allows her to accept the common lot of woman as her own.

Adam Bede dramatizes the idea that life is a struggle in which a man succeeds by practicing virtue and working hard. Adam's devotion to work is the touchstone of his success, just as Arthur's emancipation from work leads to his ruin. The life of Adam and the Poysers is a struggle against the ignorance, carelessness, vice, and arbitrary ways of their neighbors. The Poysers carry out the struggle against their hired hands, against Hetty, and against old Squire Donnithorne; Adam carries it out against the workmen in the carpenter's shop he manages, against his alcoholic father, and against Arthur. The fistfight he has with Arthur is more than a quarrel between two men over a woman: the new ethic of duty, work, and struggle represented by Adam meets an older ethic of leisure, privilege, and heredity represented by Arthur. The ultimate success of the new over the old is suggested in the return

John Blackwood, publisher of most of George Eliot's books, in 1857

of Arthur in the epilogue, where Dinah likens him to Esau, and Adam to Jacob. *Adam Bede* is the mirror of a century that saw the rise of the middle class and the decline in importance of the aristocracy. Set at the turn of the century, it seemed prophetic of things to come. The immediate success of the novel, however, was ascribed to its accurate rendering of country characters and events. Mrs. Poyser was the runaway favorite of readers and critics alike, and her sharp, witty comments on life seemed too true to be the work of a mere novelist—an opinion which led George Eliot to protest: "I have no stock of proverbs in my memory, and there is not one thing put into Mrs. Poyser's mouth that is not fresh from my own mint." Mrs. Poyser's popularity reached its climax when Charles Buxton quoted her in parliamentary debate in the House of Commons on 8 March 1859: dressing down an opponent, he remarked that no doubt the Earl of Malmesbury "would wish that his conduct, as the farmer's wife said in *Adam Bede*, could be 'hatched over again and hatched different.' " Astute critics, such as Henry James, found Hetty Sorrel more completely original: "Mrs. Poyser is *too* epigrammatic; her wisdom smells of the lamp." But Hetty Sorrel "I accept . . . with all my heart. Of all George Eliot's female figures she is the least ambitious, and on the whole, I think, the most successful." The discontent of other readers with Hetty, who embodied "the startling horrors of rustic reality," was, however, a prelude to the reception of Maggie in *The Mill on the Floss*.

By the time *The Mill on the Floss* was published on 4 April 1860, it was common knowledge that the pseudonym "George Eliot" belonged to Marian Evans Lewes; that the moral novelist was an immoral woman. The claim of Joseph Liggins to be the author of *Scenes of Clerical Life* and *Adam Bede* became too disruptive for George Eliot to ignore, and she was forced to remove the incognito. The price was high. *The Mill on the Floss* was subjected to scathing criticism: Maggie is not of "the smallest importance to anybody in the world" but herself, said Ruskin; Tom is "a clumsy and cruel lout"; and "the rest of the characters are simply the sweepings out of a Pentonville omnibus." The great critic whom George Eliot admired but whose wife divorced him because he was unable to consummate their marriage could not abide a novel whose plot, he said, "hinged mainly on the young people's 'forgetting themselves in a boat.'" Ruskin's reaction was symptomatic of that of most critics of the novel: somehow *The Mill on the Floss* affected them where they were weakest. In reading it they followed Maggie's adventures, not "the interaction of the human organism and its environment." They felt that Maggie's free will was unfairly overcome in a moment of crisis. Their simple categories of right and wrong were undermined by a "complex web of heredity, physiology, and environment." Consequently, as David R. Carroll remarks, "The Victorian reader's sympathies have been turned against his moral judgment and he feels aggrieved."

The Victorian reader who was most aggrieved was undoubtedly Isaac Evans. He was to Marian what Tom Tulliver was to Maggie—a brother whom she loved from her childhood, who early became estranged from her, and who only lately had rejected her altogether. Marian had not told her family of her life with Lewes until nearly three years after she boarded the Channel steamer *Ravensbourne* to go abroad with him. In May 1857 she had written to Isaac to inform him that she now had "someone to take

A rare photograph of George Eliot, taken by John Edwin Mayall in 1858

care of me in the world." She had referred to Lewes as "my husband," and Isaac had asked for more details. When she supplied them, he broke off all communication with her except by way of his lawyer. (He was not personally to write to his sister until her marriage in 1880.) The childhood love of sister for brother that had been strained by their different ways of thinking and acting seemed to Marian Evans in 1857 to be irreparably ended. Past and present then came together powerfully in the story of Maggie and Tom in *The Mill on the Floss*.

The novel's long beginning recounts the fortunes of the Dodson sisters and their families. The Tullivers stand apart from the Gleggs and the Pullets and are the center of the story. They have two children whose temperaments reflect Tulliver impetuosity and Dodson respectability. Maggie, like her father, is affectionate, headstrong, and rebellious. Tom, like his mother and aunts, is self-righteous and self-satisfied. More intelligent than her brother, Maggie is interested in many things that mean nothing to him. She is befriended by Philip Wakem, whose father has exacerbated Mr. Tulliver's ruin; but Tom banishes Philip from Maggie's life. Along with Philip goes an interest in art, music, and literature that she shared with the one soul that had been completely sympathetic with her own. Maggie turns to religion in an attempt to stupefy her faculties and to banish all wishing from her life, while Tom works off the debts that have resulted from his father's bankruptcy and death. When Maggie realizes, as Philip says, that "we can never give up longing and wishing while we are thoroughly alive," her conduct takes another turn in opening itself up to life. She becomes attached to Stephen Guest, her cousin's fiancé, and, caught up in the tide of her emotions, she drifts away with him in a boat until it becomes too late for them to return home the same day. When, against his pleas, she returns as soon as she can, Tom, now the model of a successful St. Ogg's businessman, repudiates her as a lost woman: "You shall find no home with me. . . . You have disgraced us all." Only in the end does Tom have a change of heart, but by then it is too late to be effectual. When the river Floss floods and Tom is trapped at the mill, Maggie rows out to save him. In the boat with his sister, Tom in the moment before his death revalues her life: "They sat mutely gazing at each other: Maggie with eyes of intense life looking out from a weary, beaten face—Tom with a certain awe and humiliation." In an instant their boat is swamped: "brother and sister had gone down in an embrace never to be parted."

The power of the book lies in an evocation of childhood that was unequaled when *The Mill on the Floss* was published, and in the onrush of the catastrophe toward the novel's end. The flood that kills Tom and Maggie has often been complained of, but it was the ending that George Eliot had intended from the beginning. It enabled her to tie the body of the novel to the history of the place where it is set. St. Ogg's has two legends associated with it: the legend of the flood speaks of a river that grows angry when the Tullivers' Dorlcote Mill changes hands. The legend of St. Ogg tells of a tenderhearted boatman who shows human sympathy in the midst of nature's anger. One legend ties natural effect to human cause and suggests a way to control the river by controlling the working of the mill. The other shows that human kindness enables man to survive nature's ravages. The legend of the flood

is one of anger and retribution, and the legend of the patron saint is one of sympathy and love. The flooding of the Floss is closely associated with Tom's anger in the novel, and his attempted rescue is closely associated with Maggie's love. The legends associated with the origin of St. Ogg's are transformed into the characters and events whose story is told as *The Mill on the Floss*.

Having finished the novel, George Eliot left with Lewes for Italy. In Florence he suggested to her the possibility of writing a novel centered on the life of Girolamo Savonarola, and she began preliminary research for it. All of George Eliot's novels are the product of research—"Whatever she has done, she has studied for," said Emily Davies—even though the earlier ones are principally indebted to recollections of her Warwickshire days. *Romola* (1863), however, was worked up from scratch, and the reading and note taking it required so entered into the author's life that she said of it, "I began it a young woman, —I finished it an old woman." On their return from Italy the Leweses stopped in Switzerland to see Charles, Thornton, and Herbert, Lewes's sons by Agnes. Charles returned home with them after they stopped in Geneva to see the D'Albert-Durades. George Eliot gave the right of translating *Adam Bede* into French to M. D'Albert, who would eventually also translate *The Mill on the Floss* (1863), *Silas Marner* (1863), *Romola* (1878) and *Scenes of Clerical Life* (1884). They returned in June to a house they had taken the year before in Wandsworth, with George Eliot thinking about her Italian novel. But having just acquired three children herself, she wrote instead a novel about a child who comes suddenly into a man's life. The labors of *Romola* were delayed, and *Silas Marner* was written. George Eliot began the novel on 30 September 1860 and finished it on 10 March 1861. It was published by Blackwood on 2 April 1861.

Silas Marner is a tale of alienation that is perched on the edge of tragedy but manages to be a comedy of the kind Demetrius called "tragedy in the disguise of mirth." Silas, a weaver, belongs to a Dissenting sect in the northern manufacturing town of Lantern-Yard. He believes in God, is engaged to a woman named Sarah, and trusts his friend William Dane completely. Dane, however, also loves Sarah and betrays Silas's trust by arranging a theft while Silas is incapacitated with catalepsy. The money is cached in Silas's dwelling, and he is accused of the crime. Silas leaves town, goes south, and settles in Raveloe. He lives there

The first page of the manuscript for Adam Bede, *inscribed to George Henry Lewes (British Museum)*

without a friend, without a woman to love, and without a God to believe in. Year in and year out he works at his loom, amassing a hoard of gold that becomes his only love until that too is taken from him by the wastrel scion of Red House, Dunstan Cass. Silas reports the theft at the Rainbow, a tavern, and the worthies who are gathered there seriously discuss the crime over their beer pots. During the Christmas season of Silas's fifteenth year in Raveloe, he awakes from a cataleptic seizure to find that a golden-haired child has crawled to his hearth. Eppie replaces his gold as something to love and live for, and he rears her as his daughter with the help of Dolly Winthrop. Having kept secret his first marriage to an opium addict who is now long dead, Godfrey Cass decides to claim the child from that marriage after the skeleton of his brother, identified by a whip, is found in a drained pit alongside Silas's gold. To prevent a similarly startling revelation of his own guilt, Godfrey confesses to his wife, and they go together to Silas's house to claim Godfrey's daughter. But Eppie refuses to recognize any father except the one who has loved and cared for her. Eventually she marries Aaron Winthrop, and the couple lives with Silas. The Rainbow society looks on in the person of its chief elder, Mr. Macey, and approves the happy outcome.

Silas in the end gets both the child and the gold; he wins at precisely those points where the Cass brothers lose. He wins because he has learned to love and to act responsibly; they lose because they act irresponsibly. Trusting in chance, Dunstan robs Silas; trusting in chance, Godfrey refuses to acknowledge Eppie until it is too late. But their moments of trust in chance are precisely those that release Silas from its grip. Because his money is taken from him, human feeling is stirred in Silas: he is, as Mr. Macey says, "mushed." Because Eppie comes to him, the stirrings of feeling burgeon into love and responsibility. The moral and emotional hardness that has encased Silas from the time Dane betrayed him is chipped away until a human being is revealed. Silas is redeemed during the Christmas season by the coming of a child for whom he makes himself responsible and whom he learns to love. A father replaces a miser when a child replaces a gold hoard. Eppie then leads Silas back to the community of his fellowmen. The novel that began so darkly thus ends brightly. *Silas Marner* finally declares itself a comedy that does not avoid tragedies but contains them: Silas loses all to find all and dies that he might live.

George Eliot had for a third time written a novel about ordinary people. She had once again done for fiction what Wordsworth had done for poetry by showing what was extraordinary in the lives of ordinary men and women. Appropriately, *Silas Marner* begins with lines from Wordsworth—George Eliot's favorite poet:

> A child, more than all other gifts
> That earth can offer to declining man,
> Brings hope with it, and forward-looking
> thoughts.

The novel was received as a relief from the moral complexities of *The Mill on the Floss*, though some reviewers complained again of its low-life realism, like that of the Dutch painters George Eliot had extolled in chapter 17 of *Adam Bede*. The novel gradually gained wide popularity, surviving in schoolrooms when George Eliot's other novels went unread. *Silas Marner* was mistaken for a simple moral fable that had a "tender religious charm" to it, when in fact it was a version of secular redemption through human love. Its disappearance from reading lists in secondary schools allowed it to find a more critical reader-ship on its own and thereby regain its place as a classic for mature readers.

When *Silas Marner* was reprinted in the Cabinet Edition of *The Works of George Eliot* (1878-1885), it appeared with two stories that had been previously published anonymously. "The Lifted Veil" had appeared in *Blackwood's Magazine* in July 1859, and "Brother Jacob," which was written in August 1860, had appeared in the *Cornhill* magazine in July 1864. These two stories round out the early fiction of George Eliot. "The Lifted Veil," the more important of the two, inverts the action of *Silas Marner*: its protagonist, Latimer, portrays what Silas would have become if he had kept his gold and not found Eppie. Silas dramatizes Carlyle's "Everlasting Yea," and Latimer his "Everlasting No." Latimer can form no bond of fellow feeling with anyone he meets because he cannot accept the mixture of good and evil in human nature. He is blessed with an artist's sensibility but cursed by his inability to create. He is the projection of what George Eliot could have become if she had not sympathetically accepted man as he is: "the only effect I ardently long to produce by my writings is," she says, "that those who read them should be able to *imagine* and to *feel* the pains and joys of those who differ from themselves in everything but the broad fact of being struggling, erring, human creatures." Latimer cannot create because he cannot feel with his fellowman. He is the opposite then of both George Eliot and the best readers of her fiction.

The early phase of George Eliot's career ends with *Silas Marner*, a novel that is generally considered to be the most rounded and balanced of her works. From "Amos Barton" to *Silas Marner*, she gathers together her powers to explore the tragedy and comedy of life as it is lived in carefully delimited rural communities. Beginning with *Romola*, her perspective widens, and she deals with the complexities of human nature as men find themselves living through turning points in the history of Western civilization. She focuses on a period of reformation in Florence in the 1490s in *Romola*; she brings alive the era of Reform in England from 1829 to 1833 in *Felix Holt, The Radical* and *Middlemarch*; and she projects an 1860s Zionist vision of a new Israel in *Daniel Deronda* (1876). George Eliot's last four novels engaged her in a great deal of historical research. "When you see her," Lewes wrote to John Blackwood concerning *Romola*, "mind your care is to discountenance the idea of a Romance being the product of an Encyclopaedia." *Romola* is so filled

Strafgericht traf die Unschuldige, da ihre Macht
gegen den Schuldigen nicht ausreichte!"

41

Instances of Heroism. In the wreck of the Rothsay
Castle, two men had hold of one plank at the same
moment. Each wished to let it go & save the other:
one because his companion in danger was old, the
other because he was young. Both let it go at the
same moment. They had previously been strangers
to each other. Both were afterwards picked up &
saved, & met again. (Told in Harriet Martineau's
History of the Thirty Years' Peace.)

41ᵃ

How to find the whereabout of the Olympiads.
Multiply the particular Olympiad by four,
& then subtract the product from 777. Thus,
if it be the 70ᵗʰ Olympiad — 70 × 4 yields 280;
subtract 280 from 777, the remainder will
be 497; & that expresses the Olympic or Grecian
period in the Christian equivalent of year B.C.

41ᵇ

"Here Greece shall stay; or, if all Greece retire,
Myself will stay, till Troy or I expire;
Myself & Sthenelus will fight for fame.;
God bade us fight, & 'twas with God we came"
　　　　　　　　　　　　　　　Pope's Iliad, B. IX, 65.

Νῶϊ δ', ἐγὼ Σθένελός τε, μαχησόμεθ', εἰσόκε τέκμωρ
Ἰλίου εὕρωμεν· σὺν γὰρ θεῷ εἰλήλουθμεν.

A page from one of George Eliot's notebooks (Beinecke Library, Yale University)

with learning that Henry James called it "a splendid mausoleum" in which George Eliot's "simplicity . . . lies buried." There was certainly nothing simple about the conception and writing of it. The idea for a novel about Savonarola had been presented to George Eliot in Florence in May 1860. After writing *Silas Marner*, she went again to Florence in May 1861 for further research. When she returned to England, reading and note taking continued. On 7 October 1861 she began writing *Romola* but by the end of the month was "utterly desponding" about it. On 1 January 1862 she began writing again and finished it on 9 June 1863, having deserted Blackwood as her publisher—which she later admitted may have been a mistake—to be paid seven thousand pounds by Smith, Elder to publish it in fourteen installments in the *Cornhill* magazine before its appearance as a three-volume novel. The encyclopedic research, the delay caused by *Silas Marner*, the false start, the change of publisher, and the serial publication altogether wore George Eliot out and made her, as she said, "an old woman."

Romola is the story of a faithful woman who marries a faithless man. Romola is faithful to her blind, scholarly father, Bardo; to her beloved godfather, Bernardo, a Medicean politician; to Savonarola, the democratic reformer of Florence; and to Florence itself. Her husband, Tito, is unfaithful to these men, to their city, and to Romola. His treachery costs the men their lives, and with nothing to live for, Romola herself wants to die. But she does not: seeking death, she finds life. *Romola* is consequently a novel about renaissance. It asks how a woman can be born again once those whom she loves are dead and once personal love itself dies within her. The question is asked in a tragic form that gives universal meaning to a unique period of history, and it is answered in a coda that points away from future tragedy. *Romola* takes up where *The Mill on the Floss* left off: *The Mill on the Floss* ends with a flood, a modern deluge that wrecks a civilization; *Romola* begins in the Renaissance, the rebirth of civilization. The historical time of *Romola* coordinates perfectly with its theme of rebirth. It suggests the intimate relationship between the individual and his civilization while both are in the process of renewing themselves. Thus, Savonarola presents to Romola the same ideal that he presents to Florence. Because she is less compromising than he in living out that ideal, she is renewed and Florence is not; she lives and he dies. Romola is reborn from water when her boat is washed

ashore, and Savonarola dies by fire when he is burned at the stake. But in his death he is purified, and his principles live on for others to follow. Renaissance is made personal; only when a sufficient number of people embrace it personally can there be a public renewal.

If the Renaissance meant the cultural rebirth of a civilization and the liberation of the individual, it did not necessarily mean the spiritual rebirth of either. A completely liberated Renaissance man such as Tito therefore dies because of selfishness, and late quattrocento Florence falls into anarchy and succumbs to tyranny because it repudiates Savonarola's reform. *Romola* is consequently centrally concerned with the birth of a spiritual ideal, in one woman who endures the loss of everyone and everything she loves and survives the license of a civilization that executes the man who gave it an ideal.

At the end of *Romola*—in the coda that George Eliot said belonged to her "earliest vision of the story"—her moral belief in fellow feeling as man's chief saving virtue achieves a new status. Bereft, betrayed, unloved, Romola wants to die, but she must live; others need her. Neither personal pleasure nor personal pain is allowed to be an adequate guide for moral action. Each man, though unique, shares with other men a common humanity that binds him to life when for personal reasons he might choose not to live. Fellow feeling is therefore a universal ethical principle that governs both life and death, and *Romola* puts it to the test. Humanity in the novel is very often deplorable, showing itself in pedantic and vengeful learned men, in faithless and treacherous lovers, in fanatical zealots, and in the bestial rich and the depraved poor. George Eliot shows in the novel that life is painful because of other human beings, but that Romola must affirm life at just that point because the very pain others cause her shows their dire need for her.

When the critics protested against the erotic attraction between Maggie and Stephen in *The Mill on the Floss*, George Eliot replied: "If the ethics of art do not admit the truthful presentation of character . . . *then*, it seems to me, the ethics of art are too narrow, and must be widened!" When the critics set up "a universal howl of discontent" over her departure in *Romola* from "the breath of cows and the scent of hay" that made *Adam Bede* so popular, George Eliot anticipated them in a letter to Sara Hennell: "If one is to have freedom to write out one's own varying unfolding self, and not be a machine always grinding out

George Henry Lewes, George Eliot's "husband," in 1859.
The pug dog was given to them by John Blackwood
after the successful publication of Adam Bede.

the same material or spinning the same sort of web, one cannot always write for the same public." In acting like an artist, George Eliot lost some of her audience. The complaint was that the setting was too remote, the evocation of time and place too learned, the "instructive antiquarianism" too lifeless. Whereas Robert Browning called *Romola* "the noblest and most heroic prose poem" that he had ever read, and a small coterie came to refer to George Eliot as "the author of *Romola*," the more general reaction to the novel was given in the *Saturday Review*: "No reader of *Romola* will lay it down without admiration, and few without regret."

The publication of *Romola* changed the way that George Eliot was generally viewed by the Victorian public. Although she was still an outsider because of her irregular union with Lewes, she came to be looked upon as a great moral teacher all the same. A new permanent residence (The Priory, 21 North Bank, Regent's Park) and Sunday af-

ternoon receptions added a sense of ritual to her life that enhanced her image as a Victorian sage. The Leweses had The Priory entirely to themselves because Lewes's sons had begun to strike out on their own: Charles, who had a position at the post office, married; Thornton and Herbert went to South Africa to farm a three-thousand acre tract of land on the Orange River (both, however, were to die young, Thornie in 1869 and Bertie in 1875). After another trip to Italy, George Eliot settled at The Priory to attempt something altogether new for her in a drama called "The Spanish Gypsy." The first try at writing was a failure, and Lewes took the manuscript away from her when physical and emotional afflictions over her inability to write became gravely debilitating. A month later, on 29 March 1865, she began work on *Felix Holt, The Radical*, which was finished on 31 May 1866. Lewes offered the manuscript to Smith, Elder for five thousand pounds; his price was not met because the firm had lost a considerable sum of money on *Romola*. *Felix Holt* was then offered to John Blackwood, who, finding it "a perfect marvel," paid what was asked, and the novel was published on 15 June 1866.

Felix Holt divides its interest between the working class as represented by Felix and the gentry of Transome Court, especially Harold Transome and his aging mother. They are linked together by Esther Lyon, who is courted by both Harold and Felix and who, though reared by the Dissenting clergyman Rufus Lyon, turns out to be the heiress to Transome Court. Felix figures in the novel as a moral catalyst for Esther. Through him she learns what she really wants to do with her life. Set in 1833 at the time of the first election following the passage of the Reform Bill of 1832, the novel presents Felix as a political Radical who accidently kills a man in the midst of a rioting mob. From the courtroom and the jail he first wins Esther's conscience and then her heart; at the same time, the elegant Mrs. Transome tries to win Esther as her daughter because Harold had repudiated his mother when he discovered that he is illegitimate. Torn between Felix and poverty on the one side and Harold and wealth on the other, Esther chooses the former, having briefly experienced the emptiness and sorrow of the latter in a stay at Transome Court.

Felix Holt is not so much Felix's novel as it is Esther's: it is the drama of her moral development. Felix leads Esther to examine the meaning of the goals that she has set for herself: riches, fin-

First page of the manuscript for The Mill on the Floss *(British Library)*

ery, and leisure. Felix forces Esther to confront her erotic impulses and to ask herself whether life is better with love or luxury if one must choose between the two. Felix is indispensable to Esther's ethical and erotic life insofar as she comes to realize that without loving him, she cannot be moral: "the man she loved was her hero," and "her woman's passion and her reverence for rarest goodness rushed together in an undivided current." Because of Felix she realizes that Transome Court is a "silken bondage" and "nothing better than a well-cushioned despair."

One of the problems that critics have found with the novel is that there is so much in it that Esther's moving back and forth between two levels of society is not a sufficient dramatic action to unify it. This is especially the case because the characterization of Mrs. Transome is so splendid an achievement that the reader tends to forget the eponymous hero, while the speech and movements of this pathetically tragic old woman linger powerfully in the memory. Mrs. Transome is so poignantly drawn that it seems inadequate to think of her as simply an instance of what Esther could become if she turned her back on Felix and took Harold's hand in marriage. The felt life in the novel comes together in Mrs. Transome while its moral intention is focused on the more forgettable Felix. As in Dickens's *Great Expectations* (1861), which anticipates a great deal that is in *Felix Holt*, Mrs. Transome, like Miss Havisham before her, draws out her creator's imaginative genius so completely that no other character is her equal.

With *Felix Holt* finished, George Eliot took up *The Spanish Gypsy* again, but she no longer thought of it as a drama to be staged; it would be a narrative poem with significant dramatic sequences in it. After a trip to Spain in the winter of 1866-1867, she was able to work more comfortably at the poem, and it was completed on 29 April 1868. After its publication, she wrote a series of poems—"Agatha," "How Lisa Loved the King," and the "Brother and Sister" sonnets—before turning her mind once more to a novel. In August 1869 she began work on a novel called "Middlemarch," which in its original conception was only part of the novel that is known by that name today. It was to have focused on Lydgate and the Vincys and to have been set in the middle-class society of the town. Work on this novel was interrupted at the end of 1870 by the writing of two more poems—"The Legend of Jubal" and "Armgart"—and by a peremptory

idea for another novel called "Miss Brooke," which would focus on Dorothea and the life of the gentry surrounding a town like Middlemarch. Early in 1871 George Eliot began to amalgamate the Lydgate and Dorothea stories into the one novel under the title *Middlemarch: A Study of Provincial Life*, which Lewes persuaded Blackwood to publish in eight parts, the first part appearing in December 1871 and the last in December 1872. *Middlemarch* was also issued as a four-volume novel in late 1872. "It treats marriage, medical progress, religious idealism, the abstruse researches of mythological Biblical scholarship, recalling Strauss and his peers, the coming of railways into agricultural communities, Reform, conservation, sex, changing fashions in art, and the eternal themes of painful discovery of truth as opposed to romantic, or conventional fantasy," says A. S. Byatt. "It is a novel, above all, about *intelligence* and its triumphs, failures, distractions, fallings-short, compromises and doggedness." The greatness of *Middlemarch* was immediately acknowledged; the novel was a classic in its own time. Not that it did not raise complaints similar to those that greeted *The Mill on the Floss*, where complexity compounded perplexed the critics: it caused confusion because it was even more complex morally and aesthetically than its predecessor. In *The Mill on the Floss* George Eliot had written a tragedy; in *Middlemarch* she wrote an epic. "If we write novels so," asked Henry James, "how shall we write History?"—a question that he answered tellingly in the same review: *Middlemarch* "sets a limit ... to the development of the old-fashioned English novel." After it, fiction must dare to be difficult. *Middlemarch* could be given too much praise, said Geoffrey Tollotson, only "by saying that it was easily the best of the half-dozen best novels in the world."

Middlemarch: A Study of Provincial Life spreads so wide a canvas that it is frequently compared with Leo Tolstoy's *War and Peace* (1862-1869). In it George Eliot weaves together four stories to make one novel. That of Dorothea Brooke shows her making a marriage on idealistic grounds to a scholarly clergyman, Edward Casaubon, who is at least twice her age. She marries him to be his helpmate but turns out to be his critic. Their marriage is a purgatory to each until Casaubon's timely death. A second story, that of Lydgate, is similar to the first. As a gentleman he seems an ideal catch to the daughter of the mayor of Middlemarch, Rosamond Vincy, whose middle-class upbringing requires her to marry

justify his insincerity by manifesting its prudence.
And ~~[crossed out]~~
~~[crossed out]~~
~~[crossed out]~~ in this point of trusting to some throw
of fortune's dice, Godfrey ~~[]~~ can hardly be called specially
old-fashioned. Favourable chance, I fancy, is
the god of all men who follow their own devices instead of obeying a law they believe in.
Let even a polished man of these days ~~[crossed out]~~
be set into a position he is ashamed to avow, to
his mind will be bent on all the possible issues that
may deliver him from the calculable results of that
position; let him live outside his income or trust
the resolute honest work that brings wages & he
will presently find himself dreaming of a possible
benefactor, a possible simpleton who may be cajoled
into being his interest, a possible state of mind in
some possible person not yet forthcoming. Let
him neglect the responsibilities of his office, & he
will inevitably anchor himself on the chance that
the thing left undone may turn out not to be of
the supposed importance; let him betray his friend's
confidence & he will adore that same cunning ~~[]~~

Manuscript for the end of chapter nine of Silas Marner *(British Library)*

into gentility. Her respectability destroys his scientific vocation and leads him to an undistinguished career and an early grave. A third story is that of Nicholas Bulstrode, a banker with a passion for preaching religion and making his favor in God's eyes felt by all—until his past reveals him to have done a dire deed of a kind that he repeats in the present. Linking these three stories together is Will Ladislaw, who learns that Bulstrode is his stepgrandfather, who is mistakenly thought to be Rosamond's lover, and who actually becomes Dorothea's second husband. Ladislaw's love for Dorothea is paralleled by Fred Vincy's for Mary Garth in a fourth story that also introduces the figures of Caleb Garth and Peter Featherstone as original instances of integrity and indulgence, respectively.

A singular note in this novel is the intelligence of the narrator and his sympathy with the human condition. There are no caricatures among the major characters. Each is known so thoroughly that whatever is reprehensible, or indeed even at times criminal, in him is understood in terms of a complex of human desires not very different from those of the reader himself. "With George Eliot, to understand is to pity," says Gordon S. Haight, "—as far as possible, to forgive." In a novel that has no epigraph of its own, one that could serve for the whole novel comes at the head of chapter 42, in which the reader is made thoroughly to understand the character of Edward Casaubon: "How much methinks, I could despise this man, / Were I not bound in charity against it!"

Middlemarch begins with a sixteenth-century prelude that presents the life of St. Teresa of Avila as an exemplum of the meeting of individual aspiration and epical opportunity: the time was right for her to become a heroine because Spain had just come to national unity by joining the kingdoms of Aragon and Castille, had just emancipated itself from the Moors at the battle of Granada, and had just begun to produce a literature that would issue in a Golden Age. The one thing it lacked was a spiritual ideal, and that was what Teresa gave it by reforming the Carmelite order, founding twenty-six convents and sixteen monasteries. She gave Spain spiritual direction by renewing its religious life. *Middlemarch* goes on to present a series of stories in which individual aspiration does not find an era of epos, but only a time of confusion. England in the Reform era is separated into factions either to support or to oppose a new organization of society. This is a pe-

riod characterized more by pettiness than by magnanimity. The individual aspiring to greatness in such a society finds no sure guidelines and becomes a victim of his lofty aspirations. *Middlemarch*, then, is a novel about individual aspiration coming face to face with social limitation and the unhappy consequences of their meeting. In *Middlemarch* men and women undergo the "varying experiments of Time" from 1829 to 1832; those who emerge as heroes and heroines become in some small way part of the larger historical movement for reform. Caleb Garth insists on reform in the management of estates; Will Ladislaw enters politics on the side of the Reform Bill and becomes a member of Parliament; and Dorothea Brooke promotes the work and ideals of each. Characterized by personal integrity, fellow feeling, and a sense of their place in history, these three characters become instances of the muted heroism open to men and women in a complex world. The novel's most notable failures, Bulstrode and Casaubon, lack all the qualities that allot man a modicum of greatness. Lydgate, a compassionate man with a sense of historical progress, is the novel's great tragic character because his heroic temper is geared to science alone; in other things, like the judgment of women, his mind is common and uncritical. His "spots of commonness" destroy the aims of his life, which were "to do good small work for Middlemarch" and "great work for the world." The failure of this noble man, understood in its every detail, is the most heartrending drama in all of George Eliot's fiction.

Daniel Deronda is a logical continuation of *Middlemarch*, which constantly emphasizes themes of quest: Dorothea seeks a spiritual ideal; Lydgate, scientific discovery and medical reform; Casaubon, scholarly recognition; Bulstrode, divine instrumentality; Ladislaw, a purposeful vocation; and English society seeks Reform. Daniel Deronda seeks his roots in those of his people; he seeks to establish a national center for the Jews so that they may have their own identity as a nation. The far-resonant action which presumed an era of epos in the prelude, and which was not apparent to George Eliot as a possibility in *Middlemarch*, became apparent to her when she wrote *Daniel Deronda*.

The novel opens in the casino at Leubronn, where Gwendolen Harleth is playing roulette. This scene is based on George Eliot's experience in the Kursaal at Homburg, where in October 1872 she saw Lord Byron's grandniece "com-

*The Priory, George Eliot's home from 1863 until
her marriage to John Cross*

pletely in the grasp of this mean, money-raking demon." The germ of Gwendolen's story was here. Mordecai's also had a German origin. Born in Silesia and educated in Berlin, Emanuel Deutsch came into George Eliot's life in 1866. He was a cataloguer of books in the British Museum by profession but a radical Jewish nationalist by preference. He taught George Eliot Hebrew and gave her the idea of a Jewish national homeland. She visited him when he was ill with cancer and mourned his death in May 1873. In June she began thinking about a new book and soon was reading in Jewish sources. Her work on *Daniel Deronda* was delayed by the publication of *The Legend of Jubal and Other Poems* (May 1874), but by June she was again at work on the novel. John Blackwood agreed to publish it in eight parts, the first book appearing on 1 February 1876 and the last on 1 September 1876. The novel was then published in a four-volume edition.

After being reared by Sir Hugo Mallinger, Daniel Deronda finds out that his parents were Jews and that his mother, the daughter of a proto-Zionist, is still alive and wishes to see him before she dies. Having already befriended Ezra Cohen

(familiarly called Mordecai) and his sister Mirah, Deronda rejoices in an ancestry that gives him a sense of himself, makes possible his marriage to Mirah, and enables him to fulfill Mordecai's prophecy that he will be a leader of his people. *Daniel Deronda* centers on this quest for self that is at the same time a quest for others; but it is anything but a simple romance. It is a story of psychological growth that is achieved by the experience of nearly unbearable pain. It has a counterpoint in another story, that of Gwendolen Harleth, in which Deronda must act as guide for a troubled soul: he must be to Gwendolen what Mordecai is to him. She has made, against her conscience, a hideous marriage to Henleigh Grandcourt—his mistress and the mother of his four children is the woman Gwendolen knows he should have married—and she involves Deronda in her miseries, falling in love with him as well. The story of Gwendolen and Grandcourt—a story of jaded aristocratic England in the 1860s—is far more thoroughly dramatized and consequential than that of Deronda and the Jewish community that surrounds him. The critics, as David Carroll says, were quick to see this: "Just as they had jettisoned the final volume of *The Mill on the Floss*, the historical background of *Romola*, and the tendentious commentary of *Middlemarch*, so now they dismiss the Jewish half of *Daniel Deronda*." Deronda is damned as "the Prince of Prigs" for not marrying Gwendolen and for imbibing too deeply the "bottled moonshine of Mordecai's mysteries." In 1948 F. R. Leavis went so far as to retitle the novel "Gwendolen Harleth." George Eliot nevertheless held her ground and insisted that she "meant everything in the book to be related to everything else there." For her, *Daniel Deronda* examines man's need to establish a rule within himself before he can effectively establish himself among other men. It treats this need in the context of a yearning for deliverance from individual and racial bondage so that men and women can live fuller and better lives. At the novel's center is the age-old Hebrew myth of the deliverance of Israel from exile to the promised land. George Eliot finds in this myth a transcendent moral impulse that encompasses Jew and Gentile alike and that leads all men to yearn for spiritual as well as political freedom. Thus, the mastery over self that Gwendolen and Deronda seek makes Daniel as integral a part of her life as Mordecai is of Daniel's. For many the ideal ending of such mutual quests would be marriage, but George Eliot denies her readers this easy conclusion. In *Daniel Deronda* the psychological development of Gwendolen and Daniel demands the emergence of moral independence for self-realization. For Gwendolen to marry Daniel would be for her to commit herself to continuous dependence on him, which would be a reversion to her childhood and a denial of maturity. Gwendolen has finally to choose for herself in accordance with the standards she has taken from Deronda and from the experience of sorrow in her awful marriage. George Eliot is finally ruthless with Gwendolen so that she may be truly free.

When Deronda learns of his heritage and accepts it, his life opens out not only beyond any future that Gwendolen could share with him, but also beyond the limits of Jewishness itself. Deronda cannot be the kind of intolerant man that his grandfather Daniel Charisi was. He tells his mother that "the Christian sympathies in which my mind was reared can never die out of me." He adds his Jewish heritage to his Christian upbringing and reconciles Jew and Christian within himself; his vocation to a Jewish cause enlarges the scope of his Christian principles. Just as Israel is meant in this novel to figure forth a universal brotherhood—it is to be the "halting-place of enmities"—Daniel Deronda is meant to figure forth a universal man. With him George Eliot's fiction had reached the limit of her moral imagination. She had written her last novel.

If George Eliot's fiction is considered from beginning to end, certain broad patterns can be seen in it. From "Amos Barton" to *Silas Marner* she concentrates on the individual in his community, conceived of as a traditional group; from *Romola* to *Daniel Deronda* she concentrates on the individual in his world, conceived of as a polity in a state of change. In *Adam Bede* a new man is created, in *The Mill on the Floss* an old world is destroyed by flood, and in *Silas Marner* a man is redeemed and a new Eden is created and presided over by Unseen Love. In the later novels these patterns of creation, destruction, and redemption are repeated more complexly. In *Romola* a Renaissance civilization is recreated, in *Felix Holt* and *Middlemarch* an old world dies and the world of reform is born, and in *Daniel Deronda* Israel, the halting-place of enmities, is the home of fellow feeling itself. Each of the last four novels reworks themes of the first three and sets them at crucial moments for civilization: Florence in the 1490s wavering between democracy and tyranny; England from 1829 to 1833 wavering between the old cor-

*John Walter Cross, who married George Eliot
on 6 May 1880*

ruption and reform; and the people of Israel nearing the end of exile from the New Jerusalem. In all the novels constant patterns of human experience are organized into constant patterns of aesthetic experience. George Eliot moves from tragicomedy (*Adam Bede*) through tragedy (*The Mill on the Floss* and *Romola*) to comedy as "tragedy in the disguise of mirth" (*Silas Marner* and *Felix Holt*) to epic (*Middlemarch* and *Daniel Deronda*). She ends her career as a novelist not with man accepted and assimilated into his community or rejected from it, but with man questing for new values and modes of existence.

Her last book, *Impressions of Theophrastus Such*, a collection of essays, was published in May 1879. It came from the press between the deaths of the two men who knew her best. George Henry Lewes died on 30 November 1878. Lewes had said of George Eliot, "She is a Mediaeval Saint with a grand genius"; she could not but grieve long and deeply over the death of the

George Eliot's grave in Highgate Cemetery, London

and referred to him as their nephew, he proposed to George Eliot, who was twenty years his senior, three times. They were married on 6 May 1880 at St. George's Church, Hanover Square. Isaac Evans, who had not written to his sister since 1857, sent his congratulations. George Eliot did not, however, live long enough to enjoy the respectability conferred upon her by a church wedding. She died on 22 December 1880 after an attack of acute laryngitis followed by an attack of kidney stones that together brought on heart failure. She was buried next to Lewes in Highgate Cemetery, a place in Westminster Abbey being denied her as a woman, in Thomas Henry Huxley's words, "whose life and opinions were in notorious antagonism to Christian practice in regard to marriage, and Christian theory in regard to dogma." In the centenary year of her death, nonetheless, George Eliot made her way to the Poet's Corner of Westminster Abbey, when a memorial stone was placed there in her honor.

Letters:

John W. Cross, ed., *George Eliot's Life as Related in Her Letters and Journals*, 3 volumes (Edinburgh & London: Blackwood, 1885);

Gordon S. Haight, ed., *The George Eliot Letters*, 9 volumes (New Haven: Yale University Press, 1954-1955; 1978).

Bibliographies:

W. J. Harvey, "George Eliot," in *Victorian Fiction: A Guide to Research*, edited by Lionel Stevenson (New York: Modern Language Association, 1964), pp. 294-323;

Constance M. Fulmer, *George Eliot: A Reference Guide, 1858-1971* (Boston: G. K. Hall, 1977);

U. C. Knoepflmacher, "George Eliot," in *Victorian Fiction: A Second Guide to Research*, edited by George H. Ford (New York: Modern Language Association, 1978), pp. 234-273;

David Leon Higdon, "A Bibliography of George Eliot Criticism, 1971-1977," *Bulletin of Bibliography*, 37: 2 (April-June 1980): 90-103;

George Levine with Patricia O'Hara, *An Annotated Critical Bibliography of George Eliot* (Brighton: Harvester, 1988).

Biographies:

Gordon S. Haight, *George Eliot: A Biography* (New York: Oxford University Press, 1968);

man who first called that genius out of the depths of her soul and supported it tirelessly all his life. George Eliot understood that no author could have had a better editor and publisher than John Blackwood. When he died on 29 October 1879, she paid him the tribute he deserved: "He has been bound up with what I most cared for in my life for more than twenty years and his good qualities have made many things easy for me that without him would often have been difficult." Bereft of the two men who were her support in life, she turned to John Walter Cross to help her with many of the things that Lewes or Blackwood would otherwise have done for her. Cross had been an intimate of the Leweses since 1869. A banker, he had handled their investments, and when they sought a country house, it was he who found The Heights at Witley for them. Although the Leweses called him Johnny

Ruby V. Redinger, *George Eliot: The Emergent Self* (New York: Knopf, 1975);

Ira Bruce Nadel, "George Eliot and her Biographers" in *George Eliot: A Centenary Tribute*, edited by Gordon S. Haight and Rosemary T. VanArsdel (Totowa, N.J.: Barnes & Noble, 1982);

Valerie A. Dodd, *George Eliot: An Intellectual Life* (New York: St. Martin's Press, 1990);

Ina Taylor, *A Woman of Contradictions: The Life of George Eliot* (New York: Morrow, 1990).

References:

Ian Adam, ed., *Essays on Middlemarch: This Particular Web* (Toronto: University of Toronto Press, 1975);

A. S. Byatt, *George Eliot 1819-1880* (Harmondsworth, U.K.: Penguin, 1980);

David R. Carroll, ed., *George Eliot: The Critical Heritage* (New York: Barnes & Noble, 1971; London: Routledge & Kegan Paul, 1971);

Gordon S. Haight, ed., *A Century of George Eliot Criticism* (Boston: Houghton, Mifflin, 1965);

Barbara Hardy, *The Novels of George Eliot: A Study in Form* (London: Athlone Press, 1959);

W. J. Harvey, *The Art of George Eliot* (London: Chatto & Windus, 1961);

U. C. Knoepflmacher, *George Eliot's Early Novels: The Limits of Realism* (Berkeley: University of California Press, 1968);

Knoepflmacher and George Levine, eds., "George Eliot, 1880-1980," *Nineteenth-Century Fiction*, 35: 3 (December 1980): 253-455;

Bernard J. Paris, *Experiments in Life: George Eliot's Quest for Values* (Detroit: Wayne State University Press, 1965);

J. Russell Perkin, *A Reception-History of George Eliot's Fiction* (Ann Arbor: University of Michigan Press, 1990);

Joseph Wiesenfarth, *George Eliot's Mythmaking* (Heidelberg: Carl Winter Universitatsverlag, 1977);

Hugh Witemeyer, *George Eliot and the Visual Arts* (New Haven: Yale University Press, 1979).

Papers:

The principal collections of George Eliot's papers are those of the British Museum and the Beinecke Rare Book and Manuscript Library, Yale University; there are also important collections in the New York Public Library, the Pforzheimer Library, the Folger Shakespeare Library, and the Princeton University Library.

Elizabeth Gaskell

(29 September 1810 - 12 November 1865)

This entry was written by Edgar Wright (Laurentian University) for
DLB 21: Victorian Novelists Before 1885.

BOOKS: *Mary Barton: A Tale of Manchester Life*,
anonymous (2 volumes, London: Chapman
& Hall, 1848; 1 volume, New York: Harper,
1848);

Libbie Marsh's Three Eras: A Lancashire Tale, as Cotton Mather Mills, Esquire (London: Hamilton, Adams, 1850);

*Lizzie Leigh: A Domestic Tale, from "Household
Words,"* attributed to Charles Dickens (New
York: Dewitt & Davenport, 1850);

The Moorland Cottage, anonymous (London: Chapman & Hall, 1850; New York: Harper,
1851);

Ruth: A Novel, anonymous (3 volumes, London:
Chapman & Hall, 1853; 1 volume, Boston:
Ticknor, Reed & Fields, 1853);

Cranford, anonymous (London: Chapman & Hall,
1853; New York: Harper, 1853);

Lizzie Leigh and Other Tales, anonymous (London:
Chapman & Hall, 1855; Philadelphia: Hardy, 1869);

Hands and Heart and Bessy's Troubles at Home, anonymous (London: Chapman & Hall, 1855);

North and South, anonymous (2 volumes, London:
Chapman & Hall, 1855; 1 volume, New
York: Harper, 1855);

*The Life of Charlotte Brontë, Author of "Jane Eyre,"
"Shirley," "Villette" etc.*, 2 volumes (London:
Smith, Elder, 1857; New York: Appleton,
1857);

My Lady Ludlow, A Novel (New York: Harper,
1858); republished as *Round the Sofa* (2 volumes, London: Low, 1858);

Right at Last, and Other Tales (London: Low, 1860;
New York: Harper, 1860);

Lois the Witch and Other Tales (Leipzig: Tauchnitz,
1861);

Sylvia's Lovers (3 volumes, London: Smith, Elder,
1863; 1 volume, New York: Dutton, 1863);

A Dark Night's Work (London: Smith, Elder, 1863;
New York: Harper, 1863);

Cousin Phillis: A Tale (New York: Harper, 1864); republished as *Cousin Phillis and Other Tales*
(London: Smith, Elder, 1865);

Elizabeth Cleghorn Gaskell

The Grey Woman and Other Tales (London: Smith,
Elder, 1865; New York: Harper, 1882);

Wives and Daughters: An Every-Day Story (2 volumes, London: Smith, Elder, 1866; 1 volume, New York: Harper, 1866).

Collections: *The Works of Mrs. Gaskell*, Knutsford
Edition, 8 volumes, edited by A. W. Ward
(London: Smith, Elder, 1906-1911);

The Novels and Tales of Mrs. Gaskell, 11 volumes, edited by C. K. Shorter (Oxford: Oxford University Press, 1906-1919).

A recent review of Mrs. Gaskell's critical reputation divided her critics into three camps. One group, now fading, still treats her mainly as the author of *Cranford* (1853). A second emphasizes her "social-problem" novels but insists that they be regarded as literature and not just as social history. The third and dominant one regards her as "a maturing artist, and considers each of her works in relation to the others and her general views, preferring the late fiction but giving all her writing respectful, and perhaps even admiring attention." To this summary should be added a recent special focus on her role and influence as a woman writer, and studies of her as a provincial novelist, relating her work to that of George Eliot and Thomas Hardy in its presentation of life in a regional community. It is also probably true to say that the reputation of her late fiction—the "nouvelle" *Cousin Phillis* (1864) and the novel *Wives and Daughters* (1866)—is still growing.

She won instant recognition with her first novel, *Mary Barton* (1848), which shocked readers with its revelations about the grim living conditions of Manchester factory workers and antagonized some influential critics because of its open sympathy for the workers in their relations with the masters; but the high quality of the writing and the characterization were undeniable. (Its accuracy as social observation has been compared to the work of Friedrich Engels and other contemporaries by critics such as John Lucas.) At the same time it presented a new world, the world of Lancashire factory people, making them the main characters and using their dialect (judiciously modified) for the dialogue. In so doing Mrs. Gaskell, with the Brontës, opened a path for George Eliot and later novelists. Yet her next success was with *Cranford*, stories that drew on memories of her childhood in the small Cheshire town of Knutsford to present an affectionate picture of a class and customs already becoming anachronisms. *Cranford* has charm, humor, and pathos without sentimentality, and no purpose other than to present and regret the passing of a community whose values are worth recalling. The two elements of Mrs. Gaskell's fiction responded to diferent elements in her nature: as her *Cranford* narrator says, "I had vibrated all my life between Drumble [Manchester] and Cranford [Knutsford]." After her biography of Charlotte Brontë (1857), it was the Knutsford side that predominated, providing the setting and the main themes for her later work.

Although she began by creating controversy with social-problem novels and by suggesting the adoption of genuine Christian conduct as a solution, it can be seen now that her real interests always lay with individuals and the underlying moral standards by which they act and are to be judged. Along with this went an appreciation of the changes in attitudes being created by the rapid social and industrial changes of the period. Knutsford and Manchester came to symbolize contrasting values and ways of life; she worked toward reconciling tradition and change, depicting traditional values while recognizing the necessity and desirability of new ideas and a new society. As a result, the direct role of religion drops away rapidly even in her social-problem novels; in the Cranford novels it appears rarely, and then only as a natural element of custom or behavior.

Her attention was also focused from her earliest work on the social and emotional problems of her women characters. She was capable of drawing fine and intelligent portraits of men, but it is the women who receive her closest and most sympathetic attention. Along with Charlotte Brontë, she gave a depth and credibility to her women characters that influenced succeeding novelists such as George Eliot.

Mrs. Gaskell achieved popular and critical esteem in her lifetime, with *Cranford* easily her most popular work. Although her reputation suffered along with those of all other Victorian writers during the period of critical reaction in the early twentieth century, some of her books were always in print; and A. W. Ward's Knutsford Edition of her work (1906-1911), still essential reading for its introductions, was reprinted in 1920. (One can get an idea of the quality of critical estimates at that time by noting that the *Cambridge History of English Literature* gathered George Eliot along with Benjamin Disraeli, Charles Kingsley, and Mrs. Gaskell into a chapter on the political and social novel.)

Besides novels, Mrs. Gaskell wrote short stories, essays, and articles for periodicals. Some of the essays deserve to be better known (for example, "French Life"), for she was a natural essayist. Her most famous work of nonfiction is *The Life of Charlotte Brontë* (1857), still recognized as among the finest biographies in English. Her letters reveal her alert, intelligent curiosity about people and events, matched by an eager eye and ear for describing everyday matters. As she says when concluding an early letter to her sister-in-law "Lizzy" Gaskell, "Now mind you write again, and none of

Knutsford, the model for Mrs. Gaskell's Cranford and Hollingford, in 1863. The women in the window of the building on the left are Mrs. Gaskell's cousins, Mary and Lucy Holland.

your nimini-pimini notes but a sensible nonsensical crossed letter as *I do. . . .*" ("Crossed" means the double use of space by writing vertically across a section written horizontally.) She is not an "intellectual" writer, though a bright and very well-read one; any comparison would relate her to Jane Austen rather than to George Eliot in terms of erudition, though she stands somewhere between them in approach and outlook. There is no longer any question about whether or not she is a major novelist; she qualifies both as an artist and in relation to the development of the English novel. The publication of the letters (1966), of the information in John Geoffrey Sharps's invaluable *Mrs. Gaskell's Observation and Invention* (1970), and of Winifred Gérin's biography *Elizabeth Gaskell* (1976) has provided scholars and critics with the material for further interpretation and reassessment.

Elizabeth Stevenson was born of Unitarian parents on 29 September 1810 in London, where her father, William, was keeper of the treasury records. He was a man of parts who had trained as a minister, tried being a farmer, and developed into a respected writer for the major journals, a ca-

reer he continued until his death. His marriage to Elizabeth Holland would bring the future novelist into the Holland family of Knutsford in Cheshire, a relationship that was to dominate her life. Mrs. Stevenson died when Elizabeth was only thirteen months old; the child was immediately "adopted" by her mother's sister, Aunt Lumb, and removed to Knutsford, where she grew up in the quiet and tranquil atmosphere of an old-fashioned country town, close to Sandlebridge Farm where her grandfather lived and her other Holland relatives visited. There seems to have been little further contact with her father until she returned to London about a year before he died.

Dissenters, and especially Unitarians, believed in education for girls as well as boys. After lessons at home that included French and dancing instruction from an émigré, she was sent at the age of twelve to the Byerley sisters' school at Barford; the school was moved in 1824 to Stratford-upon-Avon. The education was of high quality, broad in range (Latin, French, and Italian were standard in the curriculum), and liberal in outlook. She spent five years in surroundings that admirably suited her tastes, intelligence, and love of the country, leaving the school in 1827 an accomplished and—according to the evidence of friends and artists—a vivacious and attractive young woman. She returned to Knutsford, but the disappearance of her only brother brought her back to London in 1828. John Stevenson sailed for the East India Company; nothing is known of how he disappeared, but the sense of loss can be felt in the account of young Peter in *Cranford* and the Frederick episodes in *North and South* (1855). Her father had married again, and when Elizabeth met her stepmother there was antipathy rather than sympathy. (The portrait of Molly's stepmother, the incomparable Mrs. Gibson in *Wives and Daughters*, is said to reflect Mrs. Gaskell's impressions.) She stayed with her father until his death in 1829, when, after visits to a banker uncle, Swinton Holland, and a doctor uncle, Henry Holland (later Sir Henry and physician to Queen Victoria)—visits recollected in the opening of *North and South*—she returned to live in Knutsford until her marriage.

During a visit to Manchester she met the Reverend William Gaskell, newly appointed as assistant minister at the Cross Street Chapel; they were married on 30 August 1832. Manchester's Unitarian community was prominent in both commercial and cultural life; Cross Street Chapel was an important Unitarian center, and her husband became a leading figure in the community. Some early biographers have suggested that tensions developed in the marriage, but the evidence does not support this view. The Gaskells seem to have been two intelligent and sensitive people who respected each other's independence and temperament without denying the basic roles of husband and paterfamilias, wife and mother; the letters show that they cared about and supported each other's work and habits throughout the marriage. The obvious loss to Mrs. Gaskell was in exchanging Knutsford for Manchester. Knutsford is only sixteen miles from Manchester and is now a commuter suburb, but in the early nineteenth century it was an old-fashioned, sleepy little country town. Although the Gaskells lived on the country edge of Manchester, she was affected physically and mentally by its atmosphere; at the same time, she admired and respected its people and its leading place in the world. The love-hate attitude to "dear old dull ugly smoky grim grey Manchester" is reflected in the earlier social-problem fiction and in her later emphasis on the world of "Cranford."

Elizabeth Cleghorn Stevenson shortly before her marriage in 1832 (Manchester University Library)

Mrs. Gaskell spent the next fifteen years mainly in domestic and humanitarian activity. A particular grief was the death in 1837 of Aunt Lumb, who left her an annuity of eighty pounds. There were small signs of creativity: a sonnet to her stillborn child (1836), and a narrative poem (1837) in the style of George Crabbe written in collaboration with her husband and meant to be the first of a group of *Sketches among the Poor*. A friendship with the well-known writers and editors William and Mary Howitt led to a recollection of her school days, "Clopton Hall," appearing in their *Visits to Remarkable Places* (1840). These scattered creative impulses were brought into sharper focus after the death of her nine-month-old son in 1845. Ward states that her husband advised her to turn to writing as a relief from sorrow and encouraged her to begin her first novel, which was completed in 1847 and eventually taken by Chapman and Hall for one hundred pounds. *Mary Barton: A Tale of Manchester Life* was published anonymously on 25 October 1848. It created a sensation.

The tale is developed around a standard romantic plot. Mary Barton, the motherless daughter of a mill hand, is nearly seduced by young Carson, the mill owner's son. At the same time, a depression hits Manchester, and in the growing labor troubles John Barton, Mary's father, is selected by lot to kill young Carson as an act of union protest. He carries out the murder, but suspicion falls on Jem Wilson, who loves Mary. After complications and difficulties the truth is revealed with the aid of John Barton's outcast sister, Esther. Barton, dying, is reconciled with the elder Carson; Mary and Jem move away. But a summary of the plot gives little hint of the real force of the novel: the presentation of Manchester life and the pressures that turn John Barton into a murderer. A few attempts had been made to portray factory life in fiction, notably Disraeli's *Sybil* (1845), mainly with a reform intent. But *Mary Barton* is the first realistic portrayal of the phenomenon of the new major industrial city and its people, just as it is a new development in the use of regional dialect and detail. Manchester and its social context were to most readers an eye-opening revelation, whether it was to "hear of folk lying down to die i' th' streets, or hiding their want i' some hole o' a cellar till death come to set 'em free"; or to learn about self-taught operatives with scientific reputations, such as Job Legh (based on a real person); or to realize how the drive for profit and jobs was creating a type of society based not on human relationships, but on what Thomas Carlyle—an influence on Mrs. Gaskell—called the "Cash Nexus." (Carlyle wrote a letter of praise to the still-anonymous author.) At the heart of the novel is her bitter comment: "Are ye worshippers of Christ? or of Alecto? Oh, Orestes! you would have made a very tolerable Christian of the nineteenth century!"

Yet the novel is not ponderous, though at this stage Mrs. Gaskell's faith in the Christian ethic as a solution is too facilely displayed. Although critics such as W. R. Greg protested that the novel was unfair to the masters, they recognized the high quality of the writing, the humor that laced its observations and episodes, and the genuineness of the sentiment. Within a year—for the anonymity was quickly broken—Mrs. Gaskell was being lionized in literary London and pressed by Charles Dickens to contribute to his new journal, *Household Words*. Her rather Wordsworthian tale of guilt, remorse, and repentance, "Lizzie Leigh" (1850), led off the opening number and was the beginning of a long association,

The Reverend William Gaskell

often with exasperation on both sides, between Dickens as editor and Mrs. Gaskell as contributor. Some minor stories had already appeared in other periodicals before *Mary Barton* came out; by the end of 1851 ten more items were published. They included a Christmas book, *The Moorland Cottage* (1850), the first in her long short story or "nouvelle" form. Then came a story that was to become one of her finest novels as well as her most popular: *Cranford*.

"Our Society at Cranford," now the first two chapters of *Cranford*, appeared in *Household Words* on 13 December 1851 and was itself a fictional version of an earlier essay, "The Last Generation in England," first published in America in 1849. Further episodes were written at irregular intervals until 1853, when the book was published. In the process of writing it, Mrs. Gaskell's natural talent developed a rudimentary plot around Miss Matty's problems and the search for her missing brother. However, the attractiveness of *Cranford* lies in the way in which she re-creates with humor and affection a way of life that was already old-fashioned when she was a young girl, growing up among the little group of ladies of good birth but small income who constituted Cranford society. They maintained traditions of social behavior and dress by practicing "elegant economy." While their eccentricities are noted, the essential humanity of the characters is never forgotten.

The original episode was created around the formidable Miss Deborah Jenkyns and her softhearted younger sister, Miss Matty. With the Cranford setting established, the story chronicles the arrival of an elderly widower, Captain Brown, and his two daughters as newcomers to Cranford and their reception by the "Amazons," who are won over by his honest frankness even though he is a man. As the sickly elder daughter finally is dying, the captain is killed by a train while rescuing a young child. A faithful admirer returns to marry the younger daughter. Dickens, as editor of *Household Words*, pressed Mrs. Gaskell for more; at irregular intervals between January 1852 and May 1853 eight more episodes appeared (there was a hiatus in the middle while she concentrated on *Ruth*). In the process there was a shift of interest and a structural change. As Mrs. Gaskell told John Ruskin, "The beginning of 'Cranford' was *one* paper in 'Household Words'; and I never meant to write more, so killed Capt. Brown very much against my will." In expanding the episode into a series she quickly "killed off" Deborah, making the gentler Miss Matty the central figure and developing a rudimentary plot around a long-lost brother who finally returns from India. (This recollection of her own lost brother, John, has already been noted.) The novelist in Mrs. Gaskell was taking over. The interest remains fixed, however, on feelings, relationships, and social conduct. As Winifred Gérin says, "It is a tale told without apparent effort in a style of intimate confidence, like gossip exchanged with a friend"—like Mrs. Gaskell's letters, in fact, only with the vital difference that the gossip is being shaped by the imagination and control of a developing novelist. A few months before she died, Mrs. Gaskell confided to Ruskin that "It is the only one of my own books that I can read again; but whenever I am ailing or ill, I take 'Cranford' and—I was going to say, *enjoy* it! (but that would not be pretty!) laugh over it. And it is true too, for I have seen the cow that wore the grey flannel jacket...." The freshness of the telling mirrors the fresh de-

light in recollection. She would return to the Knutsford world to produce greater work, but not again anything so delightful. (In 1863 she did write one further episode, "The Cage at Cranford," now usually published as an "appendix" to the volume.)

During 1851 and 1852 Mrs. Gaskell was also at work on *Ruth*, published in January 1853, for which Chapman paid five hundred pounds. Charlotte Brontë, to whom Mrs. Gaskell had sent an early sketch of the plot, admired it sufficiently to make her own publishers delay the publication of *Villette* for a few days so that critics could concentrate on *Ruth*. Its subject was again controversial, this time prompted by anger at the moral conventions that condemned a "fallen woman" to ostracism and almost inevitable prostitution. Dickens's work on behalf of such women may have influenced her choice of subject, but she had already touched on it in the character of Esther in *Mary Barton*. As before, she drew on background and people she knew: the Reverend Mr. Turner, an old family friend, and his hometown of Newcastle provided some of the personality and the setting for the unworldly Dissenting minister Thurston Benson, who befriends the abandoned Ruth, helps her to bring up her child, then stands by her when the deception that she is a widow is revealed. The melodramatic ending, with Ruth redeeming herself as a nurse in a cholera epidemic and dying as she cares for her old lover, while grounded in medical realities of the time, still shows a somewhat desperate reliance on the dramatic conclusion for a plot. The strength of the novel lies in its presentation of social conduct within a small Dissenting community when tolerance and rigid morality clash—Mr. Bradshaw is a finely conceived study of self-righteousness that clearly influenced Dickens's caricature of Mr. Bounderby in *Hard Times* a year later. Although some element of the "novel with a purpose" is present, Mrs. Gaskell's sensitivity in portrayal of character and, even more, her feel for relationships within families and small communities, show a developing sense of direction as a novelist. At the same time, the range of character and the naturalness of the dialogue show increasing command of her material. Sally, the blunt and loyal housekeeper to the Thurstons, is the first of a line of domestic portraits that are a notable feature of Mrs. Gaskell's fiction. Mrs. Gaskell knew the Nightingale family; A. W. Ward, in the introduction to his collection of Mrs. Gaskell's works, quotes a report that Florence Nightingale

An 1851 portrait of Mrs. Gaskell by George Richmond
(National Portrait Gallery, London)

not only thought *Ruth* to be "a beautiful work" but approved of the fact that Mrs. Gaskell "had not made Ruth start at once as a hospital nurse, but arrive at it after much *other* nursing experience." Mrs. Gaskell knew the situations she wrote about; her experience as a minister's wife in Manchester during cholera outbreaks comes through in the novel.

Ruth touched off an immediate reaction from shocked moralists, though many critics and readers praised it for its courage and its quality. But Mrs. Gaskell, though such attacks made her physically ill, stood by her work. " 'An unfit subject for fiction' is *the* thing to say about it; I knew all this before; but I determined notwithstanding to speak my mind out about it . . . ," she said, though she admitted it was a prohibited book to her own daughters.

She now, somewhat unwillingly, gave in to Dickens's request for a full-length novel for *Household Words*. This would be her final "problemnovel," *North and South*; but before getting down to it she traveled and visited friends. A notable visit was to Haworth: she had met Charlotte

Brontë in 1850, and a friendship had developed. Another new friend was Mme Mohl, whose Paris home would be a regular base for future visits abroad. But finally, early in 1854, she began work on the as-yet-untitled novel and was soon anxiously inquiring to Dickens, who was publishing *Hard Times*, if he was going to "strike," a reference to the central episode of her own book. This is a scene in which a crowd of angry strikers attempts to storm the cotton mill run by John Thornton, who is employing Irish immigrants as "knobsticks" (strikebreakers). Dickens assured Mrs. Gaskell, who was concerned about apparent plagiarism, that such a detailed strike scene would not appear in *Hard Times*. The basic plot of *North and South* is straightforward. The setting is once again Manchester (here called Milton). Margaret Hale is a well-bred girl from Helstone in the rural south of England who is suddenly pitchforked, with little money or status, into the harsh world of the industrialized north. A leading manufacturer, John Thornton, falls in love with her. They finally learn to understand each other's worth, and in the process, to appreciate the qualities of social background each had initially despised in the other.

The novel is far from naive in its development, however, or in the complex structure of plot and subplots used to identify various themes and sets of social or personal relationships. *North and South* develops by stages. It begins in the south, where Margaret's father is a country clergyman who resigns his living and moves north after his conscience rejects traditional articles of faith. It is a misleading beginning, since it appears to anticipate, in the popular fashion of the period, a novel of religious doubt. Once the shift north is achieved, on the advice of a wealthy friend from Milton, the novel moves with force and purpose. Layers of social tension are revealed as men are opposed to masters, unionists to nonunionists, wealth to poverty, preconceptions to preconceptions. Mr. Hale becomes a private tutor of classics; Mrs. Hale, clinging desperately to gentility, slowly fades and dies. Nicholas Higgins, the workers' leader, is led from atheism to at least a respect for religion through Margaret's friendship with his daughter Bessie, who is dying from consumption brought on by mill conditions. Mrs. Gaskell even uses a subplot that recalls once again her own vanished brother: Margaret's brother is a naval officer forced to live abroad after standing up to a sadistic captain and being accused of mutiny; Frederick returns incognito to see his

Sandlebridge Farm, near Knutsford, the home of Mrs. Gaskell's grandfather, Samuel Holland.
It was the model for Hope Farm in Cousin Phillis.

dying mother and is suspected by Thornton of being Margaret's secret lover. The various levels of the complicated plot move to resolution through reconciliation and understanding, always Mrs. Gaskell's method and point of view. Thornton gives work to the unemployed Higgins after the strike. Margaret inherits a fortune and saves Thornton from ruin, which threatens not only his mill but his experiments with Higgins in improved working conditions. Finally, Margaret and Thornton marry.

The contrasts and themes are presented with far more power and subtlety than a plot summary can suggest. For example, the beauty of Helstone contrasts with the ugliness of Milton, but the beauty is a surface for ignorance and cruelty, while the ugliness conceals intelligence and vigor. Furthermore, the values of both Helstone and Milton are laid alongside the idleness and luxury of fashionable London. *North and South* upset preconceived ideas to create an understanding of the new industrial power that had emerged, whose reality was little known and less appreciated. At the same time, with some deliberateness,

it balanced the one-sided workingman's view of factory life that Mrs. Gaskell had been criticized for after *Mary Barton*.

North and South, for which she received six hundred pounds in all, marks a major stage in Mrs. Gaskell's development in several ways. She consciously instituted a comparison between the old rural and new industrial societies; when the problems of the rural laborer and those of the industrial hand were compared, the advantage lay with the new society, as Margaret admits: "If the world stood still it would retrograde—I must not think so much of how circumstances affect me myself, but how they affect others, if I wish to have a right judgment." Even more important is the extent to which her most complex and well-motivated plot to that time is firmly structured around the detailed and sensitive study of emotional and intellectual growth in the heroine. In *North and South* Mrs. Gaskell achieves maturity as a novelist. A mark of her confidence in herself was her quiet refusal to modify her way of writing to suit Dickens. In truth, *North and South* is not well suited to weekly serialization; one can feel sympathy with Dickens's increasing frustration—though she did compress the ending, which was rewritten for book publication. Not until the easier bondage of the *Cornhill* would she allow another major novel to be serialized.

North and South was completed by January 1855, and as usual Mrs. Gaskell recuperated by going visiting, this time to Paris and London. She was still away when she heard that Charlotte Brontë had died on 31 March. She had already begun to think of a memoir of her friend when, to her surprise, Brontë's father and husband both asked her to write an official biography. On 18 June she wrote to George Smith, Brontë's publisher, agreeing to undertake it. It was to occupy her fully for the next two years; the result was *The Life of Charlotte Brontë*, published on 25 March 1857, for which Smith paid her eight hundred pounds.

The Life of Charlotte Brontë was an immediate success and has established itself as one of the great biographies. Within the conventions of the period (she did not, for example, feel free to deal with Brontë's feelings for Constantin Heger) it is remarkably frank and full in its search for truth. Later biographies have modified but not replaced it; *The Life of Charlotte Brontë* still stands as a portrait of a remarkable family and its background, as well as being a detailed study of the development and motivation of its exceptional heroine.

For Mrs. Gaskell personally, however, the immediate result of the biography was disastrous. An initial wave of praise was quickly followed by angry protests from some of the people dealt with in the book. In a couple of cases legal action was threatened; she had in fact allowed her sympathies in these cases to color her judgment and had accepted a one-sided view. With the help of her husband and George Smith the problems were resolved without recourse to law, although in the case of Lady Scott (formerly Mrs. Edmund Robinson), where Mrs. Gaskell had accepted Branwell Brontë's version of his dismissal from his tutoring job and laid the blame on his refusal to be seduced by his employer's wife, a public retraction in the *Times* was needed. As she wrote ruefully to Ellen Nussey, Charlotte's old friend: "I am in a hornet's nest with a vengeance." A second edition had to be withdrawn and a revised third edition published on 22 August 1857; this became the standard text.

The Life of Charlotte Brontë is successful because Mrs. Gaskell could treat it as she did her nov-

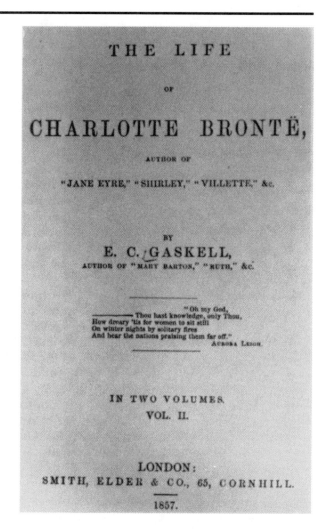

THE LIFE

OF

CHARLOTTE BRONTË,

AUTHOR OF

"JANE EYRE," "SHIRLEY," "VILLETTE," &c.

BY

E. C. GASKELL,

AUTHOR OF "MARY BARTON," "RUTH," &c.

"Oh my God,
———— Thou hast knowledge, only Thou,
How dreary 'tis for women to sit still
On winter nights by solitary fires
And hear the nations praising them far off."
AURORA LEIGH.

IN TWO VOLUMES.
VOL. II.

LONDON:
SMITH, ELDER & CO., 65, CORNHILL.
1857.

Title page for the first edition of Mrs. Gaskell's biography of Charlotte Brontë. The third edition, published the same year and revised under the threat of lawsuits, is now the standard text.

els. There is perceptive self-criticism in a comment she made that same year to George Smith when rejecting a request to do another biography, one with a political background: "I like to write about character, and the manners of a particular period—for the life of a great Yorkshire Squire of the last century I think I could have done pretty well; but I cannot manage politics." Character, manners, a given period, and a specific community constituted her natural territory. The reference to Yorkshire and the last century has, however, a particular interest, for this would be the background of her next novel, *Sylvia's Lovers* (1863), which owes something of its tone and its heightened psychological insight to the work on the biography.

Mrs. Gaskell had left England on 13 February 1857, before *The Life of Charlotte Brontë* was published, to be the guest of the American sculptor William Whetmore Story in Rome, where she arrived while the carnival was in progress. The holiday was ever afterward recalled as a high point in her life, not only for the impression made by Rome itself but also as the start of a lifelong friendship with the young Charles Eliot Norton (later professor of fine arts at Harvard), a friendship well described by Gérin as "half maternal, half platonic." The letters between them are a major source of information about Mrs. Gaskell's later years. She returned refreshed to find the "hornet's nest" and to pick up once again her life in Manchester and her work as a novelist.

During 1858-1859 she wrote rapidly, mainly items for Dickens, of which two are of more than passing interest. *My Lady Ludlow* (1858) is a short novel cut in two by a long digressive tale. But the basic narrative has something of the *Cranford* touch in its setting of a remembered past with its society and characters; it is the first evidence of a shift back to a *Cranford* approach as the vehicle for the novelist's imagination. On this occasion, however, the basis is not Knutsford, though similar; the setting of the great house and its wide-ranging domain introduces a social breadth that anticipates *Wives and Daughters*, though the period is the late eighteenth century rather than the early nineteenth. The second item, *Lois the Witch* (1861), is a powerfully somber nouvelle about the Salem witch trials whose manner prefigures, by its interest in morbid psychology, her treatment of Philip's relationship with Sylvia in her next novel. This work for Dickens provided money for travel for Mrs. Gaskell and her daughters. Meta, in particular, because of a broken engagement as well as her health in general, was of continuing concern to the anxious mother. Gérin argues that this broken engagement was one of the sources for the central episode of Sylvia's love for Kincaid in *Sylvia's Lovers*; the plot of the return of a "dead" husband had already been anticipated in a story for Dickens, "The Manchester Marriage" (1858).

Mrs. Gaskell's relationship with George Smith, begun with the biography, had by now developed on friendly as well as business terms. She was already in contact with him over "The Specksioneer" (an early title suggestion for *Sylvia's Lovers*) by the end of 1859. The appearance of his new periodical, the *Cornhill* magazine, in 1860 would provide an outlet for her later work more congenial than *All the Year Round*

(Dickens's successor to *Household Words*); the longer sections and monthly publication were better suited to her type of fiction, and she hoped to reserve her better work for it. In a revealing letter to Smith she says of a one-volume-length story (probably "A Dark Night's Work") that it "*is not good enough for the CM—I am the best judge of that please—but might be good enough for HW.*" *Sylvia's Lovers* was not, however, for serial publication.

The period between the publication of *My Lady Ludlow* and the completion of *Sylvia's Lovers* was particularly strenuous. At home, on top of the demands on the wife of a busy minister and mother of four daughters whose futures were a source of concern, there were the calls on her time as a hostess and a celebrity. (A good example is the occasion when Manchester was host to the annual meeting of the British Association for the Advancement of Science in 1861, and her house was full of visitors.) Yet the effects of Manchester on her health and spirits made holidays a necessity—even if they were usually working holidays—whether at her favorite seaside at Silverdale, or in Heidelberg or Paris. Her travels frequently supplied her with material for minor stories or articles that she could write quickly and send off, mainly to Dickens, to pay for the trips. A special visit was one to Whitby in November 1859 to research the background for *Sylvia's Lovers*.

The writing moved quickly at first, but by the end of 1860 the novel was only a quarter finished. It progressed fitfully, now provisionally named "Philip's Idol," through 1861 and 1862, much of it written when Mrs. Gaskell was away from home. Before it was finished, she was caught up in the relief efforts to deal with the depression caused by the cotton shortage in the last month of 1862, when the American Civil War cut off supplies. Her feelings come out in a letter to Smith written during a September visit to the south coast: "I believe we ought to be going back to Manchester (and very hard work, I fear, which exhausts one both bodily and mentally with depressing atmosphere of both kinds)." The depression and exhaustion can be sensed in the final volume of *Sylvia's Lovers*, where both imagination and vitality flag. The novel was finished by the end of the year, and on 31 December she received payment of one thousand pounds from Smith. *Sylvia's Lovers* was published in three volumes in February 1863, dedicated to "My Dear Husband, By Her Who Best Knows His Value."

One of the final pages from the manuscript for Wives and Daughters (The Works of Mrs. Gaskell, *Knutsford Edition*)

Many of the themes and influences in *Sylvia's Lovers* can be traced in earlier works. The wild countryside and crude habits of its people owe something to the Brontës. Several of Mrs. Gaskell's shorter pieces had used historical episodes as their bases; the background for Whitby ("Monkshaven"), its whaling industry, and the riot against the press-gang were in the sources she had used for these pieces. The story of the return of the "dead" husband, which is the climax of the plot, was taken from George Crabbe's poem "Ruth" in *Tales of the Hall* (1819). What is new is the general tone and power of what A. Easson calls a "tragical history."

Sylvia Robson is the center of a powerful, if somewhat melodramatic, story. Mrs. Gaskell created in Sylvia a portrait of passionate intensity without parallel in her work, which for three quarters of the novel is difficult to fault. The author had watched her own daughters mature, rejoice, and suffer; she had pondered over the details of Charlotte Brontë's life. All her experience is imaginatively applied to the history of Sylvia. Sylvia's early scorn for her cousin Philip, her love for the harpooner (specksioneer) Kincaid, Kincaid's removal by the press-gang and Philip's false report that presumes his death, Sylvia's weary acceptance of Philip as husband after her father's execution following the riot—these episodes are welded into a tightly structured narrative that holds the interest. As always, Mrs. Gaskell excels in presenting the setting and community life of the locality. But it is Sylvia's emotional vitality and intensity that give the book its force.

Sylvia's Lovers is a fine work that has been given a tragic ending by a novelist whose temperament and approach are not really tragic. Mrs. Gaskell's view of life accepted the tragic, but was basically melioristic. The first two volumes are full of energy; they sparkle and have humor, as does Sylvia's own character. The ending shows forced invention rather than true tragedy. Philip vanishes, returns unrecognized, and rescues his daughter from drowning before he dies, reconciled with his wife.

The novel's strength lies in the characters and in the insight into relationships between those characters in their setting. Critics vary in their views of it as tragedy but there is wide agreement on the power of the presentation. The tone was not, however, one that was finally congenial to Mrs. Gaskell. In her last works, without losing this new maturity of insight into character, she revisited and reinterpreted the Knutsford world

and the changes in attitude that had overtaken society since she was a child there.

By 1863 Mrs. Gaskell seemed to be moving into a calmer, less strenuous way of life, so that when she returned from a Paris holiday to find an appeal from George Smith for a *Cornhill* story, she was able to offer him *Cousin Phillis*, a long short story that she had already started writing. Along with some other pieces, she sold the copyright of the story for £250. *Cousin Phillis* ran from November 1863 to February 1864.

The world of the communities created by Mrs. Gaskell in *Cousin Phillis*, and later in *Wives and Daughters*, while based on the *Cranford* world, is experiencing change. The card from the man she secretly loves that shatters Phillis's hope and health is brought by the penny post (created in 1840). The railway, though not physically destructive as it is in Dickens's *Dombey and Son* (1846-1848), brings industrial progress and its new breed of men to the pastoral setting of Hope Farm, an evocation of her grandfather's Sandlebridge Farm (as Minister Holman is based on Samuel Holland himself). This is still a stable world, based on work and sound moral values. The story is an uncomplicated one; its virtues are in the manner of its development and telling. When Paul Manning, an engineer trainee on a railway development nearby, first visits his cousin, his narrative reflects the sense of having stumbled into some idyllic retreat: "I fancied that my Sunday coat was scented for days afterwards by the bushes of sweetbriar and the fraxinella that perfumed the air." Change comes from contact between the two worlds; Phillis's love for Paul's employer, Holdsworth, changes her from quiet girl to suffering woman. Holdsworth himself never quite succumbs to the idyll. His work moves him on beyond Phillis and Hope Farm: his implied failure is a lack of sensitivity, of moral discrimination. Phillis will eventually recover; but the ending has, perhaps, overtones of irony, as she agrees to a change of scene and convalescence. "Only for a short time, Paul! Then—we will go back to the peace of the old days. I know we shall; I can, and I will!"

Most critics would agree with Arthur Pollard's assessment of *Cousin Phillis* as the author's crowning achievement in the short novel; the praise is virtually unanimous. It is also recognized as a fitting prelude to her final novel, *Wives and Daughters*, the idea for which had developed in such detail that she was able to offer it to George Smith with a full synopsis on 3 May

1864. Mrs. Gaskell's wish to carry out a personal plan was also an incentive to writing it. For some time she had been considering the purchase of a house in the country which would be ready for her husband's retirement (he never did retire; he died in Manchester in 1884), and would at the same time be a retreat from Manchester. She had finally found one about fifty miles from London; the two thousand pounds that Smith paid her for the novel enabled her to make the purchase. *Wives and Daughters: An Every-Day Story* ran in the *Cornhill* from August 1864 to January 1866; the final installment was never written, yet the ending was known, and the novel as it exists is virtually complete.

Henry James, "testifying . . . to the fact of her genius" in the year the novel appeared, noted "the gentle skill with which the reader is slowly involved in the tissue of the story" and the way in which its new world presents "this seeming accession of social and moral knowledge." A comparison to Jane Austen—for its combination of humor and moral judgment in the observation of character and conduct—is often made, not unjustly, though Mrs. Gaskell's canvas is larger than Austen's bit of ivory.

The plot of *Wives and Daughters* is complex, since it relies far more on a series of relationships between family groups in Hollingford than it does on the dramatic structure, which nevertheless is well controlled and integrated with the themes. The novel is set in the same general period as *Cranford* and *Cousin Phillis*, but the Knutsford of Mrs. Gaskell's youth is now reinterpreted as a much wider community. The novelist's matured art and judgments combine with her natural interests, particularly in the portraits of her heroine and what may be called her "antiheroine." For in Cynthia Kirkpatrick, Mrs. Gaskell created a personality less tragic, yet more intriguing and sophisticated, than Sylvia Robson, possessing in W. A. Craik's words "qualities that any novelist before her would find reprehensible." While this perhaps overstates the pioneering element, it does aptly recognize a character of the complexity of Thackeray's Beatrix Esmond within the "every-day story" of Hollingford. Cynthia's less complex but equally well-observed stepsister, Molly Gibson, will marry Roger Hamley, whose career and character draw in part on Mrs. Gaskell's distant relative Charles Darwin to present a conjunction of traditional values and new conceptions. But without a doubt the finest creation is the doctor's second wife and Molly's stepmother, Mrs. Gibson. Through speech and conduct she presents, as Margaret Ganz points out, "the humorous and ironical appraisal of a vain and hopelessly petty nature" that is yet "not wholly ill-natured." It may be noted that the world Mrs. Gaskell sees is one without villains in the accepted sense; trouble and suffering are caused by life itself, by selfishness, by a failure of sensitivity to human feelings, by a lack of deeply felt moral standards. The reader is left with the feeling that even Mr. Preston, whose machinations cause the main trouble for Molly, is as much sinned against as sinning.

Hollingford is a community where society, from the great house to the tradespeople, has to grapple with a changing world, whether in technology or conduct or ideas. The length and the leisurely pace of serialization allowed the novelist to move, as James appreciated, with details of daily life and psychology; Gérin points out that Molly Gibson is distinguished from the author's previous heroines not only by her class—"she is a lady—but [by] the gradualness and naturalness of her growth." Throughout *Wives and Daughters* the humorous, ironical, and sometimes satirical view of the Knutsford generation, along with serious undertones, is developed with a heightened sense of artistic self-confidence and maturity.

Mrs. Gaskell's health was poor, and she felt fatigue at the pressure of regular stints of work. She was on a visit to her new house when, on Sunday, 12 November 1865, she collapsed and died, leaving the novel uncompleted.

Mrs. Gaskell once wrote to a friend about the contradictory elements in her own nature—her "Mes," as she called them. "One of my Mes is, I do believe, a true Christian—(only people call her socialist and communist), another of my mes is a wife and mother. . . . Now that's my 'social self' I suppose. Then again I've another self with a full taste for beauty and convenience which is pleased on its own account. How am I to reconcile all these warring members?" This self-analysis helps to explain the variety as well as the common themes to be found in her work, just as it helps to explain how she earned the respect and friendship of people from all ranks and religions. She was intensely interested in all types of human behavior and activity; it was an interest that provided her with material for essays and short stories as well as for her major fiction. Critical awareness of her as a social historian is now more than balanced by awareness of her innovativeness and artistic development as a novel-

The Gaskells' grave in the Unitarian cemetery, Knutsford

ist. James Donald Barry has commented that "she is surely among the best of the second rank of Victorian novelists and perhaps has joined the first." Since that time editions of individual works and collections of shorter pieces, properly edited, have become available; they are helping to consolidate her reputation as undoubtedly major.

Letters:
J. B. V. Chapple and Arthur Pollard, *The Letters of Mrs. Gaskell* (Manchester: Manchester University Press, 1966).

Bibliographies:
R. L. Selig, *Elizabeth Gaskell; A Reference Guide* (Boston: G. K. Hall, 1977);

Jeffery Welch, *Elizabeth Gaskell: An Annotated Bibliography, 1929-75* (New York: Garland, 1977).

Biographies:
Annette Brown Hopkins, *Elizabeth Gaskell: Her Life and Work* (London: Lehmann, 1952);

Arthur Pollard, *Mrs. Gaskell: Novelist and Biographer* (Manchester: Manchester University Press, 1966);

Winifred Gérin, *Elizabeth Gaskell: A Biography* (Oxford: Clarendon Press, 1976);

Coral Lansbury, *Elizabeth Gaskell* (Boston: Twayne, 1984);

Patsy Stoneman, *Elizabeth Gaskell* (Bloomington: Indiana University Press, 1987).

References:
James Donald Barry, "Elizabeth Cleghorn Gaskell," in *Victorian Fiction: A Second Guide to Research*, edited by George H. Ford (New York: MLA, 1978);

P. Beer, *Reader, I Married Him. . . .* (London: Macmillan, 1974);

J. A. V. Chapple, *Elizabeth Gaskell: A Portrait in Letters* (Manchester: Manchester University Press, 1980);

W. A. Craik, *Elizabeth Gaskell and the English Provincial Novel* (London: Methuen, 1975);

Deirdre David, *Fictions of Resolution in Three Victorian Novels: North and South, Our Mutual Friend, Daniel Deronda* (New York: Columbia University Press, 1981);

Enid Duthie, *The Themes of Elizabeth Gaskell* (London: Macmillan, 1980);

A. Easson, *Elizabeth Gaskell* (London: Routledge & Kegan Paul, 1979);

Margaret Ganz, *Elizabeth Gaskell: The Artist in Conflict* (New York: Twayne, 1969);

Coral Lansbury, *Elizabeth Gaskell: The Novel of Social Crisis* (New York: Barnes & Noble, 1975);

J. Lucas, "Mrs. Gaskell and Brotherhood," in *Tradition and Tolerance in Nineteenth Century Fiction*, by J. Goode, D. Howard, and J. Lucas (London: Routledge & Kegan Paul, 1966);

Pauline Nestor, *Female Friendships and Communities: Charlotte Brontë, George Eliot, Elizabeth Gaskell* (Oxford: Clarendon Press, 1985; New

York: Oxford University Press, 1985);

John Geoffrey Sharps, *Mrs. Gaskell's Observation and Invention: A Study of the Non-Biographic Works* (London: Linden, 1970);

Edgar Wright, *Mrs. Gaskell: The Basis for Reassessment* (London: Oxford University Press, 1965).

Papers:

Important collections of Mrs. Gaskell's papers include those at Harvard University, Leeds University, the Manchester Central Reference Library, Manchester University, Princeton University, and the John Rylands Library.

Thomas Macaulay

(25 October 1800 - 28 December 1859)

This entry was updated by William F. Naufftus (Winthrop College) from his entry in
DLB 55: Victorian Prose Writers Before 1867.

See also the Macaulay entry in DLB 32: Victorian Poets Before 1850.

SELECTED BOOKS: *Pompeii: A Poem Which Obtained the Chancellor's Medal at the Cambridge Commencement, July 1819* (Cambridge, 1819);

Evening: A Poem Which Obtained the Chancellor's Medal at the Cambridge Commencement, July 1821 (Cambridge, 1821);

Lays of Ancient Rome (London: Longman, Brown, Green & Longmans, 1842; Philadelphia: Carey & Hart, 1843);

Critical and Miscellaneous Essays, 5 volumes (Philadelphia: Carey & Hart, 1842-1844);

Critical and Historical Essays, Contributed to the Edinburgh Review (3 volumes, London: Longman, Brown, Green & Longmans, 1843; 5 volumes, New York: White, Stokes & Allen, 1843);

The History of England from the Accession of James II, 5 volumes; volume 5 edited by Lady Hannah Trevelyan (London: Longman, Brown, Green & Longmans, 1848-1861; New York: Harper, 1849-1861);

Speeches, 2 volumes (New York: Redfield, 1853);

The Speeches of the Rt. Hon. T. B. Macaulay, Edited by Himself, 1 volume (London: Longman, Green, Brown & Longmans, 1854);

Biographical and Historical Sketches (New York: Appleton, 1857);

The Miscellaneous Writings of Lord Macaulay, edited by Thomas Flower Ellis, 2 volumes (London: Longmans, Green, Longman & Roberts, 1860);

Biographies by Lord Macaulay Contributed to the Encyclopædia Britannica (Edinburgh: Black, 1860; New York: Macmillan, 1894);

The Indian Education Minutes of Lord Macaulay, edited by H. Woodrow (Calcutta, 1862);

Hymn by Lord Macaulay: An Effort of His Early Childhood, edited by L. Horton-Smith (Cambridge: Metcalf, 1902);

Marginal Notes, edited by George Otto Trevelyan (London: Longmans, Green, 1907);

Lord Macaulay's Legislative Minutes, edited by C. D. Dharker (London & New York: Oxford University Press, 1946);

Macaulay in 1833, portrait by S. W. Reynolds, Jr.
(Collection of Mrs. Reine Errington)

Napoleon and the Restoration of the Bourbons: The Completed Portion of Macaulay's Projected "History of France, from the Restoration of the Bourbons to the Accession of Louis Philippe," edited by Joseph Hamburger (London: Longman, 1977; New York: Columbia University Press, 1977).

Collections: *The Works of Lord Macaulay. Complete,* 8 volumes, edited by Lady Trevelyan (London: Longmans, Green, 1866; New York: Appleton, 1866);

The Works of Lord Macaulay, Albany Edition, 12 volumes (London: Longmans, Green, 1898; New York: DeFau, 1898);

The Complete Works of Lord Macaulay, Bibliophile Edition, 20 volumes (Philadelphia: University Library Association, 1910).

SELECTED PERIODICAL PUBLICATIONS—
UNCOLLECTED: "The West Indies," *Edinburgh Review,* 41 (January 1825): 464-488;
"Milton," *Edinburgh Review,* 42 (August 1825): 304-346;
"Machiavelli," *Edinburgh Review,* 45 (March 1827): 259-295;
"Major Moody's Reports: Social and Industrial Capacities of Negroes," *Edinburgh Review,* 45 (March 1827): 245-267;
"Dryden," *Edinburgh Review,* 47 (January 1828): 1-36;
"History," *Edinburgh Review,* 47 (May 1828): 331-367;
"Hallam's *Constitutional History,*" *Edinburgh Review,* 48 (September 1828): 96-169;
"Mill's *Essay on Government:* Utilitarian Logic and Politics," *Edinburgh Review,* 49 (March 1829): 159-189;
"Bentham's Defence of Mill: Utilitarian System of Philosophy," *Edinburgh Review,* 49 (June 1829): 273-299;
"Utilitarian Theory of Government, and the 'Greatest Happiness Principle,'" *Edinburgh Review,* 50 (October 1829): 99-125;
"Southey's *Colloquies on Society,*" *Edinburgh Review,* 50 (January 1830): 528-565;
"Sadler's *Law of Population, and Disproof of Human Superfecundity,*" *Edinburgh Review,* 51 (July 1830): 297-321;
"Civil Disabilities of the Jews," *Edinburgh Review,* 52 (January 1831): 363-374;
"Moore's *Life of Lord Byron,*" *Edinburgh Review,* 53 (June 1831): 544-572;
"Croker's Edition of Boswell's *Life of Johnson,*" *Edinburgh Review,* 54 (September 1831): 1-38;
"Southey's Edition of the *Pilgrim's Progress,*" *Edinburgh Review,* 54 (December 1831): 450-461;
"Lord Nugent's *Memorials of Hampden,*" *Edinburgh Review,* 54 (December 1831): 505-550;
"Nares' *Memoirs of Lord Burghley*—Political and Religious Aspects of His Age," *Edinburgh Review,* 55 (April 1832): 271-296;
"Dumont's *Recollections of Mirabeau*—The French Revolution," *Edinburgh Review,* 55 (July 1832): 552-576;
"Lord Mahon's *War of the Succession,*" *Edinburgh Review,* 56 (January 1833): 499-542;

"Walpole's *Letters to Sir Horace Mann*," *Edinburgh Review*, 58 (October 1833): 227-258;

"Thackeray's *History of the Earl of Chatham*," *Edinburgh Review*, 58 (January 1834): 508-544;

"Sir James Mackintosh's *History of the Revolution*," *Edinburgh Review*, 61 (July 1835): 265-322;

"Lord Bacon," *Edinburgh Review*, 65 (July 1837): 1-104;

"Life and Writings of Sir William Temple," *Edinburgh Review*, 68 (October 1838): 113-187;

"*Church and State* [by W. E. Gladstone]," *Edinburgh Review*, 69 (April 1839): 231-280;

"Sir John Malcolm's *Life of Lord Clive*," Edinburgh Review, 70 (January 1840): 295-362;

"Ranke's *History of the Popes*—Revolutions of the Papacy," *Edinburgh Review*, 72 (October 1840): 227-258;

"Comic Dramatists of the Restoration," *Edinburgh Review*, 72 (January 1841): 490-528;

"The Late Lord Holland," *Edinburgh Review*, 73 (July 1841): 560-568;

"Warren Hastings," *Edinburgh Review*, 74 (October 1841): 160-255;

"Frederick the Great," *Edinburgh Review*, 75 (April 1842): 218-281;

"Madame D'Arblay," *Edinburgh Review*, 76 (January 1843): 523-570;

"Life and Writings of Addison," *Edinburgh Review*, 78 (July 1843): 193-260;

"Barère's *Memoirs*," *Edinburgh Review*, 79 (April 1844): 275-351;

"The Earl of Chatham," *Edinburgh Review*, 80 (October 1844): 526-595;

"Essay on the Life and Character of King William III" (1822), edited by A. N. L. Munby, *Times Literary Supplement*, 1 May 1969, pp. 468-469.

Thomas Babington Macaulay was a public figure whose writings were inseparable from the rest of his career. His speeches made him one of the most important members of the House of Commons during the debates on the 1832 Reform Bill; his early essays for the *Edinburgh Review* were, for the most part, political polemic; and the minutes and penal code he wrote during his years as legislative member of the Supreme Council of the East India Company heavily influenced the course of education and law on the Indian subcontinent. The volumes of his essays collected from the *Edinburgh Review* were among the most popular books of the Victorian Age, making him for many modern critics the symbol of Vic-

torian philistinism and, at the very least, a useful index of Victorian assumptions and tastes. But it is as a historian that he most vigorously survives today, generally sharing with Edward Gibbon the laurels as the British man of letters who most successfully combined the demands of narrative literature and historical truth.

In his historical essays and in his *The History of England from the Accession of James II* (1848-1861), Macaulay is a watershed figure. He is the last important British historian to look consciously to the Roman, Greek, and neoclassical historians for literary models—clearly imitating the narrative techniques and stylistic devices of Thucydides; Plutarch; Tacitus; Livy; Edward Hyde, Earl of Clarendon; and David Hume. At the same time, he is a product of his own age, drawing parallels and lessons from contemporary events and indulging in Romantic sentiments and pictorial details. Finally, he looks forward to later trends in historical writing by giving the first distinguished examples of British social history, particularly in his famous third chapter of *The History of England*, with its overview of English society in 1685.

Throughout his works, Macaulay popularized—and became spokesman for—the so-called Whig view of history, a complex set of assumptions widely held in the nineteenth century and generally denigrated in the twentieth century. This Whig view can be defined in several ways, but its chief ingredients were a belief that history in general—and modern Western history in particular—was essentially the record of progress; that historical figures should be praised for having furthered the cause of progress or blamed for having opposed it; and that the moderate reformers of the Whig party were usually the servants of progress, while both Tory reactionaries and dangerous radicals threatened civilization in various ways. Macaulay did not originate this set of ideas, and he would not always have endorsed them, but in a general way he popularized assumptions of this sort among his vast readership. It was Lord Acton, another Whig historian, who said that Macaulay's writings were "a key to half the prejudices of our age."

Thomas Babington Macaulay was born on 25 October 1800 at his uncle's estate, Rothley Temple in Leicestershire, and raised in the Evangelical surroundings of Clapham Common, a London suburb where his father, Zachary Macaulay, was a prominent resident. The senior Macaulay was a prosperous merchant and shipowner involved in the African and East Indian trade, but his real interest was the abolition of slavery in the British Empire. Before his marriage he had served as the first governor of Sierra Leone, an African colony settled by freed slaves, and in later years he neglected his business firm, Macaulay and Babington, to devote his attention to editing the *Christian Observer*, the journal of the Evangelical abolitionists. Zachary Macaulay's wife, Selina Mills Macaulay, had been a student of the famous Evangelical educator Hannah More and spent most of her mature life raising her five daughters and four sons, and providing emotional support for her frequently embattled husband.

Thomas Macaulay, the eldest of these nine children, was an unusually precocious child who, at the age of ten, reminded Thomas De Quincey's mother of Samuel Taylor Coleridge. During the two days the young Macaulay spent with her, he impressed her as a "Baby genius," but she was concerned that "he says such things that he will be ruined by praise." For the fact that he was not so ruined he could bestow his thanks on his father, who was always finding some cause for complaint—Tom Macaulay's handwriting was clumsy, his habits were slovenly, he was wasting time, he was reading novels, or he was falling into dangerous political opinions. Rather surprisingly, in view of his general combativeness, Macaulay revered his father and tried constantly to please him. He did not inherit the religious faith which had made his father's life emotionally satisfying, intellectually coherent, and socially useful, but he did inherit his father's reforming zeal—a zeal which made him a champion of Catholic and Jewish emancipation, of the abolition of both slavery and pocket boroughs, of the extension of the franchise, and of the extension of Western education and Western law to Britain's Indian empire.

At Cambridge the former child prodigy failed the mathematics tripos in 1822 but was otherwise a tremendous success. He won the Chancellor's Prize for English verse in 1819 and 1821, made his mark as an orator in the University Union, won a Craven scholarship in classics, and crowned his university career by being elected a fellow of Trinity College. During this time he also became a Whig and wrote a prize essay on the "Life and Character of King William III." This essay, which was finally published in the *Times Literary Supplement* in 1969, was his most important undergraduate work because it first led

him to consider seriously the work of the monarch who would eventually become the major figure in *The History of England*. After leaving Cambridge, Macaulay read for the bar at Lincoln's Inn, spent as much time as possible with his family, and began his literary career in earnest by contributing regularly to *Knight's Quarterly Magazine*. These contributions included poetry, fiction, literary criticism, satires, and closet drama. They are now quite properly regarded as juvenilia, but in them Macaulay developed the ideas and the prose style that would soon make him the most popular writer for the *Edinburgh Review*. In *Knight's Quarterly Magazine* he advanced his notions on the nature of poetry in essays on Dante and Petrarch, made fun of an eminent Tory in his *Wellingtoniad*, and worked out his opinions on seventeenth-century English history in "A Conversation Between Abraham Cowley and Mr. John Milton, Touching the Great Civil War." Yet the differences between the articles in *Knight's Quarterly Magazine* and the *Edinburgh Review* essays are as interesting as their similarities are. The earlier pieces lack both the partisan bitterness and the almost insufferable arrogance that characterize Macaulay's *Edinburgh* reviews, a circumstance which suggests that Macaulay's *Edinburgh* essays owe some of their least attractive qualities as much to the editorial policies of the journal in which they appeared as to the personality of their author.

The *Edinburgh Review* was the quasi-official organ of the Whig party, and the period from 1825 to 1834—during which Macaulay wrote most of his reviews—was a politically acrimonious time preceding and following the passage of the Great Reform Bill of 1832. Arrogance and invective were characteristic of the *Edinburgh* reviewers as a group. In these years, Macaulay wrote twenty-seven articles—ostensibly book reviews but in fact wide-ranging essays on topics suggested, sometimes rather loosely, by the book under scrutiny. They are not today his most impressive writings, but they were the ones that established him both as a political and a literary figure. It was because of an article in the *Edinburgh Review* that Macaulay came to the attention of Henry Petty-Fitzmaurice, Lord Lansdowne, who in 1830 helped secure him a seat in Parliament through his pocket borough of Calne in Wiltshire, and it was through his three-volume collection *Critical and Historical Essays, Contributed to the Edinburgh Review* (1843) that Macaulay eventually reached the largest number of readers. The first essay (January 1825) was an abolitionist argument on the West Indies. This piece was followed by other purely political works, including a series of three attacks on James Mill and the Utilitarians in general. The general line of argument was that Mill was too theoretical and insufficiently pragmatic, that he reasoned from a priori notions rather than from observation of fact. These three essays are important in that they constituted one side of a debate between the Whig *Edinburgh Review* and the *Westminster Review*, the organ of the Benthamite Philosophical Radicals or Utilitarians. In his *Autobiography* (1873) John Stuart Mill recalls his own role in answering Macaulay's objections to his father's writings but also admits that the *Edinburgh* articles helped modify his faith in his father's views.

The three essays from this period that are still widely read today are "Milton" (August 1825); "Southey's *Colloquies on Society*" (January 1830); and "Croker's Edition of Boswell's *Life of Johnson*" (September 1831). "Milton," the essay which made Macaulay famous, is most notable for its mixed theory of progress. This theory argues that as men learn to think abstractly, they lose the ability to create the concrete images that are essential to great poetry: "Generalization is necessary to the advancement of knowledge; but particularity is indispensable to the creations of the imagination. In proportion as men know more and think more, they look less at individuals and more at classes. They therefore make better theories and worse poems." Macaulay appears to have no doubts about the beneficent nature of this change: the truth of poetry "is the truth of madness," and "poetry effects its purpose most completely in a dark age." The immediate purpose of this theory is to show Milton's greatness in producing great poetry in the polished seventeenth century, but it also suggests that Macaulay's much-maligned belief in progress was less simple than it is usually thought to have been: the wealth and freedom of the modern world were worth more than the great poetry produced by the ancients, but he was hardly unaware of the drawbacks of the scientific, democratic, and industrial revolutions.

Most of the essay on Milton is concerned, however, with politics rather than poetry. In the 1820s and 1830s, Whig and Tory controversialists were in the habit of fighting over again the battles of the seventeenth century, since it was felt that the issues of the civil war were similar to those which eventually resulted in the 1832 Re-

Thomas Flower Ellis, Macaulay's closest friend and editor of the posthumously published Miscellaneous Writings of Lord Macaulay *(Trinity College, Cambridge)*

form Bill and the rest of the reform legislation that was carried through or first proposed at this time—abolition of slavery in British colonies, Catholic Emancipation, the relief of Jewish Disabilities, Irish disestablishment, and the secularization of the universities. Tories praised Charles I, saw the Church of England in danger, and feared a return of the chaos and tyranny of the Civil War and Commonwealth. In his essay Macaulay follows the Whig tradition by damning Charles as a tyrant and Archbishop Laud as a bigot, making excuses for Cromwell and praising the Puritans in general and Milton in particular. Milton is seen as an ideal character because he shared the general Puritan characteristics of courage and hatred of tyranny and yet appreciated beauty as much as any Cavalier.

In his essay on Robert Southey's *Sir Thomas More; or Colloquies on the Progress and Prospects of Society* (1829), a recent work in which the poet laureate discussed political questions with the compliant ghost of More, Macaulay took up more obviously contemporary political questions. In keeping with the moderate reformist tradition of the Whig party, he condemns Southey both for the revolutionary opinions of his youth and the reactionary opinions of his old age. "He has passed from one extreme of political opinion to another, as Satan in Milton went round the globe, contriving constantly 'to ride with darkness.' Wherever the thickest shadow of the night may at any moment chance to fall, there is Mr. Southey." Much of the debate between Macaulay and Southey hinged on the question of whether material conditions were better or worse as a result of the industrial revolution. In his *Colloquies* Southey portrays the decay of rural England, the squalor of the new cities, and the unhealthiness of factory conditions. Macaulay cites statistics indicating greater life expectancy as well as greater material prosperity, and he ends with a peroration that is one of the best-known passages in all his works: "If any person had told the Parliament which met in terror and perplexity after the crash of 1720 that in 1830 the wealth of England would surpass all their wildest dreams . . . that London would be twice as large and twice as populous, and that nevertheless the rate of mortality would have diminished to half of what it then was . . . our ancestors would have given as much credit to the prediction as they gave to *Gulliver's Travels*. Yet that prediction would have been true. . . . On what principle is it that, when we see nothing but improvement behind us, we are to expect nothing but deterioration before us?" And the "improvement behind us" has been produced, Macaulay concludes, by "the prudence and energy of the people" and not "the intermeddling of Mr. Southey's idol the omniscient and omnipresent State."

In this essay Macaulay acknowledges Southey's good intentions, and elsewhere he praises his talents as a writer, but his review of the Tory John Wilson Croker's 1831 edition of Boswell's *Life of Johnson* is clearly a personal attack. Almost half the essay is an assault on Croker's facts—"Indeed we cannot open any volume of this work in any place and turn it over for two minutes in any direction without finding a blunder"—or his explanatory notes—"He is perpetually telling us that he cannot understand something in the text which is as plain as language can make it." Had Croker been a supporter of parliamentary reform instead of one of its most inveterate, erudite, and eloquent opponents, presumably his shortcomings as an editor would have received less attention. Boswell himself is presented by Macaulay as a puzzling set of contradictions: "Without all the qualities which made him the jest and the torment of those among whom he lived, without the officiousness, the inquisitiveness, the effrontery, the toad-eating, the insensibility to all reproof, he never could have produced so excel-

lent a book." Johnson is also depicted as a contradictory character: "He began to be credulous precisely at the point where the most credulous people begin to be skeptical. . . . He could discuss clearly enough the folly and meanness of all bigotry except his own."

Beyond their general Whig party line, several intellectual tendencies are apparent in these early essays. There is respect for empirical fact, and there is a matching suspicion for fine theories—both Southey's myth of a past golden age and Mill's myth of a rationally happy Utilitarian future. There are strong reactions to personalities, and the reaction to Milton and Johnson—writers long in their graves—are as strong as the reactions to Macaulay's contemporaries Croker and Mill. Finally, there is a clear tendency to find or create paradoxes: the theory of material progress and poetic decay in "Milton," the image of Southey's Miltonic voyage to the poles, and the presentation of Boswell and Johnson as bundles of contradictions. All of these characteristics would remain important throughout Macaulay's literary career.

The essay on Milton was something of a literary phenomenon. Macaulay's nephew Sir George Otto Trevelyan later wrote in *The Life and Letters of Lord Macaulay* (1876) that "like Lord Byron, he awoke one morning to find himself famous." The modern reader who wonders what made the essays so popular must first consider Macaulay's prose style. "The more I think, the less I can conceive where you picked up that prose style," Francis Jeffrey wrote to Macaulay after receiving the manuscript of "Milton." The style varied. It could be urbane, witty, Augustan. It could be lushly sentimental or furiously indignant. It was, however, always clear, and this clarity was certainly a large part of Macaulay's appeal to the general reader. He took great pains with his writing so that the reader should have as little trouble as possible. His journal entry for 2 July 1850 is revealing: "My account of the Highlands is getting into tolerable shape. Tomorrow I shall begin to transcribe again, and to polish. What trouble these few pages will have cost me! The great object is that, after all this trouble, they may read as if they had been spoken off, and may flow as easily as table talk." In fact, as Hippolyte Taine says in the admiring chapter on Macaulay in his history of English literature (translated into English in 1871), "it seems as if he were making a wager with his reader, and said to him: Be as absent in mind, as stupid, as ignorant as you please. . . . I will repeat the same idea in so many different forms, I will make it sensible by such familiar and precise examples . . . that you cannot help being enlightened and convinced."

Such striving for clarity could, as Taine admits, become tedious, but it should be remembered that these essays were, to a certain extent, self-help works in a society where bookishness and literacy conferred status. As John Morley observed in the *Fortnightly Review* in 1876, Macaulay's "Essays are as good as a library . . . for a busy uneducated man, who has curiosity and enlightenment enough to wish to know a little about the great lives and great thoughts . . . that have marked the journey of man through the ages." And such a reader is taught to trust the writer. Macaulay writes as if there could be no doubt about the importance of his topics or about his own competence to pass judgment. William Lamb, Lord Melbourne is supposed to have remarked that he wished he were as sure of anything as Macaulay was of everything, but most of Macaulay's readers apparently thought his confidence justified. His most impressive intellectual gift was his memory, and he used this memory throughout his writings to dredge up an enormous range of highly specific examples and analogies to illustrate every point and support every argument he made. As Jane Millgate has suggested in *Macaulay* (1973), this is both assuring and flattering to the reader. One is impressed by the writer's erudition and flattered by the writer's assumption that the reader shares this erudition, understands these allusions to literary works or historical events. When Macaulay says, as he does in his essay on the Anglo-Indian adventurer Robert Clive, that every schoolboy knows who strangled Atahualpa, the reader who finds himself innocent of this schoolboy knowledge may feel intimidated at first, but the context makes it clear that the strangler was a Spanish conqueror in the New World. So the busy, uneducated reader could take that hint and move on to the next paragraph, eventually working through a collection of essays that covers a wide range of topics.

The topics covered in Macaulay's early years with the *Edinburgh Review* include literary criticism on John Dryden (January 1828) and John Bunyan (December 1831) and character analyses of George Gordon, Lord Byron (June 1831) and Niccolò Machiavelli (March 1827). There is also a series of eight essays covering British history from the Reformation ("Nares' *Memoirs of Lord Burghley*—Political and Religious Aspects of His

Age," April 1832) to the end of the Seven Years' War ("Thackeray's *History of the Earl of Chatham*," January 1834). The literary essays show more interest in an author's life and times than in his art; the historical essays repeatedly present the Whig view that the growth of liberty has been essential to the growth of British power, wealth, and culture. The essays on Horace Walpole (October 1833) and William Pitt, Earl of Chatham, however, portray the mid eighteenth century as a period of national degeneracy when old political ideals had decayed and new ones had not yet arisen to take their place. Macaulay did not think that progress was constant or inevitable any more than he thought it was the rule in all areas of human endeavor.

Several of the *Edinburgh Review* essays were very closely connected with speeches that he delivered in the House of Commons as member for Calne. The earliest of these was a January 1831 article, "Civil Disabilities of the Jews," arguing for admitting Jews to the vote and to all public offices. Macaulay advanced this idea in two parliamentary speeches as well as in the *Edinburgh Review* essay, but such laws were not passed until several decades later. Other reform measures were more immediately successful, with Parliament spurred on by the July 1830 French revolution which brought down Charles X and ended the Bourbon dynasty.

Macaulay expressed an interest in writing an article for the *Edinburgh Review* on recent French political developments and spent the summer of 1831 traveling on the Continent and making notes. But Henry Brougham, an older and more established *Edinburgh* reviewer, claimed the subject as his own, and Macvey Napier, the new editor, reluctantly granted this claim. The fragmentary essay which Macaulay did complete was lost for more than a century until it was discovered and published in 1977 as *Napoleon and the Restoration of the Bourbons*. It concludes with the events of 1815 rather than 1830 and consequently covers much of the same ground as Macaulay's July 1832 *Edinburgh Review* essay "Dumont's *Recollections of Mirabeau*—The French Revolution." Both essays develop the same theory of revolution: "We believe it to be a rule without exception, that the violence of a revolution corresponds to the degree of misgovernment which has produced that revolution." The subjects of Charles I were less oppressed than those of Louis XVI and were less vindictive as a result; the American subjects of

Macaulay in 1832, when he stood successfully for the parliamentary seat of the newly enfranchised industrial borough Leeds; drawing by I. N. Rhodes (British Library)

George III were least violent of all because they were least oppressed.

A correct analysis of the nature of revolution seemed crucial because in the early 1830s, a revolution in England seemed a real possibility. The French church and aristocracy had failed to prevent revolution, but Macaulay thought that the British Lords and Commons could do better. The French "would not have reform; and they had revolution. . . . They would not endure Turgot; and they were forced to endure Robespierre." This passage appears in both the essay on Mirabeau and Macaulay's second speech on the Reform Bill (5 July 1831). It is, in fact, the main theme that runs through the five Reform Bill speeches that he delivered between 2 March and 16 December 1831. In the 2 March speech, he warned the Commons to reform "now while the crash of the proudest throne of the Continent is still resounding in our ears." And again on 20 September he reminded the opponents of reform that the French aristocrats were "driven forth to exile and beggary, to cut wood in the

back settlements of America, or to teach French in the school-rooms of London . . . because they refused all concession till the time had arrived when no concession would avail."

Certainly the dangers seemed real and the business at hand momentous. In a letter to his friend and future editor Thomas Flower Ellis on 30 March 1831, Macaulay recorded his excitement during the vote on the first reading of the Reform Bill, which was won by the reformers by a margin of one. "It was like seeing Caesar stabbed in the Senate-House, or seeing Oliver taking the mace from the table; a sight to be seen once only, and never to be forgotten." When the votes were counted, "the jaw of Peel fell; and the face of Twiss was as the face of a damned soul; and Herries looked like Judas taking off his necktie for the last operation." Macaulay left the House, passing through crowds cheering and throwing their hats in the air, called a cab, "and the first thing the driver asked was, 'Is the bill carried?' 'Yes, by one.' 'Thank God for it, sir.' And away I rode to Gray's Inn." The comparisons with Julius Caesar and Cromwell, as well as the conversation with the deferential cabby, suggest the sincere belief that England had just avoided a revolt of the lower classes, with resultant lawlessness and economic ruin. "Reform that you may preserve" had been the explicit or implied message of all Macaulay's speeches on the bill and was to become the main political theme of his *The History of England*. But the detail of Judas's necktie also suggests the author's obvious enjoyment of the fight. There were still some anxious moments ahead for Macaulay's party, but in the meantime, as the letter to Ellis continued, "as for me, I am . . . a lion."

The process of lionization involved invitations to Charles, Earl Grey's official residence at 10 Downing Street and also to Holland House, the seat of Henry Richard Vassall Fox, Lord Holland and unofficial headquarters of the Whig party. In a letter of 8 July 1831 to his sister Hannah, Macaulay described his reception at Downing Street: "Lady Holland . . . gave me a most gracious reception . . . and told me in her imperial decisive manner that she had talked with all the principal men on our side about my speech—that they all agreed that it was the best that had been made since the death of Fox. . . ." For a man who was only thirty years old, this praise was very flattering, but since Macaulay had neither wealth nor important family connections to help him rise in the world, such compliments had an even more important practical value.

The eventual passage of the Reform Bill meant that the pocket borough of Calne no longer had a seat in Parliament, but with Lord Lansdowne's continued support, Macaulay was appointed secretary to the Board of Trade at twelve hundred pounds per year and became Whig candidate for a new parliamentary seat in the industrial city of Leeds. Since the family firm of Macaulay and Babington was now near bankruptcy, the twelve hundred pounds and the additional lucrative offices which the government found for his father and brother were very gratifying to the promising politician. And one would expect him to have been supremely content when he won the Leeds election for the first reformed Parliament over the Tory Michael Sadler, whose theories on population he had earlier attacked with gusto in the *Edinburgh*.

But on election night he was more intensely unhappy than he had ever been—and for reasons that almost nobody guessed until Sir George Otto Trevelyan's official biography of his uncle,

The Life and Letters of Lord Macaulay, was published nearly half a century later. Macaulay's combativeness, his frequently expressed enthusiasm for common sense, and his glorification of material progress all tend to give the impression that he was a rather unemotional and insensitive man. The fact that he neither married nor carried on liaisons contributed to the same impression. His contemporary Walter Bagehot wrote, in an 1856 essay for the *National Review*, of his "inexperiencing nature . . . unalive to joys and sorrows," and the twentieth-century critic Mario Praz described him, in *The Hero in Eclipse in Victorian Fiction* (1956), as a man with "a mind free of passion and emotion."

In fact, Macaulay was emotionally quite vulnerable. This side of his character can be seen in his dealings with his father, and surely the masculine aggressiveness of his public persona was to some extent a defense mechanism. On the night of the Leeds election, he was handed a letter informing him that one of his two favorite sisters, Margaret, was to be married, and suddenly he felt that the world had ended. "I am sitting in the midst of two hundred friends," he wrote to his other favorite sister, Hannah, "all glorying over the Tories, and thinking me the happiest man in the world. And it is all that I can do to hide my tears and to command my voice. . . . Dearest, dearest, girl, you alone are now left to me.— Whom have I on *earth* but thee— . . . But for you, in the midst of all these successes, I should wish that I were lying by poor Hyde Villiers. But I cannot go on. . . . But the separation from dear Margaret has jarred my whole temper. I am cried up here to the skies as the most affable and kind hearted of men, while I feel a fierceness and restlessness within me quite new and almost inexplicable."

This passage captures both the intensity of Macaulay's feelings and the fact that he managed to keep those feelings hidden from almost everybody who knew him. Indeed modern readers with a Freudian bias will find it easy enough to account for the fierceness and restlessness which Macaulay himself found inexplicable. Obviously, Macaulay is an inviting target for the iconoclast. Some notion of his public image can be taken from the statement which Stephen Dedalus hears a priest make in James Joyce's *A Portrait of the Artist as a Young Man* (1916): "I believe that Lord Macaulay was a man who probably never committed a mortal sin in his life, that is to say, a deliberate mortal sin." A celibate Victorian sage widely believed to have been without stain or spot but inwardly tormented by incestuous passions is an appealing image for anybody bent on attacking Victorian respectability, and Macaulay's relationships with his demanding father and his two adoring young sisters were both tormented and decidedly peculiar. The examples of William Wordsworth, Charles Lamb, and many characters in Jane Austen's novels serve, however, as reminders that brothers and sisters were more often devoted to each other in early-nineteenth-century England than in most times and places. And while conflicts between fathers and sons are common in any age, the examples of Macaulay, John Stuart Mill, and Sir Edmund Gosse certainly suggest that being the son of a Victorian Evangelical or Utilitarian was a particularly uncomfortable situation. Presumably, Macaulay's conflicts with his father had some role in creating his intense feelings for Margaret and Hannah—John Clive, in his biography *Macaulay: The Shaping of the Historian* (1973), suggests that the girls allowed him to play the role of father, supplanting Zachary Macaulay—and clearly his feelings for these sisters led him into a series of traumatic experiences in the period from 1832 to 1834.

After Margaret's marriage, Macaulay's sister Hannah became her brother's favorite and confidante. His political and literary careers continued to prosper. The Whigs remained in power after the 1832 elections, so Macaulay and his relatives continued to draw their salaries. He made a successful speech on the reform of the East India Company, advocating the appointment to the company's Supreme Council of one legislative member who would not be a company employee. When the position was later offered to him, at the recommendation of his old opponent James Mill, Macaulay was definitely grateful. This office carried an annual salary of ten thousand pounds—of which at least half could be saved—giving him the prospect of the kind of financial independence he desperately wanted. Without such resources he would need to depend on either his writing or his political offices, offices which depended on his party's being in power and on his support of party policy. In 1832 he nearly had to resign from the Board of Control over his disagreements with the government's cautious policy on the abolition of West Indian slavery. Luckily, the government amended its bill so that he could support it, but such a resolution of conflict could hardly be counted on in the future.

Macaulay, of course, decided to take the position in India, but the decision was painful. The prospect of leaving his family, his friends, his country, and his promising political career was daunting, but when Hannah consented to accompany him, he felt that his exile would be entirely bearable. And after a six-month ocean voyage and his arrival in Madras on 10 June 1834, he traveled enthusiastically across the subcontinent to meet with the governor-general, Lord William Bentinck, at Ootacamund. This trip, in which Macaulay was carried in a palanquin by native bearers, is recorded in a series of letters that show his appreciation for both the natural scenery and man-made monuments of India. The ruins of Seringapatam interested him because his uncle Gen. Colin Macaulay had participated in the famous siege of 1798. The ruined courts reminded him of the college quadrangles at Oxford and Cambridge, the Indian jungles reminded him, as he wrote to his sister Margaret on 3 October 1834, of "the works of the great English landscape-gardeners," and a mountain view of the plain of Mysore moved him "almost to tears."

After this lyrical introduction to Indian life, Macaulay's situation deteriorated rapidly. When he arrived at Calcutta, he found that Hannah, like Margaret, was about to be "lost" to him through marriage to Charles Trevelyan, a young officer of the East India Company whom she had met during the voyage from England. In the shaping of Macaulay's personality, most biographers seem to give primary importance to the influence of Zachary Macaulay's paternal enormities, but the loss of his two favorite sisters was also crucial in the final forming of Macaulay's private life and consequently of his political and literary careers. For whatever reason, he never seems to have taken any step that could reasonably have led to marriage. His erotic impulses seem to have been sublimated, and his domestic affections were fully satisfied by his sisters. Obviously, such arrangements do not last, all of which was clear enough to Macaulay after the sisters he had relied on had gone. As he wrote to Margaret on 7 December 1834, "Whatever I have suffered I have brought on myself. I have neglected the plainest lessons of reason and experience . . . it is the tragical denouement of an absurd plot." In any event, he gave his full support to Hannah Macaulay's match and did his best not to let her realize how much the thought of her marriage made him suffer.

If his loss had consisted simply in his sisters' getting married, Macaulay might eventually have recovered. He moved in with the Trevelyans and, despite his considerable misgivings, the arrangement worked out well. He and Trevelyan became reasonably good friends, and when Hannah had children, he became a doting uncle. But shortly after the wedding, news arrived that Margaret had died of typhoid fever during the preceding August, four months before Macaulay had written the letter concerning Hannah's engagement. On 8 February 1835 he confessed to Thomas Flower Ellis that "I never knew before what it was to be miserable. . . . Even now, when time has begun to do its healing office, I cannot write about her without being altogether unmanned. That I have not altogether sunk under this blow I owe chiefly to literature. What a blessing it is to love books as I love them—to be able to converse with the dead and to live amidst the unreal." On 29 May he wrote again to Ellis, saying, "my time is divided between public business and books. . . . My spirits have not yet recovered—I sometimes think they will never wholly recover—from the shock which they received five months ago." Almost fifteen years later, on 8 April 1849, Macaulay recorded in his journal a visit to Lichfield Cathedral. When he looked at a statue of some children, he "could think only of one thing; that, when last I was there, in 1832, my dear sister Margaret was with me, and that she was greatly affected. I could not command my tears, and was forced to leave our party and walk about by myself." Like the letter he wrote to Hannah on the election night at Leeds, the journal passage is striking for the intensity of the feelings it expresses and for Macaulay's effort to disguise them.

His initial reaction to Margaret's death was, as he suggested in the letter to Ellis, to bury himself in work and escapist reading. He did a great deal of important official work, but his extensive private reading was perhaps even more significant. At the end of 1835 he wrote to Ellis, saying that "the tremendous blow which fell upon me at the beginning of this year has left marks behind it which I shall carry to my grave. Literature has saved my life and my reason. Even now, I dare not, in the intervals of business, remain alone for a minute without a book in my hand. . . . I am half determined to abandon politics, and to give myself wholly to letters; to undertake some great historical work which may be at once the business and the amusement of my life." So the plan of *The History of England* emerged during this pe-

riod—and in part at least because Macaulay had found literature so effective an escape from a pain that he found almost unbearable. When he told Ellis he was fortunate to be "able to converse with the dead and live amidst the unreal," he hit on the source of both much of his strength and much of his weakness as a writer.

Sir George Otto Trevelyan has noted how Macaulay and Hannah talked about books in such a way that "a bystander would have supposed that they had lived in the times which the author treated, and had a personal acquaintance with every human being who was mentioned in his pages." Margaret Macaulay, in her journal for 30 March 1831, had recorded Macaulay's admission that he owed his accuracy in facts to his habit of "castle-building": a habit of imagining conversations between historical characters. "I am no sooner in the streets than I am in Greece, in Rome, in the midst of the French Revolution. Precision in dates, the day or hour in which a man was born or died, become absolutely necessary. A slight fact, a sentence, a word, are of importance in my romance." This comment suggests one reason behind his ability to write vivid historical narrative. But the habit he described to Ellis of conversing with the dead led to his developing violent prejudices about historical figures, prejudices which sometimes distorted his understanding of historical evidence. Furthermore, the word *romance* suggests a certain escapist dimension often noted in Macaulay's historical writings. Escapist daydreams were particularly necessary to him during the painful first year in India, but they remained important throughout his life. In a late letter to Ellis he wrote that he and Hannah "indulge[d] beyond any people I ever knew" in "the habit of building castles in the air" and that he thought it significant that the Greek term for this habit translated as "empty happiness."

In 1835, however, Macaulay was quite willing to settle for happiness of any kind. Escapist castle-building and reading (for example, one of Plutarch's lives in Greek or one of Pedro Calderón de la Barca's plays in Spanish before breakfast each day plus heavy reading in the evenings) were supplemented by prodigious work during the day as legal member of the Supreme Council. In this capacity he produced two works of particular importance: the Minute on Indian Education and the Indian Penal Code. The former was perhaps the most important of the two because it decided the course of Indian higher education for at least 150 years. A considerable debate

Macaulay's sister Hannah. She and Margaret Macaulay were his favorites, and, in the words of Macaulay's biographer John Clive, "it was these two younger sisters . . . upon whom alone was focused the strongly developed emotional side of his nature."

had been waged for years before Macaulay's arrival in India over the proper subjects for such education, with two schools of thought emerging. The Orientalists favored instruction in the Sanskrit and Arabic classics; the Anglicists argued for the English language as the medium of instruction. Instruction in the modern Indian vernacular languages was not considered a viable option by either party because it was believed that there was insufficient worthwhile reading matter available in these languages. Macaulay predictably supported the Anglicist position. Since Sanskrit and Arabic were as much "foreign" languages as English, Macaulay saw the issue as a simple one: "whether, when we can patronize sound philosophy and true history, we shall countenance, at the public expense, medical doctrines which would disgrace an English farrier—astronomy, which would move laughter in the girls at an English boarding-school—history, abounding with kings thirty feet high, and reigns thirty thousand years long—and geography, made up of seas of treacle and seas of butter." Hooghly College was consequently opened in Calcutta in 1836 as an English-language institution, and English remained the primary language of instruction in In-

dian schools (and eventually universities) throughout the British period and still plays an important role today. This fact has had incalculable effects on the spread of Western thought and national consciousness in India, and it is not surprising that Indian opinion has been divided over the merits of Macaulay's position.

The Indian Penal Code, like the education minute, has been criticized for its attempt to impose a new and foreign system on Indian life. This code was a much more substantial work than the minute—running with its notes to approximately two hundred pages and being almost completely Macaulay's own work. The work was completed in May 1837, taking less than two years—compared with nine for the French Code Napoleon and three and one-half for Livingston's Code for Louisiana. Macaulay, by his own account, "changed the whole plan ten or twelve times" and yet had the vexation to find that it was not adopted in his lifetime. It was, however, adopted in 1860, providing a clear and compact guide for Indian civil servants, "the younger of whom," Trevelyan noted, "carry it about in their saddle-bags, and the older in their heads." But in 1837 the code seemed too radical and too simple, to take too little account of existing Indian laws. And Macaulay himself was not a popular public figure. He had helped pass two laws, which in combination caused him considerable trouble. The first was the "Black Act," which placed Englishmen outside Calcutta under the same courts as native Indians and was intensely resented by Anglo-Indians. Since the second law was the Censorship Act, which deregulated the Anglo-Indian press, this resentment was freely expressed. The physical climate of India seems never to have bothered Macaulay, and the political climate was an annoyance rather than a serious problem. He had been used to hostile journalists in England and had private sorrows that made Calcutta editorials seem insignificant, but he had not had a pleasant time in the East, and by the end of 1837 he was ready to leave. He had invested much of his princely salary and had inherited an additional ten thousand pounds from his uncle General Macaulay, so his purpose in going to India had been accomplished; he need never worry about money again.

While in the East he had written two more essays for the *Edinburgh Review*, the first of which placed his life in considerable danger and the second of which has been similarly disastrous for his reputation. The first, "Sir James Mackintosh's *His-*

tory of the Revolution" (July 1835), was a review of Mackintosh's fragmentary history of the Glorious Revolution of 1688, as completed and edited by a certain Mr. Wallace. Wallace had appeared to be excessively critical of Mackintosh, and since Macaulay admired and liked Mackintosh, he attacked Wallace with what he later admitted was "an asperity . . . which ought to be reserved for offences against the laws of morality and honour." When Macaulay returned to England in the summer of 1838 (having spent the long sea journey home learning German), three years after the review appeared, Wallace sent him an entirely serious challenge to a duel. Macaulay had no experience with firearms, but since the challenge had been made in a correct and gentlemanly manner, he saw no way out of a situation very likely to be fatal. Wallace was, however, persuaded to say that he had intended no disrespect to Mackintosh; Macaulay expressed regret that he had used excessive language as a result of having misunderstood Wallace's intention; and the confrontation was avoided.

The essay on Francis Bacon (July 1837), the other *Edinburgh Review* article from the Indian years, is one of Macaulay's best-known and most unfortunate writings. "Lord Bacon," wrote Walter Houghton in *The Victorian Frame of Mind* (1957), is "the *locus classicus* of Victorian anti-intellectualism," and it has certainly had a major role in creating the popular image of its author as a complacent, insensitive, and belligerent boor. In depicting Bacon, the essay presents the most exaggerated of Macaulay's antithetical characters: "the difference between the soaring angel and the creeping snake was but the type of the difference between Bacon the philosopher and Bacon the Attorney-General . . . in one line the boldest and most useful of innovators, in another one the most obstinate champion of the foulest abuses." In Macaulay's essay Bacon's moral character is blackened, while his useful, practical, limited philosophy is praised as the basis for Western progress. Plato and other ancient philosophers "promised what was impracticable; they despised what was practicable; they filled the world with long words and long beards; and they left it as wicked as they found it," but Bacon's focus on the inductive method and on practical "fruit" has done a great deal "to make imperfect men comfortable." Thus Bacon becomes in Macaulay's hands a seventeenth-century Utilitarian who gave mankind the intellectual key to progress, with the result that "the books which have been written in the languages of Europe during the last two hundred and fifty years—translations from the ancient languages of course included,— are of greater value than all the books which at the beginning of that period were extant in the world." The important parenthetical clause about translations from the ancients is often unjustly overlooked by critics eager to pillory Macaulay, and these same critics tend erroneously to assume that he is describing his own tastes. In fact Macaulay himself read ancient literature (including Plato) without benefit of translations and generally preferred it to modern work. His statements in the Bacon essay are concerned with the books—including works on medicine and the natural sciences in general—that were of most value to most people, not simply to those people who had the advantages of the classical education that he himself had enjoyed. Furthermore, this essay was written in India, when the author was miserably unhappy and even worried about losing his mind. His exaggerated praise of practical reason and reliable material progress should be seen in this context.

As soon as the threat of the duel with Wallace was out of the way, Macaulay set off for a long tour of France and Italy, leaving in October 1838 and returning in February 1839. In Italy he was vexed by the dirt and the corrupt officials but fascinated and invigorated by the classical associations. He passed scenes described by Livy and Tacitus and worked on his one collection of published poems, *Lays of Ancient Rome*. These poems, begun in India and eventually published in 1842, were attempts to reconstruct primitive Roman ballads which—the German historian Barthold Niebuhr had suggested—were the probable sources of Livy's stories in the early books of his *History*. Macaulay never took these poems very seriously, but they were widely read, and one—"How Horatius Kept the Bridge"—was memorized and declaimed by countless schoolboys over the next hundred years. In 1846 the book was already so widely circulated that the American historian Francis Parkman found a man reading it in the distinctly nonliterary setting of the Oregon Trail.

The Mackintosh essay, as well as the one on Sir William Temple (*Edinburgh Review*, October 1838) which he wrote shortly after returning from India, reflects Macaulay's lingering uncertainty about the future shape of his career. Mackintosh had so divided himself between politics and historical scholarship as to make no great figure in either field. Similarly, Temple seemed to

Macaulay to be culpably unable to stick to either politics or literature. Temple, he tells his readers, "avoided the great offices of the state with a caution almost pusillanimous . . . and while the nation groaned under oppression, or resounded with tumult and with the din of civil arms, amused himself by writing memoirs and tying up apricots." As this passage suggests, Macaulay was feeling the moral claims of public life at this point. While in India, he had written to his friend Ellis (30 December 1835) that the essence of a British political career seemed to be "pestiferous rooms, sleepless nights, aching heads, and diseased stomachs," but now he was more impressed by the demands which the embattled Whig party placed on his services. As late as 5 September 1839, Arthur Wellesley, Duke of Wellington wrote to his friend Lady Wilson, wife of Sir Robert Thomas Wilson, that Lord Melbourne "would prefer to sit in a Room with a Chime of Bells, ten Parrots and one Lady Westmoreland to sitting in Cabinet with Mr. Macaulay," but only fifteen days later, Macaulay, having been elected MP for Edinburgh, did join Melbourne's cabinet as secretary-at-war.

He held this position until the Whig ministry fell in July 1841. While in office he had the interesting task of interrogating a lunatic who had tried to assassinate Queen Victoria and the difficult duty of defending both government policy in the opium war with China and the military conduct of James Thomas Brudenell, Lord Cardigan, the same Lord Cardigan who later led the Light Brigade to disaster at Balaklava. His speeches were as persuasive as the situations would permit, but he seems not to have been particularly upset when the fall of the Whigs released him from office. He had begun *The History of England* on 9 March 1839, right after returning from his Continental tour, and was really more interested in literary work than in politics. He was completing the *Lays of Ancient Rome* and continuing his work with the *Edinburgh Review*. Meanwhile, *The History of England* was not getting enough attention so he had plenty to do without trying to run the War Office. He did not want to share the fate of Mackintosh, who never finished his history. On 12 July 1841 he took rooms in the Albany on Piccadilly, which, at different times, was also home to Byron and William Gladstone, and began to work in earnest on *The History of England*.

After his return from the Continental tour, he wrote twelve more essays for the *Edinburgh Re-* *view* before his determination to devote himself entirely to *The History of England* made him give up reviewing altogether after 1844. Two of the earliest of these essays were devoted to religious themes, one on the Church of England and the other on the papacy. The April 1839 criticism of Gladstone's *The State in Its Relations with the Church* (1838) is a useful reminder that the future Liberal prime minister was at this time a very conservative Tory and Tractarian who sought to make the British government a thoroughly Anglican institution. While Macaulay was entirely opposed to the idea of a religiously exclusive government, his essay is noteworthy for its courteous treatment of its opponent. The ad hominem attacks that had been part of Macaulay's earlier *Edinburgh Review* manner were part of the past. Perhaps Gladstone's erudition, amiable behavior, and obvious sincerity brought out Macaulay's generosity. Certainly Macaulay's own success was a factor. He was no longer an impecunious young man trying to fight his way into politics and journalism by savage attacks on eminent Tories such as Southey or Croker, nor was he a miserable exile in India venting his unhappiness in vilification of writers who had been dead for hundreds of years. He was financially independent; the Trevelyan family provided him with a good measure of the domestic happiness which he had thought lost forever; and he was about to reenter Parliament and become a minister. He could afford to treat young Mr. Gladstone generously. His other religious essay, an October 1840 review of Leopold von Ranke's *Ecclesiastical and Political History of the Popes*, published in English translation earlier that year, shows the same moderation and courtesy. He speaks of Ranke with respect and treats the rival claims of Protestantism and Catholicism fairly. He also helps define his notions about progress by making clear that he did not see religious truth to be progressive. "The ingenuity of a people just emerging from barbarism is quite sufficient to propound" the great problems of religious thought. "The genius of Locke or Clarke is quite unable to solve them."

From 1840 to 1842 three essays dealt with eighteenth-century figures who, in their combination of political and military leadership, look forward to William III in *The History of England*. Robert Clive, Baron Clive of Plassey (treated in conjunction with Sir John Malcolm's 1836 biography in January 1840) and Warren Hastings (the subject of an October 1841 piece) presumably interested Macaulay because he had been one of

"Unhappy ghosts wandering on the banks of Styx," sketch by John Doyle depicting the outcome of the 1847 parliamentary elections. Macaulay leads the defeated along the riverbank while John Bull as Charon takes the victors to their reward (British Library).

their successors in governing British India; Frederick the Great (April 1842) would, Macaulay thought, have an important role in *The History of England*, since he had been England's chief ally in the Seven Years War. All three essays show Macaulay exulting in the heroic aspects of military narrative—however much he might in theory have detested war and attributed all solid human happiness to the fruits of quiet industry and the joys of the domestic hearth. In the Cambridge lectures that were posthumously published as *A Commentary on Macaulay's History of England* (1938), Sir Charles Firth observed that Macaulay "rejoiced like the war horse in *Job*, when he sniffed a battle afar off, a thing very becoming in a former Secretary at War." British troops in a thin red line overcoming hordes of bloodthirsty Marathas or the Prussian army withstanding the combined might of France, Austria, and Russia were clearly inspiring images for him—as inspiring as they could possibly have been to Rudyard Kipling or Thomas Carlyle—despite Macaulay's relative reluctance to make excuses for the faults of military heroes.

In his 1960 essay "Macaulay: The Indian Years, 1834-38," the historian Eric Stokes remarked that the essays on Clive and Hastings show little sign that their author had lived in India, but his essays on Restoration comedy (January 1841), Fanny Burney, later Madame d'Arblay (January 1843), and Joseph Addison (July 1843) allowed Macaulay to write about the entirely congenial subject of literary life in the Restoration and eighteenth century. He had given up literary criticism because he was dissatisfied with his work—"I have never written a page of criticism of poetry, or the fine arts, which I would not burn if I had the power," he told Macvey Napier in an 1838 letter. But he was quite at home discussing the lives and times of writers and including some consideration of their works, rather in the manner of Samuel Johnson's *Lives of the Poets* (1779-1781) but with an emphasis much more biographical and historical. The writers of this period were very real to Macaulay. His castle-building never apparently involved Indian sights or sounds, but Macaulay was imaginatively an intimate of Whitehall in the days of Charles II, of the coffeehouses in the days of Queen Anne, and of Samuel Johnson's circle in the days of George III. He insisted—in opposition to Charles Lamb—that the characters of William Wycherley's and Sir George Etherege's plays were all-too-real reflections of the manners and morals of their time. Macaulay defended Joseph Addison against the attacks of Alexander Pope and seized on Fanny Burney's ill-treatment as a lady-in-waiting to Queen Charlotte to express his indignation at the tyranny of George III.

In the early 1840s unauthorized collections of Macaulay's essays were being published in America and sold in Britain. Macaulay had decided in June 1842 not to republish his essays in an authorized edition because he did not want to be judged by them. "The public judges, and ought to judge, indulgently of periodical works," he wrote to Napier on 24 June. "They are not expected to be highly finished works. Their natural life is only six weeks." Essays, he noted, often contain errors and lack structure, but "all this is readily forgiven if there be a certain spirit and vivacity in the style." Republished articles, however, must meet a higher standard, and Macaulay was not at all sure that his would measure up to such a standard. By December, however, he had changed his mind: if he collected the essays himself, he could at least make sure that the texts were correct, that the least impressive essays were excluded, that the least justifiable passages of the remainder were revised, and that the royalties were paid to the author himself. The edition of *Critical and Historical Essays, Contributed to the Edinburgh Review*, which appeared in April 1843, was something of a publishing phenomenon. It sold out quickly and was succeeded by second, third, and fourth editions—which also sold out—and each year the public bought more copies than the year before. By 1876 Trevelyan claimed that the Longman edition alone had sold 120,000 copies, with 130,000 copies of individually published essays having been sold in the Traveler's Library series as well. Indeed, Trevelyan concluded, the British market for the essays "is so steady, and apparently so inexhaustible, that it perceptibly falls and rises with the general prosperity of the nation; and it is not too much to say that the demand for Macaulay varies with the demand for coal."

In this same year in which he collected his previously published essays from the *Edinburgh Review*, Macaulay made his last contribution to the journal. In April 1844 he indignantly denounced the "Jacobin carrion" Bertrand Barère and in October 1844 wrote his second essay dealing with William Pitt, the Earl of Chatham, narrating the vicissitudes of the statesman's later years. These last few essays on eighteenth-century soldiers, writers, and statesmen are among Macaulay's most successful, but he decided that if *The History of England* was ever to be completed, he would have to stop writing for the *Edinburgh Review*. As he wrote Napier on 6 December 1844, "but for the Review I

should already have brought out two volumes at least. I really must make a resolute effort. Or my plan will end as our poor friend Mackintosh's ended." So a resolute effort was made, but while reviewing was now a thing of the past, politics was still a powerful distraction. Macaulay was still a member of Parliament and in July 1846 was persuaded to reenter the cabinet, this time as paymaster-general of the army in Lord John Russell's ministry. This position, he was relieved to discover, took up less of his time than he had expected, so progress on *The History of England* continued satisfactorily, and in July 1847 political distractions ended abruptly. To almost everybody's surprise, Macaulay lost both his place in the cabinet and his seat in the House of Commons in that month's general election.

Since this event constitutes the only serious career setback that Macaulay ever experienced, it calls for some explanation. Like many nationally prominent politicians, he had tended to neglect the voters of his own constituency. He rarely visited Edinburgh and seems to have thought that courting the voters was beneath his dignity. It never seems to have occurred to him to solicit their opinions, much less let those opinions have any effect on the speeches he gave or the votes he cast as their representative in Parliament. The single act which had apparently created the most indignation among the Edinburgh electors was Macaulay's speech on 14 April 1845 supporting a Tory bill to almost triple the annual government grant to the Roman Catholic seminary at Maynooth in Ireland. He was always willing to attack what he saw as religious bigotry and was particularly unwilling to make any political accommodation on religious matters. In the Leeds election campaign of 1832, for example, a Methodist minister asked at a public meeting for a statement of Mr. Macaulay's religious creed. For his pains he was treated like a criminal. The candidate insisted that the questioner stand up and then replied that "I have heard with the greatest shame and sorrow the question that has been proposed to me; and with peculiar pain do I learn that this question was proposed by a minister of religion." After going on to denounce the luckless clergyman at length for what he called "this disgraceful inquisition," Macaulay said only that he was a Christian and then roundly scolded the audience for having applauded his answer.

Presumably Macaulay did not get the Methodist minister's vote in the Leeds election, and by July 1847 many Edinburgh electors were concerned both by the religious policies of their M.P. and by his contemptuous dismissal of all such concerns as disgusting bigotry. The electors were not so obviously in the wrong as might now seem to have been the case. After all, Parliament routinely passed laws on religious matters, and Macaulay himself was not above being affected in his official actions by his religious biases. As paymaster-general, he had had the opportunity to award what he called "a tolerable piece of patronage," the chaplaincy of Chelsea Hospital. This position "would be an exceedingly pleasant situation for a literary man," he told Ellis, but "nothing shall induce me to take a Puseyite." The Puseyite (High Church Anglican) vote in Edinburgh was presumably small, and the electors did not have the advantage of reading Macaulay's private letters, but the Church of Scotland had recently split, and Protestant passions were running high. The Maynooth speech had used the Scottish schism to point out that even established Protestant churches could not agree on doctrine and that only one of the contending parties within such churches could possibly be right. This idea could not but give offense, and the opposition was not above making full use of Macaulay's words in its attempt to unseat him. On 30 July 1847 he finished third in the poll, and that night he wrote some verses consoling himself with the thought that he had defied "a sullen priesthood and a raving mob" amid "hate's yell, and envy's hiss, and folly's bray." No doubt the defeat rankled him, but the release from politics was welcome. He refused several offers to have his name put in nomination for other seats in Parliament and turned his full attention to *The History of England*. In November 1848 the students of Glasgow decided to show their superiority over the rival city of Edinburgh by electing Macaulay lord rector of their university, and, soon after, this vote of confidence was followed by the publication of the first two volumes of *The History of England from the Accession of James II*.

The History of England was the great, culminating work of Macaulay's career, the performance for which the *Edinburgh Review* articles had been merely rehearsals. In one of the earlier of those articles, simply called "History" and published in May 1828, he had set out his notions of how historians should write, and clearly many of these ideas were still among his shaping concepts in the 1840s when he wrote the first volumes of *The History of England*. After lamenting, in his most insufferable early *Edinburgh Review* manner, that

"we are acquainted with no history which approaches to our notion of what a history ought to be," he reviewed the classic historians from Herodotus to Hume and found them all, to varying degrees, unsatisfactory. Herodotus thought like a child; Plutarch was a revolutionary fanatic. Thucydides was an impressive narrator but did not understand the importance of social history. Modern historians, such as Hume or Gibbon, were more analytical than the ancients, but they also failed to tell the truth. Herodotus, in Macaulay's opinion, "tells his story like a slovenly witness," while "Hume is an accomplished advocate" out to win a case. The ideal historian should be an impartial judge and should combine the literary art of the ancients with the modern understanding that political revolutions "are almost always the consequences of moral changes, which have gradually passed on the mass of the community, and which originally proceed far before their progress is indicated by any public measure." The failure to emphasize social, intellectual, and economic history was what Macaulay found most unsatisfactory in other historians. "He who would understand these things rightly must not confine his observations to palaces and solemn days. He must mingle in the crowds of the exchange and coffeehouse. He must obtain admittance to the convivial table and the domestic hearth." The image of the historian walking about in a past age is clearly reminiscent of Macaulay's statements to his sister Margaret about castle-building, and there can be little doubt that already in 1828 he saw himself as the ideal historian who would give "to truth those attractions which have been usurped by fiction" and write a history that would be as popular and as sensitive to social details as Sir Walter Scott's Waverley novels.

The *Edinburgh Review* essays had already met the standard of popularity, but they did not give their author the scope he needed for the kind of social history his theories required. The later ones were, he said, after the manner of Plutarch rather than Thucydides, biographies of great men rather than histories of a whole nation. When he came to *The History of England* itself, he confided to Ellis that at least he hoped to "produce something which shall for a few days supercede the last fashionable novel on the tables of young ladies," but in his journal he admitted that "I have tried to do something that may be remembered; I have had the year 2000, and even the year 3000, often in my mind."

The History of England was, however, firmly linked to the present, stretching from "the accession of King James the Second down to a time which is within the memory of men still living," as the opening page announced, linking the Glorious Revolution of 1688, which "brought the Crown into harmony with the Parliament," and the Great Reform Bill of 1832, "which brought the Parliament into harmony with the nation." In fact, *The History of England* is actually a fragment, ending with the death of William III in 1702, but the first two volumes, published in 1848, are a complete treatment of the Glorious Revolution in ten chapters. These volumes, and *The History of England* as a whole, are structured around a conflict between James II—representing the tyranny of Stuart absolutism and the superstition of Roman Catholic bigotry—and William III, representing constitutional monarchy and freedom of conscience. William is portrayed as brave, merciful, and wise; his life with Queen Mary is presented as an admirable example of domestic affection. James, meanwhile, is depicted as a coward, a sadist, a fool, and a lecher. Finally, James and his brother Charles II are seen as having made England an international nonentity under the control of Louis XIV; William, on the contrary, rallied Europe against the threat of French militarism and began the series of wars—stretching through the eighteenth century and finally ending only at Waterloo—by which England replaced France as the first nation of Europe.

William is, however a minor character until chapter 7. The first three chapters set the scene—describing the constitutional questions of the seventeenth century, sketching the characters of the major political figures of the period, and giving a vivid account of the state of the country at the accession of James in 1685. This account, the famous third chapter, is today the most frequently read section of *The History of England* and the one in which Macaulay tries hardest to demonstrate his assertion in the opening paragraphs of chapter 1 that "the history of our country during the last hundred and fifty years is eminently the history of physical, of moral, and of intellectual improvement." The physical improvement is perhaps the easiest kind to document, something Macaulay does throughout the third chapter—and elsewhere—whenever he can compare the seventeenth-century appearance of a town or a patch of countryside with its more attractive Victorian splendor. In Victorian London, for example, the Thames is spanned by "several bridges, not inferior in magnificence and solidity to the noblest works of the Caesars. In 1685, a single line of irregular arches, overhung by piles of mean and crazy houses, and garnished, after a fashion worthy of the naked barbarians of Dahomey, with scores of moldering heads, impeded the navigation of the river." Travel between towns was agonizingly slow, prohibitively expensive, and terribly dangerous. The towns themselves were dirty, small, unlit, and infested with beggars, bullies, and footpads, while huge tracts of countryside, totaling "a fourth part of England," have, in the last two centuries, been "turned from a wild into a garden."

Intellectual progress is illustrated both by the advancement of knowledge and by its spread. "Every bricklayer who falls from a scaffold, every sweeper of a crossing who is run over by a carriage, may now have his wounds dressed and his limbs set with a skill such as, a hundred and sixty years ago, all the wealth of a great lord like Ormond . . . could not have purchased." Nor was available knowledge as widespread in the seventeenth century as in the nineteenth. "Few knights of the shire had libraries so good as may now perpetually be found in a servants' hall, or in the back parlor of a small shopkeeper. An esquire passed among his neighbors for a great scholar, if Hudibras and Baker's Chronicle, Tarlton's Jests and the Seven Champions of Christendom, lay in his hall window among his fishing rods and fowling pieces." But most important of all was the moral inferiority of old England—the cruelty which had led even good masters to beat their servants, crowds to exult at public executions, politicians to seek each other's blood, and prisons to be "hells on earth." The seventeenth century was devoid of "that sensitive and restless compassion which has, in our time, extended a powerful protection to the factory child, to the Hindoo widow, to the Negro slave . . . and which has repeatedly endeavored to save the life even of the murderer." The third chapter of *The History of England* has given much offense—both for its disparagement of the seventeenth-century clergy and gentry and for its apparent complacency concerning the Victorian scene in general and industrialism in particular. But the reduction of poverty, ignorance, and cruelty are admirable goals, and the chapter concludes with a clear expectation that life in Victorian England itself will seem very unsatisfactory when contrasted with life in the twentieth century.

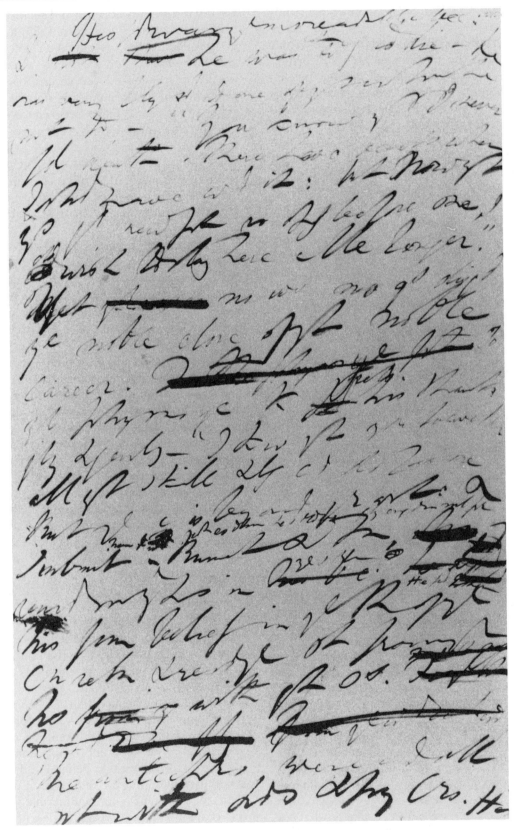

Page from the manuscript for volume five of Macaulay's The History of England *(The Pierpont Morgan Library)*

The fourth chapter begins the narrative proper, showing James II proclaimed king and beginning his first steps toward imposing Roman Catholicism and royal absolutism. Chapter 5 describes the premature rebellions of Archibald, Earl of Argyll in Scotland and James Scott, Duke of Monmouth in southwestern England. Here Macaulay continues to contrast seventeenth-century poverty with Victorian prosperity. In his account of Argyll's followers sailing up the Clyde to Greenock, the reader is informed that this community was "then a small fishing village consisting of a single row of thatched hovels, now a great and flourishing port, of which the customs amount to more than five times the whole revenue which the Stuarts derived from the kingdom of Scotland." Similarly, when the historian joins Monmouth in the steeple of Bridgewater parish church to survey the hostile royal army, he tells his audience how different the next day's battlefield of Sedgemoor looked in 1685. The sad fate of the rebels is the emotional high point of these early volumes. Argyll dies a heroic Protestant martyr prophesying deliverance for the country in the near future. Monmouth vainly begs for mercy from James, the cruel uncle whom he has wronged, and Judge George Jeffreys descends on the rebellious counties to conduct sham trials both for rebels and for those completely harmless people who sheltered them. From here James goes on hubristically to impose ever greater tyrannies until the nobility, gentry, and clergy who had rallied to his cause against Monmouth are totally alienated. Now that the time is ripe, William descends upon England, is acclaimed by large numbers, and begins his advance on London, while more and more influential men desert King James. William does everything that a wise leader can do to guarantee the success of his cause, but his final victory is possible only because James is his own worst enemy. Merciless when victorious, he proves a coward when threatened and flees England, allowing Parliament to declare the throne vacant and to offer it to William and Mary.

As one might expect from the program laid out in the 1828 essay "History," Macaulay's narrative owes a good deal to such classical models as Tacitus, Plutarch, and Thucydides, but a stronger source of the history's popular appeal for its Victorian readers was its unmistakable series of biblical echoes. The Glorious Revolution was, among other things, a religious movement. William is the Protestant hero and the Deliverer. The mar-

tyred Earl of Argyll, with his premature uprising against James, serves as John the Baptist—a voice crying in the wilderness, beheaded by a tyrant, and prophesying the national salvation which he knows he will not live to see. Judge Jeffreys's victims are holy innocents, whose Christian piety and blameless lives are prominently emphasized, and William is clearly Christ-like. In the last chapter of volume two, for example, with the Revolution all but won and William triumphantly established in London, the new king tells a Dutch friend, "Here . . . the cry is all Hosannah today, and will, perhaps, be Crucify tomorrow."

To this religious appeal is added a patriotic one. William will not only lead England back to the greatness it had known under Elizabeth and Cromwell; he will also preserve the nation from the perils which beset so many European states in the mid nineteenth century. The fact that the first part of *The History of England* appeared at the end of the revolutionary year 1848 allowed Macaulay to conclude it with his often-stated ideas about how chaos and barbarism could only be prevented by the timely adoption of reforms: "Now, if ever, we ought to be able to appreciate the whole importance of the stand which was made by our forefathers against the House of Stuart. All around us the world is convulsed by the agonies of great nations. Governments which lately seemed likely to stand during ages have been on a sudden shaken and overthrown. The proudest capitals of Western Europe have streamed with civil blood. . . . Meanwhile in our island the regular course of government has never been for a day interrupted. . . . And if it be asked what has made us to differ from others, the answer is that we never lost what others are wildly and blindly seeking to regain. It is because we had a preserving revolution in the seventeenth century that we have not had a destroying revolution in the nineteenth."

As the time of publication neared, Macaulay told his sister Hannah that "I have armed myself with all my philosophy for the event of a failure." The book was, after all, concerned with a period of British history that had never been considered particularly interesting, and there was always the danger that the author's partisan tone would alienate a great many readers. Furthermore, when Macaulay read a freshly printed copy of his own book along with a copy of Thucydides, he was reluctantly driven to the conclusion that the Greek historian's performance was, as he admitted in his journal, "much better than mine." The British reviewers and readers were, however, much more pleased with the book than its author was. By 4 December a second printing was called for, and by 12 December the author was told that "there has been no such sale since the days of *Waverley*." The second printing sold out almost as soon as it became available, and by 27 January 1849 the third printing was mostly gone. The early reviewers were universally flattering, with Tories rather unpredictably joining the Whig journals in praise of the Whig historian. Most remarkable, considering what Macaulay himself called the history's "insular spirit," was the fact that the work was also phenomenally popular in France and the United States. The author was more than a bit surprised by such enormous success but also clearly delighted, especially when he found a bookseller advertising Hume's Tory *History of England* (1754-1762) as being "highly valuable as an introduction to Macaulay."

By this time, he was already at work on volume three of his history. In August and September he took an extended trip to Ireland to examine the scenes of events which he would soon be describing, and except for similar trips to the Continent and occasional vacations in the countryside, his life was now centered in his study at the Albany and at the home of the Trevelyan family. In July 1852—without doing anything to advance his cause—Macaulay was returned to his old seat in Parliament by the contrite electors of Edinburgh, but almost immediately he suffered a heart attack which made it impossible for him to take a very active role in politics again. "Last July," he wrote in March 1853, "I became twenty years older in a week." He did not suffer much pain and did not particularly fear death, but it was now necessary for him to avoid strenuous exertion, and he hated the thought of leaving *The History of England* after only two volumes. His original goal of reaching the 1832 Reform Bill was clearly now out of the question, but he wrote in his journal, "I should be glad to finish William before I go."

The great honor done him by the Edinburgh electors was followed by others at home and abroad. In February he was elected to the French Institute and received the Prussian Order of Merit; in June he was awarded an honorary doctor of civil law degree from Oxford University. In 1853 he also began the series of five brief biographies which he wrote during the next six years for the *Encyclopædia Britannica*. The subjects were all drawn from the late seventeenth century and

the eighteenth century: John Bunyan, Francis Atterbury, Oliver Goldsmith, Samuel Johnson, and William Pitt the Younger. Johnson and Bunyan are subjects that he had already treated in *Edinburgh* reviews, and a comparison of these *Britannica* essays with Macaulay's earlier treatments of the same men shows him now adopting a less contentious persona and a less contrived prose style. These late essays are, in fact, much more in tune with *The History of England* than with the earlier reviews, and some desire to write more mature assessments of two of his favorite authors may have been Macaulay's main motive in doing the new pieces on Bunyan and Johnson. As for the others, it was now clear that *The History of England* was not likely to get far enough to allow Macaulay to deal with Atterbury, much less Goldsmith or the younger Pitt, so the essays gave him his one chance to assess men whom he found interesting and significant.

Nor were the essays for *Encyclopædia Britannica* the only literary distraction from *The History of England* in these years. By 1853 a pirated American edition of Macaulay's speeches forced him to bring out his own collection. As with the collected essays ten years earlier, he omitted his least impressive performances, but while the essays had needed only minor corrections and occasional toning down, the speeches had to be almost entirely reconstructed. Macaulay's oral delivery in Parliament was so rapid that the official records in *Hansard's Parliamentary Debates* only furnished him with what he regarded as "hints" to assist him in rewriting the speeches from memory. And rewritten they were—as faithfully to the originals as their author could manage. But readers of the published speeches should be aware that the texts were prepared in 1853. In July 1853, for example, Macaulay spent a rainy day reconstructing his great speech of 5 July 1831 on the Reform Bill. Although he believed he had "made a speech very like the real one in language, and in substance exactly the real one," he was relying on memories that were twenty-two years old. During his trip to Ireland in 1849, he had found that he could still recite about half of *Paradise Lost*, suggesting that his memory was still strong, but it would be remarkable if the printed speeches did not include some improvements over the spoken ones. In any event, these texts are the best records available of Macaulay's parliamentary oratory, and like everything he wrote, they were all well received. On the whole, however, he begrudged all the time the speeches took from *The History of En-*

gland. He knew that he could not live very many more years and was greatly relieved when volumes three and four finally appeared in December 1855.

The second installment of *The History of England* has generally been regarded as less impressive than the first, though it does contain some of Macaulay's best writing. Unfortunately, it has less obvious thematic and structural unity, and the central character of William III seems too uninteresting to carry the narrative. Volume three begins with a recasting of the Deliverer image, this time with the figure of Moses substituting for that of Christ. "From the time of the Exodus," Macaulay concedes, "the history of every great deliverer has been the history of Moses retold. Down to the present hour rejoicings like those on the shore of the Red Sea have ever been speedily followed by murmurings like those at the Waters of Strife." This passage signals the reaction which set in after the Revolution, with clergy and army having second thoughts about their desertion of King James, politicians renewing the partisan bickering which weakened England in its struggle with a unified, absolutist France, and the English people beginning to resent William's Dutch manners and Dutch favorites. Most urgent was the problem of Jacobite uprisings sweeping through the Scottish Highlands and overwhelming all of Ireland except for the two Protestant strongholds of Londonderry and Eniskillen.

The Irish and Scottish chapters of these volumes contribute the most vivid narratives. The relief of the siege of Londonderry, the Jacobite leader John Graham of Claverhouse dying at the moment of victory at Killiecrankie in the Highlands, and William leading the charge that breaks the Jacobite resistance at the Battle of the Boyne and opens the road to Dublin are dramatic, stirring events that Macaulay develops with obvious enthusiasm. The death of Queen Mary in 1694 gives him, in contrast, the material for a Victorian domestic tragedy. Mary is brave and devout, receiving the Eucharist, showing concern for her attendants' comfort, and attempting—when too weak to speak—"a last farewell of him whom she had loved so truly and entirely." William suffers "a series of fits so alarming that his Privy Councilors ... were apprehensive for his reason and his life" and is finally carried "almost insensible" from the sickroom. The queen's death is mourned by the people, gloated over by scurrilous Jacobites, and honored by the king with the building at Greenwich of "the noblest of European hospitals"—now the Royal Naval College.

William is more consistently in the forefront of these volumes than in the earlier parts of *The History of England*, but much of his work consists of the unexciting task of coping with a Parliament which would rather engage in internal squabbles and in petty sniping at him than concentrate on the war with France. In the first two volumes of the history, the Whigs—for all their duly noted faults—are clearly superior to the Tories, since they saw the danger of Stuart absolutism and recognized the fatuousness of the doctrines of divine right and passive obedience to the crown. In volumes three and four, however, the Tories are at least as good as the Whigs, reflecting both the politically untidy realities of the 1690s and a shift in Macaulay's own perspective. By the 1850s, according to Trevelyan, Macaulay had ceased to be a partisan in modern politics. He was still a "vehement ministerialist of 1698" but was progressively less enthusiastic about the Whigs as they metamorphosed into the Liberal party and seemed to be going beyond the reforms that he thought necessary. Also, Macaulay had cast John Churchill, Duke of Marlborough, a Whig, as the primary villain in volumes three and four of the history, as a traitor who gave important military secrets to the French and apparently planned to use his influence over the future Queen Anne to make himself the uncrowned ruler of England. The case against Marlborough seems today to have been convincingly refuted—as have Macaulay's vilifications of Claverhouse, Adm. William Penn, and others; and his wrongheadedness in these cases seems to reflect both the strong personal prejudices created by his habit of castle-building and his strong rhetorical need for villains to serve as foils to William.

William himself becomes a symbol of progress toward the end of volume four, when he is defeated by the French, under François Henri, Duke of Luxembourg, at Landen, his last major battle. "Never, perhaps, was the change which the progress of civilization has produced in the art of war more striking than on that day." William and Luxembourg were "two poor sickly beings who, in a rude state of society, would have been regarded as too puny to bear any part in combats," but "their lot had fallen on a time when men had discovered that strength of muscles is far inferior in value to strength of the mind." William's strength of mind had been such that he had created and maintained an alliance which

"Thomas Babington Macaulay in His Study," painting by Edward Matthew Ward, 1853 (National Portrait Gallery, London)

had checked—though not vanquished—the hitherto invincible armies of France and saved Europe from the domination of an insolent tyrant. The fourth volume of *The History of England* concludes with the 1697 Treaty of Ryswick, in which France recognized its inability to impose its will on its enemies, and the final pages echo the last scenes and reflections in volume two. Macaulay describes the reception of the treaty in London with civic rejoicing like that which seven years earlier had welcomed the Deliverer to his new capital, and the achievements of the Revolution settlement are again summarized, beginning with military accomplishments and going on to the growth of freedom and the unprecedented prosperity of the economy. "Many signs," Macaulay concludes—in 1855 as in 1848—"justified the hope that the Revolution of 1688 would be our last Revolution."

When volumes three and four of *The History of England* were published, Macaulay worried that they might disappoint the tremendous expectations of the reviewers and readers and that they might fall short of what the earlier volumes had achieved in narrative excitement. He need not have concerned himself. The reviews were again

highly favorable, and the sales soon surpassed those for the first volumes. Not surprisingly, the first two volumes now also had to be brought out in new editions to meet the new demand created by the success of volumes three and four. The phenomenal sales continued year after year so that by 1876 Trevelyan could claim that 140,000 copies of *The History of England* had been sold in Britain alone. Some idea of foreign sales can be taken from what Macaulay called "a most intoxicating letter" from Edward Everett in Massachusetts, saying that in America the history was outselling everything except the Bible.

The remainder of Macaulay's life was relatively comfortable and quiet. In January 1856 he resigned his seat in Parliament, and in May he left the Albany and moved to Holly Lodge, Camden, where he began to take an interest in gardening. In August and September of the same year, he and Ellis took a tour of Italy, and in October he was back in London and working on volume five of the history. In 1857 Henry John Temple, Lord Palmerston's government raised him to the peerage as Baron Macaulay of Rothley, marking the first time in history that such an honor had been bestowed for literary achievement.

His health, however, continued to decline, and the work on *The History of England* was slower than ever. He completed three more chapters, managing—as he had hoped—to finish the saga of William. In February 1859 his brother-in-law Charles Trevelyan left England to take up an important new post in India, and in October, Macaulay learned that Hannah would soon leave to join her husband. This news seems to have taken away his will to live. He died quietly in his study on 28 December 1859 while reading the current installment of his friend William Makepeace Thackeray's new novel, *Lovel the Widower*, in the *Cornhill Magazine*. His funeral was held in Westminster Abbey on 9 January 1860, and he was buried in the Poets' Corner.

When he died, his reputation was probably as high as it had ever been. Walter Bagehot compared him to Edmund Burke and lamented the fact that this great orator had departed without ever having addressed his new peers in the House of Lords. Thackeray bade farewell to both Macaulay and Washington Irving in an essay entitled "Nil Nisi Bonum," in which his recently deceased friends were described as the Gibbon and the Goldsmith of the nineteenth century. Having covered—in *The History of Henry Esmond, Esq.* (1852), *The English Humourists of the Eighteenth Century* (1853), and *The Four Georges* (1860)—much of the same historical ground as Macaulay, Thackeray was primarily impressed by the extent of Macaulay's reading, saying that the historian's head always reminded him of the dome of the British Museum, so full was it crammed with information: "He reads twenty books to write a single sentence." A two-volume posthumously published collection of Macaulay's miscellaneous writings (edited by Ellis, 1860) and the last three chapters of *The History of England* (edited by Hannah Macaulay Trevelyan, 1861) were eagerly received, and the first full-length biography, *The Public Life of Lord Macaulay* by the Reverend Frederick Arnold, appeared in 1862. But it was Sir George Otto Trevelyan's official biography, *The Life and Letters of Lord Macaulay* (1876), which first showed the private side of Macaulay and increased his popularity by displaying his warm family life, his sensitivity, his considerable skill as a letter writer, and his numerous acts of private charity toward anyone who chose to ask him for money.

It was just as well that his private character should receive support at this time because his reputation as a writer was already in decline. In *Friend-ship's Garland* (1871), Matthew Arnold hailed him as "the Great Apostle of the Philistines" and described his once-admired style in condescending terms: "the external characteristic being a hard metallic movement with nothing of the soft play of life, and the internal characteristic being a perpetual semblance of hitting the right nail on the head without the reality." The historian W. E. H. Lecky, in a 21 September 1876 letter to his wife, records a conversation in which he and Herbert Spencer agreed "about the especial atrocity of Macaulay, whose style 'resembles low organizations, being a perpetual repetition of similar parts.' " Meanwhile, the accuracy of *The History of England* was under constant attack. As early as 1849, the now aged John Wilson Croker had attacked volumes one and two in the *Quarterly Review*, and a Mr. Churchill Babington of Cambridge University, in *Mr. Macaulay's Character of the Clergy* (1849), had disputed the low view taken in these volumes of the seventeenth-century Anglican parsons. W. E. Forster, in *William Penn and Thomas B. Macaulay* (1849), and Hepworth Dixon, in *William Penn: A Historical Biography* (1851), conclusively showed that Macaulay had been wrong in claiming Penn was an unscrupulous agent of James II—apparently because he had confused him with a certain George Penn. William Edmonstoune Aytoun, in an appendix to his *Lays of the Scottish Cavaliers* (1849), questioned Macaulay's picture of Claverhouse, and in 1861 a barrister named John Paget published *The New "Examen,"* a wide-ranging and convincing critique of several of Macaulay's major characterizations, particularly his vilification of Marlborough. By 1886 Edward A. Freeman, the eminent historian of the Norman Conquest, could say in *The Methods of Historical Study* that "I know that to run down Lord Macaulay is the fashion of the day" and to argue that the fashion had gone too far: "I can see Macaulay's great and obvious faults as well as any man . . . but I cannot . . . speak lightly of one to whom I owe so much in the matter of actual knowledge, and to whom I owe more than to any man as the master of historical narrative." Similarly, such historians as Charles Firth (*A Commentary on Macaulay's History of England*, 1938), Herbert Butterfield (*George III and the Historians*, 1957), and Hugh Trevor-Roper (*Men and Events*, 1957) have all praised Macaulay's historical scholarship while acknowledging that it was far from infallible.

Both a popular and a scholastic audience remained for Macaulay throughout the late nineteenth century—even after much of the intelligentsia had turned away from his work. New editions of his books continued to appear, his much maligned prose style was studied diligently in countless classrooms, and William Minto gave him exhaustive attention in his 1887 *Manual of English Prose Literature*. Neither a few glaring factual errors nor the supposedly metallic and repetitive qualities of his style seem ever to have bothered Macaulay's general readers very much, and the Everyman's Library editions of his essays, poems, and *The History of England*—along with Oxford World Classics editions of the speeches and of Trevelyan's *Life and Letters of Lord Macaulay*—have kept virtually all of his works more or less constantly available in inexpensive editions. Macaulay's works were in print during years when most of the writings of Carlyle, John Henry Newman, Arnold, and John Ruskin were not so readily available, a circumstance that presumably reflects the fact that Macaulay remained the most generally popular of the Victorian sages.

But clearly he has not been as widely read in the twentieth century as he was in the nineteenth, and this decline probably has less to do with style or character judgments than with changes in basic beliefs and assumptions. Macaulay's optimism, materialism, patriotism, "manliness," sentimentalism, and admiration for the middle classes became progressively less popular after World War I. So, in a 1929 letter to his brother, C. S. Lewis would record his disgusted discovery that Macaulay "developed his full manner as a schoolboy and wrote letters home from school which read exactly like pages out of the *Essays*. He was talking about the nature of government, the principles of human prosperity, the force of the domestic affections and all that junk at the age of fourteen." Later, Lytton Strachey, in *Portraits in Miniature* (1931), would dismiss the "preposterous optimism" that "fills his pages," and Mario Praz, in *The Hero in Eclipse in Victorian Fiction*, would imagine Macaulay "greeting the advent of photography as an invention that would allow mankind to dispense with the services of men like Raphael and Titian" and thinking that "progress means to have one's whole dinner ready prepared in tins; progress is predigested food, the prefabricated house." Such comments, however, seem less criticisms of the mind and art of Thomas Babington Macaulay than visceral reactions against the pieties, beliefs, and technological achievements of bourgeois civilization.

Macaulay's influence is more difficult to trace than his reputation. Clearly his style was much imitated in his own day and for quite a few years after—as late as 1876, in the *Fortnightly Review*, John Morley lamented its baleful influence on all sorts of journalists who did not possess the great qualities which had redeemed Macaulay's own writings. The influence of his *The History of England* on the London chapters of Dickens's *A Tale of Two Cities* (1859), on Richard Doddridge Blackmore's *Lorna Doone* (1869), and most significantly on Thackeray's *History of Henry Esmond, Esq.* is clear to anyone who has read any of these novels with Macaulay in mind. And the distinguished historical works of his nephew Sir George Otto Trevelyan and of his great-nephew George Macaulay Trevelyan, Master of Trinity College, Cambridge, owe a great deal, both in conception and technique, to Macaulay's example. But the one later writer who resembles him most is Winston Churchill.

In *A Roving Commission: My Early Life* (1930), Churchill describes Macaulay's important role in gratifying the first stirrings of intellectual curiosity felt by the future prime minister when he was a young cavalry officer in India. During the hot afternoons in Bangalore, when most subalterns rested up for the evening's polo matches, he studied Gibbon and Macaulay in a belated attempt to come to terms with the world of ideas. "I had learnt The Lays of Ancient Rome by heart and loved them and of course I knew he had written a history; but I had never read a page of it. I now embarked on that splendid romance." Though Churchill found it hard to forgive the lies about his ancestor, the Duke of Marlborough, he "must admit" that he owed Macaulay "an immense debt upon the other side." The relationship between Churchill and Macaulay was much like that between Macaulay and Samuel Johnson. In each case the younger writer had a negative reaction to the personality of the older one, and yet these personalities all had a great deal in common: a gruff public manner guarding more tender private sensibilities, distinction as great talkers of a frequently pugnacious sort, and a tendency to personify for their respective generations the John Bull qualities of common sense, devotion to fair play, and love of a good fight— all combined rather improbably with extraordinary erudition. Surely Churchill's immense debt to Macaulay included some influence on Churchill's self-consciously archaic prose style, a style which Evelyn Waugh called sham Augustan and which is unlike that of any other modern politician. It also presumably included some lessons on how to tell a story. Despite the fact that Churchill's *Marlborough: His Life and Times* (1933-1938) was, in large part, an attack on Macaulay, an attempt in the author's words, "to fasten the label 'Liar' to his genteel coattails," it is just as biased—and just as convincing and engrossing—a version of English history as Macaulay's. Similarly, Churchill's histories of the two world wars and of the English-speaking people are full of ideas and narrative techniques that could have been lifted from Macaulay's pages.

Certainly Churchill, a successful politician who won the Nobel Prize for Literature, resembles Macaulay more closely than could any man of letters who had had no part in public life. Like Macaulay, he both wrote and made history, yet literary critics seldom think of either man as primarily a writer. Except for the *Lays of Ancient Rome* and Churchill's early novel *Savrola: A Tale of the Revolution in Laurania* (1900), neither wrote in belletristic modes, and literature has been redefined in the twentieth century to exclude the forms in which they (and Johnson) primarily worked. The Indian Penal Code, Churchill's letters and memos, and Johnson's dictionary are not the sort of thing often covered by English curricula, and even the speeches and historical works of Churchill and Macaulay are well outside the standard reading lists. In fact, Macaulay's eclipse as a writer probably owes as much to the kinds of writing he did as to the limitations of his style or to his unfashionable opinions.

In the first decades after Trevelyan's biography was published, several more books were written about Macaulay, but they were generally hostile or derivative. J. Cotter Morison's *Macaulay* (1882) in the English Men of Letters series and Richmond Croom Beatty's *Lord Macaulay, Victorian Liberal* (1938) are decidedly in the first category; Arthur Bryant's *Macaulay* (1932) is in the second. Almost nothing significant was written for the next thirty years, but beginning in 1968 and continuing into the 1990s, there has appeared an impressive series of articles, chapters of books, full-length studies, and new editions of Macaulay's previously unpublished work. This new interest in Macaulay presumably signals both the continuing strength of the interest in the Victorian world, which he represents as well as any single writer can, and a renewed respect for the rhetorical analysis of nonfiction prose as an enterprise quite as significant as the criticism of

poetry, fiction, and drama. As Victorian studies and rhetorical criticism continue to broaden their appeal, we can expect to hear more about Thomas Babington Macaulay.

Letters:
The Letters of Thomas Babington Macaulay, 6 volumes, edited by Thomas Pinney (London: Cambridge University Press, 1974-1981).

Biographies:
Frederick Arnold, *The Public Life of Lord Macaulay* (London: Tinsley, 1862);

Sir George Otto Trevelyan, *The Life and Letters of Lord Macaulay*, 2 volumes (London: Longman, 1876);

Arthur Bryant, *Macaulay* (London: Davis, 1932);

Richmond Croom Beatty, *Lord Macaulay, Victorian Liberal* (Norman: University of Oklahoma Press, 1938);

John Clive, *Macaulay: The Shaping of the Historian* (New York: Knopf, 1973).

References:
Walter Bagehot, "Mr. Macaulay," *National Review*, 2 (April 1856): 357-387;

J. W. Burrow, *A Liberal Descent: Victorian Historians and the English Past* (Cambridge: Cambridge University Press, 1981);

Herbert Butterfield, *History and Human Relations* (London: Collins, 1951);

Butterfield, "Reflections on Macaulay," *Listener*, 90 (13 December 1973): 826-827;

William Carleton, "Macaulay and the Trimmers," *American Scholar*, 19 (Winter 1949-1950): 73-82;

Winston S. Churchill, *Marlborough: His Life and Times*, volumes 1 and 2 (New York: Scribners, 1933);

Churchill, *A Roving Commission: My Early Life* (New York: Scribners, 1930);

Harry Hayden Clark, "The Vogue of Macaulay in America," *Transactions of the Wisconsin Academy*, 34 (1942): 237-292;

John Clive, "Macaulay's Historical Imagination," *Review of English Literature*, 1 (October 1960): 20-28;

Clive, *Not by Fact Alone: Essays on the Writing and Reading of History* (New York: Knopf, 1989);

Clive and Thomas Pinney, Introduction to *Thomas Babington Macaulay: Selected Writings*, edited by Clive and Pinney (Chicago: University of Chicago Press, 1972);

A. O. J. Cockshut, *Truth to Life: The Art of Biography in the Nineteenth Century* (London: Collins, 1974);

R. K. Das Gupta, "Macaulay's Writings on India," in *Historians of India, Pakistan and Ceylon*, edited by C. H. Philips (London: Oxford University Press, 1961), pp. 230-240;

E. S. de Beer, "Macaulay and Croker: The Review of Croker's Boswell," *Review of English Studies*, 10 (1959): 388-397;

Sir Charles Firth, *A Commentary on Macaulay's History of England* (London: Macmillan, 1938);

David Fong, "Macaulay: the Essayist as Historian," *Dalhousie Review*, 51 (Spring 1971): 27-40;

Fong, "Macaulay and Johnson," *University of Toronto Quarterly*, 40 (Fall 1970): 38-48;

G. S. Fraser, "Macaulay's Style as an Essayist," *Review of English Literature*, 1 (October 1960): 9-19;

Peter Gay, "Macaulay," in his *Style in History* (New York: Basic Books, 1974);

Peter Geyl, "Macaulay in his Essays," in his *Debates With Historians* (London: Batsford, 1955), pp. 19-34;

William E. Gladstone, "Lord Macaulay," *Quarterly Review*, 142 (July 1876): 1-50;

John R. Griffin, *The Intellectual Milieu of Lord Macaulay* (Ottawa: University of Ottawa Press, 1965);

Joseph Hamburger, *Macaulay and the Whig Tradition* (Chicago: University of Chicago Press, 1976);

Rosemary Jann, *The Art and Science of Victorian History* (Columbus: Ohio State University Press, 1985);

David Knowles, *Lord Macaulay, 1800-1859* (Cambridge: Cambridge University Press, 1960);

George Levine, *The Boundaries of Fiction: Carlyle, Macaulay, and Newman* (Princeton: Princeton University Press, 1968);

William Madden, "Macaulay's Style," in *The Art of Victorian Prose*, edited by George Levine and Madden (New York: Oxford University Press, 1968), pp. 127-151;

Jane Millgate, "Father and Son: Macaulay's *Edinburgh* Debut," *Review of English Studies*, 21 (May 1970): 159-167;

Millgate, "History versus Fiction: Thackeray's Response to Macaulay," *Costerus*, new series 2 (1974): 43-58;

Millgate, *Macaulay* (London: Routledge & Kegan Paul, 1973);

Millgate, "Macaulay at Work: an Example of his Use of Sources," *Cambridge Bibliographical Society Transactions*, 5 (1970): 90-98;

William Minto, *Manual of English Prose Literature* (Boston: Ginn, 1887);

Peter Morgan, "Macaulay on Periodical Style," *Victorian Periodicals Newsletter*, 1 (January 1968): 26-27;

J. Cotter Morison, *Macaulay* (London: Macmillan, 1882);

John Morley, "Macaulay," *Fortnightly Review*, new series 112 (April 1876): 494-513;

A. N. L. Munby, *Macaulay's Library* (Glasgow: Jackson, 1966);

Terry Otten, "Macaulay's Critical Theory of Imagination and Reason," *Journal of Aesthetics and Art Criticism*, 28 (Fall 1969): 33-43;

John Paget, *The New "Examen"* (Edinburgh & London: Blackwood, 1861);

G. R. Potter, *Macaulay* (London: Longmans, Green, 1959);

Mario Praz, "Macaulay," in his *The Hero in Eclipse in Victorian Fiction* (London: Oxford University Press, 1956), pp. 102-117;

William H. Rogers, "A Study in Contrasts: Carlyle and Macaulay as Book Reviewers," *Florida State University Studies*, no. 5 (1952): 1-9;

Bernard Semmel, "T. B. Macaulay: The Active and Contemplative Lives," in his *The Victorian Experience: The Prose Writers* (Athens: Ohio University Press, 1982), pp. 22-46;

Gerald Sirkin and Natalie Sirkin, "The Battle of Indian Education: Macaulay's Opening 'Salvo' Newly Discovered," *Victorian Studies*, 14 (June 1971): 407-428;

Vincent E. Starzinger, *Middlingness: Juste Milieu Political Theory in France and England 1815-48* (Charlottesville: University Press of Virginia, 1965);

Leslie Stephen, "Macaulay," in his *Hours in a Library*, volume 3 (London: Smith, Elder, 1879), pp. 279-324;

Eric Stokes, "Macaulay: The Indian Years, 1834-38," *Review of English Literature*, 1 (October 1960): 41-50;

Lytton Strachey, "Macaulay," in his *Portraits in Miniature and Other Essays* (London: Chatto & Windus, 1931);

Martin Svaglic, "Classical Rhetoric and Victorian Prose," in *The Art of Victorian Prose*, edited by George Levine and William Madden (New York: Oxford University Press, 1968);

William M. Thackeray, "Nil Nisi Bonum," *Corn-hill Magazine*, 1 (February 1860): 129-134;

George Macaulay Trevelyan, *Clio, a Muse and Other Essays Literary and Pedestrian* (London: Longmans, Green, 1913);

Trevelyan, "Macaulay and the Sense of Optimism," in his *Ideas and Beliefs of the Victorians* (London: Sylvan Press, 1949);

Hugh Trevor-Roper, Introduction to Macaulay's *Critical and Historical Essays* (New York: McGraw-Hill, 1965);

Trevor-Roper, "Macaulay and the Glorious Revolution," in his *Men and Events* (New York: Harper, 1957);

Jack Valenti, "Macaulay and his Critics," in his *The Bitter Taste of Glory: Nine Portraits of Power and Conflict* (New York: World, 1971);

Ronald Weber, "Singer and Seer: Macaulay on the Historian as Poet," *Papers on Language and Literature*, 3 (Summer 1967): 210-219;

Edwin Yoder, Jr., "Macaulay Revisited," *South Atlantic Quarterly*, 63 (1964): 542-551.

Papers:

The most important collection of Macaulay's papers is at Trinity College, Cambridge; it includes juvenilia, several hundred letters, and the eleven volumes of the unpublished journal that Macaulay kept from 1838 to 1859. The British Library has the manuscripts for five *Edinburgh Review* essays. Two more manuscripts for *Edinburgh Review* articles are at New York's Pierpont Morgan Library, as are large portions of the manuscript for the fifth volume of *The History of England*. An important collection of Macaulay family papers is at the Huntington Library, San Marino, California, and official papers by Macaulay are at several locations: the Public Record Office and the India Office Library in London and the West Bengal Record Office in Calcutta.

George Meredith

(12 February 1828 - 18 May 1909)

This entry was written by Michael Collie (York University) for
DLB 18: Victorian Novelists After 1885.

See also the Meredith entries in DLB 35: Victorian Poets After 1850 *and* DLB 57: Victorian Prose Writers After 1867.

BOOKS: *Poems* (London: Parker, 1851; New York: Scribners, 1898);

The Shaving of Shagpat: An Arabian Entertainment (London: Chapman & Hall, 1856; Boston: Roberts, 1887);

Farina: A Legend of Cologne (London: Smith, Elder, 1857);

The Ordeal of Richard Feverel: A History of Father and Son (3 volumes, London: Chapman & Hall, 1859; 1 volume, Boston: Roberts, 1887);

Evan Harrington; or, He Would Be a Gentleman (New York: Harper, 1860; 3 volumes, London: Bradbury & Evans, 1861);

Modern Love, and Poems of the English Roadside, with Poems and Ballads (London: Chapman & Hall, 1862); edited by E. Cavazza (Portland, Maine: Mosher, 1891);

Emilia in England (3 volumes, London: Chapman & Hall, 1864); republished as *Sandra Belloni* (London: Chapman & Hall, 1886; Boston: Roberts, 1887);

Rhoda Fleming: A Story (3 volumes, London: Tinsley, 1865; 1 volume, Boston: Roberts, 1886);

Vittoria, 3 volumes (London: Chapman & Hall, 1866; Boston: Roberts, 1888);

The Adventures of Harry Richmond (3 volumes, London: Smith, Elder, 1871; 1 volume, Boston: Roberts, 1887);

Beauchamp's Career (3 volumes, London: Chapman & Hall, 1876; 1 volume, Boston: Roberts, 1887);

The House on the Beach: A Realistic Tale (New York: Harper, 1877);

George Meredith

The Egoist: A Comedy in Narrative, 3 volumes (London: Kegan Paul, 1879; New York: Harper, 1879);

The Tragic Comedians: A Study in a Well-Known Story (2 volumes, London: Chapman & Hall, 1880; 1 volume, New York: Munro, 1881);

Poems and Lyrics of the Joy of Earth (London: Macmillan, 1883; Boston: Roberts, 1883);

Diana of the Crossways (3 volumes, London: Chapman & Hall, 1885; 1 volume, New York: Munro, 1885; Boston: Roberts, 1887);

Ballads and Poems of Tragic Life (London: Macmillan, 1887; Boston: Roberts, 1887);

A Reading of Earth (London: Macmillan, 1888; Boston: Roberts, 1888);

Jump-to-Glory Jane (London: Privately printed, 1889; London: Sonnenschein, 1892);

The Case of General Ople and Lady Camper (New York: Lovell, 1890);

The Tale of Chloe: An Episode in the History of Beau Beamish (New York: Lovell, 1890);

One of Our Conquerors (3 volumes, London: Chapman & Hall, 1891; 1 volume, Boston: Roberts, 1891);

Poems: The Empty Purse, with Odes to the Comic Spirit, to Youth in Memory and Verses (London: Macmillan, 1892; Boston: Roberts, 1892);

The Tale of Chloe; The House on the Beach; The Case of General Ople and Lady Camper (London: Ward, Lock & Bowden, 1894);

Lord Ormont and His Aminta: A Novel (3 volumes, London: Chapman & Hall, 1894; 1 volume, New York: Scribners, 1894);

The Amazing Marriage, 2 volumes (London: Constable, 1895; New York: Scribners, 1895);

An Essay on Comedy and the Uses of the Comic Spirit (London: Constable, 1897; New York: Scribners, 1897);

Selected Poems (London: Constable, 1897; New York: Scribners, 1897);

The Nature Poems (London: Constable, 1898);

Odes in Contribution to the Song of French History (London: Constable, 1898; New York: Scribners, 1898);

The Story of Bhanavar the Beautiful (London: Constable, 1900);

A Reading of Life, with Other Poems (London: Constable, 1901; New York: Scribners, 1901);

Last Poems (London: Constable, 1909; New York: Scribners, 1909);

Chillianwallah (New York: Marion Press, 1909);

Love in the Valley, and Two Songs: Spring and Autumn (Chicago: Seymour, 1909);

Poems Written in Early Youth, Poems from "Modern Love," and Scattered Poems (London: Constable, 1909; New York: Scribners, 1909);

Celt and Saxon (London: Constable, 1910; New York: Scribners, 1910);

Up to Midnight (Boston: Luce, 1913).

Collections: *The Works of George Meredith*, De Luxe Edition, 39 volumes (London: Constable, 1896-1912);

The Works of George Meredith, Library Edition, 18 volumes (London: Constable, 1897-1910);

The Works of George Meredith, Boxhill Edition, 17 volumes (New York: Scribners, 1897-1919);

The Works of George Meredith, Memorial Edition, 27 volumes (London: Constable, 1909-1911; New York: Scribners, 1909-1911).

OTHER: *The Cruise of the Alabama and the Sumter: From the Private Journals and Other Papers of Commander R. Semmes*, introductory and concluding chapters by Meredith (London:

Saunders & Otley, 1864; New York: Carleton, 1864).

Between 1856 and 1895, George Meredith published fifteen novels as well as long short stories or novellas, taking as his special subject the instability of human relationships within a sharply conceived but usually arbitrary social context. As a novelist, he was interested in the individual, not in the crowd, the events which affected his individuals occurring more in the head than in the daily traffic of exterior existence. He was, or during the course of his career became, a psychological novelist, seeming to some idiosyncratic but to others profoundly right in his rejection of the moral standards his contemporaries took for granted.

Born in Portsmouth, Hampshire, on 12 February 1828, Meredith was the grandson of Melchizedek Meredith, a well-established Portsmouth tailor; he was the son of Augustus Meredith, who took over the business when the "Great Mel" died, and of Jane Macnamara, the daughter of an innkeeper. Meredith was educated at St. Paul's (a small, probably not very distinguished, private school in nearby Southsea), at an as-yet-unidentified country boarding school (which may, however, have been near Lowestoft), and in 1843-1844 at the Moravian Brothers school in Neuwied, Germany, on the Rhine; the cost of his education was met by a small legacy from his mother's side of the family. Various attempts, none of them conclusive, have been made to assess this rather eccentric education. On the positive side, some say, was the escape from the more repressive features of the English educational system at that time. At the Protestant school in Neuwied he acquired the tolerance, self-discipline, and cosmopolitan awareness that infused all his later actions. But the circumstances of his being sent to school, first away from his own locality, then to a boarding school in another part of the country, then to a boarding school in a different country, have never been fully explained. Nor has Meredith's early family life been satisfactorily described and analyzed. His mother died in 1833. His father went bankrupt in 1838 and, moving from Portsmouth to London, married his housekeeper, Matilda Buckett, with whom he had in effect been living for years. Meredith absolutely refused in later life to talk about his youth, so it is not known whether he regarded it as happy and normal or as turbulent and unhappy, though various theories have been spun in which his feelings, indeed his traumas, are deduced from his

fiction. He may have been disturbed by the realization that his father was sleeping with his housekeeper, and George may have been sent to boarding school because of this. He may have been upset by the social airs and snobbish manner said to have been adopted by his father. He may have been ashamed to have been the son of a tailor, albeit a tailor with pretensions. He may have had the early but traumatic love affairs some critics say must be deduced from love affairs in his novels. There is in fact little direct evidence about what Meredith felt or thought during the first eighteen years of his life. It is important to say this if Meredith's fiction is to be enjoyed, because his novels, if autobiographical at all, are not naively so. He did not work out his own problems through his fiction; rather, his fiction explored with keen insight the problems of humanity, not independent of but over and above his own formative experiences.

His modest capital had been held in chancery between his father's bankruptcy and his eighteenth birthday, but in February 1845 a significant part of it was pried loose when approval was given to his being articled to a London solicitor, Richard Charnock. Although he never intended to become a solicitor himself, he was at the age of eighteen guaranteed room and board for five years, together with a small salary. During this period he began to write.

Meredith adopted as quite obviously correct those nineteenth-century assumptions about the greatness of literature which allowed an aspiring writer, without bothering overmuch about the writer's social function, to dedicate his or her life to the making of "modern" works—that is, books and poems appropriate to the times but matching in quality the masterpieces of the past. Meredith always thought of himself as a poet and indeed published more volumes of poems than novels, as well as many occasional pieces, including translations. Poetry in its nature did not require justification, thought Meredith's peer group; nor did Meredith ever provide one. But Meredith was also determined to be a novelist, because the novel was regarded, by others as well as by himself, as the literary form most appropriate to the times in which he lived. His high ambition was eventually satisfied. Among the novels he produced during his long career, some were masterworks, the fruit of his distinctive genius and a unique achievement that was marked in many ways: by three important collected editions; by a very unambiguous recognition of his greatness in North America from 1885 on; by the plaudits of suffragettes and feminists who were well pleased to see that he had written about sexual relations, matrimony, matrimonial law, and woman's position in society in a daring but essentially clearheaded way; by the admiration of his fellow writers, who elected him president of the Society of Authors after the death of Tennyson; and by the award, late in his life, of the Order of Merit, which recognized him for what he then was—a great national figure.

Although Meredith took for granted the importance of writing a good poem or a good novel, he did not immediately know how to do this. He was an extremely intelligent, sensitive, creative artist given to experimentation while a particular work was being written or revised, rather than to either a slavish imitation of what others had already done or a repetitious provision of what the public was supposed to want. He never tried to be popular. In order to be free to write, he earned his living as best he could. The struggle to establish himself as a completely independent writer was a long one. In fact, he would have to be described as a struggling author throughout the greater part of the period from roughly 1850 to 1880, and it was not until 1885, when he published *Diana of the Crossways*, that he enjoyed full public acclaim. Meredith was not the morose type of writer who separated himself from existence in order to write about it; on the contrary, he had great vitality, a zest for life, a love of good company, and a high regard for health, fitness, and physical activity. Meredith never lacked friends, least of all literary friends, who recognized his remarkable talents, enjoyed his conversation—even his monologues—and (with only one or two exceptions) gave him strong support when he needed it. It was in the company of such friends that he met his attractive, high-spirited first wife, Mary Ellen Nicolls, the widow of Lt. Edward Nicolls and the daughter of Thomas Love Peacock. Life was worth living: Meredith never really doubted this, though from the beginning he was an unbeliever—at least an agnostic—probably an atheist.

It may be that Meredith contributed significantly to the failure of his first marriage by expecting it to survive both the low standard of living that was sustained on the hope that first this, then that novel would be sufficiently well received to generate an income, and his own low tolerance of foolishness in other people—in this case, his wife. George Meredith and Mary Nicolls

Meredith's first wife, the former Mary Ellen Nicolls, the daughter of Thomas Love Peacock

were married in London in August 1849; Thomas Love Peacock was there, but Augustus Meredith was not. (In London he had recovered something of his prosperity as a tailor and on his savings had recently immigrated to South Africa.) With the duns at the door, as Meredith cheerfully put it, the young couple lived in various lodging houses and cottages in London, Surrey, Sussex, and Kent, and for a short while with Peacock. Their only child, Arthur Gryffydh, was born in June 1853. Whatever may have gone wrong with this marriage was, of course, expressed only in transmuted form in *The Ordeal of Richard Feverel* (1859) and in *Modern Love* (1862), the two works readers have thought most bear the marks of autobiographical pressure. Meredith never gave a clear account of what caused a once-carefree relationship to go sour, or at least none has survived. Edith Nicolls, Mary Meredith's daughter, who was five years old when her mother remarried, did not very much like Meredith, and he, it seems, did not very much like her. Nor did Mary like her husband's preference for male companionship and his habit (which turned out to be lifelong) of disappearing on long pedestrian expeditions with his friends. Visitors to the Meredith home reported that in domestic talk Meredith's tongue was sometimes waspish and hurtful. At the same time, evidence has come to the surface that Mary was often insensitive, coquettish, and hysterical; she once had to be restrained from throwing herself into the Thames. Gradually she became more and more impatient of his long absences and his long periods at work, while he became testy at having to labor for hours at a small table in the corner of the bedroom. Neither gave what the other wanted or needed. This was compounded when Mary became pregnant with a child Meredith knew could not be his. It has always been assumed that the father was the painter Henry Wallis, with whom she traveled in Wales in 1857 before going to live with him in Italy. She took Meredith's refusal to reply to her letters as the pretext for believing that he was indifferent to what she did. Perhaps by the time of her last known letter to him—in September 1857—he was indeed indifferent. He at any rate refused to attempt a reconciliation, as he refused to allow her to see their son until just before her death.

The breakdown of his first marriage affected Meredith in an extraordinary way: it hardened his heart, but it also made him sensitive to the position of women in Victorian society. His determination to write meanwhile did not slacken. Throughout the years of his first marriage and during the years which immediately followed its breakdown, Meredith was sustained by his own massive ego, by his equally massive intellect, by many strong and lasting friendships with literary contemporaries, and by his reading, which was extensive. Like George Gissing, that other omnivorous reader among Victorian novelists, Meredith read Latin, Greek, German, French, and Italian with equal ease, to some extent compensating for his lack of sympathy with British taste by developing a cosmopolitan awareness of what writers were thinking and doing in other places. This was reinforced by frequent expeditions to France, to Germany (where he eventually sent Arthur to school), to Switzerland, and to Italy. He brought up his son by himself, managed without help, was a survivor. His independence was above all the independence of intellect, a fact which informed everything he wrote as a particular sort of perception about what mattered in life. In a godless world, people matter; and if people matter, how they get on with each other mat-

ters. For Meredith, this getting on or not getting on was personal, not social. Because the individual human being had always to exist as an independent, self-contained, private entity, at issue was how such an individual could relate to other individuals, if he could at all. The individual human being had to manage as best he could by himself, never as part of a group. Meredith explored this problem in novel after novel, compulsively filling the imaginative space between John Stuart Mill's *On Liberty* (1859)—where self is the basic premise—and Emile Durkheim's *On Social Method* (1895)—where society is the basic premise—with fascinating, subtle, and sometimes terrifying explorations of human instabilities, both individual and social.

Meredith discovered, as he wrote, what he could do with the novel form—not starting with a theory and applying it, but learning through trial and error what would work and what would not. In this long process there were setbacks as well as gratifying successes. His first two novels were lightweight pieces, not calculated to alert the reading public to the arrival on the scene of a genius. *The Shaving of Shagpat*, written during the two years after the birth of his son, was published in December 1855 (though dated 1856) and affects a mock-oriental tone that perhaps reflects the lively but frivolous quality of Meredith's conversations with his friends. Remote from life, the young intellects sported with words and ideas. Meredith concocted a tale about a tyrannical clothier whose power over a city derives solely from the denseness of his hair and beard, and a young barber, Shibli Bagaray, who acts the part of a social reformer, eventually cutting off the hair that was the source of authority. In a loosely constructed plot, Meredith tests Bagaray's resourcefulness as he attempts to overcome, in a series of episodes, his own gullibility and pride, which he eventually does with the help of a woman, Noorna bin Noorka. This type of laughter at the absurdity of egoism later, in more subtle forms, was to become one of the hallmarks of Meredith's genius. As social allegory, however, the book's main drift was too obscure for it to be taken seriously, while it was too precious in manner to be enjoyed as a joke at the expense of orientalists. In any case, a great novel-writing career cannot very well be launched with a joke. *Farina: A Legend of Cologne* (1857) was an equally insignificant bit of storytelling: it is little more than a mannered caricature of the stock characters of romantic fiction and represents just the first stage in Meredith's disengagement from the romance convention. In what is now the standard biography, *The Ordeal of George Meredith* (1953), Lionel Stevenson said that "in this fairly brief tale Meredith was attempting a difficult type of art—the grotesque, or comic-gruesome," but that at the same time the plot of *Farina*, which concerns a "young tradesman who defies entrenched privilege and wins honour by performing great public service," reveals Meredith's lifelong preoccupation with the problem of class.

Then came two important novels which, bearing the marks of a powerful imagination at work, still hold their place among the acknowledged masterpieces of Victorian fiction, despite the fact that they were not at first well received or understood. *The Ordeal of Richard Feverel* and *Evan Harrington* (1860) represent in different ways Meredith's first serious engagements with the novel form as it had been fashioned by early Victorian novelists; by middle-class family publishers such as Frederic Chapman of Chapman and Hall; by the editors of magazines who wanted serialized fiction for family reading; and by the proprietors of circulating libraries, notably the all-powerful Charles Edward Mudie. By 1859 the multivolume novel, shaped by these forces, had come to dominate the literary scene as the medium that would best accommodate disparate factors: the novelist's independent grasp of the social reality he created for his characters, the publisher's moral and literary predispositions, the magazine editor's nervous responsiveness to weekly or monthly sales, and the public's pleasure in new fiction that might challenge but would always eventually reinforce the reader's own values. These factors in turn represented the taste of the particular social subset that read novels; that is, part of the literate middle class. Often the accommodation was achieved by means of the novelist's strategy of allowing his reader to believe that narrator, character, reader, and, by implication, novelist all subscribed to the same social values, despite interesting, even alarming, deviations from the norm by some characters. In *The Ordeal of Richard Feverel*, however, Meredith disturbed this détente. Instead of subscribing to the values of his readers, he let the narrator be ironic at the expense of the characters to the extent that the uneasy reader came to realize the author was being ironic at his expense as well. This problem of tone and style was compounded by the suspicion that the author was also withholding, somewhat maliciously, information that the reader needed. In writing about the tortured rela-

Drawing of Meredith circa 1860 by Dante Gabriel Rossetti

tionship between father and son, for example, Meredith made only oblique references to Richard Feverel's mother, despite the fact that the novel is about the boy's growth into consciousness in an unusual family environment; it is unusual because of the harshness with which Sir Austin Feverel imposes his strict, emotionally debilitating educational "system" on his son, who reacts by refusing to play the role his father has prescribed, by rebelling to the point of criminality (he burns down a neighbor's stack of wheat), and by marrying for love a woman of whom his father does not approve.

Not only does *The Ordeal of Richard Feverel* confirm Meredith's interest in the divisiveness of class and in the forces of "nature" which compensate to some degree for the inadequacies of "society," it also demonstrates, again, the author's antiromantic tendencies. Richard Feverel falls in love with Lucy in poignant early episodes that are written with a marvelous lyricism; but Richard is not represented as being an admirable person, and Meredith prevents the reader from identifying with his hero in an unthinking way. While the novel on one level is a lively, perfectly intelligible depiction of a conflict between father and son, on another it is a complex verbal exploration of human relations, the surface tensions of which imply more than is directly stated. In *The Ordeal of Richard Feverel*, Meredith adopts the technique which in later novels he refined; that is, he engages the reader's mind in a complexity of style which is an analogue of the complexity of character that is his subject.

This technique was not immediately understood by Meredith's contemporaries. Did these cryptic comments refer to a matrimonial situation that could have been described in plain terms? Was it part of Meredith's art to make the mother as elusive to the reader as to Richard Feverel? Or was Meredith disturbing the surface of plain narration for some other reason? The contemporary reader was upset by this sort of thing. He could not simply dismiss a book that was so powerfully written; on the other hand, he could not immediately cope with the techniques of subtle evasiveness, structural irony, and delayed explanation. Meredith had had to accept the constraints of the three-volume form and the expectations associated with it, but made imaginative elbowroom for himself by being ironical about the story he was telling, about the characters involved, and, in effect, about the nature of fiction itself. This anarchic attitude to a well-established, well-liked institution was not well received. One reviewer commented on the "quaint sarcastic style" and said that Meredith had "overstepped the legitimate boundaries of what is known by the adjective 'proper.' " Another spoke of the "extreme licence the author allows his pen." And in the *Athenaeum*, the reviewer wrote: "The only comfort the reader can find in closing the book is—that it is not true." An atheistic, freethinking, witty, socially disengaged and therefore irresponsible writer, as the moralist took him to be, had collided with the full force of mid-Victorian morality. Mudie refused to circulate *The Ordeal of Richard Feverel*, which, partly in direct consequence, fell dead.

This cause célèbre helped determine Meredith's attitude to the writing of fiction for the next few years. He was upset by the reception of *The Ordeal of Richard Feverel* and, in one sense, devoted much energy in later work to finding ways of neutralizing the reader's apparent appetite for a romantic story simply told. This did not mean, however, that he was willing to write the type of socially and morally acceptable fiction some middle-class readers may have wanted. It meant, rather, that he became technically devious in writing the

sort of book that would satisfy his own standards, this technical virtuosity resulting in important advances in the art of fiction. Meanwhile, it must be noted that when Meredith revised *The Ordeal of Richard Feverel* for the important second edition published by Kegan Paul (1878), he did not simplify it, or alter those parts of the novel that had been judged offensive to the British matron.

Fortunately, Meredith was already committed to the writing of *Evan Harrington* well before he experienced the public's negative reception of *The Ordeal of Richard Feverel*. After living with Arthur for about two years in Hobury Street in London, Meredith settled at Copsham Cottage in Esher in the late summer of 1859. Here he wrote his only novel that was intended primarily for magazine publication, though before the serialization in *Once a Week* had ended, he had sold the novel to Harper in the United States and to Bradbury and Evans in England. Meredith had difficulty while writing *Evan Harrington* in devising a plot appropriate to his sense of character ("To invent probabilities in modern daily life is difficult," he said), although he succeeded in writing a good story about a young man who has to come to terms with his own pretentiousness, snobbery, and false standards, and in creating some racily drawn and memorable characters (notably Evan's two uncles). The story concerns the adventures of a young man who leaves his home in the provinces to avoid a life of trade in the tailor's premises of his widowed mother, who expects him to stay with her, pay off his father's debts, and restore the family's reputation. Instead, he aspires to transcend social circumstances by becoming a "gentleman," so giving Meredith the opportunity to criticize, satirically, the class system within which Evan is trapped. Once again, and not for the last time, the novelist devises a plot in which the tough experiences of life knock some sense into a hero preoccupied with a foolish dream, experience always being preferred by Meredith to the fanciful notions with which he filled his characters' heads. He said that when the novel was finished, it disgusted him, so he passed over the opportunity to revise *Evan Harrington* when it was being prepared for book publication: "I should have had to cut him to pieces, put strange herbs to him and boil him up again—a tortuous and a doubtful process." In retrospect one can see that Meredith would have had at least two reasons for disliking a novel that others regarded as a successful comedy of manners. First, as the story of a tailor's son, it too overtly gave the impression of

Garden and rear of house at 16 Cheyne Walk, Chelsea, where Meredith lived with Rossetti and Algernon Charles Swinburne in 1862

being autobiographical. Second, in making his characters comic, he had rendered psychological analysis impossible (comedy assumes social norms and does not need psychology; psychology questions social norms and does not think deviations are fun). Once again, the writing of a novel brought Meredith face to face with a set of problems he did not immediately solve.

His next novels, *Emilia in England* (1864), *Rhoda Fleming* (1865), *Vittoria* (1866), *The Adventures of Harry Richmond* (1871), and *Beauchamp's Career* (1876), represent his attempt to satisfy at least some of his readers' desires and expectations, a problem to which he frequently referred in his correspondence. Was it possible to be a serious novelist who wrote what he felt had to be written, popular or not, *and* satisfy what Meredith regarded as the public's craving for romance? Because Meredith knew that his ideas about life were radical by comparison with those of his readers, he became somewhat obsessed by the difficulty of satisfying both himself and the general reader. Meredith did not believe life to have the

type of coherence a coherent plot implies; he did not think human beings enjoyed the psychological stability that orthodox characterization in moral terms would have the reader assume. Therefore, the kind of fiction in which the narrator, the reader, and some of the characters subscribe to the same value system was, for him, impossible: less because he himself was radical, iconoclastic, and perversely out of the common mold than because he observed that individuals did not invariably get on with one another. Was there not a fiction that dealt with broken friendship, alienation, bad faith, and human failure or inadequacy, as well as the romantic kind that dealt with harmony, reconciliation, forgiveness, and matrimonial stability? Did people meet and live in harmony, or did they sometimes meet, believe they could live in harmony, yet fail? Meredith thought failure as likely as success, but in the novels he wrote between 1861 and 1879 he tended to gloss this over, attempting by expedients to satisfy both the reader and himself: the reader by feeding him romance, or what might be taken as romance; himself by means of a covert, antiromantic, ironical style.

This means that a mere plot summary tells one very little about a Meredith novel because events are rarely represented as being important in themselves, while a sequence of events (plot) becomes only a device which demonstrates that a character's mental existence is independent of circumstance; Meredith never subscribed to the types of determinism which flourished during his lifetime. That *Emilia in England* (republished in 1886 as *Sandra Belloni*) is the story of an Italian émigré singer whose art, simplicity of manner, and democratic convictions are contrasted with the vapid social aspirations of the three daughters of Mr. Pole—a city businessman whose money, partly embezzled, supports their sentimental deviations from common sense—tells one little about a novel remarkable for its critique of materialism and its insight into the mentality of characters whose social positions are parasitic and false. In his next novel, *Rhoda Fleming*, Meredith tried to devise a plot, a "plain story" as he called it, that would satisfy the less sophisticated members of his public—"the seduction of a pretty country girl by an unscrupulous gentleman, and her rescue by her heroic sister" (this is the formula to which one critic reduced the book)—but this only convinced him, as well as his readers, that plots were not his forte, for this is the weakest of his novels. In *Vittoria* (a sequel to *Sandra Belloni*, though independent of it) he tried to compensate for the lack of a convincing plot line by placing his artistic but politically engaged heroine in the exotic setting of nineteenth-century Italian politics; this served only to underscore the fact that, while he remained interested throughout his writing career in the interface between character and politics, his mode of expression was never in the telling of a story, but in narrative structures that permitted a shift in emphasis away from "plot" toward an analysis of a character's interior existence. This is true even in *Harry Richmond*, an adventure story in which a boy travels abroad in search of his father; and it is true, remarkably, in *Beauchamp's Career*, where Meredith weakens a brilliant analysis of the dilemmas of politics as they affect both engaged and disengaged individuals, both radicals and Tories, by artificially committing his characters to an absurd sequence of events which may have added to the book the "romantic" element which Meredith despised but which certainly distracted attention from the book's center of interest. Plots, in the conven-

tional meaning of the word, are not observable in life, and Meredith did not believe in them. But the reader discovered that he was being patronized, while, by becoming a patronizer, Meredith somewhat sacrificed his position as artist. As a result, none of these books is entirely successful, though they contain fine sections and passages few other novelists could have written. The critique of materialism in *Emilia in England* is masterly, as is Meredith's depiction of Mr. Pole's nervous breakdown and disintegration of character, both of which themes anticipate later work. Many scenes in *Harry Richmond* are marvelously and humorously inventive; the spirit of antiestablishment, revolutionary European politics is almost, in *Vittoria*, adequately incorporated into a plot that sustains the reader's interest. *Beauchamp's Career*, a much stronger (because it is less squeamish) Second Reform Bill novel than George Eliot's *Felix Holt* (1866), and the most brilliant novel of Meredith's middle period, only falls short of complete success because Meredith did not allow his hero to be as socially disruptive as he would have been if his political ideas had been implemented, but instead, implausibly, killed him off.

Although in these middle years Meredith was still in the process of discovering for himself what could be done with the novel as Victorians understood it, the period was nonetheless one of real, if modest, achievement. Meredith's financial problems have perhaps been exaggerated. He was not wealthy, but nor was he poor, though like many an author he gave the impression of being in difficulties, expecting that everything he wished to do he should be able to afford. From 1860 he had a combined income from at least three part-time jobs: reading once a week for Mrs. Benjamin Wood, the cultured and wealthy widow of a member of Parliament; writing two columns and a leading article each week for the *Ipswich Journal* (without, however, having to go to Ipswich); and reading the manuscripts of aspiring authors for Chapman and Hall (this necessitated staying in London one night every week, for which purpose he for a short time shared a house with Algernon Charles Swinburne and Dante Gabriel Rossetti in Cheyne Walk). To these activities he added jobs as he could. Without telling Frederic Chapman, he secretly worked for Saunders and Otley, a new publishing house; he increased the amount of work he did for Chapman and Hall; he contributed to and became involved in the organization of various magazines

Flint Cottage, Box Hill, Meredith's home for the last forty years of his life

and journals, notably the *Pall Mall Gazette* and the *Fortnightly Review* (of which he was editor for a three-month period in the absence of John Morley); and he even accepted an assignment as special war correspondent for the *Morning Post* in Italy, despite the difficulty of getting friends to do his other work while he was away. With Arthur at boarding school in Norwich, Meredith could buckle down to work as he saw fit, and this work soon included the preparation of new editions of his earliest work. During the 1860s, there were second editions of *The Shaving of Shagpat* (1861), *Farina* (1865), and *Evan Harrington* (1866); *The Ordeal of Richard Feverel* was serialized in *Revue des deux mondes* (1865); and *Farina* went to a third edition (1868).

Whatever he may have said to friends about the difficulties he had with each new novel—and these difficulties were, of course, real—he was nonetheless an established writer and man of letters. He mixed with the most distinguished literary people of his day and enjoyed himself prodigiously in their company, particularly in after-dinner talk and in long cross-country rambles which often lasted several days and involved

convivial overnight stays at remote country pubs. He was witty, full of anecdotes and zest for existence, and always happy when out-of-doors with male friends of equal intelligence. Mary Meredith, whom he had seen only very occasionally since their separation, died in October 1861, leaving him free to put his life in order, to come to terms with the experience of his first marriage, and to consider how he would manage in the future. This last question was answered when he met Marie Vulliamy, the young daughter of a retired, anglicized French businessman. They were married on 20 September 1864, after protracted negotiations about Meredith's income and respectability. They lived in temporary homes, including (for about three years) Kingston Lodge in Kingston-on-Thames, before moving in 1868 to Flint Cottage at the foot of Box Hill, where Meredith remained for the rest of his life. Because Marie had brought to the marriage a small income of her own, the Merediths' future was reasonably secure. Though Flint Cottage was small and cramped, he now had what he wanted: a garden of his own; the marvelous woodland; the famous beauty spot, Box Hill itself, to climb before sunrise; and the still unspoiled countryside, conveniently bisected by the railway that let him travel to London but with its lanes not yet replaced by roads.

As Meredith consolidated his position during the 1860s and early 1870s, he found that because of the critique of the British way of life his ironical mode implied, his creative genius was as quickly appreciated overseas as in England. *Evan Harrington* in book form was first published in America, as was *The House on the Beach* (1877); *Emilia in England* (as *Sandra Belloni*) and *The Ordeal of Richard Feverel* were serialized in France; and *The Ordeal of Richard Feverel* was included in Tauchnitz's Collection of British Authors. This trend was to continue. Of course, other British authors were also published or republished overseas, but it was an important aspect of his career that Meredith came to feel that it was chiefly foreigners, particularly Americans, who fully appreciated and understood what he did. This feeling later on had a highly beneficial, liberating effect. Also during the 1860s and 1870s, a pattern was established: Meredith almost invariably revised a novel when a new edition was prepared, not only to remedy flaws and infelicities but also to strengthen the action by insisting upon its complexity. He corrected, added, and deleted, but he never simplified. By far the best example of the creative artist in the process of revision is the second edition of *The Ordeal of Richard Feverel*, which Meredith prepared for the publisher Christian Tauchnitz. During the course of this revision the novel first assumed its true character, though there were further minor changes when Kegan Paul published the novel in one volume, and major ones when Chapman and Hall included it in their first collected edition in 1885. Meredith was experimental in approach; his skill developed as his career proceeded; his attitude to the novel was plastic, not rigid. He was truest to himself, as artist, in the very activity of the pen on the page, the countless corrections, deletions, and additions representing an idea of the novel as a never-ending process that actively engaged the attentive reader in the turbulence of verbal activity, rather than as a fixed entity that locked the reader into one and only one response. The second English edition of *The Ordeal of Richard Feverel* (1878) is a much better book than the first of 1859; Meredith was learning as he wrote. While Marie brought up their two young children, William and Marie, in Flint Cottage, Meredith, in the little two-room wooden cabin he had

had built as his writer's den in their idyllic garden, began to imagine to himself those major works that added distinction to his later years.

The period between 1877 and 1884 was a turning point in Meredith's career, albeit a turning point open to various interpretations. Two long short stories or novellas, *The House on the Beach* and *The Case of General Ople and Lady Camper*, were published in the *New Quarterly Magazine* in 1877; in the same year *An Essay on Comedy* was published in the same magazine; *The Egoist* appeared in three volumes in 1879. The traditional view of Meredith has *An Essay on Comedy* and *The Egoist*, taken together, as so typical of his art that his other books can best be understood in the terms they establish. In this view, *The Case of General Ople and Lady Camper* is a direct reflection, through the way in which Lady Camper makes fun of her neighbor General Ople, of what Meredith thought was the purpose of fiction. Another view is that in *An Essay on Comedy*, as well as in the fiction contemporary with it, Meredith thought out something which he then largely put behind him: the idea of society as something that did not change because human nature did not change, an idea that could have little appeal for a late Victorian who could not avoid noticing the impact on behavior of science, industry, empire, education, population growth, and wealth.

An Essay on Comedy, first delivered as a lecture entitled "On the Idea of Comedy and the Uses of the Comic Spirit" at the London Institution on 1 February 1877 (published in book form in 1897), is a classic statement of the beneficial social effects of the great comedies of the Western tradition, such as Molière's: comedy rectifies the excesses of human behavior by allowing an audience to laugh at them and, in the process of enjoyment, to achieve a sort of sanity or equipoise, a return to normality. *The Egoist*, by common consent one of the most brilliant of Meredith's novels, is a highly original, but, in an important sense, orthodox comedy of manners with many theatrical features, just as *Evan Harrington* had been twenty years earlier. It is a novel, written in the spirit of *An Essay on Comedy*, about the excessive egoism of Sir Willoughby Patterne within the enclosed "society" of Sir Willoughby's own extensive estate. If the reader can believe that the aristocratic and upper-middle-class characters who occupy the stage that Willoughby's house and park represent are a credible microcosm of some other, real society, that reader can enjoy the absurdly conceited behavior of the egoist as a foible of character

Meredith's study in the garden chalet at Box Hill

which is eventually revealed for what it is and re-dressed. Meredith now had the inventiveness with character, the sure touch with dialogue, and the control of plot to write this kind of book with considerable virtuosity.

Meredith, however, called *The Egoist* a "pot-boiler." This was because he saw that the "society" of Patterne Hall was not a microcosm of England in 1879, where the stresses caused by class, poverty, urbanization, and industry were too obvious to ignore, and because he clearly understood the options in theory open to a late-nineteenth-century novelist. If the serious writer was not preoccupied with social change, he could remain within the romance tradition, as Meredith's friend Robert Louis Stevenson consciously chose to do. If he was preoccupied with social change, he had either to be a naturalist like Emile Zola (someone who concentrated on the surface detail of existence) or a psychological novelist (someone who tried to penetrate beneath surface appearance to the underlying, perhaps unconscious, springs of behavior)—character in this latter case being no longer a fixed moral entity and behavior being no longer a question of complying or not complying with a social norm.

Meredith wanted to write a modern novel, one in which the emphasis was psychological rather than moral, and devoted the next fifteen years to trying to do so. During this fifteen-year period, he published *The Tragic Comedians* (1880), *Diana of the Crossways* (1885), *One of Our Conquerors* (1891), *Lord Ormont and His Aminta* (1894), and *The Amazing Marriage* (1895), despite illness and bereavement fighting the energy in his fifties and sixties for a new set of experiments with the novel form. He also wrote *Celt and Saxon* (1910), which remained unfinished but expressed Meredith's growing conviction that the Celt, particularly the Welshman, was uncontaminated by the snobbery, prudery, haughtiness, and insensitivity that characterized the Anglo-Saxon.

The Tragic Comedians, a failure, effectively brought to an end the type of novel in which Meredith was ironical at the expense of his principal characters. Here he tried what he had tried before: to combine within the same plot an actual political concern (the career of the European socialist Ferdinand Lassalle) and an imagined love relationship (Lassalle's unconsummated, abortive affair with a young Jewess). Meredith failed to give substance and credibility to his depiction of socialism, and he trivialized both it and the relationship between the two main characters by making fun, at their expense, of the romantic convention in which he had chosen to place them. This exploration of the connection between the political and the personal, the public and the private, was one of Meredith's preoccupations. He had conducted it in *Vittoria* and in *Beauchamp's Career*; he was to renew it more subtly in *Diana of the Crossways*, as well as, obliquely, in his last three novels. He continued to write as though there *ought* to be a connection between the behavior of the individual and the political crosscurrents of the time in which that individual lived, though his sense of political reality altered as he grew older, as did his definition of individuality. *The Tragic Comedians* also placed an emphasis on a second preoccupation, that by making fun of romantic love (relationships between people based more on vague feeling than clearheadedness), he could create an opportunity of analyzing what actually went on between people, and in particular between men and women for whom the intellectual and sexual were intermingled or confused. In *The Tragic Comedians*, however, the analysis (if that is the right word for a novel in which the characters are unskillfully denied the meeting at which they might have resolved their difficulties) is quite superficial, while its banal resolution is expressed in negative terms. The characters do not overcome the barrier of race. They do not prevail over social convention. Alvan's career is not proof against the scandal of an affair. Clotilde does not have the strength of character to act upon her deepest feelings. The novel is therefore, at one and the same time, a disappointment and a clear statement of a set of as-yet-unsolved novelistic problems. Only after a long struggle did Meredith find solutions to these problems that satisfied him.

In the very difficult period between the publication of *The Tragic Comedians* in December 1880 and the serial publication of *Diana of the Crossways* in the second half of 1884, Meredith began, wrote substantial sections of, but failed to complete *Celt and Saxon, One of Our Conquerors, Lord Ormont and His Aminta*, and *The Amazing Marriage*. By 1884 multiple, partial manuscripts of these novels, as well as of *Diana of the Crossways*, filled the limited shelf space of his garden chalet, becoming so mixed up that even now passages that clearly belong in a particular book turn up in one of the others. Meredith was thinking hard about the nature of fiction, about how he could

avoid the pitfalls encountered in the writing of *The Tragic Comedians*, and about how he could modify the novel form in a way that would more satisfy his sensibility than did the traditional three-decker. Although Meredith insisted on living in the Home Counties rather than in London, he was by no means out of touch. He knew that Thomas Hardy was beginning to produce his strongest work; he knew that George Gissing was beginning to write what, in England, was a new type of fiction; he knew both men personally and exchanged books with them. He also knew as much as anyone about European fiction and the troubles and excitement caused by the work of writers such as Zola, Henrik Ibsen, Ivan Turgenev, Alphonse Daudet, Paul-Charles-Joseph Bourget, and others. He knew, in other words, that he was far from being alone in his desire to liberate the novel from its mid-century mold. But he did not immediately find his way. He had domestic problems and health problems. His wife began to feel the effects of the cancer that eventually killed her (on 17 September 1885); he began to be affected by the spinal malady that later crippled him. He had been working too hard at too many things. He had to slow down; he had to give things up, including his long walks and his wine. So a few years slipped by without his being able to publish a new work.

Out of the confusion of these years, though, Meredith found the strength to take up the manuscript of *Diana of the Crossways* and during 1884 to finish it. The novel was based on the story of Mrs. Caroline Norton, a wit and beauty, granddaughter of the Irish dramatist Richard Brinsley Sheridan: her husband had accused William Lamb, Lord Melbourne, the prime minister, of having seduced her and had taken him to law; later it was rumored that Mrs. Norton was the person who had betrayed the secret of the cabinet's decision to repeal the Corn Laws to the *Times* in December 1845, causing a crisis that obliged Robert Peel to resign as prime minister, and that she had gotten the news from Sidney Herbert, who was her lover. In the novel, Caroline Norton became Diana Warwick and Sidney Herbert became Percy Dacier. This sort of thing interested Meredith because it permitted exploration of public and private motives, the interrelationship of politics and love, and the impingement of feeling upon practical intelligence. Also, the story existed as a set of rumors: no one knew precisely what had happened. Lord Melbourne had been acquitted; Sidney Herbert had not been openly accused of treachery. Here, then, was the basis in real life for a story in which motive could be sharply analyzed at a point of crisis. Because Meredith introduced into the novel recognizable portraits of other real people, some of whom were still alive (notably his old friends Sir Alexander Cornewall Duff-Gordon and his wife Lucie), he later had to issue the disclaimer which is now to be found at the beginning of the novel: "A lady of high distinction for wit and beauty, the daughter of an illustrious Irish House, came under the shadow of calumny. It has latterly been examined and exposed as baseless. The story of *Diana of the Crossways* is to be read as fiction." This disclaimer, written to appease Meredith's friends, is of little interest now because Meredith, as usual, had transcended his source material. *Diana of the Crossways* cannot be understood by reference to the actual historical situation on which it was based. The novel is powerfully—if sometimes obscurely—written, and the characters are drawn with great vitality; in addition, Meredith at last found a means of uniting plot with the analysis of character, so that the plot could not be disposed of by the reader as mere melodrama, or the analysis of character be condemned as complexity for complexity's sake. Here the motives were complex, and Meredith's disposition of events was correspondingly subtle. So in *Diana of the Crossways* there is a necessary connection between motive and event, captured with both power and sophistication.

Meredith did not immediately see the full potential of his material: as usual, he discovered what he had to do in the course of doing it. He had the partial manuscript he had put aside a few years earlier; during the winter of 1883-1884, he took this up and tried to write the serial version for the *Fortnightly Review*. The early parts of the novel appeared in eight issues of the magazine beginning in June and ending in December 1884, at which point the reader was abruptly told: "Thus was the erratic woman stricken; and those who care for more of Diana of the Crossways will find it in the extended chronicle." In other words, the serial version would not be continued, so the reader would have to buy the novel in book form. There is no more striking example than this of a Victorian novelist breaking with a convention that had shackled him. The novel, however, had not yet been completed; indeed, Meredith had immediately started to give it a new shape as he rewrote the early magazine parts in order to create a new manuscript for his publisher. This meant that for many months different parts of the novel were not consistent with each other, Meredith having a strenuous time refashioning his material and giving it the unity it now has. Thus one can see the stages by which his imagination moved away from clever reportage to a type of fiction full of insight and compassion. Broadly speaking, in the winter of 1883-1884 Meredith wrote a novel about a woman who compromises herself with a cabinet member, a novel in which he could raise topical questions about marriage, as he said was his intention. And *Diana of the Crossways* remains one of the most challenging, disturbing marriage novels of the Victorian period. In 1884-1885 he rewrote the book, reducing the importance of the allusions to the repeal of the Corn Laws and reducing the emphasis on the moral dilemma of the woman compromised by a foolish action, but increasing the psychological interest by not concluding with her consequent breakdown and death, so that the implications of her action could be thoroughly examined. Meredith, in rewriting *Diana of the Crossways*, had achieved a breakthrough. Not only had he written a novel whose whole spirit was compatible with the recently passed "Married Woman's Property Act" and the public feeling associated with it, he had also convincingly moved his focus from the moral to the psychological, so that Diana became a person to be understood rather than to be judged. The novel was an immediate success.

With *Diana of the Crossways*, Meredith had finally achieved independence from the Victorian magazine. *Evan Harrington* had been written for *Once a Week*; *Vittoria* and *Beauchamp's Career* had both been serialized in the *Fortnightly Review*; *The Egoist* had appeared in the Glasgow *Herald*, but not on Meredith's initiative. Now with *Diana of the Crossways* he had actually written a novel that defied serialization; that is, it lacked the episodic character appropriate to a serial, having instead the unity and flow of an action that occurred much more within the heads of the characters than in sensational events. The success of *Diana of the Crossways* also coincided with Chapman and Hall's decision to publish a collected edition of Meredith's works in 1885. Technological and commercial factors had combined to reduce the unit cost of a book, with the consequence that the reader could buy the book for himself, rather than borrow it one volume at a time from a circulating library. *The Egoist* sold at thirty-one shillings and sixpence, the standard price for a three-

Lady Duff-Gordon, the model for Lady Dunstane in
Diana of the Crossways

volume novel: the volumes in Chapman and Hall's collected edition sold at six shillings or three shillings and sixpence, depending upon the quality of the paper. These volumes could be purchased separately or together. More people could afford to buy Meredith's work, and they did. This collected edition of 1885 was bought by Roberts Brothers of Boston and brought to the attention of a wide American readership by a mail-order sales technique, so much so that, having at first merely sold the copies they had bought in sheets from Chapman and Hall, Roberts Brothers began to print copies of their own and to sell large numbers. Meredith saw that he was no longer at the mercy of British moral prejudice and the cult of respectability. His popularity in the United States increased rapidly to the extent that, a few years later, American publishers' agents, stimulated by impending changes in American copyright law, began to bid for the first refusal of his new work and for the right to republish his old. Because he had work on the shelf, as well as in his head, he was able to respond to this changed situation.

Meredith had for so many years attempted to accommodate the middle-class reader that it was a great relief no longer to have to do so; now he could write as he wished. He had always avoided the explicit: very few characters in a Meredith novel fully understand the situation in which they find themselves; nor is the author often willing to offer a simple explanation for a complex situation. He did not believe in simple explanations: a character motivated only by the desire for money, position, or political power, or one guided exclusively by moral principle, would not become the subject of a Meredith novel, or if he did, his position would be represented as complicated by other factors, not all of which he would himself understand. This technique of Meredith's often left readers exasperated. "If he knows what is happening, why does he not tell us?" some would say. In the novels of the 1880s and 1890s, Meredith took this technique several stages further by writing not about what characters did, but about what other characters thought they did; not about what was understood, but what was thought to be understood; not about total and clear explanations of behavior, but about partial and opaque explanations; not about absolutes, but about that shifting, unstable, difficult world in which the relationship between one person and another is rarely fixed or totally comprehensible. In order to transfer to the page his sense of the instability of human relationships, Meredith became interested in what he frequently (in these last novels) called gossip. (In *The Amazing Marriage* one of the narrators is Dame Gossip.) The reader gets to know, not what the novelist thinks is true, but what the character thinks is true. The character, while not necessarily completely mistaken, is rarely completely right, for what people say about other people is inevitably gossip: opinion based upon insufficient evidence. By letting a novel consist of sets of half-understood events, impingements, and collisions and by letting the emphasis rest on what the characters do not understand, the novelist can remove himself from the novel, no longer disguising himself as the narrator who knows everything before it has happened. Thus is created the illusion of the characters having to thread their way through a maze of half-truths and inaccurate reports, in a world in which separation, alienation, and breakdown are at least as likely as their opposites. In *The Egoist* the narrator was supremely ironical at the expense of Sir Willoughby Patterne, who could not understand the defects of his position; in *Diana of the Crossways* the reader does not have to cope with the narrator's irony to nearly the same extent, but is made to share Diana's bewilderment as she tries to relate to the people in her life. In the novels which followed *Diana of the Crossways*, Meredith further accentuated this flight from the absolute by adopting techniques of multiple narration, two or more narrators giving quite different accounts of the same events, as—famously—in *The Amazing Marriage*. In this way, Meredith made a radical advance in the art of fiction, discovering a technique more appropriate for the analysis of unconsciously motivated behavior than for the depiction of behavior itself. Always a psychological novelist in intention, he had now found out how to be one.

A reader who believes life to be informed by moral principle will probably not enjoy Meredith's creation of an essentially secular, unstable world in these later novels, especially because of the emphasis upon acts of bad faith, breakdown, doubt, and confusion. But though his outlook was secular, antireligious, and intellectual, Meredith was not unprincipled, was not merely playing with what other people took seriously; on the contrary, he used the new type of multiple narrative to explore even more rigorously those matters which had always deeply concerned him: the springs of human character as they found expression in behavior and in relationships. On three particular concerns his emphasis was always deadly serious: the individuality which tended always to the isolation of a terribly exclusive egoism; the irredeemable nature of an action once it had been committed; and the concealed motive which could operate without its full force being understood. These three concerns were at the heart of Meredith's entire corpus, and now in his last novels he gave them a new, brilliant treatment.

First, the egoist: Meredith had given deadly portraits of egoists in *The Ordeal of Richard Feverel*, where the suffering of both Sir Austin and Richard Feverel derived from their belief in self, from their being confined within themselves, and from their inability to relate, fully or honestly, to people outside themselves. Neville Beauchamp, in *Beauchamp's Career*, had been another egoist, trapped within his consciousness of self, believing in independence of individual action rather than in the interdependence of people. Sir Willoughby Patterne, in *The Egoist*, was, of course, the supreme exemplum, the sun around which all other things in life were forced to circu-

Caricature from Punch *of Meredith testifying in an 1891 libel suit against Chapman and Hall, which ultimately cost the publishers two thousand pounds*

late. Under attack here, though only implicitly in these early novels, was that mid-century, liberal idea of the freestanding individual whose rights vis-à-vis "society" were codified by John Stuart Mill in *On Liberty*. Meredith's egoists would very much have agreed with the proposition that, provided they did no harm to others, they should be free to think and do as they wished—an attitude which disastrously cut them off from other people, both individually and in the mass, while creating, in effect, a new type of harm. The egoist is represented as being simply incapable of accepting the legitimacy of a contrary opinion: he knows how to dominate, but intimacy based upon reciprocal understanding eludes him. In the extreme case, this condition of the ego trapped within itself would give way to mental breakdown, as in the case of Mr. Pole in *Emilia in England*. In the later novels, Meredith presents a terrifyingly uncompromising psychological analysis of the tragedy of the ego. The businessman Victor Radnor in *One of Our Conquerors*, confident, ebullient, virile, masterful, marvelous in so many ways, sees only with his own eyes and, as a human being, fails: he fails to respond to his wife's love, fails to try to understand her, fails to examine his own actions and motives critically, and fails to recollect why it was so important to be a "conqueror." He loses control, goes insane, and dies. The Earl of Fleetwood, in *The Amazing Marriage*, provides an equally deadly example. Total egoism is shown in these novels to be an alienating force: Fleetwood holds himself back from his wife, tragically preferring an intact ego to the give-and-take of a love in which neither person is dominated or wholly possessed.

Meredith saw, second, that if much in life is relative, an action is not. Richard in *The Ordeal of Richard Feverel* burns down a stack of wheat and by doing so unwittingly enters the world of other people's standards, the world in which crime will be punished and good actions rewarded. Meredith rarely let his characters exist only on the level of talk, even though it was mostly through their talk that the reader got to know them. In *Beauchamp's Career* the conflict of personal and political opinion is interrupted by the brute fact of one character horsewhipping another. Diana in *Diana of the Crossways* sells a cabinet secret brought to her by her lover: the public and the private are locked together; what does such an action mean and can one recover from it? In *The Amazing Marriage*, the Earl of Fleetwood deliberately insults and degrades his wife on their wedding day and, in effect, rapes her. Can a human relationship survive such an atrocity, and if so, how? Actions of this kind are irredeemable in Meredith's novels because the characters are not allowed to behave as though the action never occurred: Meredith was a nineteenth-century psychological novelist who probed human motives in relation to events, not a twentieth-century novelist who probes personality disconnected from "real world" occurrences. Diana never recovers her ground with Dacier, whom she betrayed; and it is only as a much changed woman, after a debilitating nervous breakdown, that she can to some extent repair her life in a relationship with a different man, who distinctly requires of her some surrender of egoism. In *The Amazing Marriage*, Fleetwood remains unforgiven; although the reader knows that he has come to love his wife, not everything can be talked away or repaired. (The different treatment given to Diana and the Earl of Fleetwood in these two important novels did not, of course, escape the feminist eye.)

Third, the concealed motive: Meredith understood that what motivated men and women in many, if not all, of their more profound relationships with each other was their sexuality, though the exterior might be moral or intellectual. But whether because of Meredith's own reserve, or because of the conventions of his time, the sexual is rarely given explicit statement. The narrator does not give explicit explanations to his reader. His characters do not give explicit explanations to themselves or to each other. Indeed, they mostly do not know why they behave as they do, though they can observe easily enough that their behavior is not completely rational. They can observe their behavior, but they have no way to be articulate about the hidden springs of action. Meredith did not have the conceptual framework and the vocabulary of twentieth-century psychology, but he knew that what a man said to a woman or a woman said to a man could rarely be taken at face value, even, for example, when they believed themselves to be talking rationally about the events of the day. Thus, when Diana and Dacier talk late at night about the repeal of the Corn Laws, they are in fact making love, any subject of conversation being a possible vehicle for an intimacy that convention required should not be openly stated. Obviously, Meredith was being characteristically Victorian, albeit in a masterly way, in making an art of what could not be said openly; and his predicament was not without its advantages, since his psychological insights could be expressed metaphorically, without simplification. Richard Feverel conceals his true feelings behind an expressionless face and, with an expressionless face, the Earl of Fleetwood conceals from his companions that one of his oldest friends has blown his brains out. This mask is in Meredith the image of the repressed self. Fleetwood is incapable of breaking down and sharing his grief with his friends; in the same way, he is incapable of expressing his growing love for his wife.

The last novels significantly confirm the direction that Meredith had all the time been taking, despite his forays into the comedy of manners. They all show a heightened social awareness, an increased tendency to take a humane view of human stupidity and error, a strong preference for psychological rather than moral analysis, and a sharp focus on the underprivileged posi-

Meredith, crippled by a spinal condition, being taken for his daily ride in a donkey cart on Box Hill

tion of women. *Diana of the Crossways* is the story of a woman who thinks she can carry all before her by virtue of her wit, her beauty, her energy, in an independent existence which allows her to flout convention, prize eccentricity, and patronize others. Victor Radnor in *One of Our Conquerors*, a man who early in life married a woman for her money and then deserted her for a younger, more spirited companion, believes that he can dominate existence, manipulate it to his own ends, and ride roughshod over other people's feelings, for their own good as well as his own. In *Lord Ormont and His Aminta*, Lord Ormont considers that he can possess his wife as a chattel without bothering to get to know her as a person in her own right. And in *The Amazing Marriage*, Meredith shows brilliantly how the arrogant, excessively wealthy aristocrat, who had been brought up to take for granted the fruits of others' labor,

by a painful process learns (though too late) that his values had been ill-founded—were, in fact, wrong values. These characters are Meredith's typical egoists, but in his treatment of them there is a new emphasis: a somewhat right-wing author has moved significantly to the left; he makes his privileged characters become aware of the predicament of ordinary people, including the poor. In *The Amazing Marriage*, Carinthia Jane takes refuge in Whitechapel, where the sympathy and understanding her husband withheld are found in a greengrocer's shop. In the same novel, much hinges on her identifying with the plight of Welsh coal miners who are on strike and without means to support themselves. As the reader sympathizes with Carinthia Jane, he is moved to a democratic, not an autocratic, appreciation of events. Also, in each novel the debilitating arrogance of the egoist is counterbalanced by milder characters who, though by no means lacking in sensibility or intelligence, have settled for a more limited existence within the bounds of good sense and good feeling. So Diana is balanced by Emma Dunstane in *Diana of the Crossways*; Victor Radnor by his daughter, Nesta, in *One of Our Conquerors*; Lord Ormont and his sister by Matthew Weyburn in *Lord Ormont and His Aminta*; and Fleetwood by Gower Woodseer in *The Amazing Marriage*. Meredith addresses the psychological health of his characters, ignoring the merely moral aspects of the situations he creates for them. Diana's treachery, Victor Radnor's bigamy, Lord Ormont's incest, and Fleetwood's abuse of his wife are not the subjects of the novels: the subject is in each case what happens in the mind of the human being trapped by events. Further, Meredith ascribes to the women characters a remarkable independence, in that they are not defined in these novels by social positions or by their subservient relations to a man. Diana, Nesta Radnor, Aminta, and Carinthia Jane all break with convention or are outside it: Diana abandons her first husband; Nesta is illegitimate; Aminta clearheadedly opts for adultery; Carinthia Jane abandons her child, as well as her husband, to go to Spain with her brother. In each case, the woman defines herself not in the moral terms that would represent the opinions of others, but existentially in what she discovers to be her own personal response to whatever befalls her, irrespective of the outcome. When full understanding is at length achieved, Diana agrees to marry, as does Nesta Radnor, but Aminta chooses to live with Matthew in Switzerland while still married to Lord Ormont (symbolizing, incidentally, Meredith's emancipation from his titled characters), while Carinthia Jane rejects marriage outright and goes to Spain to work as a nurse. Meredith's contemporaries well understood that the restrictive or negative type of middle-class morality had been dealt a severe blow. He had successfully made himself a "modern" novelist.

Between 1885 and his death in 1909 Meredith enjoyed immense popularity. The collected editions—Constable's De Luxe Edition in thirty-nine volumes which began to appear in 1896, the Library Edition and its equivalent in America published by Scribners—allowed readers to assess his work as a whole. His later novels were recognized as brilliant. It was seen, retrospectively, not only that he had championed woman's rights but that he had done so in a subtle and telling way. It was seen that he had espoused radical causes

without resorting to a strident type of protest. It was seen that he had not only rejected the Evangelical morality of the period of his youth, but that he had moved his fiction toward an extremely humane but unsentimental appraisal of change, instability, uncertainty in both personal and social affairs. And it was seen that, though he had throughout his life been European in outlook and cosmopolitan in thought, he had remained a patriot, with an unquenchable love of the English countryside and an abiding concern for all matters (except party politics) that involved the welfare of the nation. Suffragettes cycled down to Box Hill to take his advice. Newspaper editors sent down messengers to obtain his views on international events. Aspiring authors sat outside his house on the lower slopes of Box Hill just to catch sight of him. Writers such as Paul Valéry came from overseas in homage and out of interest. Although Meredith in his later years went deaf, was confined to a downstairs room in Flint Cottage, and could eventually only venture out of doors in a donkey cart, with his gardener and nurse in attendance, he was nonetheless lionized, fussed over, and admired, at long last recognized for the cantankerous, willfully independent genius he had always been. Because of his lifelong agnosticism, which incorporated a pronounced abhorrence of the Church of England, he could not be buried in Westminster Abbey; a plaque was placed there as a compromise, and his ashes were buried in Dorking churchyard, next to his second wife's grave.

Finally, a word must be said about Meredith's extraordinary engagement with the English language. From the beginning, he had shown an immense liking for the well-turned phrase, the witty expression, and the complex sentence. He collected aphorisms and allowed his characters to collect them; he used them at the dinner table and made his characters do likewise. For a character to cap another character's witty remark with one that was wittier was represented as a sign of intelligence, something that distinguished him or her from lesser mortals. Sir Austin Feverel, somewhat ponderously, was addicted in this way; so, more lightheartedly, was Diana of the Crossways; so, philosophically, was Gower Woodseer in *The Amazing Marriage*. What Meredith's characters considered to be witty has often, by his readers, been considered meretricious and affected, especially when aphoristic fine talk is extended through a chapter or two until the reader longs for plain words, plain explanations. But although

Meredith too often let his love of the neatly turned phrase get the better of him, it is only a small part of a mastery of the English language so complete that what sometimes seemed to others convoluted, difficult, and wordy, was for him the essential verbal instrument for the type of psychological analysis he was practicing. When the revision of *One of Our Conquerors* would have allowed him to alter those crucial passages that critics had found obscure, impossible to work out, and perversely complex, Meredith not only declined to simplify but introduced new complexities. The complexities were not merely verbal, as perhaps they had been in some of his early novels; on the contrary, they were an integral part of the delineation of his introverted characters' minds. While he was popular, Meredith was recognized as one of the great masters of prose style; and attentive readers, prepared to engage themselves with the difficulties of the text, discovered with pleasure that he had not, after all, been merely verbose. Late in the twentieth century fewer readers, maybe, make the attempt; but for those who do, the rewards are just as great.

Letters:
The Letters of George Meredith, 3 volumes, edited by C. L. Cline (Oxford: Clarendon Press, 1970).

Bibliographies:
Michael Collie, *George Meredith: A Bibliography* (Toronto: University of Toronto Press, 1974);
John C. Olmsted, *George Meredith: An Annotated Bibliography of Criticism 1925-1975* (New York: Garland, 1978).

Biographies:
Lionel Stevenson, *The Ordeal of George Meredith: A Biography* (New York: Scribners, 1953);
Renate Muendel, *George Meredith* (Boston: Twayne, 1986).

References:
Gillian Beer, *Meredith: A Change of Masks; A Study of the Novels* (London: Athlone Press, 1970);
Ian Fletcher, ed., *Meredith Now: Some Critical Essays* (London: Routledge & Kegan Paul, 1971);
Rebecca S. Hogan, *A Concordance to the Poetry of George Meredith* (New York: Garland, 1982);
V. S. Pritchett, *George Meredith and English Comedy* (London: Chatto & Windus, 1970);
Mohammad Shaheen, *George Meredith: A Reappraisal of the Novels* (London: Macmillan, 1981);
Ioan Williams, ed., *Meredith: The Critical Heritage* (London: Routledge & Kegan Paul, 1971);
Judith Wilt, *The Readable People of George Meredith* (Princeton, N.J.: Princeton University Press, 1975).

John Stuart Mill
(20 May 1806 - 7 May 1873)

This entry was updated by Eugene R. August (University of Dayton) from his entry in
DLB 55: Victorian Prose Writers Before 1867.

BOOKS: *A System of Logic, Ratiocinative and Inductive, Being a Connected View of the Principles of Evidence, and The Methods of Scientific Investigation* (2 volumes, London: Parker, 1843; revised, 1846; 1 volume, New York: Harper, 1846; revised again, 1851, 1856, 1862, 1865, 1868, 1872);

Essays on Some Unsettled Questions of Political Economy (London: Parker, 1844);

Principles of Political Economy, with Some of Their Applications to Social Philosophy, 2 volumes (London: Parker, 1848; Boston: Little & Brown, 1848; revised, 1849, 1852, 1857, 1862, 1865, 1871);

On Liberty (London: Parker, 1859; Boston: Ticknor & Fields, 1863);

Thoughts on Parliamentary Reform (London: Parker, 1859; revised and enlarged, 1859);

Dissertations and Discussions, Political, Philosophical, and Historical. Reprinted Chiefly from the Edinburgh and Westminster Reviews (4 volumes: volumes 1-2, London: Parker, 1859; volumes 3-4, London: Longmans, Green, Reader & Dyer, 1867, 1875; 5 volumes, Boston: Spenser, 1864-1868);

Considerations on Representative Government (London: Parker, Son & Bourn, 1861; New York: Harper, 1862);

Utilitarianism (London: Parker, Son & Bourn, 1863; revised, 1864, 1867, 1871; Boston: Small, 1887);

Auguste Comte and Positivism (London: Trübner, 1865; Philadelphia: Lippincott, 1866);

An Examination of Sir William Hamilton's Philosophy and of the Principal Philosophical Questions Discussed in His Writings (1 volume, London: Longmans, Green, Longman, Roberts & Green, 1865; 2 volumes, Boston: Spencer, 1866; revised, 1867, 1872);

Inaugural Address Delivered to the University of St. Andrews, Feb. 1st, 1867 (London: Longmans, Green, Reader & Dyer, 1867; Boston: Littell & Gay, 1867);

John Stuart Mill

England and Ireland (London: Longmans, Green, Reader & Dyer, 1868);

The Subjection of Women (London: Longmans, Green, Reader & Dyer, 1869; Philadelphia: Lippincott, 1869);

Chapters and Speeches on the Irish Land Question (London: Longmans, Green, Reader & Dyer, 1870);

Autobiography (London: Longmans, Green, Reader & Dyer, 1873; New York: Holt, 1873);

Three Essays on Religion (London: Longmans, Green, Reader & Dyer, 1874; New York: Holt, 1874);

Early Essays by John Stuart Mill, edited by J. W. M. Gibbs (London: Bell, 1897);

The Spirit of the Age, edited by Frederick A. von Hayek (Chicago: University of Chicago Press, 1942);

Mill on Bentham and Coleridge, edited by F. R. Leavis (London: Chatto & Windus, 1950; New York: Stewart, 1951);

Prefaces to Liberty: Selected Writings of John Stuart Mill, edited by Bernard Wishy (Boston: Beacon, 1959);

John Mill's Boyhood Visit to France; being a Journal and Notebook Written by John Stuart Mill in France, 1820-21, edited by Anna Jean Mill (Toronto: University of Toronto Press, 1960);

Essays on Literature and Society, edited by J. B. Schneewind (New York: Collier Books, 1965);

Literary Essays, edited by Edward Alexander (Indianapolis: Bobbs-Merrill, 1967);

The Nigger Question, by Thomas Carlyle, and *The Negro Question*, by John Stuart Mill, edited by Eugene R. August (New York: Appleton-Century-Crofts, 1971);

Essays on Poetry, edited by F. Parvin Sharpless (Columbia: University of South Carolina Press, 1976).

Collection: *Collected Works of John Stuart Mill*, 25 volumes, ongoing, edited by John M. Robson and others (Toronto: University of Toronto Press, 1963-).

OTHER: *The Rationale of Judicial Evidence, From the Mss. of Jeremy Bentham*, 5 volumes, edited, with a preface, by Mill (London: Hunt & Clarke, 1827);

James Mill, *Analysis of the Phenomenon of the Human Mind, with Notes Illustrative and Critical by Alexander Bain, Andrew Findlater, and George Grote*, 2 volumes, edited, with additional notes, by Mill, second edition (London: Longmans, Green, Reader & Dyer, 1869);

Four Dialogues of Plato, including the "Apology" of Socrates, translations and notes by Mill, edited by Ruth Borchardt (London: Watts, 1947).

Like many aspects of John Stuart Mill's life and work, his literary artistry remains a subject of enduring interest and lively disagreement. Few people would now question Mill's importance as spokesman for the humane liberal tradition in the history of ideas, although considerable controversy still flares over the nature and value of his

Mill's father and mentor, James Mill; drawing by Joseph Slater dated 1831

views upon such topics as individual liberty, epistemology, Utilitarian ethics, sexual and racial equality, economic theory, and religious belief. Similarly, the question of Mill's prose artistry is far from settled.

From the day in 1873 when Thomas Carlyle in a letter to his brother John dismissed Mill's *Autobiography* as the life history of a steam engine, to the recent characterization of Mill in a widely used anthology of literature as the "least literary of the important Victorian prose writers," some readers have insisted that Mill's prose is almost entirely devoid of art. Mill has been seen by readers as a frosty rationalist without a tincture of the poet, his prose being notable chiefly for its utilitarian starkness. Other readers, however, have pointed to the extraordinary power of many of Mill's writings. In particular, the ability of these works to influence people's ideas, attitudes, and lives suggests that logic alone is insufficient to account for their impact. Thomas Hardy's citing *On Liberty* (1859) as a cure for despair is but one of many examples of Mill's influence. Also, studies in the past twenty years have convincingly traced the interweaving of imagery, metaphor, and even symbol with ratiocination in many of Mill's major texts. In the view of the authors of these pieces, Mill is one of the great Victorian sages, subtly blending argument and art, not just to win a debate but also to alter his readers' perceptions of reality and to move them powerfully to live and act on those new perceptions.

Nearly all commentators, including Mill himself, agree that his life and thought were decisively shaped by his father's forceful personality and by the extraordinary education which Mill received at his hands. James Mill, a Scotsman making his way precariously in the world of London journalism, had married Harriet Burrow in 1805. A year later, John Stuart Mill was born, the first of nine children produced by what proved to be an ill-sorted union between a dynamically intellectual male and an apparently well-meaning but ineffectual female. A disciple and protégé of the Utilitarian philosopher and reformer Jeremy Bentham, James Mill chose to educate his eldest son at home, making the boy's mind a showpiece of what empirical and logical methods could produce if they were untrammeled by social and religious preconceptions. Mill's *Autobiography* (1873) provides a memorable account of this remarkable venture in Benthamite instruction. James Mill began early, teaching Greek to his son when the boy was three. During the next four years, young Mill also studied mathematics and read widely in English books (especially histories), reporting on his reading to his father during their vigorous walks together. Between the ages of eight and fourteen, Mill studied Latin, geometry, algebra, differential calculus, experimental science, logic, and economics. Although not excluded, fiction and poetry were not strong elements in this Utilitarian education. The primary aim of the training was to enable the boy to think for himself by using empirical and rational means to arrive at truth.

Mill's education had both advantages and liabilities which manifested themselves in his later life and in his writings. At fourteen he had acquired the equivalent of a university education, as well as techniques for continuing self-learning throughout his life. His father's Benthamite bias gave Mill an unusually clearheaded and independent way of looking at controversial matters, in addition to an enthusiastic commitment to liberal reforms as a way of bettering human society. But his education at home also retarded his physical and emotional growth. Because he was kept from the "corrupting" influence of children his own age, his ability to play was arrested, and his motor skills remained underdeveloped. Although Mill was not physically punished, his father's impa-

tience and withering scorn crippled the boy's self-esteem and left him feeling unloved: the psychosexual damage evident in Mill's later life probably derives from these years of stern tutelage. According to the *Autobiography*, the tendency of his education to foster analysis at the expense of feeling also caused Mill problems in later years. Because he feared he could not love his father, inexpressiveness became second nature to Mill: high seriousness and moral indignation were the dominant modes of his personality, to the detriment of playfulness and joy.

Many characteristics of Mill's prose reflect this education. The voice in his writings is always erudite and rational; the language is more abstract than concrete. All of his major works are directed toward what Mill in the *Autobiography* called "the improvement of mankind," and the discussion in these works is conducted with unmistakable seriousness and moral purpose. The fervor of Mill's mission is often the dominant emotion in his writings, an emotion often conveyed as a strong sense of dedication and urgency. Any emotion in his writings, however, usually lies beneath the surface of a prose that seemingly acknowledges no strong feeling. Similarly, the figurative elements of his language lie embedded in a predominantly rational structure. Mill's muted language is at the opposite extreme from the dazzling blend of imagery and sound in such characteristic Carlylian works as *Sartor Resartus* (1836) and *Past and Present* (1843). Nevertheless, as if in defiance of his unpoetic education, Mill's prose exhibits an identifiable imaginative dimension.

Locale may also have played a part in shaping Mill's personality. He grew up in London, mostly in Westminster in a house located in Queen Square (now Queen Anne's Gate) and maintained with financial help from Jeremy Bentham, who lived nearby. During the summer months, Bentham sometimes hosted the Mills in the country, especially at Ford Abbey in Devonshire, a rural retreat memorialized by a uniquely poetic sentence in Mill's *Autobiography*. In 1820 Mill at fourteen went to stay for nearly a year in southern France with Jeremy Bentham's brother Samuel and his family, where he acquired a taste for French language and politics, botany, and mountain scenery. It is tempting to see Westminster (a center of London radicalism) as stimulating Mill's liberal and logical tendencies, while Ford Abbey and the Pyrenees nurtured his more romantic and affective ones. Significantly, in the latter part of his life, Mill divided his year between London and Avignon.

Mill's fifteenth through his twentieth years were dominated by his commitment to becoming the "reformer of the world" (to use his term from the *Autobiography*), the rational activist that his father and Jeremy Bentham had hoped for. Upon Mill's return to England in 1821, his formal education was completed by his reading of a French redaction of one of Bentham's treatises. This important event fixed the principle of utility ("it is the greatest happiness of the greatest number that is the measure of right and wrong") as the capstone of Mill's moral vision. Mill now had a humanistic religion to fill the place of the theological one he never had. Fired by youthful enthusiasm, he began a program of self-education, joined and formed debating societies, and was present at the founding of the *Westminster Review*. A Benthamite periodical, the *Westminster* was designed to advance such "philosophical radical" views as the need for more representative government, greater freedom of public discussion, economic and social reforms to combat population growth and poverty, and the use of associationist psychology as a means of improving education and humanity's moral qualities. Mill himself began to publish in these years—first, letters to journals on controversial topics, and later a full-scale article in the *Westminster*, "Periodical Literature: Edinburgh Review" (1824). A continuation of his father's exposé of the tepidly liberal arguments and assumptions of the Whig *Edinburgh Review*, young Mill's article seethes with zealous denunciation, including some strictures on the moral tone of Shakespeare and Sir Walter Scott. In these years Mill also began working under his father at the East India House (where the younger Mill was to continue in employment until 1858). In addition, he undertook the involved task of preparing for publication the convoluted manuscript of Bentham's *Rationale of Judicial Evidence*, published in five volumes in 1827.

In the midst of this activity, Mill in 1826 suffered what he later described as an excruciating "mental crisis." According to Mill's *Autobiography*, the onset of the crisis was his sudden discovery that crusading for radical causes was not enough. The greatest-happiness principle, ironically, was producing no happiness for one of its most zealous advocates. Left depressed and desperate by this realization, young Mill dragged through the winter of 1826-1827 until he found himself

Utilitarian philosopher Jeremy Bentham, whose principles James Mill followed in educating his son; portrait by H. W. Pickersgill (National Portrait Gallery, London)

moved to tears by reading a passage from Jean-François Marmontel's *Mèmoires d'un pére* (1804). Reinvigorated by this evidence of feeling within himself, Mill gradually began to recover. Eventually he came to fault his education for emphasizing analysis while neglecting emotion. In art, especially in the poetry of William Wordsworth, young Mill began to find the needed resources for replenishing his feelings. The combination of rural, often mountainous, scenery and placid emotion in Wordsworth's poems provided the therapy for helping Mill to exorcise the mental gloom into which he had slipped.

Mill's account of the mental crisis as a turning point in his life has been echoed by later biographers. Some, however, have added interesting speculations of their own about its causes. Overwork, the absence of love, and emotional repression have all been cited, in addition to the notion that the breakdown was partly the result of a suppressed death wish directed by Mill against his father. The crucial passage in Marmontel, it has been pointed out, deals with a son's response to his father's death, and Mill's physical and emotional collapse at his own father's death in 1836 has not escaped notice. Whatever the causes, the mental crisis of 1826 transformed Mill personally and philosophically. Although he always adhered to basic Benthamite positions, his mental crisis sent him seeking for what he termed "many-sidedness" as opposed to his father's philosophic rigidity. In the process, he transformed the greatest-happiness principle into a more complex concept of humanity's moral development. He also transformed himself from the youthful zealot of Benthamism into a more eclectic thinker and a more humane philosopher who valued poetry as well as logic.

The 1830s were marked by Mill's continuing search for many-sidedness, by the formation (amid considerable emotional distress) of the most enduring attachment of his life, and by a series of essays which reflect his intellectual and personal odyssey. These essays, many interesting in their own right, culminate at the end of the decade in two literary masterworks, "Bentham" and "Coleridge."

Attempting to correct what he described as the "half-philosophy" of his Benthamite education, Mill sought the other half of the truth from exponents of political conservatism and idealist epistemology. By the time Bentham died in 1832, Mill was already listening half sympathetically to the Romantic poet and transcendentalist philosopher whom Mill called Bentham's "completing counterpart," Samuel Taylor Coleridge. Mill was also listening so attentively to the Scots "mystic" Thomas Carlyle and to the Saint-Simonian advocate Gustave d'Eichthal that each half believed that he had enlisted Mill as a disciple. Certainly when Thomas and Jane Welsh Carlyle moved to London in 1834, Mill's friendly visits to their Chelsea home were as regular as the local church bells.

Mill's true allegiance, however, lay elsewhere. In 1831 he met Harriet Hardy Taylor, the wife of an affable London merchant and the mother of their three children. As Mill and Harriet Taylor's feelings for each other grew more intense in 1832, the emotional pressure on them and her husband John Taylor mounted. Friends and family tried to dissuade Mill, but he steadfastly refused advice. Eventually, Harriet Taylor separated from her husband, living as his wife in name only, while he continued generously to support her. In deference to his feelings,

Harriet Taylor about seven years before her marriage to Mill (British Library of Political and Economic Science)

Harriet Taylor and John Stuart Mill kept their relationship platonic, although they continued to see each other regularly and sometimes traveled together with her children. Once arrived at, this arrangement continued for years, only to be altered by John Taylor's death in 1849.

During the 1830s, while Mill was seeking philosophic many-sidedness, his relationship with Harriet Taylor apparently contributed to his interest in poetry and renewed his respect for liberty. In "The Spirit of the Age," a series of five essays published in seven installments under the pseudonym A. B. in the *Examiner* early in 1831, Mill's conservative enthusiasm had reached the point where he was capable of questioning the value of liberty of thought. At one point in the series—a lively dissection of current social unrest which stresses the need for philosophers who can reach beyond half-truths—Mill argues that because the mass of people in the age grasp only half-truths, it is pernicious to encourage them to assert their liberty of thought and to discard authority. This view of liberty is reversed dramatically, however, in the *Monthly Repository*, in an essay "On Genius," signed Antiquus, published more than a year later (October 1832) and presumably written after Mill's meeting with Harriet Taylor. After defining genius as simply the ability to know reality through one's own mental efforts, Mill in this essay extols thinking for oneself rather than relying upon authority. Apparently, Harriet Taylor's influence upon Mill was both early and decisive.

Of significance to students of literature are Mill's developing thoughts on poetry, perhaps best seen in four essays written during the 1830s, the first two using the pseudonym Antiquus— "What Is Poetry?" (1833), "The Two Kinds of Poetry" (1833), a review of Alfred, Lord Tennyson's poems (1835), and a review of Carlyle's *The French Revolution* (1837). (In 1859 Mill confused matters somewhat by revising the first two essays for publication in *Dissertations and Discussions*, combining them as a unit titled "Thoughts on Poetry and Its Varieties"; the views of poetry in the two essays, however, seem incompatible and represent different stages of Mill's developing formulation of poetry's nature and function.) Read in sequence, the four texts show Mill working out a justification of poetry against Bentham's contention that the poet betrays rational truth by "stimulating our passions and exciting our prejudices."

First published in the *Monthly Repository* (January 1833), "What Is Poetry?" defines poetry as feeling expressing itself in art—verse, music, painting, and so on. The poet, then, *is* truthful—to his feelings. But in the process of this justification, the essay practically denies poetry an audience: "eloquence is *heard*, poetry is *over*heard." Although Mill says that the poet may later display his artistry and thus reach an audience, he sets forth a view of poetry that has the effect of placing the poet *as poet* in isolation, cutting him off from the practical world of public affairs.

"The Two Kinds of Poetry" (*Monthly Repository*, October 1833) attempts to extend Mill's perception of poetry, and in the process it emerges as a far more important essay whose ideas echo throughout many of Mill's later works. Using associationist psychology, it argues that in the mind of the poet ideas are linked synchronously by emotion, whereas in a thinker's mind ideas are linked "in mere casual order," chronologically or successively. The essay then discriminates between a naturally poetic mind (like Percy Bysshe Shelley's) and a cultivated but not naturally poetic mind (like Wordsworth's). In the first, poetry overflows spontaneously; in the latter, thought is

tinged or overlaid with emotion. Mill ironically adapts Wordsworth's definition of poetry from the preface to *Lyrical Ballads* (1798) to describe Shelley, not Wordsworth, as poet. (Shelley is accorded this accolade most likely because of Harriet Taylor's preference for his work.) The essay goes on to envision the ideal of a poet-philosopher, that is, a poetic mind which has acquired logical and scientific culture.

The readers of the *Monthly Repository* were not inimical to poetry, but when Mill reviewed two volumes of Tennyson's early poetry in the *London Review* (July 1835), he was defending the utility of poetry for a large Benthamite audience. To do so, he argues that the noblest end of genuine poetry is raising human beings toward the perfection of their nature. In discussing the poems, he acutely identifies Tennyson's natural poetic ability as shown in his powerful evocation of feeling through imagery and symbol, through what later generations would call an objective correlative. Mill also astutely notices that Tennyson is cultivating logic and science as well as poetry, and he predicts that by continuing with this labor Tennyson stands a chance of becoming a poet-philosopher such as Mill advocates.

In some ways, Mill's July 1837 review of Carlyle's *French Revolution* in the *London and Westminster Review* (the new title for the merged *London Review* and the *Westminster Review*) was a repayment for friendship, insights, and a debt of another sort. After deciding that he could not publicly reveal his disbelief in Christianity, Mill had earlier abandoned his own plans to write a history of the revolution, and when Carlyle announced his intention to attempt the subject, Mill lent him books, ideas, and encouragement. Having spent five months writing book one of the history, Carlyle lent the manuscript to Mill. Somehow while in Mill's possession, it was accidentally burned as scrap paper, probably by a maid. When a badly shaken Mill broke the news to him, Carlyle magnanimously comforted Mill as best he could and immediately began rewriting the lost book one. He graciously assented to Mill's heartstricken offer of temporary financial help. When the book was published, Mill hailed it in an early review, afterwards congratulating himself that he had thereby prevented the bewildered and hostile misreadings it would most likely have received in the press. But Mill's praise of *The French Revolution* was not mere flattery or atonement; he was a man of too much integrity for that. The review clearly states his metaphysical and political differences with Carlyle, but argues that the book's greatness lies beyond such matters in its poetry, that is, in its ability to recreate the feelings that accompanied historic events. Calling Carlyle's book an epic poem, Mill asserts that it is thus all the more accurate as history. Once again, Mill is expertly "selling" the utility of poetry to a Benthamite audience.

Mill's journey toward many-sidedness is charted significantly in other writings of the 1830s, in particular "Civilisation" (*London and Westminster Review*, 1836) and "Poems and Romances of Alfred de Vigny" (*London and Westminster Review*, 1838). Unfortunately, two potentially valuable essays have been lost, namely Mill's two reviews of Robert Browning's *Pauline*. Given a copy of the poem in 1833, Mill wrote a review which proved too long for its intended publication in the *Examiner*, and its revised version, intended for *Tait's Edinburgh Magazine*, never appeared in print. Although neither version of Mill's review is extant, the copy of *Pauline* containing his marginal comments and final negative appraisal of the poem has survived. In 1833 this copy had unluckily found its way back to Browning. Although the question of its impact upon the young poet is much debated, many scholars believe that Mill's commentary jolted Browning sufficiently to make him avoid similar subjective displays in future poems.

Mill's search for many-sidedness in the 1830s bore its most impressive fruit in two essays, "Bentham" (1838) and "Coleridge" (1840), both published in the *London and Westminster Review*, of which Mill was now the proprietor. In a famous introduction to a 1950 republication of the two essays, F. R. Leavis described them as "classical" documents which constitute essential reading for the student of Victorian literature. But while Leavis saw the essays as background material for "real" literature (such as George Eliot's novels), more recent critics would argue that the essays themselves are "real" literature.

The rhetorically impressive proems which open both essays contrast Bentham and Coleridge as the two seminal minds of the age, the two men who had most influenced the practical and speculative character of the times. In Mill's estimation, they are the teachers of the teachers; they have shaped the minds of the intellectuals of the age. Bentham and Coleridge are depicted as representative of two types of mind—the one logical, analytical, and precise; the other intuitive, comprehensive, and suggestive. They are almost

archetypal opposites—the progressive versus the conservative, the skeptic versus the believer, the empiricist versus the transcendentalist. They are each other's "completing counterpart," accurate in what they affirm, wrongheaded in what they deny. Because each holds half the truth, it is necessary for those who desire wholeness to bring together the two men's visions. In these two impressive essays, Mill shows the way to achieving such a synthesis.

"Bentham" and "Coleridge" provide vivid examples of Mill's rhetorical ability to shape his text to fit his purpose and his audience. To broaden the outlook of doctrinaire liberal readers, the essays encourage a critical assessment of the limitations of Benthamism, while pointing to the positive insights which can be culled from a conservative school of thought such as Coleridge represents. Mill's purpose was no doubt reinforced by his personal awareness of the shortcomings of Benthamite thought and practice. While Mill clearly affirms in the essays his allegiance to Utilitarianism and duly notes its value, "Bentham" has the effect of stressing the limitations of the man and his thought, while "Coleridge" emphasizes the positive aspects of Germano-Coleridgean conservatism.

In "Bentham," the more rhetorically complex and personal of the essays, anticlimax dominates the discussion. Creatively borrowing language, imagery, metaphors, and allusions from Carlyle's review in *Fraser's Magazine* (May 1832) of John Wilson Croker's edition of *The Life of Samuel Johnson*, Mill's essay creates an elaborate picture of Bentham as father-teacher-hero-god figure; it then shows Bentham's inadequacies in all these roles. No distinction is made between the man and his philosophy: the successes and failures of the one are the successes and failures of the other. Much about Bentham is praised—his questioning spirit, his challenge to custom-encrusted authority, his moral integrity in the face of intimidation, his introduction of precision into philosophic and social inquiry, his attacks upon vague generalizations and prejudices, his reforms of law. But the text continually assails his failures—his narrowness of vision, his failure to learn from earlier thinkers, his lack of historical perspective, his simplified views of happiness and human nature, his too-easy dismissal of ideas he could not grasp, his preposterous rejection of poetry. In the end, Bentham's achievements seem largely overwhelmed by his absurd failures. When "Bentham" created such a run on the *Lon-*

Being about, if I am so happy as to obtain her consent, to enter into the marriage relation with the only woman I have ever known, with whom I would have entered into that state; & the whole character of the marriage relation as constituted by law being such as both she and I entirely & conscientiously disapprove, for this among other reasons, that it confers upon one of the parties to the contract, legal power & control over the person, property, & freedom of action of the other party, independent of her own wishes and will; I, having no means of legally divesting myself of these odious powers (as I most assuredly would do if an engagement to that effect could be made legally binding on me) feel it my duty to put on record a

Mill's statement, written the month before his marriage to Harriet Taylor, protesting legal rights conferred on men by Victorian marriage laws (The Letters of John Stuart Mill, edited by Hugh Elliot, 1910)

formal protest against the existing law of marriage, in so far as conferring such powers; and a solemn promise never in any case or under any circumstances to use them. And in the event of marriage between Mrs Taylor and me I declare it to be my will and intention, & the condition of the engagement between us, that she retains in all respects whatever the same absolute freedom of action, & freedom of disposal of herself and of all that does or may at any time belong to her, as if no such marriage had taken place; and I absolutely disclaim & repudiate all pretension to have acquired any rights whatever by virtue of such marriage.

J. S. Mill.

6th March 1851

don and Westminster Review that a second printing was called for, Mill added a footnote at the end of the essay depicting his subject as an irresponsible child, a final damning touch to his portrait of Bentham as man and thinker.

If "Bentham" was designed to stir a more critical attitude toward Utility among philosophical radicals, "Coleridge" was designed to foster a more sympathetic inquiry into conservative thought. The essay openly declares Mill's allegiance to Utilitarian reformers, disagrees with Coleridge's a priori metaphysics, and summarily disqualifies Coleridge's views on political economy. But most of the essay is devoted to a sympathetic survey of eighteenth-century conservative thought, showing how it operated as a corrective to the excesses of liberals and revolutionaries, and as a repository for insights which they chose to overlook. "Coleridge" is built on a pattern of thesis-antithesis-synthesis; eighteenth-century radicalism yields to eighteenth-century conservatism, which in turn leads to possible nineteenth-century synthesis. When the essay focuses specifically on Coleridge's thought, it is to emphasize its value for liberal reformers. It shows that Bentham questioned institutions from the outside (so to speak), while Coleridge entered into their origins, purposes, and spirit, asking whether they were now fulfilling their original social functions. If not, they should be reformed; only if they were beyond reform should they be eliminated. Coleridge saw that institutions often provided for important human needs and that abolishing them, as radicals often heedlessly advocated, could cause more harm than good. Mill finds in Coleridge a worthy critic of Protestant bibliolatry, or worship of the letter of the Bible. Coleridge justified the existence of a national church only if it performed an educative function for society. Even Utilitarians, Mill argues, cannot complain of a conservative philosopher who teaches that the "outward" object of virtue is "the greatest producible sum of happiness of all men." The aim of "Coleridge" is to demonstrate that a Tory philosopher, while operating as a conservator of truths which Tories have forgotten or which liberals have never known, must often be a better liberal than liberals are themselves.

Writing of Bentham and Coleridge, Mill remarks in "Coleridge": "Whoever could master the premises and combine the methods of both, would possess the entire English philosophy of his age." This passage provides the clue to the image of himself which Mill creates in the essays.

Rhetorically, in these essays Mill has found his characteristic voice, the voice of the whole philosopher who is able to transcend partial truths and achieve a comprehensive vision of reality. With minor variations, this is the voice in all of Mill's major writings.

During the 1840s the promise of Mill's earlier career came to fruition in two monumental works which established his reputation in England, *A System of Logic* (1843) and *Principles of Political Economy* (1848). While scholars in other disciplines have explored the significance of both works, literary critics have bestowed upon neither text the kind of attention which they have paid to Carlyle's writings on social conditions, Ruskin's on art and economics, and John Henry Newman's on religion. Yet both of Mill's works would repay literary analysis, for both are at one level polemical writings designed to persuade an audience through argument and imaginative rhetorical strategy. Both works project a vision of the world as flawed but improvable through rational means.

The most cautiously written of all Mill's work, *A System of Logic* began to take shape at least as far back as 1830, and the published work went through eight carefully revised editions in Mill's lifetime. Among his purposes was that of strengthening the claims of experiential philosophy by systematizing and validating its methods of observation, reasoning, and experimenting. In the process, *A System of Logic* both implicitly and explicitly undercuts transcendentalist assumptions. Although presented (perhaps somewhat disingenuously) as a neutral guide to rational processes which can be used by both a priori and experiential thinkers, *A System of Logic* is—and was perceived to be—an attack upon intuitionism. Part of the book's surprising popularity in Victorian times no doubt resulted from its being seen as a particularly weighty installment in "the omnipresent debate" (to borrow the title of Wendell V. Harris's 1981 book) between empiricism and transcendentalism in nineteenth-century England.

In this extensive survey of logic, book one clears the ground with a glance at the language used for naming and for formulating propositions. Mill seemingly skirts the issue of intuitive knowledge by ruling it outside the scope of logic: logic, he argues, is concerned not with how we know but how we judge what we think we know. Book two is devoted to deductive reasoning, including a close review of the syllogism. Although interesting, Mill's efforts here are not strikingly

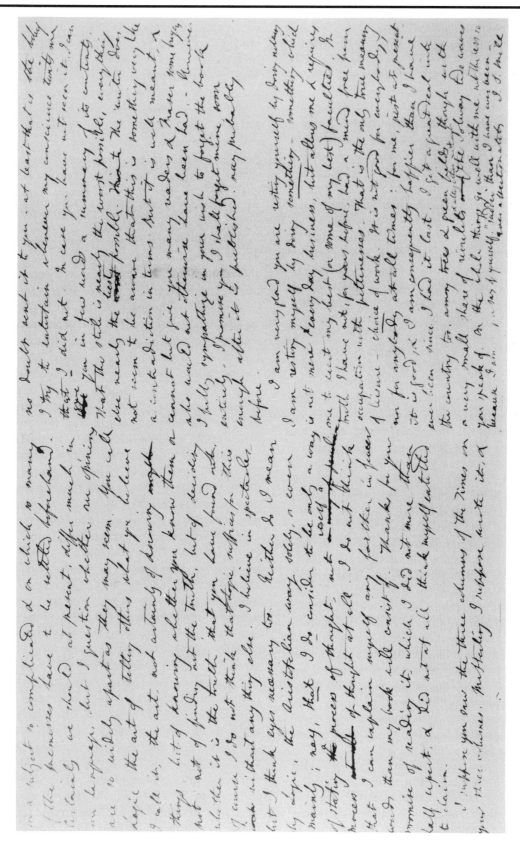

From a letter to Thomas Carlyle dated 8 August 1837, in which Mill explains his concept of "Logic," noting, "Certainly we should at present, differ much in our language, but I question whether our opinions are so widely apart as they may seem"
(*The Pierpont Morgan Library*)

original, deduction having already received considerable examination and development from the time of Aristotle onward. By contrast, induction was a comparatively neglected topic; consequently, the heart of *A System of Logic* is found in book three, an extensive and often original attempt to establish the means by which inductive reasoning can approximate an exact science. As Mill explains his position, validating inductive methods is imperative for three reasons: induction is crucial to any philosophy based upon experience, it is necessary for building reliable generalizations (and hence necessary for accurate deductive reasoning), and it is the method essential to modern science. Book four examines concerns which are "subsidiary" to induction (including, again, naming and philosophical language), and book five enjoyably enumerates the various fallacies that disrupt logic. Of most interest to students of literature is perhaps book six, "On the Logic of the Moral Sciences." Mill begins by addressing a question which deeply troubled him: does scientific predictability of human behavior negate free will? If so, then human liberty is an illusion. Mill, however, concludes that individual choice is one of the determinants of behavior. Hence, human choice is possible, and it matters. After wrestling with this demon, Mill investigates the validity of various methodologies in the social sciences. The final chapter of *A System of Logic*, "Of the Logic of Practice, or Art; Including Morality and Policy," discusses what Mill calls "Art" or the knowledge of duties, practical ethics, or morality. Art proposes the ends for which science clarifies the means. Every art requires a first principle of conduct, and (without attempting to justify his choice) Mill announces his own to be Utility—the greatest-happiness principle. But he adds a characteristic twist to this Benthamic goal: the greatest happiness of the greatest number can be best achieved by the individual's cultivation of an ideal nobility of character which must sometimes sacrifice immediate happiness or pleasure. The book, which began as a dry treatise on logic, concludes with a vision of the coming moral improvement of humanity.

Although at several points in the book Mill insists that *A System of Logic* is nonpolemical, the detached objectivity in the early part of book one yields increasingly to argumentative skirmishes with various opponents, especially intuitionists. If *A System of Logic* does not entirely rule out intuitive insights, it narrowly limits the field to which they can be legitimately applied. By the end of

the work, intuitionism seems to have been so circumscribed as to be rendered irrelevant to most human concerns. *A System of Logic*, then, bubbles with controversies, and Mill's rhetorical skill in handling opponents deserves greater attention than it has received. Moreover, the persona or image of the "speaker" Mill creates in the book develops imaginatively throughout the work. The depersonalized logician of book one is gradually humanized through several stages into the final chapter's prophet of human moral regeneration. Even in a work as abstruse as *A System of Logic*, Mill operates as an imaginative writer.

His next major work, the encyclopedic *Principles of Political Economy*, came at the end of a decade of social concern about economic matters. The "hungry forties" in Victorian England, capped by the horrors of the Irish potato famine, left political leaders and common readers equally eager for information about the "laws" of economic matters. Like *A System of Logic*, *Principles of Political Economy* is a large-scale work, designed to render a recondite science understandable to a mass audience. Its massive five books describe the laws of production, the methods of distribution, exchange and value, the impact of social progress on production and distribution, and the role of government in fostering a nation's economic well-being. By stressing that the laws of production are fixed but those of distribution are not, *Principles of Political Economy* opened the door for considerable speculation about the wisdom of many accepted economic practices. Even more than *A System of Logic*, Mill's 1848 work shows him at his best as theoretician, popularizer, and polemicist. Amid the abstract theorizing, the book includes concrete illustrations of economic life from around the world and throughout history. In a series of fascinating images, it gives the reader a view of political economy that is at once panoramic and specific. Images of primitive pastoral societies, utopian communities, ryots working on Indian farms, industrial laborers toiling in British factors, desperate Irish cotters facing rack rent and eviction, thriving American farms, and so on, bring the subject of political economy into human focus. Mill also engages once again in lively debate on controversial issues. He denounces, for example, English economic practices in Ireland, he suggests alternatives, and in later editions of *Principles of Political Economy* he inveighs against the British government's failures to act upon them.

An important clue to Mill's rhetorical method is contained in the book's full title, *Principles of Political Economy, with Some of Their Applications to Social Philosophy*. Mill, in short, is operating as both "Scientist" and "Artist." He is both describing economic laws and evaluating various economic practices in terms of a morality which posits the greatest happiness of the greatest number as its ultimate goal. Thus, *Principles of Political Economy* is also a polemical work, arguing the value of economic systems in terms of Mill's revised Utilitarian ethic. At one level, then, the book is an impassioned argument for means to improve the human lot. Once again, its rhetoric, which has been largely ignored by literary scholars, deserves at least as much attention as has been devoted to Mill's change of heart about socialism.

Three sections in *Principles of Political Economy* merit special mention for their enduring interest. The chapter "Of the Stationary State" pictures a time, dreaded by earlier theorists, when societies can no longer expand economically. Mill, however, argues that—provided population is held in check—such a state need not be feared; indeed, it is to be desired. With the necessities of life easily taken care of, humans will be able to devote their energies to the art of living, to self-cultivation. "It is scarcely necessary to remark," Mill makes a point of remarking, "that a stationary condition of capital and population implies no stationary state of human improvement." By arguing for population control, Mill shows himself a forerunner of modern ecologists: it would be catastrophic for the human spirit, he points out, for every last acre of earth to be utilized to support a vast population. With places of natural beauty and solitude lost or greatly reduced in number, individuals will lack a crucial resource for nurturing their characters.

The following chapter, "On the Probable Futurity of the Laboring Classes," is perhaps the most famous section of *Principles of Political Economy*. It predicts that eventually workers will reject upper-class paternalism in favor of their own autonomy. Ruskin, whose animosity toward *Principles of Political Economy* was great, perhaps saw himself as one of the paternalistic sentimentalists rebuked in this chapter. Also, this chapter, which originally rejected socialist schemes, was transformed in later editions (at Harriet Taylor's insistence) into an endorsement of them. As might be expected, considerable discussion has been generated among scholars about the history and implica-

tions of these changes. In the fifth book of *Principles of Political Economy*, which addresses the topic of government's legitimate role in economic matters, Mill discusses whether state-organized economies or free-enterprise systems better serve the cause of human improvement; he concludes that the preferable system is whichever one allows the greater room for individual liberty. Mill insists that, except when required by a greater good, laissez-faire or nonintervention by government "should be the general practice."

During the 1840s, as the relationship between Mill and Harriet Taylor deepened, the indignant feminism they shared increasingly influenced their thought, if not always their behavior. However radical their ideas, both contrived to live as conventionally as possible under the circumstances. Both withdrew from social life to a considerable extent, no doubt to quiet the gossip circulating about them. Harriet Taylor separated from her husband's bed but not his board, and Mill continued to live with his mother and sisters while forbidding any discussion of Harriet in his presence. In 1849, when John Taylor died of cancer, Harriet was genuinely distressed and went into a respectable period of mourning. Ever the indulgent husband, John Taylor had provided handsomely in his will for his wife's financial future, and Harriet apparently had no ideological qualms about accepting money from a husband whom she had estranged during his lifetime. Although both Mill and Harriet Taylor spent the next two years grumbling about the degenerate state of conventional matrimony, in April 1851 they slipped off to Melcombe Regis and were quietly married at the Register Office there. Later Mill went so far as to suggest that the two agnostics should remarry in a church ceremony. Before the civil ceremony Mill had written out a formal protest rejecting any legal rights which the marriage would confer upon him. Their marriage seems to have been less a partnership of equals than an acting out of chivalric male worship of the woman on the pedestal, and in this way it actually reflected certain Victorian ideals. Similarly, in retrospect the feminism that energized their social indignation often seems less a search for gender equality than an angry program designed to bolster female power by stressing the wrongs done to women and by ignoring the burdens imposed upon men and the problems faced by both sexes together. The quality of this feminism was to influence Mill's later writings, especially *The Subjection of Women*.

The announcement of his intended marriage proved to be the breaking point between Mill and his family, the separation being largely of his doing. Apparently feeling that his mother and siblings had received news of the impending nuptials with insufficient enthusiasm and respect, Mill heaped abuse on them and resolutely refused their attempts at reconciliation. Always touchy on the subject of Harriet Taylor, Mill could be vindictive when sufficiently aroused.

During their seven and a half years of married life, the couple lived quietly at Blackheath, crystallizing their thoughts in a series of works which, when published, would permanently establish Mill's fame as a thinker and writer. Although evidence is scanty, these works apparently originated in husband-and-wife conversations, were written down by him, revised by her, and rethought by both as time went on. Whatever the circumstances of composition, *On Liberty* (1859), *Utilitarianism* (1863), most of the *Autobiography* (1873), "Nature," and "Utility of Religion" (the last two published in *Three Essays on Religion*, 1874) were written during these years. Plans for other works were mapped out; these were published after Harriet Mill's death as *Considerations on Representative Government* (1861), *Auguste Comte and Positivism* (1865), and *The Subjection of Women* (1869).

Plagued by poor health, both John and Harriet Mill often resorted to travels on the Continent, together or separately. In 1858, just after Mill had retired from East India House, the couple set off for southern France. Along the way, Harriet Mill took ill and died on 3 November 1858. Emotionally devastated, Mill purchased a house within sight of the cemetery in Avignon where she was buried. For the rest of his life he spent several months of every year in southern France and often meditated for hours at her grave. Harriet Taylor Mill had become nothing less than his sacred muse in the Religion of Humanity.

No aspect of Mill studies elicits greater controversy than his relationship with Harriet Taylor. There is still little agreement about her as a person, about how and what she contributed to Mill's thought, and about whether that contribution was beneficial. In the *Autobiography* and elsewhere Mill's encomiums on his wife as a paragon of intellect and virtue are stated in such extravagant terms as almost to invite disbelief. In *John Stuart Mill and the Harriet Taylor Myth* (1960), H. O. Pappe has written of the Mill-Taylor affair, and numerous critics would agree that her saintly character and intellectual brilliance were largely figments of Mill's imagination. Others, however, would not. Commentators on Harriet Taylor range from those who depict her as Mill's intellectual equal and partner to those who depict her as a would-be bluestocking without original ideas. She has been seen by some as a liberated woman who defied Victorian conventions, by others as a pampered female who manipulated two gullible males into catering to her every whim. The destruction—at her wish—of most of her correspondence with Mill has complicated attempts to assess her character and mind. That she contributed in some way to Mill's work is clear enough, but the nature of that contribution remains uncertain despite admirable biographical and textual research in recent years. Even when the contribution is clearly established—as in the laboring-class chapter of *Principles of Political Economy*—its value remains hotly contested. Of the numerous attempts to assess Harriet Taylor's influence, perhaps the most intriguing and controversial is Gertrude Himmelfarb's *On Liberty and Liberalism: The Case of John Stuart Mill* (1974), expressing her view of "the other John Stuart Mill," whose balanced thought was skewed by Harriet into radicalism, especially in *On Liberty* and *The Subjection of Women*.

Three months after Harriet Mill's death, Mill saw to it that *On Liberty* was published. The book was, in some special way, their joint production, and Mill refused to alter it once "her all but unrivalled wisdom" was no longer there to advise him. *On Liberty* was immediately hailed as a classic, a status which it enjoys to this day despite numerous critical reservations about it. Unlike many of Mill's other works, *On Liberty* has drawn the attention of literary scholars who have analyzed its skillful weaving of argument and art. Written in Mill's most energetically cogent style, the book is both a lucid argument and a rallying cry defending the civil liberty of the individual against the pressures of the state and mass society. Coming across *On Liberty* at a bookseller's, Charles Kingsley read it through at once and insisted that it had made him "a clearer-headed, braver-minded man on the spot." Many another reader has had a similar experience. The impact of *On Liberty* on Western thought and law, as well as on personal convictions, is surely enormous.

The book opens with a historical survey of the conflict between liberty and authority. Images of struggle are effectively deployed to convey a sense of dire confrontation between forces

Mill and his stepdaughter, Helen Taylor, circa 1865

of good and evil. Mill understood that the old conflicts between rulers and populace were being replaced by a new conflict between governments of the masses and the individual. Even in democracies, the majority can become the despot that rules minorities and individuals. To defend individual liberty, Mill defines "one very simple principle" which it is the purpose of the entire book to expound: "the sole end for which mankind are warranted, individually or collectively, in interfering with the liberty of action of any of their number, is self-protection." Only to prevent harm to others can an individual's actions be legitimately restrained by the state, society, or other individuals. This principle requires that, barring harm to others, the individual be allowed to exercise freedom of conscience and opinion, freedom of thought and expression, and freedom to live life as he or she sees best. In the initial chapter of *On Liberty* Mill has defined—as succinctly as anyone has—what in fact is the guiding political principle of genuinely free societies throughout the world.

Chapter two is a vigorous defense of freedom of thought and discussion. In it Mill argues forcefully that such freedom needs to be permit-

ted for three reasons. First, if an opinion is true, prohibiting it denies its truth to humanity. Second, even if an opinion is in error, it may contain a portion of the truth which it would be pernicious to silence. Third, even if an opinion is entirely false, allowing it into the marketplace of ideas prevents truth from ossifying into dead dogma. A truth being defended is a truth kept alive. The text of the chapter gets well beyond the bare bones of this argument, however, as Mill introduces controversy and vividly re-creates historical and hypothetical examples of truth's being suppressed by force. Today, its defense of freedom of discussion remains pertinent and controversial. However, even for some twentieth-century readers sympathetic to the principle of freedom of speech, *On Liberty* can raise troubling questions, perhaps most thoughtfully articulated by Edward Alexander in his "Post-Holocaust" retrospect of Mill's liberalism in *The Victorian Experience: The Prose Writers* (1982), edited by Richard A. Levine.

Chapter three, "Of Individuality, as One of the Elements of Well Being," is at the heart of *On Liberty* and remains a classic document in Western liberal thought. It is also among the most rhetorically powerful texts Mill ever wrote. Here, Mill combines his defense of liberty with his ethical goal of the improvement of humanity. Only freedom to live as one decides is best, he argues, can produce humanity's moral development. Having the "right" way imposed upon the individual by force necessarily stunts the individual's moral growth. This chapter argues not only for "negative freedom" from coercion but also for "positive freedom" to find one's own best mode of human development. Determined to move readers by feeling as well as to convince them by logic, Mill employs a wide range of rhetorical strategies in this chapter, most notably the strikingly contrasted images of painful constriction and spontaneous energy, of mechanical deadness and natural growth. Memorable images include pollarded trees, a stagnant Dutch canal versus the magnificent outpouring of Niagara, and the painfully bound feet of a Chinese lady. In this chapter, tolerance is not enough: Mill urges a joyous acceptance of everyone's individuality as a potential path toward the overall improvement of the human race.

A stirring discourse on the tendency of government and society to interfere with the individual, chapter four excoriates the near-universal tendency of people to mistake their customs and preferences for cosmic laws. Citing examples, Mill skillfully moves from cases of irrational persecution which readers can easily recognize as such, to cases of persecution which they are likely to have countenanced. By doing so, rhetoric and logic are shrewdly deployed to achieve that most difficult of tasks—awakening the audience to awareness of its own intolerance. The fifth and final chapter presents briefly some situations in which government may legitimately interfere with individual liberty. The final pages of the work, however, are saved for another vigorous defense of freedom, thus concluding *On Liberty* with a rousing peroration.

Shortly after his wife's death, Mill had felt himself paralyzed by grief. But soon he began to revive, and indeed the 1860s were like a second spring in his life. His stepdaughter, Helen Taylor, now assumed her mother's role as his source of feminine inspiration, and agitation for a new reform bill reawakened his youthful zest for political skirmishes. During the 1860s Mill produced some of his most thought-provoking work, and—improbably enough—he was elected to Parliament.

The first work resulting from Mill's renewed interest in politics was his *Considerations on Representative Government*, apparently written mostly during 1860. The book crystallizes Mill's mature thinking on how to maximize the benefits of the new democracies while limiting their potential liabilities. Compared with the fiery rhetoric of *On Liberty*, *Considerations on Representative Government* is a mellow work. But like nearly everything else Mill wrote it generates its own interest through its display of an incisive mind probing pertinent questions. And it too has its lively polemical passages. It begins with theory, tying political matters to ethical concerns: characteristically, Mill argues that representative government is usually best because it is conducive to the improvement of humanity. The mass of people should elect their leaders, but the business of government is best left to those leaders and not to the populace itself. Although the book's suggestions were anything but foregone conclusions in 1860, many of them have since proven to be valuable components of democratic structures (for example, extension of the franchise to all tax-paying adults, woman suffrage). Other suggestions may seem quaintly reactionary (for example, opposition to the secret ballot, a plan for allowing extra votes to more educated people). Still other suggestions remain intriguing possibilities, at least in the United States (for example, limited campaign spending).

Of considerable importance to later moralists, Mill's next major work—*Utilitarianism*, published in 1863—is a compact volume which derives much of its interest from Mill's effort to accomplish a great deal in relatively few pages. *On Liberty* is the exposition of a single principle, but the aims of *Utilitarianism* are many and diverse. Because the pleasure-pain ethic of Utility was often derided in the early nineteenth century as "sensualism" and "pig philosophy," Mill adopts a tone of high seriousness in this volume, usually maintaining a loftiness which appealed enormously to Victorian earnestness. As much as he can, Mill aims at a nonpartisan discussion; usually he refrains from overt objections to intuitionist ethics and strives for an impartiality above party divisions. In addition, Mill attempts to align the old-style Benthamite calculations of pleasures and pains with his own new-style utility directed toward the moral development of the individual and the race.

In *Utilitarianism* Mill attempts other compressed reformulations which for some readers raise more questions than they answer. For example, he argues that in calculating pleasures the quality of the pleasure affects its quantity; that is, the "higher" pleasures of the more fully developed person outrank the "lower" pleasures of the ignorant sensualist. "It is better to be a human being dissatisfied than a pig satisfied," Mill writes, "better to be Socrates dissatisfied than a fool satisfied." The appeal that such a doctrine would have had to Victorian audiences is unquestionable. A similar problem arises when Mill attempts to provide supporting evidence for the idea that happiness is an ultimate good. Such ultimate aims, as Mill had pointed out in *A System of Logic*, do not admit of the usual kinds of logical proof; the best that one can do is offer "considerations" to the reason in order to elicit its assent. The "consideration" offered here is that happiness is desired; therefore, it is desirable. Likewise, because each individual desires his own happiness, the general happiness of the human race is also desirable. The chain reaction of disagreement and defense which this passage has set off is perhaps best left to professional moralists, but the student of literature should note how adroitly this same passage links "happiness" with "virtue." Mill's little book on Utilitarianism not only instigated an ongoing debate over ethical principles but also achieved its rhetorical goal of winning a

THE LADIES' ADVOCATE.

Mrs. Bull. "LOR, MR. MILL! WHAT A LOVELY SPEECH YOU *DID* MAKE. I DO DECLARE I HADN'T THE SLIGHTEST NOTION WE WERE SUCH MISERABLE CREATURES. NO ONE CAN SAY IT WAS *YOUR* FAULT THAT THE CASE BROKE DOWN."

Cartoon published in Punch, *1 June 1867, after Mill unsuccessfully attempted to legislate voting rights for women in a Reform Bill amendment*

wider respect for Utility among philosophers and lay readers alike.

The year 1865 saw the publication of two books by Mill, each an assessment of another thinker's work. The books are as different as the two men they evaluate. *Auguste Comte and Positivism* is a compact work for a popular audience; *An Examination of Sir William Hamilton's Philosophy* is exhaustive and ponderous. The book on Comte resembles Mill's earlier, lively essay on Bentham; that on Hamilton resembles a mammoth sequel to *A System of Logic*. As in "Bentham," *Auguste Comte and Positivism* employs anticlimax first to exalt and then to degrade Comte's work. This pattern fit Mill's experience of Comte's thought. He owed much to Comte's earlier writings with their discussion of the three stages of history, the concept of altruism, the methodology of sociology, and the Religion of Humanity. But Comte's later work with its advocacy of despotism was a devastating denial of all that Mill held dear. In Mill's book, fulsome praise of Comte's *Cours de philosophie positive* (1830-1842) is followed by a catalogue of his absurdities in constructing a repressive Religion of Humanity with himself as Grand

Pontiff. A favorable estimate of Comte's contribution to the philosophy of science is followed by a devastating account of his totalitarian utopia. As in "Bentham," the worst that can be said is left until last, and the text's final word is, significantly, "ridiculous." In *An Examination of Sir William Hamilton's Philosophy* Mill at last offers a full-scale critique of intuitionism through the study of one of its leading nineteenth-century practitioners. Although the book is overtly polemical, the controversy usually fizzles—except in a few memorable passages such as the one that takes issue with one of Hamilton's disciples, Henry Mansel, on the nature of God's goodness. Part of the problem may be that Hamilton, at least as this book presents him, seems hardly worth the extensive effort made to refute him. To many readers, it may seem that Mill spends most of his time flogging a dead horse. The examination of Hamilton, however, should not be underestimated, for it is the capstone of Mill's quarrel with what he regarded as the most potentially dangerous philosophy of his day. Nor should it be ignored, for it contains Mill's more mature views on several crucial philosophic questions.

In 1865, the same year that his critiques of Comte and Hamilton were published, Mill was invited to stand for Parliament as Liberal member for Westminster. Although he attached some extraordinary conditions to his consent and conducted a most unorthodox campaign, he was elected. His term in Parliament deserves closer attention than it has yet received (a book on the subject has been promised), if only for fuller accounts of his involvement in three important events. First, his participation in the tumultuous debates over the 1867 Reform Bill needs to be clarified. (Mill introduced an amendment to extend voting rights to women; although defeated, the amendment won seventy-three votes.) Second, his involvement in debates over the Irish question warrants closer scrutiny. (Mill's 1868 pamphlet *England and Ireland* succinctly presents his views on how wiser British rule could alleviate Irish troubles.) And, finally, his full role in the recall and prosecution of Governor Edward John Eyre of Jamaica needs to be chronicled. When unrest among island blacks had erupted in violence at Morant Bay, government troops under Eyre retaliated by killing and imprisoning hundreds of blacks. With dubious legality, Eyre also executed a black leader who had been one of his most outspoken critics. Although Mill's effort to prosecute Eyre for murder was unsuccessful, he effectively expressed in speeches and letters the outrage of humanitarians against Eyre's conduct. (Mill's condemnation of racism can be seen in his 1850 essay "The Negro Question," a stinging reply to Carlyle's racist tract, "Occasional Discourse on the Negro Question," published in 1849. Both appeared in *Fraser's Magazine*.)

Despite the distractions of Westminster politics, Mill took time off between parliamentary sessions to write one of his most magisterial works, the *Inaugural Address Delivered to the University of St. Andrews* (1867). Elected to an honorary post at the Scottish university, Mill was obliged to deliver a lecture on a subject relevant to university concerns. As his topic he chose the nature and value of a liberal education, and for the address he wrote one of the most impressive accounts of what a university education can be. Ironically, this tribute came from a man who had never gone to college. Like John Henry Newman's *Idea of a University, Defined and Illustrated* (1873) (with which it can be compared without embarrassment), Mill's *Inaugural Address* envisions an ideal university as a goal toward which actual universities can strive: "Let us try what conscientious and intelligent teaching can do, before we presume to decide what cannot be done." Taking an authoritative overview of the various educational disciplines in his speech, Mill discourses on the contribution which each makes toward the formation of a well-educated mind—and by extension toward the ultimate improvement of humanity. The sweep of Mill's intellect is superbly displayed as he demonstrates not only his understanding of what Newman called "the circle of the sciences" but also his judicious balancing of the various disciplines. At the outset of the address Mill rejects the notion that universities exist primarily for professional training: "Men are men before they are lawyers, or physicians, or merchants, or manufacturers; and if you make them capable and sensible men, they will make themselves sensible lawyers or physicians." Beginning with the study of language and literature, Mill goes on to consider the role of the sciences in the university, the emergence of the social sciences, and the value of mathematics, logic, ethics, politics, jurisprudence, aesthetics, and religious studies. The aim of the university is to nourish the whole person by providing an outline of human knowledge in many disciplines, by fostering an understanding of scientific methodologies and an appreciation of the arts, and by disciplining moral awareness. Mill's persona in the address is that of "the imperial in-

"A Feminine Philosopher," caricature of Mill published in Vanity Fair, *29 March 1873 (Collection of Jerold J. Savory)*

tellect" which has taken all knowledge as its province and has achieved a wisdom transcending partial views: it is perhaps Mill's most successful depiction of the whole philosopher who combines science and art. Although parliamentary duties delayed Mill's visit to St. Andrews for more than a year and although the address reportedly took three hours to deliver, students cheered Mill enthusiastically, especially his defense of the university as a place of free thought. Although not as well known as some of his other works, the inaugural address provides a brilliant epitome of Mill's thought, and it remains a stimulating challenge to later generations of educators and students alike.

In the 1868 election Mill was not returned to Parliament, voters apparently being disenchanted with some of his more quixotic endeavors. Losing no time, however, Mill—with Helen

Taylor by his side—took on his next challenge, a drive to obtain woman suffrage. To help create an atmosphere propitious to the cause, Mill decided to publish *The Subjection of Women*, which had been in manuscript for nearly a decade. An exceptionally passionate attempt to consolidate the feminist feeling and to sway public opinion, *The Subjection of Women*, which appeared in 1869, was greeted with extreme responses of outrage and adulation. Reactions to the book remain similarly divided to this day.

Like *On Liberty* (to which it might be considered a sequel), *The Subjection of Women* sets out to argue one principle, "a principle of perfect equality" between the sexes. Mill knew his rhetorical task was a formidable one: he had to dislodge from his audience's deepest feelings the "intuition" that the socially prescribed roles for women and men were "natural" ones. To win his case, he summoned his most impassioned arguments and subtle imagery. In the book Mill surveys the legal position of women, especially wives, in Victorian England and finds it analogous to that of slaves. Mill argues for equal opportunity for women in education and the professions, debunking the notion that women were intellectually inferior to men or incapable of handling positions of public authority. The final chapter focuses on the increase in human talent available to society when women are permitted to compete with men outside the home. Mill utilizes numerous rhetorical devices to win reader assent. Most notably, he depicts belief in male dominance as a form of idolatry left over from barbaric ages: it is, Mill writes, "as if a gigantic dolmen, or a vast temple of Jupiter Olympius, occupied the site of St. Paul's and received daily worship, while the surrounding Christian churches were only resorted to on fasts and festivals." As in *On Liberty*, in *The Subjection of Women* Mill uses contrasting images of the "natural" and the "artificial" and depicts history as a battle between authority and liberty, with the gradual victory of liberty ensuring the present drive for women's emancipation. As a part of this historical vision, the text includes considerable master-slave language to reinforce the concept of the legal position of wives in Victorian England. In terms which might describe an idealized version of his relationship with his wife, Mill envisages a new union of emancipated women and men working together as equals.

Predictably, *The Subjection of Women* has been hailed by feminists of both sexes. But some recent partisans, including Susan Brownmiller in her introduction to the 1971 edition of Mill's book, have faulted a few of its positions, especially Mill's chivalric attitude toward women and his traditional view of family breadwinning: "In an otherwise just state of things, it is not, therefore, I think, a desirable custom, that the wife should contribute by her labour to the income of the family." Those readers, such as John Gordon in *The Myth of Monstrous Male and Other Feminist Fables* (1982), who have more serious reservations about *The Subjection of Women* find in it many of the recurrent excesses of which radical feminist literature is often accused—the chip-on-the-shoulder stridency that generates more heat than light, the exaggerated analogy between the situation of women and the oppression of blacks, the reduction of the history of the sexes to the battle of the sexes, and the simplistic stereotyping of women as helpless victims and of men as monstrous oppressors. Even more problematic is Mill's effort in *The Subjection of Women* to address women's concerns in a vacuum, without making an equal effort to understand the social pressures and disabilities experienced by men. Keenly alive to what the Victorian age called "The Woman Question," Mill perhaps never recognized and formulated "The Man Question"—to say nothing of "The Man and Woman Question."

Despite Mill's best efforts for woman suffrage, the movement faltered, partly because of increasing resistance and partly because of internal dissension among its partisans. Mill, however, had other interests to engage his attention, including additional work on his *Autobiography* and other writings. In his mid sixties, as his health began to decline, Mill became increasingly sunny in disposition, although little of his amiableness can be glimpsed in the somewhat grim portrait which G. F. Watts painted in 1873. Shortly after the portrait was completed, Mill and his stepdaughter, Helen Taylor, set off once again for Avignon. He always seemed happiest being near his wife's grave, now marked by a marble mausoleum engraved with another of Mill's elaborate tributes to her. Early in May, Mill caught a chill after an extended walking tour, and his condition worsened rapidly. He died on 7 May 1873 and was buried beside his wife. But even after death, Mill continued to be a figure of controversy, especially as additional works appeared in print under Helen Taylor's supervision.

Of the works published posthumously, the most important is his *Autobiography*. In the 1850s, when much of "the Life" was written, Mill envi-

Portrait by G. F. Watts painted shortly before Mill's death in 1873 (National Portrait Gallery, London)

sioned it at the head of a collection of his works, and today most scholars consider it an indispensable introduction to his life and thought. Besides being a crucial social and personal document, Mill's *Autobiography* is an artistic reconstruction of his life which dramatizes his intellectual and moral development. Because manuscripts, as well as other materials, have survived for both the early draft written in the 1850s and the later, extended version completed in 1870, the *Autobiography* offers readers a rare glimpse of one of Mill's works in the process of creation. The Toronto edition of Mill's works, which began to appear in 1963, provides an invaluable service by carefully annotating and printing the parallel passages of the two manuscript versions on facing pages, thereby allowing readers to see at a glance how Mill and Harriet Taylor altered his original wording. The question of multiple authorship in the *Autobiography* has been carefully explored in Jack Stillinger's 1983 article "Who Wrote J. S. Mill's *Autobiography*?" in *Victorian Studies*. The early draft includes material which the Mills later suppressed, and the final version demonstrates the kind of material which they wanted to appear in the "official" life. The early draft is more personal; the

completed *Autobiography* is more polished. As John M. Robson noted in a 1965 article for *College Composition and Communication*, there is a shift from the "private" to the "public" voice between the two texts.

In the opening paragraph of the *Autobiography* Mill sets up a tripartite pattern which anticipates the book's structure. He lists three reasons for writing his life: first, to record for an age interested in education an account of his own unique tutelage; second, to record for an age of transition the successive stages of his mental and moral development; and third, to acknowledge the debts which his development owes to others. Those to whom Mill is indebted are classified into three groups: those who are well known, those who are less well known, and the "one to whom most of all is due, one whom the world had no opportunity of knowing." (This "one," the reader learns later, is Mill's wife.) The paragraph's tripartite pattern introduces an autobiography which presents Mill's life in three significant phases: his Benthamic education and youthful activism overseen by his father, his acquisition of broader emotional and intellectual insights during his mental crisis and the subsequent search for many-sidedness, and the achievement of full philosophic vision during his evolving relationship with Harriet Taylor Mill. This last phase of Mill's life is also divided into three sections: his intimate friendship with her, their marriage, and the communion of their spirits after her death. Mill's life is thus presented as a mental and spiritual journey, a philosophic *commedia* in which the hero begins in a loveless *inferno*, struggles through a *purgatorio* of mental crisis and striving for fuller knowledge, and enters into a *paradiso* of philosophic vision and activity presided over by a Beatrice whose powers transcend death.

Mill's account of his childhood education and youthful zealotry is marked by irony and anticlimax. James Mill's impressive achievement in educating his son is constantly undercut by details of the father's inadequacies and the drawbacks of the education. The *Autobiography* presents Mill's father as a harsh, unloving man whose emotional failures considerably undermined his accomplishment in educating his son. Repeatedly, the text stresses the moral harm done to both father and son by James Mill's failure to cultivate emotion, especially benevolent and compassionate feelings— in a word, love. Likewise, Mill presents his own radical activism as remarkable but somehow mechanical; it is rooted in no deep ability to feel and love. The inadequacy of Mill's early education becomes clear during the second phase of his life. The young Mill asks himself: "Suppose that all your objects in life were realized; that all the changes in institutions and opinions which you are looking forward to, could be completely effected at this very instant: would this be a great joy and happiness to you?" When an "irrepressible self-consciousness" honestly answers "No!" the youth is left desolate. Clearly, man cannot live by Utilitarian reform alone. During his mental crisis young Mill is assisted by a series of guides (including Wordsworth, John Sterling, and Carlyle) who lead him toward fuller philosophic vision. It is only in the third phase of his life, however, that Mill encounters his ultimate guide, Harriet Taylor, a "natural poet" seeking surer intellectuality. In the final section of the *Autobiography* Harriet and John Mill develop together toward genuine philosophic wisdom.

Although Mill describes himself as someone who grew up without religion, he uses religious language in the *Autobiography* to recount his life as a sacred quest. Indeed, this language helps to explain the embarrassed and incredulous reactions of some readers to Mill's portrait of his wife's mind and character, for the *Autobiography* presents her as a secular saint in the Religion of Humanity, a Victorian Beatrice who survives death to remain an inspiration to her lover. Those who can accept Mill's vision of his wife or who are persuaded by the text to suspend their disbelief are obviously better prepared to accept the myth of Mill's life as presented in the *Autobiography*. Those who question whether the "real" or "historical" Harriet Mill can be reconciled with the exalted portrait of her in the *Autobiography* have trouble with this myth. There is no avoiding the issue. After dramatizing the state of helpless despondency into which Harriet's death throws him, Mill depicts how her inspiration has reinvigorated his life and thought. As Helen Taylor assumes her mother's role as Mill's feminine inspiration, it is as if Harriet has been reincarnated in her daughter. Helen Taylor becomes Harriet's apotheosis, and Mill's life flourishes under her guidance. The latter pages of the *Autobiography* recount a series of episodes, each constructed upon a tripartite pattern: an announcement that Mill has a duty to perform, an account of the crisis enjoining that duty, and a statement of his success in performing it. Whether puncturing the danger-

The mausoleum at St. Véran, near Avignon, burial place of John Stuart and Harriet Taylor Mill

ously inflated reputation of Sir William Hamilton or talking sense to Hyde Park demonstrators, he succeeds unexpectedly, but behind these successes lies the guidance of Harriet-Helen. When at last the various crises have subsided, Mill's "memoir" closes with a paragraph radiating a quiet joy and contentment. The *commedia* is completed.

The second of Mill's major works published posthumously was *Three Essays on Religion* (1874), composed of "Nature," "Utility of Religion," and "Theism." The first two essays were written in the early 1850s, the third between 1868 and 1870. The three essays were not intended to form a unit, as Helen Taylor remarked in her introductory notice, and some readers have considerable difficulty reconciling the views expressed in them. For a student of literature, however, the essays are perhaps best approached as three reports from a questioning mind groping its way from angry skepticism to tentative affirmation. In this view of them, the essays form another variant of the pattern of conversion so familiar in Victorian poetry and prose. "Nature" approximates Mill's everlasting no, "Utility of Religion" his center of indifference, and "Theism" the everlasting yea—or at least a qualified version of it. One cannot help but notice, in any event, that the passionate antagonism toward supernatural belief in "Nature" and "Utility of Religion" mellows in "Theism" into quiet acceptance of "imaginative hope" concerning immortality and the goodness of God.

Containing some of the most vivid denunciations Mill ever wrote, "Nature" castigates any morality based upon a maxim enjoining humanity to "follow nature." Spectacularly violent imagery depicting nature on a rampage is used to heap scorn upon those who have urged humanity to follow such a model. "In sober truth," Mill declares indignantly, "nearly all the things which men are hanged or imprisoned for doing to one another are nature's everyday performances." From one angle, the essay represents one more expression of Victorian revulsion against the lingering Romantic tendency to worship nature; from a broader perspective, it is a biting reply to ethical prescriptions through the ages which have urged people to imitate a vaguely defined "nature." It is certainly one of the angriest depictions of "Nature red in tooth and claw" produced during Victorian times. In ringing tones, Mill proclaims that if humanity intends to improve at all its only hope is to reject entirely the insane practices of nature. (It is, incidentally, intriguing to consider how this view of nature can be reconciled with Mill's impassioned plea for the preservation of natural wilderness in the "Stationary State" chapter of *Principles of Political Economy* or with the depiction of nature as a benevolent moral force in chapter two of the *Autobiography*, a chapter apparently written around the same time "Nature" was.) The essay is a fervent refusal to worship nature and nature's God when their doings are so patently vicious.

The tone of "Utility of Religion" is only slightly less hostile in its assessment of supernatural religion. Indeed, the first part of the essay might be better titled "The Un-Utility of Religion," for it argues that belief in the supernatural is not essential for genuine morality. According to this essay, widespread acceptance of moral practices, early education, and the individual's desire to win public approval can affect ethical behavior even better than fear of hell or hope of heaven. The tone of the essay softens somewhat when Mill grants that in the past supernatural beliefs did help to keep common humanity moral, but in the latter part of the essay he argues that such supernaturalism is no longer credible to

thinking people and that the Religion of Humanity can serve even better by holding up models of human behavior for others to follow. As progress makes life more gratifying for greater numbers of people, humanity will be able to surrender more easily its hope of immortal life. "Utility of Religion" thus represents something of a midpoint between the fierce nay-sayings of "Nature" and the cautious yeas of "Theism."

After the fierce polemics of the two previous essays, the quiet rationalism of "Theism" is almost startling. Calmly setting out to review the grounds of theistic belief, in the essay Mill dispassionately examines some of the more common arguments for the existence of God. He rejects nearly all, giving only qualified support to a version of the argument from design in the universe. Propped by this thin support, the essay argues that monotheism is compatible with objective evidence. Mill eventually justifies belief in a God of limited powers who calls humanity to assist in the struggle against evil. Finally, because the evidence for and against belief in immortality is inconclusive, Mill argues that thinking people may legitimately indulge in the "imaginative hope" that human life survives death. For those who feel that Mill betrayed the apparent atheism of his earlier writings, "Theism" is seen as the last infirmity of a noble mind. For others—including Gertrude Himmelfarb in *On Liberty and Liberalism*—the essay represents a candid expression of a mind at last gathering the courage of its own beliefs. In any event, after the rhetorical storms of "Nature" and "Utility of Religion," "Theism" resembles a haven of quiet questioning and cautious affirmation.

While the debate over Mill's status as prose artist is likely to continue, additional literary analyses of his writings should help to clarify how his prose manages to achieve the strong effects it often does. Just as scholars in other disciplines have examined how Mill was able to blend Utilitarian logic and moral passion to create a philosophy of human improvement, literary scholars need to examine more deeply how he was able to fuse rational argument and imaginative artistry to create some of the most memorable prose statements of the Victorian age.

Letters:
Earlier Letters, 1812-1848, 2 volumes, edited by
    Francis E. Mineka (Toronto: University of
    Toronto Press, 1963);

Later Letters, 1849-1873, 4 volumes, edited by Mineka and Dwight N. Lindley (Toronto: University of Toronto Press, 1972).

Bibliography:

Michael Laine, *Bibliography of Works on John Stuart Mill* (Toronto: University of Toronto Press, 1982).

Biographies:

Alexander Bain, *John Stuart Mill: A Criticism, with Personal Recollections* (London: Holt, 1882);

Michael St. John Packe, *The Life of John Stuart Mill* (New York: Macmillan, 1954);

Bruce Mazlish, *James and John Stuart Mill: Father and Son in the Nineteenth Century* (New York: Basic Books, 1975).

References:

Susan Hardy Aiken, "Scripture and Poetic Discourse in *The Subjection of Women*," *PMLA*, 98 (May 1983): 353-373;

Edward Alexander, "John Stuart Mill: A Post-Holocaust Retrospect," in *The Victorian Experience: The Prose Writers*, edited by Richard A. Levine (Athens: Ohio University Press, 1982), pp. 83-111;

Alexander, *Matthew Arnold and John Stuart Mill* (New York: Columbia University Press, 1965);

Eugene R. August, *John Stuart Mill: A Mind at Large* (New York: Scribners, 1975);

August, "Mill as Sage: The Essay on Bentham," *PMLA*, 89 (January 1974): 142-153;

August, "Mill's *Autobiography* as Philosophic *Commedia*," *Victorian Poetry*, 11 (Summer 1973): 143-162;

Rise B. Axelrod, "Argument and Strategy in Mill's *The Subjection of Women*," *Victorian Newsletter*, no. 46 (Fall 1974): 10-14;

James R. Bennet, "Mill, Francis W. Newman, and Socialism: Mill's Two Argumentative Voices," *Mill News Letter*, 2 (Fall 1966): 2-7;

Richard A. Cherwitz and James W. Hilkins, "John Stuart Mill's *On Liberty*: Implications for the Epistemology of the New Rhetoric," *Quarterly Journal of Speech*, 65 (February 1979): 12-24;

Willem Remmelt De Jong, *The Semantics of John Stuart Mill*, translated by H. D. Morton (Dodrecht, Netherlands: Reidel, 1982);

Alan Donagan, "Victorian Philosophical Prose: J. S. Mill and F. H. Bradley," in *The Art of Victorian Prose*, edited by George Levine and William Madden (New York: Oxford University Press, 1968), pp. 53-72;

John B. Ellery, *John Stuart Mill* (New York: Twayne, 1964);

Andrew Griffin, "The Interior Garden of John Stuart Mill," in *Nature and the Victorian Imagination*, edited by U. C. Knoepflmacher and G. B. Tennyson (Berkeley: University of California Press, 1977), pp. 171-186;

John Grube, "*On Liberty* as a Work of Art," *Mill News Letter*, 5 (Fall 1969): 2-6;

Wendell V. Harris, "The Warp of Mill's 'Fabric' of Thought," *Victorian Newsletter*, no. 37 (Spring 1970): 1-7;

F. A. Hayek, *John Stuart Mill and Harriet Taylor* (Chicago: University of Chicago Press, 1951);

Gertrude Himmelfarb, *On Liberty and Liberalism: The Case of John Stuart Mill* (New York: Knopf, 1974);

Gordon D. Hirsch, "Organic Imagery and the Psychology of Mill's *On Liberty*," *Mill News Letter*, 10 (Summer 1975): 3-13;

Nels Juleus, "The Rhetoric of Opposites: Mill and Carlyle," *Pennsylvania Speech Annual* (September 1960): 1-7;

F. R. Leavis, Introduction to *Mill on Bentham and Coleridge* (London: Chatto & Windus, 1950); republished as *On Bentham and Coleridge*, by John Stuart Mill (New York: Harper, 1962);

Jonathan Loesberg, *Fictions of Consciousness: Mill, Newman, and the Reading of Victorian Prose* (New Brunswick, N.J.: Rutgers University Press, 1986);

Glenn K. S. Man, "Structure and Narration in Mill's *Autobiography*," *Revue de l'Université d'Ottawa*, 51 (April-June 1981): 304-314;

Charles Matthews, "Argument Through Metaphor in John Stuart Mill's *On Liberty*," *Language and Style*, 4 (Summer 1972): 221-228;

James McDonnell, "Success and Failure: A Rhetorical Study of the First Two Chapters of Mill's *Autobiography*," *University of Toronto Quarterly*, 45 (Winter 1976): 109-122;

Emery Neff, *Carlyle and Mill: An Introduction to Victorian Thought*, revised edition (New York: Columbia University Press, 1952);

H. O. Pappe, *John Stuart Mill and the Harriet Taylor Myth* (Melbourne: Melbourne University Press, 1960);

Keith Rinehart, "John Stuart Mill's *Autobiography*: Its Art and Appeal," *University of Kansas City Review*, 19 (1953): 265-273;

John M. Robson, "John Stuart Mill," in *Victorian Prose: A Guide to Research*, edited by David J.

DeLaura (New York: Modern Language Association, 1973), pp. 185-218;

Robson, "Mill's 'Autobiography': The Public and the Private Voice," *College Composition and Communication*, 16 (February 1965): 97-105;

Robson and Michael Laine, eds., *James and John Stuart Mill: Papers of the Centenary Conference* (Toronto: University of Toronto Press, 1976);

Alan Ryan, *John Stuart Mill* (New York: Pantheon Books, 1970);

David R. Sanderson, "Metaphor and Method in John Stuart Mill's *On Liberty*," *Victorian Newsletter*, no. 34 (Fall 1968): 22-25;

J. B. Schneewind, ed., *Mill: A Collection of Critical Essays* (Garden City, N.Y.: Doubleday, 1968);

Robert C. Schweik, "Mill's Analogies in *On Liberty*: The Uses of Inconsistency," *Mill News Letter*, 10 (Summer 1988): 3-7;

F. Parvin Sharpless, *The Literary Criticism of John Stuart Mill* (The Hague: Mouton, 1967);

Jack Stillinger, "Who Wrote J. S. Mill's *Autobiography?*," *Victorian Studies*, 27 (1983): 7-23;

Thomas Woods, *Poetry and Philosophy: A Study in the Thought of John Stuart Mill* (London: Hutchinson, 1961).

Papers:

Important collections of Mill's letters and papers are in the Mill-Taylor Collection, British Library of Political and Economic Science, London School of Economics; at the National Library of Scotland; at the Keynes Library, King's College, Cambridge; and in the John Stuart Mill Collection at the Yale University Library. The manuscript of the *Autobiography* is located at the Columbia University Library, and the early draft of the *Autobiography* is at the library of the University of Illinois, Urbana-Champaign. The copy of Robert Browning's *Pauline* with Mill's annotations is in the Forster and Dyce Collection at the Victoria and Albert Museum. The early draft of *A System of Logic* and the only known manuscript of *Principles of Political Economy* are located at the Pierpont Morgan Library. The press-copy manuscript of *A System of Logic* is at the British Library. Mill's will is at Somerset House, London.

William Morris

(24 March 1834 - 3 October 1896)

This entry was updated by Frederick Kirchhoff (Indiana University-Purdue University at Fort Wayne) from his entry in DLB 57: Victorian Prose Writers After 1867.

See also the Morris entries in DLB 18: Victorian Novelists After 1885 *and* DLB 35: Victorian Poets After 1850.

BOOKS: *The Defence of Guenevere and Other Poems* (London: Bell & Daldy, 1858; Boston: Roberts Brothers, 1875);

The Life and Death of Jason: A Poem (London: Bell & Daldy, 1867; Boston: Roberts Brothers, 1867);

The Earthly Paradise: A Poem, 3 volumes (London: Ellis, 1868-1870; Boston: Roberts Brothers, 1868-1870);

Love Is Enough; or, The Freeing of Pharamond: A Morality (London: Ellis & White, 1873; Boston: Roberts Brothers, 1873);

The Story of Sigurd the Volsung and the Fall of the Niblungs (London: Ellis & White, 1876; Boston: Roberts Brothers, 1876);

Hopes and Fears for Art: Five Lectures Delivered in Birmingham, London, and Nottingham 1878-81 (London: Ellis & White, 1882; Boston: Roberts Brothers, 1882);

A Summary of the Principles of Socialism Written for the Democratic Federation, by Morris and H. M. Hyndman (London: Modern Press, 1884);

Textile Fabrics: A Lecture (London: Clowes, 1884);

Art and Socialism: A Lecture; and Watchman, What of the Night? The Aims and Ideals of the English Socialists of Today (London: Reeves, 1884);

Chants for Socialists: No. 1. The Day is Coming (London: Reeves, 1884);

The Voice of Toil, All for the Cause: Two Chants for Socialists (London: Justice Office, 1884);

The God of the Poor (London: Justice Office, 1884);

Chants for Socialists (London: Socialist League Office, 1885; New York: New Horizon Press, 1935);

The Manifesto of the Socialist League (London: Socialist League Office, 1885);

The Socialist League: Constitution and Rules Adopted

William Morris, late 1870s (William Morris Gallery)

at the General Conference (London: Socialist League Office, 1885);

Address to Trades' Unions (The Socialist Platform—No. 1) (London: Socialist League Office, 1885);

Useful Work v. Useless Toil (The Socialist Platform—No. 2) (London: Socialist League Office, 1885);

For Whom Shall We Vote? Addressed to the Working-Men Electors of Great Britain (London: Commonweal Office, 1885);

What Socialists Want (London: Hammersmith Branch of the Socialist League, 1885);

The Labour Question from the Socialist Standpoint (Claims of Labour Lectures—No. 5) (Edinburgh: Co-operative Printing, 1886);

A Short Account of the Commune of Paris (The Socialist Platform—No. 4) (London: Socialist League Office, 1886);

The Pilgrims of Hope: A Poem in Thirteen Parts (London: Buxton Forman, 1886; Portland, Maine: Mosher, 1901);

The Aims of Art (London: Commonweal Office, 1887);

The Tables Turned; or, Nupkins Awakened: A Socialist Interlude (London: Commonweal Office, 1887);

True and False Society (London: Socialist League Office, 1888);

Signs of Change: Seven Lectures Delivered on Various Occasions (London: Reeves & Turner, 1888; New York: Longmans, Green, 1896);

A Dream of John Ball and A King's Lesson (London: Reeves & Turner, 1888; East Aurora, N.Y.: Roycroft, 1898);

A Tale of the House of the Wolfings and All the Kindreds of the Mark (London: Reeves & Turner, 1889; Boston: Roberts Brothers, 1890);

The Roots of the Mountains: Wherein is Told Somewhat of the Lives of the Men of Burgdale, Their Friends, Their Neighbours, Their Foemen, and Their Fellows in Arms (London: Reeves & Turner, 1890; New York: Longmans, Green, 1896);

Monopoly; or, How Labour is Robbed (The Socialist Platform—No. 7) (London: Commonweal Office, 1890);

News from Nowhere: or, An Epoch of Rest: Being Some Chapters from a Utopian Romance (Boston: Roberts Brothers, 1890; London: Reeves & Turner, 1891);

Statement of Principles of the Hammersmith Socialist Society, anonymous (Hammersmith: Hammersmith Socialist Society, 1890);

The Story of the Glittering Plain Which Has Been Also Called the Land of Living Men or the Acre of the Undying (Hammersmith: Kelmscott Press, 1891; London: Reeves & Turner, 1891; Boston: Roberts Brothers, 1891);

Poems by the Way (Hammersmith: Kelmscott Press, 1891; London: Reeves & Turner, 1891; Boston: Roberts Brothers, 1892);

Address on the Collection of Paintings of the English Pre-Raphaelite School (Birmingham: Osborne, 1891);

Under an Elm-Tree: or, Thoughts in the Country-side (Aberdeen, Scotland: Leatham, 1891; Portland, Maine: Mosher, 1912);

Manifesto of English Socialists, anonymous, by Morris, H. M. Hyndman, and G. B. Shaw (London: Twentieth Century Press, 1893);

The Reward of Labour: A Dialogue (London: Hayman, Christy & Lilly, 1893);

Concerning Westminster Abbey, anonymous (London: Women's Printing Society, 1893);

Socialism: Its Growth and Outcome, by Morris and E. B. Bax (London: Sonnenschein, 1893; New York: Scribners, 1893);

Help for the Miners: The Deeper Meaning of the Struggle (London: Baines & Searsrook, 1893);

Gothic Architecture: A Lecture for the Arts and Crafts Exhibition Society (Hammersmith: Kelmscott Press, 1893);

The Wood beyond the World (Hammersmith: Kelmscott Press, 1894; London: Lawrence & Bullen, 1895; Boston: Roberts House, 1895);

The Why I Ams: Why I Am a Communist, with L. S. Bevington's Why I Am an Expropriationist (London: Liberty Press, 1894);

Child Christopher and Goldilind the Fair (2 volumes, Hammersmith: Kelmscott Press, 1895; 1 volume, Portland, Maine: Mosher, 1900);

Gossip about an Old House on the Upper Thames (Birmingham: Birmingham Guild of Handicraft, 1895; Flushing, N.Y.: Hill, 1901);

The Well at the World's End: A Tale (Hammersmith: Kelmscott Press, 1896; 2 volumes, London: Longmans, Green, 1896);

Of the External Coverings of Roofs, anonymous (London: Society for the Protection of Ancient Buildings, 1896);

How I Became a Socialist (London: Twentieth Century Press, 1896);

Some German Woodcuts of the Fifteenth Century, edited by S. C. Cockerell (Hammersmith: Kelmscott Press, 1897);

The Water of the Wondrous Isles (Hammersmith: Kelmscott Press, 1897; London: Longmans, Green, 1897);

The Sundering Flood (Hammersmith: Kelmscott Press, 1897; London: Longmans, Green, 1898);

A Note by William Morris on His Aims in Founding the Kelmscott Press, Together with a Short Description of the Press by S. C. Cockerell and an Annotated List of the Books Printed Thereat (Hammersmith: Kelmscott Press, 1898);

Address Delivered at the Distribution of Prizes to Students of the Birmingham Municipal School of Art on 21 February 1894 (London: Longmans, Green, 1898);

Art and the Beauty of the Earth (London: Longmans, Green, 1899);

Some Hints on Pattern-Designing (London: Longmans, Green, 1899);

Architecture and History, and Westminster Abbey (London: Longmans, Green, 1900);

Art and Its Producers, and the Arts and Crafts of Today (London: Longmans, Green, 1901);

Architecture, Industry, and Wealth: Collected Papers, edited by Sydney Cockerell (London: Longmans, Green, 1902);

Communism (Fabian Tract No. 113) (London: Fabian Society, 1903);

The Hollow Land and Other Contributions to the Oxford and Cambridge Magazine (London: Longmans, Green, 1903);

The Unpublished Lectures of William Morris, edited by Eugene D. LeMire (Detroit: Wayne State University Press, 1969);

Icelandic Journals of William Morris (Fontwell: Centaur Press, 1969; New York: Praeger, 1970);

A Book of Verse: A Facsimile of the Manuscript Written in 1870 (London: Scolar Press, 1980);

Socialist Diary, edited by Florence Boos (Iowa City: Windhover Press, 1981);

The Novel on Blue Paper, edited by Penelope Fitzgerald (London: Journeyman Press, 1982); *Dickens Studies Annual: Essays on Victorian Fiction*, volume 10, edited by Michael Timko, Fred Kaplan, and Edward Guiliano (New York: AMS Press, 1982), pp. 153-220;

The Ideal Book: Essays and Lectures on the Arts of the Book, edited by William S. Peterson (Berkeley & London: University of California Press, 1982);

The Juvenilia of William Morris, edited by Boos (New York: William Morris Society, 1983).

Collections: *The Collected Works of William Morris*, 24 volumes, edited by May Morris (London & New York: Longmans, Green, 1910-1915);

William Morris: Artist, Writer, Socialist, 2 volumes, edited by May Morris (Oxford: Blackwell, 1936).

OTHER: "Mural Decoration," by Morris and J. H. Middleton, in *Encyclopaedia Britannica*, ninth edition, volume 17 (Edinburgh: Black, 1884; New York: Allen, 1888);

John Ruskin, *The Nature of Gothic: A Chapter of the Stones of Venice*, preface by Morris (London: Allen, 1892);

Thomas More, *Utopia*, foreword by Morris (Hammersmith: Kelmscott Press, 1893);

Robert Steele, ed., *Medieval Lore*, preface by Morris (London: Stock, 1893; Boston: Luce, 1907);

Arts and Crafts Exhibition Society, *Arts and Crafts Essays*, preface and three articles by Morris (London: Rivington, Percival, 1893; New York: Scribners, 1893).

TRANSLATIONS: *The Story of Grettir the Strong*, translated by Morris and Eiríkr Magnússon (London: Ellis, 1869; New York: Longmans, Green, 1901);

The Story of the Volsungs and the Niblungs, translated by Morris and Magnússon (London: Ellis, 1870; New York: Longmans, Green, 1901);

Three Northern Love Stories, and Other Tales, translated by Morris and Magnússon (London: Ellis & White, 1875; New York: Longmans, Green, 1901);

The Aeneids of Virgil Done Into English Verse (Boston: Roberts Brothers, 1875; London: Ellis & White, 1876);

The Odyssey of Homer Done Into English Verse, 2 volumes (London: Reeves & Turner, 1887);

The Saga Library, translated by Morris and Magnússon, 6 volumes (London: Quaritch, 1891-1905);

The Ordination of Knighthood, from William Caxton's translation of *The Order of Chivalry* (London: Reeves & Turner, 1892);

The Tale of King Florus and the Fair Jehane (Hammersmith: Kelmscott Press, 1893);

Of the Friendship of Amis and Amile (Hammersmith: Kelmscott Press, 1894);

The Tale of the Emperor Coustans and of Over Sea (Hammersmith: Kelmscott Press, 1894);

The Tale of Beowulf, translated by Morris and A. J. Wyatt (Hammersmith: Kelmscott Press, 1895; London & New York: Longmans, Green, 1898);

The Story of Kormak, the Son of Ogmund, translated by Morris and Magnússon, edited by Grace Calder (London: William Morris Society, 1970).

Writing is only one element of William Morris's diverse achievements. He designed textiles, wallpapers, stained glass, rugs, tapestries, and embroidery; and he founded and managed a company to produce them. He was a leading influence on the Arts and Crafts movement in England and America and, through the work of his disciples, a major force in the reform of art education. He was a pioneer in the causes of historic preservation and environmentalism. His work as a typographer and printer produced some of the finest Victorian books and encouraged the revitalization of the art of printing. His activities as a revolutionary Socialist helped shape the direction of the British party system; the example of his commitment to socialism influenced the movement even when it took directions Morris himself had not envisioned.

William Morris earned his literary reputation as a narrative poet; in recent years, however, his most popular writing has been his earlier short poems and the lectures and prose romances he wrote during the last two decades of his life. His theoretical writings on the arts and crafts have exerted a profound influence on architecture and interior design in forms very different from Morris's own; and his writings on socialism, with their faith in a Communist society determined by human desire rather than political theory, remain a significant critique of twentieth-century Marxism.

Morris is a genuinely transitional figure. His life and work are grounded in a historical past they in many respects carry to its efflorescence, yet, at the same time, he reformulates the values of that past in ways that address themselves to the modern world. For this reason, as his biographer E. P. Thompson suggests, Morris should be seen neither as a man of the past nor as a man of the present, but as "a new kind of sensibility" unique in its "reassertion at a new level and in new forms of pre-capitalist values of community" and what Morris ironically termed "barbarism."

The juxtaposition of past and present can be traced to Morris's boyhood. His father was a bill broker who commuted daily to his London office from suburban Walthamstow, where William Morris, his eldest son, was born 24 March 1834. Although living only a few miles from the center of London, the Morris family had many of the features of a medieval household: brewing their own beer, baking their own bread, and observing the fourteenth-century customs of meals at high prime and Twelfth Night celebrations. Woodford Hall, where the family moved in 1840, was located on the edge of Epping Forest. Here Morris

and his brothers wandered on foot or rode their ponies, William on occasion wearing a toy suit of armor given him by his parents.

This world with its links to the past defined the values Morris sought to preserve. The extended family, sharing the common areas of a great house and its natural environs, became his ideal community. The forest setting of his romances is grounded in the forest of his childhood: his love of nature—of flowers and foliage—has its origins in the gardens of Elm House, where Morris was born, and Woodford Hall.

Yet a home like Woodford Hall was possible only because of his father's commercial position in the city. In an 1883 letter to fellow Socialist Andreas Scheu, Morris characterized his early life as "the ordinary bourgeois style of comfort" and reported having been brought up "in what I should call rich establishmentarian puritanism; a religion which even as a boy I never took to." His boyhood may have been idyllic, but there was something false in its circumstances. The traditionalism of Walthamstow was sustained, not by its roots in a traditional culture, but by the money that flowed from London—in large amounts after 1844, when his father's lucky investment in a copper mining company increased sharply in value. Past and present met in Woodford Hall but achieved no genuine synthesis.

As the eldest son in a family of nine, Morris enjoyed a special place in his parents' affections. His father seems to have exerted slight influence over him—unless the nervous temperament they shared was hereditary. In contrast his relationship with his mother was a crucial factor in his development. Morris was a sickly child, "kept alive" by his mother on calf's-foot jelly and beef-tea. When he grew stronger, however, her attention necessarily shifted to his six younger brothers and sisters, and the loss of his mother's undivided care was a profound emotional blow to the boy. Throughout his life he hungered for a love comparable to the sheltering care he had received in his first years, fearing, at the same time, that such love would be taken from him suddenly and without reason. Typically, Morris turned the anger he felt toward his mother in other directions. As a boy—and man—he was given to violent outbursts of temper, occasionally against human beings but more often against inanimate objects, venting his frustration at a world that could not be bent to his purposes.

To some extent, his two older sisters, Emma and Henrietta, compensated for Morris's loss of maternal attention. Emma was particularly close to him. Conditioned, however, to imagine himself deprived of love, Morris seems to have regarded her marriage in 1850 as a personal betrayal.

Although Morris was to become a man of remarkable strength and physical activity, his sickly childhood had encouraged him to take up reading at an early age. He had reportedly read all of Sir Walter Scott's Waverley novels by the age of seven. Throughout his life, in consequence, he approached events through the mediation of literary romance, and his most powerful experiences were associated with reading. As Morris's nineteenth-century biographer John W. Mackail reports, Emma recalled reading Clara Reeve's *The Old English Baron* with him "in the rabbit warren at Woodford, poring over the enthralling pages till both were wrought up to a state of mind that made them afraid to cross the park to reach home."

When Morris was nine years old, he was sent to a local preparatory school, first as a day scholar, later as a boarder. After his father's death in 1847 the family moved to a smaller residence, Water House, and Morris was sent to the recently founded Marlborough College, in Wiltshire, where he remained a student until Christmas 1851.

As a result of the school's disorganization, Morris was left much on his own. "As far as my school instruction went," he later wrote, "I think I may fairly say I learned next to nothing there, for indeed next to nothing was taught; but the place is in very beautiful country, thickly scattered over with prehistoric monuments, and I set myself eagerly to studying these and everything else that had any history in it, and so perhaps learned a good deal, especially as there was a good library at the school." His schoolfellows remembered him for his solitary walks, for his invention of endless stories "about knights and fairies," and for violent but short-lived bursts of temper. They also noted his need for constant activity, which often took the form of hours spent in netting, and for his habit of talking to himself. Clearly Morris was something of an anomaly among the other boys. Writing in 1874 to Philip Burne-Jones, then a student at Marlborough, he confessed to having led "a troublous life" his first two years at the school and went on to suggest something about his sense of isolation not only as an adolescent but also as a grown man: "Alas I did not fight enough in my time, from want of

hope let us say, not want of courage, or else I should have been more respected in my earlier days; in the few fights I had I was rather successful, for a little, and thin (yes) boy as I was: for the rest I had a hardish time of it, as chaps who have brains and feelings generally do at school, or say in all the world even, whose griefs are not much shared in by the hard and stupid: nor its joys either, happily, so that we may be well content to be alive and eager, and to bear pain sometimes rather than to grow like rotting cabbages and not to mind it."

One influence of Marlborough on Morris's intellectual development was its High Church flavor, which complemented his already well-developed love of romantic literature and the Middle Ages. This bias was strengthened by his year under the private tutelage of the Reverend F. B. Guy, when Morris returned to Walthamstow in 1852. Guy turned Morris into a decent classical scholar and introduced him to such works as Euripides' *Medea* that later influenced his own narrative poetry.

Morris passed his matriculation examination at Exeter College, Oxford, in June 1852 but, because the college was full, did not go into residence until the spring of 1853. Again, Morris's autobiographical letter to Scheu is revealing: "I took very ill to the studies of the place; but fell-to vigorously on history and especially mediaeval history, all the more perhaps because at this time I fell under the influence of the High Church or Puseyite school; this latter phase however did not last me long, as it was corrected by the books of John Ruskin which were at the time a sort of revelation to me; I was also a good deal influenced by the works of Charles Kingsley, and got into my head therefrom some socio-political ideas which would have developed probably but for the attractions of art and poetry. While I was still an undergraduate, I discovered that I could write poetry, much to my own amazement; and about that time being very intimate with other young men of enthusiastic ideas, we got up a monthly paper which lasted (to my cost) for a year; it was called the *Oxford and Cambridge Magazine*, and was very *young* indeed." Most influential of Ruskin's books was *The Stones of Venice* (1851-1853), the final volume of which appeared the year Morris entered Oxford. Its chapter "On the Nature of Gothic" became a major factor in Morris's social thinking. "How deadly dull the world would have been twenty years ago but for Ruskin!" Morris wrote in 1894. "It was through him that I learned to give form to my discontent."

Foremost among the "young men of enthusiastic ideas" was Edward Burne-Jones, who was to become a lifelong friend and artistic collaborator. It was Burne-Jones who coined Morris's nickname "Topsy"—at times shortened to "Top"—after the wild-haired Topsy of *Uncle Tom's Cabin*; and through Burne-Jones, Morris became friends with a Birmingham circle—Charles Faulkner, Richard Watson Dixon, and William Fulford. The group, later joined by Cormell Price, studied—of course—Ruskin, but also Alfred, Lord Tennyson and Thomas Carlyle; discovered the beauty of medieval architecture and Pre-Raphaelite painting; and fantasized themselves as a pseudomonastic "Brotherhood." Morris had been writing poetry for a good while, but with the encouragement of his Oxford friends, he began to take himself seriously as a writer and entered wholeheartedly in their project to publish a monthly magazine.

Morris's contributions to the *Oxford and Cambridge Magazine* (January-December 1856), which he at first edited and largely financed, having come into a nine-hundred-pound-a-year income on his twenty-first birthday, included five poems, seven short romances, a contemporary love story, a review of Robert Browning's *Men and Women*, a Ruskinesque description entitled "The Churches of North France," and a brief account of two engravings by the German artist Alfred Rethel. Romances such as "The Hollow Land" and "Svend and his Brethren" are the most successful of these pieces. The critical articles, because they are almost unique in his output, deserve attention.

Morris's account of Amiens Cathedral is the only completed essay in what was to have been a series of articles treating the churches he visited during his 1854 and 1855 summer walking tours of Belgium and northern France. Because he was forced to rely on photographs to refresh his memory, the essay falls short of the precise architectural description Morris admired in Ruskin. However, Morris's naive enthusiasm defines his purpose as something more personal than Ruskin's quest for absolute values. Thinking of the medieval builders, he not only "can see through them very faintly, dimly, some little of the mediaeval times, else dead and gone from me for ever" but also professes to love "those same builders, still surely living, still real men and capable of receiving love . . . no less than the great men, poets

and painters and such like, who are on earth now; no less than my breathing friends." The cathedral, so perceived, is not an artifact of history, but an experience of timeless communion between past and present that foreshadows the dialectical conception of history in Morris's later writing.

With the exception of an 1870 review of Dante Gabriel Rossetti's *Poems*, Morris's early comments on Browning are his only published criticism of a contemporary writer. In placing Browning "high among the poets of all time, and I scarce know whether first, or second, in our own," Morris was disavowing his earlier admiration for Tennyson and declaring allegiance to the poet who was to influence strongly the poetry of his own first period. Significantly, the three poems "that strike [him] first"—"The Epistle of Karshish," "Cleon," and "Bishop Blougram's Apology"—treat questions of religious "belief and doubt" that had begun to disturb Morris. His remarks on Cleon, a figure with whom he has much in common, suggest the misgivings he may have come to have with the aesthetic elitism of his own Oxford circle: "Cleon, with his intense appreciation of beauty, is yet intensely selfish; he despises utterly the common herd; he would bring about, if he could, a most dreary aristocracy of intellect."

Morris is particularly interested in poems pertaining to art and to love. He is struck by the "intense, unmixed love; love for the sake of love" of Browning's love poems and demonstrates an unexpected sympathy for Andrea del Sarto's thankless passion for his unfaithful wife. Indeed, fulfillment seems less important to him than personal integrity in the face of loss. Fittingly, the poem he "love[s] the best of all in these volumes" is " 'Childe Roland to the Dark Tower Came,' " with its portrait of "a brave man doing his duty" in face of an uncertain outcome. In general the poems Morris singles out are the poems of disquietude and self-doubt that have continued to fascinate modern readers. More than a prescient critical judgment, however, Morris's emphasis is clearly a reflection of his own state of mind—in particular, of the inability to imagine himself a successful lover or artist that characterizes the fiction he contributed to the *Oxford and Cambridge Magazine*.

Morris had entered Oxford with the intention of becoming a clergyman. By 1855, however, he had determined to become an architect. Mackail writes that Morris's family regarded his

Jane Burden Morris, circa 1860 (Victoria and Albert Museum). She married Morris in April 1859.

says I shall be able; now as he is a very great man, and speaks with authority and not as the scribes, I *must* try." Yet even in professing Rossetti's aestheticism, Morris remained vaguely dissatisfied with a calling that had so little to do with the realities of the world: "I can't enter into politico-social subjects with any interest," he confessed to Price, "for on the whole I see that things are in a muddle, and I have no power or vocation to set them right in ever so little a degree. My work is the embodiment of dreams in one form or another."

With Burne-Jones he took lodgings at 17 Red Lion Square, furnishing them with massive, "intensely mediaeval" oak furniture of his own design. Here, amidst the chaos of bohemianism, Morris allowed his beard to grow and struggled to learn how to draw the human form. If his decision to become an architect had distressed his mother, his decision to become an artist was an even stronger blow. Yet, in estranging himself from his bourgeois family, he found new friends, including Ruskin, Rossetti, and other members of the Pre-Raphaelite circle, to take their place. Wherever Morris lived, he created a household.

In the summer of 1857 Morris and Burne-Jones joined Rossetti and a group of friends in painting Arthurian frescoes on the walls of the newly constructed Oxford Union. The experience of communal labor was much to Morris's taste. His painting—*How Sir Palomydes loved La Belle Iseult with exceeding great love out of measure, and how she loved not him again but Sir Tristram*—was the first begun and the first completed; Morris then went on to paint the roof with designs of animals and birds. However, neither Rossetti nor any of his coworkers understood the technique of mural painting, and their work, applied to an improperly prepared surface, deteriorated almost immediately.

It was in October 1857 that Morris met Jane Burden, the daughter of an Oxford stableman, whom Rossetti met at the theater and persuaded to sit as a model. Morris, who had adopted Rossetti's taste in women along with his general philosophy of life, found himself strongly attracted to her strange beauty, which he associated with the figures of Iseult and Guenevere.

In part to be near Jane Burden, Morris stayed on in Oxford, preparing for publication his first collection of verse, *The Defence of Guenevere and Other Poems* (1858). This volume contains some of Morris's most original writing and, by dint of changing tastes, most of the poems for

decision with "disappointment and almost consternation"; nevertheless, having completed his final term at the university, Morris articled himself to the successful Gothic revivalist architect George Edmund Street, then working out of Oxford. Morris remained at Street's office less than a year—enough time to become close friends with Philip Webb, Street's senior clerk; to adopt Street's belief that architecture should encompass all elements of a building's design and decoration; and to discover that architecture, even so defined, was not to be his own profession.

Burne-Jones had left Oxford without a degree in 1855 to study art in London with Dante Gabriel Rossetti. Morris visited him regularly on weekends, and, when Street moved his office to London in August 1856, Morris came increasingly under the influence of Rossetti, who soon persuaded him to become a painter. As he wrote Cormell Price, "Rossetti says I ought to paint, he

which he is known in the twentieth century. Like the best of Browning's dramatic monologues, the best of the poems in the collection—including the title poem itself—speak with a compelling realism that brings their medieval subject matter into stark immediacy. The book received a few favorable reviews and a few hostile ones largely attacking Morris for his association with Pre-Raphaelitism; however, it sold poorly, and it was not until Morris had established his reputation with later work that the volume became generally known.

By summer 1858 Morris was engaged to Jane Burden, and on 26 April 1859 they were married at Oxford. For Morris's family, his marriage to the daughter of a groom was the ultimate fall from respectability. Whether by choice or for lack of an invitation, neither his mother nor any of his brothers or sisters attended the wedding. The newlyweds spent a six-week honeymoon on the Continent and returned in June to begin a new phase of Morris's life.

Not long after his engagement Morris had commissioned Philip Webb to begin designs for a house. The site chosen was a piece of high ground ten miles south of London, near the village of Upton. Red House—so named because of its solid red brick construction—was at once Gothic and modern: a house that Morris could identify with the Middle Ages, the functionalism and simplicity of which nevertheless anticipates Modernist design.

Furnishing and decorating Red House was a problem Morris himself undertook to solve, typically enlisting the cooperation of his friends. As Mackail describes it: "Not a chair, or table, or bed; not a cloth or paper hanging for the walls; nor tiles to line fireplaces or passages; nor a curtain or a candlestick; nor jug to hold wine or a glass to drink out of, but had to be reinvented, one might almost say, to escape the flat ugliness of the current article.... Much of the furniture was specially designed by Webb and executed under his eye: the great oak dining-table, other tables, chairs, cupboards, massive copper candlesticks, fire-dogs, and table glass of extreme beauty." This experience led directly to the founding of the firm of Morris, Marshall, Faulkner and Company in 1861, "to undertake any species of decoration, mural or otherwise, from pictures, properly so called, down to the consideration of the smallest work susceptible of art beauty." In time, the firm produced stained glass, furniture, fabrics, wallpaper, tiles, embroidery, carpets, and

tapestries, all of the highest quality. The styles of Morris and Company were not always innovative; however, the firm set a standard of production that was decisive in the history of British interior design.

Morris's two daughters, Jenny and May, were born at Red House, and his years there were the happiest time in his marriage. Morris enjoyed entertaining; his friends came down regularly from London for weekends or longer stays, and there was talk of adding a wing for Burne-Jones and his wife Georgiana. In 1865, however, Morris moved his family back to London, taking up residence above the workshop of the firm at 26 Queen Square. In part Morris made this transfer to be closer to his place of work, in part because the location and northern-lighted design of Red House had proved unhealthy. Whatever its justifications, the move did not please his wife. No longer the mistress of an elegant suburban home, Jane Morris became increasingly estranged from her husband, increasingly given to poor health, increasingly involved with Rossetti, who began to imagine that it was he, not Morris, who had loved her at first sight.

The wares of the firm were beginning to become fashionable, but Morris's business earnings were as yet unable to compensate for the steadily decreasing income from his copper shares. Warrington Taylor, the firm's manager, repeatedly warned Morris that he was living beyond his means, but it was not until Taylor's death in 1870 that Morris learned how to discipline his expenditures.

During the summer of 1869, Morris took Jane to the spa at Bad-Ems in Hesse-Nassau, Germany. In the months following their return, her relationship with Rossetti apparently became a matter of public knowledge. Burne-Jones, meanwhile, had fallen desperately in love with Mary Zambaco, one of his models, and Morris found himself drawn into some kind of intimacy with Georgiana Burne-Jones, for whom he completed his first illuminated manuscript, *A Book of Verse*, in 1870.

It was during this difficult period that Morris returned to writing poetry. He had attempted "Scenes from the Fall of Troy" in the years following *The Defence of Guenevere* but found himself unequal to the task. Now, abandoning the dramatic monologue format, he began a series of extended narrative poems on traditional subjects, gathered under the title *The Earthly Paradise* and linked by the medieval device of a narrative frame. *The Life and Death of Jason*, originally intended as part of the series, outgrew the frame and was published separately in 1867. It was an immediate success; and with the publication of the four parts of *The Earthly Paradise* in the years 1868-1870, Morris found himself a major Victorian poet.

The *Sunday Times* reviewer called *The Life and Death of Jason* "one of the most remarkable poems of this or any other age"; writing in the *Nation*, the American scholar Charles Eliot Norton maintained that "no narrative poem comparable with this in scope of design or in power of execution has been produced in our generation." More widely reviewed, the successive volumes of *The Earthly Paradise* were praised for their effortless narration and for their precise descriptions of the natural world. The poems were easy to read, and so they appealed to a wide audience. Moreover, their non-Victorian subject matter was greeted as a welcome escape from mid-Victorian earnestness. (One of the few repeated objections to the work was its lack of Christian morality.)

The twenty-four tales and narrative frame of *The Earthly Paradise* for the most part reiterate the theme of a quest for happiness, often in romantic love, postponed or thwarted by the perversity of human nature. The poems have been criticized for slackness and diffusion; and Morris himself complained, "they are all too long and flabby—damn it!" However, the best of them are a remarkable achievement. Morris's versions of "The Story of Cupid and Psyche," "Pygmalion and the Image," "The Land East of the Sun and West of the Moon," "The Man Who Never Laughed Again," and "The Hill of Venus" are among the most compelling verse narratives of the Victorian period.

Although the narratives are equally balanced between classical and Germanic subjects, it is the latter that most strongly seized Morris's imagination. "The Lovers of Gudrun," the longest and perhaps the best of *The Earthly Paradise* tales, is a translation of the Icelandic Laxdale Saga. Morris had begun reading Icelandic soon after his first meeting with Eiríkr Magnússon in 1868; almost immediately they began publishing a series of translations from the sagas—*The Story of Gunnlaug the Wormtongue* (1869), *The Story of Grettir the Strong* (1869), *The Story of the Volsungs and the Niblungs* (1870), *Frithiof the Bold* (1871). The first and fourth of these translations, which originally appeared in serials, were published, along with additional material, as *Three Northern*

Edward Burne-Jones with Morris, 1874, at Burne-Jones's home, The Grange, Fulham (Victoria and Albert Museum)

Love Stories, and Other Tales (1875). And two decades later Morris and Magnússon returned to the task, with a series of Icelandic translations entitled *The Saga Library* (1891-1905), which Magnússon continued in the years following Morris's death. Morris regarded this literature of the North as a national heritage, having a relationship to English culture comparable to the relationship of Homer to the Greeks. More personally, it offered an alternative to the self-reflective melancholy of his own *Earthly Paradise*—a gust of clear, cold air that would ultimately penetrate the closed space of introspection.

The first years of the 1870s were a period in which Morris struggled to rethink his life. Instead of a romantic youth, he found himself a heavyset man of middle years, strong enough to bash in a wall with his head—and often angry enough to do it. For reasons seemingly beyond his control, he was making a living, not as an artist, but as a kind of upper-class upholsterer. His dream of married life at Red House, with an ideally beautiful wife at the center of a circle of friends, had given way to living over a shop with a woman, if not fully in love with another man, then nevertheless no longer in love with him. And the circle of friends itself had disintegrated: the idealized Rossetti was now an enemy—although Morris continued to treat him otherwise; Edward and Georgiana Burne-Jones, whom he had once imagined living with him as members of an extended family, were now as unhappily married as he and Jane. Morris's efforts to define his identity had reached a series of dead ends.

Among the signs of Morris's effort to rethink his life were his journeys to Iceland in 1871 and 1873. He kept a journal of his 1871 expedition, which he later transcribed and gave to Georgiana Burne-Jones. This journal, along with a fragmentary journal of the 1873 voyage, records his confrontation both with the harshness of the Icelandic landscape and with the place of the sagas in Icelandic culture. For Morris, the "grisly desolation" of the land, with its black volcanic mountains and icebound interior, was a lesson in the smallness of human pretensions. The backcountry trek by pony was itself challenging. The elementary need to survive in surroundings that made survival difficult placed the personal sorrows of his married life in a new perspective; the Icelanders themselves offered him a model of human endurance in the face of near overwhelming odds: "set aside the hope that the unseen sea gives you here, and the strange threatening change of the blue spiky mountains beyond the firth, and the rest seems emptiness and nothing else: a piece of turf under your feet, and the sky overhead, that's all; whatever solace your life is to have here must come out of yourself or those old stories, not over hopeful themselves."

Nor was this the only important step Morris took in 1871. A month before he set sail for Iceland, he had taken a joint lease with Rossetti on Kelmscott Manor, a gray stone Elizabethan country house near Lechlade on the upper Thames. Among Morris's motives in entering into the tenancy may have been providing his wife and Rossetti with a place in which they could be together; however, Morris quickly grew to love the "beautiful and strangely naif house" with deep affection and to identify himself with the "beautiful grey little hamlet called Kelmscott." Soon the presence of Rossetti, with his "ways so unsympathetic with the sweet simple old place," became an annoyance, but it was not until July 1874 that Rossetti gave up his share in the lease.

The need to redefine the self is the subject of the complex narrative poem *Love Is Enough;*

or, The Freeing of Pharamond, published in 1873. Its hero, Pharamond, renounces his kingdom to search for a visionary woman; he finds her—in a distinctly Icelandic landscape—only to leave her to return to his kingdom, now in the hands of a usurper. The tale ends ambiguously, with Pharamond preparing to return to Azalais, but, for the time at least, without either love or power. Despite its links to *The Earthly Paradise*, *Love Is Enough* is a major step forward in Morris's development, to a point at which he is able to imagine himself freed of the unfulfilled desires that lay beneath the malaise of the earlier work. The personal significance of the story to Morris is suggested by the elaborate framing devices surrounding the fable of Pharamond's quest, and confirmed by May Morris, in her preface for *The Collected Works*: "No glimpse of the inner life of Morris was ever vouchsafed even to his closest friends—*secretum meum mihi*. It was a subject on which he never spoke save in *Love Is Enough*." The poem was generally well received by the critics but, as Morris himself realized, was too difficult to be a popular success.

During the same period Morris also tried his hand at writing a novel, in which the love triangle characteristic of many of his romances was restated in a realistic mode, but was discouraged from completing the project. The manuscript, published in 1982 as *The Novel on Blue Paper*, suggests yet another attempt to distance himself from the melancholy of *The Earthly Paradise*.

In October 1871 Rossetti had been the object of Robert Buchanan's pseudonymous attack, "The Fleshly School of Poetry." Similar attacks continued through the following winter and spring. Rossetti's paranoia intensified, and in June 1872 he attempted suicide with an overdose of chloral. After his recovery he continued to spend time with Jane Morris both at Kelmscott and elsewhere; however, the event may have subtly changed the balance of power between Morris and Rossetti, and encouraged Morris to force Rossetti's hand by threatening to give up his share of the Kelmscott Manor lease two years later.

At the end of 1872 Morris moved his family to "a *very* little house with pretty garden" on the main road between Turham Green and Hammersmith. Jane Morris, who described it as "a very good sort of house for one person to live in, or perhaps two," was evidently less than fully satisfied with Horrington House; nevertheless, it remained the family's London home for six years.

Morris maintained a study and bedroom at Queen Square for his own use.

Despite his earnings from *The Earthly Paradise* and his other poetry, it was clear that the main source of his income would have to be the firm. Of the original partners, Burne-Jones and Philip Webb had continued furnishing designs, for which they had been paid, but the others—Rossetti, Ford Madox Brown, Peter Paul Marshall, and Charles Faulkner—had contributed no capital and had long ceased to participate in any active sense. It was clearly Morris's business, and so he determined to assume sole proprietorship. Morris handled the affair with little tact, and Brown, with the support of Rossetti and Marshall, opposed him acrimoniously, demanding an equal share in the company's assets and ultimately settling on a thousand pounds each. (Rossetti, perversely, insisted on making a gift of his share to Jane Morris.)

Once the firm had been reincorporated under his sole ownership as Morris and Company, Morris entered into its work with renewed vigor. During the summer of 1875 he began a series of experiments with vegetable dyes, attempting to replace aniline dyes, which he found unsatisfactory for quality textiles. As he wrote in his 1889 lecture, "Of Dyeing as an Art": "Any one wanting to produce dyed textiles with any artistic quality in them must entirely forgo the modern and commercial methods in favor of those which are at least as old as Pliny, who speaks of them as being old in his time." His correspondence with Thomas Wardle, owner of a Staffordshire dye works (and brother-in-law of George Wardle, who had succeeded Warrington Taylor as Morris's business manager), documents the intensity with which Morris entered into this effort. He studied early texts on dye making and visited Wardle's works in person, "even working in sabots and blouse in the dye-house myself . . . taking in dyeing at every pore."

For Morris, 1876 was a year of important changes. Jane Morris later in life told Wilfrid Scawen Blunt that she had ended her affair with Rossetti in 1875. Although she spent a fortnight with Rossetti at Bogner in March 1876, it would appear that their sexual relationship was over by the beginning of that year. Also at the beginning of 1876 Morris resigned his directorship of the mining company, an event he celebrated by sitting on the top hat he had been forced to wear to meetings of the board. In June 1876 Morris's older daughter, Jenny, "a girl of fifteen, exception-

"Rupes Topseia," drawing by Rossetti expressing his opposition to Morris's reorganization of Morris, Marshall, Faulkner and Company in 1875 (The British Museum). The original firm members are shown at top left; Jane Morris is at top right; Karl Marx and Friedrich Engels watch Morris's descent into hell.

ally bright, clever, and diligent . . . already her father's chosen companion," was stricken with epilepsy. Her health never completely recovered, and she remained an invalid until her death in 1935. Morris, it has been argued, traced her illness to his own pathological anger and thus regarded himself as in some way responsible for it.

In addition, the year 1876 saw publication of the poem Morris considered his masterpiece. Writing to Charles Eliot Norton in 1869, he had characterized the Völsunga Saga, which he was then translating into prose, as "something which is above all art." "I had it in my head to write an epic of it," he had gone on to say, "but though I still hanker after it, I see clearly it would be foolish, for no verse could render the best parts of it, and it would only be a flatter and tamer version of a thing already existing." Despite these misgivings, Morris gave way to his hankering, and in 1876 produced *The Story of Sigurd the Volsung and the Fall of the Niblungs*, the work that effectively terminates his career as a narrative poet of traditional themes. Though hailed by critics as Morris's "greatest and most successful effort," "the crowning achievement of Mr. Morris' life," the work was not popular with the public because Morris's fidelity to his sources proved an obstacle to general readers.

It is not clear whether it was his failure to win a large audience with *The Story of Sigurd* or the press of new interests that led Morris to turn from poetry in the years that followed. Although he continued to be known as "The Author of *The Earthly Paradise*," he ceased to think of himself as primarily a poet and in 1877, despite the temptation, rejected the invitation to succeed Matthew Arnold as Oxford Professor of Poetry.

In respect to his future, the most important event of 1876 may have been Morris's entry into politics. Angered at the Turkish atrocities in Bulgaria and alarmed by the rumor that England was on the verge of supporting Turkey in its war with Russia, he wrote a letter to the *Daily News*, which was printed on 24 October. With high rhetoric, he appealed to the Liberal party and to the workingmen of England "to drop all other watchwords that this at least may be heard—No war on behalf of Turkey; no war on behalf of the thieves and murderers!" Morris may not have been attuned to the subtleties of foreign policy, but he recognized that behind Benjamin Disraeli's effort to rouse support for the alliance lay the intention of exploiting Turkey economically. Joining the Liberal-Radical opposition to Disraeli, he was elected to the committee of the Eastern Question Association (EQA) and for the first time in his life encountered working-class politicians.

When war between Turkey and Russia broke out, the EQA distributed Morris's statement "Unjust War: To the Working-men of England" (1877). It is clear that he had begun to doubt the efficacy of Parliament—"the Tory Rump, that we fools, weary of peace, reason and justice, chose at the last election to 'represent' us"—and had begun to look to the working class as a source of political change. The government exerted pressure against the EQA, sending roughs to disrupt its meetings and spreading the rumor that, with the fall of Constantinople, Britain would lose its Indian Empire. William Gladstone, who had originally supported the organization,

backed down, as did nearly all other Liberal supporters of the neutrality movement. Only the Labor Representation League held firm.

In the end, the tide of jingoism prevailed, and Disraeli's maneuverings gained Britain the island of Cyprus. Morris's response was anger and frustration; however, he had experienced the excitement of political activism. He knew what it was to speak before a large audience of supporters and to hold one's own against the threat of government violence. He had gained, moreover, a profound distrust of the political system.

His experience with the EQA was complemented by his experience as founding member of the Society for the Preservation of Ancient Buildings (SPAB)—or, as its opposition to removing the weathered surface of stonework led Morris to call it, "Anti-Scrape." As with the EQA, his involvement with the SPAB began with a letter to the editor. On 5 March 1877 he addressed the *Athenaeum*, protesting the "destruction" of Tewkesbury Minster by Sir Gilbert Scott, in the name of "restoration." Morris did not object to preserving a historic building from decay; however, he objected strenuously to replacing old work with new, real Gothic workmanship with nineteenth-century stone carving. Arguing that "our ancient buildings are not mere ecclesiastical toys, but sacred monuments of the nation's growth and hope," he proposed "an association for the purpose of watching over and protecting these relics, which, scanty as they are now become, are still wonderful treasures, all the more priceless in this age of the world, when the newly-invented study of living history is the chief joy of so many of our lives."

The Society for the Protection of Ancient Buildings was organized at a meeting later in the month, with Morris as secretary. He wrote the society's manifesto, which has continued to be republished in its annual report, and drew many of his friends, including Ruskin and Carlyle, into the cause. From the start, the SPAB had two classes of enemies: the architects who made their livings by restoration, and the clergymen who regarded churches as their personal property. Beginning with the society's formal protest over the removal of the seventeenth-century choir stalls at Canterbury Cathedral, Morris found himself engaged in one controversy after another. Nor was he merely concerned with preventing inappropriate restoration; in April 1878 he wrote the editor of the *Times* opposing the bishop of London's plans to destroy some of Christopher Wren's city churches—buildings Morris disliked but recognized as irreplaceable in London's architectural history. "Surely," he declared, "an opulent city, the capital of the commercial world, can afford some small sacrifice to spare these beautiful buildings the little plots of ground upon which they stand. Is it absolutely necessary that every scrap of space in the City should be devoted to money-making. . . ?"

In time the work of the society extended beyond England, playing a major role in the effectual protest against the restoration of St. Mark's, Venice, in 1880. His experience in the organization taught Morris much about the conflict between private interests and public good. As his letter in behalf of Wren's churches suggests, he grew convinced that the enemy of "sacred memories"—of his sense of history as a living continuity with the past—was the capitalist system, with its subordination of all other values to those of the marketplace.

Although Morris had spoken at meetings of the society, his first formal public lecture, "The Lesser Arts," was delivered to the Trades Guild of Learning, London, 4 December 1877. He prepared diligently, writing the text with unusual care and practicing for delivery by reading *Robinson Crusoe* aloud to a group of friends. The lecture, like those that followed, is in fact a short essay; and, although Morris naturally became more fluent in the form as he became more practiced in it, the nearly one hundred lectures he wrote and delivered between 1877 and his death in 1896 are a notable achievement. As Bernard Shaw observed, Morris's having found time to write them in the midst of so much other activity—commercial, artistic, and political—is difficult to imagine.

"The Lesser Arts" touches on several themes that Morris was to develop in subsequent lectures. He perceived the division between the "great arts" of sculpture, architecture, and painting and "that great body of [lesser] art, by means of which men have at all times more or less striven to beautify the familiar matters of everyday life," as a phenomenon unique to the past three centuries, and he argues that this division, which is based upon a deeper division in society itself, has led to the decay of both arts. Because the two purposes of decoration are "to give people pleasure in the things they must perforce *use*" and "to give people pleasure in the things they must perforce *make*," the absence of decoration on everyday objects reflects a society in which

pleasure is largely absent from ordinary life. Even the wealthy, who fill their homes with "decoration (so-called)," have no real pleasure in their surroundings. In contrast, the high arts are "mainly kept in the hands of a few highly cultivated men, who can go often to beautiful places, whose education enables them, in the contemplation of the past glories of the world, to shut out from their view the everyday squalors that the most of men move in." Faced with this elitism, Morris would be content to "sweep away all art for awhile," in hope that it be reborn in a new, more democratic form. But as yet he admits to "a sort of faith" that so radical a solution will prove unnecessary and that the growth of leisure will in time "bring forth decorative, noble, *popular* art."

"The Lesser Arts" adumbrates a society of the future founded on "simplicity of life, begetting simplicity of taste . . . simplicity everywhere, in the palace as well as in the cottage," but falters in its explanation of just how that society will be attained. Morris's personal experience working in the lesser arts had taught him their importance; ironically, however, he saw his own decorated work contributing little to the lives of ordinary people and being bought instead by the moneyed class he was coming to deplore. Even as Morris set about putting his own life in order, the tension between his desire for a better world and his own activities remained unresolved.

Morris's public life continued to evolve. He had been appointed examiner at the School of Art, South Kensington, in 1876. In February 1878 he was invited to speak at the distribution of prizes at the Cambridge School of Art, and at about the same time was made president of the Birmingham Society of Arts for the current year.

Despite an attack of gout, in March 1878 Morris set about hunting for a new London residence. Jane Morris and the couple's two daughters were wintering in Italy, so the decision was very much his own. Morris was drawn to a three-storied, late-eighteenth-century house near the Thames in Hammersmith, and, after bringing Webb to inspect the structure, he took a lease on it in April. He now had two dwellings, connected by the Thames. To emphasize this bond, he renamed his London home Kelmscott House.

In April, Morris joined his family in Italy, planning to take them on a tour of the northern Italian cities. Again, he suffered an attack of gout. He collapsed on a street in Genoa and had to be carried to his hotel room. By this point in his life, Morris's feelings about Italy were mixed.

*Portrait of Morris in 1880, by George Frederick Watts
(National Portrait Gallery, London)*

Wandering among the olive trees above the sea at Oneglia, he felt as if he "should be well contented to stay there always." Yet, writing to Georgiana Burne-Jones three weeks later, he confessed himself "quite out of sympathy" "with the later work of Southern Europe."

The Morrises took possession of Kelmscott House at midsummer, but it was not until late October, when redecoration was complete, that they moved into their new home. Morris had a tapestry loom built in his (separate) bedroom, where he practiced hand weaving, often in the early hours of the morning. He had begun the search for a larger space for the firm's manufactory that led to the establishment of the Merton Abbey Works in 1881. As a temporary measure, the coach house and stable at Kelmscott House were converted into a room for weaving rugs and carpets—which were given the trade name Hammersmith. (Later, the coach house became a meeting room for the Hammersmith Socialists.)

On 19 February 1879 Morris delivered his presidential address, "The Art of the People," before the Birmingham Society of Arts and the Birmingham School of Design. He reiterated many of the themes sounded in "The Lesser Arts,"

sharpening the rhetoric of his attacks on art for art's sake and plutocratic luxury. But he was less sure of himself in his historical predictions. Acknowledging "how obviously this age is one of transition from the old to the new," he found himself bewildered by the "strange confusion . . . our ignorance and half-ignorance is like to make the exhausted rubbish of the old and the crude rubbish of the new." However, the language to describe historical change was not long to elude him. In February and April 1879, John Stuart Mill published his *Fortnightly Review* articles "Chapters on Socialism." Morris later described reading these articles, which set forth the general arguments for socialism "as far as they go, clearly and honestly," as an intellectual turning point in his life: his sense of a connection between the rise of capitalism and the decline of the lesser arts was vindicated, and his hitherto inchoate belief in the need for social change had now been grafted to a specific economic theory. In the years that followed, the idealistic socialism he learned from Mill would evolve, through his study of Karl Marx and association with the principal figures of late-nineteenth-century British socialism, into a unique conception of a Communist future.

In the fall of 1879 Morris was elected treasurer of the National Liberal League, a small organization that attempted to promote workingmen candidates within the Liberal party. He joined in the league's support of Gladstone in the 1880 election, but it is clear from a political lecture he wrote in the first month of 1880 that he looked to goals far more radical than those of the Liberal party: "I think of a country where every man has work enough to do, and no one has too much: where no man has to work himself stupid in order to be just able to live: where on the contrary it will be easy for a man to live if he will but work, impossible if he will not (that is a necessary corollary): where every man's work would be pleasant to himself and helpful to his neighbour; and then his leisure from bread-earning (of which he ought to have plenty) would be thoughtful and rational."

In February 1880 Morris delivered a second Birmingham lecture, "Labour and Pleasure *versus* Labour and Sorrow," later retitled "The Beauty of Life." Once more he reiterated his belief in the necessity for "an *Art made by the people and for the people, a joy to the maker and the user.*" Civilization, he argued, if it does not aim at "giving some share in the happiness and dignity of life to *all* the people that it has created . . . is simply an organized injustice, a mere instrument for oppression." Once more he reiterated his belief that "the greatest foe to art is luxury," now adding the counsel to begin the repudiation of luxury by casting out the clutter of the middle-class Victorian home: "if you want a golden rule that will fit everybody, this is it: *Have nothing in your houses that you do not know to be useful, or believe to be beautiful.*"

The early months of 1880 were a period of vague discontent because Morris sensed a need for change in his life, but was unsure of its direction. He contemplated giving up Kelmscott Manor, but instead, Kelmscott Manor took on greater significance as an image, not of the departed past, but of the continuity of the past within a historical process leading to a renewed future. In August 1880, with his family and a group of friends, Morris made a voyage up the Thames from London to Kelmscott, a trip which he was to repeat in later years and which he memorialized in the closing chapters of his utopian romance *News from Nowhere* (1890).

The following year, Morris moved the firm's works from their cramped quarters in Bloomsbury to Merton Abbey, on the banks of the river Wandle seven miles south of London. Here, amid large poplars and willows and an old-fashioned flower garden, Morris approximated the ideal working conditions he outlined in his 1884 essay "A Factory as It Might Be": "buildings . . . beautiful with their own beauty of simplicity as workshops"; "machines of the most ingenious and best approved kinds . . . used when necessary . . . to save human labour"; "no work which would turn men into mere machines." Morris allowed his workers flexible hours and a share in the company's profits, treating them as an extended family. He assigned responsibilities on the assumption that anyone could be trained to do any kind of work, and he assigned no work that he had not mastered himself. Yet, as much as he wrote about the individual worker's need to share in the creative process, he remained the chief artist, his employees simply carrying out—often laboriously—copies of his designs. Morris and Company remained a model of capitalist paternalism, rather than an experiment in Socialist production.

In a March 1881 speech before the London Institution entitled "The Prospects of Architecture in Civilization," Morris repeated his attack on the degrading ugliness of Victorian England and his call for a simple style of living. The only program for change he could suggest remained the renunciation of needless luxury; however, he recognized that this might not suffice and that there lurked a challenge he had yet to confront: "when we come to look the matter in the face, we cannot fail to see that even for us with all our strength it will be a hard matter to bring about that birth of the new art: for between us and that which is to be, if art is not to perish utterly, there is something alive and devouring; something as it were a river of fire that will put all that tries to swim across to a hard proof indeed, and scare from the plunge every soul that is not made fearless by desire of truth and insight of the happy days to come beyond."

The next year Morris collected this and four other lectures in the volume *Hopes and Fears for Art* (1882). The first period of his social activism was over. In April of the same year Rossetti, after a long period of physical decline, died, thus severing one of the few remaining threads that connected Morris with that time in the past when he denied the connection between art and social responsibility.

Morris was, in his own words, "on the look out for joining any body which seemed likely to push forward matters." And so, 13 January 1883, responding to the invitation of H. M. Hyndman, he joined the Democratic Federation (DF). Hyndman was a domineering ex-Tory who had converted to Marxism; under his leadership, the DF had held a series of conferences on "Stepping-stones" to socialism, which Morris attended, and in 1883 the federation began publishing Socialist pamphlets. Morris, once he had avowed his new political creed, adopted it with characteristic fervor. He began reading Marx's *Das Kapital* in French translation, and entered into lengthy discussions with men such as Hyndman; the exiled German anarchist and designer Andreas Scheu, who contributed a significant internationalism to the movement; and the British Marxist theorist E. Belfort Bax. Their ideas became linked with his own; what Morris had hitherto seen as remediable class differences he now saw as a class struggle to be resolved only through destruction of the class system itself. As he wrote to C. E. Maurice in July, "I believe that the whole basis of Society, with its contrasts of rich and poor, is incurably vicious."

His March lecture "Art, Wealth, and Riches," delivered at the Manchester Royal Institution, was protested in the *Manchester Examiner*. The next month Morris gave the first of his

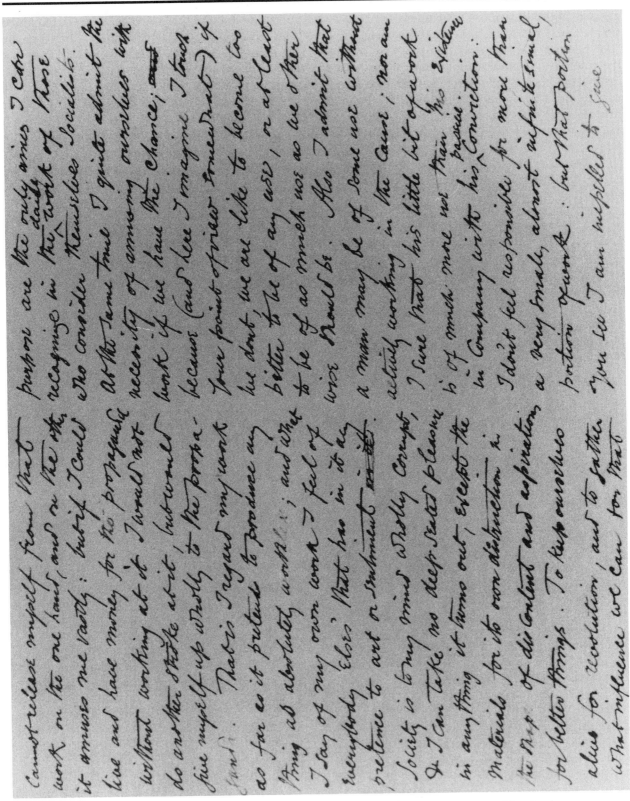

From a January 1885 letter written by Morris to fellow printer-bookbinder Thomas James Cobden-Sanderson,
explaining the Socialist mission (MA 1753, The Pierpont Morgan Library)

purely political lectures as a Socialist, and in May he was elected to the Democratic Federation Executive. In November he delivered the lecture "Art and Democracy"—later retitled "Art under Plutocracy"—to the Russell Club, at University College, Oxford, in a session chaired, appropriately, by Ruskin. Morris restated his long-standing distrust of aesthetic elitism as a notion of the common economic grounding of all human activities. Echoing Plato, he extended his definition of art to include not only the fine and lesser arts but "even the arrangement of the fields for tillage and pasture, the management of towns and of our highways of all kinds; in a word . . . to the aspect of all the externals of our life" and argued that artists of all kinds were injured "by the system which insists on individualism and forbids co-operation." "All art, even the highest, is influenced by the conditions of labour of the mass of mankind, and . . . any pretentions which may be made for even the highest intellectual art to be independent of these general conditions are futile and vain." Specifically, it is the "superstition of commerce being an end in itself, of man as made for commerce, not commerce for man, of which art has sickened."

More shocking to his audience than these arguments was Morris's public admission that he was " 'one of the people called Socialists,' " and his peroration calling upon "those of you who agree with me to help us actively, with your time and your talents if you can, but if not, at least with your money, as you can." According to a report in the *Times*, "The Master of University then said to the effect that if he had announced this beforehand it was probable that the loan of the College-hall would have been refused." For this and subsequent lectures, Morris was assailed by the press not only for his political views, but also for presenting them in the guise of a discourse on art. As he wrote to Georgiana Burne-Jones, "I have been living in a sort of storm of newspaper brickbats, to some of which I had to reply: of course I don't mind a bit, nor even think the attack unfair."

For six years after he declared himself a Socialist, Morris devoted himself with enormous energy to the movement. His *Socialist Diary*, kept during the early months of 1887 (and edited for publication in 1981) suggests the hectic pace of this period. He was willing to speak anywhere in the country to any group that wanted to hear about socialism. The Democratic Federation pioneered in open-air propaganda and initiated the

tradition of regular Sunday gatherings in Regent's Park and Hyde Park. In January 1884 the federation began publishing the weekly *Justice*. Morris regularly covered the journal's deficit and joined in selling it on the street.

The same month, before the Hampstead Liberal Club, he delivered his lecture "Useless Work v. Useless Toil" (published in 1885 as *The Socialist Platform—No. 2*). Morris was now confident that "the first step" in establishing "true Society" was the abolition of the nonproductive upper and middle classes. Already in this lecture, however, his unique contribution to Marxism is apparent. It will not suffice, he argues, that every man "reap the fruits of his labour" and "have due rest." "Nature will not be finally conquered til our work becomes a part of the pleasure of our lives." To a purely utilitarian socialism he adds the human need for taking pleasure in one's work.

From the start, Morris had recognized the contradiction in his position as a capitalist factory owner and a Socialist advocating the overthrow of capitalism. His institution of profit sharing for his workers was an effort to resolve this contradiction, but he was forced to acknowledge that "no man is good enough to be any one's master without injuring himself . . . whatever he does for the servant." While "not a capitalist in the ordinary sense of the word," he was forced to "admit to his own conscience that he was one of a class that lives upon the labour of others." For this reason, he seriously contemplated the sale of his business. Morris himself might have been able to live on a reduced income, but he had a wife—with little sympathy for his new radicalism—and two daughters to support, and he was able to use his income to advantage in support of such activities as *Justice*. After a period of soul-searching, he determined to remain the owner of Morris and Company.

In the spring of 1884 Morris addressed a meeting of textile strikers in Lancashire. Returning to London, he took part in the first annual march to the grave of Karl Marx (who had died the preceding year). In June the Hammersmith Branch of the Democratic Federation was formed. In July, Hyndman, having been forced from the presidency, nominated Morris to take his place. Morris declined, recognizing his lack of political qualifications—and attempting to distance himself from the conflict of Edward Aveling and Eleanor Marx with Hyndman. A month later, the organization changed its name to the Socialist Democratic Federation. Resentment over Hyndman's dictatorial tactics continued to grow, and in December, Morris, with the majority of the Executive, resigned from the federation and founded an alternative organization, the Socialist League, with its own journal, *Commonweal*, which Morris was to edit. Friedrich Engels, who never overcame his initial impression of Morris as a neophyte Marxist, characterized the leaders of those who resigned (Aveling, Bax, and Morris) as "the only honest men among the intellectuals—but men as unpractical (two poets and one philosopher) as you could possibly find."

Although his experience was to teach him "the frightful ignorance and want of impressibility of the average English workman," Morris at this point seems to have believed that the crisis of capitalism and rise of the proletariat were imminent. He therefore joined the leadership of the Socialist League in espousing an ideological purity that rejected parliamentary reform and any other transitional measures. He thus isolated himself not only from those friends and admirers who were unwilling to follow him into socialism but also from more moderate Socialists. (The Socialist Democratic Federation put up two candidates for the 1885 parliamentary election; the Socialist League countered with a pamphlet by Morris, *For Whom Shall We Vote?*, urging workers not to cast ballots.) Although he rejected their platform, it was difficult for Morris to counter the anarchists who in time came to dominate the Socialist League.

At the same time, the Socialist movement, which had at first been treated as a joke, was beginning to be taken as a serious threat to the political system. In "Art Under Plutocracy," Morris had called himself a representative of "reconstructive Socialism," in distinction to the "other people who call themselves Socialists whose aim is not reconstruction, but destruction." Now, in May 1885, writing to Georgiana Burne-Jones, he contemplated the end of civilization: "how often it consoles me to think of barbarism once more flooding the world, and real feelings and passions, however rudimentary, taking the place of our wretched hypocrisies." What Morris meant by "barbarism" was not chaos. His earlier reading of such historians as Edward A. Freeman had encouraged him to imagine the Germanic tribal organization underlying feudalism as a form of primitive communism. And feudalism itself he saw from the positive perspective of Ruskin's "On the Nature of Gothic," from *The Stones of Venice*. This longing for "barbarism" may have linked Morris in some ways to anarchist tendencies within the So-

cialist movement; however, as expressed in his later romances, it became the image of a renewed order, grounded in the simple life Morris found so appealing, historically explicable in terms of the Marxist notion he seems to have reached on his own that "The progress of life must be not on the straight line, but on the spiral."

Police persecution of the Socialists grew, often taking the form of harassment or arrest of public speakers. On 21 September 1885 Morris was present at the Thames Police Court for the trial of eight men arrested the previous day for speaking on the street. At the judge's sentence, the spectators, including Morris, cried "Shame," and the police began a general assault on them. Morris, defending himself, was arrested for disorderly conduct, accused by a policeman of having struck him on the chest and broken his helmet strap. He denied the charge and was dismissed, paying bail, as became his custom, for some of the working-class demonstrators.

On 8 February 1886 Socialist speeches in Trafalgar Square and Hyde Park precipitated a riot of the unemployed, with rumors of a march on the West End of London. Two weeks later a demonstration by the Socialist Democratic Federation was attacked by the police. The following July, Morris was arrested for speaking on the street and fined a shilling. (The two working-class men arrested with him were fined twenty pounds; when they refused to pay, they were sentenced to two months in jail.)

Meanwhile, Morris's other work continued. Although he could not devote himself to it with full energy, he kept a watchful eye on the firm, for which his daughter May, who had followed him into socialism, was now designing chintzes and wallpapers. In addition to his writing for *Commonweal*—which included his poem on the Paris Commune, *The Pilgrims of Hope* (serialized beginning in 1885, separately published the following year)—Morris was working on his English verse translation of *The Odyssey*, which appeared in 1887. In November 1886 his first Socialist romance, *A Dream of John Ball*, began in *Commonweal*, with separate publication following in 1888. And he continued to write lectures setting forth the goals and principles of socialism, talks now based on a fairly thorough understanding of Marxist economics. In "How We Live and How We Might Live" (1884) he established four "claims for decent life": "First, a healthy body; second, an active mind in sympathy with the past,

The Hammersmith branch of the Socialist League. Morris's daughter Jenny is seated in the center of the front row; two seats to her right is May Morris, her sister; Morris is in the second row, seventh from the right.

the present, and the future; thirdly, occupation fit for a healthy body and an active mind; and fourthly, a beautiful world to live in." In his elaboration of these claims, Morris seriously grapples with the problem of a Socialist future, addressing himself to such questions as the future of the family and the nature of education.

On 13 November 1887 ("Bloody Sunday"), Morris was present when police and soldiers brutally attacked radical demonstrators in Trafalgar Square. Well-dressed women in the surrounding houses and hotels clapped and cheered as the demonstrators were clubbed or ridden down by mounted police. Three men were killed and two hundred hospitalized. Morris confessed himself "astounded at the rapidity of the thing and the ease with which military organization got its victory. I could see that numbers were of no avail unless led by a band of men acting in concert and each knowing his part." A week later, Alfred Linnell was ridden down by the police in Northumberland Avenue. Morris wrote "A Death Song" for the benefit of his family, and was one of the pallbearers at the funeral, for which a great procession marched from Soho to Bow Cemetery.

Bloody Sunday was Morris's closest experience of political violence, and it influenced his account of revolution in *News from Nowhere*. Unlike Shaw, his companion in the march to Trafalgar Square, he was not encouraged by the experience to work within the political system. Rather, it taught him the need for strict military organization if any revolutionary force were to make a stand against the powers of the state, and therefore discouraged his belief that radical social change would take place in the near future.

The years 1888 and 1889 saw the gradual dissolution of the Socialist League. As more and more of its members rejected its antiparliamentarianism, the league became increasingly dominated by left-wing extremists. As progress in legislation and unionism was made on various fronts, the league's ideological purism seemed less and less relevant. Morris himself was attacked by the Fabians for espousing views that cast ridicule on socialism. However, there could be no doubt about the honest passion with which he advanced his opinions. E. P. Thompson quotes Edward Carpenter's assessment of Morris's speech at the International Socialist Working-Men's Congress in Paris, July 1889, as "one of the most effective in the session."

In 1888 Morris saw publication of *Signs of Change*, a collection of his most important Socialist lectures. The following year he produced *A Tale of the House of the Wolfings and All the Kindreds of the Mark*, a romance treating the confrontation of Germanic tribal society with Roman militarism. In 1890 a related work, *The Roots of the Mountains*, appeared, portraying a later stage of tribal society in conflict with invading Huns. In these recreations of the past, he attempted to portray the elements of communal society he hoped would reappear under communism. They thus foreshadow the utopian romance *News from Nowhere*, which he published in installments of *Commonweal* in 1890.

News from Nowhere is at once the summation of Morris's Socialist philosophy and a deeply personal exploration of his own desires for a future society. It is also a farewell to the Socialist League, which in May had removed Morris from the editorship of *Commonweal*. In November, the Hammersmith Branch withdrew from the league, reconstituting itself as the Hammersmith Socialist Society. Its manifesto disavowed both parliamentarianism and anarchism; however, the society was open to anyone who wanted to join and cooperated with other Socialist organizations.

For the last six years of his life Morris continued various forms of activism, but on a much reduced scale. The failure of the Socialist League taught him to distrust his abilities, and, after a serious attack of gout in February 1891, his health was broken. There were, as always, new interests. No longer devoting all his superfluous funds to socialism, he began amassing a library of early books and illuminated manuscripts. In 1891 he published a collection of short poems, *Poems by the Way*, and began publishing *The Saga Library*. Two years earlier, he had given special attention to the typography and binding of *A Tale of the House of the Wolfings*. Typically, Morris soon realized that he could do it all better if he did it himself. In 1890 he founded the Kelmscott Press, which began printing the following January.

Throughout the 1880s Morris had been at least peripherally involved with the growing Arts and Crafts movement, the chief inspiration for

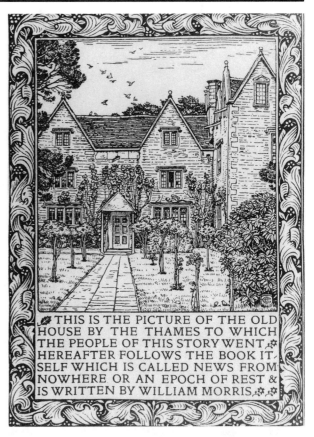

Frontispiece depicting Kelmscott Manor included in the 1892 Kelmscott Press edition of Morris's News from Nowhere

which had been his own accomplishments as a designer and artisan. He had misgivings about any reform of the arts that was not grounded in political revolution; however, he could not refuse to second the work of self-avowed disciples such as W. R. Lethaby and Walter Crane. In 1888 he had been elected a member of the recently founded Art Workers' Guild; and in the same year he had participated in the first exhibition of the Arts and Crafts Exhibition Society. It was Emery Walker's lecture on printing delivered at the 1888 exhibition—in particular, his concern with the importance of the total page—that spurred Morris's interest in the subject.

Totality was the keynote of the Kelmscott Press. Morris designed the type, ornamentation, and layout of the books, and chose their paper and binding materials with great care. He published his own works as well as a library of the writings that had meant most to him throughout his life. Altogether the Kelmscott Press printed fifty-three books, including an edition of Geoffrey Chaucer with woodcuts by Burne-Jones that is considered its masterpiece. Morris also wrote a series of prose romances for publication by the press: *The Story of the Glittering Plain Which Has Been Also Called the Land of Living Men or the Acre of the Undying* (1891), *The Wood beyond the World* (1894), *The Well at the World's End* (1896), *The Water of the Wondrous Isles* (1897), and *The Sundering Flood* (1897). The romances are deliberately escapist and, like the Kelmscott Press, represent Morris's recovered willingness to indulge himself in doing the things he liked best. They were not widely reviewed and were faulted by some critics for their archaic diction and syntax. However, some readers, including W. B. Yeats—who had attended the Socialist evenings at Hammersmith—admired their capacity to evoke an imaginary world, and twentieth-century psychological and genre criticism has come to recognize them as classic works of literary fantasy.

In 1892 Morris was considered a possible successor to Tennyson as poet laureate. He was pleased by Gladstone's support and found the idea of a Marxist courtier wryly amusing, but politely declined the offer. As a Socialist, Morris now worked toward unity of the movement and in 1893 had reached the position of hoping for the establishment of "a due Socialist party." In the same year, with Bax, he revised some earlier jointly written *Commonweal* materials into the book *Socialism: Its Growth and Outcome*. In the final years of his life, according to E. P. Thompson, "Morris stood *above* the movement—not in the sense of standing apart from it, but in the sense of comprising in his own person a point of unity above the divisions . . . he was no longer so closely engaged in the day-to-day struggle of the movement. But this very disengagement meant that he could work for the unity he so much desired with better effect."

In December 1895 he made his last open-air speech, at the funeral of Sergius Stepniak; in January 1896 he gave his last talk in the Hammersmith clubroom, and days later, his last public address. His health deteriorated steadily during the months that followed—although he continued writing and designing. In July he traveled to Norway, hoping to benefit from the sea voyage, but the journey failed to raise his spirits, and on his return in August it was clear that he did not have long to live. His friends did their best to cheer his final weeks, and Morris responded with heartfelt affection. He died quietly on 3 October and was buried three days later in Kelmscott churchyard.

While critical opinion of Morris's other writings has fluctuated radically since 1896, the lectures on art and socialism have steadily assumed greater importance and are now generally taken to be his most important literary work. In the years following his death, his two collections of lectures were supplemented by the volume *Architecture, Industry, and Wealth* (1902), edited by his literary executor, Sydney Cockerell; by volumes twenty-two and twenty-three of *The Collected Works* (1910-1915), edited by May Morris; by the two volumes of *William Morris: Artist, Writer, Socialist* (1936), also edited by May Morris; and by Eugene D. LeMire's *The Unpublished Lectures of William Morris* (1969). In addition, the best of the lectures have been republished in a variety of other editions and, with *News from Nowhere* and a handful of poems from *The Defence of Guenevere*, comprise the bulk of the various selections from Morris published in the twentieth century.

Morris's lectures continue to be read, not only as classics of Victorian prose but also as crucial statements about the nature of design and the possibility of a humane socialism. If the Modernist architecture that evolved from Morris's belief in honest simplicity has reached a dead end, it may be because his belief in the need for a human scale in building was ignored. If the communism of the twentieth century has failed to live up to Marx's hopes for the future, it may be because it has ignored Morris's belief in the value of pleasure in ordinary life and paid inadequate heed to his distrust of the centralized state. For these reasons, his lectures on art and socialism— in fact, lectures on the same subject—remain provocative. Here, as nowhere else in his writing, Morris speaks with a clarity and vigor it is difficult to resist. "There is more life in the lectures, where one feels that the whole man is engaged in the writing," Raymond Williams wrote in 1958, "than in any of the prose and verse romances. . . . Morris is a fine political writer, in the broadest sense, and it is on that, finally, that his reputation will rest."

Letters:

The Letters of William Morris to His Family and Friends, edited by Philip Henderson (London & New York: Longmans, Green, 1950);

The Collected Letters of William Morris, 2 volumes, edited by Norman Kelvin (Princeton: Princeton University Press, 1984-1987).

Bibliographies:

H. Buxton Forman, *The Books of William Morris De-*

scribed, with Some Account of His Doings in Literature and in the Allied Crafts (London: Hollings, 1897; Chicago: Way & Williams, 1897);

Temple Scott [J. H. Isaacs], A Bibliography of the Works of William Morris (London: Bell, 1897);

William E. Fredeman, "William Morris & His Circle: A Selective Bibliography of Publications," Journal of the William Morris Society, 1 (Summer 1964): 23-33; 2 (Spring 1966): 13-26;

Fredeman, Pre-Raphaelitism: A Bibliocritical Study (Cambridge, Mass.: Harvard University Press, 1965);

David and Sheila Latham, "William Morris: An Annotated Bibliography," Journal of the William Morris Society, 5 (Summer 1983): 23-41;

John J. Walsdorf, William Morris in Private Press and Limited Editions: A Descriptive Bibliography of Books by and about William Morris, 1891-1981 (Phoenix: Oryx Press, 1983);

K. L. Goodwin, A Preliminary Handlist of Manuscripts and Documents of William Morris (London: William Morris Society, 1984);

Gary L. Aho, William Morris: A Reference Guide (Boston: G. K. Hall, 1985).

Biographies:

John W. Mackail, The Life of William Morris, 2 volumes (London & New York: Longmans, Green, 1899);

E. P. Thompson, William Morris: Romantic to Revolutionary (London: Laurence & Wishart, 1955; New York: Monthly Review Press, 1955; revised, London: Merlin Press, 1977; New York: Pantheon, 1977);

Philip Henderson, William Morris: His Life, Work and Friends (London: Thames & Hudson, 1967; New York: McGraw-Hill, 1967);

Jack Lindsay, William Morris: His Life and Work (London: Constable, 1975);

Stephen Coote, William Morris: His Life and Work (London: Garamond, 1990).

References:

R. Page Arnot, William Morris; The Man and the Myth, Including Letters of William Morris to J. L. Mahon and Dr. John Glasse (London: Lawrence & Wishart, 1964);

Florence Boos and Carole Silver, eds., Socialism and the Literary Artistry of William Morris (Columbia: University of Missouri Press, 1990);

Patrick Brantlinger, "'News from Nowhere': Morris's Socialist Anti-Novel," Victorian Studies, 19 (September 1975): 35-49;

G. B. J. [Georgiana Burne-Jones], Memorials of Edward Burne-Jones, 2 volumes (London & New York: Macmillan, 1904);

Blue Calhoun, The Pastoral Vision of William Morris (Athens: University of Georgia Press, 1975);

Fiona Clark, William Morris: Wallpapers and Chintzes, revised edition (London: Academy, 1974);

G. D. H. Cole, William Morris as a Socialist (London: William Morris Society, 1960);

Gerald H. Crow, William Morris, Designer, special issue of Studio (Winter 1934);

Joseph R. Dunlap, The Book That Never Was: William Morris, Edward Burne-Jones and "The Earthly Paradise" (New York: Oriole Editions, 1971);

Peter Faulkner, Against the Age: An Introduction to William Morris (London & Boston: Allen & Unwin, 1980);

Faulkner, ed., William Morris: The Critical Heritage (London & Boston: Routledge & Kegan Paul, 1973);

Peter Floud, "The Inconsistencies of William Morris," Listener, 52 (14 October 1954): 615-617;

William E. Fredeman, ed., Victorian Poetry: An Issue Dedicated to the Work of William Morris, 13 (Fall-Winter 1975);

Bruce J. Glasier, William Morris and the Early Days of the Socialist Movement (London & New York: Longmans, Green, 1921);

John Goode, "William Morris and the Dream of Revolution," in Literature and Politics in the Nineteenth Century, edited by John Lucas (London: Methuen / New York: Barnes & Noble, 1971), pp. 221-280;

Amanda Hodgson, The Romances of William Morris (Cambridge: Cambridge University Press, 1987);

Graham Hough, "William Morris," in his The Last Romantics (London: Duckworth, 1948; New York: Barnes & Noble, 1971), pp. 83-133;

Frederick Kirchhoff, "Travel as Anti-Autobiography in William Morris' Icelandic Journals," in Approaches to Victorian Autobiography, edited by George Landow (Athens: Ohio University Press, 1979), pp. 292-310;

Kirchhoff, William Morris (Boston: Twayne, 1979);

Kirchhoff, *William Morris: The Construction of a Male Self, 1856-1872* (Athens: Ohio University Press, 1990);

Karl Litzenberg, "The Social Philosophy of William Morris and the Doom of the Gods," in *Essays and Studies in English and Comparative Literature*, University of Michigan Publications, 1 (1933): 183-203;

Paul Meier, *William Morris: The Marxist Dreamer*, 2 volumes, translated by Frank Gubb (Hassocks: Harvester Press, 1978; Atlantic Highlands, N.J.: Humanities Press, 1978);

A. L. Morton, "The Dream of William Morris," in his *The English Utopia* (London: Lawrence & Wishart, 1953), pp. 149-182;

Paul Needham, ed., *William Morris and the Art of the Book* (New York: Pierpont Morgan Library, 1976; London: Oxford University Press, 1976);

Linda Parry, *William Morris Textiles* (London: Weidenfeld & Nicolson, 1983; New York: Viking, 1983);

A. Charles Sewter, *The Stained Glass of William Morris and His Circle*, 2 volumes (New Haven & London: Yale University Press for the Paul Mellon Centre for Studies in British Art, 1975);

Carole Silver, *The Romance of William Morris* (Athens: Ohio University Press, 1982);

H. Halliday Sparling, *The Kelmscott Press and William Morris, Master-Craftsman* (London: Macmillan, 1924);

Peter Stansky, *Redesigning the World: William Morris, the 1880s and the Arts and Crafts* (Princeton: Princeton University Press, 1985);

Stansky, *William Morris* (Oxford & New York: Oxford University Press, 1983);

Paul Thompson, *The Work of William Morris* (London: Heinemann, 1967; New York: Viking, 1967);

J. M. S. Tompkins, *William Morris: An Approach to the Poetry* (London: Wolf, 1987);

Lionel Trilling, "Aggression and Utopia, A Note on William Morris's 'News from Nowhere,'" *Psychoanalytic Quarterly*, 42 (April 1973): 214-225;

Raymond Watkinson, *William Morris as Designer* (London: Studio Vista, 1967; New York: Reinhold, 1967);

Raymond Williams, *Culture and Society* (London: Chatto & Windus, 1958).

Papers:

The major collection of Morris's letters and manuscripts is held by the British Library, London. Other principal collections are at the Bodleian Library, Oxford; the Henry E. Huntington Library, San Marino, California; the Pierpont Morgan Library, New York; the Victoria and Albert Museum Library, London; the William Morris Gallery, Walthamstow; and the Sanford and Helen Berger Collection, Carmel, California.

Walter Pater

(4 August 1839 - 30 July 1894)

This entry was updated by Hayden Ward (West Virginia University) from his entry in
DLB 57: Victorian Prose Writers After 1867.

BOOKS: *Studies in the History of the Renaissance* (London: Macmillan, 1873); revised and republished as *The Renaissance: Studies in Art and Poetry* (London: Macmillan, 1877; New York: Macmillan, 1877; revised again, London & New York, 1888; revised again, London & New York, 1893);

Marius the Epicurean; His Sensations and Ideas (2 volumes, London: Macmillan, 1885; 1 volume, London & New York: Macmillan, 1885; revised, 2 volumes, London & New York: Macmillan, 1892);

Imaginary Portraits (London & New York: Macmillan, 1887; New York: Macmillan, 1899);

Appreciations, with an Essay on Style (London & New York: Macmillan, 1889);

Plato and Platonism: A Series of Lectures (London: Macmillan, 1893; London & New York: Macmillan, 1893);

An Imaginary Portrait (Oxford: Privately printed, 1894); republished as *The Child in the House: An Imaginary Portrait* (Boston: Copeland & Day, 1895);

Greek Studies: A Series of Essays (New York & London: Macmillan, 1895; London & New York: Macmillan, 1901);

Miscellaneous Studies: A Series of Essays (New York & London: Macmillan, 1895; London & New York: Macmillan, 1900);

Gaston de Latour: An Unfinished Romance (New York & London: Macmillan, 1896; London: Macmillan, 1902);

Essays from "The Guardian" (London: Privately printed, 1896; Portland, Maine: Mosher, 1897);

Uncollected Essays (Portland, Maine: Mosher, 1903);

Sketches and Reviews (New York: Boni & Liveright, 1919).

Collections: Edition DeLuxe, 9 volumes (London & New York: Macmillan, 1900-1901);

New Library Edition, 10 volumes (London: Macmillan, 1910).

Walter Pater (photograph by Elliott & Fry)

Walter Pater is important to English literary history because he combines a commitment to the romantic theory that art is essentially an expression of personality with a sympathetic response to the scientific and historical studies of the Victorian period that suggest how complex and ambiguous "personality" is. Pater's writings explore the ways in which biology, psychology, history, religion, and myth shape the individual's understanding of his own times and help him to interpret the bearing of the past upon the present. In this linking of aesthetics to religion, history, and science, Pater bridges, more subtly than any other writer of the late Victorian period, the dominant Romanticism of his own century and the dominant Modernism of the twentieth.

Few of his personal papers or anecdotal reminiscences by his acquaintances exist to provide a clear, accurate, or full biography of Pater. As Ian Fletcher has remarked in his 1959 volume, *Walter Pater*, "We must seek the inner man in the books." However, some information about Pater's early life is known. Walter Horatio Pater was born 4 August 1839 in Shadwell, a district of East London, the younger son of Richard and Maria Pater. Dr. Pater was a surgeon whose practice seems to have consisted mostly in treating the many poor people living in the neighborhood. He died when his second son was only four years old. After Dr. Pater's death, Pater's mother moved with her four children to the north London suburb of Enfield, near the home of her sister, Pater's favorite "Aunt Bessie." Pater's older brother William left home at fifteen, in 1851, and Pater lived with his mother and two younger sisters, Clara and Hester. One may suppose that the young Pater felt the absence of male companionship during the later years at Enfield and was rather isolated from his mother and sisters. Certainly, his young fictional heroes seem to be loners, seeking eagerly but tentatively for glamorous, authoritative, older male friends.

In 1853 the Pater family moved to Harbledown, near Canterbury, so that Pater could attend the King's School, attached to the famous cathedral. As a day student, Pater lived at home and does not seem to have entered fully into school life. He did form close friendships with two boys, Henry Dombrain and John Rainier McQueen. The three kept rather to themselves and were known in the school as "the Triumvirate" (Pater represents the situation fictionally in his late, uncompleted novel, *Gaston de Latour*, 1896). The boys shared the pleasure of rambling about the countryside and an intense interest in religious matters.

In 1858, the year he matriculated at Queen's College, Oxford, Pater traveled to Heidelberg, Germany, where Aunt Bessie, who had become guardian of the Pater children upon Maria Pater's death in 1854, had taken Pater's sisters to complete their education. In Heidelberg, Pater awoke to the richness of German culture, and, upon returning to Oxford, reportedly studied German so that he could read the works of Georg Wilhelm Friedrich Hegel, the great aesthetician and philosopher of history whose ideas were to influence him significantly. Indeed, one of the reasons Pater was appointed a fellow at Brasenose College seems to have been his re-

puted expertise as a Hegel scholar. He also read other German Romantics—Friedrich von Schiller, Johann Gottlieb Fichte, and Johann Wolfgang von Goethe most prominently—from whom he garnered ideas about the importance of aesthetic experience in the development of the ideal cultured man.

While at Queens, Pater developed other intellectual interests. He was tutored in Greek by Benjamin Jowett, who later became a translator of Plato and the master of Balliol College. On his own, Pater read the work of Charles-Augustin Sainte-Beuve, Théophile Gautier, Charles-Pierre Baudelaire, and Gustave Flaubert, contemporary French writers with a less than respectable reputation in staid Oxford. From them, Pater acquired a sense of the discipline and autonomy of "art for art's sake." This vague, confusing term meant to Pater that the value and pleasure of art in no way depended upon its intention or ability to inculcate morality. The aesthetic form was a good in itself, regardless of whether or not it taught one how to live. In Flaubert, Pater found the sanction for his idea that the artist's only responsibility is to insure that his work is the perfect fulfillment of his artistic intention. In Baudelaire's book of poems *Les Fleurs du mal* (1857), Pater discovered that the attraction of art can lie in its delicate images of mingled beauty and decay, that the perception of evil and death can heighten the desire for the beautiful but transient things of the world.

So, by the time he was graduated from Queen's with a second-class degree in 1862, Pater had already acquired a considerable knowledge of the literatures of ancient Greece, eighteenth-century Germany, and nineteenth-century France. With these credentials, he became a probationary fellow of Brasenose College in February 1864. In July he read to the Old Mortality, an essay society that he joined earlier in the year, a paper entitled "Diaphaneitè" (the word, though Pater incorrectly placed the accent mark from the original Greek, means "the quality of being transparent"), which, although it was not published until after his death, is the earliest surviving piece of prose that Pater wrote. It prepares the reader to understand his other early essays, including those that went into his first book, *Studies in the History of the Renaissance* (1873).

In "Diaphaneitè," Pater says that receptivity to a wide range of experience or impressions and a desire to express one's inner self fully and accurately in outward form are the leading qualities of the aesthetic personality. By implication, all

The Pater family home at Harbledown, near Canterbury, where Pater lived while he was a day student at King's School in the 1850s

truth depends on the relation of observer and experience. Self-expression is the record of that relation at one moment of its shifting existence.

In his first published essay, on Samuel Coleridge, in an 1866 issue of *Westminster Review*, Pater says that the transparency and expressiveness described in "Diaphaneitè" are the attributes with which modern humanity must confront reality. Writing enthusiastically under the influence of evolutionary theory (Charles Darwin's *On the Origin of Species* had appeared in 1859), Pater remarks that science reveals "types of life evanescing into each other by inexpressible refinements of change," not only by present physical change but also "by remote laws of inheritance, the vibration of long-past acts." As a consequence, modern humanity faces "a world of finely linked conditions, shifting intricately as we ourselves change." In this situation, Pater declares, morality can no longer be based on a presumed eternal and universal order of truths, on the belief in an "absolute spirit," which seeks "to arrest every object in an

eternal formula." Rather, morality must be based on the "relative spirit": "The relative spirit, by its constant dwelling on the more fugitive conditions or circumstances of things, breaking through a thousand rough and brutal classifications, and giving elasticity to inflexible principles, begets an intellectual *finesse* of which the ethical result is a delicate and tender justice in the criticism of human life." For Pater, Coleridge represents the futile resistance of the idealist tradition to a new epistemology based upon the empirical analysis of the physical world. Modern science, in the relative spirit, will win out over traditional philosophy on this point. Pater approves.

Relativist as he is, he still finds a use for idealism. In a *Westminster Review* essay on William Morris (1868), part of which was reprinted as Pater's conclusion in *Studies in the History of the Renaissance* and part as "Aesthetic Poetry" in *Appreciations, with an Essay on Style* (1889), he transmutes idealism into historicism. The study of the past corresponds to the recollection of important moments in the individual life; autobiography and historiography merge. One traces the influence on, or survival in, one historical age of the customs and art of earlier ages, just as one tries to understand the effect of past personal experience on one's present life. This tracing of historical survivals becomes, for the modern relativist, the equivalent of the recovery of lost perfect "forms" for the idealist. Morris's poetry is an example, because in its imitation of medieval poetry, it reveals the ancient "pagan sentiment" for beauty mingled with death that survives from Greek religion into the Christianity of the Middle Ages.

While his reading of Morris suggested to him the survival of Greek religious sentiment into the Middle Ages, Pater describes, in an important 1867 *Westminster Review* essay, the German aesthetician Johann Joachim Winckelmann (1717-1768) tracing the pagan or "Hellenic" sentiment back to its source, in his studies of the copies of Greek statues displayed at Rome, statues that express with perfect clarity the sentiment they embody. In Pater's view, by an intense empathy, Winckelmann simultaneously understands the diaphanous ideal of Greek art and works to attain it in his own writing: "This key to understanding of the Greek spirit, Winckelmann possessed in his own nature. . . . Penetrating into the antique world by his passion, his temperament, he enunciated no formal principles, always hard and one-sided. Minute and anxious as his culture was, he never became one-sidedly self-analytical. Occupied ever with himself and developing his genius, he was not content, as so often happens with such natures, that the atmosphere between him and other minds should be thick and clouded; he was ever jealously refining his meaning into a form, express, clear, objective." Again, to express one's own nature perfectly at the same time one uncovers the "secret" or "formula" of a historical culture or art form is to live the diaphanous ideal, to live in what Pater calls "the spirit of art."

This judgment of Winckelmann reflects Pater's notion of his own work as a writer. What Pater says of Winckelmann and his study of Greek art is most important as a historical analogue for the work of the scholar and artist in the nineteenth century. Not surprisingly, then, Pater concludes the essay by answering the question, "Can we bring that ideal into the gaudy, perplexed light of modern life?" He tells us that Goethe, whom Pater and many of his contemporaries (including Thomas Carlyle and Matthew Arnold) took to be the modern master spirit of self-culture, sought to impart "the blitheness and universality of the antique ideal" to art that would "contain the fullness of the experience of the modern world," as Winckelmann had done. Late in the essay on Winckelmann, Pater suggests that he and his contemporaries must continue Goethe's endeavor: modern art must "rearrange the details of modern life" so as to impart "the sense of freedom" to an age conscious of a new kind of necessity or determinism that comes from the experiments and theorizing of modern science, a biological and historical determinism that is like "a magic web woven through and through us . . . penetrating us with a network subtler than our subtlest nerves, yet bearing in it the central forces of the world."

To define that "network," and the "central forces" that it transmits, is the purpose of two of the most famous early essays that eventually went into *Studies in the History of the Renaissance*, or *The Renaissance*, as it came to be known by virtue of its 1877 retitling.

In the conclusion, Pater describes as a kind of equivalent of the ancient doctrine of "perpetual flux" the modern scientific idea of continuous physical change. Both the individual and the world he inhabits are always becoming and vanishing, each moment of life a "concurrence" of forces that meet only to part. In such a world, the individual has only "flickering" impressions of the world beyond himself, impressions that seem to disappear even before he can apprehend

them: "Every one of those impressions is the impression of the individual in his isolation, each mind keeping as a solitary prisoner its own dream of a world. Analysis goes a step farther still, and assures us that those impressions of the individual mind to which, for each one of us, experience dwindles down, are in perpetual flight; that each of them is limited by time, and that as time is infinitely divisible, each of them is infinitely divisible also; all that is actual in it being a single moment, gone while we try to apprehend it, of which it may be more truly said that it has ceased to be than that it is. . . . It is with this movement, with the passage and dissolution of impressions, images, sensations, that analysis leaves off— that continual vanishing away, that strange, perpetual weaving and unweaving of ourselves."

Pater argues boldly in the conclusion for the thesis which is latent in all his early work: that the observation and recording of sense impressions is more important than abstract thinking. The cool laser-light of perception he describes in "Diaphaneitè" and the "blitheness" and "repose" of Greek art are replaced for the modern aesthetic sensibility by the need to "burn always with a hard, gemlike flame" in a diamond-heat of the senses: "Not to discriminate every moment some passionate attitude in those about us, and in the very brilliancy of their gifts some tragic dividing of forces on their ways is . . . to sleep before evening. With this sense of the splendour of our experience and of its awful brevity, gathering all we are into one desperate effort to see and touch, we shall hardly have time to make theories about the things we see and touch."

In Pater's view, the observation not of ordinary life but of great works of art will give "the highest quality to your moments as they pass, and simply for those moments' sake." This is so because art imparts a beautiful, enduring order to experience that experience itself usually lacks.

Perhaps the numerous detractors of Pater, such as W. H. Mallock, who ridiculed him as "Mr. Rose" in his satire *The New Republic* (1877-1879), were right to see in his narrowly focused prescription for the satisfying life an abnegation of social concern or responsibility, but they were wrong to see a call to immoral thrill-seeking. Indeed, as Pater's famous image of the burning gem suggests, this life of "eager observation" necessitates a dedication, a mental toughness, a polished craft in reporting the results that are quite alien to the sloppy sensualism he was accused of inspiring.

In the preface, Pater describes the critical method and view of Western history that underlie the other essays of *Studies in the History of the Renaissance*. Beauty, he holds, is not abstract but concrete, not universal but particular, not eternal but relative to the historical conditions under which it was produced and in which it is observed. One can understand the beautiful only in terms of the "formula" of particular works of art or of the lives of individual artists. Therefore, general aesthetic theories are useless. On this point, Pater disagrees not only with eighteenth-century aestheticians but with his contemporaries John Ruskin and Matthew Arnold as well. In explaining the method of the aesthetic critic in analyzing the "formula" of each of the great artists whose lives and works he will discuss, Pater employs that analogy with physical science that he had introduced in the earlier-written conclusion: "And the function of the aesthetic critic is to distinguish, to analyze, and separate from its adjuncts, the virtue by which a picture, a landscape, a fair personality in life or in a book, produces this special impression of beauty or pleasure, to indicate what the source of that impression is, and under what conditions it is experienced."

Also in the preface, Pater asserts that the Renaissance is not a historical period, separate from the Middle Ages, but rather a cultural impulse that originated within the Middle Ages themselves, a ground swell of assertion for individual physical and moral freedom that had its roots in France in the twelfth and thirteenth centuries, reached its zenith in fifteenth-century Italy, and returned to France for its twilight in the sixteenth century.

The structure of *Studies in the History of the Renaissance* reflects this view. The first essay, "Two French Stories," treats the melding of the Hellenic "sweetness" with the "curious strength" of the Middle Ages. Pater observes that this sweetness and strength are to be seen in the "legend" of Eloise and Abelard, and that of Tannhäuser. He devotes most of the essay, however, to showing that these qualities are also exemplified by the less familiar story of Amis and Amile (like that of Palemon and Arcite in Geoffrey Chaucer's "Knight's Tale") and *Aucassin and Nicolette*, a prose tale of young lovers written in the thirteenth century. In the next six essays, Pater analyzes some of the writers and painters of the Italian Renaissance in whose work, he believes, the influence of ancient Greece transforms the cultural residue of the Middle Ages into a new humanism. Conte Giovanni Pico della Mirandola's effort to reconcile Platonic philosophy with Christianity is an early stage in this transformation, as are the pictures of Sandro Botticelli, which combine the visionary qualities of medieval painting with the definite, concrete forms Pater thinks characteristic of Greek art. Of the sculptor Luca Della Robbia, Pater notes that he combines the "pure form" of the Greeks with a considerable individual expressiveness somewhat like that of Michelangelo, only less passionate. Indeed, in his essay on Michelangelo's poetry, Pater says that the sonnet form was a stringent discipline upon the artist's emotions. In essays on Leonardo da Vinci, Giorgione, and the French poet Joachim du Bellay, Pater further considers the way in which artistic form at once expresses and controls the personality of its creator. As the eighth essay, he includes the Winckelmann piece because that classical scholar, in the eighteenth century, is "the last fruit of the Renaissance."

The most important of the essays in *Studies in the History of the Renaissance* is on Leonardo da Vinci. For the details of Leonardo's life, Pater draws on Giorgio Vasari's sixteenth-century *Lives of the Most Eminent Painters, Sculptors, and Architects* and on the 1855 study of the Renaissance by the French historian Jules Michelet, whose theories of history were an important influence generally on Pater.

As Winckelmann is for Pater the great intuitive interpreter of the surfaces of Hellenic idealism, Leonardo da Vinci is the great interpreter of depths, a seeker of "the sources of spring beneath the earth or of expression beneath the human countenance." In his studies of nature, Leonardo embodies that element in the Renaissance that anticipates the modern spirit of scientific investigation. But the science of late-fifteenth-century Italy, writes Pater, was "all divination, clairvoyance, unsubjected to our modern formulas, seeking in an instant of vision to concentrate a thousand experiences." Pater invites the reader to regard Leonardo as a magician in his way of experimenting with new materials and concepts as an inventor or painter. Using a backward, mirror handwriting to record his discoveries, sketching mysterious but wonderfully suggestive drawings and cartoons, he was ever in search, suggests Pater, of a way to free familiar subjects from tradional associations and to substitute striking and disturbing images in which corruption taints beauty.

In Pater's view Leonardo was more interested in "human personality" than in nature. "He became above all a painter of portraits," producing the disconcerting portrait of an androgynous Saint John the Baptist and the *Medusa*, with its head of snaky hair, which Pater had seen in the Uffizi Gallery in Florence during his 1865 trip to Italy. (The *Medusa* is no longer attributed to Leonardo.) There are da Vinci's chalk drawings of "clairvoyant" women, "through whom, as through delicate instruments, one becomes aware of the subtler forces of nature, and the modes of their action . . . all those finer conditions wherein material things rise to that subtlety of operation which constitutes them spiritual. . . ." Here are the "forces" at work in each individual life, of which Pater had written in the "Conclusion," symbolized in the experimental drawings of the fifteenth-century painter.

Inspired partially by an essay by Algernon Charles Swinburne entitled "Notes on Designs of the Old Masters in Florence," published in the *Fortnightly Review* for July 1868, Pater describes the *Mona Lisa* (or *La Gioconda*, as it is sometimes called) as "Leonardo's masterpiece," the perfectly diaphanous form, with "a beauty wrought out from within upon the flesh," on which "all the thoughts and experience of the world" are expressed. As Pater interprets her, "Lady Lisa" becomes the "symbol of the modern idea" of the "fancy of a perpetual life, sweeping together ten thousand experiences." She suggests the "idea of humanity as wrought upon by, and summing up in itself, all modes of thought and life." In *Art and the Creative Unconscious* (1959) the German psychiatrist Erich Neumann writes of the *Mona Lisa* and of Pater's description of it that "with Mona Lisa's smile was born the soul of modern man."

In his evocation of the *Mona Lisa*, Pater gave to the English literary world of the 1890s a kind of inspiration that led William Butler Yeats to present that passage, arranged as free verse, as the opening poem of *The Oxford Book of Modern Verse, 1892-1935* (1936) and to comment in the introduction to the volume: "I recall Pater's description of the Mona Lisa; had the individual soul of da Vinci's sitter gone down with the pearl divers or trafficked for strange webs? or did Pater foreshadow a poetry, a philosophy, where the individual is nothing, the flux of *The Cantos* of Ezra Pound . . . human experience no longer shut into brief lives, cut off into this place and that place . . . ?"

As Pater stresses the modern, symbolic qualities in Leonardo's art, so, in other essays in *Studies in the History of the Renaissance*, he emphasizes characteristics or habits of his subjects that parallel attitudes or methods of nineteenth-century scientific or historical studies. For example, Botticelli's painterly sensibility "usurps the data before it as the exponent of ideas, moods, visions of its own." In the essay on Giorgione, Pater describes a "striving after otherness" (*Anders-streben*) by which each art achieves "a partial alienation of its own limitations, by which the arts are able . . . reciprocally to lend each other new forces." This idea is the aesthetic equivalent to the evolutionary impulse in the life sciences, to which Pater finds the relative spirit attuned. Finally, in writing of the Neo-Platonic Humanism of Pico della Mirandola, Pater sees a prefigurement of the nineteenth-century predilection for discovering patterns in history. In Pico, he discerns an attitude more characteristic of nineteenth-century historicism, of the kind found in *Studies in the History of the Renaissance*, than it is of the writings of Pico himself: "Nothing which has ever interested living men and women can wholly lose its vitality— no language they have spoken, nor oracle beside which they have hushed their voices, no dream which has once been entertained by actual human minds."

In his biography of Pater, published in 1906, Arthur C. Benson emphasizes the liberating effect of the publication of *Studies in the History of the Renaissance* on 1 March 1873: "It gave Pater a definite place in the literary and artistic world. . . . The younger generation was thrilled with a sense of high artistic possibilities." But if youth was thrilled, maturity, at least within the Oxford establishment, was appalled. The Reverend John Wordsworth, grandnephew of the poet and, like Pater, a fellow of Brasenose College, wrote to Pater about his book: "Could you indeed have known the dangers into which you were likely to lead minds weaker than your own, you would, I believe, have paused."

With characteristic reticence, Pater responded publicly to neither the criticism nor the praise. He was, at least, mindful enough of John Wordsworth's stricture to have deleted the offending conclusion from the second edition of the book in 1877 and to have restored it to the third edition of 1888, with an explanatory note that, fifteen years later, echoes Wordsworth's phrasing: "This brief 'Conclusion' was omitted in the second edition of this book, as I conceived that it

Pater as a fellow at Brasenose College, Oxford, 1872; drawing by Simeon Solomon (Fondazione Horne, Florence)

might possibly mislead some of the young men into whose hands it might fall." Indeed, *Studies in the History of the Renaissance* became a kind of cult book, treasured and even rapturously recited by at least two generations of Oxford undergraduates.

The Macmillan brothers, Pater's publishers for *Studies in the History of the Renaissance* as for the subsequent books, haggled with him over the form of the book as well as the number of copies to be printed. Both the first and second editions had printings of 1,250 copies, while the third had 1,500 and the fourth, in 1893, 2,000, suggesting the book's slightly growing reputation over a twenty-year period. American editions of 1,000 copies each were published in 1887 and 1890, as Pater's reputation blossomed modestly among a transatlantic audience. The pattern of producing several editions in approximately the same number of copies as those published editions of *Studies in the History of the Renaissance* was to be more

or less the same for his later books. By modern standards, Pater was never a best-seller.

Pater soon developed a new literary form, derived from the method of his Renaissance essays, that was to characterize the most important work of the rest of his career, the fictionalized historical studies he called "imaginary portraits." His earliest portrait, "The Child in the House," was published in the August 1878 *Macmillan's Magazine*. More than fifteen years later limited editions of this work appeared in both England and the United States. On a slip of paper, among his unpublished, fragmentary writings now at Harvard University, Pater wrote: "Child in the House: voilà, the germinating, original, source, specimen of all my imaginative work."

"The Child in the House" is an autobiographical sketch to the extent that the states of mind Pater attributes to his character, Florian Deleal, were frequently Pater's own: the susceptibility to intense impressions of beauty mixed with pain or tinged with mortality, a sacramentalist sense of the beautiful holiness of the rituals of human life, the eagerness for vision of the transcendental spiritual life in actual persons and places. The minutely recorded memory of these impressions is the core of the older Florian's religious attitude: "His way of conceiving religion came then to be in effect what it ever afterwards remained—a sacred history indeed, but still more a sacred ideal, a transcendent version or representation, under intenser and more expressive light and shade, of human life and its familiar or exceptional incidents. . . . A place adumbrated itself in his thoughts, wherein those sacred personalities, which are at once the reflex and the pattern of our nobler phases of life, housed themselves; and this region in his intellectual scheme all subsequent experience did but tend still further to realize and define. Some ideal, hieratic persons he would always need to occupy it and keep a warmth there." The "process of brainbuilding" which Florian recalls in his own life is the evolution of the mythic possibility in one's own experience, the discovery of multiple, symbolic meanings that connect the individual life to the collective life of humanity across the boundaries of space and time that define history.

A more personal version of Winckelmann's discovery of the diaphanous unity of form and religious sentiment in Greek art, and of the relevance of that ideal to his own development as man and writer, this "brainbuilding" is the underlying subject of Pater's major work, *Marius the Epicurean; His Sensations and Ideas* (1885).

The book was a long time in gestation. Pater began it in the spring of 1881, and in December 1882 he went to Rome to do background research. By July 1883 he could write to his friend Violet Paget, who wrote under the pseudonym Vernon Lee: "I have hopes of completing one half of my present chief work—an Imaginary Portrait of a peculiar type of mind in the time of Marcus Aurelius—by the end of this Vacation, and meant to have asked you to look at some of the MS. perhaps. I am wishing to get the whole completed, as I have visions of many smaller pieces of work the composition of which would be actually pleasanter to me. However, I regard this present matter as a sort of duty. For, you know, I think that there is a . . . sort of religious phase possible for the modern mind . . . the conditions of which phase it is the main object of my design to convey."

Pater's purpose was to define, in the story of a young man's search for a philosophy by which to live in second-century Rome, the kind of religious belief or state of mind that he considered possible for a thoughtful person in late Victorian England. Repeatedly in the novel, Pater makes explicit and implicit parallels between his fictional world and the circumstances of modern life. In both worlds, the condition of religion is fragmented into many competing sects or cults, and old liturgies and rituals survive, divorced from their traditional dogmatic significances. Many philosophies are available to supplant traditional religion.

In the first of the four parts into which he divides the novel, Pater exposes the impressionable Marius to two materialist philosophies, the Aesculapian cult of bodily health and the sensual literary aestheticism, or "Euphuism," practiced by Flavian, the friend Marius meets in Pisa, who comes to symbolize early in Marius's life the mingled beauty and corruption of the pagan world.

While at the temple of Aesculapius, Marius learns what Pater had taught some years earlier in the conclusion to *Studies in the History of the Renaissance*: the need, throughout life, to cultivate "the capacity of the eye": "To keep the eye clear by a sort of exquisite personal alacrity and cleanliness, extending even to his dwelling place; to discriminate, ever more and more fastidiously, select form and colour in things from what was less select; to meditate much on beautiful visible objects, on objects more especially connected with the period of youth."

As an intended corrective to the perceived licentiousness of his description of diaphanous clarity in the conclusion, Pater emphasizes here, as elsewhere in *Marius*, the moral poise of his "epicurean" doctrine, a poise that Marius comes to see is lacking in his friend Flavian, in whose aestheticism there is not only an unhealthy sensualism but also an impulse to satire. Pater remarks that Flavian reads the legend of Cupid and Psyche, in which Marius innocently finds an idealized representation of love, as though he were reading the work of Jonathan Swift! For Marius, the decorous restraint of his childhood religion is preserved in an unfailing conscience that keeps him from excess.

However, in Flavian's "Euphuism" (Pater recalls in the term the most extravagant of Elizabethan literary styles), Marius finds an intriguing sublimation of religious zeal and sexual energy into the perfection of language of full and exotic self-expression. Marius himself becomes for a period (like the youthful Pater) a poet, and then a kind of diarist, as he seeks always to match the word to the idea. At this point, for Marius, literary style is a variant of ritual, the organic form or medium seeking to discover a new and adequate content.

At eighteen, with Flavian recently dead from fever, Marius ponders his need to understand, not in some doctrinal way, but in his own terms, the meaning of his life in relation to the larger world: "Still with something of the old religious earnestness of his childhood, he set himself . . . to determine his bearings, as by compass, in the world of thought; to get that precise acquaintance with the creative intelligence itself, its structures and capacities, its relation to other parts of himself and to other things, without which certainly no poetry can be masterly. . . . An exact estimate of realities, as towards himself, he must have—a delicately measured gradation of certainty in things, from the distant, haunted surmise or imagination, to the actual feeling of sorrow in his heart. . . ."

Marius's youthful readings of Heraclitus, Epicurus, and Lucretius, each in some way based upon the view of life as continuously changing, incline him to skepticism, to a "despair of knowledge" of the external world for which he tends to compensate "with a delightful sense of escape in replacing the outer world of other people by an inward world as himself really cared to have it. . . ." This tension between a "vision" of a transcendent order and the impressions of the changeful material world is continual in the novel—indeed, it is one of the common elements in all of Pater's writings.

Under the influence of the "New Cyrenaicism," the sensationalist philosophy he learns from the teachings of Aristippus, Marius develops a more focused, if still tentative, sense of his purpose in life: "To understand the various forms of ancient art and thought, the various forms of actual human feeling . . . to satisfy, with a kind of scrupulous equity, the claims of these concrete and actual objects on his sympathy, his intelligence, his senses . . . and in turn become the interpreter of them to others: this had now defined itself for Marius as a very narrowly practical design: it determined his choice of vocation to live by."

As did Winckelmann, Marius comes to equate knowing the self in the present with knowing the past; one does not precede or cause the other. The two knowledges are one, simultaneous. When one has this double vision, he must become an "interpreter . . . to others." To this end, Marius goes to Rome, as did Winckelmann, but to study rhetoric instead of statues. However, beyond learning to see and speak, Marius must learn how to live. He must discover ethics in aesthetics. The central ethical conflict for Marius is embodied in two "hieratic persons" (to recall Florian Deleal's phrase): the handsome young soldier, Cornelius, who represents "some possible intellectual formula" that turns out to be early Christianity, and the emperor, Marcus Aurelius, for whom Marius works as a kind of secretary, whose famous *Meditations* are the most admired expression of Roman Stoicism.

In contradiction of his own Cyrenaic enthusiasm for the physical life before him, Marius perceives in the emperor's oration to his court, on the theme of the evanescence and insignificance of life, only a will to indifference: "Consider how quickly all things vanish away—their bodily structure into the general substance; the very memory of them into that great gulf and abysm of past thoughts. Ah! 'tis on a tiny space of earth thou art creeping through life—a pigmy soul, carrying a dead body to its grave." Marius believes his own sense of the value of life, contingent on his perception of its fragility and brevity, to be morally superior to the willed indifference of the emperor to the spectacle of suffering, both by humans and animals. The emperor's studied apa-

thy, broken only when his own young son dies and the philosopher is overcome by the man, allows him to tolerate what to Marius is the deeply evil spectacle of the gladitorial games and their concomitant torture of animals. (Only later does Marius hear of the brutal torments of the Christian martyrs by previous emperors.) Marius thinks that "he, at least, the humble follower of the bodily eye, was aware of a crisis in life, in this brief, obscure existence, a fierce opposition of real good and real evil around him, the issues of which he must by no means compromise, or confuse; of the antagonisms of which the 'wise' Marcus Aurelius was unaware."

Marius rejects Aurelius's Stoicism because, as he understands it (not accurately, defenders of Aurelius would argue), he believes that this philosophy is based on the emperor's illusory belief in his own moral infallibility, an idea that Marius's own relativist skepticism contradicts. However, if he rejects the main teachings of the emperor, Marius does accept, in his own eclectic way, one preachment of Aurelius: " ' 'Tis in thy power to think as thou wilt .' " Here, Marius finds sanction for his own ruminations on "the will as vision," during a ride in the Sabine Hills outside Rome.

Drawing on the theory of material flux he had presented in the conclusion of *Studies in the History of the Renaissance*, Pater has Marius reason, "after the analogy of the bodily life," that his own spirit might participate in "that great stream of spiritual energy" in such a way that the "material fabric of things" might be considered as "but an element in a world of thought," and, if that were so, the "prison-wall" of the material world might actually be penetrable, "actually dissolving all around him," under the power of his own intense apprehension. Marius comes to believe, more strongly than before, in the strength of diaphanous vision to perceive the ideal in the material, described by Pater as characterizing the career of Winckelmann. With a new "quiet hope, a quiet joy," in his new belief, Marius thinks, in Pater's words: "Must not all that remained of life be but a search for the equivalent of that ideal, among so-called actual things—a gathering together of every trace or token of it, which his actual experience might present?"

Marius finds this ideal realized in the actual when he is taken by his friend Cornelius to visit the primitive Christian church in the house of the Roman matron Cecilia. Here, in the intimate presence of the dead in their catacombs, and in the decorous but joyous ritual of an early morning Mass, Marius finds a religion that combines with his recollections of the "Religion of Numa" of his childhood a promise of resurrection, of eternal life, that seems to combine the human with the divine. But the emphasis in Marius's thoughts is on the human: "It was Christianity in its humanity, or even its humanism, in its generous hopes for man, its common sense, and alacrity of cheerful service, its sympathy with all creatures, its appreciation of beauty and daylight."

Marius finds in the second-century Christian church not the asceticism that would take hold in later centuries, but the idea of culture, to which he has already given his assent. His witnessing of the Mass confirms his prior belief—Pater's own—that ritual is the element that links aesthetic philosophy to at least possible belief, especially when the ritual has been divorced from no longer credible dogma and is thereby opened up to new transcendent significance in the form of revitalized myth. The dying gods of pagan myth give way to the death and Resurrection of Christ. The early Church that Marius observes, for which he feels such a strong affinity but to which he is never converted, is a model of that "religious phase" that Pater hoped would be possible for the modern mind, a form of faith more enduring than faith itself.

At the end of the novel, Pater has Marius and Cornelius taken prisoner by anti-Christian soldiers. Marius stays behind as the supposed Christian when Cornelius is released. Falling ill with fever, Marius is left behind by the soldiers, in the care of peasants, to await his death.

Not only has Marius not become a Christian convert, but he also seems at the end to back away from his evident attraction to Christianity and to revert to an earlier Epicureanism, although it is now so elemental, so austere, so abstract, as to be unidentifiable with any doctrine, either that of Epicurus or of Aristippus: "Surely, the aim of a true philosophy must be, not in futile efforts toward the complete accommodation of man to the circumstances in which he chances to find himself, but in the maintenance of a kind of candid discontent, in the face of the very highest achievement; the unclouded and receptive soul quitting the world finally, with the same fresh wonder with which it had entered the world still unimpaired, and going on its blind way at last with the consciousness of some profound enigma in things, as but a pledge of something further to come."

Marius's closing thought is of the diaphanous sensibility described as though it were one of Plato's migrating souls, entering material form in life only to cast it off again in death, before going on to another form. Christianity, like the other philosophies and religions Marius encounters, is merely one more "aesthetic adventure." For reasons he does not explain, Pater denies his hero final faith, but leaves him a composed skepticism—a strange last reversal of the apparent direction of the entire novel.

However, the ending is ambiguous: although Marius remains unconverted at his death, the peasants who tend him do not know this and, from his circumstances, conclude that he is, in fact, a Christian. Just before he dies, they administer wafer and water, and Marius dies with the apparent sacrament if not the faith of the religion he has admired as his ideal-in-the-actual. One astute twentieth-century reader has pointed to the irony of Pater's ending, that it makes "a Christian saint out of a pagan skeptic."

That observation sets the tone for the critical reception of *Marius the Epicurean* in Pater's own time. Most of the reviewers found Pater's attention to historical detail, his inclusion of translations of classical authors—Lucius Apuleius, Lucian, and Marcus Aurelius—and his highly wrought though difficult style more worthy of praise than they did the "aesthetic" philosophy of the book. As the London *Times* reviewer put it, " 'Marius the Epicurean' may be briefly described as fine writing and hard reading."

Mrs. Humphry Ward's review in *Macmillan's Magazine* (May 1885) is analytical. She observes that the book is more about nineteenth-century England than about second-century Rome, and that it reveals an essentially "English characteristic": "As a nation we are not fond of direct 'confessions.' All our autobiographical literature, compared to the French or German, has a touch of dryness and reserve. It is in books like 'Sartor Resartus,' or 'The Nemesis of Faith,' 'Alton Locke,' or 'Marius,' rather than in the avowed specimens of self-revelation which the time has produced, that the future student of the nineteenth century will have to look for what is deepest, most intimate, and most real in its personal experience. In the case of those natures whose spiritual experience is richest and most original, there is with us, coupled with a natural tendency to expression, a natural tendency to disguise. We want to describe for others the spiritual things which have delighted or admonished ourselves, but we shrink

Sketch of Pater by Charles Holmes, a student at Brasenose College who later became director of the National Gallery in London (Constable Publishers)

from too great a realism of method. English feeling, at its best and subtlest, has always something elusive in it, something which resents a spectator, and only moves at ease when it has succeeded in interposing some light screen or some obvious mask between it and the public."

"Disguise," "screen," "mask": these terms suggest the oblique, distorting, symbolic modes of expressiveness that characterize modernist literature. Yeats later chose the term "mask" to define that antitype of the actual self through which the poet must, in one phase of his art, speak. In Pater's case, the concept of a disguise or mask for the presumably diaphanous sensibility takes the form mainly of myth as, unlike Marius, the heroes of his later imaginary portraits are seen as avatars of the dying god Dionysus. Pater uses the motif of the gods-in-exile, which he probably discovered in the German poet Heinrich Heine, as a mythic disguise in his later work, and this disguised transparency Mrs.

Ward's trenchant comment defines as it appears in *Marius the Epicurean.*

In order to work full-time on *Marius*, Pater had resigned his tutorial duties at Brasenose, although not his fellowship, in 1883. In 1885 he and his sisters moved to London, where he lived as a modest literary celebrity. The move coincided with his being rejected for the Slade Professorship in the fine arts that Ruskin had vacated; once again, Pater had been snubbed by official Oxford. In his house at 12 Earl's Terrace, London, Pater entertained what Violet Paget called a "fashionable Bohemian element," although Frank Harris was more struck by the "austere simplicity" of the Pater home: "The house might have belonged to a grocer." Another visitor thought that Pater himself looked like "a retired artillery officer in reduced circumstances"—an impression borne out by late photographs. In the summer of 1893, perhaps weary of fashionable life, Pater and his sisters moved back to Oxford, to a house at 64 St. Giles, near the famous Martyrs' Monument.

Pater's writing during the London years was diverse and extensive. In addition to revising his earlier essays, he produced seven "imaginary portraits," four of which appeared in a book of that title in 1887. These pieces are "A Prince of Court Painters," "Sebastian van Storck," "Duke Carl of Rosenmold," and "Denys l'Auxerrois."

"A Prince of Court Painters" presents the career of the French painter Jean-Antoine Watteau (1684-1721), supposedly through selective entries in the diary of the older sister of Watteau's disciple Jean Baptiste Pater, with whom Walter Pater and his sisters liked to claim a distant kinship. In Pater's sketch, Watteau, a native of Valenciennes in northern France, goes to Paris to study art and soon develops a "new manner" of painting that becomes fashionable. Despite his success as a painter of the elegant amusements of the French court, Watteau is restless, contemptuous of the brilliant but superficial world he has idealized in his art. What he experienced in his childhood and youth, his "vision within," carries over into his mature period as a genius who is master of an alien world from which he wishes to escape. As the narrator writes: "He will overcome his early training; and these light things will possess for him always a kind of representative or borrowed worth, as characterizing that impossible or forbidden world which the mason's boy saw through the closed gateways of the enchanted garden. Those trifling and petty graces, the *insignia* to him of that noble world of aspiration and ideas, even now that he is aware, as I conceive, of their true littleness, bring back to him by the power of association, all the old magical exhilaration of his dream—his dream of a better world than the real one. There, is the formula, as I apprehend, of his success—of his extraordinary hold on things so alien from himself."

The Romantic impulse to recover, amid alien circumstances, the original dream of childhood or youth underlies the behavior of most of Pater's diaphanous heroes. It is the motive of Florian Deleal, of Marius, and even, as Pater treats him, of the historical Winckelmann. It is only in the later imaginary portraits that the emphasis falls more decisively on the alienation and less on the recovery.

Most somber, perhaps, is the case of Sebastian van Storck—the son of a wealthy Dutch burgomaster and the cynosure of that seventeenth-century world depicted by the genre-painters of the time—who seeks to escape altogether from the physical world into the realm of abstract theory. Taking refuge in his tower room, he comes to think of reality as the product of "his own lonely thinking power." The symbol of this absolute thought is the sea, which, in Holland, always threatens to overwhelm the life depicted by the painters. Sebastian's love of the sea is a death wish. However, he has some residual affection for life and is partially redeemed from his aberration when he rescues a small child from the onrushing waters of a sea storm, although he himself drowns.

In contrast to Watteau and Sebastian van Storck, Duke Carl of Rosenmold has an explicit mythic identity: he is an Apollo figure, seeking to bring "enlightenment" to his sleepy little duchy in the last years of the eighteenth century. Carl has a vision of his true mission, which is to prepare the way for the *Aufklärung*, or awakening, by developing the latent cultural powers of Germany: "Here, he began to see that it could be in no other way than by action of informing thought upon the vast material of which Germany was in possession: art, poetry, fiction, an entire imaginative world, following reasonably upon a deeper understanding of the past, of nature, of one's self—an understanding of all beside through the knowledge of one's self. To understand, would be the indispensable first step towards the enlargement of the great past, of one's little present, by criticism, by imagination."

Again, as with Winckelmann and Marius, to know oneself is to know history. This passage is perhaps the most cogent statement Pater ever made of the historical role of diaphanous man as "an interpreter . . . to others." Carl's labors, Pater notes, anticipate the work of the great German thinkers of the late eighteenth and early nineteenth centuries, when German culture was the richest in Europe, the source of the cultural enhancement of England itself. Especially in Goethe, greatest of German Romantics, Duke Carl's Apollonian role as culture-bringer is fulfilled.

As "Duke Carl of Rosenmold" depicts the Apollonian side of diaphanous man, "Denys l'Auxerrois" represents the vestigial presence of Dionysian worship in medieval Christianity. We do not see the "quaint legend" of Denys—Dionysus reborn in the person of the likable but peculiar young artisan of thirteenth-century Auxerre, with special gifts for gardening, playing ball, and making music—at first hand, but rather through the fragmentary interpretation of a nineteenth-century antiquarian scholar, who pieces together the details of the legend from a fragment of stained glass (depicting Denys), an old set of tapestries that portray the legend, and certain antique priestly notes that he finds in the cathedral of Saint Etienne.

Throughout most of the portrait, Denys's Dionysian identity is handled rather playfully, but, eventually, as the mythic embodiment of irrational impulse, Denys symbolically has a maddening effect on the townspeople of Auxerre. They give themselves to drunken and violent revelry, and finally tear Denys himself to pieces in a savage ritual hunt, as the original god, or his human surrogate, was torn to pieces by ecstatic Greek worshipers, his remains being scattered to ensure a fruitful harvest. Unlike his prototype, Denys is not resurrected with the spring planting; instead, his heart is buried by a frightened monk in a dark corner of the cathedral—symbolic of Denys's alien, pagan status in a Christian world.

Imaginary Portraits was Pater's favorite among his own books. However, the volume received a more muted critical reception than either *Studies in the History of the Renaissance* or *Marius the Epicurean*. Critics disagreed about which of the portraits was most impressive. Oscar Wilde favored "Sebastian van Storck," while George Woodberry, an American admirer of Pater, thought "A Prince of Court Painters" the "most highly finished" of the pieces. A third critic,

Eleanor Catherine Price, judged *Imaginary Portraits* "the saddest book that Mr. Pater has yet written," and thought "Denys l'Auxerrois" "the most adorned with touches in Mr. Pater's own peculiar style." None of the critics was much impressed by "Duke Carl of Rosenmold," although one may think that, for Mrs. Ward's student of the nineteenth century, it is in many respects the most interesting of the four portraits.

Subsequently, three more of Pater's short imaginary portraits appeared in magazines: "Hippolytus Veiled" (*Macmillan's Magazine*, 1889), "Emerald Uthwart" (*New Review*, 1892), and "Apollo in Picardy" (*Harper's Magazine*, 1893). (Earlier, he had written a fragment, "An English Poet," that was not published until 1 April 1931 in the *Fortnightly Review*.)

"Hippolytus Veiled," based on a lost version of the *Hippolytus* of Euripides (circa 484-circa 406 B.C.), tells of the son of Theseus and Antiope, queen of the Amazons, who is raised in a remote village of ancient Greece when his father, prince of Athens, casts off Antiope and takes the sensuous Phaedra as his queen. Hippolytus grows into a chaste and devout youth, a worshiper of the stern nature goddess Artemis. When he goes to Athens, Phaedra, his stepmother, attempts to seduce him to the worship of Aphrodite, goddess of love. When Hippolytus refuses, Phaedra tells Theseus that he has seduced her, and the prince curses his son, who is eventually killed when Poseidon, god of the sea, causes Hippolytus's beloved chariot-horses to panic and drag him to death along the rough seashore stones.

Unlike Pater's earlier diaphanous heroes, Hippolytus is not so much an Apollonian symbol of light brought to illuminate the new age of cultural development as a symbol of forces and attitudes "veiled," virtually lost in the dark of history, brought to light by the penetrative light of the scholar's imagination. "Hippolytus" is Pater's most intimate and touching sketch of the remote past.

"Apollo in Picardy" is, in effect, a companion piece to "Denys l'Auxerrois" in which the mysterious god-in-exile comes among the monks of a rural monastery to shock them violently out of the torpor of abstract thought that Pater consistently regards as the besetting defect of medieval Christianity. Apparently without intent, the god kills a young novice of the monastic order, Hyacinth, as he had killed his mythic namesake. Like Hippolytus, Hyacinth is a symbol of Pater's idea that beautiful youth must die as a harbinger of, a

sacrifice to, the irresistible forces of natural or historical change.

The third of these short portraits, "Emerald Uthwart," is especially interesting, for like the earliest, "The Child in the House," it is set in England and draws upon more elements of Pater's own life than the other portraits. In fact, the immediate inspiration for its composition was a nostalgic 1891 visit that Pater made to the King's School in Canterbury.

Emerald is the promising son of an otherwise decaying rural family of Sussex, raised in perfect natural freedom but sent to school to be disciplined into an English gentleman. Mythically, he is a Dionysian figure endowed with a genius for "submissiveness," being shaped by the Apollonian ascetic rigor of the school. Emerald becomes a synthesis of just those historical and personal attributes that appealed in the early 1890s, when Rudyard Kipling was the literary rage. Indeed, Emerald seems, in historical retrospect, to be the type of that clear-eyed, idealistic youth that went off to die in World War I. However, Emerald and his friend James Stokes fight in the Napoleonic war, during which Stokes is executed for desertion and Emerald is sent in disgrace from the army. After wandering in France, he comes home, is forgiven his sin, and dies as a result of an old bullet wound close to the heart.

In this strange tale, Pater reflects the tensions between the individual's need for freedom and self-esteem and the inclination of national life to repress and subordinate those qualities for its own purposes. Pater stresses ironically the similarities and differences between the nurturing discipline of school and the mindless regimentation, conducive to restlessness and disobedience, of the army. Emerald, whose "submissiveness" makes him ideally suited to this discipline, also possesses a sensitivity and intelligence that make him resentful of and vulnerable to the destructive power of authority that is too repressive. He seems, somewhat like the hero of A. E. Housman's sequence of poems, *A Shropshire Lad* (1896), born to be a victim, one whose special aura is also the cause of his death. (*Billy Budd*, Herman Melville's posthumously published novella, also treats such a figure.) Pater's Emerald is the type of many successive youthful "dying gods" in English and American fiction.

On 15 November 1889 a collection of Pater's earlier periodical essays on English literature appeared under the title *Appreciations*. In the introductory essay, "Style," Pater asserts that imaginative prose presents not fact, but the writer's "sense of fact"; it makes "an appeal to the reader to catch the writer's spirit . . . his peculiar intuition of a world, prospective, or discerned below the faulty conditions of the present, in either case changed somewhat from the actual world." Repeatedly, Pater brings his theory back to this key point of expressiveness: literary art is the representation of "fact as connected with soul, of a specific personality, in all its preferences, its volition and power."

Pater devotes much of "Style" to describing the way the diaphanous writer acquires the language necessary for this perfect expression of the inner vision. He must be eclectic, drawing not only on the language of metaphysics and the pictorial arts, but also, and especially, on the language of science, since science gives the most precise formulation of the actual conditions of life, as the modern world knows it. Pater is the first critic wholeheartedly to assert the indispensable fusion of personal, intuitive insight with scientific method as the basis of criticism, of all literary art. The perfect style must balance "soul" with "mind." That is, the expression of personality must come in a logically cogent structure of thought attained by craftsmanship, a subject that Pater gives new emphasis in this late essay. Nowhere else does Pater speak so insistently of the necessity for intellectual effort to achieve moral significance in writing.

The other essays in *Appreciations*, written from 1874 to 1886, not surprisingly follow the method of criticism Pater defines in the preface to *Studies in the History of the Renaissance*: they seek the unique "formula" of a writer through an analysis of his life and selected works. For example, Wordsworth exhibits the habit of Romantic poets of discovering "an intimate consciousness of the expression of natural things"; "he has a power . . . of realising, and conveying to the consciousness of the reader, abstract and elementary impressions—silence, darkness, absolute motionlessness: or, again, the whole complex sentiment of a particular place, the abstract expression of desolation in the long white road, of peacefulness in a particular folding of the hills. In the airy building of the brain, a special day or hour even, comes to have for him a sort of personal identity . . . it has a presence in one's history, and acts there, as a separate power or accomplishment; and he has celebrated in many of his poems the 'efficacious spirit,' which, as he says, resides in these 'particular spots' of time." Above all, Words-

worth, as Pater interprets him, teaches that "being," rather than "doing," is "the principle of all the higher morality." Wordsworth shows that "to withdraw the thoughts for a little while from the mere machinery of life, to fix them, with appropriate emotions, on the spectacle of those great facts in man's existence which no machinery affects . . . is the aim of all culture."

Charles Lamb is a subject more amenable to Pater's ideas than is Wordsworth. Essentially a lover of old things, rather out of temper with his time, Lamb the antiquarian essayist possessed an "intellectual epicureanism" that enabled him, in *Specimens of English Dramatic Poets Contemporary with Shakespeare* (1808), to bring to modern attention the disregarded work of Elizabethan dramatists other than Shakespeare. (Although Pater does not mention the fact, Lamb and his sister, Mary, produced *Tales from Shakespeare*, 1807, a retelling of some of the plays that became a children's classic.) But Lamb's greatest triumph was to treat, in his *Essays of Elia* (1823, 1833), his own age from an antiquarian perspective; he shows how a later age will see his own: "But it is part of the privilege of the genuine humourist to anticipate this pensive mood with regard to the ways and things of his own day; to look upon the tricks in manner of the life about him with that same refined purged sort of vision, which will come naturally to those of a later generation. . . ."

This "purged sort of vision" is that of the diaphanous sensibility, which can express through itself the kind of selective or idealized apprehension of the living, contemporary world that is usually attainable only from works of art or the inert patterns of the past. In this respect, the "humor" of Lamb is like that of Walter Scott and Charles Dickens. Lamb's essays, in some ways, writes Pater, are a "mimicry" of the subjects and style of the seventeenth-century physician and writer Sir Thomas Browne. Pater does not mention Lamb in his essay on Browne, published in May 1886 in *Macmillan's Magazine*, but what he says of the "humourist" in the Browne essay is consonant with his definition of the term in the essay on Lamb. To Pater, these writers, for all their differences of personal character and historical circumstance, share the qualities of the diaphanous sensibility: "It is, in truth, to the literary purpose of the humourist, in the old-fashioned sense of the term, that this method of writing—of the humourist to whom all the world is but a spectacle in which nothing is really alien from himself, who has hardly a sense of the distinction between great and little among things that are at all, and whose half-pitying, half-amused sympathy is called out especially by the seemingly small interests and traits of character in the things or the people around him."

More than Lamb's, however, Browne's humor is tinged with a kind of cheerful if morbid curiosity in the presence of death amid the activities of daily life: one of his most noteworthy works is a treatise on a set of burial urns from the days when Britain was under Roman occupation. Browne's curious studies and his physician's vocation make him, despite his many old-fashioned habits and beliefs, a kind of precursor, along with Francis Bacon, of the modern scientific investigator. Perhaps his best-known work is the *Religio Medici* ("A Doctor's Religion," 1643), and Pater points to the relevance of this work for a nineteenth-century audience beset by the apparently hopeless conflict between scientific discovery and traditional religious belief: "He presents, in an age, the intellectual powers of which tend strongly to agnosticism, that class of minds to which the supernatural view of things is still credible."

Appreciations includes Pater's three essays on Shakespeare. The first of these, on *Love's Labour's Lost*, focuses on Shakespeare's comic treatment of the extravagant euphuistic language popular with writers in the 1590s, the period of Shakespeare's own earliest works, such as *Romeo and Juliet*, the elaborate figurative language of which is much like that of the Euphuistic writers. The essay on *Measure for Measure* is Pater's most insightful on Shakespeare. Calling the play "the central expression of his moral judgment," Pater makes it into a parable of the moral necessity for critical understanding informed by love.

In "Shakespeare's English Kings" Pater makes the history plays a "humorous" expression of sympathy for the fallibility of mere mortals, only very occasionally asserting the divinity that hedges a king. Especially, Pater focuses on King Richard II, the self-styled lyric poet, whose capricious policies and infatuation with his ability to image his own prisoner's plight in clever language, cause his overthrow by the ruthless Bolingbroke. In possibly 1853, the young Pater had seen the eminent Victorian tragic actor Charles Kean in a production of *Richard II*, and, as he says in the essay, the memory stuck. In the poeticizing and self-pity of Richard, Pater finds the most apt example for his thesis that "Shakespeare's

kings are not, nor are meant to be, great men." The view is one-sided (especially when one considers the full context of *Henry IV*, Parts 1 and 2, and *Henry V*) but supportable.

In the Pre-Raphaelite poet and painter Dante Gabriel Rossetti, Pater finds a Victorian embodiment of the diaphanous sensibility, clearly expressed in Rossetti's work. Both as a poet in his own right and as a translator of Dante's *Vita Nuova* and other works of medieval Italian poetry, Rossetti possessed the "gift of transparency in language," and Pater's description of the precise felicity of Rossetti's language anticipates what he will say, five years later, in "Style," about the disciplined eclecticism that fuses form and matter in good writing. Pater also finds in the poems of Rossetti that the "common things" of nature "are full of human or personal expression, full of sentiment," as in "The Woodspurge," in which Rossetti evokes something like the "pagan sentiment" that Pater asserts is the basis of all religious feeling. With Rossetti, we seem to enter "some revival of the old mythopoeic age," as the modern artistic consciousness seeks in the vividly imaged past, as in its minutely realized impression of the present, some form to serve as the expressive symbol of itself.

The closing essay of *Appreciations*, "Postscript" (originally titled "Romanticism" when it was published in *Macmillan's Magazine*, November 1876), was written in 1876 and is an extended definition that has affinities with Pater's description of the Renaissance spirit in his earlier book of essays. Romanticism, with a restless curiosity that leads it to seek "a beauty born of unlikely elements," elements in which strangeness and wildness are more common than familiarity and order, is an assertion of freedom in many facets of life, as it throws off or adapts older aesthetic forms to new significance. It is the dominant historical impulse of the nineteenth century, which seeks in an eclectic way to realize its characteristic art: "our curious, complex, aspiring age still abounds in subjects for manipulation by the literary as well as by other forms of art. For the literary art, at all events, the problem just now is, to induce order upon the contorted, proportionless accumulation of our knowledge and experience, our science and history, our hopes and disillusion. . . . In literature as in other matters it is well to unite as many diverse elements as may be: that the individual writer or artist, certainly, is to be estimated by the number of graces he combines, and his power of interpenetrating them in a

First page from the unfinished manuscript for "Tibalt the Albigense," one of several "imaginary portraits" begun by Pater in his later years (Houghton Library, Harvard University)

given work." That paradox, of inducing unitary, transparent order by an eclectic (that is, carefully selected but various) means, is at the heart of Pater's moral aesthetic. In many different forms, the principle of eclectic order is central to the aesthetics of modern art.

The critics especially liked the essays on Wordsworth and Lamb, although at least one critic, W. J. Courthope, writing for *Nineteenth Century* in April 1890, objected to Pater's assertion that Wordsworth teaches the supremacy of "being" over "doing" as the basis of the moral life. Courthope also felt that Pater's "sympathetic" method did not eliminate the necessary critical standards for a valid "objective" criticism. One critic, Mrs. Margaret Oliphant, who had earlier chastised Pater for his interpretation of Botticelli, took him to task again, in *Blackwood's Magazine* for January 1890, for what she believed to be his pedantry in "Style" in trying to force French models, in the shape of Flaubert, on the forms of English prose. She also found his theory of eclectic vocabulary obscure.

The matter of Pater's own style was once again debated. John Addington Symonds, to some extent Pater's rival as an interpreter of the Renaissance, wrote in a letter of 19 January 1890, during a bout of influenza, "I tried Pater's 'Appreciations' to-day, and found myself wandering about among the precious sentences, just as though I had lost myself in a sugar-plantation— the worse for being sweet." On a more positive note, Arthur Symons, in the *Athenaeum* (14 December 1889), characterized Pater's style in *Appreciations*, in contrast to the style of *Studies in the History of the Renaissance*, as having "less sensuousness, a severer ordering and ornament, more of what he calls '*mind* in style'; more freedom also." William Watson, writing in the *Academy* (21 December 1889), believed that *Appreciations* would "consolidate its author's fame as one of the most catholic of living critics, and beyond rivalry the subtlest artist in contemporary English prose."

Pater's last book published in his lifetime was *Plato and Platonism*, worked up from lectures he delivered to undergraduates in 1891. "I have tried to treat the subject in as popular a manner as possible," he assured his editor in discussing this volume, which appeared on 10 February 1893.

In the first three chapters, Pater describes the early Greek philosophies from which Plato's philosophy developed. Specifically, the doctrine of Heraclitus, that all reality is perpetual motion, is opposed by the doctrine of Parmenides that all phenomena are ultimately, absolutely one, at perpetual rest. The opinions of Heraclitus and Parmenides are combined in the "doctrine of number" taught by the mysterious Pythagoras, wherein the relative motion of all things is in accord with mathematical ratios that reflect the harmony of the "music of the spheres."

Along the way, Pater establishes some corollary terms: the doctrine of motion reflects the diversity of the centrifugal Ionian culture of Athens, its many-sidedness, the impulse of all things to go their own way, the tendency of forces to fly off in all directions. The Parmenidean doctrine of the One at perpetual rest expresses the impulse of individual persons and things to cohere to a central authority or community, the centripetal impulse that Plato found expressed in the Dorian culture of Athens's great rival city, Sparta (or "Lacedaemon," as Pater usually calls it, referring to the region to the north of Athens where Sparta was situated). These related oppositions— Heraclitean/Parmenidean, Ionian/Dorian, centrifugal/centripetal—are all ways of conceiving the opposition between the sensuous life and the ideal life. Plato's purpose was to define the way in which the changefulness of the physical world, and of Athenian society, could be brought into harmonious stability and hierarchical order of the quasi-ideal kind at Sparta.

Pater suggests that Plato stands, like Marius, as a kind of analogue for nineteenth-century thinkers, trying to balance the claims of evolutionary theory and historical relativism with the still precious but no longer wholly credible doctrines of Christian belief. The theory of ideas is almost a metaphor for traditional Christian theology, and Plato's commitment to the claims of the changeful physical world is a metaphor for the nineteenth-century intellectual's necessary allegiance to the "relative spirit" and to the many implications of the historical and scientific concept of "development."

Pater makes of Socrates, the great philosophical inspirer of Plato and the central figure in the Platonic Dialogues, a teacher who inculcates in his students the need for a self-questioning, skeptical examination of the conditions of actual experience and of the degree to which they conform to the ideal. The famed "Socratic method" of question-and-answer, the dialogue, not so much of the teacher and student but of the teacher's "mind with itself," as it explores such issues as the nature of justice and the good, becomes presumably a model for dialogues that the students may subsequently hold for themselves within their own minds. Socrates presents himself (whether he is as he says he is, is a moot point for Pater) as an inquirer after truth, not the dogmatic proponent of truths he already knows. He instills in Plato a belief in the reality of the ideal as it relates to the issue of how we are to live, and this belief makes Plato the adamant opponent of the Sophists, the Athenian school of philosophers and rhetoricians who teach that not the discovery of truth, but the ability to make other people believe that what one says is the truth, is the goal of education. The Sophists, priding themselves on the powers of argument they train in their pupils, are symptomatic of the dangerous centrifugality, of the excessive individualism, that Plato discerned in Athens—and, one may infer, that Pater discerned in late-nineteenth-century England.

Increasingly, Pater turns away from the radical, almost solipsistic individualism he had avowed in the "Conclusion" to *Studies in the History of the Renaissance*, toward an embrace of something like religious orthodoxy and, by implication, even state authoritarianism, as his account of Plato's effort to apply the Dorian spirit to the diffuse Ionian spirit of Athens suggests. In Lacedaemon, Pater finds "the very genius of conservatism" expressed. This Dorian culture, which Pater read about in the writings of the German scholar Karl Otfried Müller (1797-1840), has a social and educational structure that reminds Pater not only of "the novices at school in some Gothic cloister," but "of our own English schools" as well. His description of the ascetic training of Spartan youth blends Müller's scholarship with his own recently refreshed impressions of English public-school life, so evident in "Emerald Uthwart," which was written about the same time as the "Lacedaemon" chapter of *Plato and Platonism*.

In this Spartan education, as presumably in its modern English equivalent, the spiritual and the physical are treated as inseparable: the "outer form" of the body becomes expressive of the inner discipline of the students, who realize the ideal of humanity in the aesthetic exercises they perform—appropriately, simple, ritualistic dance set to a severe Dorian music that Pater compares to the Gregorian music of the medieval Christian church. This Lacedaemonian dancing, says Pater, perfectly exemplifies the kind of "imitative" art

that Plato believed contributed to the solidarity of the individual and the community. Ritual dance is an element in Sparta's "religion of sanity."

Perhaps because he was disturbed by the hedonistic interpretations his own earlier works had received in the popular press and among the undergraduates and academic authorities of Oxford, Pater wanted to present Plato as the source of an institutional tradition, blending the secular and the religious, that would assure the moral soundness of the individual life modeled in "the spirit of art." The final chapter of *Plato and Platonism*, "Plato's Aesthetics," attempts precisely that justification.

According to Pater, Plato is "the earliest critic of the fine arts. He anticipates the modern notion that art as such has no end but its own perfection—'art for art's sake.'" As Pater explains Plato's views on the matter in *The Republic*, the perfection of artistic technique in craft or performance is congruent with the individual's moral development, as he comes perfectly to fulfill his "function" in the communal life. "Platonic aesthetics," Pater writes, "are ever in close connection with Plato's ethics. It is life itself, action and character, he proposes to colour; to get something of the irrepressible conscience of art, that spirit of control, into the general course of life, above all into its energetic or impassioned acts."

Although *Plato and Platonism* was, on the whole, well received, individual reviewers found fault with some of Pater's points of interpretation. Richard Holt Hutton, editor of the *Spectator*, felt that Pater did not rightly represent the awesome, aloof reality of Plato's "ideas," not to be attributed to or controlled by gods or men. Plato's conception of the ideal was not that it was associated with, or embodied in, a "personality," but that it was abstract from the experiential world. Lewis Campbell, Scottish classicist, writing in the *Classical Review*, found Pater's representation of the mysticism of Plato "inadequate." Most critics praised, more warmly than they did Pater's analysis of Plato's own thought, his description of the pre-Socratic philosophies. But Pater's view of Plato as, at once, the philosopher of the "absolute" and the master spirit of skepticism was confirmed by the American classical scholar Paul Shorey of the University of Chicago, in a review for the *Dial* (1 April 1893).

After *Plato and Platonism*, Pater's reputation began to grow toward the considerable stature it would reach in the first decade of the twentieth century. However, he did not produce another book before his death the next year, only some short magazine pieces and several incomplete manuscripts, which were collected or published for the first time only posthumously, by his literary executor Charles Shadwell, who had the cooperation of Pater's sisters.

In 1895 Shadwell prepared for publication two volumes of Pater's essays, *Greek Studies* and *Miscellaneous Studies*. The first of these collections contains "A Study of Dionysus" and "Demeter and Persephone," both published originally in 1876, "Hippolytus Veiled," and several lesser essays on Greek sculpture, poetry, and coins. *Miscellaneous Studies*, as the title suggests, is a more scattered collection. "The Child in the House," "Emerald Uthwart," and "Apollo in Picardy" are included, as well as late essays on Raphael (first published in *Fortnightly Review*, October 1892) and Blaise Pascal (unfinished at Pater's death and published posthumously in *Contemporary Review*, February 1895).

The most controversial posthumous publication was *Gaston de Latour* (1896), which Pater intended to be a historical novel similar in method to *Marius the Epicurean*. He had six chapters published in periodicals: the first five appeared in *Macmillan's Magazine* from June to October 1888; the seventh was printed in the *Fortnightly Review* of 1 August 1889. Pater abandoned *Gaston de Latour* in 1891, and the rest of the novel was left in manuscript at his death. Of these manuscripts, Shadwell found only that of chapter 6 suitable for publication in the book edition. However, the remaining six manuscript chapters have recently been edited for publication, and the novel may appear soon in a complete, if unrevised, form.

The characterization and plot of *Gaston de Latour*, set in turbulent sixteenth-century France, are even more attenuated than those in *Marius the Epicurean* and the *Imaginary Portraits*. The principal figure is a young man from central France who is ordained in the Roman Catholic church and is sent for training to the great cathedral at Chartres. He is given by a friend a copy of the poems of Pierre de Ronsard, which have the effect of opening his eyes to the beauty of the physical world, much as Marius's study of Cyrenaic philosophy affected him. When he is taken by the same friend who had given him Ronsard's poems to meet Ronsard himself, Ronsard gives Gaston a letter of introduction to take to Michel Eyquem de Montaigne.

As Pater presents him, Montaigne is the skeptical philosopher and the apologist for Renaissance humanism, as against the ascetic practices of medieval religion. Montaigne is an early expositor, in Pater's view, of the modern relative spirit.

In describing Montaigne's "doctrinal egotism," Pater gives another clear statement of the skeptical attitude of belief in the sovereign power of the individual creative imagination, a central tenet of his work from the early conclusion to his late lectures on Plato, in which he stresses discipline rather than expression of individual powers. Pater's interest in Montaigne apparently subsided once he had deeply engaged himself with the study of Plato. The truth of Montaigne is the old truth of the diaphanous sensibility: "Whatever truth there might be, must come for each of us from within, not from without. To that wonderful microcosm of the individual soul, of which, for each one, all other worlds are but elements,—to himself,—to what was apparent immediately to him ... he confidently dismissed the enquirer. His own egotism was but the pattern of the true intellectual life of every one."

Gaston, however, finds a more fully compelling philosophy in the discourse at Paris, "Shadows of Ideas," given by the Italian philosopher Giordano Bruno (1548?-1600), whose "lower pantheism" becomes, in Pater's terms, the recognizable forerunner of Romantic aesthetics: "The divine consciousness has the same relation to the production of things as the human intelligence to the production of true thoughts concerning them. Nay! those thoughts are themselves actually God in man: a loan to man also of His assisting spirit, who, in truth, is the Creator of things, in and by His contemplation of them. For Him, as for man in proportion as man thinks truly, thought and being are identical, and things existent only in so far as they are known." Man participates in the creative process by virtue of his thinking power. His awareness that God is animate in all things obligates him to be ever alert in discerning the minute particularity of the "details of life and character." Reading the passing spectacle of human life and of the natural world in Bruno's philosophy, one perceives "the full revelation, the story in detail, of that one universal mind, struggling, emerging ... in various orders of being,—the veritable history of God." History as the concrete evolution of the mind of God: Pater has made Bruno a precursor of the Hegelian philosophy in which Pater's own historical and aesthetic views are rooted.

When Walter Pater died at his Oxford home on 30 July 1894, the tone of the obituaries

Pater's grave, Holywell Cemetery, Oxford

and the various eulogistic statements was respectful but rather muted, like the reviews of his publications, as though the issue of his presumed bad influence on the "aesthetic" climate of the age had still to be skirted. The London *Times* notice is representatively ambiguous: "As a teacher Mr. Pater has exercised considerable influence on modern Oxford. The picturesqueness and, to a certain extent, the mannerism of his writings possessed much fascination for youthful minds of a particular caste. That that influence was always wholesome we do not pretend to say. . . ."

Preaching a funeral sermon in Brasenose College Chapel in October 1894, Frederick William Bussell—Pater's closest friend during the writer's last years who became vice-principal of the college two years after Pater's death—stressed the personal kindness and good humor of Pater the man, qualities that, as Bussell observed, did not always come through in the writings. Further, Bussell gave a brief account of Pater's personal habits and routine day's work that must have reassured doubters: "He never smoked; rarely took

tonic or medicine of any kind; and has left an example which it would be well if every student could follow; spending his morning in writing or lecturing, some part of the afternoon in correcting the composition of noon, and, in the evening, closing his books entirely;—regarding it as folly to attempt to make up for idleness in the day by unseasonable labour at a time when reading men are best in bed."

Perhaps the two most substantial memorial essays from the 1890s are by Edmund Gosse and Lionel Johnson, the young poet and critic, member of the Rhymers' Club, a group to which Yeats belonged. (Yeats describes the influence of Pater on the group in the chapter of his 1938 *Autobiography* entitled "The Tragic Generation.") Most interesting in Gosse's biographical sketch (*Contemporary Review*, December 1894), written twelve years before Arthur C. Benson's brief "authorized" biography of 1906, is an account of Pater's method of composition: "It has been said, and repeated, that Pater composed his best sentences without any relation to a context, and wrote them down on little squares of paper, ready to stick them in at appropriate and effective places. This is nonsense; it is quite true that he used such squares of paper, but it was for a very different purpose. He read with a box of these squares beside him, jotting down on each, very roughly, anything in his author which struck his fancy, either giving an entire quotation, or indicating a reference, or noting a disposition. He did not begin, I think, any serious critical work without surrounding himself by dozens of these little loose notes." Gosse also quotes Pater's response to the proposals for toughening and regularizing the curriculum and the general discipline of undergraduate life at Oxford: " 'I do not know what your object is. At present the undergraduate is a child of nature: he grows up like a wild rose in a country lane; you want to turn him into a turnip, rob him of all grace, and plant him out in rows.' "

Lionel Johnson, like Gosse, speaks of Pater in the Oxford context: "Emphatically the scholar and man of letters, there was in his life and work a perfect expression of that single-hearted devotion to fine literature, yet without a shadow of pedantry, which is ceasing to flourish in our ancient academic places. There is yet deeper sorrow, upon which I cannot touch, save to say that to younger men concerned with any of the arts, he was the most generous and gracious of helpful friends. In due time, they will be able to think, with nothing but a reverent affection, of the admired writer at last laid to rest under the towers and trees of his own Oxford."

This identification of Pater with Oxford was also the point of attack for those critics who, in the early years of the twentieth century, denigrated the favorable reputation that Pater enjoyed in the decade following his death. The American "New Humanists" Irving Babbitt and Paul Elmer More, teachers and allies of T. S. Eliot, who himself mounted after World War I the most sustained and influential attack on Pater's reputation, were contemptuous of Pater's critical approach and scholarly knowledge. In an article in *Publications of the Modern Language Association* in 1906, Babbitt condemned "impressionist" criticism of the kind Pater wrote, because it merely records the author's pleasurable response to a work of art, with no external criteria as a guide. In a 1911 review of the New Library Edition of Walter Pater for the *Nation*, More was even more sweeping: "The simple truth is that Pater was in no proper sense of the word a critic at all. History was only an extension of his own ego, and he saw himself whithersoever he turned his eyes." Beyond dismissing Pater himself, More depicted the enthusiasm he inspired as symptomatic of the isolated, devitalized condition of Oxford itself: "Paterism might without great injustice be defined as the quintessential spirit of Oxford, emptied of the wholesome intrusions of the world—its pride of isolation reduced to sterile self-absorption, its enchantment of beauty alembicated into a faint Epicureanism, its discipline of learning changed into voluptuous economy of sensations, its golden calm stagnated into languid elegance."

T. S. Eliot's attack on Pater culminated in his 1930 essay in the *Bookman*, "Arnold and Pater," the general theme of which is the failure of the Victorians to achieve any kind of coherent or credible religious belief in reaction to the challenges of modern scientific theory and philosophic thought: "The dissolution of thought in that age, the isolation of art, philosophy, religion, ethics, and literature, is interrupted by various chimerical attempts to effect imperfect syntheses. Religion became morals, religion became art, religion became science or philosophy; various blundering attempts were made at alliances between various branches of thought. Each half-prophet believed that he had the whole truth. . . ." Speaking of *Marius the Epicurean*, Eliot sniffs, "I do not believe that Pater, in this work, has influenced a single first-rate mind of a later

generation." And *Studies in the History of the Renaissance* "propagated some confusion between life and art which is not wholly irresponsible for some untidy lives."

Along with a repudiation of things Victorian that generally characterized British and American culture between the end of World War I and the finish of World War II, the censure of Eliot, perhaps the most eminent poet and critic of the period, was enough to ensure that most of the Victorian titans would languish in obscurity or disrepute. Pater sank into total eclipse.

But, since the late 1940s, Pater has enjoyed a renewed critical interest and, for the first time, sustained discussion of the complexity of his work. This renewal began with Graham Hough's *The Last Romantics* (1949), which places Pater in a line of intellectual history that runs from Ruskin, through Dante Gabriel Rossetti and the other Pre-Raphaelites, to Yeats. The essay on Pater begins with a rejoinder to Eliot and goes on to suggest that, as much as Arnold and Pater reflect the philosophical preoccupations of the later Victorian age, Pater at least must be thought of as a precursor of literary modernism. Hough is not altogether enthusiastic about Pater, but because of Pater's "temperament" and complex version of "impressionism," his work is the matrix out of which the next great literary generation was to emerge.

In *Romantic Image* (1957), an important study of the evolution of modern symbolist poets from the work of their nineteenth-century forebears, Frank Kermode quotes Hough on Pater: "His ideal is the kind of art where thought and its sensible embodiment are completely fused." A few pages later, Kermode connects Yeats explicitly to Pater: Yeats "is the poet in whose work Romantic isolation achieves its full quality as a theme for poetry, being no longer a pose, a complaint, or a programme; and his treatment of it is very closely related to his belief in what Pater called 'vision' and the French called Symbol."

In his 1959 monograph, *Walter Pater*, Ian Fletcher, like Kermode, echoes Hough in asserting that Pater's work represents "all the triumphs and failures of a temperament." Fletcher distinguishes Pater from Arnold, against the judgment of Eliot: "Again, Pater is always a scholar as Arnold quite strikingly was not. Furthermore, Pater is perhaps the first English critic of importance to have the historical sense very profoundly developed."

Other important studies in the 1960s contributed to a deeper understanding and a fuller appreciation of Pater's writings. Among these is U. C. Knoepflmacher's *Religious Humanism and the Victorian Novel* (1965), most useful because it enables the reader to compare the religious views of Pater with those of George Eliot and Samuel Butler. In 1967 Gerald C. Monsman, in *Pater's Portraits*, for the first time discussed in systematic detail the mythic patterns in Pater's fiction. David J. DeLaura's *Hebrew and Hellene in Victorian England* (1969) treats John Henry Newman, Arnold, and Pater in a way that gives specific density to the emerging critical consensus that Pater is a major writer, in the context of his own time as well as in the context of modern literature.

In 1970 *Letters of Walter Pater*, a scholarly edition by Lawrence Evans of most but not all of Pater's extant correspondence, was published. The letters do not generally shed much light on Pater's work except occasionally to establish the chronology of composition or the climate of opinion in which Pater believed himself to be working. However, the edition is thoroughly annotated and provides much information about Pater's relations to other people.

Despite the dearth of materials noted early by Gosse and more recently by Fletcher, Michael Levey was able to write a short 1977 biography, *The Case of Walter Pater*, that clears away most of the factual and interpretive errors of Thomas Wright's 1907 *Life of Walter Pater*. In 1980 Donald L. Hill produced the first scholarly edition of Pater's work, *The Renaissance: Studies in Art and Poetry: The 1893 Text*, with thorough explanatory notes; the next year saw publication of Billie Andrew Inman's *Walter Pater's Reading, 1858-1873*, an annotated bibliography of Pater's borrowings from Oxford libraries that sheds much light on the sources of Pater's work. A second volume by Inman, covering Pater's reading from 1874 to 1877, was published in 1990.

In his 1977 introductory study of Pater for the Twayne series, Monsman discusses Pater's influence on later writers: among modern poets, Gerard Manley Hopkins (who was a student of Pater at Brasenose), Yeats, Wallace Stevens, Ezra Pound, T. S. Eliot (despite his subsequent disapproval of Pater), and W. H. Auden. Among novelists, Pater's influence can be observed in the work of Henry James, Joseph Conrad, Virginia Woolf, James Joyce, D. H. Lawrence, and Marcel Proust—virtually a pantheon of literary Modernism.

Perhaps the most comprehensive assertion of Pater's role as the bridge between Romanticism and Modernism is that of Harold Bloom in "The Crystal Man," his introductory essay to the *Selected Writings of Walter Pater* (1974): "Though Pater compares oddly, perhaps not wholly adequately, with the great Victorian prose prophets, he did what Carlyle, Ruskin, Newman, Arnold could not do: he fathered the future. Himself wistful and elaborately reserved, renouncing even his own strength, he became the most widely diffused (even though more and more hidden) literary influence of the later nineteenth upon the twentieth century."

In ways that scholars have already examined and continue to explore, through textual studies, biographical research, and critical analysis, Pater's dual role as encapsulator of the past and father to the future is becoming more fully understood, as he emerges from the limited and often prejudicial interpretations of previous generations. His place as an extremely important if highly mannered and difficult writer in the body of nineteenth-century English literature seems, at last, well established.

Letters:

Letters of Walter Pater, edited by Lawrence Evans (Oxford: Oxford University Press, 1970).

Bibliographies:

Lawrence Evans, "Walter Pater," in *Victorian Prose: A Guide to Research*, edited by David J. DeLaura (New York: Modern Language Association, 1973);

Samuel Wright, *A Bibliography of the Writings of Walter H. Pater* (New York: Garland, 1975);

Franklin E. Court, *Walter Pater: An Annotated Bibliography of Writings About Him* (De Kalb: Northern Illinois University Press, 1980).

Biographies:

Arthur C. Benson, *Walter Pater* (London: Macmillan, 1906);

Thomas Wright, *The Life of Walter Pater*, 2 volumes (London: Everett, 1907);

Germain d'Hangest, *Walter Pater: l'homme et l'oeuvre*, 2 volumes (Paris: Didier, 1961);

Michael Levey, *The Case of Walter Pater* (London: Thames & Hudson, 1977).

References:

Paul Barolsky, *Walter Pater's Renaissance* (University Park: Pennsylvania State University Press, 1987);

Harold Bloom, "The Crystal Man," Introduction to *Selected Writings of Walter Pater* (New York: New American Library, 1974);

Bloom, "The Place of Pater: *Marius the Epicurean*," in his *The Ringers in the Tower* (Chicago: University of Chicago Press, 1971);

Eugene Brzenk, "The Unique Fictional World of Walter Pater," *Nineteenth-Century Fiction*, 13 (December 1958): 217-226;

William E. Buckler, *Walter Pater: The Critic as Artist of Ideas* (New York: New York University Press, 1987);

Barbara Charlesworth, *Dark Passages: The Decadent Consciousness in Victorian Literature* (Madison: University of Wisconsin Press, 1965);

Ruth C. Child, *The Aesthetic of Walter Pater* (New York: Macmillan, 1940);

John J. Conlon, *Walter Pater and the French Tradition* (London: Associated University Presses, 1982);

Richmond Crinkley, *Walter Pater: Humanist* (Lexington: University Press of Kentucky, 1970);

David J. DeLaura, *Hebrew and Hellene in Victorian England* (Austin: University of Texas Press, 1969);

"Essays in *Marius*," *English Literature in Transition*, 27, nos.1-2 (1984): 5-155;

Ian Fletcher, *Walter Pater* (London: Longmans, Green, 1959);

Graham Hough, *The Last Romantics* (London: Duckworth, 1949), pp. 134-174;

Billie Andrew Inman, "The Organic Structure of *Marius the Epicurean*," *Philological Quarterly*, 41 (April 1962): 475-491;

Inman, *Walter Pater and His Reading, 1874-1877* (New York: Garland, 1990);

Inman, *Walter Pater's Reading, 1858-1873* (New York: Garland, 1981);

Lionel Johnson, "Notes on Walter Pater," in *Post Liminium: Essays and Critical Papers by Lionel Johnson*, edited by Thomas Whittemore (London: Matthews, 1911);

Robert Keefe and Janice A. Keefe, *Walter Pater and the Gods of Disorder* (Athens: Ohio University Press, 1988);

Frank Kermode, *Romantic Image* (London: Routledge & Kegan Paul, 1957; New York: Macmillan, 1957);

U. C. Knoepflmacher, *Religious Humanism and the Victorian Novel* (Princeton: Princeton University Press, 1965);

John A. Lester, Jr., *Journey Through Despair,*

1880-1914 (Princeton: Princeton University Press, 1968);

Gordon MacKenzie, *The Literary Character of Walter Pater* (Berkeley: University of California Press, 1967);

F. C. McGrath, *The Sensible Spirit: Walter Pater and the Modernist Paradigm* (Tampa: University of South Florida Press, 1986);

Perry Meisel, *The Absent Father: Virginia Woolf and Walter Pater* (New Haven: Yale University Press, 1980);

Meisel, *The Myth of the Modern: A Study in British Literature and Criticism after 1850* (New Haven: Yale University Press, 1988);

J. Hillis Miller, "Walter Pater: A Partial Portrait," *Daedalus*, 105 (Winter 1976): 97-113;

Gerald C. Monsman, "Pater Redivivus," in *The Victorian Experience: The Prose Writers*, edited by Richard A. Levine (Athens: Ohio University Press, 1982), pp. 203-239;

Monsman, *Pater's Portraits: Mythic Pattern in the Fiction of Walter Pater* (Baltimore: Johns Hopkins University Press, 1967);

Monsman, *Walter Pater* (Boston: Twayne, 1977);

Monsman, *Walter Pater's Art of Autobiography* (New Haven: Yale University Press, 1980);

Daniel T. O'Hara, *The Romance of Interpretation: Visionary Criticism from Pater to deMan* (New York: Columbia University Press, 1985);

Bernard Richards, "Pater as Comic Writer," *English Literature in Transition, 1880-1920*, Special Series, 4 (1990): 43-56;

Louise Rosenblatt, "The Genesis of Pater's *Marius the Epicurean*," *Comparative Literature*, 14 (Summer 1962): 242-260;

Nathan A. Scott, Jr., *The Poetics of Belief: Studies in Coleridge, Arnold, Pater, Santayana, and Heidegger* (Chapel Hill: University of North Carolina Press, 1985), pp. 62-89;

R. M. Seiler, ed., *Walter Pater: A Life Remembered* (Calgary: University of Calgary Press, 1987);

Seiler, ed., *Walter Pater: The Critical Heritage* (London: Routledge & Kegan Paul, 1980);

William F. Shuter, "Pater's Reshuffled Text," *Nineteenth Century Literature*, 43 (Spring 1989): 500-525;

Shuter, "Walter Pater and the Academy's 'Dubious Name,'" *Victorians Institute Journal*, 16 (1988): 129-147;

Ian Small, "Intertextuality in Pater and Wilde," *English Literature in Transition, 1880-1920*, Special Series, 4 (1990): 57-66;

Anthony Ward, *Walter Pater: The Idea in Nature*

(London: Macgibbon & Kee, 1966);

René Wellek, "Walter Pater," in *A History of Modern Criticism, 1750-1950*, volume 3 (New Haven: Yale University Press, 1965), pp. 381-399;

Carolyn Williams, *Transfigured World: Walter Pater's Aesthetic Historicism* (Ithaca, N.Y.: Cornell University Press, 1989);

Samuel Wright, *An Informative Index to the Writings of Walter H. Pater* (West Cornwall, Conn.: Locust Hill Press, 1987).

Papers:

Pater left few personal papers or manuscripts. However, the major collection of manuscripts is at Harvard University. Most of the material is from Pater's later years, and much of it is unpublished. Included are several fragmentary "imaginary portraits" and drafts of several lectures. Harvard also has the manuscript of the 1880 version of the Coleridge essay. The manuscript for the published chapters of *Gaston de Latour* is in the Berg Collection at the New York Public Library, while the manuscripts of the unpublished chapters are in the library of the University of Arizona. "Measure for Measure" is in the Folger Shakespeare Library, Washington, D.C., and "Diaphaneitè" is at the King's School, Canterbury. The manuscript of the essay on Pascal, Pater's last, is at the Bodleian Library, Oxford.

Dante Gabriel Rossetti
(12 May 1828 - 9 April 1882)

This entry was updated by Florence S. Boos (University of Iowa) from her entry in
DLB 35: Victorian Poets After 1850.

BOOKS: *Sir Hugh the Heron: A Legendary Tale in Four Parts* (London: Privately printed, 1843);

Poems (London: Privately printed, 1869; enlarged, 1870; revised, London: Ellis, 1870; Boston: Roberts Brothers, 1870); republished with slightly different contents as *Poems. A New Edition* (London: Ellis, 1881);

Ballads and Sonnets (London: Ellis & White, 1881; Boston: Roberts Brothers, 1882);

Ballads and Narrative Poems (Hammersmith, U.K.: Kelmscott Press, 1893);

Sonnets and Lyrical Poems (Hammersmith, U.K.: Kelmscott Press, 1894);

Jan Van Hunks (London: Printed for T. Watts-Dunton, 1912); republished as *Dante Gabriel Rossetti: Jan Van Hunks*, edited by John Robert Wahl (New York: New York Public Library, 1952);

The Paintings and Drawings of Dante Gabriel Rossetti (1828-1882): A Catalogue Raisonné, 2 volumes, edited by Virginia Surtees (London: Oxford University Press, 1971).

Collection: *The Collected Works of Dante Gabriel Rossetti*, 2 volumes, edited by William M. Rossetti (London: Ellis, 1886); republished as *The Poetical Works of Dante Gabriel Rossetti*, 1 volume (London: Ellis, 1891); enlarged as *The Poems of Dante Gabriel Rossetti with Illustrations from His Own Pictures and Designs*, 2 volumes (London: Ellis, 1904); revised and enlarged as *The Works of Dante Gabriel Rossetti*, 1 volume (London: Ellis, 1911).

TRANSLATION: *The Early Italian Poets* (London: Smith, Elder, 1861; London: Simpkin, Marshall, Hamilton, Kent / New York: Scribners, 1861); republished as *Dante and His Circle* (London: Ellis & White, 1874; Boston: Roberts Brothers, 1876).

Gabriel Charles Dante Rossetti, who assumed the professional name Dante Gabriel Rossetti, was born 12 May 1828 at No. 38 Charlotte Street, Portland Place, London, the second child and eldest son of Gabriele Rossetti (1783-1854)

Dante Gabriel Rossetti, 1867

and Frances Polidori Rossetti (1800-1886). Gabriele Rossetti was a Dante scholar, who when younger had been exiled from Naples for writing poetry in support of the Neapolitan Constitution of 1819. He settled in London in 1824, where in 1826 he married the daughter of a fellow Italian expatriate and man of letters; Frances Polidori had trained as a governess, and she supervised her children's early education. Gabriele Rossetti supported the family as a professor of Italian at King's College, London, until his eyesight and general health deteriorated in the 1840s. Frances then attempted to support the family as a teacher of French and Italian, and as an unsuccessful founder of two day schools. Few Victorian families were as gifted: Maria Rossetti (1827-1876) was described as talented, enthusiastic, and domineering as a child; in later life she published *A Shadow of Dante* (1871) and became an Anglican nun (1873); William Michael Rossetti (1829-1919) was along with his brother an active member of the Pre-Raphaelite Brotherhood and became an editor, man of letters, and memoirist; the youngest child, Christina Georgina Rossetti (1830-

1894), became an introspective lyrical poet.

Dante Gabriel Rossetti was bilingual from early childhood and grew up in an atmosphere of émigré political and literary discussion. From childhood he intended to be a painter and illustrated literary subjects in his earliest drawings. He was tutored at home in German and read the Bible, William Shakespeare, Johann Wolfgang von Goethe's *Faust, The Arabian Nights,* Charles Dickens, and the poetry of Sir Walter Scott and George Gordon, Lord Byron. At the age of eight he entered Mr. Paul's day school in Portland Place and a year later began studies at King's College School, which he attended for five years, from 1837 to 1842. From 1842 to 1846 he attended Cary's Academy of Art to prepare for the Royal Academy, which he entered in July 1846. After more than a year in the Academy Antique School, Rossetti left to apprentice himself to the historical painter Ford Madox Brown, who later became his closest lifelong friend. He also continued his extensive reading of poetry—Edgar Allan Poe, Percy Bysshe Shelley, Samuel Taylor Coleridge, William Blake, John Keats, Robert Browning, and Alfred, Lord Tennyson—and romantic and satiric fiction—Charles Robert Maturin, William Makepeace Thackeray, Friedrich Heinrich Karl de la Motte-Fouqué, Charles Wells—and in 1845 began translations from German medieval poetry (Hartmann von Ave's twelfth-century *Der Arme Heinrich*, and parts of the *Nibelungenlied*), and from the Italians (Dante's *Vita Nuova* and British Museum volumes of Dante's little-known predecessors, published as *The Early Italian Poets* in 1861). In 1847 and 1848 Rossetti began several important early poems—"My Sister's Sleep," "The Blessed Damozel," "The Bride's Prelude," "On Mary's Portrait," "Ave," "Jenny," "Dante at Verona," "A Last Confession," and several sonnets, including "Retro Me Sathana" and a trio, "The Choice." There is some evidence that Rossetti might have wished to take up poetry as a career but felt impelled to turn to painting to earn his living. In 1848 he wrote the poet and critic Leigh Hunt about the possibility of supporting himself by writing poetry, and his dual impulses toward art and poetry may have hindered his development as a painter.

In 1848 Rossetti joined with six other young men, mostly painters, who shared an interest in contemporary poetry and an opposition to certain stale conventions of contemporary academy art. Their name, Pre-Raphaelite Brotherhood,

Self-portrait in pencil and chalk by Rossetti, March 1847
(National Portrait Gallery, London)

honored Giovanni Paolo Lasinio's engravings of paintings by Benozzo Gozzoli and others who decorated Pisa's Campo Santo. In a general way, the Pre-Raphaelite Brotherhood sought to introduce new forms of thematic seriousness, high coloration, and attention to detail into contemporary British art. Talented members of the group included John Everett Millais, its most skilled painter and future president of the Royal Academy, and William Holman Hunt, a painter inclined to religious themes and dedicated to accurate representation of natural phenomena. The painter James Collinson soon left the brotherhood on religious grounds and was unofficially succeeded by the painter Walter Howell Deverell. Other members were the sculptor Thomas Woolner; the future art critic Frederic Stephens; and William Michael Rossetti, who as P.R.B. secretary kept a journal of activities and edited the six issues of its periodical, the *Germ* (1850). Associates of the group (other than Elizabeth Eleanor Siddal) included the older painter Ford Madox Brown, the painter and poet William Bell Scott, the poet Coventry Patmore, the painter Anna Mary Howitt, the woman's rights activist Barbara Leigh Smith (Bodichon), and Christina Rossetti, six of whose poems appeared in the *Germ*.

The Pre-Raphaelite Brothers provided each other with companionship, criticism, and encour-agement early in their careers and defended each other against initial public hostility. Dante Gabriel Rossetti shaped the group's literary tastes, pressed for the founding of the *Germ*, and published in it several poems, including "My Sister's Sleep," an early version of "The Blessed Damozel," and six sonnets on paintings. He also contributed an allegorical prose tale, "Hand and Soul," in which a thirteenth-century Italian painter, Chiaro dell'Erma, is visited by a woman representing his soul, who tells him, "Paint me thus, as I am . . . so shall thy soul stand before thee always . . ."—an early suggestion of Rossetti's later artistic preoccupation with dreamlike, heavily stylized female figures. In 1849 Rossetti accompanied William Holman Hunt to France and exhibited his first oil painting, *The Girlhood of Mary Virgin*, at the Free Exhibition in London; in 1850 he exhibited his *Ecce Ancilla Domini* at the National Institution. P.R.B. meetings became sporadic by 1851, and the group had disbanded by 1853; it had served its purpose, which was to provide initial professional encouragement to its members.

In 1850, at the age of twenty-two, Rossetti met Elizabeth Eleanor Siddal ("Lizzie") then about seventeen years old. According to William Michael Rossetti, she was the daughter of a Sheffield cutler and was working as a millinery shop assistant when Walter Deverell persuaded her to serve as an artist's model. After 1850 she became a model for many of Rossetti's drawings and paintings, including a series of informal sketches made in the early 1850s and a large watercolor exhibited in 1852 and 1853, *Beatrice at a Marriage Feast Denies Dante Her Salutation*. Lizzie Siddal and Rossetti became engaged about 1851 but did not marry for several years. Her recurrent respiratory illness, his financial difficulties, and some mutual ambivalence may have contributed to the delay. Lizzie Siddal shared Rossetti's poetic and artistic interests and under his tutelage produced a series of emotional lyrics and watercolors on medieval themes (collected in *The Poems and Drawings of Elizabeth Siddal*, edited by Roger Lewis and Mark Samuels Lasner, 1978).

In 1856 several university undergraduates, including William Morris and Edward Burne-Jones, began a journal modeled after the *Germ*. Entitled the *Oxford and Cambridge Magazine*, it had a run of twelve issues to which Rossetti contributed three poems—an early version of "The Burden of Nineveh," "The Staff and the Scrip," and a revised version of "The Blessed Damozel." In 1857

The Girlhood of Mary Virgin, *Rossetti's first exhibited oil painting (The Tate Gallery, London). His models were his mother, Frances; sister Christina; and brother William Michael.*

Rossetti responded to an invitation to paint murals on the Oxford Union Debating Hall and was joined in this project by Morris, Burne-Jones, and the Oxford undergraduate Algernon Charles Swinburne. While there, he also met Jane Burden and introduced her to her future husband William Morris.

In 1860 Rossetti and Lizzie Siddal were married; during twenty-odd months of married life, Rossetti painted steadily, saw publication of *The Early Italian Poets,* and cofounded the firm of designers Morris, Marshall, Faulkner, and Co. with Morris, Brown, Burne-Jones, Philip Webb, Charles Faulkner, and Peter Marshall. The firm did decorative work for churches and private houses, and Rossetti designed furniture and stained-glass windows. The birth of a dead child in May 1861 depressed Lizzie. On 10 February 1862 she and Rossetti dined with Swinburne at a hotel; afterward Rossetti left Lizzie alone, returning home later to find her nearly dead of an overdose of laudanum. She died the next day and left a final poem with a note requesting that he care for her brother. As a last tribute Rossetti placed

a manuscript of his poems in his wife's grave, a decision he later regretted.

After the death of his wife, Rossetti moved to No. 16 Cheyne Walk, Chelsea, a large house on the Thames which contained a first-floor drawing room and, according to William Michael Rossetti, "hardly less than a dozen" bedrooms above. For a while, Rossetti and his brother shared these premises with Swinburne and George Meredith. Here he helped Alexander Gilchrist's widow, Anne, complete the two-volume *Life of William Blake: Pictor Ignotus* (1863), which Gilchrist had left at his death; Rossetti edited and "regularized" many of the poems and prepared headnotes. He also continued to paint steadily, completing *Joan of Arc* (1863), *Beata Beatrix* (1864), *The Beloved* (1865-1866), *Monna Vanna* (1866), *Venus Verticordia* (1864), *The Blue Bower* (1865), and several watercolors and designs. Despite his reluctance to exhibit his paintings in public, he acquired several patrons and became relatively prosperous. One of his models, the blond and full-bodied Fanny Cornforth, became Rossetti's resident mistress, and later, housekeeper; she appears in several paintings of this period (*Bocca Baciata, The Blue Bower, Aurelia, The Loving Cup,* and *Found,* begun in 1854 but never finished). Though never publicly acknowledged, the liaison with Cornforth seems to have become the steadiest sexual relationship of Rossetti's life.

In 1868 Rossetti persuaded Jane Burden Morris, then in ill health, to begin sittings for a series of paintings, and his portraits of her—in crayon, pencil, and oil—are usually considered his most striking artistic work. William Michael Rossetti commented of Jane Morris's appearance: "in the extraordinarily *impressive*—the profound and abstract—type of beauty of Mrs. Morris, he found an ideal more entirely responsive than any other to his aspiration in art. . . . For idealizing there was but one process—to realize." In 1868 Rossetti painted *Mrs. William Morris* and *La Pia* in oil and drew *Aurea Catena* and *Reverie* in crayon; later he painted her in *Pandora, Mariana,* the large *Dante's Dream* (she was Beatrice), *Proserpine, Water Willow, Venus Astarte, Mnemosyne, La Donna della Finestra,* and *The Day-dream.* Letters from Rossetti to Jane Morris reveal that by 1869 she had become the center of his emotional life: "All that concerns you is the all-absorbing question with me . . . no absence can ever make me so far from you again as your presence did for years. For this long inconceivable change, you know now what my thanks must be." Jane Morris's health contin-

CYCLOGRAPHIC SOCIETY.
CRITICISM SHEET.

No. 1307

Subject of Picture or Quotation :—

[Margaret, having abandoned virtue and caused the deaths of her mother and brother, is tormented by the Evil Spirit at Mass, during the chaunting of the "Dies Iræ." — (Goethe's Faust.)

Evil Spirit.— How different, Margaret, it was, with thee
when, full of innocence, thou cam'st before
the altar, and didst kneel thee at its foot
Lisping thy prayers out of the well-known book,
Half in the playfulness of childhood, half
as if a sense of God were in thy soul!
How is it with thee now? Within thine heart
What pride and evil doing? &c.

Margaret.— Woe, woe, these fearful thoughts!
They seem to hold me and come over me
Spite of myself.
choir (chaunting) — "Dies iræ, Dies illa." — "Solvet sæclum in favilla."
Evil Spirit.— The glorified their countenance. They
turn away from thee: to stretch to thee the hand
the pure & thankless shudder. Woe to thee!

Date July 27 /48   Signature Gabriel C. Rossetti]

The Members of the C. S. are requested to write their remarks *in Ink*, concisely and legibly, avoiding SATIRE or RIDICULE, which ever defeat the true end of criticism, and are more likely to produce unkindly feeling and dissension.

A very clever & original ~~cast~~ design, beautifully ~~executed~~ —
The figures which deserve the greatest attention are the
four figures, praying to the left — The young girl's face is very
pretty but the head is too large; the other three are full of piety —
The Devil is in my opinion a mistake; his head wants
drawing & the horns through the cowl are common-place &
therefore objectionable — The right arm of Margaret
should have been shewn; for by hiding the Devil's right hand,
(which is not sufficiently prominent) you are impressed
with the idea that he is tearing her to pieces for a meal —
The drawing & Composition of Margaret are original &
expressive of utter prostration — The greatest objection
is the figure with his back towards to you who is
unaccountably short; the pleasing group of lovers
should have occupied his place — The Girl & child
in the foreground are exquisite in feeling — The flaming sword
well introduced & highly emblematical of the subject which is well chosen
& with a few alterations in its treatment should be painted
Chair is out of perspective —

J. E. Millais

[This design is in such perfect feeling, as to give me a far higher idea
of Goethe than I have before obtained either from a translation, or the
artificial illustrations of Retzsch, the Margaret here is wonderful, Margaret enduring the tauntings of the evil spirit who is pressing
her weight of sin into her crouching and repenting self — the children
are beautifully introduced, without in the slightest intifering with the
principal figures — and the holy heads around are beautifully devotional
through WHR never having seen the evil one, he has not got it
sufficiently grand, or near so good as the other parts, excepting the
elevated hand which most appropriately accords with the utter
prostration of Margaret

W H Hunt]

Criticism sheet with comments by John Everett Millais and William Holman Hunt of a drawing by Rossetti.
The sketching and drawing club known as the Cyclographic Society was an immediate forerunner of the
Pre-Raphaelite Brotherhood (Collection of William E. Fredeman).

Present, at Hunt's, himself, } *P. R. B.*
Millais, Stephens, & W. M.
Rosetti

13 Jan.ʸ 1851.   In consideration of the unsettled
& unwritten state of the rules guiding the
P.R.B., it is deemed necessary to determine &
adopt a recognized system.

The P.R.B. originally consisted of 7 members – Hunt, Millais, Dante & Wᵐ Rossetti, Stephens, Woolner, & another; & has been reduced
to 6 by the withdrawal of the last. It was
at first positively understood that the P.R.B.
is to consist of these persons & no others, – se-
cession of any original member not being
contemplated: & the principle that neither
this highly important rule, nor any other
affecting the P.R.B., can be ~~finally adopted,~~ repealed, or
or any finally adopted,
modified, unless on unanimous consent
of the members is hereby declared permanent.

First page of the rules drafted for the Pre-Raphaelite Brotherhood (Collection of William E. Fredeman)

No. 2. *(Price One Shilling.)* FEBRUARY, 1850.

With an Etching by JAMES COLLINSON.

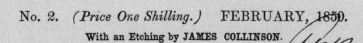

The Germ:

Thoughts towards Nature

In Poetry, Literature, and Art.

When whoso merely hath a little thought
  Will plainly think the thought which is in him,—
  Not imaging another's bright or dim,
Not mangling with new words what others taught;
When whoso speaks, from having either sought
  Or only found,—will speak, not just to skim
  A shallow surface with words made and trim,
But in that very speech the matter brought:
Be not too keen to cry—"So this is all!—
  A thing I might myself have thought as well,
  But would not say it, for it was not worth!"
  Ask: "Is this truth?" For is it still to tell
That, be the theme a point or the whole earth,
Truth is a circle, perfect, great or small?

London:

AYLOTT & JONES, 8, PATERNOSTER ROW.

G. F. TUPPER, Printer, Clement's Lane, Lombard Street.

Cover for the second of six issues of the Pre-Raphaelite journal (George Price Boyce's copy from the Collection of William E. Fredeman)

ued to trouble her throughout the 1870s; she seems to have suffered from the combined effects of a weak back, a pinched spinal nerve, and an unidentified neurological disorder. In 1866 and 1867, Rossetti also had begun to suffer from physical and mental complaints which burdened him for the rest of his life: uncertain eyesight, headaches, insomnia, a hydrocele which made sitting difficult and required periodic drainage, and growing fear of, and distaste for, the outer world. Preoccupation with Jane Morris's health sometimes seemed to provide Rossetti with an external focus for his anxieties.

Early in the 1850s Rossetti had written several poems: ballads such as "The Staff and the Scrip" (1851-1852) and early versions of "Sister Helen" and "The Burden of Nineveh." In the mid 1850s he wrote sonnets and short lyrics on themes of failed opportunity, wistful regret, or the recognition of an earlier love. Later in the decade several poems followed, on prostitution ("Jenny," completed in 1858), the failure of past love ("A New Year's Burden," 1859), and satisfied sexuality ("The Song of the Bower," 1860). In *Dante Gabriel Rossetti: His Family Letters with a Memoir* (1895), William Michael Rossetti does not record that any of the sonnets in his brother's major literary work, "The House of Life," were written between 1856 and 1861. Rossetti wrote "Lost Days" in 1862, the year of Lizzie's death, then no more until 1867.

In startling contrast, the years of Rossetti's relationship with Jane Morris coincided with his most vigorous poetic activity since the early days of the P.R.B. In 1868, for example, he wrote seven "House of Life" sonnets: four comprising the "Willowwood" sequence, two paired as "Newborn Death," and the proudly possessive "The Portrait":

> Let all men note
> That in all years (O Love, thy gift is this!)
> They that would look on her must come to me.

The year 1869 was an annus mirabilis: in addition to about seventeen "House of Life" sonnets (an exact number is difficult to determine; numbers 92 and 93, "The Sun's Shame," for example, are listed as written sometime from 1869 to 1873), Rossetti worked on revisions to "Dante at Verona," "Jenny," and "A Last Confession"; composed the highly erotic "Eden Bower" and "Troy Town"; wrote several more sonnets on pictures; and began "The Stream's Secret," which he com-

pleted the next year. In the March 1869 *Fortnightly Review*, he published the four Willowwood sonnets, whose presentation of erotic frustration and intensity exemplifies his best style, as in Love's song from sonnet three:

> "O Ye, all ye that walk in Willowwood,
>   That walk with hollow faces burning white;
> What fathom-depth of soul-struck widowhood,
>   What long, what longer hours, one lifelong
>   night,
> Ere ye again, who so in vain have wooed
>   Your last hope lost, who so in vain invite
> Your lips to that their unforgotten food,
>   Ere ye, ere ye again shall see the light!"

Rossetti decided in 1869 to publish a volume of his poems, and in October he employed Charles Augustus Howell and others to exhume the manuscript from his wife's grave. Rossetti's year of production was not without its shadows: in his 1892 *Autobiographical Notes*, William Bell Scott related that during a visit to Scotland, Rossetti showed fear at a chaffinch which he felt contained the spirit of his dead wife. In January 1870 Rossetti wrote Jane Morris: "For the last two years I have felt distinctly the clearing away of the chilling numbness that surrounds me in the utter want of you; but since then other obstacles have kept steadily on the increase, and it comes too late." The "obstacles" seem to have been their ill health, not her lack of interest or William Morris's opposition. In the spring of 1870 Rossetti rested his eyesight at the estate of Barbara Bodichon in Scalands, Sussex, near Jane Morris, at Hastings for her health. The Morrises visited Rossetti together, and Jane Morris remained with him while her husband returned to work. The fifteen 1870 "House of Life" sonnets carry such tranquil titles as "Youth's Springtribute," "A Day of Love," and "Life-in-love."

At Scalands, Rossetti also began to drink chloral with whiskey to counter his insomnia. According to William Michael Rossetti this remedy was suggested by a friend, the American journalist William Stillman, but Rossetti can hardly have been unaware of the dangers of his choice—Lizzie, after all, had died of an overdose of morphia. Chloral induces paranoia and depression, both latent traits of Rossetti's character. His suspiciousness, reclusiveness, and fear of strangers steadily worsened.

Morris seemed mildly pleased at Rossetti's fine portraits of his wife but obviously understood their titles' literary allusions to entrapped

Sent to me 4/7/6 by Dr. Williamson. This
is printed off from another photograph of
Lizzie Rossetti, wh. is coloured — as it is
stated, by Gabriel. The coloured photograph
used to belong to a monthly nurse who
attended L. in her confinement, 1861, & afterwards. She says that she saw G. in the
act of colouring it.
WmR.

Photograph of Rossetti's wife, Elizabeth Siddal Rossetti, with explanatory note by William Michael Rossetti
(Collection of William E. Fredeman)

Jane Burden, about the time Rossetti introduced her to her future husband, William Morris; detail of a portrait sketch by Rossetti made at Oxford, 1858 (National Gallery of Ireland, Dublin)

or mistreated wives (*La Donna della Finestra, La Pia, Persephone*), women pining for an absent love (*Mariana*), and a woman immortalized by a poet not her husband (*Beatrice*). From 1868 through 1870 Morris was also at work on his most ambitious poem, *The Earthly Paradise,* which he dedicated to his wife. It contains several lyrics and tales of acutely frustrated love, including the 1869 "The Lovers of Gudrun," in which Gudrun marries a man she does not love and incites her husband to murder her former lover. Gudrun scorns her obedient husband, who dies worn by guilt, frustration, and grief, while she survives to a robust if reflective old age. Morris's letters of 1870 and 1871 and several private, grieving lyrics reveal that he blamed himself for his failure to hold his wife's love, and strove to realize an ethic of unselfish friendship, suppression of self-pity, and respect for the sexual freedom of women as well as men.

Rossetti had two "trial books" of his *Poems* printed privately in late 1869 and early 1870 and revised them for publication by F. S. Ellis in April 1870. He was sufficiently worried about their reception to accept offers by Swinburne,

Morris, Sidney Colvin, and others who admired his poetry to prepare advance reviews (in his memoir, William Michael Rossetti asserts that they volunteered to do this). Quite aware of the situation's ironies, Morris wrote in the *Academy* of his friend's work: "To conclude, I think these lyrics, with all their other merits, the most *complete* of their time; no difficulty is avoided in them: no subject is treated vaguely, languidly, or heartlessly; as there is no commonplace or second-hand thought left in them to be atoned for by beauty of execution, so no thought is allowed to overshadow that beauty of art which compels a real poet to speak in verse and not in prose. Nor do I know what lyrics of any time are to be called great if we are to deny that title to these."

In May 1871 Morris leased Kelmscott Manor in southern Oxfordshire, together with Rossetti and F. S. Ellis, his publisher and Rossetti's, who seldom visited it; in July, Morris left his wife and daughters at Kelmscott and set out resolutely for Iceland, source of the Norse literature of which he had begun serious study and whose heroic exemplars may have suggested some solace. Later in July, Rossetti arrived at Kelmscott. Morris returned to London in September and visited Kelmscott for short periods, and Rossetti remained until October.

During this period Rossetti wrote "Down Stream," "The Cloud Confines," "Sunset Wings," thirty new sonnets for "The House of Life," and began a romantic ballad, "Rose Mary," in which a dark-haired, gray-eyed heroine's purity in love leads to divine forgiveness for a lapse in chastity. At age forty-two Rossetti wrote his first ballad in which an "unchaste" woman is neither a witch ("Sister Helen"), a snake ("Eden Bower"), or trivial and thoughtless ("Jenny"). Even in "Rose Mary," though, exoneration requires her death. The "House of Life" sonnets of 1871 are threatened by a sense of the brevity of love, as in "Love and Hope":

> Cling heart to heart; nor of this hour demand
>> Whether in very truth, when we are dead,
>> Our hearts shall wake to know Love's golden head
> Sole sunshine of the imperishable land;
> Or but discern, through night's unfeatured scope,
> Scorn-fired at length the illusive eyes of Hope.

Despite such pervasive fears, these sonnets' calmest moments proclaim deep appreciation of love, as in "The Dark Glass":

Beata Beatrix, *Rossetti's portrait of his wife, Lizzie,*
painted two years after her 1862 suicide
(The Tate Gallery, London)

Not I myself know all my love for thee:
    How should I reach so far, who cannot weigh
    To-morrow's dower by gage of yesterday?
Shall birth and death and all dark names that be
As doors and windows bared to some loud sea,
    Lash deaf mine ears and blind my face with
        spray;
    And shall my sense pierce love,—the last relay
And ultimate outpost of eternity?

Rossetti and Jane Morris's brief period of apparent happiness and (presumably) sexual liaison has attracted biographers by its supposed romantic unconventionality. It might be more sympathetic as well as realistic to keep in mind the situation's infirmities and constraints: Rossetti's obesity, addiction, hydrocele, bad eyesight, and growing anxieties; and Jane Morris's ever-present children, neuralgia, and bad back.

In October 1871 the *Contemporary Review* published a pseudonymous article by Thomas Maitland (Robert Buchanan), who reacted against Sidney Colvin's praise of "The Blue Bower" for its "marvellous fleshliness of the flesh," and attacked Rossetti as a leader of a school of poets of sensual lust: "he is fleshly all over, from the roots of his hair to the tip of his toes." Buchanan was a penurious minor poet who had resented a slighting reference to him in a review by William Michael Rossetti. Rossetti replied with an article in the *Athenaeum,* "The Stealthy School of Criticism," and Buchanan then expanded his views for publication under his own name in the spring of 1872 as *The Fleshly School of Poetry and Other Phenomena of the Day.* In this lucubration, he added a lengthy attack on "The House of Life" as a "hotbed" of "nasty phrases," which virtually "wheel[ed] . . ." the poet's "nuptial couch into the public streets." Of his brother's response, William Michael Rossetti wrote in his memoir:

> His fancies now ran away with him, and he thought that the pamphlet was a first symptom in a widespread conspiracy for crushing his fair fame as an artist and a man, and for hounding him out of honest society. . . .
>   It is a simple fact that, from the time when the pamphlet had begun to work into the inner tissue of his feelings, Dante Rossetti was a changed man, and so continued till the close of his life.

In an atmosphere of Victorian prudery, it was not unreasonable to fear harm from such a pamphlet. Still, most of Rossetti's poetic predecessors and contemporaries—Tennyson, Robert Browning, Elizabeth Barrett Browning, Morris, and Swinburne—had survived worse reviews, and much of Buchanan's article in fact blasted Swinburne rather than Rossetti. Almost all the reviews of Rossetti's 1870 *Poems* were favorable, and the book sold unusually well (four editions in 1870). Few in Rossetti's actual or potential audience were likely to share Buchanan's extreme prudery. Rossetti was deeply proud of the originality of his best work, which did, after all, idealize male heterosexual fantasies; yet he retained a good deal of social and sexual conservatism. His own ambivalence, heightened by the effects of his growing drug dependence, seemed to leave him unusually vulnerable to Buchanan's philistine attack.

More directly, Rossetti may also have feared public exposure of his relationship with Jane Morris. Rossetti scholar William E. Fredeman notes that the printed version of Buchanan's pamphlet applies the accusations of sensuality at greater length to "The House of Life" and identifies its "house" with the brothel of "Jenny."

In any case, after leaving Kelmscott on 2 June 1872, Rossetti suffered a complete mental

The Rossetti family photographed in 1863 by Lewis Carroll; left to right: Dante Gabriel, Christina, Frances, William Michael

breakdown with auditory hallucinations of accusing voices. He was taken to the Roehampton home of his friend Dr. Thomas Gordon Hake, where he attempted to commit suicide with an overdose of laudanum. He then spent the summer under the care of friends and associates at Roehampton, then at Ford Madox Brown's house in Fitzroy Square, and at three residences in Scotland, two of which, Stobhall and Urrard House, were lent by one of his art patrons, the Liberal M.P. William Graham. During this period he was accompanied by George Hake, the son of his friend, who served as general assistant and secretary, and he was visited by Fanny Cornforth and the Morrises.

A portion of his fine collection of Oriental china was sold for income, and his paintings were removed from his home for safekeeping. Rossetti's earnings had been high for a painter of the 1870s, but he was anxious lest knowledge of his ill health would make his clients press for completion of commissions and more reluctant to provide advance payment. By September 1872 he was able to paint again, and in the same month he returned to Kelmscott, from which he wrote his brother that experience had taught him dependence on "the society of the one necessary person." He remained at Kelmscott until the summer of 1874, employed Charles Augustus Howell as agent to sell his pictures in London, and received frequent visits from Jane Morris.

William Morris's letters of October and November 1872 show muted strain ("I have had a fit of low spirits—for no particular reason that I could tell"; "I shall not be there [Kelmscott] much now I suppose"). Perhaps partly in response, Morris completed *Love Is Enough,* a masque on the sufficiency of ideal love; in 1873 he visited Italy, then made another strenuous summer trip to Iceland.

Rossetti's poetic productivity revived once again in 1873, and he finished seven single sonnets and the double sonnet "The Sun's Shame." The sonnets of this period are melancholy and resonant, but the familiar themes of suffused passion have begun to merge with new ones—the creation of art and intimations of immortality, expressed in the following verses from "The Heart of the Night":

> Alas, the soul!—how soon must she
> Accept her primal immortality,—
> The flesh resume its dust whence it began?
>
> O Lord of work and peace! O Lord of life!
>   O Lord, the awful Lord of will! though late,
>   Even yet renew this soul with duteous breath:
> That when the peace is garnered in from strife,
> The work retrieved, the will regenerate,
>   This soul may see thy face, O Lord of death!

In 1873 Rossetti continued to paint steadily, using Jane Morris as a model for *Proserpine* and

Rossetti's revisions and additions for the ballad "Sister Helen" written in a copy of Poems *(Leipzig: Tauchnitz, 1873).*
His note on the flyleaf reads: "This copy contains alterations to be adopted in reprinting. D. G. R. 1879"
(Anderson Galleries auction catalogue, sale number 1806, 11-13 February 1924).

Alexa Wilding for *La Ghirlandata*. Jane Morris seemed to absent herself more and more frequently, and during one such absence in 1874 Rossetti left Kelmscott for Chelsea. There his health continued to decline, and in 1874 he seems to have written no "House of Life" sonnets, and only one obituary sonnet on the death of Oliver Madox Brown. His volume of *Early Italian Poets* was republished that year, under the title *Dante and His Circle*. In 1875 he wrote three sonnets, in

1876 two short poems, and in 1877 one sonnet, "Astarte Syriaca," to accompany a picture.

After Kelmscott, Rossetti rented several country residences in succession for privacy. Jane Morris visited him for an extended period at Bognor in 1875, but she became increasingly unavailable for sittings in ensuing years, and his loneliness and anxieties about his work seem to have grown. Jane's letters of the mid 1870s indicate a decline in her own health; she found it difficult to sit and suffered from faints. At one point in 1879, Rossetti chided her with reluctance to pose, since she would be no more uncomfortable with him than at home, and she assured him in response that she would be "but too happy to feel myself of use again."

In 1876, however, Jane Morris's daughter Jenny began to suffer from epileptic fits, and anxiety about Jenny's health as well as her own led to extended trips with the George Howard family to European spas. Rossetti's chief daily concern remained the production and sale of his paintings, doubtless necessary but scarcely absorbing. Rossetti's valetudinarian phobias and increasingly paranoid suspicions may also have contrasted more and more unfavorably with William Morris's energy, prosperity, affectionate goodwill, and attentive concern for the Morrises' children. In any case, Rossetti suffered further breakdowns in 1877 and 1879, and his letters of the period indicate that Jane disapproved of his most melancholy poems and his depressive statements.

In 1875 he completed the oil painting *La Bella Mano,* in 1877 *Venus Astarte* and *The Sea-Spell,* and in the next three years *La Donna della Finestra* (1879) and *The Day-Dream* (1880), modeled by Jane, and *A Vision of Fiametta* (1878), modeled by Marie Stillman. In 1878 he returned to ballads once again and began a historical ballad, "The White Ship," and in 1879 he completed a ballad begun in 1871, "Rose Mary."

A last surge of poetic energy in 1880 and 1881 anticipated the publication of his *Poems: A New Edition* in 1881. In this edition, he added six sonnets to "The House of Life," completed seventeen more sonnets and short poems, revised "Sister Helen," finished "The White Ship," and wrote a carefully developed historical ballad, "The King's Tragedy." The final sonnets and short poems reflect in sometimes eschatological language on the nature and source of art, as in the famous introductory sonnet to "The House of Life":

> A Sonnet is a moment's monument,—
> 　Memorial from the Soul's eternity
> 　　To one dead deathless hour.
> 　. . . . .
> 　A Sonnet is a coin: its face reveals
> 　　The soul,—its converse, to what Power 'tis due:—
> Whether for tribute to the august appeals
> 　Of Life, or dower in Love's high retinue,
> It serve; or, 'mid the dark wharf's cavernous
> 　breath,
> In Charon's palm it pay the toll to Death.

Fanny Cornforth, Rossetti's mistress and the model for several of his paintings, including Bocca Baciata, The Blue Bower, Aurelia, *and* Found

In "The King's Tragedy" Rossetti returned to the mingled political, literary, and romantic themes of his early "Dante at Verona," but unlike the obsessive passions of his ballads of the late 1860s and 1870s (such as "Eden Bower" and "Troy Town"), "The King's Tragedy" presents a love which, though frustated by death, is deep and sustained.

In 1881 Rossetti sold one of his largest and best paintings, *Dante's Dream,* to the Walker Art Gallery in Liverpool. Although his volumes of *Poems* and *Ballads and Sonnets* (1881) were quietly but favorably received, he had entered a final pattern of depressive ill health. A sudden decline in February 1882 caused him to move to Birchington, where he revised the comic poem *Jan Van Hunks;* was visited by his mother, William, and Christina; and died of blood poisoning from uric acid on 9 April 1882. At his death he

Rossetti's tombstone at Birchington-on-Sea, designed by his lifelong friend Ford Madox Brown

left behind the almost completed "Joan of Arc" and "Salutation of Beatrice." Rossetti was buried in Birchington churchyard, under a tombstone designed by his lifelong friend Ford Madox Brown, and near a stained-glass memorial window designed by Frederick Shields. A fountain and bust by Brown were placed in Cheyne Walk.

If one moderates them somewhat, many of Rossetti's self-estimates were accurate. Had he been able when young to choose a literary career, he would probably have been a better poet than painter; he was a more genuinely original and skillful writer than many who were more prolific. In part, his achievement was vicarious: he galvanized others in many ways not easily measured. In his youth, he was capable of infectious and gregarious enthusiasm for the work of others, however obscure, but resentment at his own lack of fame deepened gradually as he aged. Insecurity and self-reproach manifested themselves in all but his earliest poems. Behind his self-confident, even peremptory manner with artistic associates, he seemed to need a praise-filled, even sheltering environment for completion of work: first the

P.R.B.; then his intimates of the "Jovial Campaign" to paint the Oxford Union Debating Hall and, later, the members of the Firm; and, finally, Jane Morris and a few faithfully supportive friends. His final surge of poetic effort, for example, benefited from the ministrations of Theodore Watts. He withdrew from former friends in his last years, but new acquaintances formed a fresh audience, which seemed to soothe reminders of his former self.

Had Rossetti curbed his use of chloral and lived another decade, he might have doubled his oeuvre. Striking shifts in range and manner occur in the last poems, and reflections on old subjects of sexuality and failed ambition are graced by a new and mediating detachment. Even his paintings after 1870, such as the large oil *Dante's Dream*, show somewhat improved ability to arrange a complex canvas (his greatest weakness throughout his career). Some of his late designs for oil paintings, such as *The Boat of Love* and *The Death of Lady Macbeth*, were at least as good as any he had done earlier. Rossetti was haunted by a (perhaps partially accurate) private assessment of his weaknesses as a painter and was obsessed with Jane Morris as a model. Yet he was perhaps right that his intense response to such private archetypes was the chief distinction of his work. Perhaps he might have found a new focus for this intensity had he lived a few more years. Likewise, of course, he might also have improved his technical ability, or finished more of the poetry which at some level he yearned to write, had he painted fewer lucrative replicas and painted more slowly.

It would be wrong, at any rate, to sentimentalize Rossetti as a victim of "tragic loves." It seemed to serve some inner purpose for Rossetti to idealize women who were withdrawn, invalid, and/or melancholic. Their genuine alienation (literal, in the case of Elizabeth Siddal and Jane Morris, from their families, potential friends, and class origins) seems to have provided some counterpart for an inner sense of inadequacy and isolation in him. In some way he seemed to need serious emotional attachments with women who were poised on the edge of abrogation and withdrawal. In any case, a sense of this equilibration heightened the effects both of his paintings and of his poetry.

Critics have differed in assessing the quality of Rossetti's poetic achievement and in their preferences for different periods of his work. Directly after his death, the later ballads and "The House of Life" were much admired. In the early twentieth century, "The House of Life" was still considered among his best works, but attention shifted to ballads, such as "The Blessed Damozel," to which William Michael Rossetti assigned an earlier date. In fact, it is difficult to date Rossetti's work or divide it into periods, since he continually revised poems begun as a young man. The texts to many early poems—"The Blessed Damozel," "Sister Helen," "The Burden of Nineveh," "The Portrait," "Jenny," "Dante at Verona," and several of the sonnets—gradually became near-palimpsests. His revisions often do add structure and plot to the ballads and cohesion and elegance to the sonnets. Even slight verbal changes may heighten a poem's cumulative effect. Compare, for example, the 1847 and 1881 version of stanza seven of one of his most admired poems, "The Blessed Damozel":

1847: Heard hardly, some of her new friends,
    Playing at holy games,
Spake gentle-mouthed among themselves
    Their virginal chaste names;
And the souls mounting up to God
    Went by her like thin flames.

1881: Around her, lovers, newly met
    'Mid deathless love's acclaims
Spoke evermore among themselves
    Their heart-remembered names;
And the souls mounting up to God
    Went by her like thin flames.

When Rossetti was young, his bright pictorialism, concrete detail, archaisms, and sublimated sexuality reflected rather conventional aspects of contemporary poetic sensibility. His poems on grief, loss, and inadequacy in the 1850s, by contrast, were some of his best work. Consider "The Landmark" (1854):

                              —I had thought
    The stations of my course should rise unsought,
As altar-stone or ensigned citadel.

But lo! the path is missed, I must go back,
    And thirst to drink when next I reach the spring
Which once I stained, which since may have grown black.
    Yet though no light be left nor bird now sing
As here I turn, I'll thank God, hastening,
That the same goal is still on the same track.

By the late 1860s his sense of failure had evolved into an oppressive fear about identity, evident in "A Superscription":

Look in my face; my name is Might-have-been;
    I am also called No-more, Too-late, Farewell;
    Unto thine ear I hold the dead sea-shell
Cast up thy Life's foam-fretted feet between;

Unto thine eyes the glass where that is seen
    Which had Life's form and Love's, but by my
        spell
    Is now a shaken shadow intolerable,
Of ultimate things unuttered the frail screen.

Mark me, how still I am! But should there dart
    One moment through thy soul the soft sur
        prise
    Of that winged Peace which lulls the breath
        of sighs—
Then shalt thou see me smile, and turn apart
Thy visage to mine ambush at thy heart
    Sleepless with cold commemorative eyes.

In Rossetti's middle and later poetry, sexual love became a near-desperate desire to transcend time. Passion's benefit is not pleasure or mutual relaxation but a poignant hope that one moment may endure. This shift brought radical changes in themes and style. In the opening sonnet of the early triplet "The Choice" (1848) sexual attraction is an enjoyable minor distraction:

Now kiss, and think that there are really those,
    My own high-bosomed beauty, who increase
        Vain gold, vain lore, and yet might
            choose our way!
        Through many years they toil; then on a
            day
    They die not,—for their life was death,—but
        cease;
And round their narrow lips the mould falls close.

Still, the sequence ends with an admonition to aspire to "higher" ends and greater achievement: "And though thy soul sail leagues and leagues beyond, / Still, leagues beyond those leagues, there is more sea." In contrast, by 1869 love has become awesome and solemn, as in "Lovesight":

O love, my love! if I no more should see
Thyself, nor on the earth the shadow of thee,
    Nor image of thine eyes in any spring,—
How then should sound upon Life's darkening
    slope
The ground-whirl of the perished leaves of Hope,
    The wind of Death's imperishable wing?

Sexual frustration and resentment in this period have become diffused indictments of more general injustice, as in "The Sun's Shame":

Fair copy of the poem published as "The Blessed Damozel," probably made circa 1873, when Rossetti was beginning the painting of the same title (The Pierpont Morgan Library)

Beholding youth and hope in mockery caught
  From life; and mocking pulses that remain
  When the soul's death of bodily death is fain;
Honour unknown, and honour known unsought;
And penury's sedulous self-torturing thought
  On gold, whose master therewith buys his
    bane;
  And longed-for woman longing all in vain
For lonely man with love's desire distraught;
And wealth, and strength, and power, and pleasant-
ness,
  Given unto bodies of whose souls men say,
  None poor and weak, slavish and foul, as
    they:—
Beholding these things, I behold no less
The blushing morn and blushing eve confess
  The shame that loads the intolerable day.

By comparison, the final sonnets of Rossetti's life are tranquil, even celebratory. "The Song-Throe" (1880) offers assurance that real pain may eventuate in the perfection of great art:

By thine own tears thy song must tears beget,
  O Singer! Magic mirror thou hast none
  Except thy manifest heart; and save thine own
Anguish or ardour, else no amulet.
    . . . nay, more dry
  Than the Dead Sea for throats that thirst and
    sigh,
That song o'er which no singer's lids grew wet.

The Song-god—He the Sun-god—is no slave
  Of thine: thy Hunter he, who for thy soul
  Fledges his shaft: to no august control
Of thy skilled hand his quivered store he gave:
But if thy lips' loud cry leap to his smart,
The inspir'd recoil shall pierce thy brother's heart.

In several ways "The House of Life" sonnets make more sense in their roughly reconstructible chronological order than in the sequence of happiness-followed-by-loss in which Rossetti arranged them, but in any rearrangement all but the very earliest sonnets (such as the moralistic "Retro Me, Sathana") are among the finest examples of their genre in English. Some of his romantic ballads—"The Blessed Damozel," "Sister Helen," "Rose Mary," and "The King's Tragedy"—are perhaps as good as any literary ballads of the period. Rossetti also possessed a gift for the grotesque, embodied in the comic "Jan Van Hunks" and perhaps to a degree in "Sister Helen" and "Eden Bower." "Jenny" was the first major Victorian poem to present a prostitute who is sexually attractive and not entirely responsible for her fate.

If the poem now seems condescending and evasive, it took some stubbornness for Rossetti to address the issue at all, and "Jenny" remains one of the more interesting "contemporary subject" poems of its period.

It is difficult to compare Rossetti's achievement with that of the other Victorian poets. For its modest size, Rossetti's poetic work is wide in manner and subject. He was a talented experimenter, and his heightened rhythms and refrains influenced other mid- and late-century poetry. He was also an important popularizer of Italian poetry in England and a major practitioner of the sonnet. Certainly, he lacked the strong, confident range and impressively subtle lyricism of Tennyson and Browning, but his erotic spirituality and gift for the dramatic were his own, and Swinburne, George Meredith, Oscar Wilde, and Arthur Symons benefited from the liberating influence of his example. Rossetti was perhaps as significant for his effect on others as for his own work, a judgment that he himself came to make with growing bitterness. His critical remarks on Romantic and contemporary literature were often cogent and influenced all around him—the P.R.B. when he was young; later the Morris and Burne-Jones circle; and finally, Walter Pater and a later generation of poets who sought escape from moralistic art.

Rossetti's attempt to create a unified oeuvre of poetry and painting was also pioneering and extended conceptions of both arts. Through such painters as Burne-Jones, Frederick Sandys, and John William Waterhouse, Rossetti had a further indirect influence on the literature of the Decadents. He also conceived the idea of the *Germ*, the first little magazine of literature and art, and with Brown, Morris, Burne-Jones, and Webb helped cofound the movement to extend the range of decorative art and improve the quality of book design. Rossetti's poetry is not as important as that of Tennyson, Browning, or Gerard Manley Hopkins, but it would be difficult to name others who clearly excelled him at his best, and even more difficult to imagine later nineteenth-century Victorian poetry and art without his influence. His writings can be perhaps best viewed as an unusually acute expression of Victorian social uncertainty and loss of faith. Rossetti's poetry on the absence of love is as bleakly despairing as any of the century, and no poet of his period conveyed more profoundly certain central Victorian anxieties: metaphysical uncertainty, sexual anxiety, and fear of time.

Letters:

William Michael Rossetti, ed., *Dante Gabriel Rossetti: His Family Letters with a Memoir*, 2 volumes (London: Ellis, 1895);

Oswald Doughty and John Robert Wahl, eds., *The Letters of Dante Gabriel Rossetti*, 4 volumes (Oxford: Clarendon Press, 1965, 1967);

John Bryson, ed., *Dante Gabriel Rossetti and Jane Morris: Their Correspondence* (Oxford: Clarendon Press, 1976).

Bibliographies:

William E. Fredeman, "William Morris and His Circle: A Selective Bibliography of Publications, 1960-62," *William Morris Society Journal*, 1, no. 4 (1964): 23-33;

Fredeman, "Dante Gabriel Rossetti," in his *Pre-Raphaelitism: A Bibliocritical Study* (Cambridge, Mass.: Harvard University Press, 1965), pp. 90-105;

Fredeman, "William Morris and His Circle: A Selective Bibliography of Publications, 1962-63," *William Morris Society Journal*, 2, no. 1 (1966): 13-36;

Fredeman, "The Pre-Raphaelites," in *The Victorian Poets: A Guide to Research*, edited by Frederick Faverty (Cambridge, Mass.: Harvard University Press, 1968), pp. 251-316;

Francis L. Fennell, *Dante Gabriel Rossetti: An Annotated Bibliography* (New York: Garland, 1982).

Biographies:

William Michael Rossetti, *Dante Gabriel Rossetti As Designer and Writer* (London: Ellis, 1895);

William Michael Rossetti, ed., *Dante Gabriel Rossetti: His Family Letters with a Memoir*, 2 volumes (London: Ellis, 1895);

William Michael Rossetti, *Some Reminiscences*, 2 volumes (New York: Scribners, 1906);

Oswald Doughty, *A Victorian Romantic: Dante Gabriel Rossetti* (London: Oxford University Press, 1949);

William E. Fredeman, *Prelude to the Last Decade: Dante Gabriel Rossetti in the Summer of 1872* (Manchester: John Rylands Library, 1971);

Brian and Judy Dobbs, *Dante Gabriel Rossetti: An Alien Victorian* (London: Macdonald & Jane's, 1977).

References:

Florence S. Boos, *The Poetry of Dante G. Rossetti: A Critical and Source Study* (The Hague: Mouton, 1976);

Ronnalie Howard, *The Dark Glass: Vision and Technique in the Poetry of Dante Gabriel Rossetti* (Athens: Ohio University Press, 1972);

Jan Marsh, *The Legend of Elizabeth Siddal* (London: Quartet, 1989);

Marsh, *The Pre-Raphaelite Sisterhood* (London: Quartet, 1985);

Joan Rees, *The Poetry of Dante Gabriel Rossetti: Modes of Self-Expression* (Cambridge: Cambridge University Press, 1981);

James Richardson, *Vanishing Lives: Style and Self in Tennyson, Rossetti, Swinburne, and Yeats* (Charlottesville: University Press of Virginia, 1989);

David G. Riede, *Dante Gabriel Rossetti and the Limits of Victorian Vision* (Ithaca, N.Y.: Cornell University Press, 1983);

William Michael Rossetti, *P.R.B. Journal: William Michael Rossetti's Diary of the Pre-Raphaelite Brotherhood, 1849-1853*, edited by William E. Fredeman (Oxford: Clarendon Press, 1975);

David Sonstroem, *Rossetti and the Fair Lady* (Middleton, Conn.: Wesleyan University Press, 1971);

Richard L. Stein, *The Ritual of Interpretation: Literature and Art in Ruskin, Rossetti, and Pater* (Cambridge, Mass.: Harvard University Press, 1975);

Lionel Stevenson, *The Pre-Raphaelite Poets* (Chapel Hill: University of North Carolina Press, 1972);

Victorian Poetry: An Issue Devoted to the Works of Dante Gabriel Rossetti, edited by William E. Fredeman, 20, nos. 3 and 4 (1982);

Joseph Vogel, *Dante Gabriel Rossetti's Versecraft* (Gainesville: University of Florida Press, 1971).

Papers:

Collections in the United States that include manuscripts and letters by Rossetti are at the Library of Congress; the library of the Wilmington [Delaware] Society of the Fine Arts; Princeton University Library; the Pierpont Morgan Library; and the Harry Ransom Humanities Research Center at the University of Texas, Austin. In Great Britain, Rossetti manuscripts can be found in the British Library; the library of the Victoria and Albert Museum; and the Fitzwilliam Museum, Cambridge.

John Ruskin

(8 February 1819 - 20 January 1900)

This entry was written by Charles T. Dougherty (University of Missouri at St. Louis) for
DLB 55: Victorian Prose Writers Before 1867.

SELECTED BOOKS: *Salsette and Elephanta: A Prize Poem* (Oxford: Vincent, 1839);

Modern Painters, 5 volumes (London: Smith, Elder, 1843-1860; volumes 1-2, New York: Wiley & Putnam, 1847-1848; volumes 3-5, New York: Wiley, 1856-1860;

The Seven Lamps of Architecture (London: Smith, Elder, 1849; New York: Wiley, 1849);

Poems. J. R. Collected 1850 (London: Privately printed, 1850);

The King of the Golden River; or, The Black Brothers: A Legend of Stiria (London: Smith, Elder, 1851; New York: Wiley, 1860);

Notes on the Construction of Sheepfolds (London: Smith, Elder, 1851; New York: Wiley, 1851);

Examples of the Architecture of Venice, Selected, and Drawn to Measurement from the Edifices (London: Smith, Elder, 1851);

Pre-Raphaelitism (London: Smith, Elder, 1851; New York: Wiley, 1851);

The Stones of Venice, 3 volumes (London: Smith, Elder, 1851-1853; New York: Wiley, 1851-1860);

Giotto and His Works in Padua (3 parts, London: Printed for the Arundel Society, 1853-1860; 1 volume, New York: Scribners, 1899);

Lectures on Architecture and Painting Delivered at Edinburgh in November 1853 (London: Smith, Elder, 1854; New York: Wiley, 1854);

The Opening of the Crystal Palace, Considered in Some of its Relations to the Prospects of Art (London: Smith, Elder, 1854; New York: Alden, 1855);

Notes on Some of the Principal Pictures Exhibited in the Rooms of the Royal Academy: 1855 (London: Smith, Elder, 1855);

The Harbours of England (London: Gambart, 1856);

Notes on Some of the Pictures Exhibited in the Rooms of the Royal Academy, and the Society of Painters in Water Colours, No. II—1856 (London: Smith, Elder, 1856);

John Ruskin, 1882

Notes on the Turner Gallery at Marlborough House, 1856 (London: Smith, Elder, 1857);

The Political Economy of Art, Being the Substance (with additions) of Two Lectures delivered at Manchester, July 10th and 13th, 1857 (London: Smith, Elder, 1857; New York: Wiley & Halsted, 1858);

Notes on Some of the Principal Pictures Exhibited in the Rooms of the Royal Academy and the Society of Painters in Water Colours, No. III—1857 (London: Smith, Elder, 1857);

Catalogue of the Turner Sketches in the National Gallery (London: Privately printed, 1857);

The Elements of Drawing in Three Letters to Beginners (London: Smith, Elder, 1857; New York: Wiley & Halsted, 1857);

Catalogue of the Sketches and Drawings by J. M. W. Turner, R.A., Exhibited in Marlborough House in the Year 1857-8 (London: Privately printed, 1857);

Notes on Some of the Principal Pictures Exhibited in the Rooms of the Royal Academy, the Old and New Societies of Painters in Water Colours, the Society of British Artists, and the French Exhibition, No. IV—1858 (London: Smith, Elder, 1858);

Cambridge School of Art. Mr. Ruskin's Inaugural Address Delivered at Cambridge, Oct. 29, 1858 (Cambridge: Deighton, Bell / London: Bell & Daldy, 1858);

The Oxford Museum, by Ruskin and Henry W. Acland (London: Smith, Elder / Oxford: Parker, 1859);

The Unity of Art. By John Ruskin, Esq., M.A. Delivered at the Annual Meeting of the Manchester School of Art, February 22nd, 1859 (Manchester: Printed by Thos. Sowler, 1859);

The Two Paths: Being Lectures on Art, and its Application to Decoration and Manufacture, Delivered in 1858-9 (London: Smith, Elder, 1859; New York: Wiley, 1859);

The Elements of Perspective Arranged for the Use of the Schools and Intended to be Read in Connexion with the First Three Books of Euclid (London: Smith, Elder, 1859; New York: Wiley, 1860);

Notes on Some of the Principal Pictures Exhibited in the Royal Academy, the Old and New Societies of Painters in Water Colours, the Society of British Artists, and the French Exhibition, No. V—1859 (London: Smith, Elder, 1859);

"Unto this Last": Four Essays on the First Principles of Political Economy (London: Smith, Elder, 1862; New York: Wiley, 1866);

Sesame and Lilies: Two Lectures Delivered at Manchester in 1864 (London: Smith, Elder, 1865; New York: Wiley, 1865);

The Ethics of the Dust: Ten Lectures to Little Housewives on the Elements of Crystallisation (London: Smith, Elder, 1866; New York: Wiley, 1866);

The Crown of Wild Olive: Three Lectures on Work, Traffic, and War (London: Smith, Elder, 1866; New York: Wiley, 1866);

Time and Tide, By Weare and Tyne. Twenty-five Letters to a Working Man of Sunderland on the Laws of Work (London: Smith, Elder, 1867; New York: Wiley, 1868);

First Notes on the General Principles of Employment for the Destitute and Criminal Classes (London: Privately printed, 1868);

The Queen of the Air: Being a Study of the Greek Myths of Cloud and Storm (London: Smith, Elder, 1869; New York: Wiley, 1869);

Lectures on Art Delivered Before the University of Oxford in Hilary Term, 1870 (Oxford: Clarendon Press, 1870; New York: Wiley, 1870);

Fors Clavigera: Letters to the Workmen and Labourers of Great Britain (96 letters, London: Printed for the author by Smith, Elder, 1871-1884; 8 volumes, Orpington: George Allen, 1871-1884; New York: Wiley, 1880-1886);

Munera Pulveris: Six Essays on the Elements of Political Economy (London: Printed for the author by Smith, Elder, 1872; New York: Wiley, 1872);

Aratra Pentelici: Six Lectures on the Elements of Sculpture, Given Before the University of Oxford in Michaelmas Term, 1870 (London: Printed for the author by Smith, Elder, 1872; New York: Wiley, 1872);

The Relation between Michael Angelo and Tintoret: Seventh of the Course of Lectures on Sculpture Delivered at Oxford, 1870-71 (London: Printed for the author by Smith, Elder, 1872; New York: Alden, 1885);

The Eagle's Nest: Ten Lectures on the Relation of Natural Science to Art, Given Before the University of Oxford in Lent Term, 1872 (London: Printed for the author by Smith, Elder, 1872; New York: Wiley, 1873);

The Sepulchral Monuments of Italy: Monuments of the Cavalli Family in the Church of Santa Anastasia, Verona (London: Arundel Society, 1872);

The Nature and Authority of Miracle (N.p.: Privately printed, 1873);

Love's Meinie: Lectures on Greek and English Birds (3 parts: lectures 1-2, Keston: George Allen, 1873; New York: Wiley, 1873; lecture 3, Orpington: George Allen, 1881; 1 volume, Orpington: George Allen, 1881);

Ariadne Florentina: Six Lectures on Wood and Metal Engraving, With Appendix (7 parts: lecture 1, Keston: George Allen, 1873; lectures 2-6 and appendix, Orpington: George Allen, 1874-1876; 1 volume, Orpington: George Allen, 1876);

The Poetry of Architecture: Cottage, Villa, etc. To Which Is Added Suggestions on Works of Art, as Kata Phusin (New York: Wiley, 1873); republished as *The Poetry of Architecture: Or, The Architecture of the Nations of Europe Considered in its Association with Natural Scenery and National Character*, as Ruskin (Orpington: George Allen, 1893);

Val d'Arno: Ten Lectures on the Tuscan Art Directly Antecedent to the Florentine Year of Victories, Given Before the University of Oxford in Michaelmas Term, 1873 (Orpington: George Allen, 1874; New York: Alden, 1885);

Mornings in Florence: Being Simple Studies of Christian Art, for English Travellers (6 parts, Orpington: George Allen, 1875-1877; 1 volume, New York: Wiley, 1877; Orpington: George Allen, 1885);

Proserpina: Studies of Wayside Flowers, While the Air was Yet Pure Among the Alps, and in the Scotland and England which My Father Knew (10 parts, Orpington: George Allen, 1875-1886; parts 1-6 republished in 1 volume, 1879; New York: Alden, 1885);

Notes on Some of the Principal Pictures Exhibited in the Rooms of the Royal Academy: 1875 (Orpington: George Allen / London: Ellis & Bond, 1875);

Deucalion: Collected Studies of the Lapse of Waves, and Life of Stones (8 parts, Orpington: George Allen, 1875-1883; parts 1-3, 2 volumes, New York: Wiley, 1875-1877; parts 1-6, 1 volume, Orpington: George Allen, 1879);

Guide to the Principal Pictures in the Academy of Fine Arts at Venice, Arranged for English Travellers, 2 parts (Venice, 1877; Orpington: George Allen, 1882-1883);

St. Mark's Rest. The History of Venice, Written for the Help of the Few Travellers Who Still Care About Her Monuments (6 parts, including appendix and two supplements, Orpington: George Allen, 1877-1884; 1 volume, 1884; New York: Wiley, 1884);

The Laws of Fésole: A Familiar Treatise on the Elementary Principles and Practice of Drawing and Painting (4 parts, Orpington: George Allen, 1877-1879; New York: Wiley, 1877-1879; 1 volume, Orpington: George Allen, 1879; New York: Wiley, 1879);

Notes by Mr. Ruskin on His Drawings by the late J. M. W. Turner, R.A. (London: Elzevir Press, 1878);

Notes by Mr. Ruskin on Samuel Prout and William Hunt, Illustrated by a Loan Collection of Drawings Exhibited at the Fine Art Society's Galleries (London: Fine Art Society, 1879);

Letters Addressed by Professor Ruskin, D.C.L., to the Clergy on the Lord's Prayer and the Church, edited by F. A. Malleson (N.p.: Privately printed, 1879);

Elements of English Prosody for Use in St. George's Schools. Explanatory of the Various Terms Used in "Rock Honeycomb" (Orpington: George Allen, 1880);

Arrows of the Chace, Being a Collection of Scattered Letters Published Chiefly in the Daily Newspapers, 1840-1880 (2 volumes, Orpington: George Allen, 1880; New York: Wiley, 1881);

"Our Fathers Have Told Us." Sketches of the History of Christendom for Boys and Girls Who Have Been Held at Its Fonts, Part I: The Bible of Amiens (5 parts, Orpington: George Allen, 1880-1885; 1 volume, 1885; New York: Alden, 1885);

The Art of England: Lectures Given in Oxford (6 parts, Orpington: George Allen, 1883-1884; 1 volume, 1884; New York: Wiley, 1884);

The Pleasures of England: Lectures Given in Oxford (4 parts, Orpington: George Allen, 1884-1885; 1 volume, New York: Wiley, 1885);

The Storm-Cloud of the Nineteenth Century: Two Lectures Delivered at the London Institution, February 4th and 11th, 1884 (2 parts, Orpington: George Allen, 1884; 1 volume, 1884; New York: Wiley, 1884);

On the Old Road: A Collection of Miscellaneous Essays, Pamphlets, Etc., Etc., Published 1834-1885, 2 volumes, edited by Alexander Wedderburn (Orpington: George Allen, 1885);

Praeterita: Outlines of Scenes and Thoughts Perhaps Worthy of Memory in My Past Life (28 parts, Orpington: George Allen, 1885-1889; 3 volumes, Orpington: George Allen, 1886-1889; New York: Wiley, 1886-1889);

Dilecta: Correspondence, Diary Notes, and Extracts from Books, Illustrating Praeterita, 3 parts (Orpington: George Allen, 1886-1900);

Verona and Other Lectures, edited by W. G. Collingwood (Orpington: George Allen, 1894; New York & London: Macmillan, 1894);

Lectures on Landscape, Delivered at Oxford in Lent Term, 1871 (Orpington: George Allen, 1897);

The Diaries of John Ruskin, 3 volumes, edited by Joan Evans and J. H. Whitehouse (Oxford: Oxford University Press, 1956-1959);

The Brantwood Diary of John Ruskin, edited by Helen Gill Viljoen (New Haven: Yale University Press, 1970).

Collection: *The Works of John Ruskin*, Library Edition, 39 volumes, edited by E. T. Cook and

Alexander Wedderburn (London: George Allen / New York: Longmans, Green, 1903-1912).

John Ruskin was the most influential art critic to write in England between the death of Sir Joshua Reynolds in 1792 and the publications of Clive Bell and others around 1914. It is not, in fact, too much to say that his is the most important body of art criticism in the English language. It is a useful exercise to read all of his books, in order, year by year, for in a real sense Ruskin's bibliography is his biography. He wrote every day except Sunday and published everything he wrote except his diary and some hundreds of personal letters, and he wrote it all so well that he is acknowledged to be one of the great masters of English prose.

Ruskin was also a hardworking, "hands-on" art critic. He was not a painter or a sculptor; he was a critic, and he knew the difference. Besides producing a stream of books on art and artists, he taught drawing, wrote textbooks, reviewed shows, organized museums and galleries, collected paintings, gave public lectures, promoted new artists, wrote guidebooks, catalogued collections, and, finally, served as the first professor of fine art at Oxford. His architectural studies were the results of arduous observation of the details of Italian Gothic cathedrals, which demanded hours of climbing ladders and scaffolding. He illustrated most of his own books with meticulous drawings, and, after 1871 when he established in Orpington, Kent, a publishing house named for and operated by his longtime associate George Allen, he became his own publisher.

It is probable that Ruskin worked so hard because he combined a Puritan conscience with a love of beauty that was immediate and sensual. He passionately loved natural scenery and painting, but he believed that God did not approve of rich, idle young men who indulged their passions. He knew that if he were to enjoy his rapture of the eyes in this fallen world, he would have to labor and to do good works. He did both.

Ruskin was the only child of John James and Margaret Ruskin, a Scottish couple who had married late in life. His father was a prosperous sherry merchant whose work required frequent trips to the Continent and regular calls at the houses of the landed gentry in England. Before the development of the museums, the galleries in these houses were the repositories of most of the important paintings in Great Britain, and John James Ruskin became a knowledgeable connoisseur. From the time his son was six years old, he traveled with his father on occasion, thus becoming a precocious art critic.

Margaret Ruskin, in contrast, had scant interest in the arts. She was an unbending Evangelical. Almost from infancy young Ruskin read the Bible at his mother's knee, straight through, "hard names and all," as he said, over and over. He read Sir Walter Scott and Homer and learned the elements of Latin, but he had no toys and no playmates and was severely disciplined. John Ruskin attended a day school occasionally and was sometimes taught by a tutor, but his education was eccentric and irregular. In 1836, however, he qualified as a gentleman-commoner and thus was admitted without examination to Christ Church College, Oxford.

He began serious writing immediately. In 1837 and 1838 he published under the pseudonym Kata Phusin (According to Nature) a series of four articles entitled "The Poetry of Architecture" in the *Architectural Magazine*. It was a study of how cottages and villas in England, France, and Switzerland fit with their surroundings and related to the national characteristics of the inhabitants. The articles were well received and were a remarkable achievement for an eighteen-year-old.

In 1839 Ruskin received the prestigious Newdigate Prize for poetry at Oxford. The next year, however, he dropped out of the university because of illness and traveled on the Continent. In 1841, at home, he wrote *The King of the Golden River* for a girl who was visiting his parents. This classic fairy tale, which has been constantly in print since it was first published in 1851, contains in its allegory the germ of much of Ruskin's later social thought. The girl was Euphemia Gray, who, seven years later, became his bride.

In 1842 Ruskin returned to Oxford, took his examinations, and was graduated. He immediately began work on a book to defend his favorite painter, J. M. W. Turner. Turner had been a famous, well-established painter for forty years. In his later years he changed his manner of painting and therefore had been subjected to harsh criticism, but he scarcely needed the young Ruskin to defend him. Ruskin, however, plunged into the controversy. In 1843, the year he received an Oxford M.A., he produced volume one of *Modern Painters*, a work which was to extend to five volumes and to occupy him for seventeen years.

Ruskin's parents, John James and Margaret Ruskin; portraits by Henry Raeburn and James Northcote

The volume was published with the signature "a Graduate of Oxford." The argument of this volume is, first, that a painting ought to be true to life, and, second, that Turner's paintings were more nearly true than were those of the landscape painters of the previous two centuries.

The assertion that a painting ought to be true to life was made against the theory of Sir Joshua Reynolds and the practice, as Ruskin perceived it, of Claude Lorrain, Nicolas Poussin, and Salvator Rosa. Reynolds had argued that a painter should not paint the accidental qualities of a specific object, but rather that he should strive to present "the ideal form" of a natural object. This was common doctrine in the eighteenth century. Ruskin had no patience with this thinking. He was bound to nature by the scientific bias of his time. As a traveler with his parents, he had been raised in the tradition of view hunting. He loved nature with all his Evangelical fervor because God had made it. Because he lived in the age of William Wordsworth, he saw nature as a source of beneficent influences, and he had recently come to admire the abstract forms which

he found in nature. He believed that it was immoral to paint nature falsely under the delusion that one could improve upon it, and he believed that it was immoral to use nature simply as a vehicle for showing one's prowess as a painter.

The second part of his argument, that Turner painted nature more accurately than did his predecessors, is the longer part of the volume. Ruskin divides nature into categories: color, light and shade, space, clouds, mountains, water, and vegetation. In each category he describes some examples of natural scenery, then shows the accuracy of Turner's painting. It is Ruskin's descriptions, his word painting, that give this volume its distinction, though some of the prose seems too ornate even for Victorian taste. The weakness of the volume lies in its logic, because the validity of Ruskin's argument rests entirely upon the accuracy of his vision. The first installment of *Modern Painters* was praised and condemned, but no one doubted that a major new writer had appeared on the London scene. Ruskin's work was savagely attacked in an unsigned review by John Eagles for *Blackwood's Maga-*

St. Mark's Cathedral and the Ducal Palace, drawn by Ruskin at age sixteen, when he made his first trip to Venice (The Brantwood Trust, Coniston)

zine: "Self-convicted of malice, he has not the slightest suspicion of his ignorance. . . ." It fared little better in a two-part review by George Darley, also unsigned, in the *Athenaeum:* "[This work] is just not blasphemous because it is crack-brained." In contrast, volume one of *Modern Painters* was praised by Walt Whitman in the *Brooklyn Eagle* and by reviewers for the *Weekly Chronicle*, the *Churchman*, and *Gentleman's Magazine*. The critic for *Fraser's Magazine* called it "perhaps the most remarkable book which has ever been published in reference to art. . . ."

In 1844 Ruskin did some reading in art history and spent time at the Louvre. The next year he made his first trip to the Continent without his parents. He went to visit the scenes which Turner had painted, but in northern Italy he discovered the great religious and historical painters of the Renaissance. He was overwhelmed by what he saw, and especially by the canvases of Tintoretto.

He returned to England, and, after five months of concentrated writing, Ruskin's *Modern Painters*, volume two, was published in 1846. The first volume had been concerned with truth in art; the second was concerned with beauty. It is the shortest of the five volumes. The subject is difficult, and this volume is principally interesting as the record of the attempt of an Evangelical of distinct Puritan cast to come to terms with the sensuous appeal of beauty in art. It was published along with the third edition of the first volume, both by "a Graduate of Oxford."

By this time Ruskin knew much more about art than he had at the beginning of his project. He now knew that art had a history, that the Turner controversy was but an episode in that history, and that the idea of truth in art was a much simpler concept when dealing with landscape than when looking at a religious painting. It was ten years before he resumed work on *Modern Painters*.

On 10 April 1848 John Ruskin married Euphemia Gray. About this time he also turned his attention to architecture. After a tour of the cities of Normandy, he produced in 1849 *The Seven Lamps of Architecture*. This work was an application of the principles of *Modern Painters* to architecture. It differed from the earlier volumes in that for Ruskin truth in architecture meant something like an integration of form, function, and site rather than conformity to an exterior object. *The Seven Lamps of Architecture* was the first of his volumes to be illustrated. Ruskin was a superb draftsman, and he drew and sketched all the illustrations himself, a practice he was to continue. This was also Ruskin's first volume published under his own name.

Ruskin was beginning to suspect that there was a connection between the quality of the art produced at a certain time and place and the quality of the culture out of which it came, and he needed a new argument. Two volumes of *Modern Painters* had not succeeded in winning popular taste away from the Old Masters. He perceived that this taste had been corrupted by the Renaissance, though it would not be easy to make the case that the period that produced Michelangelo, Leonardo da Vinci, and Raphael had a corrupting influence because their great genius had obscured their faults. Ruskin believed that their mastery of and concentration upon technique led the viewer to contemplate not nature, or man, or God, but the artist himself. It was a self-conscious art, corrupted by pride of technique. To make his case for the relationship of art and culture and against the Renaissance, Ruskin decided to discuss architecture rather than painting. Architecture is the more social art. Individual genius does not come into play in the way that it does in painting; architecture involves many workmen, and the great buildings serve social purposes.

Ruskin chose Venice as his laboratory. He spent the winter of 1849-1850 there with his young wife. While she reveled in the brilliant society of the Austrian occupation, he toiled feverishly on high ladders and scaffolding, sketching in loving detail the decorative devices of these great buildings which he believed were inevitably to be lost to increasing industrial pollution, or to slip beneath the waves. Volume one of *The Stones of Venice* was published in 1851. It is a technical introduction to architecture. A building is an artificial arrangement of stones, and Ruskin leads readers through the process, from the quarry to the foundation, the walls, and the roof.

The same year, 1851, Ruskin's pamphlet entitled *Pre-Raphaelitism* was published. It was a defense of a group of young London artists, including John Everett Millais, Edward Burne-Jones, William Holman Hunt, and Dante Gabriel Rossetti, who called themselves the Pre-Raphaelite

Euphemia Gray Ruskin, drawn by Ruskin in 1848 or 1850 (Ashmolean Museum, Oxford). They were married 10 April 1848.

Brotherhood (PRB). They were trying to break the bondage of Renaissance tradition, and they strove to paint with meticulous accuracy. Their shows were viciously attacked, and Ruskin threw his by-now-considerable weight on their side. He defended their theory and practice, but most of the pamphlet was concerned, once more, with the paintings of Turner. Since Turner's paintings were not at all like those of the PRB, Ruskin felt obliged to explain how he could admire both styles.

The Ruskins returned to Venice for a full year in 1851 and 1852, and in 1853 the final two volumes of *The Stones of Venice* were published. In the second volume Ruskin describes and pays tribute to the Byzantine churches of early Venice and shows their superiority to pagan art. Then, in a passage that is one of the most widely republished and quoted in all Ruskin, he turns to his consideration of Gothic architecture. He concludes that the excellence of Gothic architecture lies in the way its builders solved structural problems and in the way they ornamented the buildings, but especially in the manner in which the structures, by their very irregularity, reflect a civilization whose workers were free to express themselves in their work. The contrast with the life of the factory worker in the new industries of England was evident: "You must either make a tool of the creature, or a man of him. You cannot make both."

The *Communist Manifesto* had appeared in 1848; in 1850 Karl Marx arrived in London, where he worked at the British Museum writing *Das Kapital*. A workers' revolution was in the air. Young militants seized upon Ruskin's words. "The Nature of the Gothic," a chapter in volume two of *The Stones of Venice*, was published separately and distributed as a pamphlet. Ruskin had become an important social commentator.

Volume three of *The Stones of Venice* was subtitled *The Fall*. It is an account of the Renaissance architecture of Venice. In Ruskin's view, Venice had abandoned its religious fervor; it then lost its preeminence as a trading nation and a sea power, and its architecture fell to the ministry of pride and luxury. The parallel with Great Britain was clear. It too was a great sea power and trading nation which was losing its religious fervor. For the English there were sermons in *The Stones of Venice*.

Ruskin's work was still receiving bad reviews from the established quarterlies, but he continued to receive praise from the more popular press. The *Times* gave *The Stones of Venice* a very long, generally favorable review in three installments. Ruskin was clearly a force on the London scene. His work on architecture is written in the same Latinate prose as *Modern Painters*. As in that work, the sentences are long and complex, with many subordinate clauses, self-conscious rhythms, alliterations, suspensions of the predicate, and other devices of classical rhetoric. The opening sentences of *The Stones of Venice* serve as an example: "Since first the dominion of men was asserted over the ocean, three thrones, of mark beyond all others, have been set upon its sands: the thrones of Tyre, Venice, and England. Of the First of these great powers only the memory remains; of the Second, the ruin; the Third, which inherits their greatness, if it forget their example, may be led through prouder eminence to less pitied destruction." Ruskin's powers of description are brought to bear on buildings and city streets instead of on natural scenery, but the work is more orderly, more under control than is *Modern Painters*. *The Stones of Venice* is probably the finest study of a great city ever written.

From Shakespeare to Thomas Mann, Venice has fascinated writers from what George Gordon, Lord Byron called "the moral North." Ruskin's passionate response to this seductive city and the

William Bell Scott, Ruskin, and Dante Gabriel Rossetti, 1863. Ruskin had defended the paintings of Rossetti and others of the Pre-Raphaelite Brotherhood in his 1851 pamphlet Pre-Raphaelitism.

frantic, even maniacal, pace of his work may also have had personal roots. In 1854 his wife successfully sued for an annulment of their marriage on the grounds that it had never been consummated. The decree was granted on 15 July 1854. Almost exactly one year later, on 3 July 1855, she married John Everett Millais, one of the Pre-Raphaelite painters whom Ruskin had befriended.

The episode had no visible effect on Ruskin's public life and work. He does seem, however, to have sought ways to be more effective in the practical order and to reach a broader audience. He met Dante Gabriel Rossetti in 1854. Turner had died in 1851, and it occurred to Ruskin that there might be more merit in helping a live artist than in defending a dead one. Therefore, for several years he did what he could to lift Rossetti's financial burdens so that he would be free to paint.

He also began to teach drawing at the Working Men's College and, in 1855, began to write annual reviews of the paintings hung each year at the Exhibition of the Royal Academy. These pamphlets, meant to be sold to visitors entering the gallery, were published for five years, until 1859; a final one appeared in 1875.

In 1856 Ruskin produced volumes three and four of *Modern Painters*. One reads volume three with a sense of continuity, not from volume two, but from *The Stones of Venice*. In the ten years since the second volume of *Modern Painters* had appeared, Ruskin had seen many more paintings, especially in Italy, and had learned much. He maintained steadfastly his general argument that a great painter looks at what he paints through the eyes of love, thus sees it truly and paints it truly. A bad painter paints out of pride, or self-love. Ruskin now understood, however, that there were great painters who made no attempt to paint external nature accurately— Italian primitives such as Giotto, for example. Therefore, he devoted the first part of the volume to distinguishing between good and bad use of the imagination to create "ideal" images. He had also learned that people, even in Europe, have not always seen Nature in the same way, that landscape has a history. The second part of *Modern Painters*, volume three, traces the history of landscape from Homer to Turner.

Volume four contains additional essays on Turner, a long technical discussion of the geology of mountains, and two chapters on the effects of mountains on people who live in them and visit them. These chapters carry forward brilliantly the eighteenth-century concept of the picturesque.

The opinions of the reviewers of this volume were consistent with most of those expressed concerning earlier volumes. However, Ruskin continued to have strong support in the more popular journals. George Eliot, in a review of volume three for the *Westminster*, wrote, "he who teaches . . . with such power as Mr. Ruskin's, is a prophet for his generation"; of the third and fourth volumes she declared, "[they] contain, I think, some of the finest writing of the age."

As an extension of his teaching, in 1857 Ruskin produced a textbook, *The Elements of Drawing in Three Letters to Beginners*. His study of Venice had reaffirmed his conviction that there was a connection between a society and the art it produces. He was beginning to believe that British society was in such a wretched state that little advancement in the arts was possible. If he were to reform the taste of his countrymen in art, he would have first to reform the society. All his writing on art, he suspected, may have been a waste of time.

From this time forward almost all of his writings were either public lectures or magazine articles, as he reached for a larger public. These new formats are reflected in Ruskin's radical change in style. The periodic sentences of the longer books are gone, replaced with sentences of simple structure and limpid clarity. Ruskin's shift to lectures and periodical pieces also created problems for bibliographers because the works were published at the time they were written and then gathered into books which appeared sometimes many years later, and with different titles.

An example is the two lectures Ruskin delivered in 1857 on "The Political Economy of Art." In these addresses he identified the troubles of British society as liberalism in religion and laissez-faire capitalism. The great industrial town of Manchester was the seat of both, so he gave his lectures there. He tried to talk to businessmen about art in terms that they would understand. How does one identify a good artist? How much should one pay him? Why should businessmen collect art? Why should they try to help preserve the art being destroyed by war in Italy? The lectures were printed in an inexpensive edition immediately and were published again, with additions, under the title "*A Joy for Ever*," in 1880. Newspapers carried full accounts of the lectures, and most took the view that Ruskin should stay away from social questions and confine himself to art.

The year 1858 was a decisive one in Ruskin's life. Turner had died in 1851 and had left nineteen thousand sketches, drawings, and paintings to the nation. Ruskin had been named executor and trustee of Turner's estate. Although he did not function during the prolonged litigation that followed, he did survey and catalogue the bulk of these pictures. When he had finished, he was tired of Turner; and he perceived that Turner had severe limitations. He concluded that Turner was still the greatest landscape painter who had ever lived and probably the greatest painter England could produce, but the great Venetians had captured Ruskin.

He also dated from 1858 the loss of his Evangelical faith. He did not cease to be a Christian, and he did not move toward Catholicism, but he did abandon the sectarian views of his childhood. He also abandoned some of the arguments that supported the first two volumes of *Modern Painters*. In fact, he was beginning to wonder whether there was any use in landscape painting at all. Perhaps it is better to look at real scenery than at a painting, and, if it seemed desirable to record accurately a scene, the camera was now available.

In 1859 Ruskin wrote another textbook, *The Elements of Perspective*, and he set about finishing *Modern Painters*. He no longer had enthusiasm for the project, but his father was proud of his work on art. In 1858 Ruskin had been elected an honorary scholar at Christ Church, Oxford. This was a great distinction; he was clearly succeeding in his career as an art critic, and his father did not want him to abandon this career for the rough-and-tumble world of public controversy over political and social matters.

To please his father, Ruskin plunged forward and published volume five of *Modern Painters* in 1860. It is one of the most challenging books to come out of Victorian England. Because he had lost his enthusiasm for landscape, Ruskin concentrated on Turner's paintings of mythological subjects, and, because he had given up his conventional religious beliefs, he was able to bring a freshness and vitality to his reading of the ancient myths. The result is a notable Christian statement about art as the light of the world, the redeemer from darkness and chaos.

In the same year, as a series of magazine articles, Ruskin produced "*Unto this Last*," his most successful incursion into the field of political economy. Before looking at the argument of this series, however, it is useful to consider the titles of his three principal works on the subject together: "*Unto this Last*," *Munera Pulveris*, and *The Crown of Wild Olive*.

Ruskin's fundamental insight in these works was that capitalism, guided by the economic theory of the time, defined man as a selfish being who presumably acts always in his own interest. More than that, in Ruskin's view, this selfishness is perceived not as an evil in man's fallen nature but as a positive good. Ruskin points out that nineteenth-century England represents the only culture that has ever exalted selfishness as a virtue. All other cultures in all other times have perceived it to be a vice. "*Unto this Last*" takes its title from Matthew 20:14. *Munera Pulveris* (A Little Dust) finds its title in an obscure ode by Horace—the principal Roman poet after the death of Virgil—who died a few years before the birth of Christ.

The Crown of Wild Olive is a series of three lectures delivered in different cities in 1864 and 1865. The third lecture, "War," was privately printed in 1866, the year that the complete volume was published. A fourth lecture, "The Future of England," was delivered in 1869 and added to the 1873 edition. In these lectures Rus-

kin offers a choice of pagan or Christian ethics. If the ostensibly Christian businessmen of England need a reason for abandoning their economic theories and replacing them with justice and charity, Ruskin promises them that their reward will be eternal life in Heaven. He knows that his audience may well regard this kind of talk as frothy nonsense to be listened to with patience only on Sunday morning and so pursues his point: if eternal life is not a sufficient reward, do these things as the ancient Romans did them—that you may be honored among your friends. Let your reward be a crown of wild olive placed upon your head. This is, of course, the ironic message of a man who has despaired of ever conveying his message to the middle class.

Ruskin wanted to reach that class because he was a member of it. His father was a merchant who loved the arts and was an honorable man. Ruskin wanted to show that a merchant who cared about his employees and felt a responsibility toward the community could be held in honor the way a professional man was. "*Unto this Last*" was published in four articles in consecutive issues of *Cornhill Magazine* and *Harper's New Monthly Magazine* (New York) in 1860, before the series was stopped by the editor. The essays were gathered into a book in 1862, and a second edition appeared in 1877.

The articles caused a fierce outcry when they first appeared, but the volume has been one of Ruskin's most frequently republished and most influential books. Written in clear, straightforward prose, the articles lay out a theory of a just wage and a just price, exalting the merchant as a person who devotes his life to supplying the needs of his community.

In 1862 and 1863 Ruskin published a sequel to "*Unto this Last*" under the heading "Essays on Political Economy." They appeared in four issues of *Fraser's Magazine*, and, once again, the editor halted the series. Gathered into a volume, *Munera Pulveris*, in 1872, these pieces attack the law of supply and demand as a way of determining wages and prices and attempt to redefine elementary economic concepts such as wealth, value, and money.

In 1864 Ruskin's father died. In December of that year he delivered two lectures, one week apart, at the Town Hall in Manchester. The two lectures, "Of Kings' Treasuries" and "Of Queens' Gardens," were published together the following year under the title *Sesame and Lilies*. The first lecture was delivered in connection with a fund-

An 1853 drawing of Ruskin's wedding to Euphemia Gray by John Everett Millais (Victoria and Albert Museum). In 1854 Euphemia Ruskin had the marriage annulled; the following year she married Millais. In Millais's drawing the ghostly figure behind the groom is Ruskin's grandfather John Thomas Ruskin, who committed suicide in 1817.

raising effort to establish a library, an occasion that allowed Ruskin to move away from the subjects that had occupied him for twenty years.

He had tried to change people's taste in art; he had tried to point the way toward a reformation in society itself. The first Manchester lecture provided an opportunity to step back from controversy—and to talk about books. Bad books are a terrible waste of time, he said, but good books are precisely the most precious possessions of a nation. The wisdom and moral training found in good books are essential to the stability of the state.

The occasion of the second lecture was to raise funds for schools, and Ruskin addressed himself to the education of women. If men needed wisdom and moral strength, what did women need? His answer was that women needed to learn the same things that men did (with the exception of theology!) and that their training should issue in the virtues of justice and mercy. The ideal kingdom would then be ruled by men and women, kings and queens, of strong character, fortified by the virtues of wisdom, justice, and charity.

The lectures represent a tendency that surfaced in the later chapters of *Modern Painters*, volume five. When Ruskin studied Turner's paintings of mythological subjects, he began to organize his own thoughts in mythic terms. He had begun to see Turner as a painter of the fallen world and all art as a struggle to overcome the chaos of that world. The great Venetians, he believed, strove mightily to achieve the redemption of that world, but, because their religion was ultimately false, they failed. "Of Kings' Treasuries" is an account of human wisdom, the best that can be achieved in the fallen world, the world of the Old Testament, of King Solomon. "Of

Ruskin's worksheet no. 99, on the Ducal Palace, for The Stones of Venice *(Education Trust, Ruskin Galleries, Bembridge)*

Self-caricature by Ruskin (The Pierpont Morgan Library)

Queens' Gardens" presents a Garden of Eden, where woman, or the female principle, presides over the world of the New Testament, redeemed by love and ruled by Christ.

Sesame and Lilies was Ruskin's most popular work. It went through twenty editions in forty years and is still republished from time to time. In 1868 he delivered a third lecture, this time in Dublin, which was added to the 1871 edition of *Sesame and Lilies*. He had become a very popular lecturer. More than two thousand tickets were sold to this lecture, "On the Mystery of Life and its Arts." The address is, in some ways, a sad one, for Ruskin had concluded that neither literature nor art really mattered very much. But there is no bitterness in this conclusion. He simply says that man's efforts might be better spent in feeding the hungry, clothing the naked, and housing the shelterless—those things upon which, according to Matthew's Gospel, we shall finally be judged.

Going to Ireland to deliver the lecture must have been a bittersweet occasion for Ruskin. In 1858 he had begun giving drawing lessons to a nine-year-old Irish girl named Rose La Touche. Rose was beautiful, sickly, and talented, and Ruskin, over the next six or seven years, fell hopelessly in love with her. On her seventeenth birth-

day, when he was forty-seven, he proposed marriage. Rose asked him to wait until she was twenty-one, or at least until she reached nineteen, to which Ruskin agreed. Her parents, however, were understandably concerned. It was not only Ruskin's age but also his former marriage and his new irreligion that distressed them. They did what they could to break off the relationship, and the resulting uncertainty deeply troubled Ruskin for the next ten years until, in 1875, at the age of twenty-seven, Rose died. Her memory haunted Ruskin for the rest of his life.

In 1865 Ruskin was invited to address the Royal Institute of Architects on the study of architecture in the schools. These practicing architects regarded him as an unpractical theorist, but it is significant that they did invite him to address them. He told them that they had taken but half of his message. He had freed them from the tyranny of classical art, and they had achieved the ugliness of Gothic without its freedom. Beginning in 1865 he also published "The Cestus of Aglaia," a collection of articles on the laws of art, which appeared in the *Art Journal*.

Since 1857 Ruskin had been visiting a girls' school at Winnington Hall, Cheshire. It is clear that Ruskin enjoyed these visits with the girls, who were a pleasant change from his students at the Working Men's College. The result of his time at Winnington Hall was *The Ethics of the Dust* (1866), a series of ten lectures, more or less about mineralogy, in the form of a dialogue with a group of girls. Public reception to Ruskin's book was mixed. A reviewer of *The Ethics of the Dust* in *Saturday Review*, 30 December 1865, found it "whimsical, incongruous, and silly beyond all measure." The critic for the *Guardian*, 21 February 1866, reported that "Mr. Ruskin appears to unusual advantage; playful, allegorical, and dramatic as well as instructive."

Ruskin remained in the thick of British intellectual life. In 1867 he was invited to give the Rede Lecture at Cambridge, where he received an honorary degree. The address, entitled "On the Relation of National Ethics to National Arts," was a summary of previous writings and remarks. After a brief period of discouragement, Ruskin plunged into the serious study of mythology which had its beginnings in *Modern Painters*, volume five, and *Sesame and Lilies*. He knew Max Müller, at Oxford, and he knew the work of James Fergusson. His objective was to use primitive myths of earth and air as a way of perceiving the natural world as it appeared to ancient man.

Page from the manuscript for the final chapter of Modern Painters, *volume five (The Pierpont Morgan Library)*

Drawing by Ruskin of Rose La Touche, the young Irish girl thirty years his junior to whom he proposed marriage in 1866 (Education Trust, Ruskin Galleries, Bembridge)

To understand this primitive view of nature and then to trace its development as it is reflected in the development of mythologies would be, Ruskin reasoned, a way to understand contemporary man's relation to nature.

It was evident that this kind of learning would have expanded enormously Ruskin's understanding of landscape painting, and he regretted that he had not had these insights when he had written *Modern Painters*, volume two, especially the chapters on "Typical Beauty." He produced *The Queen of the Air: Being a Study of the Greek Myths of Cloud and Storm* in 1869. It was to have been followed by a companion volume on Greek earth myths, but this work was never completed. The 1869 volume is vintage Ruskin—discursive and filled with brilliant insights—and it was also well received. Thomas Carlyle wrote Ruskin on 17 August 1869: "No such Book have I met with for long years past"; the critic for the *Westminster Review*, October 1869, similarly offered praise: "we are inclined to call this the most brilliant and successful piece of interpretation to which any set

of Hellenic myths have been subjected in England since the discoveries of philologists have set interpreters on the right road." In a private letter Ruskin said of it, "It is the best I ever wrote . . . it is the most useful and careful piece I have done."

In Ruskin's principal economic books, "*Unto this Last*," *Munera Pulveris*, and *The Crown of Wild Olive*, he had developed a devastating criticism of capitalism. He contradicted its theories and exposed the miserable lives of the working people that had been its fruit. These studies were collections of articles and lectures designed for the middle class, the winners in the economy. In 1867, however, Ruskin sought another audience—the workingman. He wrote twenty-five letters addressed to "a Working Man of Sunderland" which were published over a period of two months in newspapers in two of the great industrial cities, Leeds and Manchester. In the same year they were collected in a book entitled *Time and Tide*. In these letters Ruskin showed himself to be close to the thought of Carlyle, Matthew Arnold, and the Christian Socialists. That is, he was profoundly critical of capitalism, its injustices and the squalor in which the poor were forced to live, but he drew back from supporting communist or socialist revolutions. As a group, these Victorian thinkers urged instead the moral reformation of owners and workers in order to bring about a just society. They mistrusted the mob and bureaucracy alike and saw this conversion as society's hope.

In 1868 Felix Slade bequeathed a sum of money for the endowment of Slade professorships in fine art at the universities of Oxford and Cambridge and at University College, London. Ruskin was the unanimous choice of the electors to fill the chair at Oxford. He gave his inaugural lecture in February 1870 and began a period of intense activity. He delivered twelve courses of lectures at Oxford, all of which were published. He organized the university's art collection. He started a drawing school. He saw himself as a kind of professor of beauty, so he lectured and wrote on botany, on geology, and on ornithology. He founded a museum. He wrote guidebooks for the use of travelers in Florence and Venice.

Ruskin took rooms at Corpus Christi College and worked actively with the students. On one occasion he involved the young Alfred Milner, Arnold Toynbee, and Oscar Wilde, among others, in an arduous road-building project. It was his view that strong and healthy young men of the upper classes, instead of playing games, should try manual labor. He thought that they might get just as much exercise and, at the same time, learn about life. In spite of this activity at the university, Ruskin did not abandon his commitment to social reformation. During the years of his professorship he produced one pamphlet per month addressed to the workingmen of England. These ninety-six "letters" were eventually published together in the multivolume *Fors Clavigera* (1871-1884). He also involved himself in practical projects—cleaning the streets, selling tea at honest prices, and the forming of his Guild of St. George.

A chronological account of his writing during this period is impossible because he worked on everything at once. "Head too full, and don't know which to write first," he wrote in his diary in 1872. In 1875 he calculated that he had seven large books in press at the same time. His mother died in 1871, at the age of ninety; Rose La Touche died in 1875. It is not surprising that Ruskin suffered a severe physical and mental collapse in 1878.

Ruskin served three three-year terms as professor of fine arts, from 1870 to 1879. His lectures were models of orderly presentation in which he undertook to distill the work of a lifetime for systematic presentation to students. He later remarked that the "lectures were the most important piece of my literary work done with unabated power, best motive, and happiest concurrence of circumstance." At Oxford he had found, again, a new audience. He did not give up on the working class; he continued to address them on economic and social matters, but he had decided, as he put it in his inaugural lecture, that the sons of the nobility and gentry were best able to love landscape. This remark may have been designed to encourage his students, but he was noting a phenomenon that more recent history confirms. The love of landscape is an urban phenomenon. It coincides with the rise of great industrial cities. The laborer struggling to plow a field or to haul a load over a mountain does not enjoy the view, and people, in truth, come to treasure natural beauty only as they are in danger of destroying it. Ruskin, however, surmised that a love of beauty developed only in homes where the arts were honored, where music and the fine arts flourished. He also believed that love of landscape required a sense of history, an awareness of the human life that has passed over a scene.

In his second lecture at Oxford, "The Relation of Art to Religion," he wrestled once more with what for him were difficult questions. First, what role does religion play as a cause of art? Second, what effect does art have upon religion? His answer to the first question was simple: religious inspiration does not directly affect art. The second problem was more difficult, and in his attempt at resolution Ruskin's Evangelical heritage surfaces. Religious painting, Ruskin holds, does realize and make concrete religious doctrine, and this is good, but it also circumscribes the religious event in place and time. This is one of the two standard objections to religious art. The other is temptation to idolatry.

He continued his series of inaugural lectures with "The Relation of Art to Morals" and "The Relation of Art to Use." In the first he asserted that immorality was the love of chaos and the love of self. All bad art comes from these misguided allegiances. Morality is the love of life, of order, and of something outside the self. All good art, assuming, of course, technical competence, flows from these moral instincts. The second of these lectures can be summarized in Ruskin's phrase: "[Art] gives Form to knowledge and Grace to utility." The second series of Oxford lectures delivered in the fall term 1870, published as *Aratra Pentelici* (1872), are devoted to sculpture. In these Ruskin began with consideration of a breakfast plate, its structure and decoration, and developed a full series of addresses on Greek and Florentine sculpture, contending in a magnificent summary that "Art is the contest of life with clay."

These first two series of lectures were delivered to large audiences, including many from outside the university. In the spring 1871 term, however, Ruskin changed his forum. For this series on landscape he limited attendance to students enrolled in his course so that his work on art might be integrated into the university studies. Because he addressed a smaller gathering he was able to distribute examples of art and lift his own burden of having to prepare so many formal lectures directed toward large audiences. The spring 1871 talks were not published until many years later, as *Lectures on Landscape* (1897). The thesis of this volume is that nature is only significant in terms of its relation to human life. An interest in nature that is limited to its colors and its forms, or to the science of it, is inferior. An erupting volcano is significant, not because of its aesthetic qualities and not because it exemplifies prin-

158

A certain portion of the work of man must be for his bread — and that is his Labour; — with the sweat of his face, for accomplished as a daily task — and ended as a daily task — with the prayer — Give us each day our daily bread. But another portion of Man's work is that in which according to his separate power. gift and strength, he carries forward the purposes of God for his Race: accepts from his Sires their Knowledge and their Art; adds to it his 1 tone of true craftsmans cutting — bequeaths his own piece and a part of the Immortal of work of this World — to the Future. be it here in his own place — our work and the year — This will be done, on earth as it is in Heaven. And the toil of the hands, for the life — today is our 'Labour'.

But the toil of hand and heart, liveth — for the future of life of others — is our 'Opus; — of which when well done — the angels may say. Perfecit opus'. Perfected — Did it throughly. and of which before his eyes are closed — the promise is to every Servant of God. 'He shall see of the travail of his Soul. and shall be satisfied:'

Page from the manuscript for Fors Clavigera, *Ruskin's series of ninety-six "letters" to the workingmen of England (W. G. Collingwood,* The Life and Work of John Ruskin, *1893)*

ciples of evaporation and gravity, but because it is dangerous and lethal to men.

The series of ten lectures which Ruskin delivered in the spring term 1872, and had published that year as *The Eagle's Nest*, is as subtle and complicated as anything he ever wrote. His intention was to show the place of art in the university program by relating it to the end of a university. He argues that it is the place of art to serve knowledge. It records and makes vivid the passions of men. Great art records the "right things," so that, paradoxically, the art will be forgotten as men are led to contemplate those right things. *Val d'Arno* (1874), a collection of the fall 1873 lectures, is a series of studies of Tuscan art in relation to the history of Florence. The lectures deal mainly with architecture and are not much different from Ruskin's writing in *The Stones of Venice* except that they develop no broad social thesis.

In the spring of 1874 Ruskin went abroad, but he returned for the fall semester and offered a series of lectures which was published under the title "The Aesthetic and Mathematical Schools of Art in Florence," first collected in the Library Edition of his works. In these talks Ruskin distinguishes between those who draw the appearance of things and those who draw from measurements. He taught the latter as a beginner's technique, but always regarded it as just that. In his explanation of what he calls the aesthetic school, his position is not far from that of the Impressionists, who were flourishing by this time in Paris, and even in London.

During his university years, Ruskin also began work on some technical studies. They include *Ariadne Florentina* (1873-1876) and *The Laws of Fésole* (1877-1879), which are about engraving and drawing. He also produced *Love's Meinie* (1873-1881), *Deucalion* (1875-1883), and *Proserpina* (1875-1886), on ornithology, geology, and botany. Ruskin's approach to natural history was, first, to look carefully at an object, and then to attempt to discover what had been thought about it by wise men throughout history. Hence, a vital part of Ruskin's studies of natural objects is his investigations of the myths that had grown up around those objects. While he was at the university, Ruskin also prepared notes and prefaces for new editions of *Modern Painters* and *The Stones of Venice*.

In 1878 Ruskin suffered his severe breakdown. In letter number seventy-nine of *Fors Clavigera*, dated 18 June 1877, Ruskin had made some adverse comments on one of James Whis-

Ruskin in 1874, photograph by Lewis Carroll

tler's paintings. Whistler sued for libel, and the case came to trial in 1878. Ruskin was not well enough to attend, and he lost the case. The jury found for Whistler, but awarded him only one farthing in damages. Ruskin used the verdict as an occasion to resign his professorship in 1879. This episode marked the virtual end to his public life. He did, however, continue to produce the pamphlets published as *Fors Clavigera* until 1884. The literary interest in these "letters" comes from the fact that they contain a vein of ironic writing as rich as any to be found in Victorian England. Ruskin's target is the merchants who had been deaf to his calls to honor and to conscience.

After 1879 Ruskin gave much money and what energy he had to the Guild of St. George. This group, which he founded, was to be a kind of commune. The members were to farm, do light manufacturing, and educate their children according to the principles which he had laid down. Although attempts were made by zealous followers to begin such enterprises as far away as Australia and the United States, the project never really got off the ground, though the guild did successfully establish a small educational museum in Sheffield.

In 1883 Ruskin accepted reappointment to his professorship at Oxford. His lectures, published as *The Art of England* (1883-1884), are appreciations of whatever he could find to praise in contemporary British art. He praised Sir Edwin Landseer, William Holman Hunt, Dante Gabriel Rossetti, and some illustrators of children's books. It was his own practice, and he urged it upon all who heard him, to buy only the work of living artists.

Ruskin developed in his last years a keen awareness that the new industrialism was polluting the air and water and thus ruining the architecture and the frescoes that had survived for centuries. In 1884 he delivered a lecture entitled "The Storm-Cloud of the Nineteenth Century," in which he complained that the atmosphere had changed during his lifetime. The lecture is elegantly structured and supported, but it was ridiculed at the time. Ruskin was a keen and practiced observer of light and clouds and it is now clear that he was correct in his concerns. To save what he could, Ruskin turned to the writing of historical sketches. One of the best is *"Our Fathers Have Told Us"* (1880-1885)—or *The Bible of Amiens*, as it is known—a full exposition of the cathedral at Amiens, France. He produced *St. Mark's Rest* (1877-1884) and *The Pleasures of England* (1884-1885) in the same vein. They represent his attempts to get at the root myths and legends of Christian Europe, and thus of Christian art.

Ruskin began to produce his autobiography, *Praeterita*, in 1885, and it appeared intermittently until 1889. It is a charming, if selective, account of his life. It does not, for example, mention his marriage, but it more than fulfills Ruskin's promise in the subtitle to provide "Outlines of Scenes and Thoughts Perhaps Worthy of Memory in My Past Life." Ruskin had frequent attacks of both physical and mental illness between 1879 and 1889. In 1871 he had bought a country home, Brantwood, at Coniston, which he occupied when his schedule permitted. In 1889 he finally retired there and lived quietly, in the care of a young relative, until his death on 20 January 1900.

Ruskin's early works, in the 1840s, were vigorously attacked in the established journals, while the newer, more moderate journals were often favorable. Often a reviewer simply reflected his own estimate of Turner, rather than of Ruskin. However, Ruskin was reviewed widely, and, while still in his twenties, he was clearly a strong presence in the rather limited world of art criticism. In the 1850s his valiant defense of the Pre-Raphaelites cost him dearly in the art world, but *The Stones of Venice* was an achievement too massive to dismiss. His works were reviewed in a range of publications, from prominent quarterlies to daily newspapers. Reviews were mixed, but Ruskin was a powerful cultural influence all over England. The 1860s were the years of his lectures on social and economic subjects. Most of the press attacked him as a man out of his field, but he had his defenders, and he had a large popular following. His tenure as professor of fine art at Oxford, at least until his breakdown in 1878, must be judged as a brilliant success.

As the century closed, Ruskin's reputation as an art critic declined. The Pre-Raphaelites fell out of favor, and although he had only championed them because they were the best painters working at the time in England, Ruskin's reputation suffered with theirs. He had missed the Impressionist developments in France, and the rise of the art-for-art's-sake school made Ruskin's work seem out-of-date.

In spite of the magnificent Library Edition, which appeared from 1903 to 1912, Ruskin, along with many Victorian writers, was no longer widely read by the early twentieth century. When he was read at all, it was for his social criticism. He influenced Mahatma Gandhi, Leo Tolstoy, and many members of the early British Labour party. In the United States, where a cigar was named in his honor, he was remembered as a friend of the workingman.

Important studies of Ruskin began to appear again in the 1930s and 1940s. Much of this interest was stimulated by new information about his marriage, his loves, and his breakdown. Some of this information was simply sensational, but much of it was genuinely illuminating. Since 1950 there has been a steady stream, in both England and the United States, of biographies, studies, and editions of individual works. Though the most recent academic work on Ruskin is vigorous, much of it follows paths already marked. Studies based on Ruskin's economic, social, or political views are still scarce, although Robert Hewison's 1981 collection of critical essays by various hands contains many contributions in this area.

Jeanne Clegg's *Ruskin and Venice* (1981) is a narrowly focused, very competent study of the absolutely central episode in Ruskin's life and work—

Ruskin's study at Brantwood, the Coniston country home he purchased in 1871

the four years he spent in Venice living out his marriage and writing *The Stones of Venice*—but *Modern Painters* continues to attract most of the scholars. Elizabeth K. Helsinger's *Ruskin and the Art of the Beholder* (1982) is a valuable work in which the author traces the shifts of aesthetics and criticism that occurred in England during Ruskin's lifetime and shows his relationship to these changes, some of which he reflected and some of which he caused. Helsinger also brings to Ruskin criticism some of the insights into the role of the reader and viewer of a work of art that have been developed by recent literary criticism. Gary Wihl's *Ruskin and the Rhetoric of Infallibility* (1985) attempts to impose a large pattern on Ruskin's criticism. This task has always proved difficult and is never entirely successful, but this study has the merit of dealing with many works that are usually neglected. Another volume which approaches in a fruitful way the challenge of finding order in Ruskin's thought is Paul L. Sawyer's *Ruskins's Poetic Argument: The Design of the Major Works* (1985). A less traditional approach which is stimulating but offers its own difficulties is Jay Fellows's *Ruskin's Maze: Mastery and Madness in*

His Art (1981). Two other collections of essays on Ruskin offer a similar contrast. Robert E. Rhodes and Del Ivan Janik's *Studies in Ruskin* (1982) is a festschrift honoring Professor Van Akin Burd, the editor of several volumes of Ruskin's letters. The essays follow the lines of traditional scholarship. John Dixon Hunt and Faith Holland's *The Ruskin Polygon: Essays on the Imagination of John Ruskin* (1982), in contrast, explores less trodden paths.

It is in biography that we may expect important developments. There was a spate of Ruskin biographies between 1949 and 1954; then there was a pause for twenty years. During these years scholars devoted their energies to the editing and publishing of the diaries and of the great bulk of Ruskin's letters. Now that this material is available, new biographers will be able to take full advantage of these sources.

Two solid biographies have appeared, John Dixon Hunt's *The Wider Sea: A Life of John Ruskin* (1982) and Tim Hilton's *John Ruskin: The Early Years* (1985), the first part of a projected two-volume work. In summary, Ruskin's reputation has risen with the general increase in interest in

Ruskin and his lifelong friend Henry Acland at Brantwood, August 1893

Victorian literature. He has no popular following anymore, but those who have ranged widely through his books can assert that his is a blazing genius of the Victorian age.

Letters:

Hortus Inclusus: Messages from the Wood to the Garden, Sent in Happy Days to the Sister Ladies of the Thwaite, Coniston, edited by Albert Fleming (Orpington: George Allen, 1887; New York: Wiley, 1887);

Letters of John Ruskin to Charles Eliot Norton, 2 volumes, edited by Charles Eliot Norton (Boston & New York: Houghton, Mifflin, 1905);

John Ruskin's Letters to Francesca and Memoirs of the Alexanders, edited by Lucia Gray Swett (Boston: Lothrop, Lee & Shepard, 1931);

The Gulf of Years: Letters from John Ruskin to Kathleen Olander, edited by Rayner Unwin (London: Allen & Unwin, 1953);

Ruskin's Letters from Venice, 1851-1852, edited by John L. Bradley (New Haven: Yale University Press, 1955);

Letters of John Ruskin to Lord and Lady Mount-Temple, edited by Bradley (Columbus: Ohio State University, 1964);

Dearest Mama Talbot, edited by Margaret Spence (London: Allen & Unwin, 1966);

The Winnington Letters, edited by Van Akin Burd (Cambridge, Mass.: Harvard University Press, 1969);

Ruskin in Italy: Letters to His Parents, 1845, edited by Harold I. Shapiro (Oxford: Clarendon Press, 1972);

Sublime and Instructive, edited by Virginia Surtees (London: Joseph, 1972);

The Ruskin Family Letters, 2 volumes, edited by Burd (Ithaca, N.Y. & London: Cornell University Press, 1973);

John Ruskin and Alfred Hunt, edited by Robert Secor (Victoria, B.C.: University of Victoria, 1982);

The Correspondence of Thomas Carlyle and John Ruskin, edited by George Allan Cate (Stanford: Stanford University Press, 1982).

Bibliographies:

Thomas J. Wise and James P. Smart, *A Complete Bibliography of the Writings in Prose and Verse of John Ruskin, LL.D.*, 2 volumes (London: Privately printed, 1893);

Kirk H. Beetz, *John Ruskin: A Bibliography, 1900-1974* (Methuchen, N.J.: Scarecrow Press, 1976).

Biographies:

W. G. Collingwood, *The Life and Work of John Ruskin*, 2 volumes (London: Methuen, 1893);

E. T. Cook, *The Life of John Ruskin*, 2 volumes (London: Allen, 1911);

Derrick Leon, *Ruskin: The Great Victorian* (London: Routledge & Kegan Paul, 1949);

Peter Quennell, *John Ruskin: The Portrait of a Prophet* (New York: Viking, 1949);

Joan Evans, *John Ruskin* (London: Cape, 1954);

John L. Bradley, *An Introduction to Ruskin* (Boston: Houghton Mifflin, 1971);

John Dixon Hunt, *The Wider Sea: A Life of John Ruskin* (New York: Viking, 1982);

Tim Hilton, *John Ruskin: The Early Years* (New Haven: Yale University Press, 1985).

References:

Joan Abse, *John Ruskin, The Passionate Moralist* (New York: Knopf, 1981);

Quentin Bell, *Ruskin* (Edinburgh: Oliver & Boyd, 1963);

A. C. Benson, *Ruskin: A Study in Personality* (London: Smith, Elder, 1911; New York: Putnam's, 1911);

John L. Bradley, ed., *Ruskin: The Critical Heritage* (London: Routledge & Kegan Paul, 1984);

Van Akin Burd, "Another Light on the Writing of *Modern Painters*," *Publications of the Modern Language Association*, 68 (September 1953): 755-763;

Burd, "Background to *Modern Painters*: The Tradition and the Turner Controversy," *Publications of the Modern Language Association*, 74 (June 1959): 254-267;

Burd, "Ruskin's Defense of Turner: The Imitative Phase," *Philological Quarterly*, 37 (October 1958): 465-483;

Burd, "Ruskin's Quest for a Theory of Imagination," *Modern Language Quarterly*, 17 (March 1956): 60-72;

Kenneth Clark, *Ruskin at Oxford* (Oxford: Clarendon Press, 1947);

Jeanne Clegg, *Ruskin and Venice* (London: Junction Books, 1981);

Charles T. Dougherty, "Of Ruskin's Gardens," in *Myth and Symbol*, by Northrop Frye, L. C. Knights, and others (Lincoln: University of Nebraska, 1963), pp. 141-151;

Dougherty, "Ruskin's Moral Argument," *Victorian Newsletter*, no. 9 (Spring 1956): 4-7;

Dougherty, "Ruskin's Views on Non-Representational Art," *College Art Journal*, 15 (Winter 1955): 112-118;

John T. Fain, *Ruskin and the Economists* (Nashville: Vanderbilt University Press, 1956);

Jay Fellows, *Ruskin's Maze: Mastery and Madness in His Art* (Princeton: Princeton University Press, 1981);

Raymond E. Fitch, *The Poison Sky: Myth and Apocalypse in Ruskin* (Athens: Ohio University Press, 1982);

Kristine Ottesen Garrigan, *Ruskin on Architecture* (Madison: University of Wisconsin Press, 1973);

Katharine Gilbert, "Ruskin's Relation to Aristotle," *Philosophical Review*, 49 (1940): 52-62;

Sister Mary Dorothea Goetz, *A Study of Ruskin's Concept of the Imagination* (Washington, D.C.: Catholic University of America Press, 1947);

Frederic Harrison, *John Ruskin* (New York: Macmillan, 1902);

Elizabeth K. Helsinger, *Ruskin and the Art of the Beholder* (Cambridge, Mass.: Harvard University Press, 1982);

Robert Hewison, *John Ruskin: The Argument of the Eye* (Princeton: Princeton University Press, 1976);

Hewison, ed., *New Approaches to Ruskin: Thirteen Essays* (London: Routledge & Kegan Paul, 1981);

J. A. Hobson, *John Ruskin: Social Reformer* (Boston: Estes, 1898);

John Dixon Hunt and Faith Holland, eds., *The Ruskin Polygon: Essays on the Imagination of John Ruskin* (Manchester: Manchester University Press, 1982);

Sir William James, *John Ruskin and Effie Gray* (New York: Scribners, 1947);

Henry Ladd, *The Victorian Morality of Art* (New York: Long & Smith, 1932);

George P. Landow, *The Aesthetic and Critical Theories of John Ruskin* (Princeton: Princeton University Press, 1971);

Landow, "Ruskin's Refutation of False Opinions Held Concerning Beauty," *British Journal of Aesthetics*, 8 (1968): 60-72;

Landow, "Ruskin's Versions of 'Ut Pictura Poesis,'" *Journal of Aesthetics and Art Criticism*, 26 (1968): 521-528;

David Larg, *John Ruskin* (London: Davis, 1932);

Alice Meynell, *John Ruskin* (New York: Dodd, Mead, 1900);

Robert E. Rhodes and Del Ivan Janik, eds., *Studies in Ruskin* (Athens: Ohio University Press, 1982);

John D. Rosenberg, *The Darkening Glass* (New York: Columbia University Press, 1961);

Rosenberg, "Style and Sensibility in Ruskin's Prose," in *The Art of Victorian Prose*, edited by George Levine and William Madden (New York: Oxford University Press, 1968), pp. 177-200;

Paul L. Sawyer, *Ruskin's Poetic Argument: The Design of the Major Works* (Ithaca, N.Y.: Cornell University Press, 1985);

James Clark Sherburne, *John Ruskin, or the Ambiguities of Abundance* (Cambridge, Mass.: Harvard University Press, 1972);

William Smart, *A Disciple of Plato* (Glasgow: Wilson & McCormick, 1883);

Roger B. Stein, *John Ruskin and Aesthetic Thought in America, 1840-1900* (Cambridge, Mass.: Harvard University Press, 1967);

Francis G. Townsend, "John Ruskin," in *Victorian Prose: A Guide to Research*, edited by David J. DeLaura (New York: Modern Language Association, 1973);

Townsend, *Ruskin and the Landscape Feeling: A Critical Analysis of His Thought During the Crucial Years of His Life, 1843-1860* (Urbana: University of Illinois Press, 1951);

Helen Gill Viljoen, *Ruskin's Scottish Heritage* (Urbana: University of Illinois Press, 1956);

Donald Wesling, "Ruskin and the Adequacy of Landscape," *Texas Studies in Literature and Language*, 9 (1967): 253-272;

J. Howard Whitehouse, *Vindication of Ruskin* (London: Allen & Unwin, 1950);

Gary Wihl, *Ruskin and the Rhetoric of Infallibility*

(New Haven: Yale University Press, 1985);

R. H. Wilenski, *John Ruskin* (London: Faber & Faber, 1933).

Papers:

The Ruskin papers are scattered, but the major repositories are the Pierpont Morgan Library, New York; the Beinecke Rare Book and Manuscript Library, Yale University; the Ruskin Gallery at Bembridge School, Isle of Wight; and the John Rylands Library, Manchester.

Algernon Charles Swinburne
(5 April 1837 - 10 April 1909)

This entry was updated by David G. Riede (Ohio State University) from his entry in
DLB 35: Victorian Poets After 1850.

See also the Swinburne entry in DLB 57: Victorian Prose Writers After 1867.

SELECTED BOOKS: *The Queen-Mother. Rosamond. Two Plays* (London: Pickering, 1860; Boston: Ticknor & Fields, 1866);

Atalanta in Calydon (London: Moxon, 1865; Boston: Ticknor & Fields, 1866);

Chastelard (London: Moxon, 1865; New York: Hurd & Houghton / Boston: Dutton, 1866);

Poems and Ballads (London: Moxon, 1866); republished as *Laus Veneris, and Other Poems and Ballads* (New York: Carleton / London: Moxon, 1866);

A Song of Italy (London: Hotten, 1867; Boston: Ticknor & Fields, 1867);

William Blake: A Critical Essay (London: Hotten, 1868; New York: Dutton, 1906);

Notes on the Royal Academy Exhibition, 1868, by Swinburne and William Michael Rossetti (London: Hotten, 1868);

Songs before Sunrise (London: Ellis, 1871; Boston: Roberts Brothers, 1871);

Under the Microscope (London: White, 1872; Portland, Maine: Mosher, 1899);

Bothwell (London: Chatto & Windus, 1874);

George Chapman: A Critical Essay (London: Chatto & Windus, 1875);

Songs of Two Nations (London: Chatto & Windus, 1875);

Essays and Studies (London: Chatto & Windus, 1875);

Erechtheus: A Tragedy (London: Chatto & Windus, 1876);

Note of an English Republican on the Muscovite Crusade (London: Chatto & Windus, 1876);

A Note on Charlotte Brontë (London: Chatto & Windus, 1877);

Poems and Ballads, Second Series (London: Chatto & Windus, 1878; New York: Crowell, 1885?);

A Study of Shakespeare (London: Chatto & Windus, 1880; New York: Worthington, 1880);

Songs of the Springtides (London: Chatto & Windus, 1880; New York: Worthington, 1882?);

Studies in Song (London: Chatto & Windus, 1880; New York: Worthington, 1880);

Specimens of Modern Poets: The Heptalogia or The Seven Against Sense (London: Chatto & Windus, 1880);

Mary Stuart (London: Chatto & Windus, 1881; New York: Worthington, 1881);

Swinburne, portrait by G. F. Watts (National Portrait Gallery, London)

Tristram of Lyonesse and Other Poems (London: Chatto & Windus, 1882; Portland, Maine: Mosher, 1904);

A Century of Roundels (London: Chatto & Windus, 1883; New York: Worthington, 1883);

A Midsummer Holiday and Other Poems (London: Chatto & Windus, 1884);

Marino Faliero (London: Chatto & Windus, 1885);

Miscellanies (London: Chatto & Windus, 1886; New York: Worthington, 1886);

A Study of Victor Hugo (London: Chatto & Windus, 1886);

Locrine: A Tragedy (London: Chatto & Windus, 1887; New York: Alden, 1887);

A Study of Ben Jonson (London: Chatto & Windus, 1889; New York: Worthington, 1889);

Poems and Ballads, Third Series (London: Chatto & Windus, 1889);

The Sisters (London: Chatto & Windus, 1892; New York: United States Book Company, 1892);

Astrophel and Other Poems (London: Chatto & Windus, 1894; London: Chatto & Windus / New York: Scribners, 1894);

Studies in Prose and Poetry (London: Chatto & Windus, 1894; London: Chatto & Windus / New York: Scribners, 1894);

Robert Burns. A Poem (Edinburgh: Printed for the Members of the Burns Centenary Club, 1896);

The Tale of Balen (London: Chatto & Windus, 1896; New York: Scribners, 1896);

Rosamund, Queen of the Lombards: A Tragedy (London: Chatto & Windus, 1899; New York: Dodd, Mead, 1899);

Love's Cross-Currents: A Year's Letters (Portland, Maine: Mosher, 1901; London: Chatto & Windus, 1905);

Poems & Ballads, Second & Third Series (Portland, Maine: Mosher, 1902);

Percy Bysshe Shelley (Philadelphia: Lippincott, 1903);

A Channel Passage and Other Poems (London: Chatto & Windus, 1904);

The Poems of Algernon Charles Swinburne, 6 volumes (London: Chatto & Windus, 1904; New York & London: Harper, 1904);

The Tragedies of Algernon Charles Swinburne, 6 volumes (London: Chatto & Windus, 1905; New York: Harper, 1905);

The Duke of Gandia (London: Chatto & Windus, 1908; New York & London: Harper, 1908);

The Age of Shakespeare (New York & London: Harper, 1908; London: Chatto & Windus, 1908);

The Marriage of Monna Lisa (London: Privately printed, 1909);

In the Twilight (London: Privately printed, 1909);

The Portrait (London: Privately printed, 1909);

The Chronicle of Queen Fredegond (London: Privately printed, 1909);

Of Liberty and Loyalty (London: Privately printed, 1909);

Ode to Mazzini (London: Privately printed, 1909);

Shakespeare (London, New York, Toronto & Melbourne: Henry Frowde, 1909);

The Ballade of Truthful Charles and Other Poems (London: Privately printed, 1910);

A Criminal Case (London: Privately printed, 1910);

The Ballade of Villon and Fat Madge (London: Privately printed, 1910);

The Cannibal Catechism (London: Privately printed, 1913);

Les Fleurs du Mal and Other Studies (London: Privately printed, 1913);

Charles Dickens (London: Chatto & Windus, 1913);

A Study of Victor Hugo's "Les Misérables" (London: Privately printed, 1914);

Pericles and Other Studies (London: Privately printed, 1914);

Thomas Nabbes: A Critical Monograph (London: Privately printed, 1914);

Christopher Marlowe in relation to Greene, Peele and Lodge (London: Privately printed, 1914);

Lady Maisie's Bairn and Other Poems (London: Privately printed, 1915);

Félicien Cossu: A Burlesque (London: Privately printed, 1915);

Théophile (London: Privately printed, 1915);

Ernest Clouët (London: Privately printed, 1916);

A Vision of Bags (London: Privately printed, 1916);

The Death of Sir John Franklin (London: Privately printed, 1916);

Poems From "Villon" and Other Fragments (London: Privately printed, 1916);

Poetical Fragments (London: Privately printed, 1916);

Posthumous Poems, edited by Edmund Gosse and Thomas James Wise (London: Heinemann, 1917);

Rondeaux Parisiens (London: Privately printed, 1917);

The Italian Mother and Other Poems (London: Privately printed, 1918);

The Ride from Milan and Other Poems (London: Privately printed, 1918);

A Lay of Lilies and Other Poems (London: Privately printed, 1918);

Queen Yseult, A Poem in Six Cantos (London: Privately printed, 1918);

Lancelot, The Death of Rudel and Other Poems (London: Privately printed, 1918);

Undergraduate Sonnets (London: Privately printed, 1918);

The Character and Opinions of Dr. Johnson (London: Privately printed, 1918);

The Queen's Tragedy (London: Privately printed, 1919);

French Lyrics (London: Privately printed, 1919);

Contemporaries of Shakespeare (London: Heinemann, 1919);

Ballads of the English Border, edited by William A. MacInnes (London: Heinemann, 1925);

Lesbia Brandon, edited by Randolph Hughes (London: Falcon Press, 1952); republished in *The Novels of A. C. Swinburne* (New York: Farrar, Straus & Cudahy, 1962);

New Writings by Swinburne, edited by Cecil Y. Lang (Syracuse: Syracuse University Press, 1964).

Collection: *The Complete Works of Algernon Charles Swinburne,* 20 volumes, edited by Edmund Gosse and Thomas J. Wise (London: Heinemann / New York: Wells, 1925-1927).

Algernon Charles Swinburne is justly regarded as the major Victorian poet most profoundly at odds with his age and as one of the most daring, innovative, and brilliant lyricists to ever write in English. Less justly, his reputation still depends largely on the two early volumes, *Atalanta in Calydon* (1865) and *Poems and Ballads* (1866), with which he shocked and outraged Victorian sensibility, introducing into the pious, stolid age a world of fierce atheism, strange, powerful passions, fiery paganism, and a magnificent new lyrical voice the likes of which had never before been heard. But Swinburne must be remembered for other things as well. His radical republicanism, really a worship of the best instincts of man, pushed Victorian humanism well beyond the "respectable" limits of Matthew Arnold's writings, his critical writings on art and literature greatly influenced the aesthetic climate of his age, and his extraordinary imitative facility made him a brilliant, unrivaled parodist. Most important, the expression of his eroticism in many poems about nature, particularly about the sea, wind, and sun, makes him the Victorian period's greatest heir of the Romantic poets, and it is in Swinburne's nature poetry that the unbroken Romantic tradition running through the nineteenth century is most clearly seen.

Many of Swinburne's lifelong passions, and particularly his fierce love of sea, wind, and sun, were fostered during his early childhood at East Dene, Bonchurch, on the Isle of Wight. A descendant of two ancient, aristocratic, and highly inbred families, Swinburne was born into the highest English nobility. His mother, Lady Jane Hamilton Swinburne, was a daughter of the third Earl of Ashburnham; his father, Lady Jane's second cousin, was Admiral Charles Henry Swinburne, who could trace his ancestry back to a Swinburne peerage that had been, in his son's phrase, "dormant or forfeit since the thirteenth or fourteenth century." Swinburne's aristocratic background contributed in later life to a high-handed disdain of the lower classes, but it also contributed, paradoxically, to his rabid republicanism. He was much influenced by his colorful grandfa-

Caricature by Max Beerbohm: "Riverside Scene. Algernon Swinburne taking his great new friend [Edmund] Gosse to see Gabriel Rossetti" (© Eva Reichmann)

ther who, as the poet never tired of saying, "had enjoyed the personal friendship of Mirabeau and Wilkes." In addition, both the Ashburnhams and the Swinburnes had a long history of political rebellion, since, as Swinburne put it, his family "in every Catholic rebellion from the days of my own Queen Mary to those of Charles Edward had given their blood like water and their lands like dust for the Stuarts." Swinburne himself attributed his own rebellious streak to his family background, commenting in 1875 that "when this race chose at last to produce a poet, it would have been at least remarkable if he had been content to write nothing but hymns and idylls for clergymen and young ladies to read out in chapels and drawing-rooms." His family, at least as he romanticized it, had left him certain standards to live up to. A still more important legacy of Swinburne's early childhood, however, was his love of nature. Though he was born, by his own questionable account, "all but dead and certainly not expected to live an hour," he was a vigorous and reckless lover of the outdoors. At East Dene, and at the nearby family seats of the Swinburnes at Capheaton and of the Ashburnhams at Ashburnham Place, he rode horses with reckless abandon, reveling in the sensations of speed, wind, and sun. Most of all, he loved the sea. Later in life he accounted for the "endless passionate returns to the sea" in his poetry by recalling one of his earliest memories: "As for the sea, its

salt *must* have been in my blood before I was born. I can remember no earlier enjoyment than being held up naked in my father's arms and brandished between his hands then shot like a stone from a sling through the air, shouting and laughing with delight, head foremost into the coming wave." Swinburne's many later writings on the sea echo this childlike rapture of submission. In fact, the submission to great men that characterized his republicanism, the submission to primitive sensual passions and the masochism that characterize his erotic writings, and especially the submission to elemental forces of nature described throughout his poetry are all evoked in this illuminating comment. Indeed, the blend of masochism with incestuous love and strangely erotic descriptions of the pleasures of riding and sea-bathing in the quasi-autobiographical novels *Love's Cross-Currents* (1901) and *Lesbia Brandon* (1952) reveals the fusion of Swinburne's most intense passions. His hopeless love for his cousin Mary Gordon evidently owed much to her companionship and shared joy in the wild pleasures of nature.

Swinburne knew milder pleasures as well. His histrionic bent found an outlet in amateur theatricals with his sisters and cousin, and at an early age he was reveling in the more solitary pleasures of literature. He began to enjoy Shakespeare at the age of six and other Renaissance dramatists soon after. By the time he entered Eton in 1849, he was also a fervent admirer of Dickens, to whose works he remained devoted all his life, frequently, in fact, falling into the idiom of such comic characters as Sairey Gamp. By this time, too, his mother had taught him French and Italian, and he was soon fluent in both languages. To this early training he was ultimately to owe the distinction of being one of the most widely read men of his age in Continental literature.

Swinburne's four years at Eton seem to have had an inordinate importance for him. In his later years he would constantly begin conversations with the prologue "When I was a kid at Eton," and indeed it was at Eton that most of his lifelong interests took root. He now read not only Shakespeare but also the other Elizabethan and Jacobean dramatists with extraordinary enthusiasm and thoroughness, and he now first developed his undying hero-worship of Victor Hugo and Walter Savage Landor. It must have been at Eton also that he developed the flagellation mania that was to remain with him to a

Faustine, *oil painting by Maxwell Armfield in which Swinburne is depicted with a woman who represents his ideal of malevolent beauty (Musée d'Orsay, Galerie du Jeu de Paume, Paris). When Swinburne's poem "Faustine," about a sadistic Roman empress, was first published in the* Spectator *(31 May 1862), John Ruskin wrote, "It made me all hot, like pies with the devil's fingers in them. It's glorious!"*

greater or lesser degree for the rest of his life. He later wrote numerous letters recounting in gory detail the floggings that had left him bloody but unbowed. He no doubt was flogged, as was the custom, but his later accounts of a tutor preparing the flogging-room with "burnt scents" or choosing a "*sweet* place out of doors with smell of firwood" or allowing him to "saturate my face with eau-de-Cologne" before a beating have the ring of the fictional accounts of floggings that he enjoyed writing and reading.

Whatever Swinburne may have suffered at the hands of his tutors, he was at least, unlike Percy Bysshe Shelley, not bullied by his schoolfel-lows. Like Shelley, he had no interest in field sports and in other respects impressed his companions as rather exotic, but he did show considerable physical courage in riding, in swimming, and perhaps even in enduring the customary floggings. Swinburne was evidently left sufficiently alone to follow his own pursuits, among which one of his favorites, as his schoolmate and cousin Algernon Freeman-Mitford, Lord Redesdale, recalled, was reading: "I can see him now sitting perched up Turk-or-tailor wise in one of the windows looking out on the yard, with some huge old-world tome, almost as big as himself, upon his lap, the afternoon sun setting on fire the great mop of red hair. There it was that he emancipated himself, making acquaintance with Shakespeare (minus Bowdler), Marlowe, Spenser, Ben Jonson, Ford, Massinger, Beaumont and Fletcher, and other poets and playwrights of the sixteenth and seventeenth centuries. His tendency was great towards Drama, especially Tragic Drama. He had a great sense of humour in others. He would quote Dickens, especially Mrs. Gamp, unwearyingly; but his own genius leaned to tragedy." His genius leaned so heavily to tragedy that he wrote several Jacobeanlike tragedies before and during his stay at Eton. His juvenile tragedies were, of course, schoolboyish in many ways; Mary Gordon, later Mary Disney-Leith, recalled them as of a "bloodcurdling and highly tragic nature, in which a frequent stage direction—'stabs the king'—passed into a family joke." But one of these plays, *"The Unhappy Revenge,"* survives in manuscript to exhibit a precocious talent for imitative verse and a foretaste of Swinburne's later analysis of the coupling of pain with sensuality.

Possibly because he was becoming a disciplinary problem, Swinburne left Eton early, at the age of sixteen, to be privately tutored by the Reverend John Wilkinson at Cambo, Northumberland. He was evidently a difficult pupil, scanting his studies to ride on the moors and bathe in the sea. Wilkinson had trouble controlling him, but it was at this time that Swinburne met Lady Pauline Trevelyan, whom he came to regard as a second mother and who now and later had a calming influence on him. Nevertheless, Swinburne was not yet ready to settle down to a life of quiet study, for in 1854, motivated by the Balaklava charge in the Crimean War which, he said, "eclipsed all other visions," he declared his ambition to be a cavalry officer, a desire that his parents wisely thwarted. He would have made an unusual cavalry officer; in addition to his tiny physique, he was extremely excitable and given, from early childhood, to spastic twitching of his arms and hands. Also, though a courageous rider, he was reckless and frequently thrown. Throughout his life he was, like George Gordon, Lord Byron, defensive about his physical defects and eager to defend himself from what he called "bitterly contemptuous remarks about my physical debility and puny proportions." He often defended himself by referring to an exploit that occurred shortly after his request to join the cavalry. In the winter of 1854 he found a "chance of testing my nerve in the face of death" by scaling the reputedly inaccessible Culver Cliff on the Isle of Wight, which he did, at genuinely great peril. Swinburne's accounts of the exploit reveal what has often been called his virility complex, but they reveal also the love of primitive encounters with nature that informs much of his best verse.

In January 1856, after a final year of preparation with the Reverend Russell Woodford at Kempsford, Gloucestershire, Swinburne matriculated at Balliol College, Oxford. At Oxford the republican enthusiasm that he had more or less inherited from his grandfather became a passion. He was much influenced by a classmate, John Nichol. Nichol, the founder of the Old Mortality Society, a republican and freethinker, became a lifelong friend. Swinburne hung in his room a portrait of Felice Orsini, the would-be assassin of Napoleon III, and began to write verse in praise of regicide. Nichol also contributed to Swinburne's emerging atheism. Swinburne had been raised as a devout Anglo-Catholic and had kept his faith intact until he reached Oxford. His comments on a Catholic mass that he had seen during a visit to Cologne as recently as 1855 indicate how strong the will to worship had been in him: "I felt quite miserable, it was such a wretched feeling that while they all were praying, old men and tiny children kneeling together, I was not one of them, I was shut out as it were. I could have sat down and cried, I was so unhappy." This faith was soon shattered, but his need to worship remained: he became a worshiper of great republicans, great poets, and, interestingly, of "old men and tiny children." Throughout his later life, he never lost his devotion to the great old republican Giuseppe Mazzini, or the great old poets Landor and Hugo, or tiny children.

During the fall of 1857, when the Pre-Raphaelites and others were at Oxford on their "jovial campaign" to decorate the Oxford Union, Swinburne came under an influence even stronger than Nichol's. Delighted by the high spirits of the artistic temperament in its wildest form, he was quickly drawn into close and enduring friendships with Dante Gabriel Rossetti, William Morris, and Ned Jones (later Sir Edward Burne-Jones). The immediate attraction was mutual: on meeting Swinburne, Jones instantly remarked, "Now we are four and not *three*." Under their influence Swinburne soon began to write what might be called Pre-Raphaelite verse. Most notably, *Queen Yseult,* published in the Old Mortality Society's monthly journal, *Undergraduate Papers,* is a close imitation of William Morris's early work, both in matter and manner. Though he did not long continue to write Pre-Raphaelite pastiche, the abiding influence of Morris and Rossetti shows up in much of *Poems and Ballads*, particularly in such poems as "Laus Veneris" and "The Leper." More important, Swinburne developed a new aestheticism, which did not induce him to abandon his political poetry but did encourage him to write more for the sake of the beauty of verse itself.

After the departure of Rossetti, Jones, and Morris, Swinburne remained at Oxford, exhibiting rather more wild bohemian mannerisms but studying hard enough to earn some academic honors; riding hard enough to fall, splinter some teeth, and sprain his jaw; and writing poetry. The poetry reflected Swinburne's varied interests. "The Death of Sir John Franklin" (published in pamphlet form in 1916 and collected a year later in *Posthumous Poems),* written on a set topic for a poetry competition in 1860, effectively expresses his love for courageous exploits and for the sea. The unpublished "Laugh and Lie Down," a drama, as Swinburne later said, "after (a long way after) the late manner of Fletcher," reflects his love of the early dramatists and also, as Philip Henderson has said in *Swinburne: Portrait of a Poet* (1974), gives "full expression to the sexual ambiguity of his nature" by providing two young boys who also masquerade as girls, one of whom is whipped to death by a tyrannical woman. Swinburne also remained politically conscious. When, in 1858, he and his parents encountered Napoleon III in passing, the poet disdained to remove his hat because, as he later told Edmund Gosse "in an ecstasy of ironic emphasis," he did not wish "to be obliged to cut off my hand at the wrist the moment I returned to the hotel." A year previously, in "A Song in Time of Order," he had written of Napoleon III the rather enthusiastic lines "We shall see Buonaparte the Bastard / Kick heels with his throat in a rope."

Swinburne studied fairly hard in his last two years at Oxford, even going so far as to "break my teeth more or less for months" over the "dead constitutional records" of a work by Henry Hallam. But in the end he failed to take his examinations. Though he left Oxford without a degree through his own fault, he liked to compare himself with Shelley and observe that "Oxford has turned out poets in more senses than one."

Shortly after leaving Oxford, Swinburne published his first plays, with financial backing from his father. *The Queen-Mother* and *Rosamond*

Swinburne, Dante Gabriel Rossetti, Fanny Cornforth, and William Michael Rossetti at Tudor House, Cheyne Walk, Chelsea, circa 1863 (Collection of Mrs. Virginia Surtees)

(published together in 1860) are not entirely successful, but they anticipate the strengths and weaknesses of many of Swinburne's later plays. Certainly they were a great advance on his earlier efforts, though they remain too strongly reminiscent of the drama of an earlier age. The verse is often excellent, but like John Keats, Shelley, Robert Browning, and Alfred, Lord Tennyson, Swinburne remained enslaved to the nineteenth-century view of Elizabethan models: his emphasis was too much on long set speeches and characterization and too little on dramatic action, so the dramas, especially *The Queen-Mother,* move slowly, awkwardly, and sometimes too predictably. Both plays are concerned with the pleasures of sadistic violence, the overwhelming power of passionate love, and the terrible, destructive power of passionate women.

The Queen-Mother is set in the court of Charles IX, at the time of the murder of the Huguenots in 1572. As the title suggests, the queen mother is the power behind the throne in a court in which, Swinburne later wrote, "debauchery of all kinds, and murder in all forms, were the daily matter of excitement or of jest." The setting provided a perfect opportunity for Swinburne to revel in Grand Guignol, and he made the most of it. *Rosamond,* shorter and less gruesome, is somewhat more successful than *The Queen-Mother.* Through the characters of King Henry's mistress, Rosamond, and his wife, Queen Eleanor, Swinburne more subtly explores the theme of the fatal woman and the destructive power of love. The play is best remembered for one speech, in which Rosamond projects her female fatality into mythic proportion: "Yea, I am found the woman in all tales / The face caught always in the story's face. . . ."

The publication of the plays did not make much of a stir despite two brief but hostile reviews, but by this time Swinburne, newly settled in London with a four-hundred-pound annuity from his father, was already becoming known in artistic and literary circles. In 1860, after leaving Oxford, he had moved into rooms at 16 Grafton Street, Fitzroy Square, near Rossetti, Morris, and Burne-Jones. Through them he met several other artists and writers, including George Meredith, Ford Madox Brown, John Ruskin, Simeon Solomon, and eventually James McNeill Whistler. In addition, through Richard Monckton Milnes (later Lord Houghton), he met a rich mix of people, including Browning, Tennyson, and the adventurer Richard Burton. He was especially intimate at this time with Burne-Jones and his wife Georgie, and still more with Rossetti and his wife Elizabeth ("Lizzie") Siddal Rossetti. He enjoyed a close and boisterous friendship with Lizzie in particular, and had in fact dined with Lizzie and Rossetti at the Sablonière Hotel on 10 February 1862, the night on which Lizzie killed herself with an overdose of laudanum. After her death, Rossetti, Swinburne, and, on an occasional basis, George Meredith and Rossetti's brother William, took up communal living at Tudor House, Cheyne Walk, in Chelsea. Both Rossetti and Swinburne were creatures of flamboyant habits, so life at Tudor House was, to say the least, irregular. Swinburne contributed in no small degree. Even before reading Milnes's copy of the Marquis de Sade's *Justine* in 1862, he had declared his discipleship to the "divine" Marquis de Sade, and he delighted in shrilly declaiming the joys of Sadic eroticism. More seriously, he was beginning to drink excessively, perhaps through the influence of Richard Burton, who is credited with introducing him to brandy in 1862. By 1864 or 1865 Swinburne, in Edmund Gosse's words, was a drunkard. With increasing regularity, he was being deposited dead drunk on the doorstep of Tudor House. One incident of 1863 seems characteristic: at three in the morning, by Gosse's account, Rossetti was "wakened by a tremendous knocking, and on looking out of the window, he saw Algernon being held up in the arms of a policeman, with a whole bevy of gutter-boys accompanying; he had been out on a spree, and no one knew where. Rossetti went out and let him in, and had a fearful time with him, 'screaming and splashing about,'" before he got him to bed. Within the house his antics included sliding down bannisters and dashing naked around the house with Simeon Solomon. One less than sympathetic observer recalled that Swinburne was almost as strange when sober, since "his one idea of rational conversation was to dance and skip all over the room, reciting poetry at the top of his voice, and going on and on with it." Such a description is an exaggeration, of course, but he was extremely excitable, especially when reciting verse or talking politics. The impression that the "demoniac boy," as Ruskin called him, was making on literary London in the early 1860s can be seen in the impression he made on Henry Adams in 1862. Adams's famous description compares Swinburne to "a tropical bird, high-crested, long-beaked, quick-moving, with rapid utterances and screams of humor, quite unlike any English lark or nightingale. One could hardly call him a crimson macaw among owls, and yet no ordinary contrast availed." But this strange apparition, this exotic bird, Adams noted, was remarkably impressive in the prodigious range of his learning and memory, and was also "astonishingly gifted, and convulsingly droll."

Swinburne's convulsing drollery appears in several burlesques in French and English that were written in the early 1860s but not published until Cecil Y. Lang's *New Writings by Swinburne* appeared in 1964. In both the French tale *La Fille du Policeman* and the French play *La Soeur de la Reine,* Swinburne brilliantly parodied Victor Hugo's productions on English topics and brilliantly pilloried Queen Victoria. Swinburne's description, in a letter, of a now missing part of the play gives the flavor of both the play and the tale. He describes how the queen had been seduced by Wordsworth, "who had scandalously abused his privileged position as Laureate to se-

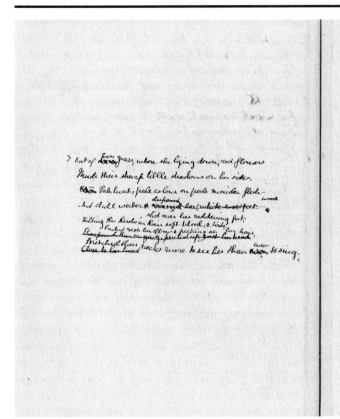

From the manuscript for Swinburne's "At Eleusis," written circa 1864 and collected in Poems and Ballads, 1866
(The Pierpont Morgan Library)

duce her by means of recitations 'de cette poésie fièvreuse et palpitante de sensualité—cette excursion' " and of "sa chanson érotique de Betty-Foy!" *La Fille du Policeman,* described by Meredith as "the funniest rampingest satire on French novelists dealing with English themes that you can imagine," depicts an attempt by Prince Albert, "le prince prolétaire," to supplant Victoria. Swinburne summed up the themes in a letter to William Bell Scott: "Rape, perjury, murder, opium, suicide, treason, Jesuitry, are the mildest ingredients." As the ingredients indicate, Swinburne's broad and bawdy humor in these immensely funny farces was not far dissociated from his more serious concerns, and it has occasionally been suggested that under cover of persiflage he was able to liberate his deepest feelings.

The impressive ability to mimic that made *La Fille du Policeman* and *La Soeur de la Reine* superb parodies of Hugo later surfaced in superb parodies of Tennyson, Browning, Rossetti, Swinburne himself, and others collected in *Specimens of Modern Poets: The Heptalogia or The Seven Against Sense* (1880), a volume that conclusively proves Swinburne, as Lang has said, "quite sim-

ply (to use his own kind of phrase), the greatest parodist who ever lived." In 1862 Swinburne's talent very nearly enabled him to perpetrate two brilliant hoaxes. In a series of critical articles on Hugo in the *Spectator* he planted references to two nonexistent French writers and then submitted critical essays on their recent works. The first of these, a review of *Les Amours Etiques* by Félicien Cossu, was actually set in type, but after receiving the second, on *Les Abîmes* by Ernest Clouët, the editor of the *Spectator,* perhaps suspecting a hoax or perhaps appalled by the obscene subject matter of Cossu and Clouët, declined to print either. And the subject matter assuredly was offensive, for Swinburne had used his unrivaled gift for parody to produce such remarkable "excerpts" from decadent French poetry as the appalling couplet in which Cossu admires his mistress's charms: "Sa crapule a l'odeur fraiche et chaste du lait; / Et son vomissement quelque chose qui plait." Swinburne's tone in describing such works as "Une Nuit de Sodome" and "Spasme d'Amour" is one of controlled outrage as he ironically undermines the strict Victorian ideas of propriety: "Accusations are often put forward, at home and abroad, against the restrictions imposed by a possibly exaggerated sense of decency on the English literature of the present day. We have seen what are the results of a wholly unfettered license; base effeminacy of feeling, sordid degradation of intellect, loathsome impurity of expression, in a word every kind of filth and foolery which a shameless prurience can beget on a morbid imagination." These were, of course, precisely the charges that would soon be aimed in earnest at Swinburne's own work.

A much more important prose work of 1862 is the satiric epistolary novel *A Year's Letters* (pseudonymously serialized in the *Tatler* in 1877 and published as *Love's Cross-Currents* in 1901 by Mosher of Portland, Maine). Both *A Year's Letters* and *Lesbia Brandon* (not published until Randolph Hughes's edition in 1952), begun soon after but never finished, are masterful quasi-autobiographical accounts of the aristocratic Victorian world that shaped Swinburne's character, "a world," wrote Edmund Wilson in *The Novels of A. C. Swinburne* (1962), "in which the eager enjoyment of a glorious out-of-door life of riding and swimming and boating is combined with adultery, incest, enthusiastic flagellation and quiet homosexuality." The subtle analysis of characters and relationships, the close portraits of an aristocratic way of life, the power of description, and the precise, beautifully cadenced prose of these works reveal Swinburne's genuine but often unrecognized talents as a novelist.

Swinburne was, of course, primarily a poet, and during the prolific years from 1860 to 1862 he was a very busy one. In addition to a large body of lyrics, many of which were to appear in *Poems and Ballads*, Swinburne completed at this time his tragedy *Chastelard* (not published until 1865), the first play in the eventually massive trilogy about Mary Queen of Scots that would include *Bothwell* (1874) and *Mary Stuart* (1881). Swinburne was drawn to the history of Mary Stuart both by his family's historic attachment to the Stuart cause and by his attraction to the character of Mary, whom he saw as a strong and fatal woman. Chastelard's bitter expression of his love for the queen pithily expresses Swinburne's main concern: "men must love you in life's spite; / For you will always kill them, man by man / Your lips will bite them dead; yea, though you would, / You shall not spare one; all will die of you." Though weakened, as were *The Queen-Mother* and *Rosamond*, by Swinburne's penchant for sacrificing dramatic movement to long, lyric speeches,

Chastelard is a considerable poetic achievement. Since Swinburne's deep emotional involvement with the theme of painful, fatal love infuses his verse with passionate lyricism, his faults as a dramatist are largely redeemed by his powers as a poet. *Bothwell* and *Mary Stuart* are far less successful. By the time they were written Swinburne had become immersed in historical scholarship aimed at vindicating the character of Mary Stuart by proving her "the most fearless, the most keen-sighted, the most ready-witted, the most high-gifted and high-spirited of women." Unfortunately, the plays became clotted with historic detail as Swinburne, in his own words, became "choked and stifled with the excessive wealth of splendid subjects." In his effort to include all significant events he lost much of the inspired lyricism of *Chastelard*. *Bothwell* in particular swelled to colossal proportions. Though the two later plays were well received on publication, they are rarely read today.

In the summer of 1863 Swinburne left London for East Dene to be present at the death of his favorite sister, Edith. While there he began writing *Atalanta in Calydon*, which he continued to work on during a subsequent long visit to neighboring Northcourt, the home of his cousin Mary Gordon. At Northcourt he was enraptured by Mary's piano performances of George Frideric Handel, which he said influenced the impassioned cadences of *Atalanta*, and still more enraptured with reckless gallops across the moors with Mary, during which he recited the magnificent first chorus of *Atalanta*, beginning "When the hounds of spring are on winter's traces." In the winter of 1864 he left Northcourt to visit Italy, where he saw the paintings that he described in his splendid essay "Notes on Designs of the Old Masters at Florence" (published in the *Fortnightly Review* in July 1868 and collected in *Essays and Studies*, 1875), an essay that significantly influenced British art criticism by helping to mold the critical style of Walter Pater. After this prolonged absence, Swinburne finally returned to London, where he once again saw much of Mary Gordon. Though he never told his love, by this time his childhood affection for her had evidently deepened into intense passion. Mary's failure to reciprocate in kind was the major tragedy of his life.

Late in 1864 Mary Gordon announced her impending marriage to Colonel R. W. Disney-Leith, sending Swinburne into bitter agonies of despair and long darkening his outlook on life. Apparently alluding to this experience years later,

Theodore Watts-Dunton and Swinburne in the garden of Watts-Dunton's home, the Pines

he remarked that it had left his "young manhood a 'barren stock.'" His desolation is movingly recorded in one of his greatest lyrics, "The Triumph of Time": "I have put my days and dreams out of mind, / Days that are over, dreams that are done." The same stoical note is sounded in the beautiful companion poems, "Les Noyades" and "A Leave-Taking," but what is perhaps most interesting in all of these poems is a startling transference of passion from the woman to the sea. These poems, like all of Swinburne's great nature poems, express a kind of oceanic eroticism in which the poet's passion and despair are fused in a longing to merge utterly with oblivious elemental nature: "I will go back to the great sweet mother, / Mother and lover of men, the sea. / I will go down to her, I and none other, / Close with her, kiss her and mix her with me."

He was, no doubt, stoical in his further relations with Mary Gordon, though he later described in "Notes on Poems and Reviews" another spiritual refuge for a man "foiled in love and weary of loving": "refuge in those 'violent delights' which have 'violent ends,' in fierce and frank sensualities which at least profess to be no more than they are." Swinburne resumed with a vengeance the dissolute London life he had previously led. He passed from heavy drinking to chronic alcoholism and became a more ardent and more serious devotee of flagellation and other "fierce and frank sensualities." The next fifteen years of Swinburne's life are full of incidents, some funny and all sad, in which he paid the price for debauchery. But in the first few years following 1864, before his alcoholism had physically debilitated him, Swinburne had more pleasure than pain from his antics. He became increasingly intimate with Richard Burton who, after long evenings of drinking, would carry him out, unconscious, under one arm, and send him home in a cab. Burton, like other intimates of this period, including Simeon Solomon, George Powell, Charles Augustus Howell, and Lord Houghton, shared and encouraged his mania for flagellation and other unorthodox sexual practices, though Swinburne's deviance remained confined to conversation, flagellation literature, and letters exchanging tales of whippings at Eton.

In 1865 and 1866 Swinburne became a literary lion and a literary scandal with the publication of *Atalanta in Calydon, Chastelard* and *Poems and Ballads. Atalanta in Calydon,* still justly regarded as one of Swinburne's supreme achievements, became a masterpiece partly because his choices of subject and form were perfectly adapted to his concerns and talents. The imitation of Aeschylean tragedy gave him an opportunity to exercise his superb lyrical gifts; the choice of the pagan Greek setting enabled him to express his virulent antitheism convincingly; and the Meleager myth provided a vehicle with which to express his obsession with the fatal power of passion and of women. The play centers on the conflict between Meleager and his mother, Althaea, over his passionate love for the chaste huntress Atalanta. During the hunt for the wild boar that is ravaging Calydon, Meleager kills both of Althaea's brothers, who had abused Atalanta. At Meleager's birth, the Fates had prophesied that he would die when the brand then burning the fire was fully burnt; Althaea, who had extinguished and saved it, burns it after the death of her brothers, slaying her own son in compliance with the ancient code of retribution for blood spilled.

Meleager's love for Atalanta, who has taken a vow of virginity and upholds the ideal of chastity, constitutes a denial of natural cycles of generation, of the fertility associated throughout the play with Althaea. His love, which forsakes, in effect, the natural and inevitable for the ideal and unattainable, epitomizes the bleakly pessimistic dictum of the gods that "Joy is not, but love of joy shall be." Perhaps the clearest expression of the play's nihilistic theme comes from Althaea:

> The gods have wrought life, and desire of life,
> Heart's love and heart's division; but for all
> There shines one sun and one wind blows till
>   night.
> And when night comes the wind sinks and the
>   sun,
> And there is no light after, and no storm,
> But sleep and much forgetfulness of things.

Man should recognize and accept the only certainties: elemental nature and death. Swinburne's play is clearly to be understood not merely as a refutation of the Greek gods and ideals but also as a refutation of any idealism or religion that endorsed chastity, a Blakean code word for moral repression. Theism, as Swinburne saw it, represses man's primitive, pagan impulses, denies man's role in nature, and so the play couples erotic love with the poet's equally erotic, in a larger sense, love of elemental nature. Consequently *Atalanta in Calydon* is a forceful attack on traditional Christianity, which Swinburne, like Blake, saw as an instrument of moral repression that sets the ideals of the soul in conflict with the needs of the body. The message is summed up in the famous antitheistic chorus that denounces "The supreme evil, God," who "shapes the soul, and makes her a barren wife / To the earthly body and grievous growth of clay."

Atalanta in Calydon, however, is not merely a play with a message; it also represents a masterful rebirth of the powerful lyricism of Greek tragedy. Rejecting all belief in a beneficent scheme of things and even in the possibility of joy, it is Swinburne's most pessimistic major work, yet in its surging rhythms, in its fusion of the imagery of natural cycles, it achieves the intensity that Keats saw as the essential quality of tragic art, the intensity that is "capable of making all disagreeables evaporate, from their being in close relationship with Beauty & Truth."

Before the publication of *Atalanta in Calydon* in March 1865, Swinburne had been known only among the artistic circles of Rossetti and Lord Houghton. His critical articles in the *Spectator* had been published anonymously, and *The Queen-Mother* and *Rosamond* had been virtually unnoticed. But the reviews of *Atalanta* saluted him as a major new poet, raising him instantly near to the status of Tennyson and Browning. The critics caviled about the extent to which the tragedy was truly Greek and about the lushness of imagery and obscurity of diction, but they recognized Swinburne's great lyrical power and mastery of language. Somewhat surprisingly, the moral tone, the savage antitheism, of the play went almost unnoticed. Swinburne's position as a ranking poet was further consolidated the following autumn with the publication of *Chastelard*, which was considered by some reviewers superior to *Atalanta*. On the whole, however, the notices of *Chastelard* were somewhat less complimentary than those of *Atalanta*. Critics were disposed to admire the poetry but objected to what they saw as an ungenerous treatment of Mary Stuart. Worse, troubled by its sensuality and irreverence, the reviewers were becoming uneasy about Swinburne's moral tone. The *Spectator*, for example, complained that a "want of moral and intellectual relief for the coarseness of passion, and for the deep physical instincts of tenderness or cruelty on which he delights to employ his rich imagination, strikes us as a radical deformity of his poetry."

The stage, clearly, was being set for the outraged reception of *Poems and Ballads*, which Swinburne was then preparing for publication. Such friends as Rossetti, Ruskin (through Swinburne's "good angel," Hannah More Macaulay, Lady Trevelyan), and Meredith, hearing " 'low mutterings' from the lion of British prudery," as Meredith put it, urged him to cut some of the more offensive verses for the sake of his reputation, but in vain. Contending that he had "written nothing to be ashamed of" (though he had himself described "Dolores" as "boiling and gushing infamy"), Swinburne determined to face the teeth of the British lion as the volume was published in

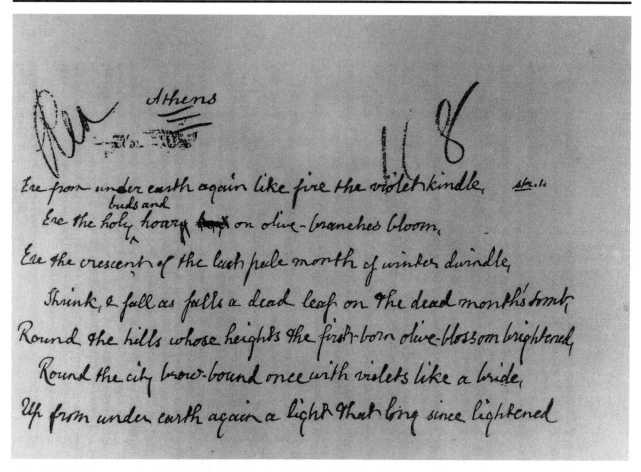

First lines of the manuscript for Swinburne's "Athens: An Ode," collected in Tristram of Lyonesse and Other Poems, *1882 (Anderson Galleries auction catalogue, sale number 1820, 17-20 March 1924)*

August 1866. The result was one of the most savage critical barrages in literary history. Critics called the author of "Anactoria" and "Dolores" the "libidinous laureate of a pack of satyrs" and compared him to "Gito, seated in the tub of Diogenes, conscious of the filth and whining at the stars." His poems are "prurient trash," the product of "the spurious passion of a putrescent imagination." So great was the outrage that the publisher, Moxon, withdrew the book from circulation, and Swinburne was able to have it republished only through the disreputable firm of J. C. Hotten, the publisher of a line of sordid flagellation literature.

Unfortunately, the howls of outraged Victorian propriety have too often distracted readers from the real merits of *Poems and Ballads*. For example, "Dolores," the most blatantly shocking of the poems, has received a disproportionate share of attention ever since the mid-Victorian students at Oxford used to walk arm in arm across the lawns, chanting its blasphemous litany to the sadis-

tic antivirgin, "Our Lady of Pain." Yet even "Dolores" has a serious point, for Swinburne is singing the nihilistic theme of *Atalanta in Calydon* in a different key: "For the crown of our life as it closes / Is darkness, the fruit thereof dust / No thorns go as deep as a rose's, / And love is more cruel than lust." "Dolores" describes the phase that Swinburne himself evidently passed through, when a man "foiled in love and weary of loving" takes refuge in "fierce and frank sensualities which at least profess to be no more than they are."

In fact, none of the poems, written in the early and mid 1860s, were designed merely to shock. Even the perverse eroticism of "Dolores" and "Faustine," the necrophilia of "The Leper," and the sadistic lesbianism of the masterful "Anactoria" analyze and pay tribute to a part of human nature that may not be genteel but is at least genuine. The volume links frank and fierce eroticism, moreover, with Swinburne's violent but philosophically acute antitheism, for the pleasures of the flesh are consistently viewed as a response to the moral repression of Christianity, which chastens the flesh and denies the pleasures of mortal life for the hope of a dubious immortal reward and so enforces the maxim that "Joy is not, but love of joy shall be." Christianity, for Swinburne as for William Blake and Friedrich Wilhelm Nietzsche, had robbed modern life of its passionate energies, and so he attacked it in the famous couplet of "The Hymn to Proserpine" in *Poems and Ballads*: "Thou hast conquered, O Pale Galilean; the world has grown grey from thy breath; / We have drunken of things Lethean, and fed on the fullness of death." For Swinburne, the one solace for the wretched human condition is that it ends, and so, as he beautifully expresses it in "The Garden of Proserpine":

> From too much love of living,
> 　　From hope and fear set free,
> We thank with brief thanksgiving
> 　　Whatever gods may be
> That no life lives for ever;
> That dead men rise up never,
> That even the weariest river
> 　　Winds somewhere safe to sea.

In a few poems, most notably "Hesperia" and "Sapphics," Swinburne's pessimism is lightened as he begins to form the new faith that was to sustain him for the rest of his life. Annihilation of the old faiths, of the accepted verities, brought for Swinburne, as for Nietzsche, a belief in renewed scope for creation. After the fierce passions had been spent, they could be transmuted into compassion for the human condition and eternally memorialized in song. The savage lust of Sappho celebrated in "Anactoria," for example, could be preserved in her song, passed on down through the ages to Swinburne and transformed into the gentler compassion of his "Sapphics." Man could attain a measure of immortality by linking his consciousness in a communion of song with past and future generations; Swinburne could share the consciousness of Sappho, as future generations of poets could share the consciousness of Swinburne and of all who had contributed to the human spirit.

Not surprisingly, most of Swinburne's finest poetry after *Poems and Ballads* is elegiac, and also not surprisingly, his first full expression of his new faith was to come in his elegy for Charles-Pierre Baudelaire, the magnificent "Ave atque Vale," written in July 1867 after Swinburne had heard premature rumors of his French con-

A. C. Swinburne, 1895 (photograph by Elliott & Fry, Bassano & Vandyck Studios, London)

temporary's death and published in the *Fortnightly Review* in January 1868 after Baudelaire obligingly died on 31 August 1867. The greatest consolation for Baudelaire was that the life of passion and pain, "Fierce loves, and lovely leaf-buds poisonous" in Swinburne's phrase, was over, that he had found the peace of oblivion, but the greatest consolation for Swinburne is that because the poet lived life intensely, he passed on works that reproduced the sound of his "sad soul." Clasping a book by Baudelaire (*Les Fleurs du Mal*, although the title is not mentioned), Swinburne is in communion with his spirit, "As though a hand were in my hand to hold." Baudelaire is able to reach out from oblivion to comfort the mourner: death is defeated not by the ascetic repression of the body by the soul but by energetic life and creation. The void left by Christianity is filled with a religion of art, and human life is given significance. As the metaphorical clasping of hands implies, the lonely isolation of the individual is overcome by communion in art.

Swinburne's life during these years reflects both the wildness of his erotic writings and the more chastened mood of his elegiac poems. His life in London was occasionally interrupted by visits to the Continent and to the sea, but when in the city he continued to drink, now so heavily that he was falling into a pattern of chronic illness. From the mid 1860s until 1879 his life fell into a depressing routine of alcoholic dissolution in London, collapse, rescue by his parents, and drying-out periods at his family's new home in Holmwood. The wildest anecdotes about Swinburne—those by which he is most often judged— all date from this period. In addition to the drinking, he was doing his best to live a sexually dissolute life. Late in 1867, Rossetti and others, thinking it a shame that Swinburne should write so well of love and have so little experience of it, contrived to set him up with an American circus performer, Adah Menken. Menken did her best and inspired some genuine affection in Swinburne, who referred to her as his mistress, but she had no chance of real success, for as she remarked to Rossetti, "I can't make him understand that biting's no use!" According to Edmund Gosse the affair only lasted about six weeks. It was also in the late 1860s that Swinburne actually put his flagellation mania into practice with frequent visits to Verbena Lodge, a specialized brothel where, as Gosse put it, "two golden-haired and rouge-cheeked ladies received, in luxuriously furnished rooms, gentlemen whom they consented to chastise for large sums." The sums charged were evidently too large, for Swinburne quarreled over the money in 1869 and never returned. His obsession with flagellation, though certainly reflecting an important part of his psychic life, was mostly a lark for him and never brought him any real grief. His alcoholism was a different matter and was becoming an inconvenience in more ways than one. Though he vigorously denied it, his many illnesses during these years were almost certainly caused by the undermining of his constitution by alcohol. He preferred to blame his sickness on the flu, or indigestion, or even, as he put it in a letter, the "perfume of Indian lilies in a close bedroom." He was also becoming a public scandal, as the famous incident of his ejection from the Arts club, cited by Gosse, illustrates. In the spring of 1870, extremely drunk after dinner at the club, Swinburne had trouble finding his hat, "which, on account of the great size of his head, was of excessive capacity. He tried one hat after another, and as each pinched his brows he

flung it to the floor; finally in a towering and ungovernable rage, he danced and stamped upon the hats." When sober, Swinburne was every inch a gentleman, forgot what he had done when drunk, and vehemently denied that he might ever have done anything unworthy of a gentleman. Swinburne's most bizarre tastes were vicariously indulged, but because he spoke of them indiscreetly he developed an international reputation for profligacy of all kinds. In response to the uproar over his immorality in *Poems and Ballads* and to continuing journalistic abuse of his writings and his character, Swinburne declared that he had an image to live up to, and he seems, like Baudelaire, to have encouraged rumors about his own vice. The strangest rumors had him engaging in pederasty and bestiality with a monkey, which he is said to have eaten later. But as Oscar Wilde said, Swinburne was "a braggart in matters of vice, who had done everything he could to convince his fellow citizens of his homosexuality and bestiality, without being in the slightest degree a homosexual or a bestializer." Even Swinburne's physical appearance and innocent mannerisms told against him. His diminutive size and an apparently innate tendency to tremble violently when excited looked like the result of debilitating alcoholism, and his voluble enthusiasm gave the impression that he was raving insanely. But despite all of his wildness, Swinburne's friends during this period remembered quieter moments, when his innate generosity of spirit and deeply affectionate nature more than made up for his flamboyance. In fact, the libidinous satyr of the press was actually something of a lost innocent: his friends seem to have particularly loved him for his childlike incapacity to cope with the world.

Even before the publication of *Poems and Ballads,* much of Swinburne's poetry was beginning to take a new direction. His aesthetic dogma in the early 1860s, best expressed in the critical masterpiece *William Blake* (begun in 1863 and published in 1868), had been an unqualified expression of art for art's sake, but he had never abandoned his ardent republicanism, and in 1866 he began to write rather shrill political lyrics. He repudiated his earlier aesthetic doctrines in a letter to William Michael Rossetti—"It was only Gabriel and his followers in art (l'art pour l'art) who for a time frightened me from speaking out"—and dedicated himself passionately to the cause of European republicanism. In this mood he wrote *A Song of Italy* (published in pamphlet form in 1867) and his "Ode on the Insurrection in Candia," which inspired the republican leader Mazzini's exhortation to Swinburne to abandon "songs of egotistical love" and write "a series of Lyrics for the Crusade." Swinburne's meeting with Mazzini, one of the major events in his life, was apparently brought about by his old master at Oxford, Benjamin Jowett, and other friends in an effort to bring his life under some control. On meeting Mazzini he dropped to his knees to kiss his hero's hands and felt that he would willingly die for him, and for the cause—but he did not reform.

He did, however, proudly write the series of "Lyrics for the Crusade," eventually publishing two volumes of republican lyrics, *Songs before Sunrise* (1871) and *Songs of Two Nations* (1875). Of all his works, Swinburne had the highest regard for *Songs before Sunrise,* the volume he most wanted to be remembered for, but with few exceptions the republican poems are too verbose, too dogmatic, too mechanically allegorized, and too shrill for most readers. Swinburne was a master of invective, but calling the church a putrescent, leprous, "haggard harlot" and the Trinity a "triple-headed hound of hell" and instructing a dead king to "Go down to hell" does not make great lyric poetry. *Songs of Two Nations* has no saving moments, but *Songs before Sunrise* is partially redeemed by several fine lyrics in which the verse is more controlled and in which Swinburne is inspired by more than spleen or a vague adoration of an allegorical goddess of liberty. The occasional flashes of power and beauty most often result from Swinburne's central doctrine—a doctrine central also to *Atalanta in Calydon* and most of all to his best late poetry—that the eternal spirit of nature and the eternal spirit of humanity are one. Liberty is associated with the free forces of elemental nature, to which the human spirit must submit itself, rejecting the shackles of all inhibiting creeds. Significantly, however, the submission to elemental forces reflects the same psychic need as in the erotic poetry, a longing for merger with an identity greater than the poet's own. Even Swinburne's abstract abasement before the "Spirit of Man" and actual abasement before such heroes as Mazzini, Landor, and Hugo reflect a deep need to submit his identity to some greater force.

Songs before Sunrise received a very mixed reception when first published. Not surprisingly the reviewers who had been shocked by the blasphemy in Swinburne's earlier volumes were shocked once again. Delight in "the reddest of

Swinburne in 1900, by R. P. Staples (National Portrait Gallery, London)

Red Republicanism" was now added to the list of Swinburne's other sins: blasphemy, atheism, sensualism, and vacuousness bordering on insanity. Further, the criticisms that were to be aimed at much of Swinburne's later work now began to be clearly heard: his mastery of verse disguised a paucity of thought in the endless, sonorously alliterated cadences, his verse was monotonous, and he did not know when to stop. *Songs before Sunrise* eventually found, and continues to find, enthusiastic admirers, and even when first published it found defenders. The liberal and radical journals praised Swinburne for submitting his lyrical genius to a higher cause than love and lust, and even many of the hostile reviewers conceded his poetic powers. All in all, the critical climate in the 1870s became far more congenial to Swinburne than it had been in the previous decade. *Bothwell*, which Swinburne had labored on for many years and had published in 1874, finally convinced his contemporaries that he had reformed and left them free at last to praise his art without disparaging his character. A new respect for Swinburne's intelligence and learning was also emerging, perhaps partly because he was beginning to be recognized as an important critic by the mid 1870s; both his fine book on George Chapman and his splendid *Essays and Studies* appeared in 1875. Swinburne's literary criticism, like his art criticism, is too much neglected in our time, so it is perhaps worth noting that his studies of Elizabethan and Jacobean dramatists, groundbreaking in their own time, retain their usefulness and importance in ours, and that his estimates of the early dramatists and of his French and English contemporaries have stood the test of time better than, say, those of Matthew Arnold. Swinburne's fellow critics recognized the merit of his studies, but they also recognized the faults: a tendency to praise too extravagantly what he liked, to attack too vituperatively anyone who disagreed with him, and to overload his long and sometimes clogged and convoluted sentences with alliteration. Swinburne's vituperation is often amusing, and his extravagant praise shows a real generosity of spirit, but his overloaded prose, still usually beautiful and effective in the 1870s, eventually became so marred by meretricious mannerisms as to become almost unreadable. Nevertheless, his studies of Blake, Chapman, John Ford, Shakespeare, Byron, Keats, Rossetti, and Arnold remain not only readable, but also essential to serious students of those authors.

Swinburne's career was generally on the rise in the 1870s for several reasons, but it was the publication of *Erechtheus* in 1876 that brought him all but universal praise and established him firmly and unquestionably, in the eyes of his contemporaries, as a great living poet. The praise of *Erechtheus* was well merited, for Swinburne was at the height of his lyrical powers. It would be easy to neglect the play's depth of thought or its intensely focused construction but difficult in the extreme to deny the sonorous and majestic lyricism exemplified in the second chorus:

Out of the north wind grief came forth,
    And the shining of the sword out of the sea.
Yea, of old, the first-blown blast blew the prelude of
    this last,
The blast of his trumpet upon Rhodope.

Reverting to the Aeschylean model that he exploited so brilliantly in *Atalanta in Calydon*, Swinburne chose as his subject the legend of the saving of Athens, the first republic, the seat of Greek culture, the perfect type of the eternal City of Man. The legend was perfectly designed to express both the noblest ideals of his republicanism and his faith in the holiness of undying art, the truest expression of the spirit of man. The central event, the sacrifice of the maiden Chthonia for the salvation of Athens, epitomizes Swinburne's newfound faith that the nobility of submission to a larger cause, the nobility of dying for freedom, enables mankind to overcome the tyranny of death, for Chthonia "dead, shalt live / Till Athens live not." And Athens, Swinburne knew, would live as long as the race of man in the hearts of all great republicans and all great poets.

As with *Atalanta in Calydon,* the triumph of *Erechtheus* is in its perfect fusion of form and content. The thematic concerns are not baldly stated, as they too often are in the dogmatism and facile allegories of the republican lyrics, but are implicit in the dramatic conflict and subtly drawn out by the deft synthesis of imagery. The images associated with Chthonia, for example, link her death with sexual consummation, birth, and, in general, acceptance of cyclical change and individual mortality. The complex of imagery associating Chthonia and Athens with suffering, wisdom, song, and the indomitable spirit of man, moreover, points to Swinburne's antitheistic belief that accepting the finality of individual mortality liberates the creative energies that enable Athens and all great civilizations to triumph over time and the annihilation of oblivion. The nihilism of *Atalanta in Calydon* is gone, as though Atalanta had surrendered her maidenhead to Meleager, accepting with Althaea the place of the individual in nature's cycles.

Erechtheus, published a turbulent decade after *Atalanta,* is a more mature and, in its more serene power, arguably a greater achievement, yet something is missing. The tone of clamorous insistence of the demoniac boy of 1866 has vanished. The positive outlook of Swinburne's republican and aesthetic faith is partly responsible, no doubt, but so too are the depressant qualities of aging and of alcohol. After repeated cycles of alcoholism and collapse, Swinburne was in fact aging rapidly, declining into serious ill health, melancholy, and loneliness. At times the demoniac boy continued to emerge in the old exuberant blasphemy and obscenity, and more important in declamations of poetry and of republican indignation, but fits of deep depression were becoming more and more common. Even with the praise of *Erechtheus* fresh in his ears, Swinburne was lamenting the "rather dull monotonous puppet-show of my life, which often strikes me as too barren of ac-

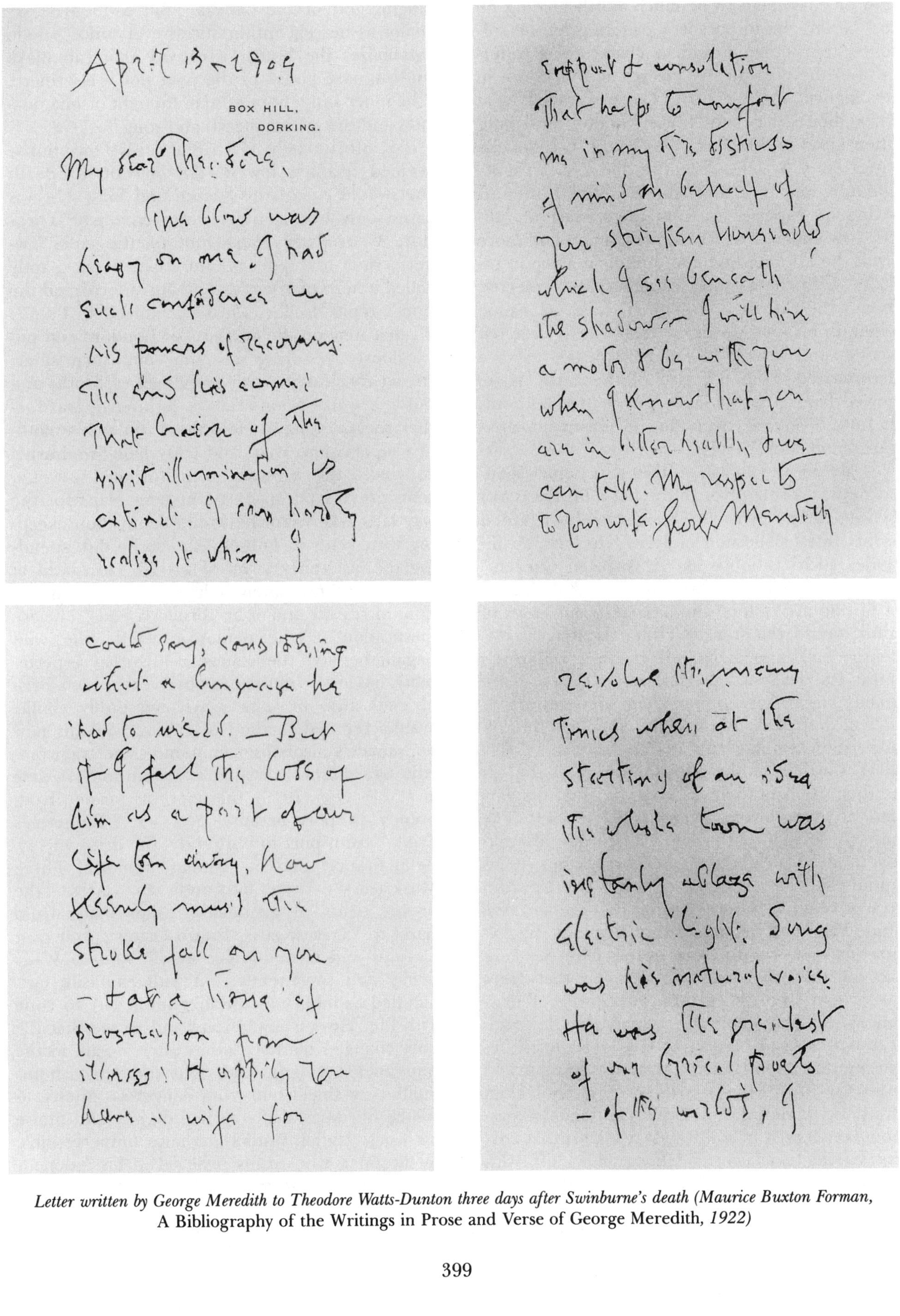

April 13 ~ 1909

BOX HILL,
DORKING.

My dear Theodore,

The blow was
heavy on me. I had
such confidence in
his powers of recovery.
The end has come!
That beacon of the
vivid illumination is
extinct. I can hardly
realize it when I

support & consolation
that helps to comfort
me in my sick sickness
of mind on behalf of
your stricken household
which I see beneath
the shadow. I will hire
a motor & be with you
when I know that you
are in better health, & we
can talk. My respects
to your wife. George Meredith

could say, considering
what a language he
had to wield. — But
if I feel the loss of
him as a part of our
life torn away, how
keenly must the
stroke fall on you
— at a time of
prostration from
illness. Happily you
have a wife for

resolve this many
times when at the
starting of an idea
the whole town was
instantly ablaze with
electric light. Song
was his natural voice.
He was the greatest
of our lyrical poets
— of the world, I

Letter written by George Meredith to Theodore Watts-Dunton three days after Swinburne's death (Maurice Buxton Forman,
A Bibliography of the Writings in Prose and Verse of George Meredith, *1922)*

tion or enjoyment to be much worth holding on to." Never one to parade a private grief, he softened the comment with a characteristic reference to the pleasures of the sea and of "verse in its higher moods," but Gosse recalled that throughout the late 1870s Swinburne would often lapse into melancholy silences, occasionally interrupted by tales "plaintive and rather vague, about his loneliness, the sadness of his life, the suffering he experiences from the slander of others." Swinburne was withdrawing more and more from the London high life, huddling alone in his rooms with the alcoholic dysentery he preferred to call the flu. At one point in 1878, at a time when, in his own words, he had "hardly ever felt wearier and weaker," Swinburne seemed to have disappeared from the face of the earth as he moved from 3 Great James Street to new rooms in Russell Square, neglecting to inform his anxious family and friends.

Yet in the midst of this depression Swinburne was seeing through the press his *Poems and Ballads, Second Series* (1878). Generally regarded as his finest collection of lyrics, the volume includes such triumphs as "A Forsaken Garden," "At a Month's End," "Ave atque Vale," "A Vision of Spring in Winter," and a magnificent series of translations from François Villon. Alcohol had evidently had a sedative effect on Swinburne's muse, for the lyrics, magnificent as they are, are quieter, more serene than their predecessors. A note of despair does, assuredly, creep into the volume, most emphatically in the famous "A Forsaken Garden," which uses the image of the sea eroding the land to describe the death of the garden, of young lovers, and even of love itself. The only consolation is that once all earthly life and love is dead, death, with no more victims, turns upon itself: "As a god self-slain on his own strange altar, / Death lies dead." Yet as "Ave atque Vale" and the many other elegies in the volume express, comfort can be taken in the very fact of the inevitability of oblivion that frees every man from the painful vicissitudes of existence. Also throughout the volume the other comfort expressed in "Ave atque Vale" is set forth, revealing the theme that was to be Swinburne's most fruitful for the next thirty years: individual death is, thankfully, inevitable, but human passions, redeemed in song, endure: "Dust that covers / Long dead lovers / Song blows off with breath that brightens." As "The Last Oracle" makes clear, the faith in song is a genuine religion, a worship of Apollo, the "sun-god and the singing-god of the Greeks." But Swinburne remains as fiercely antitheistic as ever, since Apollo symbolizes the human creativity that can make and unmake gods—as the poet put it elsewhere, "the inner sunlight of human thought or imagination and the gift of speech and song."

Unfortunately, in 1878 and 1879 Swinburne seemed heading toward the oblivion of death that would cut off his speech and song. He was saved only by the timely intervention of Theodore Watts (later Watts-Dunton), the stolid lawyer, critic, and poet whom Rossetti once aptly called a hero of friendship. Watts interrupted the poet's rapid decline, whisking him off to Putney (at that time on the outskirts of London) and miraculously restoring his tiny but surprisingly strong constitution with a regimen of broths and outdoor walks. Soon after, as Swinburne was further recuperating at Holmwood under his mother's supervision, Watts and Lady Jane Swinburne, convinced that a return to his former life would soon prove fatal, made permanent plans for the wayward Dionysian: he would set up housekeeping with Watts in Putney. And so he did, spending the last thirty years of his life ensconced at No. 2, the Pines, safely isolated from the temptations of city life and of his former friends. The domestication of the demoniac youth, the wild pagan, the satyr, the scourge of Victorian respectability, has always impressed observers as both terribly sad and, in some ways, irresistibly comic. Watts's reputed method of coping with his new housemate's alcoholism epitomizes the tragicomedy. By Coulson Kernahan's account in *Swinburne as I Knew Him* (1919), the poet was weaned from brandy to port because port was "Tennyson's drink," from port to burgundy, the drink of "La Belle France" and of "Dumas' immortal Three Musketeers," from burgundy to claret, "the proper drink of gentlemen," and finally from claret to "Shakespeare's brown October, our own glorious and incomparable beer!" And so Watts firmly and consistently, but with exquisite tact, handled Swinburne's childlike incapacity to cope with life. He was always on hand to see that the poet changed his wet clothes after a walk in the rain, to get him on the right train to visit his mother, to shield him from dangerous guests, to soothe his occasionally ruffled dignity and praise his work. Under Watts's guidance (imperceptible to the poet, who firmly believed in his independence), Swinburne gradually fell into a monotonous but pleasant routine. Because Watts said it would be unbecoming, Swinburne had promised never to go into any of the pubs "in the village," but every morning at precisely eleven o'clock he would leave the Pines, walk briskly across Putney Heath to the neighboring village of Wimbledon, and drop into the Rose and Crown tavern. With the same regularity he would return for lunch and his ration of one glass of beer, ascend to his room for a nap, return at 6:30 to read aloud from Dickens and eat dinner, and at 10:00 retire to his books and work late into the night. At first the routine was broken by visits from old friends, but these gradually grew less frequent as Swinburne's advancing deafness made conversation more difficult and as his old friends began to die off. He did not usually like to meet new people, but as the years passed literary pilgrims occasionally were brought to lunch at the Pines, and some of them, most notably Max Beerbohm, have left bemused accounts of the comfortable domesticity of Watts fussing over Swinburne like a protective maiden aunt.

The routine sounds stultifying, but Swinburne was genuinely happy. His health was excellent, he had a deep affection for Watts, he immensely enjoyed his evening readings of Dickens, and he loved the neighboring heath which, with its glorious hawthorn, seemed to him an unrivaled landscape. The routine was broken by annual excursions with Watts to the sea, by visits to his mother and sisters, and by occasional visits to Jowett at Oxford. The most notable break in the routine occurred in 1882, when Watts and Swinburne went by invitation to a celebration in honor of Victor Hugo in Paris. Swinburne's first meeting with his idol should have been a great occasion, but both poets were by now so deaf that they could not quite understand one another. The visit was something of a fiasco, but Swinburne remembered it fondly.

Yet another alleviation came in the form of young Bertie Mason, Watts's nephew who had come with his parents to live at the Pines. Swinburne had always loved children, but at the Pines his love grew to a passion. He loved all babies, frequently peering into their prams as he passed them on his morning walks, but Bertie was special to Swinburne, who described him as "the sweetest thing going at any price." So great was Swinburne's devotion that Bertie's parents may have become a little unsettled about it, and perhaps in an attempt to curb it, they sent the child away on an extended holiday. Absence only made the heart grow fonder, and Swinburne wrote *A Dark Month,* a series of intolerably mawk-ish poems commemorating each day of loneliness.

A Dark Month (incongruously bound with *Tristram of Lyonesse,* 1882) and multitudes of other "baby poems" account in part for the widespread belief that though Watts saved Swinburne's life, he helped to kill his inspiration. There were other signs of Swinburne's artistic decline. His republicanism was gradually turning to jingoistic imperialism. Poems such as "The Commonweal," "The Armada," and "England: An Ode" make it all too clear that Mazzini's poet, the poet of regicide, had become Victoria's poet. Seemingly "born and baptized into the church of rebels," as he said Blake was, Swinburne was now the rankest of apostates. There is a certain consistency in his views, since a strain of intolerance and of cultural monism had always run through his republicanism. In 1886 he condemned the "anarchists and intriguers whose policy is to break up the state" with the observation that "the first principle of a Republican is and must be Unity." He consistently flattered himself with the strange observation that Mazzini would have agreed with him. He unabashedly supported the British effort in the Boer War, and he was among the most fervent celebrants of Victoria's jubilee. Part of his turnabout was probably due to sheer ignorance, since in his isolation at the Pines his only informants were the newspapers and the conversation of the patriotic Watts. He evidently believed that the British were the most benevolent of despots, and it is worth remembering that earlier, upon hearing of the savagely brutal, sadistic despotism of Governor Edward Eyre in Jamaica, he had allied himself against such defenders of Eyre as Carlyle, Ruskin, Dickens, Charles Kingsley, and Tennyson.

The baby poems, the imperialism, and a steady stream of clumsily vituperative prose naturally enough disillusioned the admirers of the magnificent pagan of earlier days and led to a general disparagement of Swinburne's late work. The monotony of his life, it is said, is reflected in the tediousness of his verse; the diminished sphere of activity is apparent in a diminished range of thought and feeling in the poetry. To a great extent the charges are accurate. Much of the late poetry is uninspired, a haze of words, and Swinburne was becoming quite unnecessarily prolix: as his mother complained, he never knew when to stop. In addition, his late plays, *Mary Stuart* (1881), *Marino Faliero* (1885), *Locrine* (1887), *Rosamund, Queen of the Lombards* (1899), and *The*

Duke of Gandia (1908), did not significantly add to his stature as a dramatist, since, despite frequent fine passages of verse, they retained the structural weakness and artificiality of his earlier plays in the Elizabethan manner. Only the strange autobiographical play, *The Sisters* (1892), broke new ground by bringing verse drama into a modern setting, but the dialogue is awkwardly artificial, and the melodramatic plot is only intriguing because it closely reflects what must have been a recurring fantasy for the aging poet. Young Reginald Clavering has become the cavalry officer that young Algernon Swinburne had dreamed of being, has been wounded at Waterloo, and has been too modest to declare his love to the beautiful cousin with whom, as a boy, he had enjoyed wild gallops. But in the fantasy world of the play, the cousin, a surrogate Mary Gordon, declares her love for him, and after a short period of ecstatic bliss, the two are accidentally murdered and die with a kiss. The play, significantly dedicated to Mrs. Disney-Leith, is oddly touching in its transparent revelations of the poet's unfulfilled wish for happiness.

The Sisters is not a successful work, but in many ways it suggests that Swinburne was not, as is often said, cut off from his old sources of inspiration. The celebration of passionate love and the desire for death with the beloved recall the themes of "Anactoria," "The Leper," "The Triumph of Time," "Les Noyades," and many other early poems; the oceanic eroticism suggested in Reginald Clavering's splendid description of the sea is reminiscent of countless passages in earlier poems, letters, and especially in the novels. Even the conviction that the great literature of the past impinges constantly on the present is suggested by the inclusion of a Jacobean interlude that mirrors the main plot.

All of these sources of inspiration, so strangely expressed in *The Sisters,* are brilliantly fused in many great lyrical achievements written during the thirty years at the Pines, for the many volumes of poetry produced in this period contain, mixed in with the baby-worship and the imperialism, many more important poems than has generally been thought. Only a sampling of these poems can be mentioned, but they include "Thalassius" and "On the Cliffs" from *Songs of the Springtides* (1880); "Off Shore," "Evening on the Broads," and "By the North Sea" from *Studies in Song* (1880); the masterful title poem of *Tristram of Lyonesse and Other Poems* (1882); many of the lyrics in *A Century of Roundels* (1883); "A Bal-

lad of Sark" and the title poem of *A Midsummer Holiday and Other Poems* (1884); "To a Seamew" and "Neap-Tide" from *Poems and Ballads, Third Series* (1889); "A Nympholept" and "Loch Torridon" from *Astrophel and Other Poems* (1894); the fine Arthurian narrative, *The Tale of Balen* (1896); and "The Lake of Gaube," "The Promise of the Hawthorn," "Hawthorn Tide," and "The Passing of the Hawthorn" from *A Channel Passage and Other Poems* (1904). These noteworthy poems, written over twenty-five years, form a unit because they all express, with consummate artistry, variations on themes from Swinburne's most enduring sources of inspiration—the sea, the wind, human passions, and the great poetic tradition from Sappho and Aeschylus to Shakespeare and Shelley. Swinburne had certainly never been inspired by London—he is the least urban of poets—so his rescue by Watts could not, and did not, remove him from his sources of inspiration. The years at Putney may not have been tragic after all.

One of Swinburne's finest poems, "On the Cliffs," was written at Holmwood in 1879, shortly after Watts had rescued Swinburne from his rooms on Guildford Street. It is a sort of spiritual autobiography which expresses the themes of *Poems and Ballads, Second Series* in the most richly complex and precise syntax that Swinburne ever achieved. The setting, as in "A Forsaken Garden" and later "By the North Sea," is a crumbling cliff that is being slowly eaten away by the sea—Swinburne's favorite image for his belief that all earthly life, even the earth itself, is destined for oblivion. But looking over the desolate scene, the poet recalls certain words of Sappho and in doing so realizes that she has not died wholly, that her words and therefore her very passions are alive as they influence his own perception of nature. Further, nature can no longer be viewed as indifferent or hostile, for in the unchanging sea, the sea that inspired Sappho, the heart of Sappho is preserved. Nature and the divinity in man, incarnate in the word—not Christ but the song of Sappho—are brought into harmony, and human existence is given meaning. Swinburne came to see a divinity in nature that could bring all things into harmonious unison, but he was no pantheist, for as he puts it in "On the Cliffs," the divinity Apollo was simply "man's live breath," the "ruling song" "wherein all earth and heaven and sea / Were molten in one music." Though he was embarking on the quiet, secluded life of the Pines, Swinburne's faith in the redemptive powers of song interestingly included a belief in the necessity of the hot passions of love expressed in his demoniac youth, for he insisted that redeeming song must be "kindled," as he said in "Thalassius," by the "love / That life and death are fashioned of."

His fierce antitheism had survived as virulently as ever. In "By the North Sea" he is more quietly and also more thoughtfully and thoroughly blasphemous than he had been in "Dolores." In "By the North Sea" the sea devours a church in which man, ironically, "Hailed a God more merciful than Time" and graves where the dead futilely "awaited / Long the archangel's re-creating word." He had not lost the desire to shock his prim contemporaries either, for as he worked on the erotic scenes of *Tristram of Lyonesse* he gleefully anticipated their likely effect on British matrons. Far from being designed merely to shock, however, *Tristram* expresses Swinburne's deepest artistic impulses and shows plainly how his early eroticism merged with his late love of nature. The poem perfectly exemplifies what John D. Rosenberg, in the 1968 Modern Library edition of Swinburne's *Selected Poetry and Prose*, calls the "erotic interpenetration of nature and man," a fusion of human love and song in "multitudinous unison" with nature. In a description that recalls the erotic death-wish of "Les Noyades" and the settings of "A Forsaken Garden," "On the Cliffs," and "By the North Sea," in *Tristram* Tristram and Iseult do not merely die but are fused together as "their four lips become one silent mouth," and, buried on a crumbling sea-cliff, they are ultimately made one in the peace and "The light and sound and darkness of the sea." The eroticism, the longing for oblivion, the love of nature are present, and so, too, is the faith in redemptive song: "And one deep chord throbs all the music through, / The chord of change unchanging." Like many of the late poems, *Tristram of Lyonesse* deepens Swinburne's affirmation of passionate life, his unblinking acceptance of death, his love for elemental nature, and his faith that the imaginative power of poetry can fuse nature and man in beauty in the undying song of man.

Unlike most of his contemporaries, Swinburne never lost the Romantic faith in the redemptive power of imagination; he never forsook the bardic role of the poet. It is true that he remained remarkably consistent in his chief sources of inspiration. Yet despite persistent criticisms that his art was consistent because stagnant—that his art ceased to develop—his ideas did deepen and mature, and at least occasionally he rose, in

his later years, to heights of unsurpassed lyrical virtuosity. The first stanza of the very late "The Lake of Gaube" reveals his undiminished lyrical skill and verbal precision, as well as his vision of the "erotic interpenetration" of man and nature:

> The sun is lord and god, sublime, serene,
>   And sovereign on the mountains: earth and air
> Lie prone in passion, blind with bliss unseen
>   By force of sight and might of rapture, fair
>   As dreams that die and know not what they
>   were.
> The lawns, the gorges, and the peaks are one
> Glad glory, thrilled with sense of unison
> In strong compulsive silence of the sun.

Though his major achievements over the last thirty years of his life went largely unrecognized, though his most perceptive critics were offended by his often fatuous effusions, and though the sales of his works declined, Swinburne was generally recognized toward the end of his life as England's greatest living poet. His jingoism had atoned for his earlier "Red Republicanism," and his baby poems had reconciled him to the British matron. In fact, after the death of Tennyson in 1892, Queen Victoria, considering the empty post of poet laureate, is reputed to have been told that Swinburne was the greatest poet in her realm. Perhaps in view of Swinburne's earlier regicidal principles, the honor went instead to Alfred Austin. Swinburne would have scorned it, as he scorned an honorary degree from Oxford in 1908 and as he was prepared to scorn a Nobel Prize that was falsely reported to be coming his way in the same year. Nevertheless, the consensus was clear that he was unsurpassed, and that opinion was not surprising, since his rebelliousness and consummate artistry had contributed mightily to forming the cultural climate of the late Victorian age. He had, after all, greatly influenced the style and thought of Pater, Wilde, and a host of other writers of the yellow 1890s, and his work was greatly admired by such very different writers as W. B. Yeats, Thomas Hardy, and the young Ezra Pound.

Swinburne's death in 1909 was the result of the reckless childishness that Watts had tried to protect him from for thirty years. With the ever vigilant Watts seriously ill in bed and for once not at his post, Swinburne sallied out for his morning walk on a particularly cold and rainy day and caught a cold that quickly turned into double pneumonia. After a period of delirious declamations in Greek—probably recitations from his beloved Aeschylus—he died on the morning of 10 April shortly after his seventy-second birthday. "Up to his last moment," according to Watts-Dunton, "he cherished the deepest animosity against the Creed," and according to his wish, the Burial Service was not read over his grave. As he was quietly interred in the churchyard on his native Isle of Wight, the rector of Bonchurch, in the interests of decorum, did let drop a few Christian sentiments, but his last words were more apt and more truly decorous, as he bade farewell to "a creative art-genius of the first order, one of the most lovable great men of the later Victorian age, and one of the sweetest and most musical English poets who ever lived."

Swinburne's death brought the eulogies generally attendant on the death of a great poet, but posterity has not been kind to his reputation. The reasons are not difficult to understand. In the first place, his very great influence on the late nineteenth and early twentieth centuries has not always been appreciated. He had many imitators, but no good ones, for his virtuosity was inimitable. Yet his bittersweet paganism had significantly altered the flavor of his age, and the sensibilities of authors as diverse as Hardy, D. H. Lawrence, Yeats, Eugene O'Neill, and Pound were saturated by Swinburne. In addition, he was among the last of the great Victorians, and in the reaction against Victorianism his early rebelliousness could not atone for his late conformity and political apostasy. But most serious, his verse, despite its undeniable virtuosity, impressed readers as diffuse and devoid of intellectual content. Swinburne was aware of such charges in his own lifetime and brilliantly parodied his own supposedly vacuous virtuosity in "Poeta Loquitur" (written in 1889 and published posthumously in *The Italian Mother and Other Poems*, 1918):

My philosophy, politics, free-thought!
  Are worth not three skips of a flea,
And the emptiest of thoughts that can be thought
  Are mine on the sea.

Thanks to his sense of irony and his gift of mimicry, Swinburne could make fun of himself with greater skill than any of his critics could show, but he always wanted to be remembered not only as a great poet, but as a great poetic thinker as well. He would be gratified that the most recent critical assessments of his poetry are beginning to recognize that in his best work a vigorous and courageous intellect shines through the complex imagery and majestic music of his song. He would also have been gratified by T. S. Eliot's recognition that at his best Swinburne's music and intellect cohere in a perfect aesthetic fusion of form and content, that even his diffuseness, as Eliot says, "requires what there is no reason to call anything but genius.... What he gives is not images and ideas and music, it is one thing with a curious mixture of suggestion of all three." Eventually, perhaps, Swinburne's profundity of thought will gain full recognition, but in the meantime his stature as a major poet rests securely on his daring and skillful metrical innovations, his astonishing versatility in the use of lyric forms, and his frank and fierce paganism. Though it is sometimes taken as disparagement, Tennyson's famous remark that his contemporary was "a reed through which all things blow into music" expresses the enduring quality of Swinburne's achievement. The winds of primitive, savage, and joyous passions from love, from the elemental forces of nature, the sea and sky, and from the "ruling song" of man blew through Swinburne's remarkably open, responsive sensibility, and came forth in sophisticated yet joyous and primitive song. Tennyson's comment not only does justice to Swinburne's indubitable talent for lyrical beauty, but also, perhaps accidentally, to his less-recognized gift for translating the immediacy of experience into verse.

Letters:

The Swinburne Letters, 6 volumes, edited by Cecil Y. Lang (New Haven: Yale University Press, 1959-1962).

Bibliographies:

Thomas James Wise, *A Bibliography of the Writings of Swinburne,* 2 volumes (London: Privately printed, 1919, 1920); revised as *A Bibliography of the Writings in Prose and Verse of Algernon Charles Swinburne,* volume 20 of *The Complete Works of Algernon Charles Swinburne* (London: Heinemann / New York: Wells, 1927);

William E. Fredeman, "Algernon Charles Swinburne," in his *Pre-Raphaelitism: A Bibliocritical Study* (Cambridge, Mass.: Harvard University Press, 1965), pp. 216-220;

Clyde K. Hyder, "Algernon Charles Swinburne," in *The Victorian Poets: A Review of Research,* revised edition, edited by F. E. Faverty (Cambridge, Mass.: Harvard University Press, 1968), pp. 227-250;

Kirk H. Beetz, *Algernon Charles Swinburne: A Bibliography of Secondary Works, 1861-1980* (Metuchen, N.J. & London: Scarecrow Press, 1982).

Biographies:

Edmund Gosse, *The Life of Algernon Charles Swinburne* (New York: Macmillan, 1917);

Coulson Kernahan, *Swinburne as I Knew Him* (London: Lane, 1919);

Clara Watts-Dunton, *The Home Life of Swinburne* (London: Philpot, 1922);

Georges Lafourcade, *La Jeunesse de Swinburne, 1837-1867,* 2 volumes (London: Oxford University Press, 1928);

Lafourcade, *Swinburne: A Literary Biography* (London: Bell, 1932);

Mollie Panter-Downes, *At the Pines* (London: Hamilton, 1971);

Ian Fletcher, *Swinburne* (Harlow: Longman, 1973);

Philip Henderson, *Swinburne: Portrait of a Poet* (New York: Macmillan, 1974);

Donald Thomas, *Swinburne: The Poet in His World* (New York: Oxford University Press, 1979).

References:

Julian Baird, "Swinburne, Sade, and Blake: The Pleasure-Pain Paradox," *Victorian Poetry,* 9 (Spring-Summer 1971): 49-75;

Max Beerbohm, "No. 2, The Pines: Reminiscences of Swinburne," in his *And Even Now* (New York: Dutton, 1921), pp. 55-88;

C. M. Bowra, "*Atalanta in Calydon,*" in his *The Romantic Imagination* (Cambridge, Mass.: Harvard University Press, 1949), pp. 221-244;

Leslie Brisman, "Of Lips Divine and Calm: Swinburne and the Language of Shelleyan Love," in *Romanticism and Language,* edited by Arden Reed (Ithaca, N.Y.: Cornell University Press, 1984), pp. 247-262;

Brisman, "Swinburne's Semiotics," *Georgia Review,* 31 (Fall 1977): 578-597;

E. K. Brown, "Swinburne: A Centenary Estimate," *University of Toronto Quarterly,* 6 (January 1937): 215-235;

Samuel C. Chew, *Swinburne* (Boston: Little, Brown, 1929);

T. E. Connolly, *Swinburne's Theory of Poetry* (Albany: State University of New York Press, 1964);

David A. Cook, "The Content and Meaning of Swinburne's 'Anactoria,'" *Victorian Poetry,* 9 (Spring-Summer 1971): 77-93;

T. S. Eliot, "Swinburne as Critic" and "Swinburne as Poet," in his *The Sacred Wood* (London: Methuen, 1920), pp. 17-24, 144-150;

Leonard M. Findlay, "Swinburne and Tennyson," *Victorian Poetry,* 9 (Spring-Summer 1971): 217-236;

Robert A. Greenberg, "Swinburne and the Redefinition of Classical Myth," *Victorian Poetry,* 14 (Autumn 1976): 175-195;

H. J. C. Grierson, *Swinburne* (London: Longmans, 1953);

Anthony H. Harrison, "The Aesthetics of Androgyny in Swinburne's Early Poetry," *Tennessee Studies in Literature,* 23 (1978): 87-99;

Harrison, *Swinburne's Medievalism: A Study in Victorian Love Poetry* (Baton Rouge: Louisiana State University Press, 1988);

Lafcadio Hearn, "Studies in Swinburne," in his *Pre-Raphaelite and Other Poets* (New York: Dodd, Mead, 1922), pp. 122-179;

Clyde K. Hyder, *Swinburne's Literary Career and Fame* (Durham, N.C.: Duke University Press, 1933);

Hyder, ed., *Swinburne: The Critical Heritage* (London: Routledge, Kegan Paul, 1970);

John O. Jordan, "Swinburne on Culver Cliff: The Origin of a Poetic Myth," *Biography: An Interdisciplinary Quarterly,* 5 (Spring 1982): 143-160;

Cecil Y. Lang, "Swinburne's Lost Love," *PMLA,* 74 (March 1959): 123-130;

Margot K. Louis, *Swinburne and His Gods: The Roots and Growth of an Agnostic Poetry* (Montreal & Kingston: McGill-Queen's University Press, 1990);

F. L. Lucas, "Swinburne," in his *Ten Victorian Poets* (Cambridge: Cambridge University Press, 1948);

Richard Mathews, "Heart's Love and Heart's Division: The Quest for Unity in *Atalanta in Calydon,*" *Victorian Poetry,* 9 (Spring-Summer 1971): 35-48;

Jerome J. McGann, *Swinburne: An Experiment in Criticism* (Chicago: University of Chicago Press, 1971);

Richard D. McGhee, " 'Thalassius': Swinburne's Poetic Myth," *Victorian Poetry,* 5 (Summer 1967): 127-136;

Kerry McSweeney, "Swinburne's *Poems and Ballads* (1866)," *Studies in English Literature,* 11 (Autumn 1971): 671-685;

McSweeney, *Tennyson and Swinburne as Romantic Naturalists* (Toronto: University of Toronto Press, 1980);

Thais E. Morgan, "Swinburne's Dramatic Monologues: Sex and Ideology," *Victorian Poetry*, 22 (Summer 1984): 175-195;

Ross C. Murfin, "Athens Unbound: A Study of Swinburne's *Erechtheus*," *Victorian Poetry*, 12 (Autumn 1974): 205-217;

Murfin, *Swinburne, Hardy, Lawrence and the Burden of Belief* (Chicago: University of Chicago Press, 1978);

Harold Nicolson, *Swinburne* (London: Macmillan, 1926);

Morse Peckham, *Victorian Revolutionaries: Speculations on Some Heroes of a Cultural Crisis* (New York: Braziller, 1970), pp. 250-305;

Robert L. Peters, *The Crowns of Apollo: Swinburne's Principles of Literature and Art* (Detroit: Wayne State University Press, 1965);

Ezra Pound, "Swinburne versus Biographers," *Poetry*, 11 (March 1918): 322-329;

Mario Praz, *The Romantic Agony*, translated by Angus Davidson (London: Oxford University Press, 1933), pp. 413-433;

Meredith B. Raymond, *Swinburne's Poetics: Theory and Practice* (The Hague: Mouton, 1971);

John R. Reed, "Swinburne's *Tristram of Lyonesse*: The Poet-Lover's Song of Love," *Victorian Poetry*, 4 (Spring 1966): 99-120;

Paul de Reul, *L'Oeuvre de Swinburne* (London: Oxford University Press, 1922);

George M. Ridenour, "Swinburne on 'The Problem to Solve in Expression,'" *Victorian Poetry*, 9 (Spring-Summer 1971): 129-144;

Ridenour, "Time and Eternity in Swinburne: Minute Particulars in Five Poems," *English Literary History*, 45 (Spring 1978): 107-130;

David G. Riede, *Swinburne: A Study of Romantic Mythmaking* (Charlottesville: University Press of Virginia, 1978);

Rikky Rooksby, "Swinburne without Tears: A Guide to the Later Poetry," *Victorian Poetry*, 26 (Winter 1988): 413-430;

John D. Rosenberg, "Swinburne," *Victorian Studies*, 11 (December 1967): 131-152;

William R. Rutland, *Swinburne: A Nineteenth-Century Hellene* (Oxford: Blackwell, 1931);

George Saintsbury, "Mr. Swinburne," in his *Corrected Impressions* (New York: Dodd, Mead, 1895), pp. 60-78;

Richard Sieburth, "Poetry and Obscenity: Baudelaire and Swinburne," *Comparative Literature*, 36 (Fall 1984): 343-353;

Mark Siegchrist, "Artemis's Revenge: A Reading of Swinburne's *Atalanta in Calydon*," *Studies in English Literature*, 20 (Autumn 1980): 895-912;

Arthur Symons, "Swinburne," in his *Studies in Strange Souls* (London: Sawyer, 1929), pp. 50-83;

Geoffrey Tillotson, "Swinburne," in his *Mid-Victorian Studies* (London: Athlone Press, 1965), pp. 209-215;

T. Earle Welby, *A Study of Swinburne* (New York: Doran, 1926);

Welby, *The Victorian Romantics: 1850-1870* (London: Howe, 1929);

William Wilson, "Algernon Agonistes: 'Thalassius,' Visionary Strength, and Swinburne's Critique of Arnold's 'Sweetness and Light,'" *Victorian Poetry*, 19 (Winter 1981): 381-395;

Wilson, "Behind the Veil, Forbidden: Truth, Beauty, and Swinburne's Aesthetic Strain," *Victorian Poetry*, 22 (Winter 1984): 427-437;

Thomas L. Wymer, "Swinburne's Tragic Vision in *Atalanta in Calydon*," *Victorian Poetry*, 9 (Spring-Summer 1971): 1-16;

Melissa Zeiger, "'A Muse Funereal': The Critique of Elegy in Swinburne's 'Ave atque Vale,'" *Victorian Poetry*, 24 (Summer 1986): 173-188.

Papers:

The largest single collection of manuscripts and letters is at the British Library. Large collections of letters are at the Beinecke Rare Book and Manuscript Library, Yale University; Rutgers University Library; the National Library of Wales; and the Brotherton Library, Leeds University. Extensive collections of manuscripts are at the Harry Ransom Humanities Research Center, University of Texas, Austin; the New York Public Library; the Mayfield Library, Syracuse University; the Brotherton Library, Leeds University; the Huntington Library, San Marino, California; the Public Library of New South Wales; the Pierpont Morgan Library; the Free Library of Philadelphia; Trinity College, Cambridge University; the Library of Congress; and the libraries of Rutgers, Harvard, Yale, and Princeton universities, and the University of Michigan.

Alfred, Lord Tennyson

(6 August 1809 - 6 October 1892)

This entry first appeared in DLB 32: Victorian Poets Before 1850.

BOOKS: *Poems by Two Brothers,* anonymous, by Tennyson and Frederick and Charles Tennyson (London: Simpkin & Marshall / Louth, U.K.: Jackson, 1827);

Timbuctoo: A Poem (in Blank Verse) Which Obtained the Chancellor's Gold Medal at the Cambridge Commencement (Cambridge: Smith, 1829);

Poems, Chiefly Lyrical (London: Effingham Wilson, 1830);

Poems (London: Moxon, 1832);

Poems, 2 volumes (London: Moxon, 1842; Boston: Ticknor, 1842);

The Princess: A Medley (London: Moxon, 1847; Boston: Ticknor, 1848);

In Memoriam, anonymous (London: Moxon, 1850; Boston: Ticknor, Reed & Fields, 1850);

Ode on the Death of the Duke of Wellington (London: Moxon, 1852);

Maud, and Other Poems (London: Moxon, 1855; Boston: Ticknor & Fields, 1855);

Idylls of the King (London: Moxon, 1859; Boston: Ticknor & Fields, 1859);

Enoch Arden, etc. (London: Moxon, 1864; Boston: Ticknor & Fields, 1865);

The Holy Grail and Other Poems (London: Moxon, 1869; Boston: Fields, Osgood, 1870);

Gareth and Lynette Etc. (London: Strahan, 1872; Boston: Osgood, 1872);

Queen Mary: A Drama (London: King, 1875; Boston: Osgood, 1875);

Harold: A Drama (London: King, 1876; Boston: Osgood, 1877);

Ballads and Other Poems (London: Kegan Paul, 1880; Boston: Osgood, 1880);

Becket (London: Macmillan, 1884; New York: Dodd, Mead, 1894);

The Cup and The Falcon (London: Macmillan, 1884; New York: Macmillan, 1884);

Tiresias and Other Poems (London: Macmillan, 1885);

Locksley Hall Sixty Years After, Etc. (London & New York: Macmillan, 1886);

Demeter and Other Poems (London & New York: Macmillan, 1889);

Alfred Tennyson (Tennyson Research Centre)

The Foresters, Robin Hood and Maid Marian (New York & London: Macmillan, 1892);

The Death of Oenone, Akbar's Dream, and Other Poems (London: Macmillan, 1892; New York: Macmillan, 1892);

The Poems of Tennyson, edited by Christopher Ricks (London: Longmans, Green, 1969).

More than any other Victorian writer, Alfred, Lord Tennyson has seemed the embodiment of his age, both to his contemporaries and to modern readers. In his own day he was said to be—with Queen Victoria and Prime Minister William Gladstone—one of the three most famous living persons, a reputation no other poet writing in English has ever had. As official poetic spokesman for the reign of Victoria, he felt called upon to celebrate a quickly changing industrial and mer-

Tennyson's parents, the Reverend George Clayton Tennyson and Elizabeth Fytche Tennyson (Tennyson Research Centre)

cantile world with which he felt little in common, for his deepest sympathies were called forth by an unaltered rural England; the conflict between what he thought of as his duty to society and his allegiance to the eternal beauty of nature seems peculiarly Victorian. Even his most severe critics have always recognized his lyric gift for sound and cadence, a gift probably unequaled in the history of English poetry, but one so absolute that it has sometimes been mistaken for mere facility.

The lurid history of Tennyson's family is interesting in itself, but some knowledge of it is also essential for understanding the recurrence in his poetry of themes of madness, murder, avarice, miserliness, social climbing, marriages arranged for profit instead of love, and estrangements between families and friends.

Alfred Tennyson was born in the depths of Lincolnshire, the fourth son of the twelve children of the rector of Somersby, George Clayton Tennyson, a cultivated but embittered clergyman who took out his disappointment on his wife Elizabeth and his brood of children—on at least one occasion threatening to kill Alfred's elder brother Frederick. The rector had been pushed into the church by his own father, also named George, a rich and ambitious country solicitor intent on founding a great family dynasty that

would rise above their modest origins into a place among the English aristocracy. Old Mr. Tennyson, aware that his eldest son, the rector, was unpromising material for the family struggle upward, made his second son, his favorite child, his chief heir. Alfred's father, who had a strong streak of mental instability, reacted to his virtual disinheritance by taking to drink and drugs, making the home atmosphere so sour that the family spoke of the "black blood" of the Tennysons.

Part of the family heritage was a strain of epilepsy, a disease then thought to be brought on by sexual excess and therefore shameful. One of Tennyson's brothers was confined to an insane asylum most of his life, another had recurrent bouts of addiction to drugs, a third had to be put into a mental home because of his alcoholism, another was intermittently confined and died relatively young. Of the rest of the eleven children who reached maturity, all had at least one severe mental breakdown. During the first half of his life Alfred thought that he had inherited epilepsy from his father and that it was responsible for the trances into which he occasionally fell until he was well past forty years old.

It was in part to escape from the unhappy environment of Somersby rectory that Alfred began writing poetry long before he was sent to school,

Somersby rectory, home of the Tennysons (Tennyson Research Centre)

as did most of his talented brothers and sisters. All his life he used writing as a way of taking his mind from his troubles. One peculiar aspect of his method of composition was set, too, while he was still a boy: he would make up phrases or discrete lines as he walked, and store them in his memory until he had a proper setting for them. As this practice suggests, his primary consideration was more often rhythm and language than discursive meaning.

When he was not quite eighteen, his first volume of poetry, *Poems by Two Brothers* (1827), was published. Alfred Tennyson wrote the major part of the volume, although it also contained poems by his two elder brothers, Frederick and Charles. It is a remarkable book for so young a poet, displaying great virtuosity of versification and the prodigality of imagery that was to mark his later works; but it is also derivative in its ideas, many of which came from his reading in his father's library. Few copies were sold, and there were only two brief reviews, but its publication confirmed Tennyson's determination to devote his life to poetry.

Most of Tennyson's early education was under the direction of his father, although he spent nearly four unhappy years at a nearby grammar school. His departure in 1827 to join his elder brothers at Trinity College, Cambridge, was due more to a desire to escape from Somersby than to a desire to undertake serious academic work. At Trinity he was living for the first time among young men of his own age who knew little of the problems that had beset him for so long; he was delighted to make new friends; he was extraordinarily handsome, intelligent, humorous, and gifted at impersonation; and soon he was at the center of an admiring group of young men interested in poetry and conversation. It was probably the happiest period of his life.

In part it was the urging of his friends, in part the insistence of his father, that led the normally indolent Tennyson to retailor an old poem on the subject of Armageddon and submit it in the competition for the chancellor's gold medal for poetry; the announced subject was Timbuctoo. Tennyson's *Timbuctoo* is a strange poem, as the process of its creation would suggest. He uses the legendary city for a consideration of the relative validity of imagination and objective reality; Timbuctoo takes its magic from the mind of man, but it can turn to dust at the touch of the mundane. It is far from a successful poem, but it shows how deeply engaged its author was with the Romantic conception of poetry. Whatever its shortcomings, it won the chancellor's prize in the summer of 1829.

Probably more important than its success in the competition was the fact that the submission of the poem brought Tennyson into contact with the Trinity undergraduate usually regarded as the most brilliant man of his Cambridge generation, Arthur Henry Hallam. This was the beginning of four years of warm friendship between the two men, in some ways the most intense emotional experience of Tennyson's life. Despite the too knowing skepticism of the twentieth century about such matters, it is almost certain that there was nothing homosexual about the friendship: definitely not on a conscious level and probably not on any other. Indeed, it was surely the very absence of such overtones that made the warmth of their feelings acceptable to both men, and allowed them to express those feelings freely.

Also in 1829 both Hallam and Tennyson became members of the secret society known as the Apostles, a group of roughly a dozen undergraduates who were usually regarded as the elite of the entire university. Tennyson's name has ever since been linked with the society, but the truth is that he dropped out of it after only a few meetings, although he retained his closeness with the other members and might even be said to have remained the poetic center of the group. The affection and acceptance he felt from his friends brought both a new warmth to Tennyson's personality and an increasing sensuousness to the poetry he was constantly writing when he was supposed to be devoting his time to his studies.

Hallam, too, wrote poetry, and the two friends planned on having their work published together; but at the last moment Hallam's father, perhaps worried by some lyrics Arthur had written to a young lady with whom he had been in love, forbade him to include his poems. *Poems, Chiefly Lyrical* appeared in June 1830. The standard of the poems in the volume is uneven, and it has the self-centered, introspective quality that one might expect of the work of a twenty-year-old; but scattered among the other poems that would be forgotten if they had been written by someone else are several fine ones, such as "The Kraken," "Ode to Memory," and—above all—"Mariana," which is the first of Tennyson's works to demonstrate fully his brilliant use of objects and landscapes to convey a state of strong emo-

A sketch of Alfred (left) and Charles Tennyson by their younger brother Arthur, indicating the gloomy atmosphere at the rectory brought on by their father's mental instability (Tennyson Research Centre)

tion. That poem alone would be enough to justify the entire volume.

The reviews appeared slowly, but they were generally favorable. Both Tennyson and Hallam thought they should have come out more quickly, however, and Hallam reviewed the volume himself in the *Englishman's Magazine*, making up in his critical enthusiasm for having dropped out of being published with his friend.

The friendship between the young men was knotted even more tightly when Hallam fell in love with Tennyson's younger sister, Emily, while on a visit to Somersby. Since they were both so young, there was no chance of their marrying for some time, and meanwhile Hallam had to finish his undergraduate years at Trinity. All the Tennyson brothers and sisters, as well as their mother, seem to have taken instantly to Hallam, but he and Emily prudently said nothing of their love to either of their fathers. Dr. Tennyson was absent on the Continent most of the time, sent there by his father and his brother in the hope that he might get over his drinking and manage Somersby parish sensibly. Arthur's father, the distinguished historian Henry Hallam, had plans for his son that did not include marriage to the daughter of an obscure and alcoholic country clergyman.

In the summer of 1830 Tennyson and Hallam were involved in a harebrained scheme to take money and secret messages to revolutionaries plotting the overthrow of the Spanish king. Tennyson's political enthusiasm was considerably cooler than Hallam's, but he was glad to make his first trip abroad. They went through France to the Pyrenees, meeting the revolutionaries at the Spanish border. Even Hallam's idealistic fervor scarcely survived the disillusionment of realizing that the men they met were animated by motives as selfish as those of the Royalist party against whom they were rebelling. Nonetheless, in the Pyrenees, Tennyson marked out a new dimension of the metaphorical landscape that had already shown itself in "Mariana," and for the rest of his life the mountains remained as a model for the classical scenery that so often formed the backdrop of his poetry. The Pyrenees generated such marvelous poems as "Oenone," which he began writing there; "The Lotos-Eaters," which was inspired by a waterfall in the mountains; and "The Eagle," which was born from the sight of the great birds circling above them as they climbed in the rocks. Above all, the little village of Cauteretz and the valley in which it lay remained more emotionally charged for Tennyson than any other place on earth. He came again and again to walk in the valley, and it provided him with imagery until his death more than sixty years later.

Early the following year Tennyson had to leave Cambridge because of the death of his father. Dr. Tennyson had totally deteriorated mentally and physically, and he left little but debts to his family, although he had enjoyed a good income and a large allowance from his father. Alfred's grandfather naturally felt that it was hardly worth his while to keep Alfred and his two elder brothers at Cambridge when it was only too apparent that they were profiting little from their studies and showed no promise of ever being able to support themselves. The allowance he gave the family was generous enough, but it was not intended to support three idle grandsons at the university. Worse still, neither he nor Dr. Tennyson's brother Charles, who was now clearly marked out as the heir to his for-

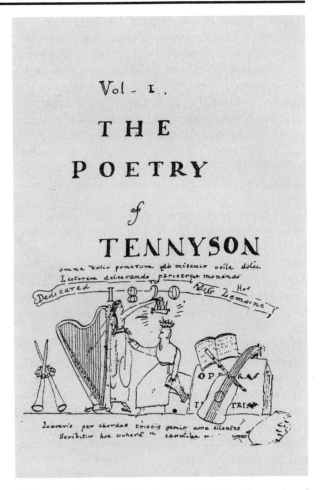

Title page for a notebook volume of Latin poetry, composed and illustrated by Tennyson at about age twelve (American Art Association/Anderson Galleries auction catalogue, sale number 4283, 10 December 1936)

tune, attended the rector's funeral, making the division in the family even more apparent. The widow and her eleven children were so improvident that they seemed incapable of living on the allowance, and they were certainly not able to support themselves otherwise.

This began a very bitter period of Tennyson's life. An annual gift of one hundred pounds from an aunt allowed him to live in a modest manner, but he refused his grandfather's offer to help him find a place in the church if he would be ordained. Tennyson said then, as he said all his life, that poetry was to be his career, however bleak the prospect of his ever earning a living. His third volume of poetry was published at the end of 1832, although the title page was dated 1833.

The 1832 *Poems* was a great step forward poetically and included the first versions of some of Tennyson's greatest works, such as "The Lady of

Shalott," "The Palace of Art," "A Dream of Fair Women," "The Hesperides," and three wonderful poems conceived in the Pyrenees, "Oenone," "The Lotos-Eaters," and "Mariana in the South." The volume is notable for its consideration of the opposed attractions of isolated poetic creativity and social involvement; the former usually turns out to be the more attractive course, since it reflected Tennyson's own concerns, but the poems demonstrate as well his feeling of estrangement in being cut off from his contemporaries by the demands of his art.

The reviews of the volume were almost universally damning. One of the worst was written by Edward Bulwer (later Bulwer-Lytton), who was a friend of Tennyson's uncle Charles. The most vicious review, however, was written for the *Quarterly Review* by John Wilson Croker, who was proud that his brutal notice of *Endymion* years before was said to have been one of the chief causes of the death of John Keats. Croker numbered Tennyson among the Cockney poets who imitated Keats, and he made veiled insinuations about the lack of masculinity of both Tennyson and his poems. Tennyson, who was abnormally thin-skinned about criticism, found some comfort in the steady affection and support of Hallam and the other Apostles.

Hallam and Emily Tennyson had by then made their engagement public knowledge, but they saw no way of marrying for a long time: the senior Hallam refused to increase his son's allowance sufficiently to support both of them; and when Arthur wrote to Emily's grandfather, he was answered in the third person with the indication that old Mr. Tennyson had no intention of giving them any more money. By the summer of 1833, Hallam's father had somewhat grudgingly accepted the engagement, but still without offering further financial help. The protracted unhappiness of both Arthur and Emily rubbed off on the whole Tennyson family.

That autumn, in what was meant as a gesture of gratitude and reconciliation to his father, Arthur Hallam accompanied him to the Continent. In Vienna, Arthur died unexpectedly of apoplexy resulting from a congenital malformation of the brain. Emily Tennyson fell ill for nearly a year; the effects of Hallam's death were less apparent externally in Alfred but were perhaps even more catastrophic than for his sister.

The combination of the deaths of his father and his best friend; the brutal reviews of his poems; his conviction that both he and his family

were in desperate poverty; his feelings of isolation in the depths of the country; and his ill-concealed fears that he might become a victim of epilepsy, madness, alcohol, and drugs, as others in his family had, or even that he might die like Hallam, was more than enough to upset the always fragile balance of Tennyson's emotions. "I suffered what seemed to me to shatter all my life so that I desired to die rather than to live," he said of that period. For a time he determined to leave England, and for ten years he refused to have any of his poetry published, since he was convinced that the world had no place for it.

Although he was adamant about not having it published, Tennyson continued to write poetry, and he did so even more single-mindedly than before. Hallam's death nearly crushed him, but it also provided the stimulus for a great outburst of some of the finest poems he ever wrote, many of them connected overtly or implicitly with the loss of his friend. "Ulysses," "Morte d'Arthur," "Tithonus," "Tiresias," "Break, break, break," and "Oh! that 'twere possible" all owe their inception to the passion of grief he felt but carefully hid from his intimates. Most important was the group of random individual poems he began writing about Hallam's death and his own feeling of loneliness in the universe as a result of it; the first of these "elegies," written in four-line stanzas of iambic tetrameter, was begun within two or three days of his hearing the news of Hallam's death. He continued to write them for seventeen years before collecting them to form what is perhaps the greatest of Victorian poems, *In Memoriam* (1850).

The death of his grandfather in 1835 confirmed Tennyson's fear of poverty, for the larger part of Mr. Tennyson's fortune went to Alfred's uncle Charles, who promptly changed his name to Tennyson d'Eyncourt and set about rebuilding his father's house into a grand Romantic castle, with the expectation of receiving a peerage to cap the family's climb to eminence. His hopes were never realized, but his great house, Bayons Manor, became a model for the home of the vulgar, nouveau-riche characters in many of Tennyson's narrative poems, such as *Maud* (1855). Charles Tennyson d'Eyncourt's inheritance was the final wedge driving the two branches of the family apart; he and his nephew were never reconciled, but Alfred's dislike of him was probably even more influential than admiration would have been in keeping Charles as an immediate influence in so much of Alfred's poetry.

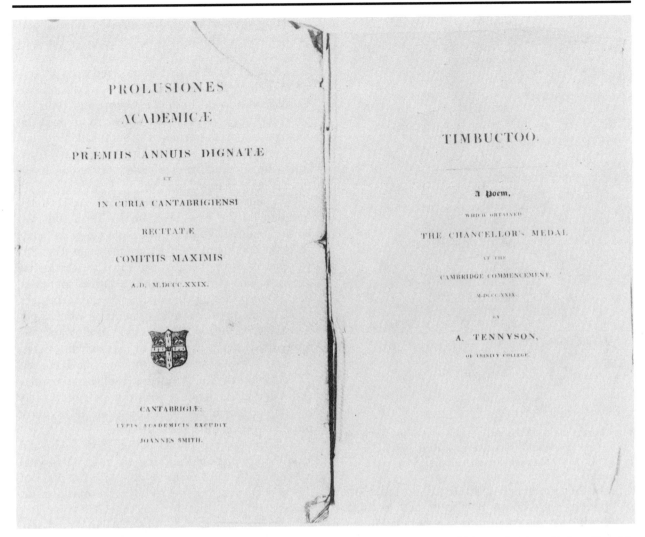

Title pages for 1829 book of Cambridge University prize poems and for Tennyson's poem, which won the chancellor's gold medal
(Tennyson Research Centre)

The details of Tennyson's romantic attachments in the years after Hallam's death are unclear, but he apparently had at least a flirtation with Rose Baring, the pretty young daughter of a great banking family, some of whose members had rented Harrington Hall, a large house near Somersby. Tennyson wrote a dozen or so poems to her, but it is improbable that his affections were deeply involved. The poems suggest that her position made it impossible for him to be a serious suitor to her, but she may have been more important to him as a symbol of wealth and unavailability than as a flesh-and-blood young woman. Certainly, he seems not to have been crushed when she married another man.

In 1836, however, at the age of twenty-seven, Tennyson became seriously involved with Emily Sellwood, who was four years younger than he. By the following year they considered themselves engaged. Emily had been a friend of Tennyson's sisters, and one of her own sisters married his next older (and favorite) brother, Charles. Most of the correspondence between Tennyson and Emily has been destroyed, but from what remains it is clear that she was very much in love with him, although he apparently withheld himself somewhat in spite of his affection for her. He was worried about not having enough money to marry, but he seems also to have been much concerned with the trances into which he was still falling, which he thought were connected with the epilepsy from which other members of the family suffered. To marry, he thought, would mean passing on the disease to any children he might father.

Rosa Baring, the wealthy young woman with whom Tennyson was romantically involved in the early 1830s (Tennyson Research Centre)

In the summer of 1840 Tennyson broke off all relations with Emily. She continued to think of herself as engaged to him, but he abandoned any hope of marriage, either then or in the future. To spare her further embarrassment, the story was put out that her father had forbidden their marriage because of Tennyson's poverty; this legend has been perpetuated in the present century.

Through the second half of the 1830s and most of the 1840s Tennyson lived an unsettled, nomadic life. Nominally he made his home with his mother and his unmarried brothers and sisters, who continued to rent Somersby rectory until 1837, then he moved successively to Essex and to Kent; but he was as often to be found in London, staying in cheap hotels or cadging a bed from friends who lived there. He was lonely and despondent, and he drank and smoked far too much. Many of those who had known him for years believed that his poetic inspiration had failed him and that his great early promise would remain unfulfilled; but this was to neglect the fact that when all else went wrong, he clung to the composition of poetry. He was steadily accu-

mulating a backlog of unpublished poems, and he continued adding to his "elegies" to Hallam's memory.

One of the friends who worried away at Tennyson to have his work published was Edward Fitz-Gerald, who loved both the poems and their author, although he was too stubborn to hide his feelings when a particular poem failed to win FitzGerald's approval. "Old Fitz" nagged at Tennyson, who in the spring of 1842 agreed to break his ten long years of silence.

The two volumes of the 1842 *Poems* were destined to be the best-loved books Tennyson ever wrote. The first volume was made up of radically revised versions of the best poems from the 1832 volume, most of them in the form in which they are now known. The second volume contained new poems, among them some of those inspired by Hallam's death, as well as poems of widely varying styles, including the dramatic monologue "St. Simeon Stylites"; a group of Arthurian poems; his first attempt to deal with rampant sexuality, "The Vision of Sin"; and the implicitly narrative "Locksley Hall," dealing with the evils of worldly marriages, which was to become one of his most popular poems during his lifetime.

After the reception of the 1832 *Poems* and after being unpublished for so long, Tennyson was naturally apprehensive about the reviews of the new poems; but nearly all were enthusiastic, making it clear that he was now the foremost poet of his generation. Edgar Allan Poe wrote guardedly, "I am not sure that Tennyson is not the greatest of poets."

But the bad luck that Tennyson seemed to invite struck again just as the favorable reviews were appearing. Two years earlier, expecting to make a fortune, he had invested his patrimony in a scheme to manufacture cheap wood carvings by steam-driven machines. In 1842 the scheme crashed, taking with it nearly everything that Tennyson owned, some four thousand pounds. The shock set back any progress he had made in his emotional state over the past ten years, and in 1843 he had to go into a "hydropathic" establishment for seven months of treatment in the hope of curing his deep melancholia.

This was the first of several stays in "hydros" during the next five years. Copious applications of water inside and out, constant wrappings in cold, wet sheets, and enforced abstinence from tobacco and alcohol seemed to help him during each stay; but he would soon ruin any beneficial effects by his careless life once he had left the estab-

The red light falls on mountain walls
        And snowy summits old in story
The long beam shakes across the lakes
        And the wild cataract leaps in glory
    Blow bugle blow, set the wild echoes
                                    flying
Blow bugle, answer echoes, dying dying dying

    O hark O hear O thin & clear!
        O thinner clearer, farther going!
O sweet & far from cliff & scar
        The horns of Elfland faintly blowing
    Blow bugle blow set the wild echoes flying
And answer echoes answer dying dying dying

    O love they die in yon rich sky
        They faint on hill or field or river
But ours roll from soul to soul
        And grow for ever & for ever
    Blow bugle blow set the wild echoes flying
Blow bugle answer echoes dying, dying, dying.

                                    A. T.

Manuscript for three stanzas of "The Princess," written by Tennyson for presentation to a friend, and containing variations from the published version (American Art Association/Anderson Galleries auction catalogue, sale number 4098, 5 April 1934)

Tennyson's wife, Emily Sellwood Tennyson, with their sons Hallam (left) and Lionel (Tennyson Research Centre)

lishment, resuming his drinking and smoking, to the despair of his friends. A rather more effective form of treatment was the two thousand pounds he received from an insurance policy at the death of the organizer of the wood-carving scheme. In 1845 he was granted a government civil list pension of twelve hundred pounds a year in recognition of both his poetic achievements and his apparent financial need. Tennyson was in reality released from having to worry about money, but the habit of years was too much for him; for the rest of his life he complained constantly of his poverty, although his poetry had made him a rich man by the time of his death. In 1845 the betterment of his fortunes brought with it no effort to resume his engagement to Emily Sellwood, showing that it was not financial want that kept them apart.

The Princess, which was published on Christmas 1847, was Tennyson's first attempt at a long narrative poem, a form that tempted him most of his life although it was less congenial to him temperamentally than the lyric. The ostensible theme is the education of women and the establish-ment of female colleges, but it is clear that Tennyson's interest in the subject runs out before the poem does, so that it gradually shifts to the consideration of what he thought of as the unnatural attempt of men and women to fulfill identical roles in society; only as the hero becomes more overtly masculine and the heroine takes on the traditional attributes of women is there a chance for their happiness. Considerably more successful than the main narrative are the thematic lyrics that Tennyson inserted into the action, to show the growth of passion, and between the cantos, to indicate that the natural end of the sexes is to be parents of another generation in a thoroughly traditional manner. The subtitle, *A Medley,* was his way of anticipating charges of inconsistency in the structure of the poem. As always, the blank verse in which the main part of the poem is written is superb, and the interpolated lyrics include some of his most splendid short poems, such as "Come down, O maid," "Now sleeps the crimson petal," "Sweet and low," "The splendour falls on castle walls," and "Tears, idle tears." The emotion of these lyrics does more than the straight narrative to convey the forward movement of the entire poem, and their brief perfection indicates well enough that his genius lay there rather than in the descriptions of persons and their actions; this was not, however, a lesson that Tennyson himself was capable of learning. The seriousness with which the reviewers wrote of the poem was adequate recognition of his importance, but many of them found the central question of feminine education to be insufficiently considered. The first edition was quickly sold out, and subsequent editions appeared almost every year for several decades.

Tennyson's last stay in a hydropathic hospital was in the summer of 1848, and though he was not completely cured of his illness, he was reassured about its nature. The doctor in charge apparently made a new diagnosis of his troubles, telling him that what he suffered from was not epilepsy but merely a form of gout that prefaced its attacks by a stimulation of the imagination that is very like the "aura" that often warns epileptics of the onset of a seizure. The trances that he had thought were mild epileptic fits were in fact only flashes of illumination over which he had no reason to worry. Had it been in Tennyson's nature to rejoice, he could have done so at this time, for there was no longer any reason for him to fear marriage, paternity, or the transmission of disease to his offspring. The habits of a lifetime, however, were too ingrained for him to shake them off at once. The real measure of his relief at being rid of his old fear of epilepsy is that he soon set about writing further sections to be inserted into new editions of *The Princess,* in which the hero is said to be the victim of "weird seizures" inherited from his family; at first he is terrified when he falls into trances, but he is at last released from the malady when he falls in love with Princess Ida. Not only this poem, but his three other major long works, *In Memoriam, Maud,* and *Idylls of the King* (1859), all deal in part with the meaning of trances, which are at first frightening but then are revealed to be pathways to the extrasensory, to be rejoiced over rather than feared. After his death Tennyson's wife and son burned many of his most personal letters, and in those remaining there is little reference to his trances or his recovery from them; but the poems bear quiet testimony to the immense weight he must have felt lifted from his shoulders when he needed no longer worry about epilepsy.

Tennyson's luck at last seemed to be on the upturn. At the beginning of 1849 he received a large advance from his publisher with the idea that he would assemble and polish his "elegies" on Hallam, to be published as a whole poem. Before the year was over he had resumed communication with Emily Sellwood, and by the beginning of 1850 he was speaking confidently of marrying. On 1 June *In Memoriam* was published, and less than two weeks later he and Emily were married quietly at Shiplake Church. Improbable as it might seem for a man to whom little but bad fortune had come, both events were total successes.

The new Mrs. Tennyson was thirty-seven years old and in delicate health, but she was a woman of iron determination; she took over the running of the externals of her husband's life, freeing him from the practical details at which he was so inept. Her taste was conventional, and she may have curbed his religious questioning, his mild bohemianism, and the exuberance and experimentation of his poetry, but she also brought a kind of peace to his life without which he would not have been able to write at all. There is some evidence that Tennyson occasionally chafed at the responsibilities of marriage and paternity and at the loss of the vagrant freedom he had known, but there is nothing to indicate that he ever regretted his choice. It was probably not a particularly passionate marriage, but it was full

IN MEMORIAM.

LONDON:
EDWARD MOXON, DOVER STREET.
1850.

Title page for the anonymously published tribute to Arthur Hallam that made Tennyson famous

of tenderness and affection. Three sons were born, of whom two, Hallam and Lionel, survived.

After a protracted honeymoon of some four months in the Lake Country, Tennyson returned to the south of England to find that the publication of *In Memoriam* had made him, without question, the major living poet. It had appeared anonymously, but his authorship was an open secret.

This vast poem (nearly three thousand lines) is divided into 131 sections, with prologue and epilogue; the size is appropriate for what it undertakes, since in coming to terms with loss, grief, and the growth of consolation, it touches on most of the intellectual issues at the center of the Victorian consciousness: religion, immortality, geology, evolution, the relation of the intellect to the unconscious, the place of art in a workaday world, the individual versus society, the relation of man to nature, and as many others. The poem grew out of Tennyson's personal grief, but it attempts to speak for all men rather than for one. The structure often seems wayward, for in T. S. Eliot's famous phrase, it has "only the unity and continuity of a diary" instead of the clear direction of a philosophical statement. It was bound to be somewhat irregular, since it was composed with no regard for either chronology or continuity and was for years not intended to be published. The vacillation in mood of the finished poem, however, is neither haphazard nor capricious, for it is put together to show the wild swoops between depression and elation that grief brings, the hesitant gropings toward philosophical justification of bereavement, the tentative little darts of conviction that may precede a settled belief in a beneficent world. It is intensely personal, but one must also believe Tennyson in his reiterated assertions that it was a poem, not the record of his own grief about Hallam; in short, that his own feelings had prompted the poem but were not necessarily accurately recorded in it.

To the most perceptive of the Victorians (and to modern readers) the poem was moving for its dramatic re-creation of a mind indisposed to deal with the problems of contemporary life, and for the sheer beauty of so many of its sections. To a more naive, and far larger, group of readers it was a work of real utility, to be read like the Bible as a manual of consolation, and it is surely to that group that the poem owed its almost unbelievable popularity. Edition followed edition, and each brought Tennyson more fame and greater fortune.

William Wordsworth, who had been poet laureate for seven years, had died in the spring of 1850. By the time Tennyson returned from his honeymoon, it must have seemed to many a foregone conclusion that he would be nominated as Wordsworth's successor. Tennyson knew that the prince consort, who advised the queen on such matters, was an admirer of his, and the night before receiving the letter offering the post, he dreamed that the prince kissed him on the cheek, and that he responded, "Very kind but very German." Early the following year he was presented to the queen as her poet laureate and kissed her hand, wearing the borrowed and too-tight court clothes that Wordsworth had worn for the same purpose on the occasion of his own presentation. The straining court suit was emblematic of the passing of the office from the greatest

Title page for the volume whose title poem is Tennyson's most experimental work

of Romantic poets to the greatest of the Victorians.

At the end of November 1853 Alfred and Emily Tennyson moved into the secluded big house on the Isle of Wight known as Farringford, which has ever since been associated with his name. Emily loved the remoteness and the fact that their clocks were not even synchronized with those elsewhere, but her husband sometimes had a recurrence of his old longing to be rattling around London. Most of the time, however, he was content to walk on the great chalk cliffs overlooking the sea, composing his poems as he tramped, their rhythm often deriving from his heavy tread.

It was perhaps his very isolation that made him so interested in the Crimean War, for he read the newspapers voraciously in order to keep current with world affairs. "The Charge of the Light Brigade" was one result in 1854 of his fascination with the heroism of that unpopular war. *Maud,* in which the hero redeems his misspent life by volunteering for service in the Crimea, was published the following year. In spite of that somewhat conventional-sounding conclusion, the poem is Tennyson's most experimental, for it tells a thoroughly dramatic narrative in self-contained lyrics; the reader must fill in the interstices of the story by inference. The lyrics are not even like one another in scansion, length, or style. The narrator of the poem is an unnamed young man whose father has committed suicide after being swindled by his partner. The son then falls in love with Maud, the daughter of the peccant partner; but since he is poor and she is rich, there is no possibility of their marrying. When he is bullied by her brother, he kills him in a duel. After Maud also dies, the narrator goes temporarily insane; he finally realizes that he has been as selfish and evil as the society on which he has blamed his bad fortune. In an attempt to make up for his wasted life, he goes to the Crimea, with his subsequent death hinted at in the last section of the poem.

As always, Tennyson is not at his best in narrative, but the melodramatic content of the plot finally matters little in comparison with the startling originality of his attempt to extend the limits of lyricism in order to make it do the work of narrative and drama, to capitalize on his own apparently circumscribed gift in order to include social criticism, contemporary history, and moral comment in the lyric. In part it must have been a deliberate answer to those who complained that his art was too self-absorbed and negligent of the world around him.

The experimental quality of *Maud* has made it one of the most interesting of his poems to modern critics, but to Tennyson's contemporaries it seemed so unlike what they expected from the author of *In Memoriam* that they could neither understand nor love it. An age that was not accustomed to distinguishing between narrator and poet found it almost impossible not to believe that Tennyson was directly portraying his own thoughts and personal history in those of the central figure. The result was the worst critical abuse that Tennyson received after that directed at the 1832 *Poems.* One reviewer went so far as to say that *Maud* had one extra vowel in the title, and that it made no difference which was to be de-

Photograph of Tennyson taken by his Isle of Wight neighbor Julia Margaret Cameron in 1865. Tennyson called it the "Dirty Monk" portrait (Tennyson Research Centre).

leted. Tennyson's predictable response was to become defensive about the poem and to read it aloud at every opportunity in order to show how badly misunderstood both poem and poet were. Since it was a performance that took between two and three hours, the capitulation to its beauty that he often won thereby was probably due as much to weariness on the part of the hearer as to intellectual or aesthetic persuasion.

Ever since the publication of the 1842 *Poems* Tennyson had been something of a lion in literary circles, but after he became poet laureate he was equally in demand with society hostesses, who were more interested in his fame than in his poetic genius. For the rest of his life Tennyson was to be caught awkwardly between being unable to resist the flattery implied by their attentions and the knowledge that their admiration of him usually sprang from the wrong reasons. It was difficult for him to refuse invitations, but he felt subconsciously impelled when he accepted them to behave gruffly, even rudely, in order to demonstrate his independence. His wife's bad health usually made it impossible for her to accompany him, which probably increased his awkwardness. It all brought out the least attractive side of a fundamentally shy man, whose paroxysms of inability to deal with social situations made him seem selfish, bad-mannered, and assertive. In order to smooth his ruffled feathers, his hostesses and his friends would resort to heavy flattery, which only made him appear more arrogant. One of the saddest aspects of Tennyson's life is that his growing fame was almost in inverse ratio to his ability to maintain intimacy with others, so that by the end of his life he was a basically lonely man. All the innate charm, humor, intelligence, and liveliness were still there, but it took great understanding and patience on the part of his friends to bring them into the open.

Idylls of the King was published in 1859; it contained only four ("Enid," "Vivien," "Elaine," and "Guinevere") of the eventual twelve idylls. The matter of Arthur and Camelot had obsessed Tennyson since boyhood, and over the years it became a receptacle into which he poured his deepening feelings of the desecration of decency and of ancient English ideals by the gradual corruption of accepted morality. The decay of the Round Table came increasingly to seem to him an apt symbol of the decay of nineteenth-century England. It was no accident that the first full-length idyll had been "Morte d'Arthur," which ultimately became—with small additions—the final idyll in the completed cycle. It had been written at the time of the death of Arthur Hallam, who seemed to Tennyson "Ideal manhood closed in real man," as he wrote of King Arthur; no doubt both Hallam's character and Tennyson's grief at his death lent color to the entire poem.

Like *The Princess, In Memoriam,* and *Maud,* the idylls were an assembly of poetry composed over a long time—in this case nearly half a century in all, for they were not finished until 1874 and were not all published until 1885. Taken collectively, they certainly constitute Tennyson's most ambitious poem, but not all critics would agree that the poem's success is equal to its intentions.

For a modern reader, long accustomed to the Arthurian legend by plays, musicals, films, and popular books, it is hard to realize that the story was relatively unfamiliar when Tennyson wrote. He worked hard at his preparation, reading most of the available sources, going to Wales and the West Country of England to see the actual places connected with Arthur, and even learning sufficient Welsh to read some of the original documents. "There is no grander subject in the world," he wrote, and he meant his state of readi-

William Ewart Gladstone, with whom Tennyson maintained an uneasy relationship (Tennyson Research Centre)

ness to be equal to the loftiness of his themes, which explains in part why it took him so long to write the entire poem.

Although Tennyson always thought of the idylls as allegorical (his word was "parabolic"), he refused to make literal identifications between incidents, characters, or situations in the poems and what they stood for, except to indicate generally that by King Arthur he meant the soul and that the disintegration of the court and the Round Table showed the disruptive effect of the passions.

In all the time that he worked on the idylls Tennyson constantly refined their structure—by framing the main action between the coming of Arthur and his death, by repetition of verbal motifs, by making the incidents of the plot follow the course of the year from spring to winter, by making different idylls act as parallels or contrasts to each other, and by trying to integrate the whole poem as closely as an extended musical composition. Considering how long he worked on the poem, the result is amazingly successful, although perhaps more so when the poem is represented schematically than in the actual experience of reading it.

As always, the imagery of the poem is superb. It is less successful in characterization and speech, which are often stilted and finally seem more Victorian than Arthurian. Even Arthur, who is meant to be the firm, heroic center of the poem, occasionally seems merely weak at the loss of his wife and the decay of the court rather than nobly forgiving. Individual idylls such as "The Last Tournament" and "Gareth and Lynette" have considerable narrative force, but there is an almost fatal lack of forward movement in the poem as a whole.

The reviewers were divided between those who thought it a worthy companion of Malory and those who found it more playacting than drama, with the costumes failing to disguise Tennyson's contemporaries and their concerns. The division between critics still maintains that split of opinion, although it is probably taken more seriously in the 1990s than it was earlier in the twentieth century. Whether that attitude will last is impossible to predict.

In spite of the adverse reviews and the reservations of many of Tennyson's fellow poets, the sales of *Idylls of the King* in 1859 were enough to gladden the heart of any poet: forty thousand copies were printed initially, and within a week or two more than a quarter of these were already sold; it was a pattern that was repeated with each succeeding volume as they appeared during the following decades.

The death of his admirer Prince Albert in 1861 prompted Tennyson to write a dedication to the *Idylls of the King* in his memory. The prince had taken an interest in Tennyson's poetry ever since 1847, when it is believed that he called on Tennyson when the poet was ill. He had written to ask for Tennyson's autograph in his own copy of *Idylls of the King,* and he had come over unannounced from Osborne, the royal residence on the Isle of Wight, to call on Tennyson at Farringford. In spite of the brevity of their acquaintance and its formality, Tennyson had been much moved by the prince's kindness and friendliness, and he had greatly admired the way Albert behaved in the difficult role of consort.

Four months after Albert's death the queen invited Tennyson to Osborne for an informal visit. Tennyson went with considerable trepidation, fearful that he might in some way transgress court etiquette, but his obvious shyness helped to make the visit a great success. It became the first of many occasions on which he vis-

Aldworth, Tennyson's home on a high hill near Haslemere

ited the queen, and a genuine affection grew up on both sides. The queen treated Tennyson with what was great informality by her reserved standards, so that the relationship between monarch and laureate was probably more intimate than it has ever been before or since. She had an untutored and naive love of poetry, and he felt deep veneration for the throne; above all, each was a simple and unassuming person beneath a carapace of apparent arrogance, and each recognized the true simplicity of the other. It was almost certainly the queen's feeling for Tennyson that lay behind the unprecedented offer of a baronetcy four times beginning in 1865; Tennyson each time turned it down for himself while asking that if possible it be given to Hallam, his elder son, after his own death.

His extraordinary popularity was obvious in other ways as well. He was given honorary doctorates by Oxford and Edinburgh universities; Cambridge three times invited him to accept an honorary degree, but he modestly declined. The greatest men in the country competed for the honor of meeting and entertaining him. Thomas Carlyle and his wife had been good friends of Tennyson's since the 1840s, and Tennyson felt free to drop in on them unannounced, at last even having his own pipe kept for him in a convenient niche in the garden wall. He had met Robert Browning at about the same time as he had met Carlyle, and though the two greatest of Victorian poets always felt a certain reserve about each other's works, their mutual generosity in acknowledging genius was exemplary; Browning, like most of the friends Tennyson made in his maturity, was never an intimate, but their respect for each other never faltered. Tennyson was somewhat lukewarm in his response to the overtures of friendship made by Charles Dickens, even after he had stood as godfather for one of Dickens's sons. It is tempting to think that some of his reserve stemmed from an uneasy recognition of the similarity of their features, which occasionally led to their being confused, particularly in photographs or portraits, which can hardly have been welcome to Tennyson's self-esteem.

Tennyson maintained a reluctant closeness with William Gladstone for nearly sixty years. It was generally accepted in London society that if a dinner was given for one of them, the other ought to be invited. Yet the truth was that they were never on an easy footing, and though they worked hard at being polite to each other, their edginess occasionally flared into unpleasantness before others. It is probable that some of their difficulties came from their friendship with Arthur Hallam when they were young men; Gladstone had been Hallam's best friend at Eton and felt left out after Hallam met Tennyson. To the end of their days the prime minister and the poet laureate were mildly jealous of their respective places in Hallam's affections so many years before. The feeling certainly colored Gladstone's reactions to Tennyson's poetry (which he occasionally reviewed), and nothing he could do ever made Tennyson trust Gladstone as a politician. The relationship hardly reflects well on either man.

Almost as if he felt that his position as laureate and the most popular serious poet in the English-speaking world were not enough, Tennyson deliberately tried to widen his appeal by speaking more directly to the common people of the country about the primary emotions and affections that he felt he shared with them. The most immediate result of his wish to be "the people's poet" was the 1864 volume whose title poem was "Enoch Arden" and which also contained another long narrative poem, "Aylmer's Field." These are full of the kinds of magnificent language and imagery that no other Victorian poet

could have hoped to produce, but the sentiments occasionally seem easy and secondhand. The volume also contained some much more experimental translations and metrical innovations, as well as such wonderful lyrics as "In the Valley of Cauteretz," which was written thirty-one years after he and Hallam had wandered through that beautiful countryside, and "Tithonus." There was no question that Tennyson was still a very great poet, but his ambition to be more than a lyricist often blinded him to his own limitations. His hope of becoming "the people's poet" was triumphantly realized; the volume had the largest sales of any during his lifetime. More than forty thousand copies were sold immediately after publication, and in the first year he made more than eight thousand pounds from it, a sum equal to the income of many of the richest men in England.

Popularity of the kind he had earned had its innate disadvantages, and Tennyson was beginning to discover them as he was followed in the streets of London by admirers; at Farringford he complained of the total lack of privacy when the park walls were lined with craning tourists who sometimes even came up to the house and peered into the windows to watch the family at their meals. In 1867 he built a second house, Aldworth, on the southern slopes of Blackdown, a high hill near Haslemere, where the house was not visible except from miles away. Curiously, the house resembles a smaller version of Bayons Manor, the much-hated sham castle his uncle Charles Tennyson d'Eyncourt had built in the Lincolnshire wolds. To his contemporaries it appeared unnecessarily grand for a second house, even slightly pretentious; today it seems emblematic of the seriousness with which Tennyson had come to regard his own public position in Victorian England, which was not his most attractive aspect. For the rest of his life he was to divide his time between Farringford and Aldworth, just as he divided his work between the essentially private, intimate lyricism at which he had always excelled and the poetry in which he felt obliged to speak to his countrymen on more public matters.

In the years between 1874 and 1882 Tennyson made yet another attempt to widen his poetic horizons. As the premier poet of England, he had been compared—probably inevitably—to Shakespeare, and he determined to write for the stage as his great predecessor had done. At the age of sixty-five he wrote his first play as a kind of continuation of Shakespeare's historical dra-

Crossing the Bar.

Sunset & evening star,
    And one clear call for me.
And may there be no moaning of the bar,
    When I put out to sea,

But such a tide as moving seems asleep,
    Too full for sound & foam,
When that which drew from out the boundless deep
    Turns again home.

Twilight & evening bell,
    And after that the dark;
And may there be no sadness of farewell,
    When I embark!

For tho' from out our bourne of Time &
    The flood may bear me far,   Place
I hope to see my Pilot face to face,
    When I have crost the bar.

Manuscript for the poem that Tennyson asked to be placed at the end of all editions of his poetry (Tennyson Research Centre)

mas. *Queen Mary* (1875) was produced in 1876 by Henry Irving, the foremost actor on the English stage; Irving himself played the main male role. It had been necessary to hack the play to a fraction of its original inordinate length in order to play it in one evening, and the result was hardly more dramatic than the original long version had been. In spite of the initial curiosity about Tennyson's first play, the audiences soon dwindled, and it was withdrawn after twenty-three performances; that was, however, a more respectable run than it would be today.

His next play, *Harold* (1876), about the early English king of that name, failed to find a producer during Tennyson's lifetime, although he had conscientiously worked at making it less sprawling than its predecessor. *Becket* (1884), finished in 1879, was a study of the martyred Thomas à Becket, Archbishop of Canterbury; Tennyson found the subject so fascinating that he once more wrote at length, in this case making a play considerably longer than an uncut *Hamlet. Becket* was, not surprisingly, not produced until 1893, the year after Tennyson's death. Following *Becket* in quick succession came *The Falcon* and *The Cup* (published together in 1884), *The Foresters* (1892), and *The Promise of May* (published in *Locksley Hall Sixty Years After, Etc.* in 1886), all of which abandoned the attempt to follow Shakespeare. On the stage only *The Cup* had any success, and that was in part due to the lavish settings and the acting of Irving and Ellen Terry. After the failure of *The Promise of May* (a rustic melodrama and the only prose work in his long career), Tennyson at last accepted the fact that nearly a decade of his life had been wasted in an experiment that had totally gone amiss. Today no one would read even the best of the plays, *Queen Mary* and *Becket,* if they were not the work of Tennyson. They betray the fact that he was not profound at understanding the characters of other persons or in writing speech that had the sound of conversation. Even the flashes of metaphor fail to redeem this reckless, admirable, but failed attempt to fit Tennyson's genius to another medium.

The climax of public recognition of Tennyson's achievement came in 1883, when Gladstone offered him a peerage. After a few days of consideration, Tennyson accepted. Surprisingly, his first thought was to change his name to Baron Tennyson d'Eyncourt in an echo of his uncle's ambition, but he was discouraged by the College of Arms and finally settled on Baron Tennyson of Aldworth and Freshwater. Since he was nearly seventy-five when he assumed the title, he took little part in the activities of the House of Lords, but the appropriateness of his being ennobled was generally acknowledged. It was the first time in history that a man had been given a title for his services to poetry. Tennyson claimed that he took the peerage on behalf of all literature, not as personal recognition.

The rest of his life was spent in the glow of love that the public occasionally gives to a distinguished man who has reached a great age. He continued to write poetry nearly as assiduously as he had when young, and though some of it lacked the freshness of youth, there were occasional masterpieces that mocked the passing years. He had always felt what he once described as the "passion of the past," a longing for the days that had gone, either the great ages of earlier history or the more immediate past of his own life, and his poetic genius always had something nostalgic, even elegiac, at its heart. Many of the finest poems of his old age were written in memory of his friends as they died off, leaving him increasingly alone.

Of all the blows of mortality, the cruelest was the death from "jungle fever" of his younger son, Lionel, who had fallen ill in India and was returning by ship to England. Lionel died while crossing the Red Sea, and his body was put into the waves "Beneath a hard Arabian moon / And alien stars." It took Tennyson two years to recover his equanimity sufficiently to write the poem from which those lines are taken: the magnificent elegy dedicated "To the Marquis of Dufferin and Ava," who had been Lionel's host in India. Hauntingly, the poem is written in the same meter as *In Memoriam,* that masterpiece of his youth celebrating the death of another beloved young man, Arthur Hallam. There were also fine elegies to his brother Charles, to FitzGerald, and to several others, indicating the love he had felt for old friends even when he was frequently unable to express it adequately in person.

Lionel's death was the climax of Tennyson's sense of loss, and from that time until his own death he became increasingly troubled in his search for the proofs of immortality, even experimenting with spiritualism. His poetry of this period is saturated with the desperation of the search, sometimes in questioning, sometimes in dogmatic assertion that scarcely hides the fear underlying it. Yet there were moments of serenity, re-

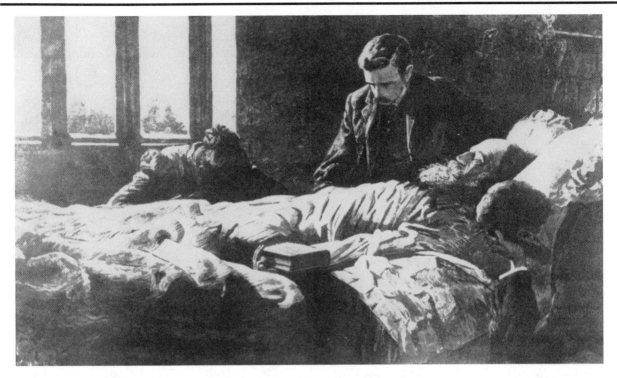

Illustration from a contemporary periodical of the death of Tennyson. Hallam Tennyson and his wife, Audrey, are on either side of the bed; Tennyson's physician, Dr. Dabbs, is beside Audrey Tennyson (Tennyson Research Centre).

flected in such beautiful poems as "Demeter and Persephone," in which he uses the classical legend as a herald of the truth of Christianity. And there was, of course, "Crossing the Bar," written in a few minutes as he sailed across the narrow band of water separating the Isle of Wight from the mainland. At his request, this grave little prayer of simple faith has ever since been placed at the end of editions of his poetry.

Tennyson continued to compose poetry during the last two years of his life; when he was too weak to write it down, his son or his wife would copy it for him. When he had a good day, he was still able to take long walks or even to venture to London. The year before his death he wrote a simple and delicate little poem, "June Heather and Bracken," as an offering of love to his faithful wife; to her he dedicated his last volume of poetry, which was not published until a fortnight after his death. His friends noticed that he was gentler than he had been for years, and he made quiet reparation to some of those whom he had offended by thoughtless brusquerie.

On 6 October 1892, an hour or so after midnight, he died at Aldworth with the moon streaming in at the window overlooking the Sussex Weald, his finger holding open a volume of Shakespeare, his family surrounding the bed. A week later he was buried in the Poets' Corner of Westminster Abbey, near the graves of Browning and Geoffrey Chaucer. To most of England it seemed as if an era in poetry had passed, a divide as great as that a decade later when Queen Victoria died.

One of the most levelheaded summations of what he had meant to his contemporaries was made by Edmund Gosse on the occasion of Tennyson's eightieth birthday: "He is wise and full of intelligence; but in mere intellectual capacity or attainment it is probable that there are many who excel him. This, then, is not the direction in which his greatness asserts itself. He has not headed a single moral reform nor inaugurated a single revolution of opinion; he has never pointed the way to undiscovered regions of thought; he has never stood on tip-toe to describe new worlds that his fellows were not tall enough to discover ahead. In all these directions he has been prompt to follow, quick to apprehend, but never himself a pioneer. Where then has his greatness lain? It has lain in the various perfections of his writing. He has written, on the whole, with more constant, unwearied, and unwearying excellence than any of his contemporaries. . . . He has expended the treasures of his native talent on broadening and deepening his own hold upon the English language, until that has become an instrument upon which he is able to play a greater variety of melodies to perfection than any other man."

But this is a kind of perfection that is hard to accept for any one who is uneasy with poetry and feels that it ought to be the servant of something more utilitarian. Like most things Victorian, Tennyson's reputation suffered an eclipse in the early years of this century. In his case the decline was more severe than that of other Victorians because he had seemed so much the symbol of his age, so that for a time his name was nearly a joke. After two world wars had called into question most of the social values to which he had given only the most reluctant of support, readers were once more able to appreciate that he stood apart from his contemporaries. Now one can again admire without reservation one of the greatest lyric gifts in English literature, although it is unlikely that he will ever again seem quite the equal of Shakespeare.

When the best of his poetry is separated from the second-rate work of the kind that any writer produces, Tennyson can be seen plainly as one of the half-dozen great poets in the English language, at least the equal of Wordsworth or Keats and probably far above any other Victorian. And that is precisely what his contemporaries thought.

Letters:

The Letters of Alfred Lord Tennyson, 3 volumes to date, edited by Cecil Y. Lang and Edgar F. Shannon, Jr. (Cambridge, Mass.: Harvard University Press / Oxford: Oxford University Press, 1981-1990).

Bibliographies:

T. J. Wise, *A Bibliography of the Writings of Alfred, Lord Tennyson,* 2 volumes (London: Privately printed, 1908);

Charles Tennyson and Christine Fall, *Alfred Tennyson: An Annotated Bibliography* (Athens: University of Georgia Press, 1967);

Nancie Campbell, *Tennyson in Lincoln: A Catalogue of the Collections in the Research Centre,* 2 volumes (Lincoln, U.K.: Tennyson Research Centre, 1971-1973);

Kirk H. Butz, *Tennyson: A Bibliography, 1827-1982* (Metuchen, N.J.: Scarecrow Press, 1984);

Marion Shaw and Clifton N. Smith, *An Annotated Critical Bibliography of Alfred, Lord Tennyson* (New York: St. Martin's Press, 1989).

Biographies:

Hallam Tennyson, *Alfred Lord Tennyson: A Memoir,* 2 volumes (New York & London: Macmillan, 1897);

Tennyson, ed., *Tennyson and His Friends* (London: Macmillan, 1911);

Charles Tennyson, *Alfred Tennyson* (New York & London: Macmillan, 1949);

Andrew Wheatcroft, *The Tennyson Album: A Biography in Original Photographs* (London, Boston & Henley, U.K.: Routledge & Kegan Paul, 1980);

Robert Bernard Martin, *Tennyson: The Unquiet Heart* (New York: Oxford University Press / Oxford: Clarendon Press / London: Faber & Faber, 1980);

Christopher Ricks, *Tennyson* (Berkeley: University of California Press, 1989).

References:

Jerome H. Buckley, *Tennyson: The Growth of a Poet* (Cambridge, Mass.: Harvard University Press, 1960);

A. Dwight Culler, *The Poetry of Tennyson* (New Haven & London: Yale University Press, 1977);

John Olin Eidson, *Tennyson in America: His Reputation and Influence from 1827-1858* (Athens: University of Georgia Press, 1943);

Elaine Jordan, *Alfred Tennyson* (Cambridge & New York: Cambridge University Press, 1988);

James R. Kincaid, *Tennyson's Major Poems: The Comic and Ironic Patterns* (New Haven & London: Yale University Press, 1975);

Robert Bernard Martin, *Tennyson: The Unquiet Heart* (New York: Oxford University Press, 1980);

W. D. Paden, *Tennyson in Egypt: A Study of the Imagery in His Earlier Work* (Lawrence: University of Kansas Press, 1942);

Norman Page, ed., *Tennyson: Interviews and Recollections* (Totowa, N.J.: Barnes & Noble, 1983);

F. B. Pinion, *A Tennyson Companion: Life and Works* (New York: St. Martin's Press, 1984);

Valerie Pitt, *Tennyson Laureate* (London: Barrie & Rockliff, 1962);

Ralph Wilson Rader, *Tennyson's "Maud": the Biographical Genesis* (Berkeley, Los Angeles & London: University of California Press, 1963);

Christopher Ricks, *Tennyson* (New York & London: Macmillan, 1972);

Edgar F. Shannon, Jr., *Tennyson and the Reviewers: A Study of His Literary Reputation and the Influ-*

ence of the Critics upon His Poetry, 1827-1851 (Cambridge, Mass.: Harvard University Press, 1952);

Alan Sinfield, *Alfred Tennyson* (Oxford & New York: Blackwell, 1986);

Herbert F. Tucker, *Tennyson and the Doom of Romanticism* (Cambridge, Mass.: Harvard University Press, 1988);

Paul Turner, *Tennyson* (Boston & London: Routledge & Kegan Paul, 1976).

Papers:

Tennyson materials are scattered around the world. The major collection of correspondence and manuscripts is at the Tennyson Research Centre, Lincoln, England. A vast family archive is housed at the Lincolnshire Archives Office, Lincoln. Among other important collections are those at Trinity College, Cambridge University; Houghton Library, Harvard University; Beinecke Library, Yale University; Perkins Library, Duke University; and the British Library.

William Makepeace Thackeray
(18 July 1811 - 24 December 1863)

This entry was updated by Edgar F. Harden (Simon Fraser University) from his entry in
DLB 21: Victorian Novelists Before 1885.

See also the Thackeray entry in DLB 55: Victorian Prose Writers Before 1867.

BOOKS: *Flore et Zéphyr: Ballet Mythologique par Théophile Wagstaffe* (London: Mitchell, 1836);

The Yellowplush Correspondence, as Charles J. Yellowplush (Philadelphia: Carey & Hart, 1838);

Reminiscences of Major Gahagan, as Goliah O'Grady Gahagan (Philadelphia: Carey & Hart, 1839);

An Essay on the Genius of George Cruikshank (London: Hooper, 1840);

The Paris Sketch Book, by Mr. Titmarsh, 2 volumes (London: Macrone, 1840; New York: Appleton, 1852);

The Second Funeral of Napoleon, in Three Letters to Miss Smith of London; and The Chronicle of the Drum, by Mr. M. A. Titmarsh (London: Cunningham, 1841); republished as *The Second Funeral of Napoleon, by M. A. Titmarsh and Critical Reviews* (New York: Lovell, 1883);

Comic Tales and Sketches, Edited and Illustrated by Mr. Michael Angelo Titmarsh, 2 volumes (London: Cunningham, 1841);

The Irish Sketch Book, by Mr. M. A. Titmarsh (2 volumes, London: Chapman & Hall, 1843; 1 volume, New York: Winchester, 1843);

Jeames's Diary (New York: Taylor, 1846);

Notes of a Journey from Cornhill to Grand Cairo, by Way of Lisbon, Athens, Constantinople, and Jerusalem, Performed in the Steamers of the Peninsular and Oriental Company, by Mr. M. A. Titmarsh (London: Chapman & Hall, 1846; New York: Wiley & Putnam, 1846);

Mrs. Perkins's Ball, by Mr. M. A. Titmarsh (London: Chapman & Hall, 1847);

Vanity Fair: A Novel without a Hero (19 monthly parts, London: Bradbury & Evans, 1847-1848; 2 volumes, New York: Harper, 1848);

The Book of Snobs (London: Punch Office, 1848; New York: Appleton, 1852);

Our Street, by Mr. M. A. Titmarsh (London: Chapman & Hall, 1848);

The Great Hoggarty Diamond (New York: Harper, 1848); republished as *The History of Samuel Titmarsh and the Great Hoggarty Diamond* (London: Bradbury & Evans, 1849);

The History of Pendennis. His Fortunes and Misfortunes, His Friends and His Greatest Enemy (23 monthly parts, London: Bradbury & Evans,

1848-1850; 2 volumes, New York: Harper, 1850);

Doctor Birch and His Young Friends, by Mr. M. A. Titmarsh (London: Chapman & Hall, 1849; New York: Appleton, 1853);

Miscellanies: Prose and Verse, 8 volumes (Leipzig: Tauchnitz, 1849-1857);

The Kickleburys on the Rhine, by Mr. M. A. Titmarsh (London: Smith, Elder, 1850; New York: Stringer & Townsend, 1851);

Stubbs's Calendar; or, The Fatal Boots (New York: Stringer & Townsend, 1850);

Rebecca and Rowena: A Romance upon Romance, by Mr. M. A. Titmarsh (London: Chapman & Hall, 1850; New York: Appleton, 1853);

The History of Henry Esmond, Esq., a Colonel in the Service of Her Majesty Q. Anne, Written by Himself (3 volumes, London: Smith, Elder, 1852; 1 volume, New York: Harper, 1852);

The Confessions of Fitz-Boodle; and Some Passages in the Life of Major Gahagan (New York: Appleton, 1852);

A Shabby Genteel Story and Other Tales (New York: Appleton, 1852);

Men's Wives (New York: Appleton, 1852);

The Luck of Barry Lyndon: A Romance of the Last Century, 2 volumes (New York: Appleton, 1852-1853);

Jeames's Diary, A Legend of the Rhine, and Rebecca and Rowena (New York: Appleton, 1853);

Mr. Brown's Letters to a Young Man about Town; with The Proser and Other Papers (New York: Appleton, 1853);

Punch's Prize Novelists, The Fat Contributor, and Travels in London (New York: Appleton, 1853);

The English Humourists of the Eighteenth Century: A Series of Lectures Delivered in England, Scotland, and the United States of America (London: Smith, Elder, 1853; New York: Harper, 1853);

The Newcomes. Memoirs of a Most Respectable Family, Edited by Arthur Pendennis Esqre. (23 monthly parts, London: Bradbury & Evans, 1853-1855; 2 volumes, New York: Harper, 1855);

The Rose and the Ring; or, The History of Prince Giglio and Prince Bulbo: A Fireside Pantomime for Great and Small Children (London: Smith, Elder, 1855; New York: Harper, 1855);

Miscellanies: Prose and Verse, 4 volumes (London: Bradbury & Evans, 1855-1857);

Ballads (Boston: Ticknor & Fields, 1856);

Christmas Books (London: Chapman & Hall, 1857; Philadelphia: Lippincott, 1872);

The Virginians: A Tale of the Last Century (24 monthly parts, London: Bradbury & Evans, 1857-1859; 1 volume, New York: Harper, 1859);

The Four Georges: Sketches of Manners, Morals, Court and Town Life (New York: Harper, 1860; London: Smith, Elder, 1861);

Lovel the Widower (New York: Harper, 1860; London: Smith, Elder, 1861);

The Adventures of Philip on His Way through the World; Shewing Who Robbed Him, Who Helped Him, and Who Passed Him By (3 volumes, London: Smith, Elder, 1862; 1 volume, New York: Harper, 1862);

Roundabout Papers (London: Smith, Elder, 1863; New York: Harper, 1863);

Denis Duval (New York: Harper, 1864; London: Smith, Elder, 1867);

Early and Late Papers Hitherto Uncollected, edited by J. T. Fields (Boston: Ticknor & Fields, 1867);

Miscellanies, Volume IV (Boston: Osgood, 1870);

The Orphan of Pimlico; and Other Sketches, Fragments, and Drawings, with notes by A. I. Thackeray (London: Smith, Elder, 1876);

Sultan Stork and Other Stories and Sketches (1829-44), Now First Collected, edited by R. H. Sheppard (London: Redway, 1887);

Loose Sketches, An Eastern Adventure, Etc. (London: Sabin, 1894);

The Hitherto Unidentified Contributions of W. M. Thackeray to Punch, with a Complete Authoritative Bibliography from 1845 to 1848, edited by M. H. Spielmann (London & New York: Harper, 1899);

Mr. Thackeray's Writings in the "National Standard" and the "Constitutional," edited by W. T. Spencer (London: Spencer, 1899);

Stray Papers: Being Stories, Reviews, Verses, and Sketches 1821-47, edited by "Lewis Melville" (Lewis S. Benjamin) (London: Hutchinson, 1901; Philadelphia: Jacobs, 1901);

The New Sketch Book: Being Essays Now First Collected from the "Foreign Quarterly Review," edited by R. S. Garnett (London: Rivers, 1906);

Thackeray's Contributions to the "Morning Chronicle," edited by Gordon N. Ray (Urbana: University of Illinois Press, 1955).

Collections: *The Works of William Makepeace Thackeray,* Library Edition, 22 volumes (London: Smith, Elder, 1867-1869);

The Works of William Makepeace Thackeray, Biographical Edition, 13 volumes (London: Smith, Elder, 1898-1899);

The Works of William Makepeace Thackeray, 20 volumes, edited by "Lewis Melville" (Lewis S. Benjamin) (London: Macmillan, 1901-1907);

The Oxford Thackeray, 17 volumes (London: Oxford University Press, 1908);

The Works of William Makepeace Thackeray, Centenary Biographical Edition, 26 volumes (London: Smith, Elder, 1910-1911);

The Works of William Makepeace Thackeray, A Critical Edition (New York & London: Garland, 1989-   ).

SELECTED PERIODICAL PUBLICATIONS—
UNCOLLECTED:

FICTION

"The Professor," as Major Goliah O'Grady Gahagan, *Bentley's Miscellany* (September 1837);

"The Yellowplush Correspondence," as Charles J. Yellowplush, *Fraser's Magazine* (November 1837 - August 1838; January 1840);

"Some Passages in the Life of Major Gahagan," as Major Goliah O'Grady Gahagan, *New Monthly Magazine* (February 1838 - February 1839);

"Catherine: A Story," as Ikey Solomons, Esq., Junior, *Fraser's Magazine* (May 1839 - February 1840);

"The Bedford-Row Conspiracy," anonymous, *New Monthly Magazine* (January-April 1840);

"A Shabby Genteel Story," anonymous, *Fraser's Magazine* (June-October 1840);

"The History of Samuel Titmarsh and the Great Hoggarty Diamond," as Michael Angelo Titmarsh, *Fraser's Magazine* (September-December 1841);

"The Luck of Barry Lyndon: A Romance of the Last Century," as George Fitz-Boodle, *Fraser's Magazine* (January-December 1844);

"Lovel the Widower," as Batchelor, *Cornhill Magazine* (January-June 1860);

"The Adventures of Philip," as Arthur Pendennis, *Cornhill Magazine* (January 1861 - August 1862);

"Denis Duval," as Denis Duval, *Cornhill Magazine* (March-June 1864).

NONFICTION

"Il était un Roi d'Yvetot—Béranger—The King of Brentford," anonymous, *Fraser's Magazine* (May 1834);

"Carlyle's *French Revolution,*" anonymous, *Times* (London), 3 August 1837;

"Our Batch of Novels for Christmas 1837," anonymous, *Fraser's Magazine* (January 1838);

"A Diary Relative to George IV and Queen Caroline, by Lady Charlotte Bury," anonymous, *Times* (London), 11 January 1838;

"Strictures on Pictures," as Michael Angelo Titmarsh, *Fraser's Magazine* (June 1838);

"A Second Letter on the Fine Arts," as Michael Angelo Titmarsh, *Fraser's Magazine* (June 1839);

"A Pictorial Rhapsody," as Michael Angelo Titmarsh, *Fraser's Magazine* (June-July 1840);

"George Cruikshank's Works," anonymous, *London and Westminster Review* (June 1840);

"Going to See a Man Hanged," anonymous, *Fraser's Magazine* (August 1840);

"Fielding's *Works,*" anonymous, *Times* (London), 2 September 1840;

"Memorials of Gourmandizing," as Michael Angelo Titmarsh, *Fraser's Magazine* (June 1841);

"Sultan Stork," as Major Goliah O'Grady Gahagan, *Ainsworth's Magazine* (February-March 1842);

"Fitz-Boodle's Confessions," as George Fitz-Boodle, *Fraser's Magazine* (June 1842 - November 1843);

"The Legend of Jawbrahim-Heraudee," anonymous, *Punch* (18 June 1842);

"The Last Fifteen Years of the Bourbons," anonymous, *Foreign Quarterly Review* (July 1842);

"Mrs. Tickletoby's Lectures on English History," anonymous, *Punch* (2 July - 1 October 1842);

"Bluebeard's Ghost," as Michael Angelo Titmarsh, *Fraser's Magazine* (October 1843);

"The History of the Next French Revolution," anonymous, *Punch* (24 February - 20 April 1844);

"Jesse's *Life of George Brummell, Esq.*," anonymous, *Morning Chronicle*, 6 May 1844;

"Greenwich—Whitebait," as Lancelot Wagstaff, *New Monthly Magazine* (July 1844);

"Wanderings of our Fat Contributor," as the Fat Contributor, *Punch* (3 August 1844 - 8 February 1845);

"Picture Gossip," as Michael Angelo Titmarsh, *Fraser's Magazine* (June 1845);

"A Legend of the Rhine," anonymous, *George Cruikshank's Table Book* (June-December 1845);

"Jeames's Diary," as C. Jeames De La Pluche, *Punch* (8 November 1845 - 7 February 1846);

"The Snobs of England. By One of Themselves," anonymous, *Punch* (23 February 1846 - 27 February 1847);

"Proposals for a Continuation of *Ivanhoe*," as Michael Angelo Titmarsh, *Fraser's Magazine* (August-September 1846);

"*Punch*'s Prize Novelists," anonymous, *Punch* (3 April - 9 October 1847);

"Travels in London," as Spec, *Punch* (20 November 1847 - 25 March 1848);

"Mr. Brown's Letters to a Young Man about Town," as Mr. Brown, *Punch* (24 March - 18 August 1849);

"The Dignity of Literature," *Morning Chronicle*, 12 January 1850;

"The Proser," as Dr. Solomon Pacifico, *Punch* (20 April - 3 August 1850);

"Roundabout Papers," as Mr. Roundabout, *Cornhill Magazine* (January 1860 - November 1863);

"The Four Georges," anonymous, *Cornhill Magazine* (July-October 1860).

Like many of his fellow Victorian novelists, William Makepeace Thackeray is noted for his ability to create memorable characters—such as Major Gahagan, Charles Yellowplush, Becky Sharp, Major Pendennis, Henry and Beatrix Es-

mond, Colonel Newcome, and, not least of all, the roundabout commentator who addresses the reader in Thackeray's nonfiction as well as in his fiction. In spite of giving such prominence to character delineation, Thackeray also came to develop an important new kind of novel, the "novel without a hero." Such a novel may have a chief figure: one who is neither a romantic hero nor a rogue hero but a flawed, recognizable human being like Arthur Pendennis or Philip Firmin. In the case of several of Thackeray's masterpieces, such as *Vanity Fair* (1847-1848) and *The Newcomes* (1853-1855), however, the center of interest is the complex of relationships among the characters—an analogue of society itself.

Thackeray's writing is important for being governed by an intense historical awareness that constantly reveals itself in the precise, concrete detail of an evoked visible world, but also in a persistent consciousness of the flow of time, which ages both things and human experience, diminishing both and calling the value of both into question. Here Thackeray gives eloquent and pronounced articulation to several of the most deeply rooted Victorian, and indeed modern, concerns. In creative tension with this historical awareness, moreover, is Thackeray's satire, which is not limited and local but beyond time and place, radically challenging the reader's most fundamental assumptions about human life, but doing so in a voice that always evokes a personal· human presence alongside the reader. He therefore gave a new prominence to the commentary of narrative personae and so offered a permanently valuable counterstance to what later came to be their pronounced opposites in the impressive dramatic novels of Henry James. Finally, one can see the importance of the wit and philosophical irony of Thackeray's fictional voices, with the constant shifting of perspective that alone can mediate to the reader the profound indeterminacy at the heart of his writing—an indeterminacy that finds its counterpart in much subsequent literature.

Service with the British East India Company's Bengal establishment characterized Thackeray's immediate male ancestors on both sides of his family. Thackeray himself was born in Calcutta in 1811 to a well-to-do official of the company. The first major shock of the child's life came not long after his fourth birthday with the death of his father at the age of thirty-three. The second trauma occurred fifteen months later, when he was sent out of the dangerous Indian climate to England for schooling, his twenty-four-

Thackeray, about three years old, with his parents in India

year-old mother remaining behind with the man she was to marry three months later, an officer in the company's military service. In recalling the event years later, Thackeray generalized about this aspect of Anglo-Indian experience: "What a strange pathos seems to me to accompany all our Indian story! Besides that official history . . . should not one remember the tears, too? . . . The lords of the subject province find wives there: but their children cannot live on the soil. . . . The family must be broken up. . . . In America it is from the breast of a poor slave that a child is taken: in India it is from the wife, and from under the palace, of a splendid proconsul."

The pain was intensified at Thackeray's school at Southampton, "which was governed by a horrible little tyrant, who made our young lives so miserable that I remember kneeling by my little bed of a night, and saying, 'Pray God, I may dream of my mother!' " Eventual transfer to a school at Chiswick provided some relief until the separation from his mother ended after three

and a half years, when she and her husband arrived in England just before Thackeray's ninth birthday. After only a month of vacation together, however, Thackeray was sent off to Charterhouse, his stepfather's former school in London. Six rather unpleasant years at Charterhouse constituted what Thackeray later called "that strange ordeal" of life in an early-nineteenth-century English boarding school, which seemed chiefly notable for the emotional privation and physical brutality a young boy had to endure, together with "the foolish old-world superstitions . . . the wretched portion of letters meted out to him . . . the misery, vice, and folly, which were taught along with the small share of Greek and Latin."

Thackeray managed to find some solace during his last three years at Charterhouse by boarding in a private house nearby and being fortunate enough to associate there with a small group of talented boys of lively interests that ranged from literature and private theatricals to the periodicals of the day and the comical prints of artists such as George Cruikshank. Their companionship, and active private reading of his own, proved more emotionally and intellectually educative than Charterhouse, where the headmaster's increasing indulgence in satire and ridicule of Thackeray made the boy feel "bullied into despair," as he later wrote to his mother. Weekend excursions into London also proved liberating, especially when Thackeray could attend the theater, imaginatively participate in the romance or boisterous comedy of the stage, and enjoy the fantasy of being in love with a particularly fascinating actress.

Emotionally, however, the chief antithesis to Charterhouse was the home to which he could now go during vacations—especially Larkbeare House, near Ottery St. Mary in Devon, where his mother and stepfather lived between 1824 and 1835. Here he dawdled about the house and grounds, drawing hundreds of caricatures, scribbling verses—partly in the style of George Gordon, Lord Byron and Thomas Moore—and reading widely, his favorite novels being the romances of Sir Walter Scott, James Fenimore Cooper, and other popular writers of the period. His most energetic activity was apparently horseback riding, which allowed him to visit nearby Exeter with its fine cathedral, ruined castle, excellent inns, and theater. He became a published author in 1828 with the appearance in an Exeter newspaper of a comical poem on an Irish politician, fol-

Larkbeare, the Devonshire home of his mother and stepfather, where Thackeray spent happy vacations away from Charterhouse

lowed by a translation of an amatory ode by Anacreon. Years later he gave some of these experiences imaginative expression in the opening of *The History of Pendennis* (1848-1850), the most emotionally compelling vignette being the engraving "Calm Summer Evenings" and its accompanying prose rendering of "a profusion of . . . embraces" between mother and son alone together on a terrace at sunset.

After entering Trinity College, Cambridge, in early 1829, Thackeray came to find its emphasis upon classical studies and especially mathematics rather stultifying. Intermittent efforts at studies that he found uncongenial turned more and more desultory; his chief pleasures came in reading modern literature, in contributing comical pieces to undergraduate magazines (the *Snob* and the *Gownsman*), in joining a debating society, and in mingling socially with his fellows. The first of what were to be many Continental trips took place during the summer of 1829, which was spent chiefly in Paris, where Thackeray developed a fascination for gambling. After sixteen months' residence at Cambridge, he gave up formal study as a waste of time and left without his degree. Besides expensive habits of personal living,

he left Cambridge with gambling debts of fifteen hundred pounds, having been victimized by two professional card players.

Germany attracted him for the next eight months, much of which was spent pleasantly at Weimar, where he studied German, read, translated, and mingled with the local society (including the aged Johann Wolfgang von Goethe) and its foreign visitors—a period he later spoke of as "days of youth the most kindly and delightful." Since Thackeray's gambling days at Paris and his debacle at the university, his mother's reproaches and his own feelings of guilt had made him both defensive and penitent. On the one hand, he could tell his mother that her letters "always make me sorrowful . . . for there seems some hidden cause of dissatisfaction, some distrust which you do not confess & cannot conceal & for which on looking into myself I can find no grounds or reason," yet on the other hand he could acknowledge still being "too open" to "idleness irresolution & extravagance," and having "*deserved*" her dissatisfaction with his "unworthiness." As part of his effort to win from her "one day . . . something like satisfaction & confidence in me," he agreed to study for the bar, and after his return to London he was admitted to the Middle Temple in June 1831.

At the time, law seemed a much more plausible profession to him than the church, the army, or medicine, but by January 1832 he was calling preparatory legal education "certainly one of the most cold blooded prejudiced pieces of invention that ever a man was slave to." As his legal studies became more occasional, they were succeeded by miscellaneous reading, leisurely dining, frequent visits to the opera and the theater, intermittent gambling, and late hours that typically led to ensuing days of "seediness repentance & novel reading." He had become one of that group he was later to term "the Temple Bohemians." Although he dallied with various schemes for producing income—drawing for a print seller, writing for a newspaper, and composing a novel—the only enterprise he actually took up was an electioneering campaign in Devon and Cornwall for a friend during part of June and July 1832. By this time he had told his mother of a formal decision to give up the study of law and briefly mentioned an implausible alternative: "I am thinking of turning Parson & being a useful member of society."

A more characteristic decision took him to France, where he remained from August until November 1832, mainly at Paris. By this time— evidently out of guilt and shame at the repeated failure of his attempts to resist gambling— Thackeray resorted to the practice of shifting from English to German when making diary entries recording his fortunes at play; the foreign language seemed to serve the function of a private cipher. Thus he would laconically note: "spielte und verlierte acht pfund" ("gambled and lost eight pounds"), "spielte und winnte fünf pfund" ("gambled and won five pounds"), and more unhappily, "spielte und wie gewohnlich verlierte" ("gambled and, as usual, lost"). In France his play continued: "have in these latter days been to Paris wo ich spielte."

Aside from occasional serious reading, he spent much of his time sketching, dining, imbibing, dancing, theatergoing, and dawdling about in idle company. He found himself "growing loving on every pleasant married woman I see," and although "talking of debauchery & consequences" made him "long for a good wife, & a happy home," he also found himself recording a new transgression in his private "cipher": "spielte und fegelte" ("gambled and fornicated"). More lawful pleasures included burning a collection of salacious books ("meine schlechte Bucher") and

A sketch by Thackeray of two professional cardsharps, like those who cheated him at Cambridge

engaging in further musings about writing a novel, which he felt would be witty in nature, though he still had no idea of a possible plot. He also had the more immediately practicable notion of extending his knowledge of modern French writing, so that he could compose an article for one of the English reviews.

Back in London by the end of the year, he engaged for several months in bill discounting, with indeterminate results, and in May 1833 bought a recently founded two-penny weekly newspaper, the *National Standard and Journal of Literature, Science, Music, Theatricals, and the Fine Arts*. The paper served as a natural sequel to his undergraduate involvement with the *Snob* and the *Gownsman*, calling forth from him comic verses and sketches—both verbal and pictorial—of French and English political and theatrical figures. The lightheartedness of Thackeray's efforts also reflected itself in the casualness of his participation: much of the newspaper's copy was edited from other publications with the help of a subeditor. Within a few weeks of buying the paper, he settled in Paris, serving for several months as correspondent for the *National Standard*, before again taking up the study of painting as his main activity. Although the newspaper venture did not draw significantly upon Thackeray's talent, it was an important experience, for it marked the beginning of his involvement with periodical journalism.

But 1833 proved even more crucial to Thackeray's fortunes by being the year in which he lost his patrimony. His payment the previous year of gambling losses and his comfortable style of living had begun the process of dissipating his inheritance, but the resounding failure of Indian financial houses at this time accounted for most of the depletion, so that at the end of October he alluded to the loss of eleven thousand pounds, and by the end of the year he accurately described himself as poor. He reluctantly left Paris for London, where he struggled to keep the *National Standard* alive; but he gave up in February 1834, losing several hundred more pounds. During the fall of 1834 he returned to Paris with his maternal grandmother to resume once again the study of painting, which he had described a year previously as "the only metier I ever liked." Taking advantage of the low cost of living and enjoying the pleasures of being an art student in Paris, the twenty-three-year-old Thackeray experienced what he later recalled as "a very jolly time. I was as poor as Job: and sketched away most abominably, but pretty contented: and we used to meet in each others little rooms and talk about Art and smoke pipes and drink bad brandy & water."

His failure to make any significant progress in his studies came to be depressing, but after a year of frustrated, sometimes desultory effort, his spirits were lightened when he fell in love during the summer of 1835 with "a girl without a penny in the world," Isabella Shawe. The daughter of a deceased Irish army officer, Isabella was an uncomplicated seventeen-year-old living in a Paris boardinghouse with her domineering mother, who became the prototype for unpleasant mothers-in-law throughout Thackeray's fiction. At first Mrs. Shawe tolerated Thackeray's courtship of Isabella, but later she tried to disrupt the relationship as Thackeray worked to improve his financial prospects. First, he apparently took employment with an English newspaper published in Paris, but this venture seems to have had a quick demise in early 1836. Then, the finan-

A sketch by Daniel Maclise of Thackeray in 1832 (Garrick Club)

cial support of a friend helped arrange the appearance in London and Paris during March or (more likely) April 1836 of Thackeray's first separate publication: a series of eight tersely captioned lithographs, together with an illustrated title page, called *Flore et Zéphyr: Ballet Mythologique*. This venture of Thackeray's also seems to have been a failure, however, for it attracted no significant notice. Finally, he became involved in another newspaper enterprise.

Meanwhile, the appearance of *Flore et Zéphyr* under the pseudonym "Théophile Wagstaffe" showed not only Thackeray's interest in ballet and his humble skills as a draftsman but also the fact that his abilities as a graphic artist expressed themselves best in the form of burlesque and caricature. Even more, in retrospect one can see *Flore et Zéphyr* as a quintessential expression of his artistic vision. To begin with, it is a work that Thackeray drew and captioned under one of his many pseudonyms—a self-conscious, waggish role that itself combines various perspectives, psychological and social, generalizing and personal.

434

The work is also quite allusive, adopting the title of a neoclassical ballet, choreographed by Charles Didelot, that had been given its London premiere in 1796, had been restaged at the Paris Opéra in 1815, and had been revived thereafter. One of Thackeray's favorite dancers, Marie Taglioni, had used it as a vehicle for her London debut in June 1830; Thackeray may have seen it at that time, especially because his enthusiasm for Taglioni had been aroused eleven months previously when he saw her dance in Jean Aumer's *La Fille mal Gardée* at the Paris Opéra. Since Taglioni repeated her role in the ballet during 1831 in Paris and London, and again in London during 1833, when Thackeray was in residence, his allusions would have been readily understandable to audiences in both cities where his series of caricatures was published.

In *Flore et Zéphyr*, however, Thackeray does more than burlesque Taglioni's aging vehicle and her costars. The caption of the first lithograph, "La danse fait ses offrandes sur l'autel de l'harmonie" ("The dance makes its offerings at the altar of harmony"), reveals in fact that Thackeray is burlesquing ballet itself. As his art was characteristically to do, *Flore et Zéphyr* focuses upon a series of fundamental ironic discrepancies. For one thing, Thackeray emphasizes the disjunction between the conventions of artistic behavior (here the poses or gestures of the dance) and the actual human emotions meant to be expressed by those conventions, especially grave emotions of sorrow and despair. For another thing, he directs comic attention to the discrepancy between the ethereal costumes, settings, and whole mythological dimension of the ballet on the one hand, and the human reality of the performers, with their unravishing features and unclassical figures, on the other. Similarly, he stresses the disjunction between the ideal beings enacted upon the stage and the crude, everyday human beings who witness them from the theater seats. Finally, Thackeray takes the dancers offstage after the ballet has ended; to modify the language of his final caption, "Les Délassements de Zéphyr," he "declasses" them by showing the discrepancies between the ennobled stage roles of the performers and their own everyday selves amid the mild sordidness of their real lives and those of their unprepossessing admirers. The final resting point of the series, then, is an ironic awareness of the limiting conditions of everyday human life.

Thackeray's third effort to establish a financial basis for marriage to Isabella Shawe was as-

A self-portrait of Thackeray in 1835. The inscription indicates the financial difficulties he was having at the time (Huntington Library).

sisted by his stepfather, Major Carmichael-Smyth, who agreed to invest in the revival of a London newspaper that was to be renamed the *Constitutional and Public Ledger* and was to be an organ of political Radicalism. Thackeray, in addition to the yearly income of £100 saved from the wreck of his fortune, was to draw eight guineas a week (£450 a year) as Paris correspondent of the *Constitutional*. With the prospect of such an income, he understandably felt himself not only financially able to marry Isabella but to have a happy prospect of "competence & reputation." He was mistaken, however, for instead of being free of "a doubtful future, a precarious profession, and a long and trying probation," he was to find that those grim phrases described exactly what he would have to endure.

If the art of the mature Thackeray can be discerned in work of these Paris years, so too can

Title page of Thackeray's first published book

his psychic habit of considering himself old before his time. Thus, while still twenty-four, he told Isabella that he was "a sulky grey headed old fellow" and in spite of his comic overstatement conveyed the sense not only of being jaded by experience but also of being especially attracted by Isabella's naive, childlike nature. After a great and protracted struggle with her mother, Thackeray and Isabella were married in August 1836 in Paris; he was twenty-five and she five and a half years younger. Within a month Isabella was pregnant, and though Thackeray's contributions to the *Constitutional* now began, the prospect of a family goaded him to make efforts to discover additional outlets for his talents in the fields of journalism and illustration. Earlier that year, while plans were still being formulated for the *Constitutional*, he had unsuccessfully applied to Charles Dickens for the job of illustrating *The*

Pickwick Papers to replace the recently deceased Robert Seymour. Additional schemes as etcher, Paris correspondent for a second English newspaper, contributor to a friend's periodical, and illustrator of W. Harrison Ainsworth's *Crichton* (1837) all came to naught, as did a proposal to minor publisher John Macrone for a two-volume work with illustrations to be called "Rambles & Sketches in old and new Paris"—though the latter project would eventually culminate in *The Paris Sketch Book* (1840).

Meanwhile, as the *Constitutional* remained unable to attract enough subscribers and Major Carmichael-Smyth assumed more and more financial responsibility for the newspaper, whose Radical views he warmly endorsed, Thackeray moved to London in March 1837 to help consolidate their affairs. He brought Isabella with him, and their first child, Anne, was born in June. For all Thackeray's journalistic and entrepreneurial efforts, however, the *Constitutional* ceased publication on 1 July, placing Major Carmichael-Smyth in financial difficulties and leaving Thackeray unemployed once again—indeed, poorer than ever, for he transferred all of the income from the small remainder of his inherited capital to his stepfather. The Carmichael-Smyths in turn migrated to Paris, where living expenses were significantly cheaper and where creditors could not have them imprisoned for debt.

Thackeray's career as an independent writer, free of familial subsidy, now necessarily began. The first of a dozen anonymous reviews for the *Times* appeared in August 1837 with a favorable notice of *The French Revolution* by Thomas Carlyle, who shortly thereafter spoke of Thackeray as "now writing for his life in London." The following month, the first of Thackeray's magazine tales, "The Professor"—a comic extravaganza about Dando, an impostor fond of oysters and ladies—came out pseudonymously in *Bentley's Magazine*. Although no more of Thackeray's stories were published in *Bentley's*, November 1837 marked the beginning of a sustained relationship with *Fraser's Magazine* as Thackeray's first series of tales, "The Yellowplush Correspondence," began to appear. The first paper was occasioned by a recently published book of fashionable etiquette, the vulgarity of which induced Thackeray to invent as an appropriate reviewer an illiterate footman, Charles J. Yellowplush, who mocked the book from the posture of his more "knowing" experience of the fashionable world—thereby not only undermining the book's claims but also exposing his own naïveté.

Thackeray's sense of the possibilities of the Yellowplush persona was such that he went on to write seven more papers under that name, with occasional illustrations. Most of them were completely fictional, especially the extended accounts of Yellowplush's corrupting service with the Honorable Algernon Percy Deuceace, a disreputable nobleman who was partly modeled upon gamblers and other raffish types whom Thackeray had met in England and on the Continent. Several of the papers, however, reverted to the review format in satirizing Lady Charlotte Bury's gossipy, pretentious *Diary Illustrative of the Times of George the Fourth* and Dionysius Lardner's ponderous *Cabinet Cyclopaedia*, as well as Edward Bulwer-Lytton's literary pretensions. With an adieu in August 1838, Yellowplush's correspondence broke off, except for the appearance in January 1840 of the final paper, "Epistles to the Literati," which satirized Bulwer-Lytton's inept drama *The Sea Captain* (1839) and its apologetic preface.

After publishing the first two Yellowplush papers in *Fraser's Magazine* during November 1837 and January 1838, Thackeray began what grew into another series, which came out irregularly in the *New Monthly Magazine* between February 1838 and February of the following year. Reviving the pseudonym loosely attached to "The Professor," Thackeray developed the name into a true persona: Major Goliah O'Grady Gahagan, the autobiographical narrator of what came to be known as "The Tremendous Adventures of Major Gahagan," another extravaganza—this time of love and war in British India during the time of Richard Colley, Marquis Wellesley. Combining amusing Irish braggadocio with the naive self-revelations of the narrator, Thackeray also found a vehicle for burlesquing military narratives; he accomplished this with extensive use of oral and written Anglo-Indian materials that had come to him through relatives, especially his stepfather, and through avid reading about the country where his father had prospered and died.

Thackeray spent March 1838 in France, mostly Paris, where he combined pleasure with business—recounting Yellowplush's adventures abroad, doing an article for the *Times*, and drawing a caricature for *Fraser's*—but also reading and gathering visual impressions for what he described as "the book"—the work about Paris he had proposed to Macrone more than a year be-

Thackeray's mother with his stepfather, Major Carmichael-Smyth, who invested in one of Thackeray's ill-fated business ventures

fore. On his return to London he submitted a long Yellowplush paper to *Fraser's*, "Mr. Deuceace in Paris," which was printed in three installments. He also began planning a short, twelve-part rogue's autobiography called *Stubbs's Calendar; or, The Fatal Boots*, relating the multifarious failed schemes of Bob Stubbs; illustrated by his friend George Cruikshank, it appeared shortly before Christmas in the *Comic Annual for 1839*, published by Charles Tilt.

Perhaps Thackeray's most significant nonfictional work of 1838, "Strictures on Pictures," appeared in the June issue of *Fraser's* under what was to become Thackeray's favorite pseudonym, "Michael Angelo Titmarsh," the persona of an artist and critic of art whose chief resemblance to his famous namesake is a broken nose, which Thackeray had himself received during a fight at Charterhouse. As in Thackeray's own case, Titmarsh's appreciation of painting far exceeds his capacity to execute it. As Thackeray's first critical article for *Fraser's* on the annual May exhibition of pictures at the Royal Academy, "Strictures on Pictures" gave him an opportunity to express not only his judgments on the work of contemporary painters but also some of the central principles of his aesthetic outlook. The first of these he states immediately: the necessity of an artist's "feeling for the beauty of Nature, which is . . . neither more nor less than Art." Hence, Thackeray's is a credo of realism limited by the artist's feeling for the beauty of what he observes around him in everyday life. On the one hand, therefore, a heartless verisimilitude is found wanting by Thackeray; on the other hand, certain technical shortcomings in the painter's rendering are overshadowed by an ability to render his sympathetic response to observed beauty. Thus the figures are wooden in the painting *Crusaders Catching a First View of Jerusalem* by Keats's friend Joseph Severn, but the work embodies a "majestic and pious harmony." The religious nature of the subject is important, for Thackeray uses this particular picture to emphasize that there "is a higher ingredient in beauty than mere form; a skilful hand is only the second artistical quality, worthless . . . without the first, which is *a great heart*. This picture is beautiful, in spite of its defects." Citing Severn's picture of Ariel merrily riding through the evening sky on a bat's back, Thackeray argues that Severn "possesses that solemn earnestness and simplicity of mind and purpose which makes a religion of art"—by which Thackeray does not mean that art is an end in itself, but that the spiritual qualities of an artist such as Severn make the practice of his calling a religious act by its worship of the Creator. Such beliefs about art were maintained by Thackeray to the end of his career.

The essay is also remarkable for the way in which it reveals Thackeray's imagination responding to a certain picture of William Etty's that evidently deeply stirred memories of his own experience: "the prodigal kneeling down lonely in the stormy evening, and praying to Heaven for pardon." Not only does Thackeray vividly enter the picture and feel the atmospheric and spiritual powers manifesting themselves there—from the howling and chill of the wind, and the oppressive emblematic presence of the goat and boar, to the comforting promises of the star above—but, even more, he compulsively imagines the ongoing life of the prodigal as the promise is fulfilled and he is welcomed home. One can observe in this entire response Thackeray's lifelong tendency, derived especially from his eighteenth-century and classical heritage, to see human life in terms of a few

Thackeray's portrait of his wife, Isabella

central, ever-repeated patterns—fables, in fact, like that of the prodigal son, which his own life seemed to reflect. Even more, one notices in the narrative of the kneeling figure's subsequent life how closely "home and hope" are linked for Thackeray, and how the terrors of isolation and a sense of personal unworthiness are largely overcome by the figures who greet the wandering son: most immediately, "a good father, who loves you," and "a dear, kind, stout, old mother." (The narrator's direct address to the returning prodigal is also notable.) Realistically, there must also be "an elder brother, who hates you" and a prosperous childhood rival, but more than adequate compensation is imagined in the mother, "who liked you twice as well as the elder," and especially in the figures of the girl left behind but still faithful and the future mother-in-law who is not hostile but welcoming.

As Thackeray continued to write for his livelihood and to hope that better employment might gain him "a little durable reputation," his family grew with the birth in July 1838 of a second daughter, Jane. Following the appearance of "Mr. Yellowplush's Ajew" in August, Thackeray saw evidence that his recent work, at least, had attained an American reputation of sorts, for a Philadelphia publisher pirated some of it, publishing *The Yellowplush Correspondence* before the end of the year; ironically, it was the first separate volume of Thackeray's fiction to be published. Meanwhile, gleanings from the French journey began to appear in the *New Monthly Magazine* and in *Fraser's* during 1838, and in a new magazine for Thackeray, the *London and Westminster Review* of April 1839.

The following month's issue of *Fraser's* then brought out the first installment of a new illustrated serial, "Catherine: A Story," which appeared somewhat irregularly in seven installments between May 1839 and February 1840 and marked Thackeray's first use of an eighteenth-century setting, being based upon the life of a famous murderess, Catherine Hayes. Thackeray invented a new persona, "Ikey Solomons, Esq. Junior," the alleged son of a notorious London receiver of stolen goods who had been tried, convicted, and transported earlier in the 1830s. In "Catherine," however, the persona seems largely nominal; because of the educated nature of his language and a certain heaviness of irony in his addresses to the reader, one tends to feel that he gives direct expression to Thackeray's satirical anger. Hence, any awareness one may have of the distinction between narrator and author comes to be obliterated.

Another anomaly of "Catherine" is its eagerness to place itself in the context of literary controversy. Critics have often identified "Catherine" as an ironic version of a then-popular genre, Newgate fiction—narratives of the 1830s based upon eighteenth-century criminals and their adventures, which had been starkly reported in the Newgate Calendar but were now being treated in a manner that Thackeray satirically termed a reflection of "the present fashionable style and taste," since these "low" and "disgusting" subjects were made to seem "eminently pleasing and pathetic." In that context, the choice of Ikey Solomons as a narrative persona seems designed to make the

Frontispiece drawn by Thackeray for
The Paris Sketch Book

ironic point that Newgate novelists of the 1830s are in fact the willing heirs of criminals, whose morally and socially disruptive exploits they emulate with their novelistic adulation and encourage in their audiences.

Indeed, the burgeoning effects of such novels were some of Thackeray's most urgent concerns. He was therefore satirizing not simply Newgate novels but a variety of contemporary fictive creations that had in common their romanticizing of evil, whether it came from the Newgate Calendar and was being "fenced" to willing buyers, or whether it was being freshly invented in analogous works. From the sympathetic use of a rogue hero as well as a highwayman near the beginning of the decade by Bulwer-Lytton in *Paul Clifford* (1830) and *Eugene Aram* (1832)—to be followed by *Ernest Maltravers* (1837)—had come novels such as William Harrison Ainsworth's *Rookwood: A Romance* (1834), with the highwayman Dick Turpin for a hero, and Dickens's *Oliver Twist* (1837-1839), which encouraged its readers, Thackeray believed, to follow the crimes of Fagin breathlessly, with a morally anesthetized, merely narrative interest; to sympathize with the "errors" of Nancy; to respond with "a kind of pity and admiration" for Sikes; and to feel "an absolute love for the society of the Dodger."

Even more, the success of these novels caused theatrical entrepreneurs to exploit the public admiration still further by offering stage representations of the novels' characters. Inevitable results ensued, the most striking contemporary example being another highwayman romance of Ainsworth's—*Jack Sheppard*, which began appearing serially in January 1839 (four months before "Catherine") and which by the end of the year had been out on the stage, Thackeray emphasized, in "four different representations." As Thackeray wrote to his mother that December, the exploitation was carried so far that a receptive public was being offered "*Shepherd-bags*" [*sic*] in the lobby of one of these theaters, "a bag containing a few picklocks . . . [and] one or two gentlemen have already confessed how much they were indebted to Jack Sheppard who gave them ideas of pocketpicking and thieving wh. they never would have had but for the play." Accordingly, Thackeray intended "Catherine" not as a romance but as a realistic "cathartic" which depicted the viciousness of its rogues and concluded with an emphatic account of their gruesome fates. For all his aim to purge the public of its taste for the corrupting aspects of contemporary fiction, however, Thackeray also found himself intermittently engaged by the personages he was creating and came to acknowledge privately that he felt "a sneaking kindness for his heroine" that interfered with a full working out of his satirical intention.

During the late summer of 1839, Thackeray revisited Paris, this time with Isabella and their daughter Anne (Jane having died at the age of eight months in March of that year). One result of the visit was a two-month hiatus in the serial appearance of "Catherine," but another was a renewed impetus to write short articles on Paris that could be sent to *Fraser's Magazine* and later gathered into his long-planned book. Thackeray also worked on another twelve-part tale illustrated by Cruikshank in the *Comic Annual for 1840*, "Barber Cox and the Cutting of his

Comb," which relates the bumbling misadventures of a hero misled by the imperious pretensions of his wife until his happy fall back into his humble calling. France also provided Thackeray with a tale of a minor writer, Charles de Bernard, that Thackeray used as the basis of a three-part piece that appeared during early 1840 in the *New Monthly Magazine*, "The Bedford-Row Conspiracy," an amusing tale of one couple's successful love and marriage amid the social and political maneuvering of others. In its implicit defense of the hero's "idleness, simplicity, enthusiasm, and easy good-nature," and in its endorsement of the heroine's struggle against aggressive female dominance, the tale seems to reflect important aspects of Thackeray's and Isabella's lives, but the future is also anticipated as Thackeray turns away from rogue narrative toward greater dramatization of social behavior generated by the interaction of middle- and upper-class characters.

Between March and September 1840, Thackeray was "in a ceaseless whirl and whizz from morning to night, now with the book, now with the drawings, now with articles for Times, Fraser, here and there." His miscellaneous pieces included a sixty-page essay on Cruikshank's works for the *London and Westminster Review* (soon published separately as well); his annual review of the May Royal Academy exhibition for *Fraser's*; the beginning of a new serial for *Fraser's* called "A Shabby Genteel Story"; a memorable article on François Benjamin Courvoisier's execution— "Going to See a Man Hanged"—also for *Fraser's*; a review of Henry Fielding's *Works* for the *Times*; and especially the two-volume book on Thackeray's French experiences, published by Cunningham for the recently deceased Macrone, entitled *The Paris Sketch Book* and published under the Titmarsh pseudonym.

The latter work, which appeared in July 1840, more or less equally mixed previously published articles and stories with new material. Of the nineteen pieces, eight were fictional (including adaptations from the French); one was a group of translations of Pierre-Jean de Béranger's poems; and the rest were reviews of French art and literature and sketches of French manners and customs. Thackeray also illustrated the book, which he comically dedicated to his French tailor, who had lent him money during its composition. The book had a modest success, though only the *Spectator* and Thackeray seemed to like the illustrations. The most important results of

Thackeray's success with *The Paris Sketch Book*, however, seem to have been the encouragement of the author, the growth of his reputation, and the finding of an additional publisher.

Following the birth in May of another daughter, Harriet Marian, Isabella seemed to recover normally from her confinement. Consequently, at the beginning of August, Thackeray enthusiastically dashed over to Belgium for a two-week stay that was intended both as a holiday and as a preparation for "a little book on Belgium & the Rhine." By the time of his departure he had also made plans for a two-volume work to be called "Titmarsh in Ireland," and he looked forward to being freed from "that odious magazine-work, wh. wd. kill any writer in 6 years." Upon his return to England, he found his wife in "an extraordinary state of languor and depression" that persisted in spite of his efforts to cheer her up and that also resisted medical diagnosis. It diminished somewhat during a recommended holiday at a seaside resort, but resumed on their return to London. Thackeray therefore held in abeyance his plans for the travel book on Belgium and the Rhine, turning instead to his Irish project. He made plans to take Isabella and the children to her mother and sister, who were living at Cork, and on 8 September 1840 he signed a contract for the Irish book with his new publishers, Chapman and Hall, that provided him with a much-needed advance of £120. He also completed the fourth installment of "A Shabby Genteel Story" for *Fraser's*, suspending it in a manner that permitted him to resume at some undetermined future date. (He was never to complete the work but in 1861-1862 wrote a sequel, *The Adventures of Philip*, which summarizes the earlier tale and draws upon the ending he had intended to write for it.)

On the boat to Ireland, Isabella tried to commit suicide by throwing herself into the sea, but she was rescued and prevented from making another attempt. For the remaining fifty-three years of her life, though there were periods of improvement, she remained insane. Eventually, she had to be put away, but not before Thackeray had explored the best means of restoring her that he could discover. An Irish doctor seemed at first to provide assistance, but after a month spent enduring Isabella's ceaselessly aggressive mother, whom Thackeray came to consider somewhat deranged herself, he made for Paris and the help of his own mother; passing through London, he arranged with Cunningham for publication of his

Thackeray's title page showing Charles J. Yellowplush and Major Goliah O'Grady Gahagan leading Michael Angelo Titmarsh "to the very brink of immortality"

"comic miscellanies." In Paris he entrusted his children to his mother and grandmother; placed his wife in the care of Esquirol's, one of the leading mental hospitals in Europe; and set about writing once more, mainly to provide for her upkeep.

A contemporary event furnished a ready subject, so that during a portion of December, Thackeray quickly wrote a humorous version of it, *The Second Funeral of Napoleon*, and a poetic epilogue, *The Chronicle of the Drum*. The two works were published together by Cunningham in January 1841, with a cover designed by Thackeray, in a small paper-covered format under the pseudonym of M. A. Titmarsh. Sales remained very low, however, and Thackeray soon prepared an article for the March issue of *Fraser's*—his first contribution to that periodical in five months.

By this time he was completing work for the comic miscellanies that were to be issued by Cunningham during April 1841 in two volumes under the title *Comic Tales and Sketches*, with new illustrations by Thackeray, including a title page showing Yellowplush and Gahagan leading Titmarsh "to the very brink of immortality" (that is, to the edge of a cliff). Besides reprinting Gahagan's adventures and the correspondence of Yellowplush (with the exception of "Fashnable Fax"), Thackeray included in this collection "The Professor," "The Bedford-Row Conspiracy," and "Stubbs's Calendar." Whether for reasons of space or by deliberate choice, *Flore et Zéphyr*, "Barber Cox," and "Catherine" were not included. With *Comic Tales*, however, Thackeray still failed to achieve notable success.

After writing the opening of a never-to-be-finished novel of the fifteenth century, "The Knights of Borsellen," Thackeray put it aside to earn immediate money. An improvement in Isabella's condition caused him suddenly to remove her from the mental hospital in late March and to have renewed hope for her eventual recovery. One result, however, was that he had to devote most of his time to her for the next six weeks. Ultimately, he hired an attendant for Isabella and took up writing again, notably for *Fraser's*, publishing four articles during the summer. Now free to travel, he visited England, the most important experience there being a visit to the country seat of a friend, John Bowes, during the general election of 1841. During this visit Thackeray learned about an ancestor of Bowes's who became the inspiration for Thackeray's novel *The Luck of Barry Lyndon* (1852-1853). Thackeray immediately proposed writing the novel for *Fraser's*, but the project was postponed.

Arrangements had evidently been made already for Thackeray's newest serial, *The History of Samuel Titmarsh and the Great Hoggarty Diamond*, which began to appear in the September *Fraser's*, concluding at the end of the year. Here again, Thackeray used a naive autobiographical persona, though in this case the narrative is not a rogue autobiography but in certain essential details a fable of Thackeray's own life and of his hopes for the future. Samuel Titmarsh, Michael Angelo's cousin, unexpectedly receives a diamond pin that enables him to marry the simple girl he loves, but the pin also leads him into a life of expensive habits and an illusory pursuit of success. Duped and self-deluded, separated from his wife, and faced with ruin, he pawns the diamond

pin, escapes from his follies, is reunited with his wife, accepts his humbled existence, and comes to enjoy modest circumstances. As Thackeray looked back ten years later, he characterized himself as "a boy . . . bleating out my simple griefs in the Great Hoggarty Diamond." He also bleated out some of his hopes—hopes that implicitly chastised his past life, for as he wrote in a diary that summer, "there is not one of the sorrows or disappointments of my life, that as I fancy I cannot trace to some error crime or weakness of my disposition."

In early 1842 Thackeray continued his attempts to sell magazine articles and succeeded in placing his first contribution with the *Foreign Quarterly Review* and several with the newly founded *Ainsworth's Magazine*. A series of miscellaneous sketches published under a new pseudonym, "George Fitz-Boodle," began to appear in the *Fraser's* issue for June, the same month in which began a long series of contributions to *Punch*, which he described privately as "a very low paper," but one that offered "good pay, and a great opportunity for unrestrained laughing sneering kicking and gambadoing." Finally, also in June, he set out for Ireland, where he spent four months gathering material for his postponed book and beginning to write it. *The Irish Sketch Book* finally appeared in May of the following year, during which Thackeray continued to write miscellaneous works for the magazines—chiefly *Fraser's* and *Punch*. Thackeray wanted to give *The Irish Sketch Book* the title "Cockney in Ireland," but though his publishers overruled him, the planned title reveals that the London narrator is as central to the book as Ireland itself. Given the unity provided by the book's subject matter—the "manners and the scenery" of Ireland—its narrator, and its generally sober narrative tone, the work has much more coherence than *The Paris Sketch Book*. Thackeray illustrated the book and attributed it to M. A. Titmarsh, but for the first time in his career he added his own name as well by signing a dedication to Charles Lever, the Irish novelist who had befriended him on his tour. By signing his name, Thackeray acknowledged the transparency of his mask but also implied his opinion of the book's merits. Except for Lever, Irish reviewers generally attacked the book—as Thackeray knew they would, and as he indicated in the dedication—for they resisted the depiction of Irish dirt, dilapidation, rhetoric, superstition, and quarrelsomeness that formed a part of Thackeray's sketch. The English reception was much more favorable, however, both with reviewers and the public. The book represented Thackeray's widest success so far in his career; it even went into a second edition two years later.

During the rest of 1843 Thackeray continued his contributions to *Punch* and wrote additional sketches for *Fraser's* under the name of Fitz-Boodle, a pseudonym he also attributed to the author of his ensuing work of fiction. Toward the end of the year he prepared for a new serial novel, which had been on his mind since the visit to Bowes more than two years before, and which began to appear in the January 1844 *Fraser's*: "The Luck of Barry Lyndon: A Romance of the Last Century." Here Thackeray returned not only to the eighteenth century but to the rogue autobiographer, who naively reveals himself as he unfolds the egotistical narrative of his rapacious adventures on the Continent, in Ireland, and in England. Soldier, gambler, brutal husband and stepfather, prodigal dissipator of his wife's fortune, and finally broken-down prisoner, Barry never falters in his devotion to the fortunes available through luck and cunning and to the values of success. Thackeray not only sustains more coolly than ever the ironic discrepancy between Barry's values and the standards violated by his misdeeds but also permits Barry degrees of "success" sufficient to emphasize increasingly the hollowness of his achievements. Objections from members of Thackeray's audience to the immorality of Barry's views apparently prompted the novelist gradually to expand the almost imperceptible editorial presence of Fitz-Boodle by having him repeatedly point out the viciousness of Barry's principles and behavior and emphasize his disapproval of them. As this expedient may suggest, Thackeray's serial was not popular, and his initial hopes of publishing the novel in "a handsome saleable volume" were not fulfilled at the end of its serial appearance in the December 1844 issue of *Fraser's*. (The novel was brilliantly adapted by Stanley Kubrick for the 1975 film *Barry Lyndon*.)

By that time, Thackeray already had another travel book under way, for when the Peninsular and Oriental Company suddenly in August offered him free passage on one of their ships sailing to Cairo, with many stops along the way throughout the Mediterranean, he accepted forthwith and was at sea four days later. Throughout the cruise and during a stay of several months in Rome on the return journey, Thackeray kept busily at work—finishing *Barry Lyndon*, writing his travel book as well as sketching for it, sending contributions to *Punch*, and beginning a Christmas book. During 1845 his miscellaneous writings for *Punch* supplied most of his income, supplemented by occasional contributions to the *New Monthly Magazine*; several to *Fraser's Magazine*, including his last annual review of the Royal Academy exhibition; and several to *George Cruikshank's Table Book* and the *Morning Chronicle*. In June he grumbled, "I can suit the magazines (but I can't hit the public, be hanged to them)." He continued to try to hit the public, nevertheless, for earlier in the year he had given to Colburn "the commencement of a novel"—which is generally understood to be the beginning of what later became *Vanity Fair*. Colburn, however, failed to respond, leading Thackeray to recall that manuscript, together with the commencement of another tale, and to busy himself with "scores of little jobs comme à l'ordinaire."

For several years Thackeray had wished to have his children with him in London, but he did not want to separate them from his mother, who was extremely attached to them. Furthermore, Major Carmichael-Smyth did not wish to move to London because of greater expenses and because of writs against him relating to debts from the collapse of the *Constitutional*. Mrs. Carmichael-Smyth's visit to London with the two girls in June 1845 brought matters somewhat closer to a resolution, as did Thackeray's decision to bring his wife to England, where she was placed under what became permanent care in Camberwell in south London. His efforts to persuade the Carmichael-Smyths failed even when he rented a house in June 1846, but his mother finally brought the children to him in the late autumn, afterward returning alone to her husband in France. After an interval of six years, Thackeray had reconstituted his family life, having his daughters permanently under his own roof.

The year 1846 had opened with the appearance of his illustrated Eastern travel book, *Notes of a Journey from Cornhill to Grand Cairo*, published by Chapman and Hall. As in *The Irish Sketch Book*, Thackeray writes in the persona of a London traveler humorously content with his national ignorance but delightedly responding to scenes of natural beauty and human idiosyncrasy. The style, somewhat less sober than in the Irish book, is even more fluent and polished. By this time Thackeray had achieved a prose of notable flexibility and range. His success among critics

TO

CHARLES LEVER, Esq.

OF TEMPLEOGUE HOUSE, NEAR DUBLIN

MY DEAR LEVER,

HARRY LORREQUER needs no complimenting in a dedication; and I would not venture to inscribe this volume to the Editor of the *Dublin University Magazine*, who, I fear, must disapprove of a great deal which it contains.

But allow me to dedicate my little book to a good Irishman (the hearty charity of whose visionary red-coats, some substantial personages in black might imitate to advantage), and to a friend from whom I have received a hundred acts of kindness and cordial hospitality.

Laying aside for a moment the travelling-title of Mr. Titmarsh, let me acknowledge these favours in my own name, and subscribe myself, my dear Lever,

Most sincerely and gratefully yours,

W. M. THACKERAY.

London, April 27, 1843.

The dedication of The Irish Sketch Book, *marking the first time Thackeray's name appeared on any of his works*

and the public was also more pronounced. A second edition again followed, this time within eight months of original publication. Later that year, Thackeray published his first Christmas book, *Mrs. Perkins's Ball*, organized essentially as a group of character sketches centering on an evening entertainment, which sold more than fifteen hundred copies by the end of December and led to an immediate second edition. (Although Thackeray's Christmas books appeared in December, their publication date was often given for the following year. Hence, Chapman and Hall listed the publication date of *Mrs. Perkins's Ball* as 1847, although it appeared in December 1846.)

But 1846 was more important for the appearance of Thackeray's longest and most notable series of contributions to *Punch*: "The Snobs of England. By One of Themselves," which began in February and ran anonymously for fifty-three weeks, with accompanying illustrations. Taking the term "snob," which at that time denoted someone of the lower class, Thackeray extended its meaning to include members of the middle and upper classes—his reading audience—by defining a snob as one *"who meanly admires mean things."* Fol-

lowing the progress of the social year, and ranging from the Snob Royal to the lowest orders but concentrating upon the middle class, Thackeray examines the influence of the aristocracy and "respectability" upon snobs and characterizes "City" snobs together with military, clerical, university, literary, political, country, and club snobs, among others. Through the prose and through illustrations like that of a liveried court footman asking a startled social superior in court dress, "Am I not a man and a brother?" (the appeal made famous by those working for the abolition of slavery), Thackeray emphasizes how much emancipation remains to be undertaken. Although the series was published anonymously, and only a small group of knowing readers could identify the author from the writing or from his artistic "signature" on the illustrations—a pair of spectacles with crossed earpieces—Thackeray's authorship of the series was publicly made known in December 1846, when Bradbury and Evans, the publishers of *Punch*, began to advertise the fact in announcing the appearance of *Vanity Fair*, which they were about to issue in separate monthly installments. The Snob papers thus

Cover of the collected edition of the Snob papers, with the "man and brother" illustration

became an important work in establishing Thackeray's public reputation as a leading satirist of his day—a reputation that increased when the Snob papers were published in 1848 in a single volume, which carried Thackeray's name (as did all his subsequent publications) and the "man and brother" illustration on its paper cover.

Eighteen forty-six was also to have been the year of *Vanity Fair*, for by January, Thackeray had reached a publishing agreement with Bradbury and Evans; but like many of his other projects, this too had to be postponed from its planned appearance in May—presumably because Thackeray was too busy with other matters to reimmerse himself in the novel, which he had evidently begun after his return from his Eastern and Italian journey in February 1845. Toward the end of 1846 he began to take up the novel again and suddenly recalled the phrase *Vanity Fair*, from John Bunyan's *The Pilgrim's Progress* (1678, 1684); it gave him the title for his major work, but can aptly be said to characterize all his narratives, and indeed his view of human life. His own brief summary of his subject, paraphrased from St. Paul (Ephesians 2:12), was "a set of people living without God in the world." Though at the last minute he wanted to change its subtitle to *A Novel without a Hero*, the first monthly installment for January 1847 and subsequent installments bore the heading *Vanity Fair: Pen and Pencil Sketches of English Society*, thereby suggesting the satirical influence of the Snob papers, which still had eight weeks to run in *Punch*. The revised subtitle appeared on the title page when the novel came out in book form during 1848, however, and served to suggest that with *Vanity Fair* Thackeray was offering not a series of sketches, like the Snob papers or *Mrs. Perkins's Ball*, but a carefully planned and well-executed whole. The revised subtitle also emphasized Thackeray's disinterest in creating a romantic hero or in narrating the adventures of a central personage. His subject was a whole society and the unheroic lives of people who lived in it, following for the most part their worldly, illusory aims.

As Thackeray was revising his manuscript of the third installment, he inserted several passages that alluded to his novel's new title of *Vanity Fair*. The first of these insertions deserves special mention, for in it Thackeray now proclaimed the narrator's intention "as a man and a brother" not merely to introduce the characters in his narrative but also at times "to step down from the platform, and talk about them"; the latter constitutes the famous Thackerayan narrative commentary. Here he also reveals a dual function of the narrator that is crucial to an adequate understanding of the novel. On the one hand, as the term "platform" shows, the narrator is what Thackeray elsewhere called "the Manager of the Performance," a stage manager who is also a puppeteer, distinct from his puppets and in a basic sense superior to them. From another perspective, however, as the phrase "a man and a brother" indicates, he is their equal, for he is also a character in the narrative, and like all men is not simply acted upon by others but is also the puppet of his own desires and illusory aims. This interplay of perspectives is the source of the narrative complexity in *Vanity Fair*, one of the sources of its intermittent melancholy, and one of the reasons for doubt as to its efficacy as a morally instructive fiction.

Depending structurally upon a complex series of contrasts and pairings within individual installments and from one installment to another, *Vanity Fair* has five main characters who are also contrasted and paired: Becky Sharp, Amelia Sedley (modeled partly on Isabella), George Osborne, William Dobbin (modeled partly on Thackeray himself), and Rawdon Crawley. From the start, as the gentle, subdued Amelia and the witty, determined Becky emerge from school into the world, it is the latter who especially captures the reader's attention with her rebellious rejection of the school's "diploma"—a copy of Johnson's *Dictionary*. As George and William depart from their school to take up military careers, the girls contemplate marriage—Amelia to George and Becky to anyone she can conquer. Amelia's real education comes only when she can grow sufficiently to emerge from her failed marriage to George, recognize the superior merits of the outwardly unprepossessing William, and find whatever happiness remains to them from their saddening growth. Becky, after failing to ensnare Amelia's wealthy brother but succeeding with Rawdon, who is the younger son of a baronet, appears to have made the more successful marriage. The false expectations in her case, however, are of monetary inheritance, for her husband is impoverished, and Becky's famous attempts "to live well on nothing a-year" by creating and sustaining the illusions of other people lead only to inevitable downfall, followed by exiled wandering and eventually a determined, partial recovery of the appearance of "respectability."

Opening in Regency England, the novel follows the intertwined relationships of these five characters amid a wide range of supplementary characters, from a chimney sweep to the king, and in settings extending from London and Brighton to Belgium, France, and Germany. With the victory of the British and their allies at Waterloo (treated in a few brief paragraphs) comes the death of George and the novel's first climax at the end of part nine; the spatial and especially the temporal scope of the novel widen even further thereafter, as it traces the fortunes of Becky, Rawdon, Amelia, and William in England and post-Napoleonic Europe, concluding in the early 1830s with a typically Thackerayan ending that stabilizes the plot but resolves very little in a conclusive way. The idea of a happy ending to a fiction was unpalatable to Thackeray, except as a joke. His kind of moral realism required that the

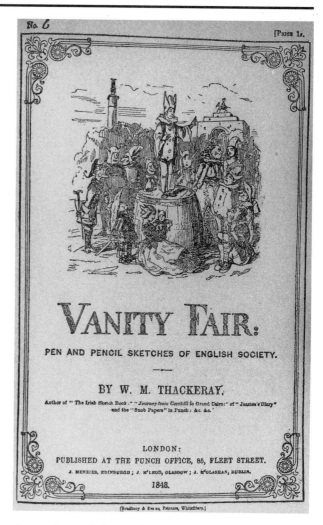

Cover of one of the monthly numbers of Thackeray's major work, showing its original subtitle

novelist not flatter the reader's ego, or leave him satisfied with his earthly condition: "I want to leave everybody dissatisfied and unhappy at the end of the story—we ought all to be with our own and all other stories."

The form of the serial novel, issued in separate monthly installments of thirty-two pages at one shilling a copy, with an illustrated paper cover and two full-page etched plates, had been initiated by Dickens with *The Pickwick Papers* (1836-1837). Such works were typically planned as twenty installments in nineteen issues, the last issue being a double number priced at two shillings, with forty or so pages of text and four plates, plus a bound novel's usual preliminaries. A subscriber could thereby have his own set of serial parts bound; at the end of serial publication other readers could buy a bound volume from the publisher or from booksellers. In reaching agreement with Bradbury and Evans, who were also publishing Dickens, Thackeray came to work in the same format. Instead of Dickens's green covers, however, *Vanity Fair* and ensuing novels of Thackeray's appeared in yellow covers—leading to a Thackerayan joke about his more bilious novelistic outlook. Thackeray also supplemented the two etched plates with wood engravings inserted directly into the text, and he, unlike Dickens, drew his own illustrations. The yellow numbers sold rather slowly for the first twelve months; but during 1848, when the novel became available in a single bound volume, sales more than doubled, though they were still far from spectacular. Favorable critical opinion already began to be published early in the novel's serial run, reviews of the published volume extending this reception. Among fellow novelists, the most notable tribute was offered by Charlotte Brontë, who dedicated the second edition of *Jane Eyre* to Thackeray and praised the intellectual, prophetic, Old Testament power of the satire in *Vanity Fair*, which she ranked above Fielding's. By July 1848, then, Thackeray had emerged into recognition not simply as a clever magazine writer but as one of the best of contemporary novelists—the rival of Dickens in excellence, if not in popularity.

For some time, however, Thackeray continued his magazine work. With an article for the January 1847 issue of *Fraser's*, Thackeray's contributions to that magazine almost entirely halted; but concurrently with the installments of *Vanity Fair* he continued his submissions to *Punch*, notably a series of parodies called "*Punch's* Prize Novelists." Beginning with "George de Barnwell," a satire on Bulwer-Lytton's novels (particularly *Eugene Aram*, which had recently been reprinted), Thackeray went on to direct gentler mockery at the fiction of Benjamin Disraeli, Catherine Gore, and other novelists of fashionable life, G. P. R. James, Charles James Lever, James Fenimore Cooper, and French writers on English life. In addition, the "Fat Contributer" now reported not on the pyramids of Egypt, as during 1844, but on Brighton; he was succeeded by "Spec," who made his "Travels in London." In December 1847 Chapman and Hall published Thackeray's second Christmas book, another illustrated series of sketches, *Our Street*. As usual, then, Thackeray found it both congenial and profitable to busy himself with more than one task. His income was still not notable, but he was finally able to settle with the last of Major Carmichael-Smyth's creditors.

By the time *Vanity Fair* appeared in one-volume form during July 1848, Thackeray had agreed with Bradbury and Evans to do another twenty-part monthly serial. First, however, he took advantage of his freedom to make for the Continent and enjoy a month's solitary holiday in Belgium and Germany. One of his favored correspondents while on this trip was Jane Brookfield, the wife of an old college friend, William Brookfield, who had become a clergyman in London. Thackeray had first met Jane in early 1842 and a year afterward jokingly told his mother that "pretty Mrs. Brookfield" was the latest woman with whom he had fallen in love. More soberly in 1846 he wrote his mother that Mrs. Brookfield was his "beau-ideal. I have been in love with her these four years—not so as to endanger peace or appetite but she always seems to me to speak and do and think as a woman should." To his good friend, her husband, he acknowledged in early 1847 that Jane's "innocence, looks, angelical sweetness and kindness charm and ravish me to the highest degree," but called it "a sort of artistical delight (a spiritual sensuality so to speak)." By November the unconcerned Brookfield had proposed that they share Thackeray's house and housekeeping expenses and that Jane supervise care of the children, but Thackeray knew *that* arrangement would be dangerous—for him, at least—and arranged to keep his love within manageable bounds. Thackeray told Jane that he had modeled Amelia in *Vanity Fair* upon her as well as upon his wife and mother; but Jane, while responding to Amelia's affectionateness, was put off by the character's selfishness and apathy toward her loving admirer, William Dobbin, and thereby failed to realize the degree to which Thackeray was drawing upon her own traits (as well as Isabella's) to a greater extent than upon his mother's.

In early August 1848, while still on the Continent, Thackeray began his next novel, which started its run in November 1848 under the title *The History of Pendennis. His Fortunes and Misfortunes, His Friends and His Greatest Enemy.* He now received one hundred pounds per part instead of sixty pounds, and the publishers felt confident enough to make the size of the initial printing (nine thousand per part) double the figure for *Vanity Fair*. By this time too, Bradbury and Evans had republished the Snob papers in a single paper-covered collection entitled *The Book of Snobs* (1848), and a shrewd entrepreneur offered unsold copies of the old 1841 edition of *Comic Tales*

The Reverend William Brookfield and his wife, Jane, with whom Thackeray was in love

and *Sketches* with a new title page identifying Titmarsh as the "Author of 'Our Street,' 'Vanity Fair,' etc." Thackeray also wrote a Christmas book for 1848, *Doctor Birch and His Young Friends*; and he continued his contributions to *Punch* during the run of *Pendennis*, his most notable series being the topical "Mr. Brown's Letters to a Young Man about Town." Other signs of his growing success were the republication of *Samuel Titmarsh and the Great Hoggarty Diamond* (1849) from *Fraser's Magazine* by Bradbury and Evans, and of *Vanity Fair* in a Continental edition (1849) by Tauchnitz of Leipzig. In addition, Tauchnitz published the first volume (1849) of a series called *Miscellanies: Prose and Verse*, the initial volume containing *The Great Hoggarty Diamond* and *The Book of Snobs*.

This surge of publication and republication came to a temporary end following the appearance of the eleventh number of *Pendennis* (September 1849), for Thackeray contracted a serious illness diagnosed as cholera, which dangerously afflicted him between mid September and mid October, leaving him to face a slow recovery thereafter. As a result, there was a hiatus of three months in the publication of *Pendennis*, which reappeared at the end of December 1849; shortly aferward, Bradbury and Evans published a volume containing the first twelve parts of the novel, as did Tauchnitz on the Continent. As this

publishing decision suggests, Thackeray had decided to extend his serial novel from the Dickensian length of twenty installments to twenty-four. These new dimensions seemed to be congenial, for his next two serials for Bradbury and Evans came to be of a similar length.

Although Thackeray's serious illness and extended recovery delayed his resumption of *Pendennis*, he found it did not prevent the less tiring occupation of composing *Rebecca and Rowena*, which became his Christmas book for 1849, published again by Chapman and Hall (this time, however, with illustrations by Richard Doyle). Long-standing dissatisfaction with the ending of a favorite work, Scott's *Ivanhoe* (1819), prompted Thackeray to resurrect an old piece written in 1846 for *Fraser's*, "Proposals for a Continuation of *Ivanhoe*," and to enact them more fully. Hence, Ivanhoe finally manages to get free of the dull, conventional Rowena and to find and marry the attractive Rebecca, who converts to Christianity for his sake, thus defeating Rowena's calculating deathbed exaction of his promise not to marry a Jewess. The ending, however, is a typically Thackerayan anticlimax: "Of some sort of happiness melancholy is a characteristic, and I think these were a solemn pair, and died rather early."

Thackeray's own melancholy, however, diminished as he began to write once more for

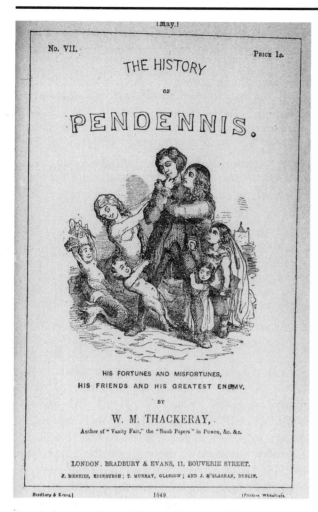

HIS FORTUNES AND MISFORTUNES,
HIS FRIENDS AND HIS GREATEST ENEMY.

Cover of one of the monthly installments of Thackeray's novel about a young man torn between worldly temptation and domesticity

Punch and resumed work again on *Pendennis*, which concluded with the double number for December 1850. Its title figure, Arthur Pendennis, has more prominence than any single character in *Vanity Fair*; and the emblematic illustration on the monthly wrappers identifies the narrative subject as Pen's making of a choice between two female figures, one representing worldly temptation and the other, domesticity. In tracing Pen's progress, Thackeray drew upon his own memories of Larkbeare in Devon; of Cambridge; and of bohemian, Grub Street, and fashionable life in London. People Thackeray had known tended to be models for the main characters—especially Pen's mother, Helen, but also his friend George Warrington and the two girls between whom Pen must choose: Blanche Amory and Laura Bell. After considerable vacillation, and partial yielding to the two main competing influences upon him, represented by his mother and his worldly

uncle, Major Pendennis, Pen finally chooses Laura—thereby basically committing himself to a guiding set of moral values. *Pendennis* is Thackeray's version of the great nineteenth-century theme of the young man from the provinces—impoverished, simple, and undereducated but intelligent and full of high hopes—who comes to a disillusioning but also maturing understanding of himself and of his place in the world.

As the latter statement may suggest, therefore, the novel gives as much prominence to Pen's context as to Pen himself. All of the characters live in Vanity Fair, have the inevitable limitations of their virtues, require the giving up of enriching possibilities, and, though they may represent desirable values, make possible only a limited happiness. In Thackerayan fashion, Pen is a quite flawed character, a crucial aspect of Thackeray's presentation of him being the ironic relationship between Pen's hopes and enthusiasms and the narrator's more mature perspectives. At the same time, as Thackeray reveals that Laura's love is a partial renewal of Helen Pendennis's love for her son ("and arms as tender as Helen's once more enfold him"), the novelist implies his awareness that he is dramatizing his own repeatedly frustrated need for domestic affection.

Pendennis was in fact written during the closest and most intense period of his relationship with Jane Brookfield. During his younger days, he had used German in confiding to his diary matters about which he felt reluctant to speak; now, in verbalizing his love for Jane, he used French. Thus, when he wrote her a letter during November 1848 confessing his longing to tell someone, anyone, that he loved her, he wrote in French throughout, carrying the letter with him for days, trying to decide whether or not he should send it. Not long afterward, he did tell a friend and again used French, speaking of being "moitié fou" ("half mad"), of suffering from "horribles peines de coeur qui sans cesse me poursuivent" ("horrible anguish of the heart that ceaselessly pursues me"), and of not having his love returned: "Elle ne m'aime pas. Elle me plaint" ("She does not love me. She complains of me"). Thackeray apparently did finally send Jane the French letter and received an expression of her husband's confidence in him, so that Thackeray began to write her in English of his love—but he placed it in a religious context ("By love I believe and am saved"), and connecting her with his mother, he said that the pair of them kept him "straight and honest."

A sketch by Thackeray of himself at the foot of Jane Brookfield's sofa (Rosenbach Museum and Library)

Thackeray and Jane agreed to call each other "friend," "sister," and "brother," but while this distant fondness seems to have been as strong an emotion as Jane Brookfield ever felt toward Thackeray, he was constantly having to restrain the power of his feelings for her and the language with which he gave them utterance.

Some measure of his feelings may be seen in a letter he wrote to a friend in early 1850, when his response to Jane's first pregnancy caused him to allude to his own poetic circumlocution for sexual intercourse: "A comic poet once singing of an [attractive] Irishwoman said 'Children if she bear blest will be their daddy.' " Thackeray then went on to speak of Jane and, in effect, of his own fantasy: "And indeed I can conceive few positions more agreeable than his who is called upon to perform the part of husband to so sweet a creature." Thackeray's relationship with Jane, however, was always one-sided and never even remotely close to being consummated. At the same time, Thackeray found a certain fulfillment as well as frustration and anguish in the relationship—indeed, he even enjoyed sardonic laughter at his predicament and received as well some fresh material for his next novel.

Before writing that novel, however, Thackeray completed what was to be his next-to-last Christmas book, *The Kickleburys on the Rhine*, for which he asked more than Chapman and Hall were willing to pay, and which therefore came out in late 1850 under the imprint of an eager publishing house that was new to Thackeray: Smith,

Elder. The book's success immediately led to a second edition. Meanwhile, made anxious by the threat of death a year before, Thackeray determined to endow a suitable legacy for his wife and especially his daughters. Accordingly, he began preparations for a series of lectures on the English humorists of the eighteenth century that he hoped would bring him a good income as he delivered them in England, Scotland, and America. Beginning in May 1851, he read the six lectures to a responsive audience in London that consisted not only of notable literary figures but also of prominent members of fashionable society; Thackeray had been regularly welcomed into the homes of the latter upon the serial appearance of *Vanity Fair*, with which his reputation was prominently established.

In his lectures Thackeray explained his belief that humor was the response of a moral sensibility, revealing a manly, pious, feeling heart. Making a familiar Victorian distinction between levity and gravity, Thackeray found in humor an underlying sense of weightiness and seriousness. For him humor is rooted in a profound recognition of the human condition and of mankind's immortal destiny, and it reminds the humorist's audience of the moral imperatives implied by that common destiny. Hence humor is separate from mere laughter or wit, for they imply an egoistic sense of superiority, and thereby they separate human beings; while humor, with its deep awareness of human communality, draws people together in sympathetic understanding. As he had

450

Caricature by an unknown artist of Thackeray preparing to give one of his lectures

written at the end of his previous novel, the claim of Arthur Pendennis upon the reader is the recognition not that he is a hero but that he is "a man and a brother." Correspondingly, Thackeray emphasized in his lectures the humorist's role as "week-day preacher"—not only by his language but by the example of his life. Therefore, of the figures upon whom he lectured—which included Jonathan Swift, Joseph Addison, William Congreve, Richard Steele, Alexander Pope, William Hogarth, Henry Fielding, Laurence Sterne, and Oliver Goldsmith—Thackeray is hardest upon Swift and Sterne, who were ordained clergymen but seemed to him guilty not only of religious skepticism but of blasphemy. Some members of his audience immediately disagreed with the severity of these judgments, as subsequent readers have increasingly done, but there was a general consensus about the brilliance, grace, and power of his lectures. Thackeray thereby had another notable success, and a quite profitable one as well. The lectures are also significant because in giving them over a period of two years, Thackeray established a direct relationship between himself and his audiences, to whom he spoke no longer through a mask but with re-

peated, personal testimony.

Immediately after completing the lectures, Thackeray signed an agreement with Smith, Elder for his next novel, which was not to be a serial fiction but—for the only time in his career—was to be completed before publication. For agreeing to provide matter to fill three post octavo volumes, Thackeray was to receive twelve hundred pounds. He celebrated with a six-week holiday on the Continent, for the first time taking his two daughters with him. A month after his return he quarreled with Brookfield over his friend's frequently insulting treatment of Jane; this allowed Brookfield to terminate Thackeray's association with her, though friends brought about a nominal reconciliation among the three. It was the third in the lifetime series of agonized separations—the first from his mother when he was five; the second from his wife, upon the outbreak of her madness, when he was twenty-nine; and now the third, from Jane Brookfield, when he was forty.

In mid November 1851, when he could speak somewhat calmly about himself, he acknowledged the sexual desire implicit in his love for Jane but recognized its absurdity: "for say I got my desire, I should despise a woman; and the very day of the sacrifice would be the end of the attachment." He observed: "Very likely it's *a* woman I want more than any particular one. . . . It is written that a man should have a mate above all things[.] The want of this natural outlet plays the deuce with me." Referring to himself by the generic name of Tomkins, he asked, "Why cant I fancy some honest woman to be a titular Mrs. Tomkins?" He was able to do that, however, only in his fiction—especially in his next novel, *The History of Henry Esmond, Esq.* (1852), with the figure of Rachel, Lady Castlewood, who is partly modeled upon Jane.

Thackeray appears to have begun *Henry Esmond* at about the time of his rupture with the Brookfields in September 1851. In October he wrote a "frightfully glum" portion but a month later was getting on "pretty well & gaily" with his novel and finding diversion no longer in writing for *Punch*, which he ceased doing by the end of November, but in delivering his lectures from time to time around the country. Steady advancement with *Henry Esmond* brought it to a conclusion in May 1852, following which he made an unaccompanied tour on the Continent. *The History of Henry Esmond, Esq.*, which marked Thackeray's return to historical fiction, finally appeared in

Portrait by Samuel Laurence that made Thackeray's face almost as well known as his name. Charlotte Brontë hung an engraving of the portrait at Haworth Parsonage.

three volumes, handsomely printed in eighteenth-century Caslon type, and with a degree of archaic spelling meant to help give the book the physical appearance of an earlier age.

Cast in the form of Esmond's autobiography, Thackeray's novel takes place amid Jacobite plotting during the reigns of William III and Anne to restore the Stuarts and prevent the Hanoverian succession. It also reflects Thackeray's own life, as would be expected from so autobiographical an author. To his mother he confessed that Esmond was in part "a handsome likeness of an ugly son of yours." Ignorant of his father, separated early from his mother, and mistreated by those looking after him, Esmond feels his early days "cast a shade of melancholy over the child's youth, which will accompany him, no doubt, to the end of his days." Later, after the happily married Lord and Lady Castlewood make him a part of their home, complications develop that mirror aspects of Thackeray's relationship with the Brookfields—including painful rejection by Lady Castlewood.

Because Esmond is isolated from his parents, and because manipulative people conceal his legitimacy, the question of personal identity be-

comes the central problem and quest of his life. His attempt to discover himself, moreover, becomes entwined with his efforts to find fulfillment in a truly self-expressive love, a part of Esmond's confusion being an attraction both to Lady Castlewood and to her daughter, Beatrix. Even in this deeply personal novel, however, the historical circumstances of Esmond's searches are inseparable from the searches themselves; for Thackeray fuses Esmond's personal story with the religious, military, and political events of Esmond's day and requires that his growth be seen in the context of those larger historical developments. Hence, as the reader follows Esmond in his military and civilian careers through a thicket of plottings and counterplottings, he becomes aware of how questions of personal legitimacy, for example, are illuminated by questions of kingly legitimacy, and vice versa. When Esmond finally gives up his plotting for the Jacobite cause, he also gives up his pursuit of Beatrix and burns the papers that prove his legitimacy and his right to a title. Having understood that his identity is defined by his own character and actions, he destroys the pretense that anything else can define him—whether a piece of paper, an empty title, a political cause, or a brilliantly fashionable wife. Hence, he chooses the widowed Lady Castlewood and moves to family estates in Virginia, where he devotes himself to a love that he sees as offering the best of earthly fulfillments and partaking of religious devotion: "To have such a love is the one blessing, in comparison of which all earthly joy is of no value; and to think of her, is to praise God."

The definiteness of this ending, perhaps motivated in part by the intensity of Thackeray's own need for such a love, gives the appearance of a somewhat uncharacteristic conclusion for a Thackeray novel. Much of the rest of the novel implies, however, that the definiteness comes more from Esmond than from Thackeray, who gives frequent evidence of his distance from his narrator, and who completed his composition of the novel by writing a preface showing the decided imperfections of the love apostrophized by Esmond at the end. The ending of *Henry Esmond*, given its context, is therefore generally consistent with Thackeray's practice of writing deliberately tempered conclusions. As this discussion may suggest, *Henry Esmond* has come to be seen as a work of tantalizing complexity. It has also been given just praise for its shapely coherence and the grave eloquence of its style.

Sarah (Sally) Baxter, with whom Thackeray flirted during his visits to New York. She later married into a prominent South Carolina family and died of tuberculosis about a year before Thackeray's death.

The History of Henry Esmond, Esq. was published at the end of October 1852, just as Thackeray was leaving for the United States, where he successfully delivered his lectures on the English humorists in the major cities of the east coast from Boston to Savannah. He was also fortunate in receiving payment from American publishers such as Harper, who had been pirating his works, and Appleton. Many invitations kept him socially busy and produced lasting friendships with prominent men of letters and with an especially congenial family in New York, the Baxters, where he found a place always ready for him—which was enlivened by an attractive daughter, Sally, whom he addressed as Beatrix and with whom he played at being in love. After his departure, Sally and her mother came to be among his favorite correspondents—who were, revealingly, all women, for Thackeray told Mrs. Baxter that he never wrote "to any man except on business."

Upon his return to London in May 1853, Thackeray set about correcting errors in proofs of *The English Humourists*, which Smith had prematurely set up in type before Thackeray could make revisions. A faulty text with an incomplete list of errata resulted, which was only partly corrected when a second edition appeared in July. Another Continental holiday followed, again with his daughters, prior to the appearance of a new serial novel for Bradbury and Evans that commenced with the number for October 1853: *The Newcomes. Memoirs of a Most Respectable Family*, illustrated by Richard Doyle and narrated by "Arthur Pendennis"—one of many characters who reappear in Thackeray's works. For *The Newcomes* Thackeray received £150 per serial installment, a total of £3,600 for the twenty-four numbers, plus £500 from Harper and Tauchnitz. Thackeray called 1853 the first "year of putting money away" and, with the prospect of a good income from *The Newcomes* before him, bought his first house.

Thackeray began composing the novel while on his Continental holiday, completing four numbers before the beginning of serial publication. Although he supplied Doyle with ideas for the illustrations, giving the artist most of the responsibility for them left Thackeray free to travel—all the more because he continued to write the text well before it was needed by the printers. Consequently, he spent October in Paris and took his daughters to Italy during the winter of 1853-1854. During his travels, however, Thackeray's health became increasingly troublesome. From August until December 1853 he was ill once a month and then was stricken in Rome with malarial fever, which not only prostrated him but left him weak for days afterward and completed the permanent damaging of his health. Emotionally, too, he felt debilitated, telling his mother, "A man who has been a pleasuring for twenty years begins to settle down as a sort of domestic character . . . [with] a sort of mild melancholy. . . . By the time I am fifty I shall be a good deal older than you are." At the time, Thackeray, who had long been gray-haired, was only forty-two, but his sense of aging was to grow markedly as the periods of sickness recurred with increasing regularity. Though his illnesses significantly reduced his lead time in completing installments of *The Newcomes*, he had time to compose a final Christmas book during 1854: *The Rose and the Ring*, a mock fairy tale that Smith, Elder published at the end of the year, became a long-lasting, popular favorite.

With the final number of *The Newcomes*, for August 1855, Thackeray completed one of his largest-scaled works, and his most richly allusive one. Again, the central dramatized reality is the selfishness of the human heart—here, as brought to a focus by the manipulations that characterize the arranging of marriages, especially fashionable ones. The Newcomes themselves epitomize

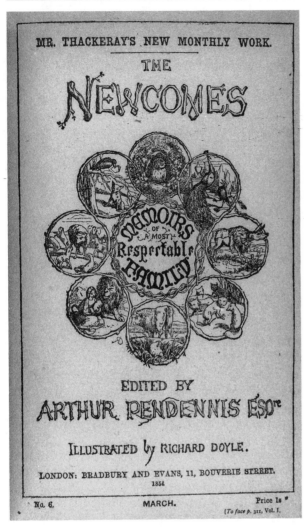

MR. THACKERAY'S NEW MONTHLY WORK.

THE

NEWCOMES

MEMOIRS
OF A MOST
Respectable
FAMILY

EDITED BY
ARTHUR PENDENNIS ESQre

ILLUSTRATED by RICHARD DOYLE.

LONDON: BRADBURY AND EVANS, 11, BOUVERIE STREET.
1854

No. 6.   MARCH.   Price 1s *
                            [To face p. 311, Vol. I.

Cover of one of the monthly parts of Thackeray's novel about the Newcome family

the way in which an upper-middle-class English family seeks to increase its wealth and satisfy its social ambition by means of aristocratic marriages and attendant benefits, including political ones. Thus, of three brothers, one marries Lady Ann Kew, eventually becoming a baronet and member of Parliament. The second brother marries a woman of his own station and manages the family bank. The third brother, however, falls in love and has his love match broken up; he goes to India, follows a military career, and comes to have a marriage both undistinguished and empty. The latter brother, Colonel Newcome, then comes back to England to be with his son, Clive, and reenters the London world. From this central web of relationships come most of the novel's conflicts, in their internal as well as external manifestations. Thus, the Colonel's old love is for-

cibly married to a French count but still loves the Colonel; Sir Brian's daughter, Ethel Newcome, is attracted to an aristocratic cousin, Kew, as well as to Clive, and later seems on the verge of rejecting Clive for a marquis; and Lady Clara Pulleyn forsakes her impoverished lover to marry Ethel's brother, Sir Barnes Newcome, but later leaves her unpleasant husband and her children for an unhappy relationship with her former lover. Though Clive has the advantage of a father who denounces marriages of convenience, he nevertheless marries Rosey Mackenzie to please his father and is miserable for it. In short, all of the family relationships are difficult, even with the love existing between Clive and his fond, upright, eccentric father, who became one of Thackeray's most noted creations.

Thackeray's own experience can, as usual, be readily seen in *The Newcomes*—for example, in Clive's unfashionable and disillusioning attempts to be a painter. Colonel Newcome was partly taken from Major Carmichael-Smyth, Rosey from Isabella, and the terrible Mrs. Mackenzie from Mrs. Shawe, while aspects of Ethel came from Lucy Baxter, and accounts of the fashionable marriage market came from Thackeray's considerable experience in well-to-do society. His critics praised the work for its authentic depiction of its contemporary subject, and they responded warmly to the benevolence of Colonel Newcome—not commenting very extensively, however, on his decided excesses and partial moral collapse. His pathetic ending as transfigured child indeed became one of the most famous death scenes in Victorian fiction. Thackeray, however, continued to resist happy endings and made any marriage between Clive and Ethel the responsibility of readers who wished to create their own fairyland. As in *Vanity Fair*, Thackeray wanted to leave his readers with the instructive dissatisfaction that seemed to him to characterize profound awareness of the human condition.

After a month's holiday abroad, Thackeray returned to London to prepare a new series of lectures intended for delivery in America, and later in England and Scotland, on the lives and times of the first four Hanoverian kings of England. Between August and October he composed the first three lectures, completing the one on George IV just prior to delivering it in November 1855. For the next six months he renewed old friendships and lectured in most of the same cities as before but also extended his itinerary as far west as New Orleans, St. Louis, and Cincinnati. Again he found good income from audiences who receptively responded to his brilliant verbal sketches of the Georges and the society of their times.

As in Thackeray's travel books and in his earlier series of lectures, *he*, as responsive spectator, is the central figure of the discourses, who seeks, affirms, doubts, speculates, welcomes lovable human presence, and passes judgment—upon himself as well as upon others. As in Thackeray's fiction, there are frequent shifts between limited and omniscient narration, especially as specific, individual perspectives alternate with panoramic views. In evoking the past, Thackeray assumed his audiences were knowledgeable about his subject and frequently drew upon this shared knowledge, especially through the use of allusion. Hence, the lectures were not as fully successful in some of the American cities as they were in England and Scotland, where Thackeray, after returning to Europe in May 1856, gave them during the winter and spring of 1856-1857.

While he was still in America, however, Bradbury and Evans followed the example of Tauchnitz in Leipzig and Appleton in New York by beginning a collection of Thackeray's previously published shorter prose works, including *The Yellowplush Correspondence*, *Barry Lyndon*, and *The Book of Snobs*, as well as some of his comic verse. These were gathered into four volumes of *Miscellanies: Prose and Verse* that appeared between November 1855 and May 1857. Each work within these volumes was also available separately in paper covers, while cheap editions of longer novels such as *Pendennis* and *Henry Esmond* (published by Smith, Elder) were also issued in a format uniform with that of the *Miscellanies*. Chapman and Hall also participated in this republication, with new editions of the Christmas books and *The Irish Sketch Book*. Hence, Thackeray's income from these older works was renewed.

By the end of 1857, moreover, a new, twenty-four-part serial novel was beginning its appearance—*The Virginians*, for which he received his largest sum ever: £250 for each installment, a total of £6,000, with further income from Harper and Tauchnitz. By a cruel irony, however, Thackeray's financial success was accompanied by the beginning of an artistic decline. Although there are plenty of vital characters and incidents in *The Virginians*, there is an overall loss of concreteness and specificity, together with signs of a loss of inventiveness. Intended as a sequel to *Henry Esmond*, the novel was meant to center on Colonel Esmond's two grandsons during the American Revolution, when one served the king and the other fought as a republican soldier, as Thackeray's cover illustration for the serial installments emphasized. On the one hand, however, an overdeveloped beginning helped defer Thackeray's treatment of the war until the novel's very end; on the other hand, he did not manage to intertwine the narratives of Harry and George Warrington so much as he simply divided the novel between them.

Thackeray's greatest successes are with Beatrix, whom he daringly brings back as stout and elderly, but still domineering; and with Harry, a likable young prodigal, like Pendennis, whose misadventures in love and gambling—with his aging English cousin, Lady Maria; with her rascally family; and with veterans of the bottle and the card tables—form the most entertaining part of the novel. In other details where Thackeray draws upon his past, he is less successful—notably as George Warrington (grandfather of the George Warrington in *Pendennis*) finds unexpected poverty and struggles in the profession of authorship to support his young wife and child. As these details suggest, Thackeray continues to explore his own history, but with somewhat failing imaginative powers. There is a corresponding increase of narrative commentary, but without all of its earlier sparkle and caustic wit. Readers seemed to respond accordingly; the book had large printings but only mediocre sales, and the publishers failed to recover their investments.

While writing *The Virginians*, Thackeray lectured in England and Scotland on the Georges, as he had done on the humorists during the writing of *Henry Esmond*. Some of this income was dissipated when Thackeray took time during July 1857 to stand as an Independent candidate for Parliament from the city of Oxford, for he was defeated by a Liberal and had little to show for his efforts except election expenses of £900. A new source of income opened in 1859, however, when the publisher George Smith made plans to begin a new monthly magazine. Thackeray agreed to write one or two serials for it, receiving £350 per month; and then, as *The Virginians* was moving toward its conclusion in the installment for October 1859, he was named editor of the new periodical, drawing a yearly salary of £1,000. When the *Cornhill Magazine* appeared with the issue for January 1860, it sold a record number of copies for such a periodical: 120,000, with a readership perhaps three or four times larger. Thackeray's success in attracting prominent and

Page from the manuscript for Thackeray's lecture on George III

knowledgeable contributors held most of that original audience, one immediate result of his success being the doubling of his salary as editor. With the guarantee of such an opulent income, Thackeray began to build himself a new home, which he constructed in the red-brick style of Queen Anne, thereby helping to initiate a revival of that architectural style in London.

For his first serial contribution to the *Cornhill*, Thackeray reworked a play he had written in 1855 called "The Wolves and the Lamb," but for which he had not been able to find a producer. The fictional result was a six-part narrative called *Lovel the Widower* (1860), which rather uneasily mingles a serious narrative tone with farcical events. The circuitous mental processes of the narrator, Batchelor, constitute the main inter-

est of the work—especially as he mingles memories of the past with his current observations of the quietly maneuvering governess, Elizabeth Prior, who shrewdly captures Lovel—but Batchelor tends at times to be displaced by the comical eruptions of minor characters. Thackeray's novelistic contributions to the *Cornhill* began in a low key, for he gave pride of place to Anthony Trollope's novel *Framley Parsonage*; but Thackeray reserved for himself the final portion of the monthly issues, where he began to publish a series of familiar essays that became known as the *Roundabout Papers* from their characteristic mode of proceeding.

These engaging works represent the culmination not only of the increasing narrative commentary in his fiction but of the discursive per-

Cover of a monthly number of Thackeray's unsuccessful novel about the American Revolution

sona at the center of his travel books and his many periodical essays. Whether writing "On a Lazy, Idle Boy," "On Ribbons," on "Thorns in the [Editorial] Cushion," "De Juventute," "On Being Found Out," on "Ogres," "On a Pear-Tree," or "On Some Carp at Sans-Souci," as Thackeray looks "Autour de Mon Chapeau" ("around my hat"), he finds objects, events, and aspects of the human condition that provoke his musing, his laughter, and his irrepressible urge to communicate his processes of thought and feeling. As Thackeray's difficulty in writing novels seemed to increase, and as his health deteriorated so as constantly to threaten his ability to complete his month's installment, he found in the "Roundabout Papers" an especially congenial form of utterance, one in which his humor, his rich allusiveness, and his stylistic ease are especially notable.

After *Lovel the Widower* completed its run, Thackeray published "The Four Georges" in successive installments of the *Cornhill* and then waited two months before opening what was to be his last completed novel, which came out in twenty installments, beginning with the *Cornhill* for January 1861: *The Adventures of Philip on His Way through the World, Shewing Who Robbed Him, Who Helped Him, and Who Passed Him By.* Drawing partly upon material from the unfinished "Shabby Genteel Story" of 1840 and from his struggling days as a writer in the first years of his married life, Thackeray intended *The Adventures of Philip* as a novel of contemporary life that would recapture readers who had been disappointed with *Lovel the Widower.* In spite of protracted efforts, however, Thackeray wrote a dull novel, managing often to repeat himself rather than to render the past in a new imaginative vision. In spite of another horrendous mother-in-law, Mrs. Baynes, who helps provide animation, and Dr. Firmin, who interestingly combines emotional anarchy with polished hypocrisy, the novel generates only an intermittent liveliness. Pendennis is again the narrator, but he is increasingly under the influence of his rigidly moralistic wife. Except for Mrs. Baynes, the female characters tend to be uninteresting, while Philip himself manages to be rebellious and boring at the same time.

Increasingly feeling the pressures focused upon the editorial chair and unhappy with the necessity of reading, evaluating, and often refusing the submissions of other people—duties that of course interfered with the writing of his own works—Thackeray resigned from his editorship of the *Cornhill* in March 1862. A few weeks later, he moved into his new, opulently furnished home in Kensington, in the quiet surroundings of which he enjoyed his remaining months of life accompanied by his two daughters and his recently widowed mother. Following the completion of *The Adventures of Philip* in the August 1862 issue of the *Cornhill* came a visit to Paris and a period of nine months during which he published nothing but a half-dozen Roundabout papers. Then, in May 1863, he began his final novel, *Denis Duval* (1864), set in the late eighteenth century. During the next seven months he completed only four serial installments, but the writing is unusually fresh and accompanies a surprising return to the novel of adventure. The events are recalled by the narrator, Denis, living

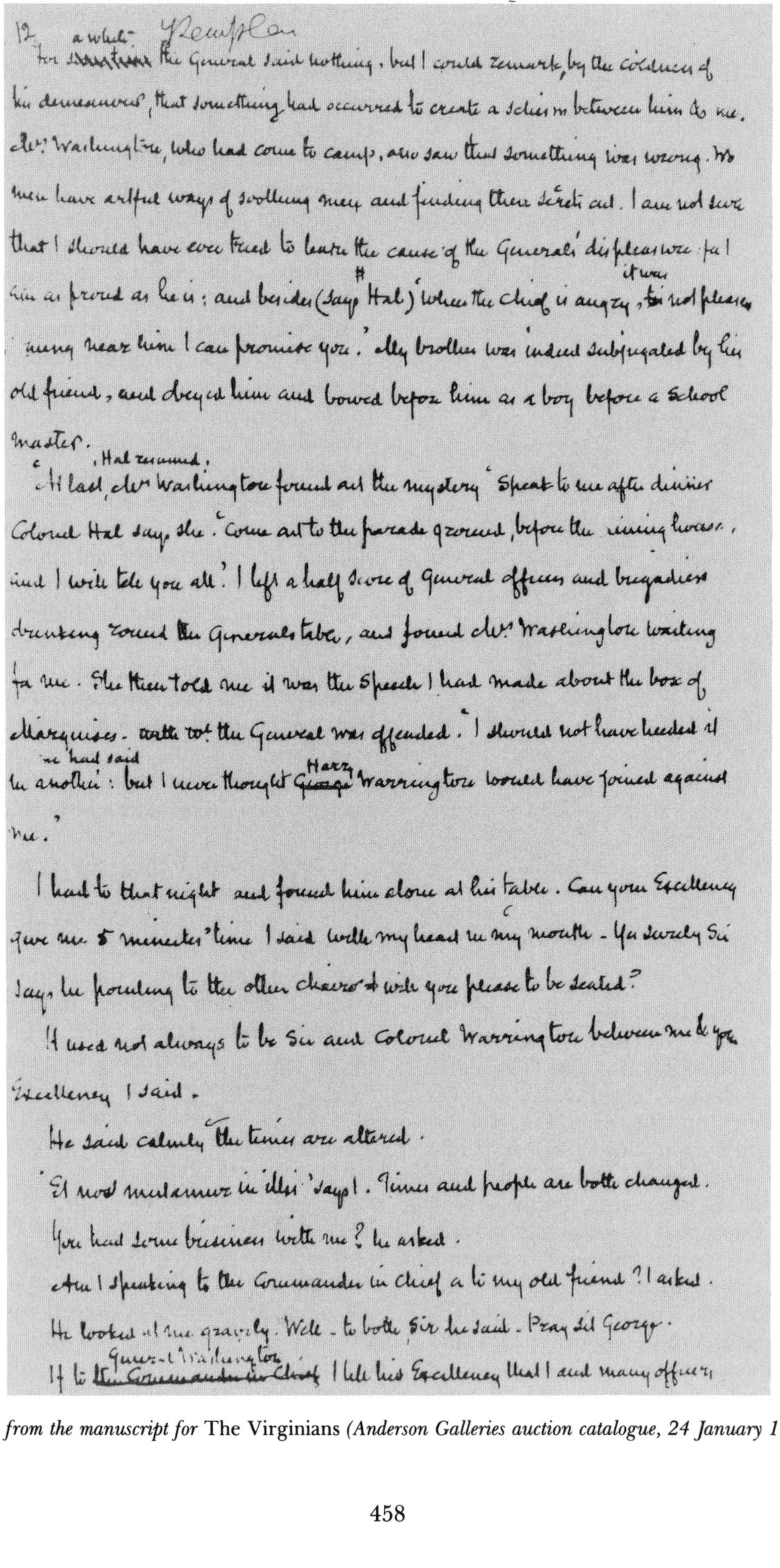

12   a white   Newplan

For sometime the General said nothing, but I could remark, by the coldness of his demeanour, that something had occurred to create a schism between him & me. Mrs Washington, who had come to camp, also saw that something was wrong. We men have artful ways of soothing men and finding their secrets out. I am not sure that I should have even tried to learn the cause of the General's displeasure ; for I know him as proud as he is: and besides (says Hal) when the chief is angry, [it was] is not pleasant being near him I can promise you.' My brother was indeed subjugated by his old friend, and obeyed him and bowed before him as a boy before a schoolmaster.

, Hal resumed,

'At last, Mrs Washington found out the mystery' Speak to me after dinner Colonel Hal says she 'Come out to the parade ground, before the evening hours, and I will tell you all.' I left a half score of General officers and brigadiers drinking round the General's table, and found Mrs Washington waiting for me. She then told me it was the Speech I had made about the box of Marquises. with wh. the General was offended. I should not have heeded it [he had said] in another: but I never thought George [Harry] Warrington would have joined against me.'

I had to that night and found him alone at his table. Can your Excellency give me 5 minutes' time I said with my heart in my mouth - Ye surely Sir says he pointing to the other chairs & will you please to be seated?

It used not always to be Sir and Colonel Warrington between me & your Excellency I said.

He said calmly the times are altered.

'Et nos mutamur in illis' says I. Times and people are both changed.

You had some business with me? he asked.

Am I speaking to the Commander in chief a [or] to my old friend? I asked.

He looked at me gravely. Well - to both Sir he said. Pray Sir George.

If to the [General Washington] Commander in chief I told his Excellency that I and many officers

Page from the manuscript for The Virginians *(Anderson Galleries auction catalogue, 24 January 1929)*

458

in contented maturity with his former child-lover, Agnes, now his wife.

Feeling like "an old gentleman sitting in a fine house like the hero at the end of a story," Thackeray had attained ease and comfort, but his ever more prostrating gastric and urinary attacks had made him pale, drawn, and frequently unable to enjoy what he had won. Yet he was able to make a short Continental trip during part of August, to enjoy a certain amount of nightlife, and to write two final papers for the *Cornhill*. During the latter part of the year, social pleasures and illnesses regularly alternated, his death coming quickly on 24 December 1863 of a ruptured blood vessel in the brain that followed ten days of gastric upset. He was only fifty-two years of age.

Thackeray's daughter Harriet married Leslie Stephen in 1867, dying eight years later in childbirth. His daughter Anne, who had published a short novel before her father's death, went on to develop a career as a professional writer, producing additional novels as well as critical and biographical works, which included biographical introductions to her father's collected writings. Since Thackeray had asked that no biography of him be written, Anne's introductions to each of the volumes discuss the circumstances in which his individual works were composed and thereby provide biographical commentary on the writings rather than a formal biography of the man himself.

Thackeray left behind a massive body of work—lyric and dramatic as well as narrative and expository—including criticism of art, of travel books, of historical writing, of fiction, of biography, and of memoirs, in addition to his own travel writings, historical and biographical sketches, illustrations, familiar essays, tales, and of course his novels, among which *Vanity Fair*, *Pendennis*, *Henry Esmond*, and *The Newcomes* remain preeminent. In all his work the motive is to increase the reader's moral awareness. Such a task includes the satirical attempt to modify the expectations of his readers, which is accomplished with burlesques of fictional conventions of his day that pretend "to represent scenes of 'life,'" with recurrent instances of mock-heroic deflation, and with a complex, powerful narrative irony. Similarly, by means of frequent structural parallels, of telling metaphorical linkages, and of actions and gestures that are emblematically resonant, he seeks to reveal the observable qualities of actual life. To use his own words, he seeks "to

Thackeray's Queen Anne-style house at
2 Palace Green, Kensington

convey as strongly as possible the sentiment of reality," the feel of it, thereby abjuring the sham substitute and evoking instead the consciousness of experienced actuality. Hence, his characters, whether recurring in different works or not, all seem to cluster in a single, continuous world thick with solid, palpable objects; and they carry within them an immense power of memory that can instantly evoke their densely populated past lives. Indeed, Thackeray's deeply felt view of human life as the reflection of the past in the present causes him to be one of the preeminent novelists of memory.

With a man of such wide and diverse reading habits, criticism has tended to concentrate on the one obvious literary relationship: that between Fielding and Thackeray. Minor English and Continental figures seem to have had as much influence upon him as major ones, but among the latter should be mentioned his favorite classical author, Horace; his nineteenth-century predecessor, Sir Walter Scott; familiar essayists such as Michel Eyquem de Montaigne,

Thackeray, near the end of his life, in the library of his home (National Portrait Gallery, London)

Addison, and Steele; and the pictorial satirist William Hogarth, together with Hogarth's followers, James Gillray and George Cruikshank.

Although Charlotte Brontë praised the author of *Vanity Fair* as a satirist, other Victorian commentators felt that the satirical outlook was too deeply grounded in Thackeray's novels. Even George Eliot was discomfited by the revelation of secret, partly unconscious motives in *Henry Esmond*, though she later judged that for "the majority of people with any intellect" Thackeray was probably "the most powerful of living novelists." The charges of "cynicism" persisted well into the twentieth century, by which time the sentiment intermittently present in his fiction came to be called "sentimentality," and one formulator termed him a "sentimental cynic." By contrast, more recent criticism has begun to emphasize the witty intellectual play of his language and to challenge the often-repeated charge of "carelessness" made by Trollope and others. One quality, however, has been continuously recognized: the masterfulness of his style.

Letters:

The Letters and Private Papers of William Makepeace Thackeray, 4 volumes, edited by Gordon N.

Ray (London: Oxford University Press, 1945-1946).

Bibliographies:

Henry S. Van Duzer, *A Thackeray Library* (Port Washington, N.Y.: Kennikat Press, 1965);

Edward M. White, "Thackeray's Contributions to *Fraser's Magazine*," *Studies in Bibliography*, 19 (1966): 67-84;

Dudley Flamm, *Thackeray's Critics: An Annotated Bibliography of British and American Criticism 1836-1901* (Chapel Hill: University of North Carolina Press, 1967);

John C. Olmsted, *Thackeray and His Twentieth-Century Critics: An Annotated Bibliography, 1900-1975* (New York & London: Garland, 1977);

Sheldon Goldfarb, *William Makepeace Thackeray: An Annotated Bibliography, 1976-1987* (New York & London: Garland, 1989).

Biographies:

"Lewis Melville" (Lewis Benjamin), *William Makepeace Thackeray: A Biography*, 2 volumes (London: John Lane, 1910);

Lionel Stevenson, *The Showman of Vanity Fair* (New York: Scribners, 1947);

Gordon N. Ray, *William Makepeace Thackeray: The Uses of Adversity* (New York: McGraw-Hill, 1955);

Ray, *William Makepeace Thackeray: The Age of Wisdom* (New York: McGraw-Hill, 1958);

Ann Monsarrat, *An Uneasy Victorian: Thackeray the Man* (New York: Dodd, Mead, 1980);

Catherine Peters, *Thackeray's Universe: Shifting Worlds of Imagination and Reality* (London & Boston: Faber & Faber, 1987).

References:

John Carey, *Thackeray: Prodigal Genius* (London: Faber & Faber, 1977);

Robert A. Colby, *Fiction with a Purpose* (Bloomington: Indiana University Press, 1967);

Colby, *Thackeray's Canvass of Humanity* (Columbus: Ohio State University Press, 1979);

Colby, "William Makepeace Thackeray," in *Victorian Fiction: A Second Guide to Research*, edited by George H. Ford (New York: Modern Language Association of America, 1978), pp. 114-142;

Philip Collins, ed., *Thackeray: Interviews and Recollections*, 2 volumes (New York: St. Martin's Press, 1983);

Costerus, special Thackeray issue, new series 2 (1974);

G. Armour Craig, "On the Style of *Vanity Fair*," in *Style in Prose Fiction*, edited by Harold C. Martin (New York: Columbia University Press, 1959), pp. 87-113;

John W. Dodds, *Thackeray: A Critical Portrait* (New York: Oxford University Press, 1941);

A. E. Dyson, "*Vanity Fair*: An Irony Against Heroes," *Critical Quarterly*, 6 (1964): 11-31;

Spencer L. Eddy, Jr., *The Founding of "The Cornhill Magazine"* (Muncie, Ind.: Ball State University Press, 1970);

Martin Fido, "*The History of Pendennis*: A Reconsideration," *Essays in Criticism*, 14 (1964): 363-379;

Philip Gaskell, "Thackeray, *Henry Esmond*, 1852," in his *From Writer to Reader: Studies in Editorial Method* (Oxford: Clarendon Press, 1978), pp. 156-182;

John Hagan, " 'Bankruptcy of His Heart': The Unfulfilled Life of Henry Esmond," *Nineteenth-Century Fiction*, 27 (1972-1973): 293-316;

Hagan, "*Vanity Fair*: Becky Brought to Book Again," *Studies in the Novel*, 7 (1975): 479-506;

Edgar F. Harden, "The Discipline and Significance of Form in *Vanity Fair*," *PMLA*, 82 (1967): 530-541;

Harden, *The Emergence of Thackeray's Serial Fiction* (Athens: University of Georgia Press, 1979);

Harden, "The Fields of Mars in *Vanity Fair*," *Tennessee Studies in Literature*, 10 (1965): 123-132;

Harden, "A Partial Outline for Thackeray's *The Virginians*," *Journal of English and Germanic Philology*, 75 (1976): 168-187;

Harden, "The Serial Structure of Thackeray's *Pendennis*," *Revue de l'Université d'Ottawa*, 45 (1975): 162-180;

Harden, ed., *Annotations for the Selected Works of William Makepeace Thackeray*, 2 volumes (New York & London: Garland, 1990);

Barbara Hardy, *The Exposure of Luxury: Radical Themes in Thackeray* (London: Owen, 1972);

John Harvey, " 'A Voice Concurrent or Prophetical': The Illustrated Novels of W. M. Thackeray," in his *Victorian Novelists and their Illustrators* (London: Sidgwick & Jackson, 1970), pp. 76-102;

Keith Hollingsworth, *The Newgate Novel* (Detroit: Wayne State University Press, 1963);

Wolfgang Iser, "The Reader as a Component Part of the Realistic Novel: Esthetic Effects in Thackeray's *Vanity Fair*," "Self-Reduction: The Self-Communication of Subjectivity in Autobiographical Fiction. Wm. Thackeray: *Henry Esmond*," in his *The Implied Reader* (Baltimore & London: Johns Hopkins University Press, 1974);

John A. Lester, Jr., "Thackeray's Narrative Technique," *PMLA*, 69 (1954): 392-409;

George Levine, "Thackeray: 'The Legitimate High Priest of Truth' and the Problematics of the Real," "Thackeray: Some Elements of Realism," "*Pendennis*: The Virtue of the Dilettante's Unbelief," in his *The Realistic Imagination* (Chicago & London: University of Chicago Press, 1981);

John Loofbourow, *Thackeray and the Form of Fiction* (Princeton: Princeton University Press, 1964);

Michael Lund, *Reading Thackeray* (Detroit: Wayne State University Press, 1988);

William H. Marshall, "Dramatic Irony in *Henry Esmond*," *Revue des Langues Vivantes*, 1 (1961): 35-42;

Juliet McMaster, *Thackeray: The Major Novels* (Toronto: University of Toronto Press, 1971);

McMaster, "Thackeray's Things: Time's Local Habitation," in *The Victorian Experience*, edited by Richard A. Levine (Athens: Ohio University Press, 1976), pp. 49-86;

Rowland D. McMaster, " 'An Honorable Emulation of the Author of *The Newcomes*': James and Thackeray," *Nineteenth-Century Fiction*, 32 (1977-1978): 399-419;

McMaster, "The Pygmalion Motif in *The Newcomes*," *Nineteenth-Century Fiction*, 29 (1974-1975): 22-39;

J. Hillis Miller, *The Form of Victorian Fiction* (Notre Dame & London: University of Notre Dame Press, 1968);

Miller, "*Henry Esmond*: Repetition and Irony," in his *Fiction and Repetition: Seven English Novels* (Cambridge, Mass.: Harvard University Press, 1982);

Isadore G. Mudge and M. Earl Sears, *A Thackeray Dictionary* (New York: Dutton, 1910);

Lidmila Pantŭčková, "Thackeray as a Reader and Critic of French Literature," *Brno Studies in English*, 9 (1970): 37-126;

Pantŭčková, *W. M. Thackeray as a Critic of Literature* (Brno, Czechoslovakia: Purkyne University Press, 1972);

Pantŭčková, "W. M. Thackeray's Literary Criticism in the *Morning Chronicle* (1844-1848)," *Brno Studies in English*, 2 (1960): 79-111;

K. C. Phillipps, *The Language of Thackeray* (London: Deutsch, 1978);

Arthur Pollard, ed., *Thackeray. "Vanity Fair." A Casebook* (London & Basingstoke: Macmillan, 1978);

Jack P. Rawlins, *Thackeray's Novels: A Fiction That Is True* (Berkeley, Los Angeles & London: University of California Press, 1974);

Gordon N. Ray, *The Buried Life: A Study of the Relation between Thackeray's Fiction and His Personal History* (London: Oxford University Press, 1952);

Ray, *"Vanity Fair*: One Version of the Novelist's Responsibility," *Essays by Divers Hands*, new series 23 (London: Oxford University Press, 1950);

Winslow Rogers, "Thackeray's Self-Consciousness," in *The Worlds of Victorian Fiction*, edited by Jerome H. Buckley (Cambridge, Mass.: Harvard University Press, 1975), pp. 149-163;

George Saintsbury, *A Consideration of Thackeray* (London: Oxford University Press, 1931);

M. Corona Sharp, "Sympathetic Mockery: A Study of the Narrator's Character in *Vanity Fair*," *ELH*, 29 (1962): 324-336;

Robin Ann Sheets, "Art and Artistry in *Vanity Fair*," *ELH*, 42 (1975): 420-432;

Peter L. Shillingsburg, "The First Edition of Thackeray's *Pendennis*," *Papers of the Bibliographical Society of America*, 66 (1972): 35-49;

Shillingsburg, "*Pendennis* Revised," *Etudes Anglaises*, 34 (1981): 432-442;

Shillingsburg, "The Printing, Proofreading, and Publishing of Thackeray's *Vanity Fair*," *Studies in Bibliography*, 34 (1981): 118-145;

Shillingsburg, "Textual Problems in Editing Thackeray," in *Editing Nineteenth-Century Fiction*, edited by Jane Millgate (New York & London: Garland, 1978), pp. 41-60;

Joan Stevens, "A Roundabout Ride," *Victorian Studies*, 13 (1969-1970): 53-70;

Stevens, "Thackeray's *Vanity Fair*," *Review of English Literature*, 6 (1965): 19-38;

Lionel Stevenson, "William Makepeace Thackeray," in *Victorian Fiction: A Guide to Research*, edited by Stevenson (Cambridge, Mass.: Harvard University Press, 1964), pp. 154-187;

Studies in the Novel, special Thackeray issue, 13 (1981);

Jean Sudrann, " 'The Philosopher's Property': Thackeray and the Use of Time," *Victorian Studies*, 10 (1966-1967): 359-388;

M. G. Sundell, ed., *Twentieth Century Interpretations of "Vanity Fair"* (Englewood Cliffs, N.J.: Prentice-Hall, 1969);

John A. Sutherland, "*Henry Esmond:* The Shaping Power of Contract," in his *Victorian Novelists and Publishers* (London: Athlone Press, 1976), pp. 101-116;

Sutherland, *Thackeray at Work* (London: Athlone Press, 1974);

Henri-A. Talon, "Time and Memory in Thackeray's *Henry Esmond*," *Review of English Studies*, 13 (1962): 147-156;

Myron Taube, "Contrast as a Principle of Structure in *Vanity Fair*," *Nineteenth-Century Fiction*, 18 (1963-1964): 119-135;

The Thackeray Newsletter (1975-present);

John Tilford, "The Love Theme of *Henry Esmond*," *PMLA*, 67 (1952): 684-701;

Geoffrey Tillotson and Donald Hawes, eds., *Thackeray: The Critical Heritage* (London: Routledge & Kegan Paul, 1968);

Tillotson, *Thackeray the Novelist* (London: Cambridge University Press, 1954);

Kathleen Tillotson, "Introductory," "*Vanity Fair*," in her *Novels of the Eighteen-Forties* (Oxford: Clarendon Press, 1954), pp. 1-156, 224-256;

Alexander Welsh, ed., *Thackeray: A Collection of Critical Essays* (Englewood Cliffs, N.J.: Prentice-Hall, 1968);

James H. Wheatley, *Patterns in Thackeray's Fiction* (Cambridge & London: M.I.T. Press, 1969);

Ann Y. Wilkinson, "The Tomeavesian Way of Knowing the World: Technique and Meaning in *Vanity Fair*," *ELH*, 32 (1965): 370-387;

Ioan M. Williams, *Thackeray* (London: Evans, 1968);

George A. Worth, "The Unity of *Henry Esmond*," *Nineteenth-Century Fiction*, 15 (1960-1961): 345-353.

Papers:

The British Library has notebook and page proofs for *Denis Duval*, manuscripts for *The Second Funeral of Napoleon* and "The Wolves and the Lamb," diaries, notebooks, and correspondence; the Charterhouse School Library has much of the manuscript for *The Newcomes*; Harvard University has portions of the manuscripts for *The Four Georges*, *Pendennis*, *Roundabout Papers*, and *Stubbs's Calendar*, and correspondence; the Huntington Library has parts of the manuscripts for *The Adventures of Philip*, *The English Humourists*, *The Four Georges*, *Lovel the Widower*, *Our Street*, and *Roundabout Papers*, fragments of minor unpublished manuscripts, and correspondence; the Pierpont Morgan Library has partial or complete manuscripts for *Denis Duval*, *The Four Georges*, *Lovel the Widower*, *The Rose and the Ring*, *Vanity Fair*, and *The Virginians*, fragments of minor unpublished manuscripts, diaries, notebooks, and correspondence; the National Library of Scotland has a small portion of the manuscript for *Denis Duval* and correspondence; at the New York Public Library, the Arents Collection has a small amount of page proofs for *The Adventures of Philip*, while the Berg Collection has partial manuscripts for *The English Humourists*, *The Newcomes*, and *Roundabout Papers*, fragmentary portions of other published works, fragments of minor unpublished manuscripts, diaries, notebooks, and correspondence, and the Manuscript Division has a notebook for *The History of Henry Esmond, Esq.* and fragments of minor unpublished manuscripts; at New York University, the Fales Collection contains fragmentary portions of published works and correspondence; at Princeton University, the Parrish Collection has correspondence, and the Taylor Collection contains fragmentary portions of published and unpublished works and correspondence; the *Punch* office has correspondence; the Rosenbach Foundation Museum contains a notebook for *The Four Georges* and correspondence; Trinity College, Cambridge University has almost all of the manuscript for *The History of Henry Esmond, Esq.;* the Harry Ransom Humanities Research Center of the University of Texas, Austin has a small portion of the manuscript for *Our Street*, proof plates for *Doctor Birch*, *The Kickleburys on the Rhine*, and *Mrs. Perkins's Ball*, fragmentary portions of published works, and correspondence; and Yale University has a small portion of the manuscript for *The Adventures of Philip*, galley proofs for *The Four Georges*, *Lovel the Widower*, and *The Adventures of Philip*, a notebook for *The Virginians*, and correspondence.

Anthony Trollope

(24 April 1815 - 6 December 1882)

This entry was updated by Juliet McMaster (University of Alberta) from her entry in
DLB 21: Victorian Novelists Before 1885.

See also the Trollope entry in DLB 57: Victorian
Prose Writers After 1867.

BOOKS: *The Macdermots of Ballycloran* (3 volumes,
London: Newby, 1847; 1 volume, Philadelphia: Peterson, 1871);

The Kellys and the O'Kellys; or, Landlords and Tenants: A Tale of Irish Life (3 volumes, London:
Colburn, 1848; 1 volume, New York:
Munro, 1882);

La Vendée: An Historical Romance, 3 volumes (London: Colburn, 1850);

The Warden (London: Longman, Brown, Green &
Longmans, 1855; New York: Dick & Fitzgerald, 1862);

Barchester Towers (3 volumes, London: Longman,
Brown, Green, Longmans & Roberts, 1857;
1 volume, New York: Dick & Fitzgerald,
1860);

The Three Clerks: A Novel (3 volumes, London:
Bentley, 1858; 1 volume, New York:
Harper, 1860);

Doctor Thorne: A Novel (3 volumes, London: Chapman & Hall, 1858; 1 volume, New York:
Harper, 1858);

The Bertrams: A Novel (3 volumes, London: Chapman & Hall, 1859; 1 volume, New York:
Harper, 1859);

The West Indies and the Spanish Main (London:
Chapman & Hall, 1859; New York: Harper,
1860);

Castle Richmond: A Novel (3 volumes, London:
Chapman & Hall, 1860; 1 volume, New
York: Harper, 1860);

Framley Parsonage (3 volumes, London: Smith,
Elder, 1861; 1 volume, New York: Harper,
1861);

Tales of All Countries, 2 volumes (London: Chapman & Hall, 1861-1863);

Orley Farm (20 monthly parts, London: Chapman
& Hall, 1861-1862; 1 volume, New York:
Harper, 1862);

*The Struggles of Brown, Jones, and Robinson, by One
of the Firm* (New York: Harper, 1862; London: Smith, Elder, 1870);

North America (2 volumes, London: Chapman &
Hall, 1862; unauthorized edition, 1 volume,
New York: Harper, 1862; authorized edition, 2 volumes, New York: Lippincott,
1862);

Rachel Ray: A Novel (2 volumes, London: Chapman & Hall, 1863; 1 volume, New York:
Harper, 1863);

The Small House at Allington (2 volumes, London: Smith, Elder, 1864; 1 volume, New York: Harper, 1864);

Can You Forgive Her? (20 monthly parts, London: Chapman & Hall, 1864-1865; 1 volume, New York: Harper, 1865);

Hunting Sketches (London: Chapman & Hall, 1865; Hartford, Conn.: Mitchell, 1929);

Miss Mackenzie (2 volumes, London: Chapman & Hall, 1865; 1 volume, New York: Harper, 1865);

The Belton Estate (3 volumes, London: Chapman & Hall, 1866; unauthorized American edition, 1 volume, New York: Harper, 1866; authorized American edition, 1 volume, New York: Lippincott, 1866);

Travelling Sketches (London: Chapman & Hall, 1866);

Clergymen of the Church of England (London: Chapman & Hall, 1866);

The Claverings (New York: Harper, 1867; 2 volumes, London: Smith, Elder, 1867);

Nina Balatka: The Story of a Maiden of Prague, 2 volumes (Edinburgh & London: Blackwood, 1867; London & New York: Oxford University Press, 1951);

The Last Chronicle of Barset (32 weekly parts, London: Smith, Elder, 1867; 1 volume, New York: Harper, 1867);

Lotta Schmidt and Other Stories (London: Strahan, 1867; London & New York: Ward & Lock, 1883);

Linda Tressel (2 volumes, Edinburgh & London: Blackwood, 1868; 1 volume, Boston: Littell & Gay, 1868);

He Knew He Was Right (32 weekly parts, London: Virtue, 1868-1869; 1 volume, New York: Harper, 1870);

Phineas Finn: The Irish Member (2 volumes, London: Virtue, 1869; 1 volume, New York: Harper, 1869);

Did He Steal It? A Comedy in Three Acts (London: Privately printed, 1869);

The Vicar of Bullhampton (11 monthly parts, London: Bradbury & Evans, 1869-1870; unauthorized American edition, 1 volume, New York: Harper, 1870; authorized American edition, 1 volume, New York: Lippincott, 1870);

An Editor's Tales (London: Strahan, 1870);

The Commentaries of Caesar (Edinburgh & London: Blackwood, 1870; Philadelphia: Lippincott, 1870);

Ralph the Heir (19 monthly parts, London: Hurst & Blackett, 1870-1871; 1 volume, New York: Harper, 1871);

Sir Harry Hotspur of Humblethwaite (London: Hurst & Blackett, 1871; New York: Harper, 1871);

The Golden Lion of Granpère (London: Tinsley, 1872; New York: Harper, 1872);

The Eustace Diamonds (New York: Harper, 1872; 3 volumes, London: Chapman & Hall, 1873);

Australia and New Zealand, 2 volumes (London: Chapman & Hall, 1873);

Lady Anna (2 volumes, London: Chapman & Hall, 1874; 1 volume, New York: Harper, 1874);

Phineas Redux (2 volumes, London: Chapman & Hall, 1874; 1 volume, New York: Harper, 1874);

Harry Heathcote of Gangoil: A Tale of Australian Bush Life (London: Low, Marston, Low & Searle, 1874; New York: Harper, 1874);

The Way We Live Now (20 monthly parts, London: Chapman & Hall, 1874-1875; 1 volume, New York: Harper, 1875);

The Prime Minister (8 monthly parts, London: Chapman & Hall, 1875-1876; 1 volume, New York: Harper, 1876);

The American Senator (3 volumes, London: Chapman & Hall, 1877; 1 volume, New York: Harper, 1877);

Christmas at Thompson Hall (New York: Harper, 1877; London: Low, 1885);

The Lady of Lannay (New York: Harper, 1877);

Is He Popenjoy? A Novel (3 volumes, London: Chapman & Hall, 1878; 1 volume, New York: Harper, 1878);

How the "Mastiffs" Went to Iceland (London: Virtue, 1878);

South Africa, 2 volumes (London: Chapman & Hall, 1878);

An Eye for an Eye (2 volumes, London: Chapman & Hall, 1879; 1 volume, New York: Harper, 1879);

John Caldigate (3 volumes, London: Chapman & Hall, 1879; 1 volume, New York: Harper, 1879);

Cousin Henry: A Novel (2 volumes, London: Chapman & Hall, 1879; 1 volume, New York: Munro, 1879);

Thackeray (London: Macmillan, 1879; New York: Harper, 1879);

The Duke's Children: A Novel (3 volumes, London: Chapman & Hall, 1880; 1 volume, New York: Munro, 1880);

Frances Trollope's unsuccessful Cincinnati emporium

The Life of Cicero, 2 volumes (London: Chapman & Hall, 1880; New York: Harper, 1881);

Dr. Wortle's School: A Novel (New York: Harper, 1880; 2 volumes, London: Chapman & Hall, 1881);

Ayala's Angel (3 volumes, London: Chapman & Hall, 1881; 1 volume, New York: Harper, 1881);

Why Frau Frohmann Raised Her Prices, and Other Stories (London: Isbister, 1882; New York: Harper, 1882);

The Fixed Period: A Novel (2 volumes, Edinburgh & London: Blackwood, 1882; 1 volume, New York: Harper, 1882);

Lord Palmerston (London: Isbister, 1882);

Marion Fay: A Novel (3 volumes, London: Chapman & Hall, 1882; 1 volume, New York: Harper, 1882);

Kept in the Dark: A Novel (2 volumes, London: Chatto & Windus, 1882; 1 volume, New York: Harper, 1882);

The Two Heroines of Plumplington (New York: Munro, 1882; London: Deutsch, 1953);

Not if I Know It (New York: Munro, 1883);

Mr. Scarborough's Family (3 volumes, London: Chatto & Windus, 1883; 1 volume, New York: Harper, 1883);

The Landleaguers (3 volumes, London: Chatto & Windus, 1883; 1 volume, New York: Munro, 1883);

An Autobiography (2 volumes, Edinburgh & London: Blackwood, 1883; 1 volume, New York: Harper, 1883);

Alice Dugdale and Other Stories (Leipzig: Tauchnitz, 1883);

La Mère Bauche and Other Stories (Leipzig: Tauchnitz, 1883; New York: Munro, 1884);

The Mistletoe Bough and Other Stories (Leipzig: Tauchnitz, 1883);

An Old Man's Love (2 volumes, Edinburgh & London: Blackwood, 1884; 1 volume, New York: Lovell, 1884);

The Noble Jilt: A Comedy, edited by Michael Sadleir (London: Constable, 1923);

London Tradesmen, edited by Sadleir (London: Mathews & Marrot, 1927; New York: Scribners, 1927);

Four Lectures, edited by M. L. Parrish (London: Constable, 1938);

The Tireless Traveller: Twenty Letters to the "Liverpool Mercury" 1875, edited by Bradford Allen Booth (Berkeley & Los Angeles: University of California Press, 1941);

Novels and Tales, edited by J. Hampden (London: Pilot Press, 1946);

The Parson's Daughter and Other Stories, edited by Hampden (London: Folio Society, 1949);

The Spotted Dog and Other Stories (London: Pan, 1950);

Mary Gresley and Other Stories, edited by Hampden (London: Folio Society, 1951);

The New Zealander, edited by N. John Hall (London: Oxford University Press, 1972);

Miscellaneous Essays and Reviews (New York: Arno, 1981);

Writings for Saint Paul's Magazine (New York: Arno, 1981).

Collections: *The Oxford Illustrated Trollope*, 15 volumes, edited by Sadleir and F. Page (Oxford: Oxford University Press, 1948-1954);

Selected Works of Anthony Trollope, 62 volumes, edited by Hall (New York: Arno, 1980).

OTHER: *British Sports and Pastimes*, edited, with contributions, by Trollope (London & New York: Virtue, 1868).

"I do lay claim to whatever merit should be accorded to me for persevering diligence in my profession," Anthony Trollope wrote in one of the concluding paragraphs of *An Autobiography* (1883). No one has ever been able to deny him that claim: as the author of some forty-seven novels, and many further volumes of travels, sketches, criticism, and short fiction, he was fully justified in his pride in the quantity of his production. He was more modest about claiming quality; but the continued sale of his many novels through a century after his death, and the increasing testimony among critics as to the power and subtlety of his work, make it clear that he did indeed achieve "the permanence of success" to which he would not himself lay claim. Among the great nineteenth-century novelists of England, he stands in critical reputation close after Jane Austen, Charles Dickens, and George Eliot; and perhaps on a level with Charlotte and Emily Brontë, and with Sir Walter Scott and William Makepeace Thackeray, whom he admired and emulated. He certainly wrote more than any of them.

Success was particularly important to him because of a grinding sense of failure in his childhood. The narrative shape that he gives to his life in his *Autobiography* is the story of an ugly duckling who through great trials and great feats came to be recognized as a swan. (Biographers have questioned the historical accuracy of the *Autobiography*, but it must be respected as his own construction of his life and responses.) His childhood was unhappy, by his own account miserable. His father was a down-at-heel gentleman and scholar who failed at the law, failed at scholarship, and then took to farming and failed at that, too. Anthony was sent as a day-student to Harrow, where the boarders sneered at him for the muddy boots he incurred by his long walk to school; then as a boarder to Winchester, where he was often beaten; and then back to Harrow. He was insufficiently supplied with money and suffered deep embarrassment among his peers and before the masters. Though coveting popularity, he felt like a pariah, and left school with the conviction that he had "been flogged oftener than any human being alive."

During his school years the family was in poor circumstances. His father was unable to support them, so his mother, the vigorous Frances (Fanny) Trollope, took matters into her own hands. In 1827 she made an excursion to America, where she set up a bazaar in Cincinnati, Ohio, with the intention of making money by selling gewgaws and objets d'art. This enterprise failed, but her experience prompted her to write; and on her return she sold her book, *The Domestic Manners of the Americans* (1832), which was not the less a success for being highly critical of American mores. Thereafter she supported the

Rose Heseltine, Trollope's wife

family by her pen, even when they had to escape ahead of the bailiffs to Bruges in Belgium. Here she continued to write in the intervals of nursing a tubercular son and daughter and her husband, who had long been subject to bouts of illness. All three died between 1834 and 1835. Fanny Trollope continued to write through a long career, during which she produced over a hundred books. She was an inspiration to her children, particularly her surviving sons, Thomas Adolphus and Anthony, who both took to "the family business" of writing in due course.

Anthony seems to have been viewed as a burden in the family, being in Bruges "that most hopeless of human beings, a hobbledehoy of nineteen." In 1834 he became an usher at a school in Brussels, but then returned to England to become a junior clerk in the post office. Although he had now found a career, his life did not immediately improve. From 1835 to 1841 he got into various scrapes over money and women. Some of these are described in the chapters on Charley Tudor, Johnny Eames, and Phineas Finn in his novels *The Three Clerks* (1858), *The Small House at Allington* (1864), and *Phineas Finn* (1869). Aside from these novels and some of his short stories that are similarly based on his own experience,

Lord Lufton and Lucy Robarts of Framley Parsonage, *as depicted by Sir John Everett Millais*

Trollope's fiction does not in any direct way re-create his life. At a conscious level, at least, he worked on a principle of abstracting himself from his fiction, laying his own identity aside.

In the summer of 1841, when he was twenty-six, he took the chance of changing his unsatisfactory life by successfully applying for the position of a post office surveyor's clerk in Ireland. Ireland was for Trollope what the fairy godmother was for Cinderella; it transformed him and opened out new vistas in his life. "There had clung to me a feeling that I had been looked upon always as an evil, an encumbrance, a use-less thing,—as a creature of whom those connected with him had to be ashamed. . . . But from the day on which I set my foot in Ireland all these evils went away from me." In Ireland he became good at his job and valued it; he married Rose Heseltine, who was his devoted wife and literary assistant for the rest of his life; he began to hunt; and he wrote his first novels.

Trollope did not, like Dickens, find his métier and his public at once. His first three nov-

els were tentative and experimental, and did not sell well. He tells how he conceived the idea for his first novel, *The Macdermots of Ballycloran* (1847), in a preface to it and in the *Autobiography*. Being delayed in the small Irish town of Drumsna, he took a walk with his friend John Merivale and came across "the modern ruins of a country house. It was one of the most melancholy spots I ever visited. . . . We wandered about the place, suggesting to each other causes for the misery we saw there, and while I was still among the ruined walls and decayed beams I fabricated the plot of *The Macdermots of Ballycloran*." (It is characteristic that Trollope should first have his imagination stirred by a place, a country residence which prompted the creation of its residents: the same thing was subsequently to happen with *The Warden*, 1855.) The tumbledown estate led Trollope to envisage a set of characters and a situation that would lead to its desolation; and his first novel is in the tragic, not the comic mode. Euphemia Macdermot, the daughter of an old Irish family that has seen better days, is seduced by an English police captain, Ussher. Finding the couple together, her outraged brother, Thady, strikes Ussher, who dies as a result. Thady is put on trial and condemned to death, and his sister rather improbably dies in the courtroom from complications of pregnancy. The plot is enlarged by Thady's dealings with a group of Irish nationalist conspirators.

Trollope's publisher was T. C. Newby of Mortimer Street, who also published Emily Brontë's *Wuthering Heights* and Anne Brontë's *Agnes Grey* at about the same time. Such a crop seems to have been due to luck rather than good management on Newby's part, for he did not treat his authors courteously. The Brontë novels were published without benefit of proofreading, and Trollope received no remuneration and no accounting for the sales of his first novel. As Charlotte Bronte said in a letter of 1847, "If Mr. Newby always does business in this way, few authors would like to have him for their publisher a second time." It is not surprising that Trollope went to another publisher, Henry Colburn, with his next novel.

The Kellys and the O'Kellys (1848) is also set in Ireland, and presents high and low Irish life and the relations of landlords and tenants, fortunes and fortune-hunters. This novel also deals sympathetically with the Irish and their problems, but it sold only one hundred forty copies in the first edition, in spite of being briefly noticed in the *Times*. "It is evident that readers do not like novels on Irish subjects as well as on others," his publishers told him. Eager to take advice, Trollope altogether changed his subject matter for his next novel, *La Vendée* (1850), a historical romance set in eighteenth-century France; on this work he made his first twenty pounds by writing, but he still found no substantial readership. *The Macdermots of Ballycloran* and *The Kellys and the O'Kellys* were later discovered and enjoyed by readers who had learned to admire Trollope's subsequent works, but *La Vendée* has never been much read.

In the early 1850s Trollope's post-office work absorbed all his energies. He was assigned to work out the routes for rural deliveries, first in a district in Ireland and then in some counties in England, particularly in the west. He did his work with zeal, riding over all the routes himself, and determined to make it possible that a letter could be delivered to every remote residence in his district. It was while visiting the close of Salisbury Cathedral that he conceived the story of *The*

Warden, the first in the series of novels about his invented county of Barsetshire, which was to make him famous.

The Warden was published in 1855, and its success, and that of its sequel, *Barchester Towers* (1857), marked the public's recognition of a new major novelist. In *The Warden* appear many of the characteristics that were to distinguish his work as a whole: his delicacy in the handling of nuances of character, his reservations about moral zeal, his propensity to view his characters in their public and professional capacities as well as in their private and domestic roles, and his qualified conservatism according to which the High Church and landowning classes are portrayed with affectionate sympathy as well as irony. The warden himself, Mr. Harding, a gentle, middle-aged innocent, has accepted a sinecure administering charitable monies for the maintenance of twelve bedesmen. A zealous young man, John Bold, who is in love with the warden's daughter Eleanor, nevertheless brings public attention to the fact that the warden, rather than the bedesmen, is the main beneficiary of the charity. Sides are taken, legal proceedings are instituted, the daily *Jupiter* (a satirical representation of the *Times*) and even the attorney-general are drawn into the burgeoning issue. The book is to some extent a mock epic, making fun of the "heroes" John Bold and Tom Towers, who arm themselves in the conflict against doughtily clad ecclesiastics, and humorously dwelling on battles at tea parties and campaigns conducted at whist. In the midst of this war, the warden, whose conscience has been touched even though he is told his side will win, simply resigns his position. As the furor dies down, no new warden is appointed, and the twelve bedesmen are left uncared for. The zeal of the reformers, despite the apparent justice of their cause, has done nobody any good.

In *Barchester Towers* Trollope reintroduced many of the same characters, including Mr. Harding and his vigorous son-in-law Dr. Grantly, an archdeacon and a pillar of the church establishment. The plot turns on the machinations of the greasy, Low Church Mr. Slope, chaplain to the mild new bishop of Barchester, Dr. Proudie, and favorite of the bishop's domineering wife. Mr. Slope's marital and professional ambitions become amusingly involved as he dangles after two attractive ladies, Eleanor Bold, now a widow, and the sirenlike Signora Vesey Neroni, while trying at the same time to stay in the good graces of his exacting patroness. Eleanor, the heroine, similarly has more than one marital prospect: besides the persistent Mr. Slope himself—whom finally she can dismiss only by administering a resounding slap in the face—she has Bertie Stanhope as a hopeful suitor. He is a good-natured dilettante, brother to the seductive signora, and he too likes the thought of getting Eleanor and her money. The reader is induced to interest himself in this matter of Eleanor's choice among rogues, and at one point the narrator addresses the reader directly: "But let the gentle-hearted reader be under no apprehension whatsoever. It is not destined that Eleanor shall marry Mr. Slope or Bertie Stanhope. And here, perhaps, it may be allowed to the novelist to explain his views on a very important point in the art of telling tales. He ventures to reprobate that system which goes so far to violate all proper confidence between the author and his readers, by maintaining nearly to the end of the third volume a mystery as to the fate of their favourite personage. . . . Our doctrine is, that the author and the reader should move along together in full confidence with each other." Such an authorial intrusion was offensive to Henry James, who took Trollope to task for his propensity to give himself away, to admit while telling his story that the story is merely a fiction. More recent critics, however, such as James Kincaid, have found much to praise in Trollope's art of maintaining an intimate relation with his reader.

The other novels in the Barset series, with which Trollope was engaged intermittently over the next decade, were *Doctor Thorne* (1858), *Framley Parsonage* (1861), *The Small House at Allington* (1864), and *The Last Chronicle of Barset* (1867). Each of these novels is distinct and separable from the rest, with its own plot and new major characters. So far as the series has a unity, it is supplied by the setting, the quiet cathedral city of Barchester with its surrounding town, villages, and ancestral estates of Barsetshire; by its continuing concern with ecclesiastical matters; and by a few recurring characters. Mr. Harding, the perpetual innocent, is in the tradition of Miguel de Cervantes' Don Quixote, Laurence Sterne's Uncle Toby, Dickens's Mr. Pickwick, and Thackeray's Colonel Newcome. His son-in-law the archdeacon, vociferous and bigoted, is nonetheless unable to dominate the gentle old man. The Barsetshire aristocrats are the arrogant De Courcys of Courcy Castle and the duke of Omnium of Omnium Gatherum Castle (Trollope has often been criticized for his facetious names). In

the henpecked Bishop Proudie and his outspoken virago of a wife, Trollope first developed a continuing concern with the distribution of power in marriage, and indeed in all human relations. Later in the series, as a result of overhearing at his club an impatient comment on the everpresent Mrs. Proudie, he killed her off—not without many regrets, as he explained: "It was not only that she was a tyrant, a bully, a would-be priestess, a very vulgar woman, and one who would send headlong to the nethermost pit all who disagreed with her; but that at the same time she was conscientious, by no means a hypocrite, really believing in the brimstone which she threatened, and anxious to save the souls around her from its horrors." The description typifies Trollope's habitually careful weighing of opposites, his exact measurement of the good even in his worst characters and of the shortcomings even in his best.

The plot of *Doctor Thorne* is on a favorite theme of Trollope's: a courtship that is complicated by the unequal social status of the lovers. Mary Thorne, who as a penniless and illegitimate orphan became the ward of her uncle, Dr. Thorne, is loved by Frank Gresham of Greshamsbury Park, but will not marry him because she has not the money he needs to unburden the encumbered family estate. Her maternal uncle, however, is the railway magnate Sir Roger Scatcherd, a capricious alcoholic with an invalid son. He does not know of his relation to Mary, since she was illegitimate and Dr. Thorne was sworn to secrecy. The doctor, who could resolve Mary's love troubles by telling what he knows, is sore beset by his conscience, particularly as he is Sir Roger's medical attendant. Eventually Sir Roger and his rickety son both die, and Mary and Frank can be prosperously married. Trollope records that his brother Thomas Adolphus Trollope, who was also a successful professional writer at this time, supplied him with the plot for *Doctor Thorne*. It is a rare instance of any kind of collaboration in his work. For the most part he was reticent about his writing, never discussing his work in progress except with his wife and never reading it aloud.

Framley Parsonage is similarly concerned with a scrupulous girl, Lucy Robarts, who refuses to marry a lord (even though she loves him) because his mother disapproves of the match. Trollope handles such issues with great delicacy. The scene in which Lucy refuses Lord Lufton's propo-

Waltham House in Hertfordshire, Trollope's home from 1859 until 1871

sal is a fine specimen of Trollope's many court-ship scenes:

> "It is impossible that I should be your wife."
>
> "Do you mean that you cannot love me?"
>
> "You have no right to press me any fur-ther," she said; and sat down upon the sofa, with an angry frown upon her forehead.
>
> "By heavens," he said, "I will take no such answer from you till you put your hand upon your heart, and say that you cannot love me."
>
> "Oh, why should you press me so, Lord Lufton?"
>
> "Why, because my happiness depends upon it; because it behoves me to know the very truth. It has come to this, that I love you with my whole heart, and I must know how your heart stands towards me." She had now again risen from the sofa, and was looking steadily in his face.
>
> "Lord Lufton," she said, "I cannot love

you," and as she spoke she did put her hand, as he had desired, upon her heart.

> "Then God help me! for I am wretched. Good-bye, Lucy," and he stretched out his hand to her.
>
> "Good-bye, my lord. Do not be angry with me."
>
> "No, no, no!" and without further speech he left the room and the house and hurried home. . . .
>
> And when he was well gone—absolutely out of sight from the window—Lucy walked steadily up to her room, locked the door, and then threw herself on the bed. Why—oh! why had she told such a falsehood?

"There must be love in a novel," Trollope de-clared; and he became an acknowledged expert in handling a character's intricate vacillations be-tween love and social constraints. It was for such portraits as that of Lucy Robarts that Henry

471

Millais's title-page illustration for the fifth of Trollope's Barset novels (C. P. Snow, Trollope: His Life and Art, *1975)*

James remembered Trollope as an author who celebrated the "simple maiden in her flower.... He is evidently always more or less in love with her." Another such maiden is Grace Crawley in *The Last Chronicle of Barset*, who resists the suit of Major Grantly, the son of the archdeacon, because her father is under suspicion of theft. Perhaps—in the scene where he shows how the archdeacon has all his resistance to the marriage charmed away by Grace's quiet goodness—Trollope was dramatizing his own susceptibility to the simple maiden.

With *Framley Parsonage* Trollope had reached a new stage of success. The novel was solicited for the much-advertised and eagerly awaited new journal, the *Cornhill Magazine*, which was launched as a new venture in 1860 by the enterprising publisher George Smith. The editor was Thackeray, whom Trollope regarded as the greatest living writer and author of the best novel in the English language, *The History of Henry Esmond, Esq.* (1852). Recognition from such a quarter, of which he was very proud, gave him occasion to make some adjustments in his post-office work. He obtained a transfer from Ireland to England and settled in Waltham House in Hertfordshire, within easy distance of London and the publishers, as well as of good hunting country. *The Small House at Allington* also ran serially in the *Cornhill*. John Everett Millais was engaged as the illustrator for both novels, and a mutually satisfactory relation of novelist and illustrator was established between the two and maintained in *Orley Farm* (1861-1862) and *Phineas Finn*. For subsequent novels Trollope had several other illustrators, including George Thomas, Marcus Stone, Frank Holl, Luke Fildes, and (briefly and abortively) Hablôt Browne, or "Phiz"; but he regarded Millais as his best illustrator.

The Small House at Allington varies the courtship situation by introducing a heroine, Lily Dale, who engages herself to a plausible suitor, Crosbie, and is subsequently jilted by him when he pursues the more fashionable Lady Alexandrina De Courcy. Lily comes to recognize that Crosbie is a scoundrel not worth pining over, but is unable to cure herself or to accept a more worthy and persistent suitor, Johnny Eames (in whom may be recognized some characteristics of the young Trollope). Trollope prolonged Lily's ultimately unreasonable resistance to Johnny not only through *The Small House at Allington* but to the end of *The Last Chronicle of Barset*, though many of his readers wrote letters begging him to marry her happily to Johnny at last. It is always difficult for Trollope's women—at least for his *good* women—to form a second attachment, but in the case of Lily Dale he suggests that her continuing loyalty to the man who deserted her is an almost morbid condition.

The Last Chronicle of Barset is typical of Trollope's copious, variegated kind of novel. Its concerns unfold amply and progressively, its characters are numerous and diverse, and its world is composed of several plots and different milieux. Although he wrote some relatively short novels in which a classic unity of action is clearly preserved, his greatest works are the "big ones"— such as *The Last Chronicle of Barset, The Eustace Diamonds* (1872), *The Way We Live Now* (1874-1875), and *Mr. Scarborough's Family* (1883)—in which the main plot is amplified by subplots and the themes are enlarged and qualified. "Though [the

*Cover for the first installment of Trollope's final Barset novel
(C. P. Snow,* Trollope: His Life and Art, *1975)*

novelist's] story should be all one, yet it may have many parts," he explained. "Though the plot itself may require but few characters, it may be so enlarged as to find its full development in many. There may be subsidiary plots, which shall all tend to the elucidation of the main story, and which will take their places as part of one and the same work." Some critics, including several of his original reviewers, have found fault with his subsidiary plots and have wished them away. More patient critics, however, have shown Trollope's impressive art in the orchestration of plot with subplot. Gordon N. Ray, in an article entitled "Trollope at Full Length," showed how Trollope "knew exactly how to assign each set of characters its proper part in the story, to time his shifts from one plot to another so as to obtain maximum emphasis, contrast, and change of pace,

and to bring the whole to a smooth conclusion within the space allotted. Trollope, in fact, made himself a great master of the contrapuntal novel long before anyone had thought of the term." In *The Last Chronicle of Barset*, for instance, the main story of Josiah Crawley—the proud and poverty-stricken curate of Hogglestock and a man of intense moral integrity though limited practical acumen—is set off against the shabby, self-interested doings of London characters who dabble in financial and sexual intrigues and constitute a cynical society in strong counterpoint to Crawley's intense intellectual, moral, and religious commitment. Crawley is suspected on circumstantial evidence of having stolen a check for twenty pounds. He is unable to account for his possession of it and is threatened with the loss of his ministry and his living, and attendant shame and degradation. The sufferings of this proud, unaccommodating, intensely sensitive man reach tragic dimensions. It is chiefly for the characterization of Josiah Crawley that *The Last Chronicle of Barset* has been labeled by many—including the author himself—Trollope's best novel.

Trollope's numerous readers and reviewers loudly lamented his decision to make this chronicle of Barset the last. His progressively emerging novels with their familiar characters had firmly lodged themselves in the public's affection. "What am I to do without ever meeting Archdeacon Grantly?" pathetically asked one reader who was quoted in the *Spectator*; "he was one of my best and most intimate friends, and the mere prospect of never hearing his 'Good heavens!' again when any proposition is made touching the dignity of Church or State, is a bewilderment and pain to me."

Trollope wrote several novels besides the Barset ones during these years. In *The Three Clerks* he drew on his experience as a civil servant to delineate the careers of his clerks. The story of the bright and successful Alaric Tudor is one of moral degeneration, while Charley Tudor, the prodigal (recognizable as a self-portrait), is morally redeemed. The novel contains some satire against the newly instituted civil service examinations, which Trollope always hated.

In *Orley Farm* the central character, Lady Mason, is—like Mr. Crawley—a figure of considerable moral rectitude who is suspected of an act of fraud, but—unlike Mr. Crawley—she is guilty. During the infancy of her son, Lucius, she had forged a codicil to her husband's will in order to provide for the child. As a widow she keeps her secret for years as Lucius grows up, but is at last constrained to confess. Trollope, who believed "a novel should give a picture of common life enlivened by humour and sweetened by pathos," was proud of his handling of the confession scene in which Lady Mason owns her guilt to her elderly fiancé, Sir Peregrine Orme; but to modern taste the pathos is perhaps overwrought.

The publication of *Rachel Ray* (1863) involved Trollope in an unexpected disagreement with his publishers. The book was solicited by Norman Macleod, who was editor of the evangelical publication *Good Words*, as well as being chaplain to Queen Victoria. Macleod invited Trollope to "let out the *best* side of your soul in *Good Words*—better far than ever in *Cornhill*." Trollope set a price of one thousand pounds for the proposed novel and accordingly wrote *Rachel Ray*. But on reading the manuscript Macleod was dismayed. Trollope had shown clearly enough his views on Low Church zealots in such figures as Obadiah Slope in *Barchester Towers*; but he was perhaps rather tactless in producing further satire on evangelical self-righteousness in a story commissioned for such a journal as *Good Words*. Here the heroine Rachel is subjected to tyranny by her puritanical relations, who object to her dancing and other social activities; and another unctuous Low Church clergyman, Mr. Prong, is roundly exposed as mercenary and hypocritical. In some embarrassment Macleod backed out of his agreement, more afraid of offending his readership than Trollope. Ruefully amused, Trollope wrote to Millais, who might have illustrated the story, "X (a Sunday magazine) has thrown me over. They write me word that I am too wicked." He let *Good Words* off their full contractual obligation of one thousand pounds but exacted five hundred pounds for his trouble. He subsequently published *Rachel Ray* with his usual publishers, Chapman and Hall.

Also concurrent with the Barset novels appeared *Miss Mackenzie* (1865), a muted tale of a spinster on the threshold of middle age who suddenly comes into money and so enters the marriage market. It is a sensitive handling of what its reviewers recognized as an unusual choice of a central character, and Trollope shows himself able to touch even a humdrum story with romance. *The Belton Estate* (1866) tells of Clara Amedroz and her two suitors, the effete member of Parliament Frederick Aylmer and her more virile cousin Will Belton, who inherits her father's estate and finally persuades her to stay on it as his wife. Be-

sides these and other novels, Trollope wrote short stories, tales, sketches, and books of travel during the Barset period. Meanwhile, he still worked full-time with the Post Office.

Also during his highly successful years of the 1860s he tried a curious experiment. He wanted to test his theory that "a name once earned carried with it too much favour," and so wrote some stories which he insisted on publishing anonymously; this action was to his considerable financial disadvantage, as John Blackwood, who accepted the stories for *Blackwood's Magazine*, would not pay as much for them as he would for work with Trollope's name attached. The experiment certainly proved that an earned name does indeed carry favor, for those who did not recognize the stories as Trollope's scarcely noticed them. But Trollope perhaps had other motives for his experiment: he had begun to discover that his great productivity was sometimes to the detriment of his reputation. "I quite admit that I crowded my wares into the market too quickly," he wrote; but he was inclined to blame the publishers: so long as George Smith kept demanding novels for the *Cornhill*, and Chapman and Hall contracted for more, what was a good-humored and energetic novelist to do but oblige them? "Could I have been two separate persons . . . of whom one might have been devoted to Cornhill and the other to the interests of the firm in Piccadilly, it might have been very well; but as I preserved my identity in both places, I myself became aware that my name was too frequent on title-pages." It seems likely that he thought an answer to this dilemma was to remove his name from some title pages, and by publishing anonymously to succeed "in obtaining a second identity." It is yet another testimony to his enormous energy that, while maintaining two distinct and highly demanding professions, he could contemplate subdividing himself yet again to become two novelists.

He made moderate attempts to disguise himself in his new identity. He was best known as a delineator of English life and English character, but *Nina Balatka* (1867) and *Linda Tressel* (1868), both serialized anonymously in *Blackwood's Magazine* between 1866 and 1868, are set abroad, in Prague, Czechoslovakia, and Nuremberg, Germany, respectively; and Trollope permitted himself more than usual in the way of romance. The first involves a Christian girl who engages herself to a Jew, and the horrified reactions of the families of both principals. *Linda Tressel* deals with the woes of a girl whose pious aunt tries to force her into

An illustration by Millais for Orley Farm. *The model for the picture is Julians, the farm near Harrow where Trollope lived as a boy.*

marriage with an elderly and repulsive suitor. In spite of Trollope's attempts at disguise, he was discovered by Richard Holt Hutton, the shrewd reviewer for the *Spectator*, so he did not succeed in creating his new literary identity.

"I have long been aware of a certain weakness in my own character," said Trollope, "which I may call a craving for love." His relatively loveless childhood and awkward youth now behind him, and his meed of success achieved, he delighted in the chance to be visible and popular. He joined clubs, becoming one of the pillars of the Garrick Club ("the first assemblage of men at which I felt myself to be popular"), and was elected to the Athenaeum. The ugly duckling had at last become a swan among swans, and he reveled in their company. He joined with others in founding such journals as the *Fortnightly*, the *Pall Mall Gazette*, and *Saint Paul's Magazine*; he gave speeches; he dined out and talked loudly. At social gatherings he was a bluff and blustering

presence, and people were often astonished at the contrast between the delicacy of his novels and the aggressive assertiveness of their author: "The books, full of gentleness, grace and refinement; the writer of them, bluff, loud, stormy, and contentious," wrote his friend W. P. Frith. He was likened to Dickens's Mr. Boythorn in *Bleak House* (1852-1853), the good-hearted but litigious neighbor whose bark is worse than his bite. George Augustus Sala characterized him at the end of his life as "crusty, quarrelsome, wrongheaded, prejudiced, obstinate, kind-hearted and thoroughly honest old Tony Trollope." His appearance, bald and bushy-bearded and heavy, was of a piece with his dominating social presence. In commenting on a photograph of himself of 1860, Trollope said, "I think the portrait as it now stands will do very well. It looks uncommon feirce [*sic*], as that of a dog about to bite; but that I fear is the nature of the animal portrayed."

His immense energy found an outlet in foxhunting as well as in his active social life. In the years between 1859 and 1871, when he was at Waltham House, he generally kept four hunting horses and hunted regularly during the season. He could not fully account for his unfailing love of the sport, since he was not a good horseman: he was heavy and shortsighted, and frequently came to grief when in the field. "I am also now old for such work," he confessed when writing the *Autobiography* at sixty-one, "being so stiff that I cannot get on to my horse without the aid of a block or a bank. But I ride still after the same fashion, with a boy's energy." He delighted in incorporating hunting scenes into his novels and frequently made the action turn on some obstacle or accident of the field: as in *Ralph the Heir* (1870-1871), where the hero inherits an estate when his uncle is killed at a ditch. Hunting also provided a fruitful source of metaphor, particularly for courtships; the sadistic Sir Griffin Tewett in *The Eustace Diamonds* pursues Lucinda Roanoke as a vixen: "There are men in whose love a good deal of hatred is mixed;—who love as the huntsman loves the fox, toward the killing of which he intends to use all his energies and intellects." In *The American Senator* (1877) the woman is the huntress and the man the prey. Arabella Trefoil sees Lord Rufford as a desirable husband and sets out to catch him, doing much of her work of subduing his resistance and engaging his affections in the hunting field. Lord Rufford is a wily quarry and manages to elude her. But when he has escaped he almost regrets

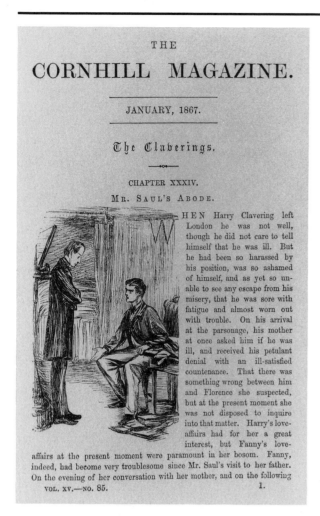

THE

CORNHILL MAGAZINE.

JANUARY, 1867.

The Claverings.

CHAPTER XXXIV.

MR. SAUL'S ABODE.

HEN Harry Clavering left London he was not well, though he did not care to tell himself that he was ill. But he had been so harassed by his position, was so ashamed of himself, and as yet so unable to see any escape from his misery, that he was sore with fatigue and almost worn out with trouble. On his arrival at the parsonage, his mother at once asked him if he was ill, and received his petulant denial with an ill-satisfied countenance. That there was something wrong between him and Florence she suspected, but at the present moment she was not disposed to inquire into that matter. Harry's love-affairs had for her a great interest, but Fanny's love-affairs at the present moment were paramount in her bosom. Fanny, indeed, had become very troublesome since Mr. Saul's visit to her father. On the evening of her conversation with her mother, and on the following

VOL. XV.—NO. 85.   1.

The magazine serialization of one of Trollope's novels. The fact that it begins on page one indicates that it was the most popular novel running in the Cornhill *at the time.*

it, recognizing her beauty and cleverness and skill at the game. "As for hunting him,—that was a matter of course. He was as much born and bred to be hunted as a fox." Though he escapes Arabella, he is presently captured by another kind of huntress, a patient lady with a baited hook. Trollope saw his own working habits in hunting terms, too, and often wrote in the same way he rode: in beginning a new novel, he confesses, "I have rushed at the work as a rider rushes at a fence which he does not see. Sometimes I have encountered what, in hunting language, we call a cropper."

Another of Trollope's activities that added to the number of his volumes was travel. He traveled as a tourist on holiday all over Europe and frequently set scenes of his novels in foreign cities. He also traveled professionally, on post-office business and as a writer. His extensive travels in England and Ireland laying out postal delivery routes occupied what he called two of the happiest years of his life. His gusto was unquenched by a visit to Egypt in 1858 and a long voyage to the West Indies beginning in the winter of the same year, on missions for the post office. The latter journey, however, also gave him the opportunity to contract with Chapman and Hall for a book, which he published in 1859 as *The West Indies and the Spanish Main.* His next trip, for which he obtained a leave of absence from his post-office duties, was to the United States in 1861-1862 and was solely for the purpose of writing a book. He regarded the substantial volumes that resulted, *North America* (1862), as in some sense a peace offering to the New World that his mother had so excoriated in *The Domestic Manners of the Americans.* His tone in his travel books is engagingly personal: instead of dividing his subject into abstract categories such as politics, commerce, and so on, he typically provides a narrative that follows his own itinerary, so that his general reflections arise from the immediate personal occasion. A late train that caused him a four-hour delay at Crossline, Ohio, for instance, moves him to characteristic impatience and reflection: "There were many others stationed there as I was, but to them had been given a capability for loafing which niggardly Nature had denied to me. . . . Idle men out there in the West we may say there are none. . . . But they all of them had a capacity for a prolonged state of doing nothing, which is to me unintelligible, and which is very much to be envied."

However much he may have envied such a capacity, Trollope did not cultivate it in himself. Before he had written his last chronicle of Barset, he had already launched into the first of a new series of interconnected novels, the Palliser or Political novels. Young Plantagenet Palliser, a dedicated politician and the heir to the duke of Omnium, was first introduced as a minor character in *The Small House at Allington* in the Barset series; he is reintroduced with some éclat, along with his vivacious and headstrong young wife, Lady Glencora, as a major character in *Can You Forgive Her?* (1864-1865). This couple, with their marital problems and their growing power and prestige in the social and political spheres, supply the unity in the next series. Where the clergy are the focus of interest in the Barset novels, politicians and their business are the concern of the Palliser novels; and the major scene of action shifts from the quiet though sufficiently busy rural county of Barsetshire to the more hectic bustle of the metropolis. Trollope had maintained an amused if affectionate distance from his clergymen; but he was more apt to identify with his politicians, and the tone of the novels is by and large more serious. "It is the highest and most legitimate pride of an Englishman to have the letters M.P. written after his name," he wrote without irony in the opening novel of the series. The Palliser novels comprise *Can You Forgive Her?*, *Phineas Finn* (1869), *The Eustace Diamonds* (1872), *Phineas Redux* (1874), *The Prime Minister* (1875-1876), and *The Duke's Children* (1880). Like the Barset novels, they all have separate plots and are complete in themselves, but the characters introduced in one novel are apt to recur in subsequent ones.

The main plot of *Can You Forgive Her?* concerns the complicated love life of Alice Vavasor, who is first engaged to her cousin George—a dangerous and unpredictable man who expects her to pay for his campaign to enter Parliament—then to the safe and respectable John Grey, and then again to George, and finally again to Grey, whom this time she does marry. Her vacillations result partly from her feminist principles, which prompt her to support her cousin and share in his political career, even though she finds him physically repellent. In the subplot the young Lady Glencora, newly married to the rather dull but highly admirable Plantagenet Palliser, is tempted to elope with a romantic ne'er-do-well, Burgo Fitzgerald, whom she had loved before her marriage. To complete the pattern, a comic third plot shows a widow similarly hesitating between a wild man and a worthy man. It is only the widow, not the girl or the wife, who resolves the conflict by uniting herself with the wild man; Alice and Lady Glencora sensibly realize that they love where they approve and cast off their wild men. Alice's story had been one of continuing interest to Trollope, as he first wrote it in 1850 as a play, "The Noble Jilt," which was rejected and set aside. (It was finally published in 1923.) Although he took considerable trouble over her characterization, his readers found her vacillations exasperating, and she was not popular. Lady Glencora, however, the racy aristocratic wife with a high ambition, a powerful but touchy husband, and a talent for managing other people's lives, was recognizably a character whom his readers would like to meet again, and she and her husband became the major figures whose continuing saga was to occupy Trollope for more than the next decade and almost to the end of his life.

Kate Field, the American writer and feminist befriended by Trollope

Phineas Finn and its sequel *Phineas Redux* are concerned with the political and marital aspirations of a personable but impecunious young Irishman. Largely by good luck, Phineas manages to enter Parliament early in life; he hopes eventually to make his living by politics, if he can get a salaried position in the Liberal government. Lady Laura Standish, a clever daughter of a cabinet minister, takes him under her wing and introduces him to influential people. He duly falls in love with her and proposes; but she tells him they should both make more financially profitable marriages and engages herself to a rich Scottish landowner, Mr. Kennedy. Her marriage is a disaster, as she comes to hate her dour and exacting husband and finally separates from him. Her uncontrollable love for Phineas and Kennedy's jealousy, violence, and eventual insanity form a powerful continuing interest in the two books. Phineas, meanwhile, has other ambitions and other women. He succeeds in getting his place in the government but is obliged to resign it when he chooses to vote against his party on the issue of Irish tenant right. At the same time he withdraws from the marriage stakes, rejecting the rich and attractive Mme Max Goesler for a youthful Irish sweetheart.

Phineas Finn's parliamentary career allowed Trollope to pursue certain topics that are of perennial interest in his political novels: the interaction of the private with the public life; the balance between a politician's individual conscience and his allegiance to party policy; and the financing of a political career, which ideally should be open to the best men regardless of their means, yet pursued only from pure and disinterested motives.

Between the writing of *Phineas Finn* and *Phineas Redux* Trollope made an attempt to enter Parliament himself. This had been a lifelong ambition, but before he could pursue it seriously he had to clear the decks and make some decisions about his two existing professions. His career in the post office was inevitably onerous as his literary commitments increased, and he made tentative plans to leave the service when he had saved enough to replace his pension. When he was passed over for a promotion to under secretary for which he had applied, he had additional reason to "sigh for liberty," as he put it. In 1867, not without many regrets, he wrote his letter of resignation.

New activities quickly took up his new free time. At the invitation of an ambitious printer, James Virtue, he undertook the editorship of a new journal, *Saint Paul's Magazine*, at the salary of one thousand pounds a year. It was here that *Phineas Finn* had its serial run. (The journal was not a success, and Trollope gave up the editorship in 1870.) Then, despite his recent resignation, he undertook a special mission for the post office that took him in the spring of 1868 on a second visit to the United States. Besides negotiating a postal agreement in Washington, D.C., he tried to effect some literary business for himself and his English colleagues: like other English writers he had long been exasperated by the flagrant piracy of his works across the Atlantic, and he tried to arrange an international agreement on copyright. In this he failed.

When he returned to England, he had his chance to pursue his political ambition. "I have always thought that to sit in the British Parliament should be the highest object of ambition to every educated Englishman," he declared. After the dissolution of Parliament in 1868, Trollope stood as a Liberal candidate for Beverley, in Yorkshire;

A self-portrait of Sir John Everett Millais, Trollope's favorite illustrator (Aberdeen Art Gallery and Museum)

and he swiftly found that the process of getting into Parliament was enough to discourage him. He spent, he said, "the most wretched fortnight of my manhood" in canvassing, found that nobody was interested in his political ideas, and finished at the bottom of the poll. Some of his humiliating experience at Beverley is recalled in *Ralph the Heir* in the campaign of Sir Thomas Underwood at Percycross: "The desire for the seat which had brought him to Percycross had almost died out amidst the misery of his position. Among all the men of his party with whom he was associating, there was not one whom he did not dislike, and by whom he was not snubbed and contradicted."

It was perhaps now that Trollope may have conceived of his parliamentary novels as a continuing series. He had intended in any case to bring Phineas Finn back into the political arena, but he was now conscious of a new motive for writing his political fictions: "As I was debarred from expressing my opinions in the House of Commons, I took this method of declaring myself. And as I could not take my seat on those benches where I might possibly have been shone upon by the Speaker's eye, I had humbly to crave his permission for a seat in the gallery, so that I might thus become conversant with the ways and doings of the House in which some of my scenes were to be placed." One might expect from such a statement that Trollope would have written novels that strongly advocated certain topical measures and opposed others, but although he does include episodes in which actual issues of the day are introduced and debated in *his* House of Commons—for instance, the ballot, parliamentary reform, Irish tenant right, and the disestablishment of the church—he seldom either advocates or opposes them. His interest is primarily in the *process* of parliamentary government—the manning of committees, the working of personal influence, and the strategy of debate and human management—rather than in advancing his own political opinions. Nevertheless, he occasionally permits himself some onstage electioneering. He describes his own political position, with habitually careful qualification, as that of "an advanced, but still a conservative liberal." He advocated a slow and controlled progress toward equality—or rather, "I will not say equality, for the word is offensive, and presents to the imaginations of men ideas of communism, of ruin, and insane democracy,—but a tendency towards equality." So much he says in *An Autobiography*. In *The Prime Minister* he allows his liberal statesman, Plantagenet Palliser, now duke of Omnium and prime minister, to enlarge on the basic principles of liberalism to his friend Phineas Finn as the two stroll in the ample acres of the duke's estate:

> "The Liberal, if he have any fixed idea at all, must I think have conceived the idea of lessening distances,—of bringing the coachman and the Duke nearer together,—nearer and nearer, till a millenium shall be reached by—"
>
> "By equality?" asked Phineas, eagerly interrupting the Prime Minister, and showing his dissent by the tone of his voice.
>
> "I did not use the word, which is open to many objections. In the first place the millenium, which I have perhaps rashly named, is so distant that we need not even think of it as possible. . . . Equality would be a heaven, if we could attain it. How can we to whom so much has been given dare to think otherwise? How can you look at the bowed back and bent legs and abject face of that poor ploughman, who winter and summer has to drag his rheumatic limbs to his work, while you go a-hunting or sit in pride of place among the foremost few of your country, and

say that it all is as it ought to be? You are a Liberal because you know that it is not all as it ought to be, and because you would still march on to some nearer approach to equality."

But such statements of principle, clearly carrying the authority of the writer as well as the speaker, are relatively rare in the political novels. The duke himself acknowledges that "when a man has to be on the alert to keep Ireland quiet, or to prevent peculation in the dockyards, or to raise the revenue while he lowers the taxes, he feels himself to be saved from the necessity of investigating principles"; and Trollope, too, usually gets on with his immediate business of activating his characters and managing his incidents.

The Palliser novels were by no means all that Trollope was writing in the second half of his literary career. His novels were appearing constantly and often concurrently as they were serialized in such journals as the *Cornhill*, the *Fortnightly Review*, *Blackwood's Magazine*, *Saint Paul's Magazine*, *Macmillan's Magazine*, the *Graphic*, and *All the Year Round*. Some novels, such as *Can You Forgive Her?* and *He Knew He Was Right*, emerged in separate shilling or monthly parts. The reading public was not likely to forget him.

The Claverings (1867), which had its serial run in the *Cornhill*, occupies an interesting place between the Barset series and the Palliser series in that it presents in its two heroines an example each of the good girl of the early novels and the experienced woman typical of the later ones—here Florence Burton and Julia, Lady Ongar, who are the rival claimants of the hand of Harry Clavering, the vacillating hero. It is a well-constructed tale of English life, with only a little visible manipulation of plot by which two brothers are conveniently drowned in order that Harry may inherit a title and an estate. The marriage of the hard and loveless Sir Hugh Clavering and his feebly dependent wife is a fine study in the deterioration of a relationship.

In *He Knew He Was Right* (1868-1869) Trollope shows a new mastery of morbid psychology. In Kennedy in the *Phineas* novels he also presents a study in the progress toward insanity, but in Louis Trevelyan he is able to examine the process in more detail. Trevelyan is a loving young husband of a rather headstrong woman, Emily. The initial disagreement between them seems trivial enough: a middle-aged man-about-town, Colonel Osborne, tries to engage Emily in a flirtation, and Trevelyan resents his attentions. Emily re-

An illustration by Luke Fildes for
Anthony Trollope's *The Way We Live Now*

An illustration by Sir Luke Fildes for
The Way We Live Now

sents his resentment, they fail to come to a satisfactory explanation, and they separate. As his obsession grows, he convinces himself that she is guilty of adultery and goes to the length of kidnapping their little son and taking him to a remote villa in Italy. The distraught mother is ultimately able to reclaim the child, and Trevelyan, now wasted physically as well as mentally, returns to England under her care; but he does not audibly recant his accusation before he dies. It is for such studies as those of Trevelyan and Kennedy that A. O. J. Cockshut has characterized Trollope as a novelist who became increasingly interested in obsessive and morbid states of mind and followed a "progress to pessimism" in his later novels.

In *The Vicar of Bullhampton* (l869-1870), Trollope based one part of his plot on the story of a fallen woman. He was conscious of dangers in handling such a theme for a Victorian public and showed his nervousness in a preface where he jus-

tifies bringing this subject before "our sisters and daughters ... the sweet young hearts of those whose delicacy and cleanliness of thought is a matter of pride to so many of us." But his plea was for understanding and compassion: "Cannot women, who are good, pity the sufferings of the vicious, and do something perhaps to mitigate and shorten them, without contamination from the vice?" To the modern ear there is not much that is daring in the presentation of Carry Brattle, the fallen woman, but her condition and its motives and consequences are certainly more deftly handled than those of Dickens's Martha or Little Em'ly in *David Copperfield* (1849-1850).

Trollope quarreled with his publishers over *The Vicar of Bullhampton*, not because of his controversial subject, but because they subordinated his interests to those of Victor Hugo. The novel was completed in 1868 and scheduled to begin its serial run in *Once a Week* in July 1869. Victor Hugo had long delayed the writing of *L'Homme Qui Rit (The Man Who Laughs)*, a translation of which was also booked for *Once a Week*, and the result was that his novel conflicted with Trollope's, and Trollope was asked to publish his in the *Gentleman's Magazine* instead. His reaction is characteristic: "My disgust at this proposition was, I think, chiefly due to my dislike to Victor Hugo's latter novels, which I regard as pretentious and untrue to nature. To this perhaps was added some feeling of indignation that I should be asked to give way to a Frenchman. The Frenchman had broken his engagement. He had failed to have his work finished by the stipulated time. . . . And because of these laches on his part,—on the part of this sententious French Radical,—I was to be thrown over! . . . I would not come out in *The Gentleman's Magazine*, and as the Grinning Man could not be got out of the way, my novel was published in separate numbers." It was not the only occasion on which the punctual Trollope was impatient of the dilatory and unmethodical habits of other writers. He took even his hero Thackeray to task for "that propensity to wandering which came to [him] because of his idleness."

The pattern of Trollope's life seems to have changed in the late 1860s, when he left the post office and had his fling as an editor and in politics. He called the years 1867 and 1868, the years of his resignation, editorship, second trip to America, and political campaign, "the busiest of my life." With the new decade he seemed to slow down a little. He continued to be busy, but he was perhaps less cheerfully ebullient than in the

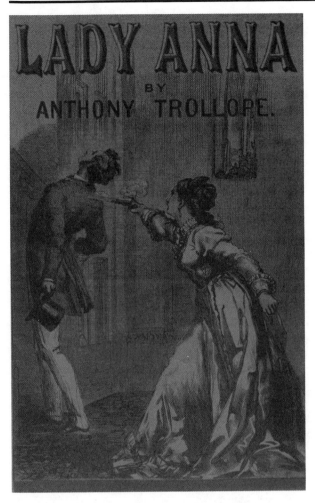

Cover design for a "yellowback" edition of one of Trollope's novels (David Magee Antiquarian Books)

triumphant days of the 1860s. He resigned from the editorship of *Saint Paul's*, he resolved that he would observe parliamentary business only from the Stranger's Gallery, and he even began to think about giving up hunting. The age of fifty-five (Trollope's in 1870) often appears in his novels as a turning point, after which a man is considered old.

His sons were now grown up and needed help in their walks of life. The elder, Henry, who was of a literary turn, studied law and was called to the bar in 1869. Success seemed uncertain, however, and Trollope instead bought him a partnership with his most constant publisher, Frederic Chapman of Chapman and Hall. His younger son, Fred, had early departed to pursue a career as a farmer in Australia, and after a visit home in 1868-1869 decided to return there for good. His parents now contemplated taking the long journey to visit him, and Trollope characteristically de-

termined that he would write a book on Australia while he was about it. The proposed long absence from home led the Trollopes to wonder what to do with their house; and in 1871, before they left, they sold it. Its convenience for Trollope's post-office work, which had been the main reason for its purchase, was no longer an issue, and they resolved to settle in London on their return. Trollope speaks of leaving Waltham House as though it were the end of an era: "The work I did during the twelve years that I remained there, from 1859 to 1871, was certainly very great. I feel confident that in amount no other writer contributed so much during that time to English literature. Over and above my novels, I wrote political articles, critical, social, and sporting articles, for periodicals, without number. I did the work of a surveyor of the General Post Office, and so did it as to give the authorities of the department no slightest pretext for fault-finding. I hunted always at least twice a week. I was frequent in the whist-room at the Garrick. I lived much in society in London, and was made happy by the presence of many friends at Waltham Cross. In addition to this we always spent six weeks at least out of England. Few men, I think, ever lived a fuller life."

In May 1871 Trollope and his wife sailed from Liverpool for Melbourne. He had his business well in hand. He had turned his editorship to good account by writing a series called *An Editor's Tales* (1870), and these were just completing their run in *Saint Paul's Magazine*, where *Ralph the Heir* was also coming out. *Sir Harry Hotspur of Humblethwaite* (1871) had just begun in *Macmillan's Magazine*, and *The Eustace Diamonds* was written and already contracted to start its serial run in the *Fortnightly Review*. *Phineas Redux* and *An Eye for an Eye* (1879) were complete and awaiting publishers; and during the voyage to Australia he wrote the whole of *Lady Anna* (1874).

He was away for nineteen months. A few weeks he spent with his son and his new daughter-in-law on their sheep farm, but most of the time he was traveling about the country and beyond it to New Zealand, with his headquarters at Melbourne. He duly produced his book *Australia and New Zealand* (1873), which was published by Chapman and Hall after his return. He arrived home in December 1872 and immediately began to think again about hunting. Although he had intended to give up the sport when he left his country house, he had not in fact disposed of his horses, and he soon settled to hunting three times a week from London. The Trollopes now lived at 39, Montagu Square, and it was here that he wrote many of his novels of the 1870s.

The changes in Trollope's career at the end of the 1860s affected his life in the next decade. He had reached a peak of success, after which some downward trend was inevitable. The visible failures of his editorship of *Saint Paul's Magazine* and the electoral campaign at Beverley perhaps did him bad service with his readership; but in any case, he began to fall off in popularity. For *Phineas Finn* and *He Knew He Was Right* he received the very substantial sums from his publishers of £3,200 each; but sales were disappointing, and he could not again command such prices. His contracts with his publishers maintained for a few years a fairly even price—"£600 for the quantity contained in an ordinary novel volume, or £3,000 for a long tale published in twenty parts, which is equal in length to five such volumes"—but sales were not as good as before, and in the mid 1870s his price likewise sagged. A melancholy footnote to the above passage in *An Autobiography* reads, "Since the date at which this was written I have encountered a diminution in price." It was a hard admission for the old stager to have to make, for he had greatly prized success— and success if possible in a visible, tangible, and quantifiable form. His loss of immediate popularity, however, was not an indication of failing artistic powers: although many of his contemporaries loved him primarily as the chronicler of Barset, and even a reader such as Henry James confessed to being unable to wade through the political novels, the criticism of the second half of the twentieth century has by and large found more to admire in Trollope's late novels than in his early ones. But for his last dozen years his name on title pages did not draw readers as it had, and his novels began to be considered rather dated.

He continued to be very prominent on the literary scene, and indeed on many others. He was on intimate terms with other writers, including Robert Browning, Alfred Austin, George Eliot, and G. H. Lewes; and, since Thackeray's death in 1863, with his daughters, particularly Anne Thackeray, who was now a novelist herself. He was over many years a devoted friend of Kate Field, a vivacious American journalist and author, to whom he gave a great deal of advice (which she did not follow) on her literary labors and her feminist activities. He knew many artists, including W. P. Frith, Samuel Laurence, and

Trollope, circa 1880

John Everett Millais, his best illustrator. And of course, as his letters show, he was well known among the publishers, particularly George Smith, John Blackwood, and Frederic Chapman. One memorable anecdote of Trollope in the 1870s is given by Thomas Hardy, who was present at a conference in 1876 on the Eastern question. Trollope, who was by now quite used to "speechifying," as he called it, was on the platform with other prominent men, including William Gladstone, Anthony Ashley Cooper, seventh earl of Shaftesbury, and Hugh Lupus Grosvenor, Duke of Westminster: "Trollope outran the five or seven minutes allowed for each speech, and the Duke, who was chairman, after various soundings of the bell, and other hints that he must stop, tugged at Trollope's coat-tails in desperation. Trollope turned round, exclaimed parenthetically, 'Please leave my coat alone,' and went on speaking."

Between the two *Phineas* novels in the Palliser series comes *The Eustace Diamonds*, a lively novel about the machinations of a devious and unscrupulous woman; Lady Glencora and other familiar characters appear as spectators and commentators on the main action. Lizzie Eustace, an attractive young widow who had ensnared a dying baronet into matrimony for the sake of a handsome settlement, lays claim to a diamond necklace which the family lawyers insist belongs, as an heirloom, to the family estate and not to the widow. Even though she is frightened by the marshaling of the lawyers, she cannot bring herself to hand over her plunder, and when the box in which the diamonds are kept is stolen by burglars during a journey, she lets it be known that they have been stolen, thinking to rid herself of trouble by that means. In fact the diamonds were under her pillow, not in the box, at the time of the burglary, and in swearing to their loss she has become guilty of perjury. Lizzie's diamonds are ultimately dispersed and utterly lost, like Pip's great expectations in Dickens's novel; but the wily Lizzie herself escapes punishment, marrying a suitably unpleasant character who is even better than she is at lying. As she clings to diamonds, so she clings to men, and her behavior with her suitors is of a piece with her behavior with other people's property. *The Eustace Diamonds* is a sparkling novel, though it is unusual in the Trollope canon in developing a central character with whom the reader can hardly sympathize. Lizzie is entertaining but so thoroughly sham that she cannot make the devil's party attractive, as does Thackeray's Becky Sharp (whom she somewhat resembles) in *Vanity Fair* (1847-1848). *The Eustace Diamonds* was favorably reviewed and sold well. This was a relief to Trollope, who was aware that he was becoming less popular than he had been.

Phineas Redux, perhaps because it was written after his unfortunate campaign at Beverley, reflects a more somber view of politics than *Phineas Finn*. Phineas, now a widower, who in the first novel had led a charmed life in which beautiful and powerful women favored him and parliamentary seats were always fortunately available, is dogged by misfortune, at odds with his party, denounced by the press, and finally put on trial for a murder he did not commit. He is charged with killing a political opponent, an unpleasant minister named Bonteen, on strong circumstantial evidence. He is acquitted largely due to the heroic efforts of Mme Max Goesler, who bravely collects

evidence on his behalf, and he is at last offered the place in the government that he has coveted. But his experience has deeply shaken him, and he refuses the post and so maintains his independence of party. His marriage to the rich and enterprising widow Mme Max means that he will still be able to stand for Parliament and serve his country without subservience to party interest.

A powerful recurring antagonist in the two *Phineas* novels and in the Palliser novels at large is Quintus Slide, the editor of the *People's Banner*. In this slimy journalist, who terrorizes public figures in the name of public morality, Trollope continues his attack on the self-righteous pursuit of power: Slide is like Tom Towers in *The Warden*, Slope in *Barchester Towers*, and the squinting evangelical curate Maguire in *Miss Mackenzie*, all of whom use the popular press as their weapon. It is characteristic of Trollope, who was always carefully qualifying his statements and modulating his judgments, that he should have the least patience in his fiction with those whose mode is ruthless overstatement. Yet even to Quintus Slide, as to Mrs. Proudie, Trollope does meticulous justice: he is "not altogether without a conscience, and intensely conscious of such conscience as did constrain him." Trollope was thoroughly at home with such fine distinctions.

The first novel that Trollope wrote from his new home in London was *The Way We Live Now* (1874-1875), his most fully developed satire on modern life. It shows a world of self-seekers busy about their business of getting rich quickly at the expense of others and justifying themselves by the cynical declaration that everybody does it. In the comprehensiveness of its satire it invites comparison with such far-reaching novels as *Vanity Fair* and Dickens's *Little Dorrit* (1855-1857), which similarly anatomize a corrupt society. Through its different plots and subplots, *The Way We Live Now* exposes the moral and spiritual bankruptcy in high and low life; in commerce, politics, religion, and the arts; and in the relations of men and women, landlords and tenants, parents and children, English and Americans. In a later estimation of what he had written, Trollope was rather apologetic for his satirist's stance, admitting with the habitual honesty of the convinced realist that "the accusations are exaggerated." But he effectively conveys his vision of a society in which dishonesty has reached high places and so becomes "rampant" and "splendid."

The main plot concerns the meteoric rise to fortune and fashion of a large-scale financier and

Trollope's working calendar for Nina Balatka, *which he completed two and a half weeks ahead of his self-imposed deadline*
(Bodleian Library)

swindler, Melmotte, a figure who promotes greed in others and a fever of speculation, as Merdle does in *Little Dorrit*. Melmotte entertains on a grand scale, forms fictional companies, acquires a country estate by means of forgery, and is even elected to Parliament before his empire of deceit collapses and he shoots himself. As usual, Trollope manages to create a good deal of interest in and even sympathy for a rogue and his machinations. Other prominent characters through whom Trollope varies and enlarges his theme are Lady Carbury, a writer of potboilers who shamelessly coaxes reviewers for favorable notices of her books; her ne'er-do-well son Sir Felix, who arranges to elope with Melmotte's daughter in order to get her money and then leaves her waiting at the railway station; Mr. Longstaffe, a squire who is ready to sell his family estate to

Melmotte; and Paul Montague, who, though honest in intent, maintains compromising relations with two women and lends his name to one of Melmotte's swindles. The wilder of his two women is a bold American, Mrs. Hurtle, who admits to having shot her boor of a husband. The honest norm of the book is Roger Carbury, a quiet and ineffectual country gentleman who lives appropriately in an outmoded house with a moat, and who loses both his beloved estate and the girl he loves to inferior men. He is one of the few who manage to avoid being drawn into the vortex of Melmotte's spectacular progress: when his relative Hetta Carbury, whom he loves, proposes to visit the Melmottes, he remonstrates, and her justification is the usual one:

"Everybody goes there, Mr. Carbury."
"Yes,—that is the excuse which everybody

makes. Is that sufficient reason for you to go to a man's house? Is there not another place to which we are told that a great many are going, simply because the road has become thronged and fashionable?"

Such is our destination if we continue to live the way we live now.

The reception of the last two of the Palliser novels reflects the decline in Trollope's popularity. *The Prime Minister*, his longest novel and one that was perhaps intended to be a masterpiece, drew a good deal of hostile criticism, and its sales did not recover the sum of twenty-five hundred pounds that Chapman and Hall had paid for the copyright. And *The Duke's Children*, which he had made as long as its predecessor, was declared by Chapman to be too long to be marketable, and Trollope was obliged with tedious labor to reduce it from four volumes to three.

The penultimate volume of the series, *The Prime Minister*, has a bifurcated plot. The half that Trollope and his readers best liked is devoted to Palliser business. Plantagenet Palliser, now the duke of Omnium, whose political career has taken many turns since he filled the office most dear to his heart, chancellor of the exchequer, is now called upon to be the prime minister of a coalition government. The duchess, who has gained in status though not in prudence since her wild days as the wayward Lady Glencora, is delighted at his promotion and at once resolves to use all the resources of their vast wealth and huge estates to celebrate the new glory. The duke, a dedicated statesman with a taste for parliamentary and domestic tranquillity, views his new position as a solemn trust; the duchess sees it as a grand opportunity for social triumph. "I should like to put the Queen down," she says exultantly. "No treason; nothing of that kind. But I should like to make Buckingham Palace second-rate. And I'm not quite sure but I can." The marriage and the ministry are in equally parlous condition. The duke, highly scrupulous and intensely sensitive to criticism, suffers agonies both from adverse publicity in the *People's Banner* and from his wife's social panoply. Although the power has been painful to him, he nevertheless becomes reluctant to lay it aside, and when the coalition is defeated he is unwilling to submit himself as a subordinate minister in a new government. The second plot concerns the marriage and fortunes of Lopez, an unscrupulous adventurer who marries Emily Wharton for

her money but fails to extract her fortune from her tightfisted father. He is ruined, and, in a scene that may well have inspired the denouement of Leo Tolstoy's *Anna Karenina* (1873-1876), he throws himself under an express train at Tenway Junction.

The reviewers were severe with *The Prime Minister*, particularly on the Lopez part of the plot. "*The Prime Minister* represents a decadence in Mr. Trollope's powers," announced the critic for the *Saturday Review*. "The hand begins to falter where it once was cunning, and even as a picture of manners the work is no longer free from reproach. To whatever part of the story he may turn, the reader of *The Prime Minister* is unable to escape the all-pervading sense of artistic vulgarity." By contrast, Geoffrey Harvey, in *The Art of Anthony Trollope* (1980), makes a strong case for the same novel as the summit of Trollope's achievement. Trollope's readers have always differed as to the merits of his many novels.

Trollope had not finished with traveling in the 1870s. In 1875 he went via the Mediterranean and Brindisi, Italy, to Ceylon, sending letters on his travels back for publication in various newspapers, and then on to a second visit with his son in Australia, returning across America to complete his second circuit of the world. In 1877 he went to South Africa and wrote a book on it. The following year he went on an excursion to Iceland, of which he wrote an account in *How the "Mastiffs" Went to Iceland* (1878). Some of these exotic locations were useful in his fiction as well as for travel books. *Harry Heathcote of Gangoil: A Tale of Australian Bush Life* (1874), written in four weeks and published as a Christmas story in the *Graphic*, drew on his experience on Fred's sheep farm, and much of the action of *John Caldigate* (1879) is likewise set in Australia.

His literary activities also included scholarship and critical commentary. By his own assertion he had learned little of the classics in all the years of having them drilled into him at Harrow and Winchester; but he had found time to apply himself to them as an adult and began to read Latin and Greek for pleasure. In 1870 he wrote a little book on *The Commentaries of Caesar*; it cost him great pains but went virtually unnoticed by the scholars. His *Thackeray* (1879) is still quoted as an interesting early treatment of Thackeray as man and writer. In 1880 he published *The Life of Cicero*. *An Autobiography*, completed in 1876, contains a good deal of shrewd criticism of his own and others' novels, testifying to wide and careful

Harting Grange, Trollope's country home in Sussex

reading. He had contemplated a book on English prose fiction and even one on the history of English literature, but these ambitious projects are among the few he did not accomplish.

The American Senator (1877) is a lively story that returns in some ways to the Barset mode but is still touched with some satirical bitterness. Set in the country in the invented county of Rufford, it concerns the love and marriage of a young and innocent girl, Mary Masters, who eventually marries the squire; and of a not-so-young and far-from-innocent fortune huntress, Arabella Trefoil, who cunningly hunts the eligible Lord Rufford and his fifty thousand pounds per annum. The novel takes its name from the American senator from Mickewa, Elias Gotobed, who is Trollope's vehicle for social criticism. After a naive but conscientious scrutiny of such hallowed English institutions as fox hunting, church patronage, and class distinctions, the senator comes to the conclusion that "the want of reason among Britishers was so great, that no one ought to treat them as wholly responsible beings."

Trollope's readers continued to wish that he would recover from "the attack of misanthropy from which he was suffering when he wrote *The Way We Live Now*"; but his next novel, *Is He Popenjoy?* (1878) did not satisfy them, and his new worldly churchman, Dean Lovelace, was not as popular as the public's old favorite, Archdeacon Grantly. This is another story of inheritance, turning on the legitimacy of the infant son of the evil marquis of Brotherton. The heroine is the dean's daughter, Mary Germain, who is married to the conscientious but dull younger brother of the marquis. The marquis and his dubious little Lord Popenjoy both die, and the birth of Mary's son, an indubitably legitimate Popenjoy, solves her marital problems and causes great rejoicing to her father and husband. The novel includes some satire on the woman's rights movement, which is represented by the terrible Baroness Banmann.

In the last of the Palliser series, *The Duke's Children*, the duchess does not appear in person, as she has died in the interim since *The Prime Minis-*

ter. She is present in spirit, however, as the duke, mourning her absence, seeks to make his children reenact in their marriages his own union with Lady Glencora. His daughter, Lady Mary, has fallen in love with Frank Tregear, an impecunious young man who reminds him of his wife's old flame, Burgo Fitzgerald; so he tries to detach her from Tregear and marry her instead to another such tame young aristocrat as he had been himself. At the same time his son, Lord Silverbridge, who had first considered marrying the suitably aristocratic and lively Lady Mabel Grex, falls in love instead with an American girl, Isabel Boncassen. The duke's children are troublesome in other ways: Silverbridge deserts the family party and joins the conservatives, to his father's dismay; besides this, he contracts enormous debts in owning and betting on a racehorse in the Derby. The duke's younger son, Lord Gerald, is sent down from Cambridge for undisciplined behavior. Though he is generous with his children in many ways, the duke clings doggedly to his plans for their marriages and opposes both Silverbridge's and Mary's choices. In this process he even quarrels with Mrs. Finn, Phineas's wife and the cherished friend of Lady Glencora. At last, however, she persuades him to relinquish his plan to reenact his past through his children, and he is reconciled to Isabel Boncassen and Frank Tregear as daughter- and son-in-law. The book is a moving study of an old man confronting youth and of the process by which his longing for self-justification makes him insist on imposing his will on others.

There are several comparable features in Trollope's two major series, the Barset and the Palliser novels. The first offers a combination of love and ecclesiastical business, and the second a similar combination of love and political business; both focus on the fascinating interaction of the domestic with the professional life. A major character in each is a dominating woman who competes with her husband for power and then dies toward the end of the series. A noticeable change is in the presentation of the other female characters. Where in the Barset novels "the simple maiden in her flower" had predominated—such girls as Mary Thorne, Lucy Robarts, and Grace Crawley—in the Palliser novels the interest shifts from innocent girls to experienced women: Lady Laura Kennedy, who deserts her husband and declares her adulterous passion for another man; Mme Max Goesler, who having married once for a settlement pursues a handsome young man for

love and actually proposes to him; and Lady Glencora herself, who not only is much more sympathetically handled than Mrs. Proudie, but also breaks the standard Trollope code by abandoning her first love and devoting herself to a second. The treatment of the male characters also develops between Trollope's early and late periods. In *Rachel Ray* (1863) Trollope had expressed a view of character as essentially set and unchanging: "A man cannot change as men change. Individual men are like the separate links of a rotatory chain. The chain goes on with continuous easy motion as though every part of it were capable of adapting itself to a curve, but not the less is each link as stiff and sturdy as any other piece of wrought iron." But in the later novels, and particularly in the long series with a spread of years that allowed for aging, Trollope was deliberately considering "the state of progressive change" in his characters. In writing the two *Phineas* novels, he records, "I had constantly before me the necessity of progression in character,—of marking the changes in men and women which would naturally be produced by the lapse of years." In observing minutely these changes as they occurred in Lady Glencora and Plantagenet Palliser over many years and through several long novels, he created characters who on occasion seem to transcend the limitations of the books in which they belong and assume a life of their own. "I do not think it probable that my name will remain among those who in the next century will be known as the writers of English prose fiction," he admits modestly; "—but if it does, that permanence of success will probably rest on the character of Plantagenet Palliser, Lady Glencora, and the Rev. Mr. Crawley."

The most considerable novel of the end of Trollope's career is *Mr. Scarborough's Family* (1883), which was still running at his death. Mr. Scarborough is old and dying but has a fierce determination to manage his own affairs until the end. His estate is entailed, but his eldest son Mountjoy is so deeply in debt that the estate would go straight into the hands of the creditors at the father's death. The old man, by a series of cunning and unscrupulous maneuvers, is able to prove Mountjoy illegitimate; and then, when the creditors have settled for a song, to prove him legitimate after all. It is a remarkable story of a roguish and power-hungry old man who is determined to beat the system, and, to the dismay of his lawyer, succeeds in doing so.

Trollope, who had so often celebrated the stability of the country estate in his fiction, was himself comparatively nomadic. He moved again before he died, leaving Montagu Square for Harting Grange, a house in the country near Petersfield in Sussex. He was now aging and troubled with asthma, deafness, and other ailments. But the Phoenix Park murders in Dublin in 1882 spurred him to write another Irish novel, and his last journeys out of England were again to Ireland, to gather material for *The Landleaguers* (1883). For that winter his wife took him to lodgings in London, so as to be within easy reach of the doctors. During a convivial evening with his old friends, the Tilleys, in the midst of laughter at a reading of F. Anstey's new comic novel *Vice Versa*, Trollope had a stroke. He lingered a few weeks, but died on 6 December 1882.

His prudent habit of keeping a manuscript or two on hand meant that the novels kept coming for a while. *Mr. Scarborough's Family* finished its run in 1883; *The Landleaguers*, which he had not lived to finish, was published incomplete; and *An Old Man's Love*, a moving little story about a man of fifty who releases the girl he loves from her engagement to him so that she can marry a younger man, came out in 1884. Even in this century books have continued to emerge: the two works his publishers rejected—*The Noble Jilt*, a play in blank verse, and *The New Zealander*, a book of social criticism—at last saw the light in 1923 and 1972 respectively.

His major posthumous publication, however, was undoubtedly *An Autobiography*, which he finished in 1876 and consigned to his son Henry to see through the press after his death. This engagingly frank account of his professional life and work habits has continued to shock and delight his readers in almost equal measure. His principal biographer, Michael Sadleir, explained how Trollope's blunt alignment of novel writing with shoe making and his undisguised interest in the financial rewards of his trade did much to damage his reputation with the aesthetes of the 1880s and caused a "tempest of reaction against his work." But Sadleir perhaps exaggerated the reaction: many of the reviews were favorable, and Trollope had in any case made no secret during his lifetime of his habits of writing. His practice was methodical, not to say mechanical: the process of literary creation has never been so completely divested of glamour. He rose early and started his labors at 5:30 A.M. "It had at this time become my custom ... to write with my watch before me,

and to require from myself 250 words every quarter of an hour. I have found that the 250 words have been forthcoming as regularly as my watch went." He would work for three hours before breakfast, producing "ten pages of an ordinary novel volume a day" and "three novels of three volumes each in the year," and still have his days free for post-office or other business. He carried his "self-imposed laws" to elaborate lengths. Besides his watch, he had a ruled diary, drawn up in days and weeks, in which he calculated in advance the time a given work should take him and recorded the number of pages written per day. To complete this working calendar exactly became a kind of game with him. "*Finis coronat opus*," he sometimes wrote triumphantly at the end of a calendar; "Finished in 24 weeks to the day" is recorded at the end of the calendar for his longest novel, *The Prime Minister*. On the other hand, where travel or committees or a sore throat prevented his usual stint, he records against the pageless day a melancholy "Ah me!"

Besides writing at home before breakfast, he wrote in clubs, on trains, and on ships—in the latter case occasionally interrupting his labors to throw up. He would frequently begin a new novel the very day after completing the last. And so by observing his self-imposed laws he piled up the novels. He was not unaware of the dangers to his reputation of producing too much, but he claimed that the quality of his work had never suffered for the quantity's being ample. "The work which has been done quickest has been done the best," he insisted.

His enormous energy, gusto, and delight in labor are perhaps the most memorable characteristics of Trollope the man. His lonely childhood and unsatisfactory youth probably had much to do with creating an appetite for success; but work in itself seems to have been as necessary to his well-being as love or nourishment. Until he found a means of directing his energies, he was miserable. "I hated the office," he writes of his early days in the London General Post Office. "I hated my work. More than all I hated my idleness." Work, and an orderly manner of going about it, were for him moral necessities. "The first impression which a parent should fix on the mind of a child is I think love of order," he wrote in his commonplace book of the same period. "It is the reins by which all virtues are kept in their proper places—& the vices, with whom the virtues run in one team, are controlled."

He was legendary in his own day for industry, punctuality, and reliability. When Thackeray failed to produce the major novel that was needed for the first issue of the *Cornhill*, Trollope was applied to and stepped in at short notice to fill the breach. He completely mastered the special difficulties of serial publication. He scorned the hand-to-mouth methods of Dickens and Thackeray, who completed the month's copy with the printer's devil waiting at the door, and made a rule—which he broke only occasionally—that every novel of his should be finished before the first number went to press. When Trollope was on his tour of Australia and New Zealand, Arthur Locker, the editor of the *Graphic*, wrote to him in Wellington to engage him for a new novel: "I should not trouble you during your antipodal tour," he apologized, "only that I know you are a man of such unflagging industry that probably you will write a tale on the homeward voyage. If you do, will you give us the offer of it?" Trollope's reply, by return from Wellington, is characteristic: "I have a novel already written called *Phineas Redux*.... My price for the copyright would be £2,500." He must frequently have staggered his publishers by his almost superhuman promptitude.

He took the pleasure of a good tradesman in serving his customers well. A quarrel with one of his publishers arose from the latter's shrewd maneuver in stretching a one-volume work, *Lotta Schmidt and Other Stories* (1867), to two volumes and raising the price accordingly. On seeing the proof Trollope indignantly protested: "I cannot allow the tales in your hands to be published in two volumes.... I have always endeavoured to give good measure to the public—The pages, as you propose to publish them, are so thin and desolated, and contain such a poor rill of type meandering thro' a desert of margin, as to make me ashamed of the idea of putting my name to the book." He applied his own high standards of honesty to himself.

Notwithstanding his frankly declared interest in the proceeds of his novels, money was not the motive but only the welcome result of his more pressing need to work for work's sake. He wrote to his old friend John Tilley, "You say of me;—that I would not choose to write novels unless I were paid. Most certainly I would;—much rather than not write them at all." The penalty of Adam in having to work in the sweat of his brow he regarded as a blessing rather than a curse. His principal worry about dying was about what he would be able to work at afterward: "My only doubt as to finding a heaven for myself at last arises from the fear that the disembodied and beatified spirits will not want novels." It is to be hoped that in the "Good heavens" so often invoked by Archdeacon Grantly there is still an appetite for good fiction, so that Trollope will not have had to face the hell of enforced leisure.

Trollope's enormous productivity has had much to do with a patronizing dismissal of his work by some critics and a rather apologetic attitude adopted even by his admirers. In a review of *Miss Mackenzie* the young Henry James admitted, "We have long entertained for Mr. Trollope a partiality of which we have yet been somewhat ashamed." It has been a recurring attitude. Even his first major biographer, Sadleir, writing in 1927, and his next major critic, Bradford A. Booth, were tentative and cautious in their praise and partly adopted the stance of apologists. Critics have found his elusive but undoubted quality difficult to analyze: "His work resists the kind of formal analysis to which we subject our better fiction," Booth admitted. His pellucid style has not invited critical exegesis. Compared with George Eliot or Meredith he seemed lowbrow, and compared with Dickens and Hardy his unemphatic social commentary seemed mild.

If it has taken time for critics to claim a place for Trollope among the greatest novelists, the readers have kept faithful to his books. He has continued to be "obsessively readable," in C. P. Snow's phrase. He lost some readers during his lifetime and some more after his death; but after the 1890s reprints of his many novels have proved sound investments for many publishers. During the two world wars Trollope and Barset were in enormous demand. In the 1970s his second series was adapted by the BBC as a highly successful television serial, *The Pallisers*. And increasingly in the two decades before the centenary of his death, the critics ceased to be apologists. Trollope has been recognized as a major novelist: a subtle delineator of character and an acute observer of normal and abnormal psychology; a shrewd social commentator; a knowing moralist; a successful humorist who can also on occasion stretch to tragedy; and a master of his art as well as of his craft. "Trollope did not write for posterity," James conceded in his classic essay, written shortly after Trollope's death; "he wrote for the day, the moment; but these are just the writers whom posterity is apt to put into its pocket.... Trollope will remain one of the most trustworthy, though not one of the most eloquent, of the writers who have helped the heart of man to know itself."

Letters:

Letters of Anthony Trollope, edited by Bradford A. Booth (London: Oxford University Press, 1951);

The Letters of Anthony Trollope, 2 volumes, edited by N. John Hall (Stanford: Stanford University Press, 1983).

Bibliography:

Michael Sadleir, *Trollope: A Bibliography* (London: Constable, 1928).

Biographies:

Michael Sadleir, *Trollope: A Commentary* (London: Constable, 1927);

Lucy Poate Stebbins and Richard Poate Stebbins, *The Trollopes: The Chronicle of a Working Family* (London: Secker & Warburg, 1947);

James Pope Hennessy, *Anthony Trollope* (Boston: Little, Brown, 1971);

C. P. Snow, *Trollope: His Life and Art* (London: Macmillan, 1975);

R. H. Super, *The Chronicler of Barsetshire: A Life of Anthony Trollope* (Ann Arbor: University of Michigan Press, 1988);

Richard Mullen, *Anthony Trollope: A Victorian in His World* (London: Duckworth, 1990).

References:

Ruth ApRoberts, *Trollope: Artist and Moralist* (London: Chatto & Windus, 1971); republished as *The Moral Trollope* (Athens: Ohio University Press, 1971);

Bradford A. Booth, *Anthony Trollope: Aspects of His Life and Art* (Bloomington: Indiana University Press, 1958);

A. O. J. Cockshut, *Anthony Trollope: A Critical Study* (London: Collins, 1955; New York: New York University Press, 1968);

P. D. Edwards, *Anthony Trollope: His Art and Scope* (St. Lucia: University of Queensland Press, 1977);

N. John Hall, ed., *The Trollope Critics* (London: Macmillan, 1981);

John Halperin, *Trollope and Politics: A Study of the Pallisers and Others* (London: Macmillan, 1977);

Geoffrey Harvey, *The Art of Anthony Trollope* (New York: St. Martin's Press, 1980);

Christopher Herbert, *Trollope and Comic Pleasure* (Chicago: University of Chicago Press, 1987);

Henry James, "Anthony Trollope," in his *Partial Portraits* (London: Macmillan, 1888), pp. 97-133;

Walter M. Kendrick, *The Novel-Machine: The Theory and Fiction of Anthony Trollope* (Baltimore: Johns Hopkins University Press, 1980);

James R. Kincaid, *The Novels of Anthony Trollope* (Oxford: Clarendon Press, 1977);

Juliet McMaster, *Trollope's Palliser Novels: Theme and Pattern* (London: Macmillan, 1978);

J. Hillis Miller, *The Form of Victorian Fiction: Thackeray, Dickens, Trollope, George Eliot, Meredith, and Hardy* (Notre Dame, Ind.: University of Notre Dame Press, 1968);

Deborah Denenholz Morse, *Women in Trollope's Palliser Novels* (Ann Arbor: UMI Research Press, 1987);

Jane Nardin, *He Knew She Was Right: The Independent Woman in the Novels of Anthony Trollope* (Carbondale: Southern Illinois University Press, 1989);

Robert M. Polhemus, *The Changing World of Anthony Trollope* (Berkeley & Los Angeles: University of California Press, 1968);

Gordon N. Ray, "Trollope at Full Length," *Huntington Library Quarterly*, 31 (1968): 313-340;

Donald Smalley, ed., *Trollope: The Critical Heritage* (London: Routledge & Kegan Paul / New York: Barnes & Noble, 1969);

R. C. Terry, *Anthony Trollope: The Artist in Hiding* (London: Macmillan, 1977).

Papers:

Trollope's working papers are collected in the Bodleian Library, Oxford University. Many of the manuscripts of his novels are at the Beinecke Library, Yale University.

Index to Volume 4

Index

This index includes proper names: people, places, and works mentioned in the texts of entries for Volume 4. The primary checklists, which appear at the beginning of each entry, are not included in this index. Also omitted are the names London and Dublin, because they appear so frequently. Volume 8 of the *Concise Dictionary of British Literary Biography* includes a cumulative proper-name index to the entire series.

Cumulative Index of Author Entries for
Concise Dictionary of British Literary Biography

Cumulative Index
of Author Entries

ISBN 0-8103-7984-8